TEXTILE FABRICS
AND
THEIR SELECTION

Cherokee Alphabet
Alexandria, Virginia 1967

This scarf was first unveiled at the Virginia Museum and portrayed the Cherokee heritage of Frankie Welch. Mrs. Dean Rusk (wife of the Secretary of State in 1967) requested an all-American design for President and Mrs. Johnson to give to visiting Heads of State. The Secretary and Mrs. Rusk also used this scarf as an official gift. For the first time, an American theme, the Cherokee alphabet printed on a textile, was used as a presidential gift.

8th edition

TEXTILE FABRICS AND THEIR SELECTION

ISABEL B. WINGATE

A.B. and M.S. in Retailing, Ph.D.
Professor Emeritus of Retail
  Management
Institute of Retail Management
New York University

JUNE F. MOHLER

B.S., M.A., and Ph.D.
Dean and Professor of Textiles
School of Consumer Science
  and Allied Professions
Winthrop College, Rock Hill,
  South Carolina

PRENTICE-HALL, INC., Englewood Cliffs, New Jersey 07632

Library of Congress Cataloging in Publication Data

Wingate, Isabel Barnum.
  Textile fabrics and their selection.

  Bibliography: p.
  Includes index.
  1. Textile industry. 2. Textile fabrics. I. Mohler,
June F. II. Title.
TS1449.W5 1984   677   83-11243
ISBN 0-13-912865-4

Editorial/production supervision and
  interior design: Barbara Grasso
Cover design: Lundgren Graphics, Ltd.
Manufacturing buyer: Ed O'Dougherty

Printed in the United States of America

10 9 8 7 6 5 4 3 2 1

ISBN 0-13-912865-4

Prentice-Hall International, Inc., *London*
Prentice-Hall of Australia Pty. Limited, *Sydney*
Editora Prentice-Hall do Brasil, Ltda., *Rio de Janeiro*
Prentice-Hall Canada Inc., *Toronto*
Prentice-Hall of India Private Limited, *New Delhi*
Prentice-Hall of Japan, Inc., *Tokyo*
Prentice-Hall of Southeast Asia Pte. Ltd., *Singapore*
Whitehall Books Limited, *Wellington, New Zealand*

CONTENTS

12 Wool and the Consumer   **297**

History of Woolen Cloth / Wool Production / Interpretation of the Wool Products Labeling Act / Characteristics of the Wool Fiber / Manufacture of Worsted Yarns / Manufacture of Woolen Yarns / Wool Blends / Weaving, Knitting, and Felting Fabrics / Finishes for Worsted and Woolen Fabrics / Buying Points of Wool Fabrics / Minor Hair (Specialty) Fibers / Summary / Review Questions / Project / Experiments / Glossary

13 Rayon and Acetate and the Consumer   **332**

Rayon / Acetate and Triacetate / Characteristics of Rayon, Acetate, and Triacetate Fibers / Rayon, Acetate, and Triacetate Yarns / Construction of Rayon, Acetate, and Triacetate Fabrics / Rayon, Acetate, and Triacetate Fabrics: Regular Finishes / Rayon, Acetate, and Triacetate Fabrics: Functional Finishes / Alginate Fiber / Desirability of the Cellulosic Man-Made Fibers / Fiber Producers' Concern for Consumer Satisfaction / Trends in the Output of the Cellulosic Fibers / Summary / Review Questions / Experiments / Glossary

14 General-Purpose Noncellulosic Fibers and the Consumer   **357**

Nylon / The Polyesters / The Acrylics / The Modacrylics / Summary / Review Questions / Experiments / Project

15 Special-Purpose Noncellulosic Fibers and the Consumer   **382**

Glass Fibers / Aramid / Olefin / Saran / Vinyon / Elastomeric Fibers and Yarns / Anidex / Metallic Fibers / Fluorocarbon Fibers / Other Man-Made Noncellulosic Fibers Produced Abroad / Bicomponent and Biconstituent Fibers / Current Status and Trends in Man-Made Fibers / Cost Relationship Between That of the Fiber and the Retail Price of Apparel / Trends in Technology / Review Questions / Experiment / Projects / Glossary

16 The Care of Textile Fabrics   **410**

Cleaning of Textile Products / Refreshening / Storage / Dry Cleaning / Products Used in Cleaning / Spot and Stain Removal / Consumer Claims for Unserviceable or Lost Textile Articles / Summary / Review Questions / Project / Glossary

Part Two
SELECTION OF APPROPRIATE FABRICS

17 Women's and Girls' Wear   **428**

Styles and Fabrics in Women's and Girls' Outer Apparel / General Requirements for Serviceability of Outer Apparel / Points in Selecting Women's and Girls' Ready-to-Wear / Points in Selecting Underwear, Sleepwear, Loungewear, and Intimate Apparel / Hosiery and Panty Hose / Selection of Clothing Accessories / Infants' Wear / Adult Diapers / Summary / Projects / Glossary

FOREWORD

As a former student of Dr. Wingate's at the New York University School of Retailing, I was delighted to be asked to review the eighth edition of *Textile Fabrics and Their Selection*, a book that has long been regarded as the most comprehensive textile consumer-oriented college text published.

And now, as a retailer, I find the new edition even more relevant. In this edition, Dr. Wingate is joined by co-author Dr. June Mohler, the dean of the School of Consumer Science and Allied Professions, Winthrop College, who provides valuable insight as the former fashion director for Fieldcrest Mills.

The new edition incorporates all the organizational qualities I found so useful in the earlier volume, but now it is updated to reflect the rapidly changing technology of textiles and the ever-increasing market and consumer demands. A new chapter has been added on the distribution of textiles from fiber to consumer and on the career opportunities the textile field provides.

To complete the picture, this new book also includes not only apparel textiles but also much needed input in the rapidly expanding home textile field. Coupled with such background is an industry-sponsored update on new generic fibers and finishes, new methods of computerized control of fabric construction, and of vital importance to any future merchant, the new Federal Trade Commission's law on care labeling and the Flammable Fabrics Act.

Today, fiber and fabrics—their selection, design, and ultimately, their consumer care—form a major building block for the retailer and manufacturer to work within the structuring of a profitable business.

In an age where relevance is constantly being challenged, Dr. Wingate's new edition has earned an honored place, not only in the classroom but also as a business reference. As with many of the earlier editions, this new volume will not be traded in but will be kept as a handy sourcebook, one that can provide a real edge in the competitive market.

Mark S. Handler
President, R. H. Macy & Co., Inc.

PREFACE

The textile industry continues to be a rapidly changing one, creating new fiber and yarn modifications and manufacturing them into functional and decorative products for apparel and home furnishings as well as for industrial purposes.

In 1776, except for imports from abroad, virtually all clothing and home furnishings were made in the home. The farmer raised the raw material and his wife spun the yarn, wove the cloth, colored it, and made it into garments and household textiles.

But the Industrial Revolution with its factory production brought a dramatic change. In 1791, Samuel Slater brought to America the secret English methods of carding and combing of yarns; and in 1814, Francis Cabot established the first completely power-operated textile plant where all steps in the manufacture of cloth were performed. For over one hundred years, although there were great improvements in mechanical methods, the raw materials used were the natural fibers, particularly cotton, wool, linen, and silk. Late in the nineteenth century, chemists created the first man-made fiber, rayon, which assumed commercial importance early in the twentieth century. But in the post–World War II era of the 1940s, the genius of the chemical industry led to a wide variety of man-made fibers that in the United States, at least, surpasses the natural fibers in importance. The spectacular changes in production have been supported by changes in customer demand, growing out of increases in population and in per capita income, by changes in life-styles, and by the demand for new end uses to which textile products might be put.

Consumer demand for new products has resulted in new creations in fibers, yarns, and finishes of textile fabrics. To illustrate, one of the creative style developments in textiles is the old familiar staple twill denim with its blue warp and white filling, originally used for jeans. It has now become a fashion fabric. It may now be striped, checked, plaid, embroidered, or printed, have a brushed surface, or a faded look. It will even stretch.

The consumer's right to know has led to new and revised government regulations. Accordingly, the text discusses federal laws and Federal Trade Commission rulings intended to inform the consumer of the fiber content of each article: the Flammable Fabrics Act to protect the consumer from dangerously flammable fabrics and the Permanent Care Labeling Act to provide information for proper care permanently attached to articles of clothing and many home furnishings.

Merchandise knowledge can be acquired by the consumer from experience in buying, using, and caring for textile articles. It can be learned from reading informative advertisements and labels on merchandise, from well-informed salespeople, from knowledgeable friends and associates, and from formal classroom study.

Many years of experience in teaching textiles have proved that, of all methods, formal instruction can most quickly and accurately organize and present product information. This, coupled with an emphasis on the selling points of textile fabrics, will aid the retail salesperson in helping the consumer to make a wise selection.

But a mere presentation of the facts is not enough. The reader must assimilate the facts and apply them through study and experimentation. To assist in learning these facts, the first edition of this book was published in 1935. Subsequent editions have attempted to keep its content up to date.

THE EIGHTH EDITION

For the first time in the forty-eight years of the life of this text, the senior author has selected a joint author for this the eighth edition. She is June F. Mohler, dean of the School of Consumer Science and Allied Professions and professor of textiles at Winthrop College in Rock Hill, South Carolina. She holds the degree of Ph.D. in textiles and clothing from the University of North Carolina at Greensboro. Formerly, she was associate professor in the School of Education at New York University.

Her career in business has been impressive. For nine years, she was fashion director for Fieldcrest Mills, Inc., and following that vice president of Design Research International, developing manufacturing and marketing systems for Marimekko textile products. In 1977, the Marimekko furnishings collection received the Tommy Award for the best design in home furnishings in the United States. She continues to be active in professional societies, especially the Association of College Professors of Textiles and Clothing and the Fashion Group of Charlotte.

Since the preparation of the seventh edition in 1976, the textile industry has had to face up to challenging changes. The following in particular are reflected in the current edition, together with the points made by Mr. Handler in the Foreword:

1. Technological advances, including automation, in the spinning of yarns, the construction of fabrics, and their dyeing and printing.
2. The expanded use of man-made specialty fibers, some entirely new and some associated with space travel.

3. The efforts of the cotton industry to increase the demand for its products relative to that of the man-made fibers.
4. The growing use of nonwoven fabrics by industrial and institutional consumers.
5. The demand to eliminate pollution in connection with cotton dust, asbestos, and chemicals used in the production of man-made fibers.
6. A growing recognition that the acceptance of finished textile products by the consumer depends not only upon their serviceability but also upon their styling to suit the life-styles of individual groups along with the dictates of fashion.

The new edition gives special attention not only to the changes listed, but it also expands on former treatment in view of new information from the various segments of the textile industry. The publications of the International Fabricare Institute have been especially useful in connection with the points the consumer should look for in the selection and care of apparel.

As before, the text is divided into two parts. Part One covers the intrinsic characteristics of fabrics. This information is basic to judging the grade of a fabric, to estimating its probable performance, and to determining the care required to get maximum performance. Part Two emphasizes the importance of the selection of appropriate fabrics for specific uses in apparel and home furnishings and describes the factors to be considered in examining the construction of garments and household textiles.

The plan for use of this text is flexible. It can provide for a year's course in textiles, with Part One covering the subject matter for the first semester and Part Two the second semester. The text can also be used for two separate courses in fashion fabrics: "Fashion Fabrics in Apparel" and "Fabrics in Home Furnishings." For the apparel class, subject matter may include Chapters 1 to 8, 16 to 18, and 22. For the home furnishings class, the subject matter may include Chapters 1 and 2, 8, 10 to 16, and 19 to 22. It will be noted that Chapters 1 and 2 are repeated in both programs. Since one course should not be prerequisite for the other, students in both courses must familiarize themselves with the terminology from the beginning. For adult education, ten two-hour lectures the first term and eight the second term have proved effective.

The Laboratory Swatch Book for Textile Fabrics, published by W. C. Brown, Dubuque, Iowa, now in its seventh edition, endeavors to give readers the opportunity to apply the information in the text to actual cloths. The organization of the experiments follows the table of contents of the text except in the case of the new Chapter 22 on Marketing and Career Opportunities that requires no samples.

The following listing presents the names of the many experts who have read critically one chapter or parts of a chapter or have submitted new write-ups on a specific topic. The authors are deeply indebted to these people for the care and dedication each has provided freely to make the new edition again authoritative.

The authors also wish to express their warm appreciation to Mary Ellen Holmes, to Dianne Walters, to Maggie Elliott, and to Patricia Schmidt, graduate students at Winthrop College, for their dedicated assistance in the research, editing, and typing of the manuscript for this edition.

Contributors to the Text of the Present Edition

Contributor	Title (at time of assistance)	Topic
Horace Adams, Jr.	Technical director, Man-Made Fiber Producers Association	Biconstituent and bicomponent fibers
Walter H. Ayers	Marketing research analyst, Textile Fibers Department, DuPont	Textile product data
*Walter J. Bartlett	Manager, Marketing Services, Fibers Division, American Cyanamid	Man-made fibers
Hans Baumann	Vice president, Rudolph-Desco Co.	Silk
*Bernard F. Bertland	Director of public affairs and communication, Phillips Fibers Corp.	Specialty man-made fibers and nonwoven fabrics
Edward Borg	Marketing manager, Hoechst Fibers	Nonwoven fabrics
W. A. Britton	Manager, Polymer Products Department, DuPont	Plastic netting
James Byler	Executive vice president, Gear	Household textiles
Pauline V. Delli-Carpine	Director of promotion for the U.S.-Belgium Linen Association	Linen
James M. Donovan, Jr.	Associate director, Communications Division, American Textile Manufacturers' Institute	Spinning and shuttleless loom
Patricia Eels	Public relations manager, Mohasco Corp.	Rugs and carpets
Paul Ellis	Product development coordinator, Springs Industries	Dyeing and printing
Geraldine Emmert	Merchandise manager for intimate apparel, Celanese Corp.	Women's undergarments
Rudolph C. Geering	Textile engineer; member of AATT	Textile education and career opportunities
J. A. Genereux	Marketing representative, Engineered Industrial Applications, DuPont	Teflon
Thomas Haas	Vice president of advertising and public relations, The Wool Bureau	Wool
Alan Huston	Assistant Professor of interior design, Winthrop College	Draperies, curtains, and upholstery
*John L. Kelly	Director of communications and public relations, Avetex Fibers	Rayon and acetate
Joyce Lambert	Public relations consultant, Fieldcrest Mills	Period styles
Gloria Lang	Vice president, Sheet Department, Fieldcrest Mills	Household textiles
Hurdle Lea	Vice president, Cannon Mills	Cotton
David H. Lipkin	Vice president, Home-furnishings Division, American Silk Mills	Basic and fancy weaves
John Lomartire	Former member of the Fabric Development Division, Monsanto Fibers and Intermediates Co.	Flammability
Bettie McClasky	Assistant professor of textiles, Winthrop College	Fancy weaves and yarns
*Carl Moskowitz	Director, Public Relations, Monsanto Fibers and Intermediates Co.	Man-made fibers

Contributor	Title (at time of assistance)	Topic
Norman Oehlke	Chief analyst, International Fabricare Institute	Plastic coatings
Albert Paghini	Manager, Product Publicity, Celanese Corp.	Rayon and acetate
James B. Phillips	Manager, Quality Assurance, Springs Industries	Inspection of gray goods
Janet Racy	Fashion director, Associated Dry Goods Corp.	Women's and men's wear
Charles Reichman	Former chairman of Technical Advisory and Education Committee, National Knitted Outerwear Association	Knitting
*Fisher A. Rhymes	Director of public affairs, Man-Made Fiber Producers Association, and chairman of the Education Committee	Coordinator or revision of chapters on man-made fibers
R. J. Richardson	Manager, Marketing Systems, Allied Fibers & Plastic Co.	Man-made fibers
Mort Rochelle	President, North Carolina Finishing Co.	Finishing fabrics
Adaline T. Ryan	Product information manager, DuPont	Man-made fibers
Barbara Starke	Chairperson, Department of Micro-environmental Studies and Design, Howard University	Women's and men's wear
Daniel M. Thornton III	Manager, Textile Economy & Environment, DuPont	Fiber price trends
George Todd	Technical superintendent, Springs Industries	Dyeing and printing
J. C. Troy	Director, Creative Products Research, Carpet & Rug Division, Fieldcrest Mills	Karacrest and Karaloc construction
John M. Wright, Jr.	Strategy development manager, Textile Fibers Department, DuPont	Noncellulosic man-made fibers

*Members of the Education Committee of the Man-Made Fiber Producers Association, Inc. These contributors provided a careful revision of the three chapters on man-made fibers.

Photography, artwork, and many charts have been completely revised to present a new edition of updated graphics. The authors are grateful also to the following manufacturers, trade associations, magazines, and others for their assistance in providing illustrations and answering questions about their products.

Allied Chemical Corporation
American Association of Textile Chemists and Colorists (AATCC)
American Association of Textile Technology (AATT)
American Cyanamid Company
American Enka Corporation
American Fabrics Magazine
American Silk Mills
American Textile Manufacturers Institute, Inc.
America's Textiles, Reporter/Bulletin and Knitter/Apparel editions

The American Yarn Spinners Association, Inc.
Appropriate Technology Corp.
Arnold, Hoff & Associates Inc.
Arthur T. Gregorian, Inc.
The Asian Society
Atlas Electric Devices Co.
Avtex Fibers, Inc.
Bassett Furniture Industries, Inc.
The Belgian Linen Association
Bigelow Sanford Carpet Co., Inc.
Dick Blick (identification of parts of the loom)
Burlington Industrial Fabrics Co.
Carbide and Carbon Chemical Company
Carborundum Company
Carleton Voice, Carleton College (Minn.)
The Carpet and Rug Institute, Inc.
Catalina, Inc.
Celanese Fibers Marketing Company
Chatham Research and Development Corporation
The Chemstrand Corporation
Cheyney Brothers, Inc.
Ciba-Geigy Corporation
Cone Mills, Inc.
Consumers' Research, Inc.
Consumers' Union of the U.S., Inc.
Cotton Incorporated
Cranston Print Works Company
Dan River, Inc.
David Gessner Co.
Deering Milliken Research Corporation
Dubied Machinery Co.
E. I. DuPont de Nemours & Company, Inc.
Eastman Chemical Products, Inc.
Fieldcrest Mills, Inc.
Formfit Rogers
Forstmann Woolen Company
Franklin Process Company, a division of Indian Head Yarn Company
Gimbels
Good Housekeeping Consumers' Guaranty Administration
Jonas Grushkin (photos)
Hanes Corporation
Hercules, Inc.
Hoechst Fibers Industries
Hoover Company
Industrial By-Products and Research Corporation
International Fabricare Institute (IFI)

International Nonwoven and Disposables Association (INDA)
International Silk Association
Irish Linen Guild
Ivey's (Carolinas)
John Stickley & Co.
Karastan Rug Mills
Kent-Kostikyan, Inc.
Knitted Outerwear Times
Lands' End
Levi Strauss & Co.
Lowenstein & Sons
Man-Made Fiber Producers Association, Inc.
Max Mandel Laces, Inc.
Men's Fashion Association of America
Mobay Chemical Corporation
Mohawk Carpet Mills, a division of Mohasco Corp.
Monsanto Fibers and Intermediates Co.
NASA
National Plastic Products Company
New Process Company
North American Rayon Corporation
Owens-Corning Fiberglas Corporation
J. C. Penney Company
Perfect Fit Industries, Inc.
Phillips Petroleum
Jack Pitkin (photos)
Polylok Corp.
Quaker Lace Company
The Sanforized Company, a division of Cluett Peabody & Co., Inc.
Scalamandré Silks, Inc.
Soap and Detergent Association
Southern Research Laboratory of the U.S. Department of Agriculture
Springs Industries, Inc.
Southern Furniture Manufacturers Association
Teri Leigh Stratford (photos)
Sulzer Brothers, Inc.
Textile Economics Bureau, Inc.
Textile Organon
Textile World
Uniroyal, Inc.
United States Testing Company, Inc.
Warwick Dyeing Corporation
Weave Corp.
Wellington Sears Co., Inc.
Whirlpool Corporation
The Wool Bureau, Inc.

Chapter 1

WHY STUDY TEXTILES

INTRODUCTION—THE CHANGING TEXTILE SCENE

A woman experienced both as a homemaker and as a teacher of textiles made this comment to a friend: "I've discarded my electric iron; I haven't used it for over a year. You know, I never miss it. The permanent- and durable-press clothing, towels, sheets, and table linens come out so smooth from the dryer that they don't need pressing. Yes," she went on, "I do follow the instructions on care labels that are now required by law, and I remember the rules in the instruction booklets for setting my washer and dryer. I remember to take the wash out of the dryer as soon as the machine stops and to take out each article separately, since static sometimes makes one article stick to others. If it's a towel, I fold it. If it's a shirt, I hang it on a hanger or fold it for a drawer. No, I haven't missed my electric iron. When I have things dry-cleaned, the dry cleaner presses them for me."

The teacher may have overstated the lack of need for an iron, since "touching up" is sometimes required and since consumers may have special fabrics that still require ironing. Nevertheless, her view reflects a major change in the characteristics of apparel and home furnishings in the late part of the twentieth century.

No wonder that when the first no-iron fabrics were introduced in the 1950s they were quickly dubbed "miracle fabrics" by their advertisers; for they were just that to most American consumers—a "miracle" of easy care and improved wear performance.

Our forebearers knew only of cotton, wool, linen, and silk and were well acquainted with at least the first two fiber names. They spun and dyed yarns, wove fabrics on home looms, and sewed their clothing frequently in their own homes. Thus, they had ample firsthand experience to make wise decisions even after production moved from the home to factories.

But today most of the basic fibers used in construction of apparel and home furnishings are a product of chemistry, and the finishing and dyeing of the cloth represents elaborate chemical treatments. The test-tube fibers and finishes often have a specific end use in view. Accordingly, to be a wise buyer in the marketplace, consumers must acquire a great deal of knowledge that their predecessors did not need to know. The same is true of those who sell to those customers: salespeople, advertisers, and all those who market textiles. Much of this essential knowledge must come from the producers of the fibers, yarns,

Textile Products:

5 CONSUMER RIGHTS AND RESPONSIBILITIES

1. The Right to INFORMATION
and the RESPONSIBILITY to seek it out and to use it when buying

2. The Right to SELECTION
and the RESPONSIBILITY to buy wisely from the wide variety available

3. The Right to PERFORMANCE
and the RESPONSIBILITY to follow care recommended on the hangtag

4. The Right to SAFETY
and the RESPONSIBILITY to guard against carelessness, especially around fire hazards

5. The Right to RECOURSE
and the RESPONSIBILITY to let legitimate dissatisfactions be known

PLUS . . . a right to give a vote of confidence when you find satisfaction with textile products . . . best expressed through loyalty to retail stores and brands of merchandise which suit your standards of style, performance and service.

CELANESE®
CELANESE FIBERS MARKETING COMPANY

Figure 1.1 Consumer rights and responsibilities. (Courtesy of Celanese Fibers Marketing Co.)

fabrics, and the finished product; but it must also come from the experience of knowledgeable consumers who observe closely how the products perform in relation to their intended use.

Sources of information are many; but few consumers and sales personnel have the time to undertake an elaborate research study. To take a course in school, college, or place of business, supplemented by a text, such as this book, which can be used as a future reference guide, is an excellent way in which to be better informed. Consumers and sellers alike should understand the rights and responsibilities of the consumer in connection with the selection of textile products (see Fig. 1.1) and be armed with the knowledge to assure the realization of these rights.

TEXTILE EDUCATION

A distinction may be made between providing *information* for the customer or the consumer that the former may represent and acquiring an *education*. Information provides the customer with knowledge about a particular product or service offered for sale, whereas education teaches the individual how to make an intelligent choice among the many products and services available in the market. Ways in which customer education are provided are discussed in the sections that follow.

Teaching Salespeople

In the small dry-goods store, salespeople still acquire much textile information through experience. This method of learning is often a slow and discouraging process. A shortcut to learning is the classroom instruction in textiles that training departments in retail stores may give their salespeople, supplemented by regular meetings conducted by the buyer of the department.

In the larger department stores and chains, the prime source of textile information comes from pamphlets, films, and fact cards provided by the manufacturers, vendors, and textile associations. More sophisticated electronic communications systems, such as closed-circuit television, which may be beamed throughout a store's branch units from a central television studio in the main (or flagship) store, are used in larger retail chains. The essential information is usually provided by the buyer or department manager at morning meetings. Emphasis is naturally given to new items added to the assortment. In chain stores, the pertinent information may be compiled at headquarters and distributed to the department managers in the various units. The store's training department may be responsible for writing informative booklets and providing the buyers with teaching materials for the main store and branches and for chain store units. Sometimes, the training department gives "reinforcement" instruction. When a new product appears in stock, the manufacturer's representative may present pertinent facts about it to salespeople. Part-timers are usually given the same textile information as the regular salespeople by the same executives.

The main difficulty lies in training part-time salespeople and contingents who come in only for the busy season, when all the store's efforts must be concentrated on sales volume and when formal training can, at best, be for only one or two hours. One solution to the problem is the sponsor system in which a person is named by the management to assist in training a new salesperson. The sponsor may be credited with the sales of the new person for the first two days, or receive remuneration for each person trained, or both.

Part-time as well as full-time selling personnel will also benefit from the videotaped sales training information now regularly used in larger stores to train and update salespeople.

To improve salesmanship, one store has used a "show-tell skit" for its salespeople, the purpose being to emphasize dramatically the value not only of showing the customer the merchandise but of telling the prospective user the pertinent facts in an accurate way. A few days following the skit, store shoppers checked with customers to determine the effectiveness of the information communicated by the salespeople. Several other motivational and situational methods have been used by progressive stores, including role playing and quiz-show-format training sessions.

Many progressive stores encourage their sponsors and junior executives to take textile courses in high schools, colleges, museums, and other outside institutions. Stores may pay part or all of their employees' tuition if they complete the courses successfully. Textile experts from outside organizations also conduct courses in retail stores. Unfortunately, retail management's interest in training programs varies with the times—emphasized in periods of profitable growth and curtailed in periods of recession. Perhaps it would be more effective (and thus more profitable) to stress sales training as a means of increasing the productivity of selling personnel, regardless of the state of the retail economy.

Education in the High School and College

Most vocational high schools that offer programs in retailing include the subject of textiles as an important part of that program. Many feature actual store experience, in which part of the student's school day is spent in a retail store performing numerous routine tasks, such as wrapping, packing, and marking stock arrangement, in addition to on-floor selling. In a typical retail setting, such as in a specialty apparel shop or department store, the vast majority of products sold are textiles or textile-related. Thus, a knowledge of textiles is important to the student even at the entry level of retailing. For the student who hopes to advance to a higher position such as buyer, the study of textiles is even more important. The continuing search for the latest and most relevant product information will not only help to improve selling skills, but also will be viewed by management as a positive indication of career commitment on the part of the student.

It is important to note to prospective retailing students that even in large department stores, where they may be placed for "field experience," it is possible that they will not receive much on-the-job training, especially in stores where training sessions are held in morning hours. The typical high school student spends afternoon hours in the store or, in some instances, Saturdays only. Thus, he or she is likely to miss regularly scheduled store training; accordingly, merchandising courses in the school program are of immeasurable help, most especially, the textile courses.

High school and other secondary vocational programs with retailing as a major emphasis can be found in many departments of the schools; the majority are located in Business Education, Distributive Education, and Distributive Education and Marketing divisions, while in some states the programs are also found in Home Economics and Industrial Arts areas. Wherever located, it is likely that the retailing courses are taught by teachers who have special funding for both their training and teaching under a federal law, the Vocational Education Act of 1963. These special funds provide also for cooperative-type training, thus encouraging the vocational student to combine work and study.

At the four-year college level, as well as in many junior and community colleges (two-year programs), the study of textiles is an integral part of the retailing curriculum. Quite often these programs are in the home economics, human ecology, and consumer science areas of the college and carry such names as fashion merchandising, fashion retailing, and consumer marketing. Although generally not found as a major program in business schools, retailing also is and has been for many decades a traditional course offering in business curricula.

Collegiate Internship Programs

The concept of cooperative or internship business training at the college level was first used over sixty years ago and grew steadily until the 1950s. About that time, a curriculum movement toward theoretically based courses created a backlash away from offerings in more practical field experience. More recently, the pendulum has swung back as college administrators and faculty are coming to realize that experience in the "real world" is a valid educational experience. Moreover, some colleges grant academic credit for prior experiences if proper documentation can be provided. Students are encouraged to find part-time related employment, often being urged by faculty advisors to acquire "on-the-job" summer work experiences to supplement their regular college program. The student with textile background knowledge will obviously have an edge over others while competing in this expanding part-time job market. (See. Fig. 1.2.)

Place of Industrial Research and Government
Direction in Textile Education

This era of man-made fibers and the competition among them, plus the advent of blends (mixtures of various fibers), has caused those in the textile industry to realize the need for more and better consumer research and for improvement in textile training for the industry.

Figure 1.2 On-the-job training is invaluable to students. In cooperative education college students spend part of their time in store service, where a knowledge of textiles is essential. (Photo courtesy of The Center for Career Development, Winthrop College, South Carolina.)

The industry is constantly trying to determine what fiber, mixture, or blend is best suited for an intended use; how the fabric can be dyed so that it will serve most satisfactorily; and how the consumer should care for it. When, through research, the textile manufacturer can say, for example, "We have proved that a blend of 55 percent wool and 45 percent Dacron polyester is the most satisfactory blend for a man's business suit," and can give consumers logical reasons why, one of the consumer's most confusing problems in clothing selection will have been solved. Only through a vast amount of research would this decision be possible. Any research necessitates trained men and women. For textile training, the industry supports education and research in numerous institutions.[1]

The dry-cleaning industry is an important segment of the textile industry, with the International Fabricare Institute providing dry-cleaning and laundry plants throughout the world with training aids both for production workers and sales personnel. (See Fig. 1.3.) These include training cassettes and slides on handling customers' problems (such as spotting) and on finishing (ironing and smoothing) of garments and other textile products. It also conducts management courses, both resident and correspondent, and provides scholarships for certain of these educational programs.

The federal government has also played an active role in the development of industrial standards and public education. In 1962, a National Consumer

[1]See Appendices F and G for a list of schools and research organizations active in the field.

Figure 1.3 Certified washable and dry-cleanable seal. (Courtesy of the International Fabricare Institute.)

Advisory Council was appointed by President John F. Kennedy to concern itself with consumer welfare, protection, education, and labeling (see Fig. 1.4), with Dr. Helen Connoyer as chairwoman. Subsequently, in President Lyndon Johnson's administration, this post was held by Esther Peterson and later by Betty Furness. Betty Furness was succeeded by Virginia H. Knauer as President Richard Nixon's consumer aide. Knauer continued under President Gerald Ford as special assistant to the president on consumer affairs, and under the Carter administration, Esther Peterson returned to the post. Once again, Virginia H. Knauer has returned to serve President Ronald Reagan in a consumer affairs post. These people have arranged conferences of executives in the textile industry, scientists, and consumer representatives to help eliminate consumer complaints involving factual content or lack of it on labels and the loss of care labels in washing. The mandatory labeling regulations discussed in this chapter are the result of joint efforts of the federal government and the textile industry.

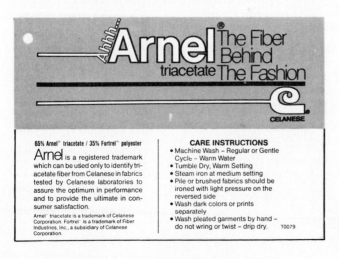

Figure 1.4 Fiber content label with care instructions. (Courtesy of Celanese Fibers Marketing Co.)

ASSISTING AND GUIDING THE CONSUMER

Big business has brought the consumer many lines of improved goods and new goods. The complex processes used in their production have disguised the old products completely, and many new goods are so utterly novel that the consumer does not know whether they can be washed without shrinkage and without changing color, whether the color is sunfast, of what fiber the material is made, and how to care for the finished article so that it will give its money's worth.

The American Home Economics Association has been an important instrument in consumer education and protection. In cooperation with technical societies, it assists in the setting of standards and is a major instrument in educating the consumer to make an intelligent choice.

For the typical consumer without ready access to the more technical and professional sources of information, the label now attached to most textile products is the major supplement to the personal inspection of the product. Other guides also available are seals of approval, ratings and guarantees, advertisements, and the presence of an informed and intelligent sales force.

Informative Labels

Mandatory Content and Performance Labels

A tag or label attached to the merchandise usually gives the consumer information about qualities inherent in the merchandise. Under federal law, the Textile Fiber Products Identification Act (TFPIA),[2] a tag or label must give the name of the raw material (fiber content) of which the fabric is made. Such a label must remain affixed to the merchandise until it is sold to the ultimate consumer.

This law, which was passed by the Congress of the United States in August 1958, became effective March 3, 1960 and has been amended to February 1, 1981. It requires that the label include not only fiber content but also percentage by weight, in order of importance, of each fiber used in an article. The manufactur-

---

[2]The term "textile fiber product," as currently defined by the TFPIA, means (1) any fiber, whether in the finished or unfinished state, used or intended for use in household textile articles; (2) any yarn or fabric, whether in the finished or unfinished state, used or intended for use in household textile articles; (3) any household textile article made in whole or in part of yarn or fabric, except that such term does not include a product required to be labeled under the Wool Products Labeling Act of 1933 (discussed in a later section in this chapter).

Since the purpose of the TFPIA is to educate the consumer, the definition does not include textile products designed for industrial use.

Section 12 of the TFPIA and its interpretation by the FTC also exempts from the provisions of the act certain textile fibers in finished goods ready for the consumer. Among others, these include used, secondhand products, fabrics used in essentially nontextile products, such as shoes and handbags; sewing threads; coated fabrics; interlinings, filling, and padding used for structural purposes, not for warmth; and nonwoven fabrics intended for one-time use.

er's (sponsor's) name and address or registered identification number also must be given on the label, and the country of origin must be given for imported fabrics. A list of generic or family names of fibers and their definitions compiled by the Federal Trade Commission is included in the act. Unfortunately, however, because of the technical nature of the definitions, some generic terms like "polyester" and "acrylic" cannot be readily comprehended by the consumer. These requirements are a step in the right direction to guide consumer purchases. But fiber content is not the sole criterion for judging how a fabric will perform. Of equal significance affecting use and performance are the following factors: (1) type and quality of the yarn, (2) type of fabric construction, (3) quality of the finishes including the coloring of the fabric, and (4) features of the construction of the garment or home furnishing.

The label may be made up by the manufacturer or by the retailer. The retailer's label must subscribe to the TFPIA, and the retailer must keep a record of the data that appeared on the label together with the vendor's name. In fact, department stores, retail chain organizations, wholesalers, manufacturers, and the federal government have contributed to informative labels. But it is difficult to standardize data that appear on a label. The TFPIA, in requiring fiber content and the sponsor's name, has taken a valuable step in that direction. In so doing, the government has imposed a mandatory standard. The Wool Products Labeling Act, passed in 1939 and later amended, is also mandatory; it requires that the types of wool (new wool and recycled wool) be disclosed on labels.

Since fur fibers may be used in textile blends, the Fur Products Labeling Act of 1951, amended in 1961, should be included here. The act requires that, in advertising a fur, the name of the animal from which the fur comes must be used. The use of the name of any other animal is not permissible. The name of the animal and the country of origin must appear on the label. An original pelt cannot be altered without naming the pelt that was used in the alteration. A simile to describe a fur quality, or a deceptive use of the adjectives "domestic" or "imported," is not permissible.

The Flammable Fabrics Act, passed in 1953 and amended since, is also mandatory. The objective in this case is to prohibit the sale of fabrics or clothing that would be so flammable as to be dangerous when worn.

In 1967 Congress passed the Consumer Product Safety Act, setting up a Consumer Product Safety Commission. The responsibilities for implementing the Flammable Fabrics Act as well as other hazardous substance and safety acts were assigned to the new commission, which requires that many textile products carry labels indicating that they meet the flammability standards set. (See Chapter 7.)

The Wool Products Labeling Act, the Flammable Fabrics Act, and the Textile Fiber Products Identification Act were intended to protect the consumer against deception in labeling and, with the exception of the Wool Act, against the misrepresentation of merchandise in advertising. These laws are also

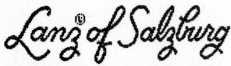

MADE IN U.S.A. WITH LOVE
MACHINE WASH TUMBLE DRY MODERATE
TEMP. MINIMAL SHRINKAGE IF IRONED.
DO NOT USE BLEACH

RN 37566

Figure 1.5 A permanent care label. (Courtesy of Lanz of Salzburg.)

intended to protect the manufacturer against unfair methods of competition. The Federal Trade Commission administers these laws. A retailer who fails to follow the regulations may receive cease-and-desist orders from the commission and unpleasant publicity. The Wheeler-Lea Act of 1938 made violation of a cease-and-desist order punishable by a fine up to $5,000. Appeals for review of the case may be made to a circuit court of appeals.

Mandatory Care Labels

The rules just discussed do not require that information on how to care for textile products be included. While many manufacturers did provide such information, the tags were easily removable and were frequently not available for future guidance. Accordingly in 1972, with a revision in 1981, the Federal Trade Commission put into effect a regulation requiring that most apparel, carpets and rugs, upholstered furniture, draperies, and bedding and bath towels (and also the nontextiles: leather and suede garments) carry permanently attached labels, good for the life of the article, giving care and maintenance information. These may be woven or printed labels, sewn, glued, or fused to the products themselves. (See Fig. 1.5.) In the case of yard goods, except remnants, the care instructions are to be printed on labels that carry a code that corresponds to the label at the end of each bolt. These labels are given to the customers at the time of purchase and may be sewn to the finished garments. Products that are exempt from the foregoing requirements include those that do not require routine cleaning, such as hats and gloves, and articles sold for $3 or less that are completely washable, such as undershorts containing no wool. The standard terminology appearing on labels is discussed in Chapter 16.[3]

Informative Labels Voluntarily Applied

Grade standards and labels of the ABC variety, often used on canned foods, are not applied to textile products. To the consumer, a combination of various features, including style, is more important than a narrow definition of

---

[3]See Appendix D for details of the federal regulations.

quality. However, many voluntary labels and advertisements do provide information that denotes quality. For example, the phrase *pima cotton, 2 × 2 mercerized broadcloth, sanforized* can mean a great deal to the trained consumer. *Pima* means that the cotton fibers are extra long, except for Sea Island, the best quality. The term *2 × 2* means the yarns are made of two single-stranded yarns twisted together; they are more durable than are single yarns of the same diameter. *Mercerized* means that the cloth has been treated with chemicals to give added strength and luster. *Sanforized* means that there is not more than 1 percent residual shrinkage (one-fourth of an inch to a yard). Thus, with good-quality cotton fiber, strong yarns, luster, and minimum shrinkage, this broadcloth should prove serviceable for a tailored blouse or shirt.[4]

Voluntary Industry Standards

There are standards voluntarily developed by industry that are used as a basis for labeling consumers' goods. Such standards may be set up by a manufacturer for a product he or she makes. The purpose is to make products that are uniform and quality controlled. Most of these voluntary standards in the textile industry are the result of the general consensus of the parties involved. For example, USA Standard L22 was the result of a voluntary agreement of almost thirty trade associations representing various segments of the textile industry, technical societies, and consumer groups. Minimum requirements based on features deemed essential to the satisfactory performance of various types of textile merchandise in their respective end uses were specified in L22.

An example is the suggested standard for girls' blouse or dress woven fabrics. It includes breaking and tearing strength; dimensional change in laundering and dry cleaning; absence of odor; colorfastness to light, perspiration, crocking, atmospheric gas, laundering, and dry cleaning; yarn shifting or slippage; retention of hand (feeling of fabric); character and appearance; seam strength; and features of the garment other than the fabric.

Textile merchandise that meets these voluntary standards may bear a tag with an L22 designation, signifying the kind of performance guaranteed for the item in question. These standards form the basis for care labeling discussed earlier in this chapter.

Standards and methods of testing have been established by various technical societies and trade associations, particularly the United States American Standards Institute (USASI) (formerly the American Standards Association), the Association for Textile Technology (AATT), the American Society for Testing and Materials (ASTM), the American Association of Textile Chemists and Colorists (AATCC), and the International Fabricare Institute (IFI).

---

[4]Brief mention should be made of the British "Tel Tag" system designed to provide useful, accurate, and readily comprehensible information for products at the point of sale. Performance or wear information is provided, but not care. The information furnished on the tags must be substantiated by official tests.

Seals of Approval Based on Standards and Guarantees

The National Bureau of Standards of the U.S. Department of Commerce has worked out commercial standards for (1) testing a fabric's colorfastness to sunlight, perspiration, laundering, and crocking (rubbing off of color); (2) control of shrinkage; and (3) crease resistance. (See Chapter 8 for a discussion of standardized methods of testing and reporting.) Although manufacturers are encouraged by the National Bureau of Standards to use self-identifying quality-guaranteeing labels or tags to indicate that a set of specifications has been met or exceeded, these guarantees are not enforced.

Conformity to Quality

Standards set by the USASI in cooperation with technical societies and with groups of manufacturers, retailers, dry cleaners, and consumers permit the manufacturer to label goods as meeting the Institute's standards. These standards cover many phases of quality.

Laboratories may give goods that pass their tests certified seals of approval for use in labeling and advertising. One of the best known consumer protection programs is that of the *Good Housekeeping* magazine. Since 1885, the magazine has exercised strict editorial judgments in the consideration of products it will accept for advertising and for use of its seal. These judgments, based on investigations by the technical staff of the Institute, comprise the basis of the *Good Housekeeping* consumers' refund or replacement policy.

Under this policy, if any product or service advertised in any issue of the magazine is defective, *Good Housekeeping* will, upon verification of the complaint, replace such product or service or refund to the consumer the price paid for it. The details of this consumers' policy are stated in each issue of the magazine.

Should certain advertisers wish to use the seal beyond the pages of *Good Housekeeping* magazine, such as on labels or in advertisements in other media, they may do so. (See Fig. 1.6.) The use of the seal is contingent upon the advertiser's signing an agreement governing its use. Again, endorsement of a product and the claims made for it are based on investigations made by the Good Housekeeping Institute.

Figure 1.6 *Good Housekeeping* consumers' seal. (Reproduced courtesy of *Good Housekeeping.*)

There are also some well-known textile manufacturers' guarantee programs. A guarantee, in strictly legal terms, means that if an article has not lived up to its promise of performance, the guarantor (company) will replace the item or return its original price to the consumer within a stated period of time. The Everfast color guarantee was the first program of this type. In 1921 Everfast Fabrics, Inc., guaranteed money back on the purchase price of the fabric plus the construction cost of the garment. In 1962 Monsanto introduced its Wear-Dated program, which guaranteed the replacement of a garment or refund of money if it failed to give normal wear for a year. The Badische Corporation has apparel certification for a full 365-day warranty on fabrics made with its Zefran acrylic and nylon products. Should the product fail to give normal wear for 365 days from date of purchase, it will be replaced or the full purchase price will be refunded. The Allied Corporate Technology's program has a three-year guarantee for commercial or contract carpets. J. P. Stevens & Co., Inc., offers a ten-year guarantee for its fiber glass screening.

The Celanese licensed trademark program attempts to develop the confidence of the trade and the consumer in Celanese's good fabric performance. It strives to make known that a Celanese hangtag means exactly what it says. To qualify for a licensed fiber trademark, a company's fabric must pass specific Celanese tests for specific end uses. Since the Celanese Corporation is a fiber manufacturer, it must make sure that the quality of its fiber in the tested fabric has been maintained. In guiding the fiber into the appropriate end uses, the fiber company must work with the mill, converter, finisher, dyer, printer, manufacturer, and retailer. Celanese must assure the members of the textile industry and the quality-conscious consumer that the nature and quality of the product are controlled through testing for the promised performance. The company feels that this assurance is worth the price because it protects profitability and insures the consumer against false claims.

Ratings and Testing

Textile research laboratories are generally of two kinds: (1) public laboratories that test fabrics for anyone on a fee basis (the United States Testing Company organized in 1880 represents this type), and (2) private laboratories that test fabrics for manufacturers and retailers (in some cases the laboratory may serve as a quality-control agent for certain manufacturers). Better Fabrics Testing Bureau is an example of a private organization.

In addition, large chain stores may have their own laboratories for research and quality control. Large department stores may also maintain testing bureaus for analyzing customers' complaints and for maintaining standards of quality. (See Fig. 1.7.)

When informative labeling is lacking, the consumer often consults *Consumer Reports* or the *Consumers' Research* magazine for guidance about the purchase of textiles and other products. *Consumer Reports* is a monthly publication of

Figure 1.7 Textile testing then and now. Today the J. C. Penney Co. tests many types of merchandise in a large laboratory in New York City and in a huge field testing site in Connecticut to assure high quality. (Photo courtesy of J. C. Penney Co.)

Consumers Union (P.O. Box 1949, Marion, Ohio), a nonprofit organization established in 1936. *Consumers' Research* magazine is published monthly by Consumers' Research, Inc., a nonprofit organization established in 1929 in Washington, New Jersey. These organizations are testing agencies established for the purpose of making science more effectively serve the interest of the consumer. They provide the buyer with the same type of advisory service that the technical staff provides for its own industrial establishment. The Consumers Union, in its *Consumer Reports,* rates items that have been tested. For example, when Consumers' Union judges the test samples to be of high overall quality and appreciably superior to other rated items tested for the same report, they are grouped in order of overall preference. A rating of one item sold under a brand name is not to be considered a rating of other items sold under the same brand name, unless so noted. "Best buy" ratings are given to products that rate high in overall quality but are also priced relatively low; they should provide more quality per dollar than acceptable items in that set of ratings.

Most retailers believe that consumers are entitled to know what they are buying and how an article will perform in use. This knowledge ideally should be carried from the mills through garment manufacturing plants to the retailer and right on to the consumer. To this end, the National Retail Merchants Association and the USASI developed the washing and dry cleaning instructions previously described.

Informative Advertisements

One of the most powerful tools for consumer education can be advertising. Informative advertising goes hand in hand with informative labeling.

The TFPIA specifies that the required information for labels be shown in the advertisement of textile fiber products *in those instances* where the advertisement uses terms that are descriptive of a method of manufacture or construction, which is customarily used to indicate a textile fiber or fibers or by the use of terms that constitute or connote the name or presence of fiber or fibers. In contrast to the labeling requirements, advertising does not have to specify percentages of fiber present but simply list fibers in order of predominance by weight. Fiber or fibers amounting to 5 percent or less shall be listed as "other fiber" or "other fibers." This regulation applies to display signs used as advertising media, but it does not apply to signs merely directing customers to the location of the merchandise.

A fiber trademark may be used in an advertisement of a textile fiber product, but the use of such trademark requires a statement of fiber content in at least one instance in the advertisement. When a trademark is used, it must appear in immediate proximity and in conjunction with the generic name of the fiber. The generic name of the fiber shall appear in plain, legible type or lettering of the same size or conspicuousness as the trademark in the copy of the ad. (See

Trademark information from ad at right

Action tests prove Hi-Bulk ORLON˙ gets the sweat out twice as fast as cotton.

Hi-Bulk ORLON ᴿ doesn't retain sweat like cotton. It "wicks" sweat away from the foot. So feet stay drier. And socks stay softer...don't get matted or hard during play. Look for the name Hi-Bulk ORLON✳ acrylic. You'll find it on all the best labels.

Figure 1.8 An informative and educational ad promoting the fiber manufacturer's trademark. (Photo courtesy of E. I. DuPont de Nemours & Company, Inc.)

Fig. 1.8.) Also, when a fiber trademark or generic name is used together with nonrequired information, it must in no way be false, deceptive, or misleading as to fiber content. Nonrequired information is permissible in conjunction with an advertisement of a textile fiber product if it is truthful, nondeceptive, not misleading, or not detracting from the required information.

Swatches and samples used in display or to promote textile fiber products are not subject to labeling requirements provided that

1. Samples and swatches are less than 2 inches in area and the data otherwise required on the label appears in the accompanying promotional piece.
2. Samples and swatches are related to a catalog to which reference must be made to make a sale and such catalog nondeceptively gives information required for labels.
3. Samples and swatches are not used to make sales to the ultimate consumer and are not in the form intended for sale or delivery to the ultimate consumer.

Labeling or advertising of textile fiber products may *not* employ any names, directly or indirectly, of fur animals. Names symbolizing a fur-bearing animal through custom or usage may not be employed, for example, "mink," "mutation," "broadtail." However, references may be made to furs which are not in commercial use, such as "kitten soft" or "bear brand."

Should a textile fiber product contain the hair or fiber of a fur-bearing animal in an amount exceeding 5 percent of the total weight, the name of the animal producing the fur is permissible, provided that the name is used in conjunction with the words "fiber," "hair," or "blend," as, for example, "80% Rabbit hair/20% Nylon."

The term "fur fiber" may be used to describe the hair or fur fiber or any mixtures of any animals other than sheep, lamb, Angora goat, Kashmir goat, camel, alpaca, llama, or vicuña where such hair or fur fiber or mixture exceeds 5 percent of the total fiber weight of the textile fiber product, and no direct or indirect reference is made to the animals involved, for example, "60% Cotton/40% Fur fiber" or "50% Nylon/30% Mink hair/20% Fur fiber."

But mere facts used without their application to consumer needs and without emotional appeal are not usually so successful as a combination of the three. Newspaper advertising that is truthful and at the same time educational builds customer confidence in the store. Mail-order houses have tried to improve their catalog through more informative descriptions of their merchandise.

Broadcasters communicate consumer education via consumer quizzes, lectures by educational speakers, and talks by merchandising store executives. Television demonstrates merchandise in use. Fashion shows, informative interviews on how to select merchandise, and programs with a women's magazine format are a few of the ways in which television brings consumer education into the home. Women's and men's fashion publications, decorating magazines, and fashion columns in newspapers are read by an increasing number of consumers.

The advertising media often share with the advertisers responsibility for the accuracy of claims made and the safety of products, refraining from publishing or broadcasting ads until sponsors present evidence that their products present no health or safety problems.

An Intelligent Sales Force

Even when an adequate label is appended to the merchandise, the salesperson is the chief disseminator of merchandise information, since many customers never read the label. Suppose that a customer wants a pair of boy's jeans for a seven-year-old. Before the advent of nylon or polyester blends, the customer had only a choice of all-cotton in navy blue. Nowadays, the choices are loden green, light blue, wheat, and other fashion colors. Jeans also come in regular, slim, and husky cuts. Most of them are durable press. Weights range from 10 to 14 ounces per square yard. There is a choice of all-cotton or cotton plus an appropriate percentage of polyester or nylon. Some manufacturers even offer jeans with "reinforced knees" for extra durability in high-wear areas.

The salesperson who serves this customer has had instruction from the department's buyer and therefore can be of real assistance. For example, the salesperson could communicate information on all cotton jeans: the heavier the better for tear and bursting resistance. But a lighterweight material, say an 11-ounce blend of cotton with 20 percent nylon or 50 percent polyester, will be about as durable as a 14-ounce all-cotton denim. As for color, yes, dark colors may darken the wash water. Durable-press blends are usually more resistant to abrasian, owing to a high percentage of man-made fiber. The salesperson can also point out strength features, such as reinforced bar tacks at each end of the hip pockets; the stitching of the side pockets for maximum security; the reinforcement of the fly at the bottom by rivets and bar tacks; the self-locking pull tab and double-stitched zipper tape; the waistband joined to the body by multiple rows of stitching; and double or triple seams wherever there is stress and strain.

Terminology on labels that requires interpretation resolves into a training problem for the retailer. Buyers are the logical interpreters of such information because they are in a position, if they do not know all the terms themselves, to get the correct meaning from (1) the manufacturer who sold them the goods, (2) the store's testing laboratory, or (3) a textile consultant outside the store. In some stores, a textile expert in the training department assists the buyer in training salespeople and helps in other ways when necessary.

Recognition of Consumers' Buying Motives

For some consumers, a brand name of merchandise may be a motivating factor in selection. For other consumers, factual information is demanded for satisfaction.

If consumers can judge the wearing quality of a fabric, they are more likely to get their money's worth. To determine wearing quality, one must recognize the inherent characteristics of a fabric, such as the kind of raw material (fibers) used, the strength and evenness of the yarns, the construction or weave, and the permanency of the dye or the finish. Textile education attempts to teach the consumer (1) to recognize and interpret the inherent characteristics of a fabric in light of its intended use and (2) to judge the wearing quality in relation to the price.

A customer who comes to purchase a textile fabric may not ask a single question; yet the salesperson who can determine the customer's likes and dislikes through conversation and sales talk will usually make a sale. The salesperson can also determine whether the customer is trying to satisfy physical and social needs. The customer's self-image is a consideration. Customers who believe themselves to be fashion leaders may want something new, different, high style; others will conform to what they recognize as acceptable.

The discriminating consumer has at least some of the following questions in mind when buying a fabric:

1. Is this suitable to my needs and wants? (suitability)
2. Can it be worn for a number of different occasions or purposes? (versatility)
3. Will it conserve time and effort? (convenience)
4. Will it wear well? (durability)
5. Will it be warm in winter? Is the texture suitable? (comfort)
6. Will this material be easy to dry-clean, launder, protect from moths, mildew, and so forth? (care)
7. Is the article safe to use, either flame-resistant or nonirritating to the skin? (safe)
8. Is the fabric good-looking? Will it look good on me? Will it go well with other garments or with the surroundings in which it will appear? (becomingness)
9. Is it in fashion? (appearance)
10. Does the price come within my means? Is it a "good buy"? (price)
11. Do I want to buy this merchandise because of associations it calls to mind? because someone else has something like it and because I don't want to be out of style? (sentiment)
12. Will ownership of this merchandise give me a sense of possessing something unique and of great rarity? (pride of ownership)
13. Will people be impressed with my selection? Is it in line with what my group recognizes as acceptable? (recognition)
14. Does this merchandise satisfy a creative urge, particularly in buying yard goods and accessories? (creativity)

In question 8 the customer is considering the "ensemble idea"—the harmonious relationship of fabrics, color, and fashion-rightness, not only among various units of apparel worn together, but also among home furnishings. The customer may also ask, "Is my selection in line with my self-image?"

In answer to question 9, if the fabric is in accord with prevailing tendencies and modes of expression, if it has beauty, becomingness, and fashion-rightness, it looks good in use.

In question 10, the customer is also asking, "Am I getting my money's worth?" If the customer is limited in the amount of money that can be spent for an article, the price is of great importance as a buying motive.

Many people buy old tapestries, laces, and rugs, not necessarily because of durability, but for the satisfaction of acquiring collections of fabrics. Other purchasers want materials that call to mind pleasant associations. For example, to a man whose childhood was spent in Asia Minor, where beautiful rugs are woven, rugs would recall boyhood. Such a person's buying motive is based on sentiment.

Rivalry is an instinct, and the striving to equal or excel forms an appeal to the customer who buys to "keep up with the Joneses." This customer thrives on recognition.

Few consumers need to consider all these factors before making a purchase. To one customer, price is paramount; to another, style; to another, becomingness; to another, possibly comfort. Knowing the factors inherent in the merchandise, the salesperson can relate the factors to the buying motive. For the man who wants comfort, durability, and ease of care in a shirt, the salesperson can recommend a polyester and cotton blend, emphasizing the strength (durability) and convenience of polyester (no starching or ironing required; quick drying) and the absorptive value of cotton (absorbs perspiration without feeling clammy).

SUMMARY

The well-informed consumer is the one who can recognize and interpret the inherent characteristics of a textile fabric in the light of its intended use. With knowledge of facts about the goods, consumers can judge its probable wearing quality and can determine whether they are getting their money's worth. Consumer education in textiles may be obtained through courses in merchandise information given by high schools or colleges. The consumer is being protected and informed as a result of federal legislation. The government has also realized the value of courses in retailing that are now given in high schools and department stores with federal support under the Vocational Education Act of 1963.

Furthermore, progressive retailers have established the policy of informative newspaper, radio, and television advertising. Likewise, mail-order houses have rewritten their catalogs so that the consumer may have better informative descriptions of their merchandise.

Retailers have also realized that the consumer depends upon the salesperson for merchandise information, and therefore they have developed training programs toward that end. It is the salesperson who must determine the consumers' buying motives and, knowing the factors inherent in the merchandise, relate those factors to the buying motives.

Discriminating consumers are those who plan to get their money's worth. A person who gets value for the price paid is the one who knows the characteristics inherent in a fabric that affect the qualities of *suitability, versatility, durability, convenience, comfort, care, safety, becomingness, appearance, price, sentiment, pride of ownership, recognition, and creativity.*

REVIEW QUESTIONS

1. With what aims are courses in textiles given to salespeople in department stores?
2. By what means may the new salesperson acquire a knowledge of the textiles that he or she is selling?
3. What practical value has a textile course to a high school student?
4. Why are individual research and education important for the textile industry?
5. (a) Why is a knowledge of textile fabrics important to the consumer?
   (b) How can he or she acquire such merchandise information?
6. (a) Of what value is an informative label to the consumer?
   (b) What limitations do informative labels have?
7. (a) Name the federal laws pertaining to textiles.
   (b) What are the objectives of each law?
   (c) How are these laws enforced?
   (d) Are the provisions of the TFPIA sufficient to give the consumer adequate information about the inherent qualities of a fabric to enable him or her to decide how it will perform in a given use? Why?
8. What is the responsibility of the buyer in training salespeople in the selling points of certain merchandise?
9. (a) What is the chief objective of the Flammable Fabrics Act?
   (b) To what textile products does this act apply?
   (c) What are the functions of the Consumer Product Safety Commission?
10. (a) Describe the application of mandatory care labels.
    (b) How do these labels aid the home sewer?
11. In what ways is the government attempting to control textile standards?
12. What is the educational value of advertising to the consumer?
13. What is meant by the phrase "getting your money's worth"?
14. (a) List the questions a customer may have in mind when he or she comes to purchase a textile fabric.
    (b) Which question or questions are the most important to you when you plan to buy (1) underwear, (2) hosiery, (3) a dress, (4) a suit, (5) a coat, (6) handkerchiefs, (7) curtains?
15. Explain what is meant by *sentiment* as a buying motive; by *recognition* as a buying motive.
16. Give an example, preferably from your own experience, in which the salesperson related the inherent factors in the merchandise to the buying motive.

PROJECTS

1. (a) Clip an advertisement for a particular item of clothing, such as a dress, suit, hosiery, underwear, or hat.
   (b) Underline all terms descriptive of the merchandise.
   (c) List any terms that you believe a consumer would have difficulty in understanding.
   (d) What are the chief merits of the advertisement?
2. Locate another advertisement that not only provides facts about the goods but is also educational in the sense that it helps the customer to make a wise choice, giving certain advantages of superiority, other than price, that are of importance to the reader of the ad (or the listener of a television or radio presentation).

3. Visit the yard-goods department of a department or fabric store in your community. Observe one salesperson. Notice how he or she displays the goods and the way in which he or she cuts it from the bolt. Observe the measuregraph (the device fastened to the farther side of the counter) and the way in which it is used by the salesperson to measure the goods and to compute the sale.

   (a) When you leave the store, recall your observations and rate the salesperson as excellent, good, fair, or poor. Give 60 points if the salesperson gave the customer intelligent information about the merchandise; 10 points if the salesperson displayed the goods attractively; 20 points if he or she cut the goods straight and with no apparent difficulty; and 10 points if he or she computed the sale quickly by reading the figures on the measuregraph.

   (b) Judging from the rating you have given the salesperson, what type of training would help to improve his or her selling job?

4. (a) Visit a large department store and check at least five articles of apparel and five of home furnishings made of textiles. Determine whether the federally required care labels are attached and note whether the piece-goods regulations are followed. Review this chapter to determine what articles are exempt.

   (b) Talk to five consumers to determine their attitude toward the use of care labels. Do they read care labels? Do they feel that the value gained exceeds some increased prices to cover the cost of the research involved and the cost of preparing the labels?

   (c) If the entire class will make an extensive survey of consumer attitude toward care labels, it is suggested that the results be sent to the U.S. Consumer Product Safety Commission in Washington, D.C., which re-evaluates its regulations from time to time.

GLOSSARY

Broadcloth   A tightly constructed cotton fabric in plain weave with a fine crosswise rib.

Buying motives   Reasons why consumers select a certain product for an intended use.

Buying points   Facts that the consumer considers important in selecting merchandise.

Cloth   See *fabric*.

Consumer   The purchaser of merchandise for personal and household uses—such as wearing apparel, household textiles, food, and all consumable goods.

Consumer education   The process of assisting the consumer in becoming a more informed buyer and user of goods and services, a more prudent manager of financial resources, and a more intelligent consumer-citizen.

Cooperative program (in school or college)   A program in which the student spends part of his or her program time in store service.

Customer   The person making the purchase decision who may be the consumer or the representative of the consumer.

Delamination   The separation of the layers of fabric in bonded goods.

Fabric (textile)   A material formed of fibers and/or yarns by the interlacing method of weaving, by the interlooping of knitting and lacemaking, by braiding, or by felting, bonding, fusing, or interlocking of web fibers.

Gray goods   Textile merchandise as it comes from the loom (where it has been constructed but before it is finished).

Informative label   A tag that gives a description of qualities inherent in the merchandise to aid consumers in appropriate selection for their needs and to give instructions for proper care of their purchase.

Merchandise Any finished good ready for consumer purchase.

Merchandise information Facts about products that will aid the consumer in selecting suitable articles.

Nylon A man-made textile fiber largely derived from petroleum, chemically combined with air and water.

Role playing A method of instructing trainees in selling situations in retail stores.

Selling points Product facts that are stressed by the salesperson in selling and advertising that help the consumer make a suitable selection.

"Show-tell" skit Method by which the salesperson demonstrates and explains pertinent facts about the merchandise.

Textiles Originally, a woven fabric (from the Latin verb *textere,* meaning "to weave"). Now the generic name for natural and man-made fibers and yarns used to construct fabrics and also the fabrics and the finished goods that retain to a degree the properties of the original fibers. See *fabric.*

Chapter 2

FIBER CONTENT
OF TEXTILE FABRICS

A salesperson in a specialty shop was assisting a young businesswoman in coordinating a blazer and skirt. The latter seemed favorable but hesitated. "Can I wash it or must I send it to the cleaners? And will it wear well?" she asked.

The salesperson had studied the federally required labels and knew that the material was polyester and cotton and was machine washable. She replied, "It's a combination of polyester and cotton. The cotton launders easily, absorbs moisture, and is comfortable. The polyester is durable, crease-resistant, and retains its shape well." This specific information about the *fiber content* of the material cinched the sale.

FIBERS, YARNS, AND CONSTRUCTION

A fiber is a hairlike unit of raw material of which cloths are made—for example, cotton, linen, rayon, silk, wool, nylon, and polyester.[1] To see what a fiber looks like, unravel a thread, called a *yarn*, from a sample of sheer cotton cloth. Untwist the thread. Each of the tiny hairs that make up the yarn is a fiber. To make a yarn, several fibers are grouped (often twisted) into a strand.

Cloth can be constructed from fibers or yarn in nine different ways:

1. *Weaving* is the interlacing of two sets of yarns usually at right angles.
   a. *Warp* (end) is yarn that runs lengthwise in a woven fabric.

[1]The TFPIA defines a "fiber" or "textile fiber" as a "unit of matter which is capable of being spun into yarn or made into fabric by bonding or by interlacing in a variety of methods including knitting, weaving, braiding, felting, twisting, or webbing, and which is the basic structural element of textile products."

Figure 2.1 Fibers are shown at the loose end of a yarn that has been pulled away from the piece of cloth shown below. (Photo by Jack Pitkin.)

    b. *Filling* (woof, weft, pick, shot) is yarn that runs crosswise in a woven fabric. These fillings are carried over and under the warp yarns. (See Fig. 2.1.)

    c. *Selvage* is the outer finished edge on both sides of the fabric. The selvage is formed by the filling yarn, which loops around the outside warp yarn to form an edge that does not ravel. Warp yarns always run parallel to the selvages. (See Fig. 2.2.)

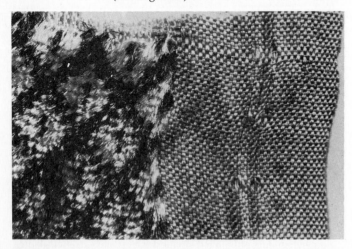

Figure 2.2 The selvage is the plain strip of fabric shown in the right half of the picture. (Photo by Jack Pitkin.)

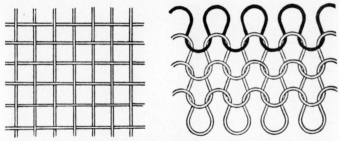

Figure 2.3   Left: Construction of a plain woven fabric. Right: Construction of a plain knitted fabric.

2. *Knitting* is the construction of an elastic, porous fabric by means of needles. One or more yarns form a series of connecting loops that support one another like a chain. (See Fig. 2.3.)

3. *Felting* is the process of matting fibers together (especially wool) by heat, steam, and pressure to form a fabric.

4. *Nonweaving* is the process of laying out a web of fibers into thin webs or mats that are held together by various applications: adhesive, plastic, solvents, heat fusion, entanglement of the fibers, stitching the fibers together, and stretching a plastic film to form fibers. (See Chapter 6.)

5. *Crocheting* is a construction made from yarn with just one hook or needle: a chain of loops is made from a single yarn.

6. *Braiding* (or *plaiting*) is the interlacing of three or more yarns or strips of cloth over and under one another to form a narrow tubular fabric.

7. *Knotting* (or *netting*) is the process of forming an open-work fabric or net by tying yarns together where they cross one another as in lace. Tatting is a form of knotted lace that is made with a shuttle filled with yarn.

There are two other forms of constructions based on a woven or knitted cloth:

8. *Bonding* is a process of joining two, or more layers of cloth with a layer of adhesive.

9. *Laminating* is a process of uniting a piece of fabric to a sheet of urethane foam (a plastic, frothy mass), especially the joining of a surface fabric to a foam plastic back.

Cloths or fabrics are known as "textile fabrics" when they are made from fibers by one of the aforementioned methods into pliable cloths.[2] (See Fig. 2.4 for constructions 3 through 9 in the listing.) Leather is not a textile fabric because it is not made of fibers and is not constructed into a fabric by any of the nine methods listed here. (Sometimes, however, leather is cut into narrow strips and is woven into the uppers of sport shoes and handbags. In such cases, it has been made into a textile fabric.) Paper used for stationery is not a textile fabric for the previously mentioned reason. A man's panama hat, however, is a textile fabric because it is woven from straw. A disposable pillowcase is made of bonded web—a nonwoven cloth (textile).

[2]According to the TFPIA, "Fabric means any material woven, knitted, felted or otherwise produced from, or in combination with, any natural or manufactured fiber, yarn, or substitute therefor."

Figure 2.4 Types of fabrics: (a) felted; (b) nonwoven; (c) bonded, with piece of cloth folded over and with back layer removed; (d) crocheted; (e) braided—three strips of knitted jersey; (f) unbonded; (g) knotted; and (h) laminated.

The term textiles includes both fabrics and fibers from which fabrics are made. (See Fig. 2.5.) Although the term originally applied only to woven fabrics, the present definition includes fabrics made by other methods of construction.

All other consumer merchandise is frequently called "nontextile goods." China, glassware, leather shoes and riding boots, stationery, wooden and steel furniture, jewelry, and silverware are some nontextile items.

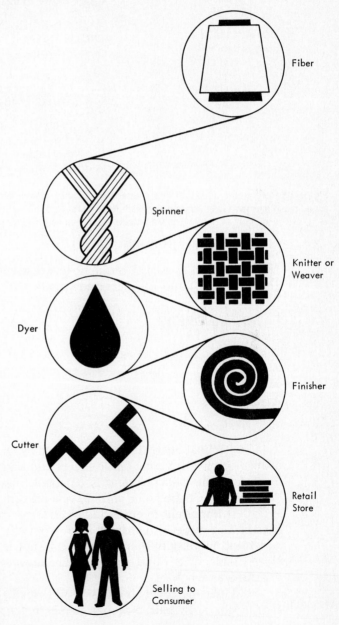

Fiber

Spinner

Knitter or Weaver

Dyer

Finisher

Cutter

Retail Store

Selling to Consumer

Figure 2.5 How most fabric is made and moved from source to consumer. (Courtesy of *Textile World* magazine.)

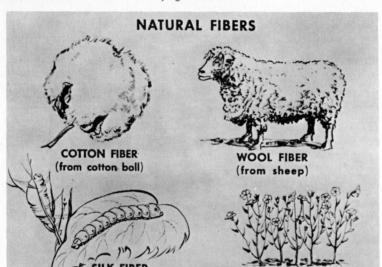

Figure 2.6 Before the advent of man-made fibers, clothing and other textile goods could be made only from fibers which nature provided, mainly, cotton, wool, silk, and linen. (Courtesy of Man-Made Fiber Producers Association.)

Classification of Textile Fibers

Two main classes of textile fibers are used in consumer goods: (1) natural fibers (Fig. 2.6) and (2) man-made fibers.

NATURAL TEXTILE FIBERS

These fibers that grow in nature can be divided into three groups: (1) animal, (2) vegetable, and (3) mineral.

Animal Fibers

Wool and Silk

The animal fibers that are most used in consumers' goods are wool, which is the protective covering of the sheep, and silk, cultivated or wild, which is the product of the silkworm and is obtained from its cocoon. Silk and wool are discussed in Chapters 11 and 12, respectively.

Less important fibers include hair fibers from camels, rabbits, goats, cats, horses, and cattle. They differ microscopically from wool and, as a rule, are stiffer and more wiry than wool and do not felt well. Cashmere, a goat fiber, vicuña and alpaca, and camel's hair, however, are quite soft and may be classified as wool.

Cat hair and cow hair can be used as textile fibers, but they are used mostly for fur felts. Cow hair, although harsh and coarse, can be made into blankets and carpets, but it should be mixed with other fibers. The sources and properties of hair fibers are discussed in Chapter 12.

Vegetable Fibers

Vegetable fibers are found in the cellulosic structure of many plants. Some are on the coverings of seeds, such as cotton, kapok, and coir. Others are in the outer layer of stalks, such as linen, ramie, jute, and hemp. Some are in the leaves, such as sisal, and some are grasses and reeds.

Cotton is the world's most important textile fiber, and Chapter 9 is wholly devoted to it.

Kapok

A vegetable fiber that comes from a plant or tree grown chiefly in Java, the West Indies, Central America, India, Africa, South Asia, and Brazil, kapok is a silky fiber, finer than cotton but not as adaptable to spinning; hence, it is not used in woven cloth. Mattresses and pillows are filled with kapok. Kapok dries quickly and is serviceable for life preservers because it is buoyant and light in weight. After a season's use the kapok filling can become heavy and nonbuoyant.

Coir

This is a hard, reddish-brown fiber obtained from the outer shell of the coconut. Coir is prepared by hand or by machines with fluted iron rollers that crush the husks. Broken fibers are dried in the sun, then cleaned, and are used for mattresses. The finer grades of mattress fiber can be made into rope and cocoa matting. The stronger, coarser fibers are made into hanks and sold for brushes, primarily to the European market. From strips of leaves of the coconut palm, a thread can be made that is elastic, lightweight, and waterproof. It is used in mats, bags, hats, and slippers.

The Bast Fibers

Flax fibers, the source of linen yarns and cloth, are the most important. These and the minor bast fibers, ramie or rhea, jute, and hemp, are discussed fully in Chapter 10.

Sisal

Sisal, from the leaves of a tropical plant, is often called *sisal hemp*. This is a hard fiber larger and stiffer than the bast fibers, flax, hemp, jute, and ramie. Sisal grows on large planatations in Java, Haiti, Kenya in East Africa, West Africa, and Central America. We import most of our sisal from the first three countries.[3] White fibers are obtained from the leaves of the agave plant (*Agave sisalana*). Principal uses are for cordage, ropes, and binder twine.

[3]J. M. Matthews, *Textile Fibers*, ed. H. R. Mauersberger, 6th ed. (New York: John Wiley & Sons, Inc., 1954).

The uses for sisal.[4]   The main use for sisal fiber is in the manufacture of strings, twines, and ropes. Low-grade fiber is used for sacks, but these are not very popular because of their coarseness. In agriculture, baler and binder twines use a considerable amount of sisal fiber. Low-grade fiber is used in the mat and carpet industries. Pile carpets are being manufactured successfully in Holland. And on the continent of Europe and in England, the use of sisal for matting is beginning to supersede the better known coir matting.

Grass, Rush, and Straw

Cured prairie grass from Minnesota and Wisconsin is bound together into a rope for weaving into grass rugs for sun rooms, porches, and summer homes. Rush, generally made of reeds that grow in sluggish waters of Europe and the Far East, is similarly used in rugs.

Straw fibers are obtained from stems, stalks, leaves, and bark of natural plants. Following are names of straws, many of which are woven into hats: baku (fibers of bari palm of Ceylon and the Malabar Coast), balibuntal (from unopened palm leaf stems), leghorn (from a kind of wheat grown in Tuscany), milan (from Milan, Italy), panama (from toquilla straw of Ecuador), toquilla (from jippi-jappa leaves), and tuscan (from bleached wheat stalks grown in Tuscany).

Paper

Made mainly from linen, cotton, and hemp rags, and from straw, bamboo, jute, and wood, in sheet form paper is a nontextile. But fine strips of paper made of wood pulp can be twisted into yarn and used in floor coverings and porch furniture. Ordinarily, paper used in the manufacture of so-called "fiber" rugs is weak when wet, and if thoroughly drenched will become mush.

Although paper may be so treated as to present a good appearance as textile fabric, it is not durable, comfortable, or serviceable as a textile yarn. Consumers should consider carefully before they purchase fabrics containing paper.

Disposable items come under the classification of *throwaway fabrics* and are really nonwoven goods usually made of webs of cotton, rayon, nylon, or polyester that are fused or bonded with a cementing medium or by entanglement.[5]

Mineral Fibers

Asbestos is said to be the only fibrous mineral found in nature, although it is true that fabricated sheets of gold, silver, and aluminum are cut into narrow strips and are used as yarn for luxury fabrics.

[4]Result of research written especially for *Textile Fabrics* by Tongoni Plantations Ltd., Christo Galanos, director, Nairobi, Kenya.

[5]See Chapter 6.

Asbestos is obtained from rocks primarily in Quebec, Canada; Southern Rhodesia (Zimbabwe); South Africa; and Russia. It is noncombustible and reisistant to all liquids except strong acids. Its major uses are in the automotive equipment field and now flights into the stratosphere, any point where great heat must be resisted.

Because asbestos fibers are long enough (about one-fourth of an inch), they can be spun and woven into cloth and used for protective clothing, gloves, stove pads (to place over the flame), insulation for hair dryers, and safety curtains for theaters.

But asbestos has one serious drawback. In the production process and in use, the fibers may become airborne and be inhaled into the lungs, causing serious respiratory disease among both mill workers in the plants and consumers exposed to these fibers. Examples are hair dryers of a few years back that were insulated with asbestos and that blew the fibers directly onto the users, and schoolroom ceilings, coated with asbestos as a fire protective measure, where, with age, the asbestos flaked off and was inhaled by students. The attendant legal problems probably account in part for the demise of some major manufacturers of asbestos.

Where the danger of airborne particles is eliminated asbestos is still used, although a recently developed ceramic fiber (made from clay) may replace asbestos for some industrial applications, especially where high heat must be withstood.

Status of Natural Fibers

The natural fibers that we have been discussing continue in top place from the standpoint of world production, even though they have dropped from 68 percent of total production in 1966 to 53 percent in 1979, with man-made fibers increasing from 32 percent to 47 percent. In the United States natural fibers are relatively much less important, with only 25½ percent of total production.

Cotton is by far the major natural fiber, accounting for over 90 percent of the world's natural fiber production. Its production is still on the increase; wool production has been declining slowly; and silk is about holding its own in actual poundage but not in percentage of the total.[6]

MANUFACTURED OR MAN-MADE FIBERS

According to the TFPIA, the term *manufactured fiber* means "any fiber derived by a process of manufacture from a substance which, at any point in the manufacturing process, is not a fiber." This act lists the generic or family names

---

[6]Data on world production from the *Textile Organon* for July 1980 and November 1982. Percentage of natural fiber production in the United States based on poundage of mill consumption reported in the *Man-Made Fiber Fact Book* (for 1980) of the Man-Made Fiber Producers Association.

and definitions for manufactured fibers established by the FTC for use in labeling and advertising consumer goods. No other names may be substituted for these generic names unless and until established by the FTC.

Rule 7 of this act names twenty generic names of manufactured fibers (see Table 2.1), along with their respective definitions. (See Chapters 13, 14, and 15 for technical definitions.) It will be noted that the definitions of these generic names by the FTC are couched in technical, chemical terminology that a salesperson or consumer would not be likely to understand. Yet these terms must be used by labelers and advertisers just as the generic names of the natural fibers—cotton, linen, silk, wool—are used. Familiarizing consumers with these terms requires considerable training of salespeople so that they can explain the terms adequately. Simplification of these definitions should be most helpful in this training.

Table 2.1 Classification of Man-Made Fibers

Fibers Derived from Pure Cellulose	Chemically Derived Fibers	Fibers Derived from Nonfibrous Natural Substances
Rayon (purified cellulose)	Nylon (polyamide)—largely derived from petroleum, chemically combined with air and water	Rubber (natural or synthetic rubber including lastrile)
Acetate (cellulose acetate)		Glass (molten glass)
Triacetate (modified acetate—higher ratio of acetate to cellulose)	Acrylic (resin)—coal, air, water, petroleum, limestone	Metallic (metal, plastic coated metal, metal coated plastic, or core covered completely by metal)
	Modacrylic (modified acrylic)—acrylonitrile, and other materials	
Alginate[a] (from seaweed)	Polyester (resin)—coal, air, water, petroleum	
	Saran (vinylidene chloride)	Azlon (protein—casein, peanuts, corn)
	Vinyon (vinyl chloride)	
	Olefin (propylene gas and ethylene gas)	Ceramic[a] (clay)
	Vinal (polyvinyl alcohol)	
	Nytril (vinylidene dinitrile)	
	Spandex (polyurethane)	
	Anidex (elastomeric acrylate)	
	Aramid (elastomeric aromatic polyamide)	
	Novoloid (phenolic)	
	Fluorocarbon[a] (fluorine and carbon)	
	Carbon[a]	

[a]Even though these are generic names for textile fibers, they have not been recognized by the Federal Trade Commission, probably because they are used primarily for industrial, not consumer, goods. Ceramic and carbon are still experimental.

To comprehend the meanings of the generic terms, a general description of broad bases for classification of manufactured fibers should be helpful.

Fibers Derived from a Cellulosic Base

Some fibers, such as rayon and acetate, have a base of natural plant cellulose, the same as cotton. Other fibers are based on protein found in milk, soybeans, or corn meal. Others are based on natural rubber from the rubber tree. Cellulosic fibers are treated fully in Chapter 13.

Fibers Derived Synthetically from a Noncellulosic Base

Nylon, Polyester, Acrylic, Modacrylic

The fibers in this classification may be called general-purpose fibers since they are widely used for many kinds of clothing and for many industrial purposes. The fiber-forming substances are chemical compounds created largely from petroleum and natural gas. These compounds are also used for plastic materials. They are extruded through a spinneret to form fibers. (See Fig. 2.7.) They are treated fully in Chapter 14.

Other noncellulosic man-made synthetic fibers may be called special-purpose fibers. They are included in Table 2.1 and are discussed in Chapter 15 and defined in the glossary at the end of that chapter.

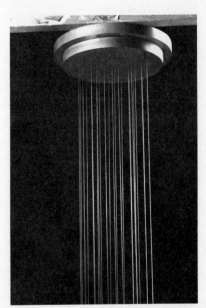

Figure 2.7 A spinneret in action. A chemically developed solution is being extruded through a spinneret to form fibers that are promptly hardened. (Photo courtesy of Man-Made Fiber Producers Association.)

Hydrophilic and Hydrophobic Fibers

From the point of view of water absorbency, textile fibers are classified as "hydrophilic" and "hydrophobic." The former absorbs and retains water and the latter absorbs little or no water. These terms are derived from the Greek words *hydro*, meaning "water," *philic*, meaning "to favor," and *phobos*, meaning "fear." The term "hydroscopic" denotes the property of certain fibers to retain moisture.

The natural fabrics (cotton, linen, silk, and wool) and the cellulosic-based man-made fabrics (rayon and the acetates) are hydrophilic; the noncellulosic man-made fibers (such as nylon, polyester, and the acrylics) are hydrophobic. Since the hydrophilics absorb perspiration, they are more comfortable for summer clothing, whereas the hydrophobics tend to feel clammy. However, a hydrophilic finish can be applied to clothing made of hydrophobic fibers to make them water-absorptive and provide "breathability."

The Economic Status of Man-Made Fibers

The genius of researchers in the field of chemistry, especially in the United States and England, accounts for two great modern industries—man-made textiles and plastics. The two fields are closely related, with the chemical composition from which nylon and polyester are extruded into textile fiber being the same as that molded, cast, or laminated in plastic materials of many sorts.

In the United States, man-made fibers account for about 75 percent of all textile fibers consumed, leaving only about 25 percent for the natural fibers. The older cellulosic fibers (rayon and acetate) account for only some 10 percent of the man-made fiber production, with the rest represented by the noncellulosic fibers.[7]

The price of cotton yarn ready for the fabric mill is much higher than the price of raw cotton. In late 1980, the mill price for cotton clothing yarn was about $1.20 a pound and for polyester filament about 80 cents a pound. It takes about 6.9 pounds of crude oil to produce 1 pound of polyester. When oil prices rise more rapidly than the price of cotton yarn, cotton can become more competitive on a price basis.[8] (See Table 2.2.)

In Appendix B, the table entitled "Fiber Trademarks Listed by Generic Fiber Names" presents the generic names of the manufactured fibers, trademarks, features, and producers. In general, the companies listed in the table make both fibers and yarns. Most do not make fabrics.

A classification according to the man-made material from which each class of fiber is derived appears in Table 2.1. With this guidance, the generic classification of manufactured fibers established by the FTC under the TFPIA should be more meaningful.

[7]The percentages calculated from Table 1433 of the *1980 Statistical Abstract of the United States* (Washington, D.C.: Government Printing Office, 1980).

[8]International Fabricare Institute, *Fabricare News,* October 1980.

Table 2.2 Average Annual Market Prices of Selected Textile Fibers ($/lb), Selected Years 1965–1982

	1965	1971	1973	1974	1975	1977	1979	1982
Polyester staple[a]	$0.84	$0.38	$0.38	$0.46	$0.48	$0.56	$0.60	$0.77
Rayon staple[b]	0.72	0.27	0.33	0.51	0.51	0.58	0.65	0.85
Cotton[c]	0.31	0.31	0.58	0.60	0.49	0.66	0.69	0.68
Wool[d]	1.25	0.67	2.47	1.62	1.55	NA	NA	NA
Wool[e]	1.19	0.66	1.58	1.13	0.88	NA	NA	NA
Polyester filament[f]	1.55	1.15	0.88	0.93	0.82	0.70	0.73	0.89

[a]1.5 denier 1½" staple, delivered (fibers cut short for spinning).

[b]1.5 and 3.0 denier regular rayon staple, delivered (fibers cut short).

[c]Strict low middling, 1 1/16" Group B mill points.

[d]Graded territory, 64s, good French combing.

[e]Graded fleece, ⅜ blood, 56s–58s.

[f]150 denier on tubes (prices from trade sources), delivered (lengthy man-made fiber used without spinning).

NA–Not available.

Source: U.S. Department of Agriculture, *Cotton and Wool Situation* (Washington, D.C.: USDA, 1982).

THE CONSUMER'S INTEREST IN FIBERS

The consumer is not usually interested in identifying fibers per se. Consumers are interested in how certain fibers will perform in use in a finished cloth. They want to know how the use of certain fibers in a cloth will affect its durability, suitability, comfort, ease in care, and attractiveness. These factors are the consumers' buying criteria. The Permanent Care Labeling Act of 1972 requires that finished articles of wearing apparel must have a permanently attached label.

The use of more than one fiber in a fabric might (1) give the fabric more uses than if it had one fiber, (2) give it a different feeling or "hand," (3) overcome a definite drawback of the other fiber or fibers, (4) lower the cost, or (5) give it a different appearance or style value.

There is an increasing amount of mixing of fibers. A fabric is a *mixture* if each individual yarn is composed of a particular fiber. For instance, the warp might be made of acetate, and the filling might be of rayon. The acetate is more dimensionally stable than the rayon. The rayon filling provides the texture with surface interest of the fabric.

A fabric is a *blend* if each yarn is composed of two or more different fibers. To make a blend, different fibers are mixed together before the yarn is spun. There is an increasing amount of blending being done today. The technical problem lies in the percentage of man-made fibers that must be added to make the fabric best suited to the particular use for which it is intended. Nylon blended with wool adds strength to the wool. One technologist states that each 1 percent of nylon increases the strength of a woolen yarn 3 percent. But the consumer might want to know about a specific use: "Is the presence of nylon in a wool blend advantageous for use in upholstery, for example?" The answer would be affirmative, because nylon adds strength and abrasion resistance—two important factors in this end use.

Sense of Touch

While the sense of touch is not very reliable in helping the consumer to identify textile fabrics (because of the man-made fibers and blends), one can still learn much from the hand, or feeling, of a cloth. Such factors as warmth, coolness, pliability, texture, bumpiness, smoothness, or strength of a fabric can be discerned by the sense of touch.

To develop a sense of touch, grasp the edge of a cloth between the thumb and index finger, with the thumb on top. Rub the thumb and forefinger across the cloth, then lengthwise, then in a circle. Each time a fabric is felt, words that best describe the feel should be brought to mind: pliability, elasticity or "give," warmth, softness, smoothness, and so on.

When is a cloth pliable and when is it elastic or resilient? Pliability is the degree of flexibility or "give" a fabric possesses. If a fabric is gripped by the thumb and forefinger of each hand and is pulled crosswise and then lengthwise, it will give, and is said to be pliable. A fabric that returns to its original shape and form after stretching is said to be elastic or resilient.

Smoothness is the ease with which the fabric slips if pulled between the fingers.

Sense of Sight

Luster (or sheen), fuzziness, fineness, and coarseness of a fabric may be observed. A Qiana nylon satin has a rich luster; a cotton flannel has a fuzzy surface; a linen table damask has a flat, smooth surface; a silk chiffon is fine and sheer; an acetate shantung looks bumpy. Texture of a fabric is easily observed.

On the basis of fiber content, sight, and touch, a consumer can decide whether the fabric has the suitability, attractiveness, ease in care, durability, and style-rightness that he or she requires in a given use. The informed salesperson should be able to help the customer make a decision.

THE INDUSTRIAL AND INSTITUTIONAL CONSUMER

Textile fabrics and the finished goods made from them are bought and consumed not only by the "ultimate" consumer but also by industrial and institutional consumers: hospitals, hotels, eating establishments, builders of roadways and embankments, and manufacturers of upholstered furniture and automobile bodies. Nonwoven fabrics are especially well suited for many of these uses. See Chapters 6, 14, and 15 for additional discussions.

FIBER IDENTIFICATION

Interest of the Manufacturer

To the manufacturers of cloth garments and household textiles, the TFPIA has made fiber identification a *must*. It is they who are responsible for seeing that the fiber content is specified on labels or tags. Who knows better what fibers went into a fabric than the manufacturer of the gray goods?

Interest of the Retail Buyer

Retailers are legally responsible for subscribing to the TFPIA. They rely on their vendors to supply them with merchandise that is labeled to conform to the act. Should the labels become detached from the merchandise or should imported merchandise be unlabeled, it becomes the retail buyer's responsibility to have labels made and affixed to the goods.

　　If the buyer is unable to identify fiber content, and most buyers do not have either the time or the equipment to do so, then the merchandise must be sent to a testing bureau. With the advent of two or three different fibers in a blend and the variety of man-made fibers that can be blended with each other or with natural fibers, fiber identification is not easy.

Laboratory Methods of Fiber Identification

Thirteen different classes of fibers (acetate, acrylic, modacrylic, nylon, olefin, polyester, rayon, saran, spandex, cotton, flax, silk, and wool) can be identified with certain modifications by seven tests.[9] The tests and a summary of the procedures follow.

　　1. *Effects of heat and flame.* A preliminary inspection is made to obtain information on the fabric's distinct characteristics. The heat and flame test should be applied to note the effects of heat, the burning characteristics, and the burning odor of the sample. The results of this test can be used in determining what subsequent tests are to be made.

Test Procedure

Slowly move a specimen of the fiber to be tested toward a small flame and observe the reaction of the fiber to heat. Then push one end of the specimen directly into the flame to determine the burning characteristics of the fiber. After removal from the flame, observe the fiber's burning characteristics again and note the burning odor. (Burning odor can be compared with that of known fibers.) Then allow the specimen to cool and check the characteristics of the ash.

　　You can use groups of fibers, short lengths of yarn, or small pieces of fabric as test specimens, unless the product to be tested contains a combination of yarns or a

---

[9]See *Textile World*, Vol. 3 (December 1961), 47–59. Procedures for all fiber identification are given in this section.

blend of fibers. In such cases, select individual fibers as test specimens from the textile material with the aid of a magnifying glass.

2. *Microscopic examination* (see Appendix A for longitudinal and cross-sectional photomicrographs of various fibers). It is advisable to make the first microscopic examination with low magnification (50 to 60X). The results of this test should verify or modify the conclusions reached in the preliminary inspection. If more microscopy is needed, groups of fibers (ASTM Test D 276-60T) from the specimen should be mounted and examined at a higher magnification (250 to 500X). The longitudinal appearance of the fibers should be compared with photomicrographs of known fibers. If further examination is needed, the cross-sectional appearance of the fibers should be studied.

3. *Solubility tests.* After completing the microscopic test, fibers are divided into groups for identification by solubility. If one already knows the identity of one or more fibers, one can verify this by testing a specimen to determine whether fibers dissolve or disintegrate in selected liquids (organic solvents as well as acids and alkalis).

4. *Stain tests.* Various manufacturers of dyes make special stains for fiber identification. The manufacturer provides test procedure and cards showing typical colors resulting from staining the principal fibers. The procedure is simple, but identification may be difficult because in an intimate blend all fibers may be stained about the same color. In this case, a stain from another manufacturer may prove more suitable, or examination under a microscope may prove helpful.

5. *Melting-point test.* A single fiber is placed between 19-millimeter microcover glasses on a calibrated Fisher-Johns melting-point apparatus. The fiber temperature is raised to the melting point.

6. *Moisture-regain test.* In this test, the specimens are all made of one kind of fiber or of two fibers that can be easily separated from each other. A specimen of fiber is first dried, weighed, and conditioned in air at 70° F, 65 percent relative humidity. To determine the moisture regain, record the percentage increase in weight of the fiber specimen during conditioning.

7. *Specific gravity test.* A fiber specimen is placed in a liquid of known specific gravity and is observed to determine whether it sinks or floats. This is a method of differentiating among some fibers.

Other tests for identification include a refractive index test and an infrared spectrum test (an infrared spectrophotometer is used to scan the spectrum of a solvent cast or melt-pressed film or potassium bromide disk made from a specimen of the fiber). These spectra can also be used to identify fibers within a generic classification. Another test is heat discoloration. A fiber specimen is exposed for a specified time in air at 350° F. The discoloration of this specimen is to be used as a standard for comparison with discoloration of an unknown specimen. Since mechanical properties of fibers vary with different classes (such as breaking strength and breaking elongation), these properties can sometimes be used as means of fiber identification.

SUMMARY

Although consumers are not particularly interested in the fibers themselves, they are interested in the effect that different fibers will have on the use and care of a fabric. A knowledge, then, of the classification of textile fibers is the first step in the study of textile fabrics. A knowledge of their classification will help in recognizing them in use.

Blends of various fibers will probably increase in importance because the blending of proper amounts of certain fibers will give the consumer a fabric that should serve his or her purpose better than one fiber alone. The noncellulosic manufactured fibers, particularly, can do much for giving "plus" qualities to blends; the public is learning that these man-made fibers can give increased wearing quality, crease and wrinkle resistance, and ease in the care of fabrics in which they are used. The consumer should realize that these manufactured fibers are not "miracle fibers." Each fiber has certain advantages and drawbacks, and the selection of one fiber or fibers over others for an intended use is the problem of the technologist. There is no one all-purpose fiber. In later chapters, the reader will discover what each fiber can do in use.

REVIEW QUESTIONS

1. (a) What is a natural fiber?
   (b) What is a man-made fiber?
2. (a) Name the most widely used natural fibers.
   (b) List the man-made fibers derived from cellulose.
   (c) How do acetate fibers differ from rayon?
3. What is Orlon, Dacron, Verel? (See Appendix.)
4. What laboratory tests are used to determine content?
5. Explain the difference between a mixture and a blend.
   (a) What are the advantages of the use of more than one kind of fiber in a fabric?
   (b) What do you think the future of blends will be?
6. (a) What is the importance of a knowledge of textile fibers to the consumer?
   (b) To the textile manufacturer?
   (c) To the retail buyer?
7. How may a good sense of touch be developed?

PROJECT

For one month check the advertisements in a daily newspaper to determine the end uses for each of the classes of generic fibers. Also check the trademark of each generic fiber. Compile the data to show for what articles the manufactured fibers are being used. Analyze the data and come to some conclusions as to where the fiber and yarn companies have markets for their various products.

GLOSSARY

Blend   A mixture of different fibers in the same yarn.

Bonded face fabric   The side of a bonded fabric used as the face (right side) of the cloth in a garment or other end use.

Bonding   Combining fibers into sheets or webs to form a nonwoven fabric or a process of joining two or more layers of cloth with a layer of adhesive.

Braiding (plaiting)   Forming a narrow band by intertwining several strands of cotton, wool, or other materials.

Cellulosic fiber   A fiber having a cellulose base. Includes natural fibers from plants and the man-made fibers, primarily rayon, acetate, and triacetate.

Crimp   A term referring to the wavy appearance of a fiber or yarn.

End use   Intended use by the consumer.

Felting   A method of producing fabric or interlocked fibers by an appropriate combination of mechanical work, chemical action, moisture, and heat. Processes of spinning, weaving, or knitting are not employed.

Fiber content   Amount of basic unit (raw material), such as cotton, polyester, wool, nylon, and so on, used in the fabrication of a textile fabric.

Finish   Treatment of a cloth after the gray goods come from the loom or knitting machines.

Generic names   Names in the public domain for the classes of natural and man-made fibers. See the glossaries in Chapters 13 and 15 for specific definitions.

Hand   A general term referring to the feeling of a fabric or yarn obtained by touching or handling, that is, soft, smooth, pliable, springy, stiff, cool, warm, rough, hard, and limp.

Hydrophilic fiber   An absorptive fiber with a great affinity for water.

Hydrophobic fiber   A nonabsorptive fiber with no or little affinity for water.

Knitting   The construction of a porous, elastic fabric by means of two or more needles. One or more yarns form a series of connecting loops that support one another, as in chaining.

Knotting   A process of forming an open-work fabric or net by tying yarns together where they cross one another.

Laminating   Bonding a foam or sheet of plastic to a cloth.

Mineral fibers   Textile raw material obtained from minerals in the earth, such as asbestos (natural) and silver, gold, copper, and glass.

Mixture   A fabric composed of two or more kinds of yarns, each yarn being made of one kind of fiber.

Natural fibers   Textile raw materials that grow or exist in nature: cotton, linen, hemp, jute, ramie, kapok, silk, wool, hair fibers, asbestos, and others.

Nonwoven fabric   A cloth made from a web of fibers that is held together by various methods (other than felting) such as the interlacing or intertwining of yarns.

Nylon   A generic name for manufactured fibers derived from polyamide resin.

Staple   A term descriptive of the average length of a cotton fiber in a sample or bale.

Synthetic fibers   Man-made textile fibers derived from natural bases or chemical bases.

Texture   The appearance of the surface of the fabric.

Tow   A continuous loose rope of man-made filaments drawn together without twist.

Warp   The yarns running lengthwise in a woven fabric parallel with the selvage.

Weaving   The interlacing of two sets of yarns, usually at right angles, to form a fabric.

Yarn   A generic term for a group of fibers or filaments, either natural or synthetic, twisted or laid together to form a continuous strand suitable for use in weaving, knitting, or some other method of intertwining to form textile fabrics.

See the glossary in Chapter 15 for a listing of other manufactured fibers.

Chapter 3

TEXTILE YARNS: THEIR MANUFACTURE AND USES

In Chapter 2 our consumer learned that fibers of which textile fabrics are made are very important for judging how a fabric will perform in a given use. But kind of fibers used is not the sole criterion. Yarns, construction, and finish must also be considered. In this chapter, yarns are discussed, and in subsequent chapters, construction and finishes are considered.

A yarn is a strand of natural or man-made fibers or filaments that have been twisted or grouped together for use in weaving, knitting, or other methods of constructing textile fabrics. The type of yarn to be manufactured will depend on the fibers selected; the texture, or hand, of the fabric to be made; and qualities such as warmth, resiliency, softness, and durability required in the fabric's end uses. In addition, the weave and the finish used will depend on kinds of fibers and yarns, end use of the fabric, and price.

The final fabric can be thought of as a linked chain, each link representing a process in the manufacturing of the chain. One link is fibers, another yarn, another construction, another finish. The final fabric can be of no better quality than the links of which it is composed. If, however, the fibers, construction, and finish of the fabric were not of the same excellence as the yarn, then the fabric could not be excellent in quality.

CLASSIFICATION OF YARNS ACCORDING TO USE

Yarns may be divided into two classifications according to their use: weaving yarns and knitting yarns. Thread, a special-purpose yarn, is discussed later in this chapter.

Weaving Yarns

Yarns for woven cloth are prepared for the intended end use. Yarns to be used in the warp, the lengthwise direction of a cloth, are generally stronger, have a tighter twist, and are smoother and more even than are yarns used for filling, the crosswise direction of a cloth. Novelty yarns may be used in the warp, but they are generally found in the filling. Highly twisted crepe yarns are usually found used as filling yarns.

Knitting Yarns

These may be divided into yarns for hand knitting and yarns for machine knitting. Knitting yarns are more slackly twisted than yarns for weaving. Hand-knitting yarns are generally ply, whereas those for machine knitting can be either single or ply. The following are some of the yarns used for hand knitting:[1]

1. *Knitted worsted.* The four-ply all-around yarn used for accessories, for the house, and for apparel. This is the most common weight of hand-knitting yarn, comprising 90 percent of the handmade yarn business.
2. *Fingering (baby or sock) yarn.* The fine yarn that was originally wool, but is found most commonly in acrylic for comfort and ease of care.
3. *Sport yarn.* The three-ply yarn used for socks, sweaters, and hats.
4. *Shetland yarn.* The two-ply yarn used for sweaters.
5. *Fashion or novelty yarn.* Any novelty structure.

All the yarns listed may be found in any fiber. Of the major fibers, rayon is the least likely to be used in the handmade yarn business.

YARN MAKING

Physical Structure

Yarn making is generally the second step in the manufacture of textile fabrics. Methods of manufacturing yarn depend on the type of fibers used and the type of yarn required. However, certain terminology is common to all yarns.

For instance, a single yarn is a single strand of strip or a strand of fibers and filaments twisted or grouped together. When two or more single yarns are twisted together the final yarn is called *ply*. Two-ply yarn is composed of two singles, three-ply of three singles, and so on. A cord is the result of twisting together ply yarns in a third operation. The types of yarn just described are regular yarns. Then there are novelty yarns that may be either single or ply. When plied, there is often a core or center yarn with other yarns twisted about it to give textural effect. Frequently these yarns are bound to the core by other strands to hold all yarns together. Furthermore, there are *textured* yarns— continuous-filament man-made fibered yarns that have been modified to change their appearance and hand. (See Fig. 3.-1.)

[1]This information is from Mary Colucci, National Needlework Association, New York City.

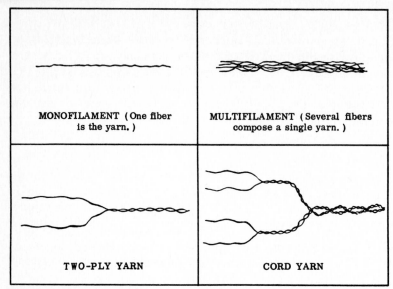

Figure 3.1 Yarn construction.

Methods of Yarn Manufacture

Raw fibers arrive at the yarn manufacturers in different forms. For example, cotton is in bales; wool in fleeces; cultivated raw silk in strands and waste and wild silk in bales; flax in bundles; rayon, acetate, nylon, and the other manufactured fibers on tubes, cones, cops, spools, or skeins.

The natural fibers are restricted in length. For example, cotton staple ranges from ¾ to 1½ inches long; linen averages 18 to 20 inches long in best grades. Man-made fibers are continuous or are cut up into predetermined lengths called *staple fibers*. If a fabric is to resemble cotton, the *tow* (groups of continuous filaments) is cut up into staple. Obviously, the basic processes for making yarn will vary. However, certain fibers are prepared for yarn by similar processes.

Carding and Combing

In general, fibers are blended or mixed before yarn manufacture actually begins. Cotton, wool, spun or waste silk, spun rayon, spun acetate, spun nylon, and many of the noncellulosics are made into yarn by carding and combing with little or no spinning. Although these processes vary with the fibers and from mill to mill, the terms and purpose of the operations are comparable.

Carding separates the fibers and puts them in a filmy sheet that is funneled into a soft mass called a *sliver*. Sheets of fiber are passed between rollers that are covered with card cloth with fine wires that perform a brushing function.

In cotton, this operation removes dirt and short fibers. Wool fabrics are made of woolen yarn, which is carded only, or of worsted yarn, which is both carded and combed. For woolen yarn, three carding operations put the fibers into a thin sheet or sliver suitable for yarn.[2] Staple man-made fibers are made into yarn in the same manner as cotton or wool, depending on the intended use of the fabric.

For waste, clippings, and rags, rather than sheets of fibers, a process similar to carding, called *garnetting,* is used. The material is passed through rollers covered with heavy wires that break up the material into fiber form.

Not all wool yarn is combed. Yarns that are carded only are called woolen yarns. These yarns are used for such fabrics as blankets, tweed coating and suiting, wool flannel, and wool broadcloth. Worsted yarns are both carded and combed, and longer fibers are selected for worsteds than for woolens. One long combing machine, operating slowly to avoid breaking the long fibers, makes the sliver. In combing worsteds, the short fibers are removed and the fibers laid parallel. The sliver is drawn out to its desired width and thickness. Worsted yarns are used in fabrics such as tropical worsted, gabardine, whipcord, worsted flannel, and wool sharkskin.

Combing of cotton is necessary when fine, uniform yarns are needed to give sheerness, luster, smoothness, and possibly durability. All cotton yarns are carded, but not all cotton yarns are combed. Only a small percentage of cotton yarns are combed. For combing, longer-staple cottons are selected. Combing makes the fibers parallel in the sliver and removes the shorter fibers. The sliver is drawn out narrower and narrower, depending on the fineness of the yarn to be made. Spun-silk fibers are also combed to lay fibers parallel and to remove the short ones. Man-made staple fibers intended to resemble combed cotton or worsted yarns would be combed.

Hackled and Well-Hackled Yarns

Hackling is the process by which flax is prepared for linen yarn. The purpose of hackling is to disentangle the flax fibers and to lay them parallel. For fine, even yarns, the fibers must be long and parallel; hence, more hackling is necessary. When yarns are well hackled, those in the trade may say that the yarns are combed. At any rate, the purpose of the operation and the results are similar to combing.

Reeling and Throwing

Raw silk is the long-fibered silk that is reeled from the cocoon and twisted into yarn. Several yarns are combined and twisted onto bobbins. If ply yarns are required, the strands are combined and twisted together. The combining and

---

[2]See carding of cotton in Chapter 9, carding of wool in Chapter 12, combing of cotton in Chapter 9, combing of worsted in Chapter 12, hackling of flax in Chapter 10, and reeling of silk in Chapter 11.

Figure 3.2 A woman spinning drawn from a scene painted on an ancient Greek vase. The tradition in Greece of spinning and weaving and of garment making goes back thousands of years. The epic story of *The Odyssey* relates that Penelope worked away at her loom for 20 years while awaiting Odysseus' return. (Courtesy of Olympic Airways.)

twisting is called *throwing*. The machine that performs this operation is a *throwster*. (See the glossary.)

Rayon, acetate, nylon, polyester, glass, and other man-made filament ply yarns, hard-twist voile, and crepe yarns are thrown. The term "thrown," then, applies to reeled-silk ply yarn and to man-made filament ply yarns in high twist. Regular filament yarns result from grouping fibers together so they lie parallel.

Spinning

The spinning operation draws out the *roving* (very slackly twisted sliver) and puts in the required amount of twist. (See Figs. 3.2 and 3.3.) The purpose of twist is to bind the fibers together and to hold in the ends of fiber. Generally speaking, the tighter the twist, the stronger the yarn. This is true to a certain point; then the yarn weakens and may finally break. Long fibers like linen and long-fibered raw silk do not require so much twist to give strength as do cotton and short rayon staple fibers. A low or slack twist makes a more lustrous, softer yarn than a tight twist. Slack-twisted yarn is needed when the fabric is finished with a nap (fuzzy surface). When a yarn is twisted to the point of knotting, a crepe yarn results. Warp yarns are usually twisted tighter than filling yarns because warp yarns have to stand tension in the loom in weaving. (See Fig. 3.4.) One way to identify warp and filling yarns is to compare amounts of twist in each yarn. Warp is frequently tighter. There are exceptions, however. Warps are generally stronger and therefore harder to break.

Figure 3.3 The old-time art of spinning with a wheel is not dead. This college girl is housed with a group of students who are interested in arts and crafts and natural history. (Photo courtesy of *Carleton Voice*, Carleton College, Summer 1974.)

Twist may be put into yarn in spinning or in subsequent plying operations. The direction of twist (right or left) and number of twists (turns) to the inch may be determined by a testing device called a twist counter. The number of turns to the inch can also be determined by very nontechnical means—a real rule-of-thumb method. Although the result may not be very accurate, the test will serve to compare amount of twist of other yarns tested by the same method. Unravel from a fabric about a 2-inch length of yarn. Grasp the yarn between the thumb and index finger of each hand. Leave about 1 inch of yarn in tension between the hands. A right-handed person should keep his or her left hand stationary. With the right hand, turn the yarn slightly until the direction in which the yarn untwists is evident. Then, still holding the yarn taut, roll the end between the thumb and index finger of the right hand. Each time the yarn rolls over constitutes a twist. A single yarn will pull apart when it is untwisted. When a ply yarn is untwisted, stop counting the twists when the single yarns lie parallel. The fibers will not pull apart in a ply yarn.

Single yarns are made in two directions of twist, right and left. The right

Figure 3.4 Chiffon, showing crepe yarns. (Photo by Jack Pitkin.)

twist is effected by twisting the sliver clockwise, and the left twist results from a counterclockwise motion. Right-twisted yarns are identified as Z twist, and left-twisted yarns as S twist. (See Fig. 3.5.) If a paper clip is attached to the end of a single yarn, and the end is allowed to hang free, the end will rotate. If the end rotates in a clockwise direction, the inherent twist is S; if in a counterclockwise direction, the yarn is Z twist. To make a ply yarn, the singles are usually twisted in one direction and the final ply twist in the opposite direction; for example, Z/S (Z is the direction of the twist for the singles and S is the ply twist). But a ply yarn may be S/S or Z/Z. A cable cord is S/Z/S or Z/S/Z; a hawser cord is S/S/Z or Z/Z/S. Cords, in addition to being made by twist, may be braided, woven, or knitted. A ply yarn is stronger than the combined strength of the single yarns composing it. Similarly, a cord is stronger than a ply yarn of the same size.

A practical illustration of how alternate direction in twist is used is in the filling yarns of rough and flat crepes. These crepes are often identified in the trade by their filling yarns as "2 × 2," which means 2 S alternating with 2 Z twists in the fillings of these fabrics. Two-by-two broadcloth, however, means two-ply yarn in warp and filling, not alternate direction in twist.

Figure 3.5 "S" and "Z" twists.

The word "spun" refers to a yarn that has been twisted by spinning. It is also applied to a yarn made of man-made staple fibers that have been twisted into yarn. Hence, nylon yarn made of staple fibers is called spun nylon. "Spun-dyed" has another connotation. This term is synonymous with "solution-dyed," which means that the dyestuffs are put into the viscous solution before extrusion, and then the dyestuff is locked in the fiber when the fiber hardens. In the same manner, man-made fibers which have a high luster may have dulling agents added to the fiber-forming substance before spinning.

Industrial Methods of Spinning Staple Fibers

Early Methods of Spinning

Staple fibers are the short fibers that have to be spun so as to hold together as yarn or thread. They are *natural* in the case of cotton and wool and the short broken fibers of silk and flax and *man-made* in the case of continuous fibers extruded through a spinneret that are then cut into short lengths for spinning purposes. The continuous fibers if not cut up need little twisting before weaving but are generally textured, as explained later in this chapter.

In about the middle of the eighteenth century, James Hargreaves of England invented the *spinning jenny,* and a few years later Sir Richard Arkwright designed an *automatic upright frame* that drew the cotton and wool into a spun yarn. Based on these developments, Samuel Crompton in 1779 created the *muel spinning frame* that could twist over 1,000 ends of yarn and wind them on tubes of paper or other material. The tubes could be withdrawn, leaving the package solely of yarn, ready for weaving. This machine was used for spinning wool and fine counts of cotton. No man-made fibers existed at that time.

Modern Methods of Spinning

Ring spinning.   The ring spinner automatically reduces the bulk and weight per inch of the roving, particularly of wool, cotton, and rayon, twists it into yarn, and winds it on a bobbin or spindle. The roving is fed through rollers that elongate it and carry it to a traveler. This is a small clip that carries the fiber rapidly around a stationary ring that is placed over a spindle that turns. The traveler, carrying the fiber as it is converted into yarn, whirls around the ring at thousands of revolutions a minute. The movement of the traveler and the turning of the spindle twist the roving into yarn, which, as a part of the same process, is wound on the spindle as it turns. Changes made in the diameter of the ring and the speed of the traveler, controlled by the spindle, change the diameter of the yarn.

Open-end spinning.   This is a relatively new process that makes a yarn directly from the sliver, which is elongated and brought together in a spinning unit that forms the yarn in a single continuous operation. The slivers of fiber are laid out in a thin stream by a rotary beater and are moved by air to a twisting device, commonly a rotating disk, that carries the fibers in a groove inside the circumference of the disk. As the fibers are drawn off, they become attached to the *open end* of the yarns already formed. The centrifugal force of the rotary movement causes the fibers to twist into yarn. In some installations, the operation is enhanced by giving a negative electric charge to the fiber and a positive charge to the twisting device.

Open-end spinning is gradually replacing ring spinning, since the increase in automation decreases the labor cost. Also, the yarns are more even, without thick and thin places. They have greater elongation potential than do ring-spun yarns but less length recovery.

Most of the newer machines are made abroad, some in connection with German-made robots. These cruise along the many positions in the spinning room, piecing strands of yarn together wherever there is a break and testing the yarn tension. The entire operation takes only 20 seconds and can be repeated 80 times an hour.

Figure 3.7 shows a robot taking the place of the live attendant in Fig. 3.6, where the open-end method is used.

New Specialized Methods of Spinning

With the rapid advancements in technology, newer methods of spinning are being developed. Some of these are reviewed briefly in the paragraphs that follow.

Figure 3.6 The spinning room attended by a person. Yarn can be spun by the new open-end method or in the older ring spinning system. Both methods twist the fibers into the yarn, but the open-end process uses air suction to draw fibers through a small opening to produce yarn whereas ring spinning is done mechanically with a series of rollers. The open-end method takes sliver directly from drawing and skips several steps used prior to ring spinning. Both methods twist the strands ten to thirty turns per inch to produce a strong, firm yarn. The amount of twist depends upon the eventual use of the finished yarn. (Photo courtesy of American Textile Manufacturers Institute.)

Figure 3.7 A robot-attended open-end spinning machine. (Photo courtesy of the American Textile Manufacturers Institute.)

No-twist yarn system. Yarns are twisted directly from the carded web and are held together by a binder, for example, resin. The quality of the yarn varies with the quality of the carding.[3]

Self-twist yarn system. Two rovings of fibers are manipulated to twist themselves to form a two-ply yarn. The rovings are passed between rollers that both rotate and oscillate in such a way that two rovings twist themselves together. The process is suitable for wool and relatively long-staple man-made fibers.

Direct spinning. One method of making yarn from man-made continuous filaments breaks them into staple fibers of various lengths by stretching. The fibers are then drawn into a sliver that is twisted and wound, all in one operation. These fibers are subject to shrinkage, which for some fabric constructions may be an asset.

Neo-spun (Toray) engineering. Using a false-twist method (see page 57), these fibers are entangled by air jets, while suction is used to make the outer fibers act as binders.[4]

Split film. Split film fibers result from fibrillation (drawing which increases strength in the direction of the stretch) so that the film breaks down into a

[3]"The Southern Regional Research Center (SRRC) No-Twist Yarn System," *America's Textile Reporter*, November 1980, pp. 36–40.

[4]Ibid., p. 40.

fibrous state. While fibers may be spun of the splits, they more commonly become a nonwoven fabric. See Chapter 6 for a detailed explanation.

Split or tape yarns. These yarns are formed by splitting film into ribbons or tapes. Some yarns may exhibit fibrillation.

Size of Yarns

To distinguish differences in weight and fineness, yarns are given size numbers called counts, lea, or denier. The term "count" applies to the size of cotton, wool, and spun yarns. The term "lea" applies to linen yarn, and "denier" applies to reeled-silk and filament man-made yarns.

For cotton and spun yarns, the standard used is 840 yards of yarn to the pound. If 840 yards of cotton yarn weigh 1 pound, the count is #1. If it takes 8,400 yards to weigh a pound, the count is #10, and so on. The higher the numerical count, the finer the yarn.

There are two methods of computing sizes of woolen yarns: one method, the American run count, is discussed here. If 1,600 yards weigh 1 pound, the count or size is #1, a very coarse yarn. The higher the number, the finer the yarn. The size of worsted yarns is determined by the number of hanks of 560 yards weighing 1 pound. If one 560 yard hank weighs 1 pound, the count or size is #1. If 5,600 yards weigh 1 pound, the count is #10, and so on. Yarns numbered 30s to 40s ("s" means single yarn) are very coarse. (See Chapter 12.) The higher the number, the finer the yarn.

Linen yarns use a lea of 300 yards as a base for figuring size. To find the size of the yarn, divide the number of yards weighing a pound by 300 yards. For example, if 3,000 yards weigh 1 pound, the count of the yarn is 3,000 ÷ 300, or 10. The higher the number, the finer the yarn.

The size of filament man-made yarns and reeled-silk yarns is designated in terms of denier. Denier (pronounced den´yer) is equal to the weight in grams of 9,000 meters of yarn. In yarns, 9,000 meters = 9,842.4 yards. If 9,842.4 yards of yarn weigh 150 grams, the yarn is 150 denier. If 9,842.4 yards weigh 75 grams, the denier is 75. Since the length of the yardage weighed is always the same, the yarns that weigh more must be larger in size. The lower the denier number, the finer the yarn. The number of filaments in a given filament yarn is indicated with the denier number; that is, 100—74 means 100 denier yarn composed of 74 filaments (See chapter 11 for the computation of International Denier in reeled silk.) A proposed universal yarn numbering system called "Tex" expresses the weight in grams of 1 kilometer length of yarn. Such a system was suggested in 1873 at an international conference in Vienna. But it was not until 1956 that action was taken when ten nations attending an International Conference for Textiles unanimously voted to adopt the system. Tex can be applied to all fibers. It is intended to replace the many diverse yarn numbering sytems. As the metric system is more widely adopted here, the use of Tex measurements should increase accordingly.

Sizing of Yarn

Even though sizing, the application of a finishing and protective agent, is often a finishing process applied to a fabric after weaving, it is also a similar process applied to the yarn, especially to the warp yarn. The sizing process applied to the warp yarn is called *slashing*. The warp yarn is coated by immersion in a liquid that contains the sizing material, such as starch (especially potato starch derivatives). The yarn is then dried by heat application prior to weaving. This treatment protects the warp yarn against injury in the weaving process and adds temporary strength and abrasion resistance to withstand the stress of weaving.

One of the major problems encountered with slashing has been the great amount of energy required to dry the yarn. A process called *high-pressure squeezing* has been developed to reduce the water "take-up" from the solution absorbed into the yarn. A squeezing process is employed as the yarn is immersed into the solution that reduces and controls the amount of water absorbed into the yarn. This greatly reduces the amount of energy required to dry the yarn. It also keeps the sizing at a required constant level.

Other methods to solve the problem are in the experimental stages. One is the use of a foam that substitutes air for water. Another, called *hot melt sizing*, melts the sizing and reapplies it with a roller. Again, there is no water to evaporate.[5]

Coloring of Yarn

When a yarn is dyed before it is woven, it is said to be yarn-dyed. Plaid ginghams are good examples of this method of dyeing. In the case of man-made fibers, where a chemical solution is extruded through a spinneret, the coloring is often added to the solution.

Yarns can also be printed before weaving. It is common practice to print warp yarns before they are woven into cloth. By the use of a white or solid-colored filling with the printed warp yarns, a hazy grayed effect is produced in the design. A cloth with the warp printed before weaving is called a warp-printed fabric.

Space-dyed fabric is made of yarns that have color applied by dipping or spotting various places along the yarn. This is done to warp and/or filling yarns.

HOW TO IDENTIFY ORDINARY OR CONVENTIONAL YARNS

Yarns used in clothing and home furnishings may be classified in two general types: (1) ordinary or conventional and (2) novelty.

[5]*America's Textiles* (R/B edition), February 1981, pp. 11, 18.

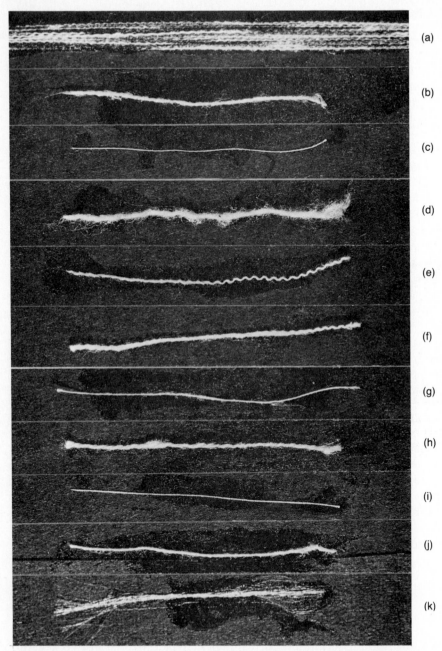

Figure 3.8 Types of yarns. Top to bottom: (a) space-dyed yarn; (b) carded cotton; (c) combed cotton; (d) carded woolen; (e) combed worsted; (f) tow linen; (g) line linen; (h) spun silk; (i) reeled silk; (j) spun rayon; and (k) filament rayon. (Photo by Jack Pitkin.)

Carded and Combed Yarns

It is important to know the fiber content of a yarn first in order to tell what has been its processing. If the fibers are cotton or wool or a blend of these fibers, carding and combing will be the processing required in manufacture. If man-made staple fibers are spun into yarn to resemble cotton or wool, these yarns will be spun on the cotton or wool systems and therefore will be carded and combed, too. (See Fig. 3.8.)

To identify a carded cotton yarn, untwist the yarn to the point where it pulls apart. Discard one piece of the yarn that has pulled apart. From the broken end of yarn, pluck out several fibers. Note whether the fibers are very short—less than 1 inch. Also note whether the fibers seem to branch out in all directions—are not parallel. If this is the case, the cotton yarn is probably carded only. If the yarn pulls apart and does not separate ino two or three distinct yarns, then the yarn is a single. If the cotton yarn has long fibers (approximately 1 inch or over), all about the same length and lying parallel, the yarn is probably combed.

After identifying the yarns, the whole cloth should be studied. Notice whether the diameters of the yarns are quite even and smooth. If so, the yarns are probably combed. A very fine, even yarn, like one found in organdy, is combed.

Line and Tow Linen Yarns

Everyone is familiar with dish towels that are 100 percent linen but are bumpy in texture. These towels are made of tow linen, which is poorly hackled yarn made of short fibers that are removed from the sliver in the hackling process. When a yarn is untwisted, short fibers of varied lengths branching out from the yarn will identify tow.

Handkerchief linen is a good example of line yarn made of long fibers that lie parallel in the sliver to make a smooth, even-diameter, fine yarn. Such yarns have been well hackled.

Woolen and Worsted Yarns

To identify a woolen yarn used for clothing and home furnishings, excluding rugs, proceed as for cotton by untwisting it. Note whether the fibers average less than 2 inches and branch out from the yarn in all directions. If so, the yarn is carded only and is a woolen.

To identify a worsted yarn, proceed as before by untwisting the yarn. Note whether the fibers average more than 2 inches, are all about the same length, and lie parallel. If so, the yarn is combed and is a worsted.

Silk Yarns

Reeled-Silk Yarns

The term "reeled" applies to long-fibered silk. Again, the fiber content is important to know first. If silk is reeled, the yarn is often lustrous, and there is usually less twist than for spun silk. The fibers will fan out or shred apart when the yarn is untwisted.

Spun-Silk Yarns

Short lengths of silk fibers may be twisted (spun) into yarn called "spun silk." The yarns of spun silk are generally dull and cottony and usually have considerable twist to hold in the short ends (the fibers of spun silk are shorter than are those of reeled silk). When the yarn is untwisted, fibers do not lie parallel and are of varied short lengths. (See Fig. 3.9.)

Yarns of Man-Made Fibers

Filament Yarns

Filament yarns of man-made fibers have features similar to those of reeled silk. The fibers are continuous, and they lie parallel and fan out when the yarn is untwisted. These yarns may be dull or lustrous, depending on their end use. When various types of monofilament yarns are combined and twisted together, a "combination" filament yarn is formed.

Generally speaking, the greater the number of filaments in a yarn, the stronger and more pliable and supple the yarn. Some yarns may consist of one filament, as in nylon hosiery or saran fabric for beach chairs. Such yarns are called monofilament, as opposed to multifilament yarns.

Spun Yarns from Staple

Short man-made fibers of cut or broken filaments of desired lengths, called staple fibers, may be spun into yarn, as are cotton, wool, and worsted. Spun yarns are more irregular, more fuzzy, and more bulky than are filament yarns of the same weight. Therefore, these yarns are suitable for warm, porous fabrics and nonsmooth textured cloths.

Spun yarns of man-made fibers have fibers of the same lengths, because the tow (a strand of continuous filaments) is cut all one length: the length of cotton, if the yarn is to resemble cotton, wool to resemble wool, and so on. The texture of the cloth and evenness of the yarn should help in determining what processes have been used to manufacture the yarn.

A type of spun yarn called a "blend" is a combination of two or more staple fiber types (either man-made or natural) that are blended together before the fibers are spun into yarn. Fabrics made of such blended spun yarns are called "blends."

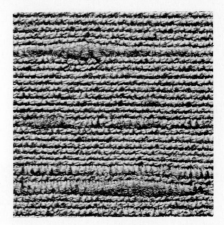

Figure 3.9 Shantung, showing slub fillings. (Photo by Jack Pitkin.)

Textured Yarns

Texturing is a process that gives the normally smooth, continuous-filament yarns, of the noncellulosic fibers, crimps, loops, coils, and crinkles. (See Fig. 3.10.) Thus, the rugged performance of these fibers is augmented with luxurious bulk and/or stretch. These fibers are made more closely to resemble the natural fibers they simulate for clothing purposes. They are made suitable for a wide range of apparel for which smooth, continuous-filament yarns are not appropriate. The yarns most often texturized are nylon and polyester. In fact, about half the nylon yarns now used for apparel are textured, and of the fibers used in knitting yarns, polyester is in the lead, especially for double-knit fabrics and, to a lesser extent, tricot.

There are a great many highly ingenious techniques for texturing the noncellulosic yarns. These may be considered under two headings: mechanical methods and chemical methods.

Mechanical Methods

Classical or three-staged method. This is the oldest technique; it was developed by the Heberlein Company in Switzerland. There are three stages in production:

1. Twisting of the yarn.
2. Heat-setting the yarn in its twisted form.
3. Untwisting the yarn.

Such yarns are bulky. They have loft and a small amount of stretch (10 to 15 percent). Familiar brands of yarn made by this method are the original Helanca and Cheveux d'ange (Billion & Cie, France).

False twist. This process is essentially the same as the classical process but is a refinement, since it is a continuous operation, not three separate ones. (See Fig. 3.11.) Notice the false-twist spindle. This is the most widely used process in the

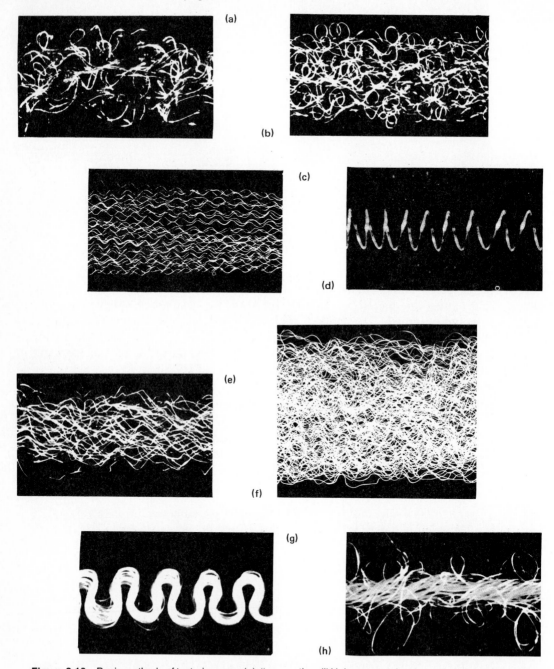

Figure 3.10 Basic methods of texturing yarn: (a) "conventional" Helanca stretch nylon yarn; (b) a typical "false-twist" stretch nylon yarn; (c) Miralon gear-crimped nylon yarn; (d) Agilon (crimped-type) nylon monofil yarn; (e) spunize textured yarn nylon; (f) producer-textured "Blue C" nylon yarn; (g) knit-deknit-textured nylon yarn; (h) Taslan-textured nylon yarn. (Courtesy of Monsanto Company.)

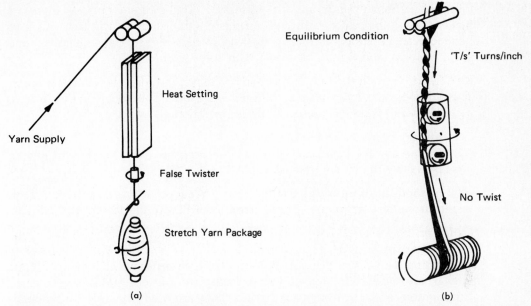

Heat Setting

Yarn Supply

False Twister

Stretch Yarn Package

(a)

Equilibrium Condition

'T/s' Turns/inch

No Twist

(b)

Figure 3.11   (a) This figure shows schematically how a false twister is used to produce stretch yarn. (b) Yarn is twisted above the false twister, heat-set and relaxed while in the twisted condition, and then completely untwisted as it leaves the false twister. A continuous, delicate balance is maintained wherein downstream twist exactly cancels upstream twist. (Courtesy of *Textile World*.)

world. The same basic false-twist process produces both a heat-set and a stretch yarn. Actually, the stretch yarn is simpler to produce because it is made in three stages: twist, set, and untwist. The set yarn is made in four stages: twist, set, untwist, and heating to stabilize or destroy the twist in the yarn. Trademarked names of stretch yarn of the false-twist type are Fluflon, Superloft, and some Helanca. A similar duo-twist process, which uses no spindle, makes a yarn with a lower twist. Two yarns are then twisted together, heat-set, separated, and wound on individual cones.

Drawn-textured.   This is a process wherein a partially oriented, or undrawn, yarn is drawn and textured in the same manufacturing step, usually on a false-twist texturizing machine. It is primarily used to make polyester and nylon apparel yarns.

Crimped yarns.   In one method, yarns are made by a stuffer-box technique. Straight filaments are "stuffed" tightly into a heated box. When removed, the yarn resembles a "v" or sawtooth. Ban-Lon and Tycora are two registered yarns made by this method. Uses of the yarns include women's dress fabrics, sweaters, and men's knitted sport shirts. "Spunized" yarns by the Allied Corporate Technology Fibers Division are crimped by the teeth of two heated gears which mesh, so that the configuration of the yarn is like the gear teeth. Instead of texturing a single end of yarn, J. P. Stevens & Co., Inc., textures a multiple number of ends in warp formation. The crimping process therefore makes the crimps uniform throughout the length of these warp yarns. Crimps per inch can be varied according to the end use. Blouse, pajama, dress, and tricot lingerie fabrics may be made with these yarns.

Knit deknit. Any hand knitter has had the experience of unraveling her work. The raveled yarn resembles a rounded sawtooth. The steps in the process include three stages in one continuous operation:

1. Knitting of a tubular fabric.
2. Heat-setting the fabric.
3. Deknitting (unraveling) the fabric.

This method does not make a stretch yarn. A crepe or bouclé textured fabric results from this technique. Brand names are Bucaroni and Antron Crinkle.

Curled or edge-crimped yarns. The filament passes over a heated blade that causes alternate surfaces of the yarn to be flattened, much as one curls a ribbon by running it over the blade of scissors. Curled yarns, which have moderate stretch, are produced chiefly under a license from Deering Milliken Research Corporation, with the trademark Agilon. They are used primarily for women's nylon hosiery.

Air-bulked (air-jet) or looped yarns. A filament yarn is subjected to an air jet that blows a number of loops per inch into the individual filaments, both on the surface and in the *yarn bundle.* Textures of smooth, silky, or worsted-like textures, as well as woolen and heavy chenille types, can be achieved. Core and effect yarns are obtainable under the registered trademark Taslan by DuPont. (See Fig. 3.12.) The yarn so formed does not have stretch properties, but it has increased bulk and texture not unlike spun yarn. Another brand name for air-jet yarns is Skyloft, by American Enka.

Thick and thin yarns. Yarns of varying diameters are produced by varying the diameters of man-made fibers. (See Chapter 12.)

Chemical Methods

If the two polymers extruded through a spinneret are of the same generic family, it is a *bicomponent* yarn. If the two polymers are of different generic families, the yarn is a *biconstituent* yarn. (See Chapter 14.)

In the mechanical processes described, texturizing depended on twisting and the application of heat, the exception being the thick and thin yarns. In some instances, texturizing is chemical. Generally two polymers with different ratios of shrinkage are used. Upon the application of heat, one polymer shrinks more that the other, in the solution forced through the spinneret, thus crimping the whole yarn. Since texturizing is done at the source, it is said to be "producer-textured." A yarn of this type is Cantrece, made by DuPont.

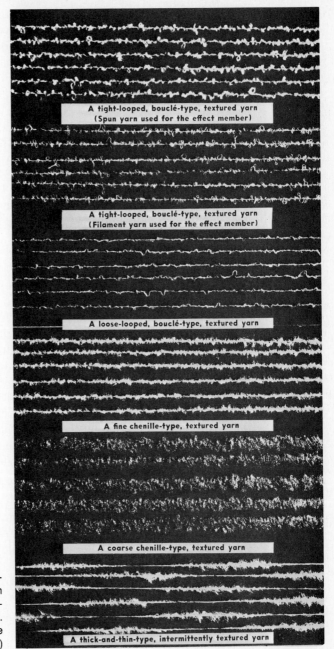

A tight-looped, bouclé-type, textured yarn
(Spun yarn used for the effect member)

A tight-looped, bouclé-type, textured yarn
(Filament yarn used for the effect member)

A loose-looped, bouclé-type, textured yarn

A fine chenille-type, textured yarn

A coarse chenille-type, textured yarn

A thick-and-thin-type, intermittently textured yarn

Figure 3.12 Examples of Taslan-textured specialty yarns produced from continuous-filament yarns (note exception at top) by multiend texturing. (Photo courtesy of E. I. DuPont de Nemours & Company, Inc.)

A bright future seems indicated for textured yarns. There are new markets in men's knitted suits, children's wear, outerwear, and textured tricot and full-fashioned knits. Textured polyesters, so important today in clothing, may be in short supply during any energy crisis because about 1 percent of the nation's petroleum is used by the man-made fibers industry.[6]

Merits, Problems, and Uses
of Textured Yarns

Bulked-yarn fabrics are more comfortable than are fabrics made from filament yarn. Bulked-nylon fabrics, for example, tend to approach the general physical characteristics of cotton and wool staple knit fabrics with respect to thickness, weight, opacity, density, packing factor, surface characteristics, and thermal conductivity. Some men may remember the coldness and clamminess of the first filament nylon shirts. Synthetic yarns now used in woven shirts are often textured.

Furthermore, in addition to improved comfort, textured yarns have a better appearance, better resistance to pilling (unless filaments break), greater durability and evenness, and improved covering power because of their bulk. Problems of fuzzing from abrasion, matting, or breaking of the filaments, which may result in pilling, have confronted the technician.

The quality of textured yarn has improved owing to the increase in production speed and the continuous and automatic processing from start to finish. These improvements are noted in the texturing equipment of the United States, France, the United Kingdom, Germany, Italy and Japan.

"Converters" of man-made fibers have reached a new and higher status. They are the throwsters who used to be twisters of silk. Now they twist continuous-filament man-made fibers. Originally, they performed only a commission service, but now they are responsible for custom designing of yarns for specific markets. Their goal is variety and flexibility of the products.

Kinds of Novelty Yarns

Fabric designers are constantly bringing out fabrics with novelty yarns to stimulate sales through a wider, more diversified variety of fabrics. Textural effects obtained by use of novelty yarns would be impossible with any ordinary yarn.

Novelty yarns are made on a novelty yarn-twisting machine by combining different types of yarns in various ways. The weight of novelty yarns may vary from a few hundred yards per pound to as fine as 20,000 yards per pound or more.[7]

Novelty yarns are used in knitted sweaters and dresses, contemporary drapery and upholstery fabrics, and the decoration of men's and women's

---

[6]Man-Made Fiber Producers Association, *Man-Made Fiber Fact Book*, 1980, p. 10.
[7]*Novelty Yarns* (pamphlet), by Philadelphia Penn Worsted Company.

suiting fabrics. Such yarns are often made with blends of natural and man-made fibers. In any case, they are designed for a specific end use, and they can be varied by numerous possible combinations of fibers, twist, ply, and color.

These novelty yarns are popular:

1. *Bouclé* is one of the most used novelty yarns. It is characterized by tight loops that project from the body of the yarn at fairly regular intervals. It is often made of a combination of rayon and cotton or wool. Bouclé is used in knitted sweaters, both knitted and woven dresses, and upholstery fabrics. Ratiné is similar in construction to bouclé, but the loops are twisted continuously and are not spaced.

2. *Chenille* is a term derived from the French, meaning "caterpillar." It refers to a special soft, fuzzy, loft yarn with pile protruding on all sides. The yarn is constructed on any fiber or blend by first weaving a cloth in which the crosswise or filling yarns are battened down tightly. The cloth is then cut lengthwise into narrow strips, with each strip containing a few warp yarns. Each strip is twisted to form the yarn with the fuzzy ends of the cut filling yarns protruding. The yarn can be identified by the running of one's fingernail along the yarn; the pile consisting of filling is removed readily, revealing the warp yarns. Chenille yarns are used for both woven and knitted women's and men's outerwear, including sweaters, jackets, and skirts, to obtain prominent effects. A type of chenille yarn, often called chenille fur, is used for chenille rugs.

3. *Metallic yarn* is metal foil or steel, aluminum, gold or silver, coated on both sides with plain or plastic colored film, and then cut into narrow strips. Metallic yarns coated with plastic do not tarnish. Recent metallic yarns have been produced by bonding aluminum foil between two clear layers of plastic film. This is called the *foil* type of yarn. A second kind, called the *metallized* type, uses a layer of polyester film (Mylar) treated with vaporized metal that is subsequently bonded between two clear layers of film. Polypropylene, acetate, and cellophane films may also be used. For colors other than silver, color pigment can be added to the bonding adhesive. The quality of these two types of metallic yarn depends on the type of clear film used, plus the resistance it and the adhesives have to stretching and wet processing. To provide the strength and to prevent stretching, these yarns are often wrapped with nylon or high-tenacity rayon.[8]

4. *Nub yarn* is made by twisting one end around another many times within a short space, causing enlarged places (nubs) on the surface of the yarn. Sometimes a binder is used to hold the nub in place. Nubs are generally spaced at varied intervals. Nub yarns are sometimes called knap yarns.

5. *Paper yarns*[9] are made by slitting and wet-twisting paper to form individual strands of yarn that are then knitted or woven like other yarns. Since

---

[8]These yarns should not be confused with nonwoven cloth.
[9]See fiber rugs, Chapter 20.

these yarns have strength, they are suitable for bagging, fiber rugs, automobile seat covers, hats, and handbags.

6. *Plastic yarns* are coated yarns made of natural or synthetic fibers that have been dipped into a protective coating of plastic.

7. *Splash yarn* is really an elongated nub that has been tightly twisted about a base yarn. A *seed yarn* is a very small nub, often made of man-made yarns applied to a dyed or natural base yarn.

8. *Slub* is a soft, elongated nub. The yarn forming the slub may be continuous or may be made of tufts of roving inserted at intervals between binder yarns.[10]

WHAT IS THREAD?

The chief difference between yarn and thread lies in the method of twisting strands together. Thread is plied for extra strength, with the third and sixth being the most common plies. Each strand is balanced in twist, and the finished thread approximates a perfect circle in cross section. Like yarn, thread is inspected and reeled into hanks. A thread has a higher twist than a yarn. It is highly specialized with a definite purpose such as sewing or embroidery.

In hank form, thread can be mercerized, bleached, or dyed. It is then wound on spools, inspected, and boxed.

A good thread must be (1) even in diameter, to move under tension easily and quickly through the eye of the needle; (2) smooth, to resist friction caused by sewing; (3) strong enough to hold seams firmly in laundering and in use; and (4) elastic enough to make stitches that will not break or pucker.

Sewing threads are made of cotton, linen, silk, rayon, nylon, and polyester. Nylon and polyester may be monofilament, multifilament, spun, or core spun with a cotton or rayon outer wrap. The size of cotton and linen thread is indicated on the end of the spool. As we have already mentioned, the higher the number, the finer the thread. For special uses such as luggage, shoes, carpets, bookbinding, gloves, umbrellas, upholstery, and awnings, special sewing threads are made. Special thread called *buttonhole twist* is made for buttonholes. Just a few yards of thread are wound on a spool for this purpose. Special thread in gold is made for crocheting and tatting.

Research has revealed that apparel made from water-repellent fabrics gives the wearer better protection when the seams are sewed with a thread that has been made water-repellent.

Threads should be selected for use on fabric of like generic families. Some threads may be too strong and cut the fabric. Methods of caring for the garment fabrics may weaken threads from unlike generic families.

[10]For *roving,* see the glossary in this chapter.

IMPARTING STRETCH TO CLOTHING FABRICS

As we have seen in connection with texturing, stretch may be imparted to yarns by certain of the texturing methods in use. But there are other ways in which to provide the quality of stretch in clothing and other finished goods. The whole question may be logically considered at this point since the yarn used is an important consideration.

Stretch garments have the ability to extend and recover rather than to remain rigid. Stretch garments are akin to skin. Just as our skin moves freely as we bend or twist, so do stretch garments move with the body. Nonstretch garments may be so rigid as to be uncomfortable because they constrict bodily movements. See Fig. 3.13 for a specialized use of stretch.

Fabrics, then, are made to stretch for three reasons: comfort, control, and fashion. Freedom of movement is desirable in active sportswear, in suit jackets, and in straight skirts. For foundation garments, ski pants, and swimsuits, body control or support is needed. For a trim, slim, sleek look in ski pants, jumpsuits, and slacks, fashion plays an important role.

Stretch woven fabrics, which originated in Europe in the early 1950s, were used principally for ski pants. Originally they were made of Helanca yarn with stretch nylon warp and acrylic filling. In 1960 Pucci, the Italian designer, introduced sportswear made of a fabric with stretch nylon warp and silk Dupioni filling. The stretch concept grew in importance. But with the advent of durable press, stretch was eclipsed for a time. However, durable press has helped to bring back stretch. Pants manufacturers added stretch to their durable-press offerings. One men's shirt manufacturer employed stretch as a durable-press principle in stretch batistes for shirts. Another manufacturer added all-rayon stretch dresses to the line. With the increased use of textured yarns, many of which are of the stretch type, an upward trend in stretch fabrics has been evidenced.

Figure 3.13. Medical dressings reduce pain from burns, fight infection, and control fluid loss. Dressings are made of stretchable BioBrane burn dressings. (Photo courtesy of American Convertors, a division of American Hospital Supply.)

Stretch may be imparted to the end product in the fiber stage, the yarn stage, the fabric construction, or the finishing stage.

In the Fiber Stage

Of the natural fibers, wool has the most stretch. Its natural crimp can be increased by the application of certain chemicals and by the twist, set, and untwist method (already explained in connection with texturizing), when done in the wet state at a temperature of 212° F or higher. This treatment has been found to increase the stretch of two-ply worsted yarn to about 100 percent. A resin application on the yarn prior to untwisting has been found in a laboratory test to increase the amount of stretch significantly.

Elastometric fibers, particularly rubber and spandex, stretch much more than wool. Natural rubber was one of the first materials used to give stretch to clothing. The familiar trade name Lastex is still in use. Another trade name is Contro. Rubber deteriorates from exposure to oxygen in the air, continuous flexing, chlorine, salt water, sunlight, contact with body oil, perspiration, cosmetics, and repeated laundering. Rubber's usage includes surgical supports, tops of men's socks, support hosiery, bindings, foundation garments, swimsuits, trimmings and sewing thread.

Spandex, a man-made polyurethane fiber, has supplanted rubber for most uses. Its stretchability is comparable to that of rubber. It is one-third lighter in weight than rubber and twice as strong. Hence, it can be made much finer—a reason why fabrics of spandex are lighter and more sheer with the same control features and stretch properties as fabrics made with rubber. Furthermore, spandex is unaffected by sunlight, water, most oils and oil-based cosmetics, salt water, and dry-cleaning agents. However, white spandex may yellow in usage, and chlorine bleach may degrade and yellow the fiber quickly and severely. Trade names of spandex fibers include Blue "C," Lycra, Numa, and Vyrene.

Spandex and rubber, covered or uncovered, may be woven or knitted into fabrics. Uncovered yarns give good elasticity but an undesirable rubbery feel to the fabric. When spandex is used as the core of a yarn, with other fibers wrapped spirally around it, the yarn has considerable stretch, a bulkier hand, and a more pleasant feel than uncovered yarns. Core-spun yarn, as these covered yarns are called, are used in such fabrics as batiste, flannel, gabardine, lace, poplin, seersucker, taffeta, and twills. Yarns stretch about 25 to 40 percent on the average in these fabrics. (See Fig. 3.14.)

The TFPIA has been amended to allow "the disclosure of any fiber present in a textile product which has clearly established definite functional significance." Prior to the amendment, the act required that all fibers constituting over 5 percent of a fabric be listed on the label or hangtag according to the generic name. Frequently a small percentage of spandex in a yarn was unidentified. Since as little as 1 percent spandex in a yarn gives stretch, it is highly desirable to have the generic name specified.

Figure 3.14 To determine the degree of stretch on a fabric, the stretch board illustrated has been developed. It has been adopted by other testing centers. (Photo courtesy of J. C. Penney Co.)

In the Yarn Stage

It has been noted that some of the three-stage textured yarns may stretch, that the false-twist method is the dominant stretch yarn process in use today, and that the curled or edge-crimped technique develops a certain degree of stretch in the yarn. Uses for heat-set stretch yarn include infants' wear, ski wear, lingerie, sportswear, and swimsuits.

The stretch yarns used in a woven fabric may be either in the warp, in the filling, or in both, depending upon whether stretch is desired in the length of the fabric, the width, or in both dimensions.

In the Fabric Finishing Stage

Knitting as contrasted to weaving imparts a great deal of stretch to the finished garment and will be discussed in Chapter 6. In woven fabrics, the simplest and least expensive method of imparting stretch is called "slack mercerization." Mercerization was described in Chapter 2 as a treatment of cotton yarns or fabrics under tension in a bath of caustic soda. When only warp yarns are held in tension, the loosely held filling yarns shrink. This shrinkage is permanently set by a chemical treatment that provides stretch and recovery properties ranging from 13 to 22 percent beyond its finished width. To be sure, this range is lower than stretch from elastomeric fibers and heat-set yarns. Also, recovery is said to diminish with wear and repeated laundering. The care of stretch fabrics is considered in Chapter 16.

CURRENT ADVANCES IN MANUFACTURE

Great advances have been made recently in the manufacture of yarns. They are gradually being adopted by the industry, such as an air jet spinning machine, and a mechanical yarn spinner that repairs broken yarns with an almost invisible yarn splint.

The spinning process is approaching automation. Perhaps unfortunately, most of the new machines are made abroad. There is a need in the United States for more research and development of both the mechanical and electronic methods of manufacturing yarns and fabrics. College textile programs have tended to neglect the technical side of the field where there are great opportunities for cost savings.[11]

SUMMARY

The type of yarns used has an effect on the fabric's texture, hand, warmth, weight, resiliency, durability, and luster.

Specifications for a particular yarn are determined by the fabric's end use. Ply yarns, for instance, are desirable in men's broadcloth shirts, in tropical worsted suitings, and in women's cotton voile dresses. In the first two uses, ply yarns give strength to the fabrics; in the third use, ply yarns in tight voile twist give the characteristic thready feel of voile and also give strength.

Yarns differ in weight and fineness, and in sheerness, smoothness, fuzziness, nubbiness, and elasticity—all varied to create qualities required in the final fabric.

Yarns may be classified according to structure (single or ply, direction of twist, size, or count) or use (as warp, filling, or other purposes). The present text has considered three classifications: (1) ordinary yarns, (2) textured and/or stretch yarns, (3) novelty yarns.

There have been innumerable pluses built into stretch fabrics. (See Figs. 3.15 and 3.16.) Therefore, stretch should be a plus factor and not a sole selling point. Stretch fabrics should be used only where their properties are genuinely useful and beneficial to the consumer. The degree of stretch must be adequate to the function.

[11]*America's Textiles*, November 1982, pp. 20, 32.

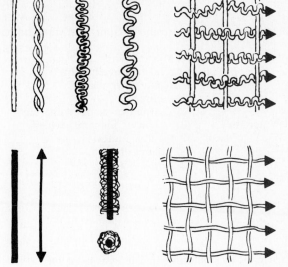

Figure 3.15 Twist texturing induces a coil or crimp in filament yarns. Yarns then provide stretch characteristics to the woven or knit fabric. Degree of stretch is both high and long-lasting. (Courtesy of E. I. DuPont de Nemours & Company, Inc.)

Figure 3.16 Core-spun yarns incorporate the stretch of a core of Lycra spandex inside a bundle of staple fibers. Performance and esthetics are those of the covering yarn; the stretch is high; recovery properties are strong and permanent. (Courtesy of E. I. DuPont de Nemours & Company, Inc.)

REVIEW QUESTIONS

1. (a) Define core-spun yarn, textured yarn, solution-dyed yarn, bouclé yarn.
   (b) Describe the methods of making textured yarn. Give a trade name of each type.
2. (a) What yarns are carded?
   (b) What yarns are combed?
   (c) Give the advantages of combed cotton yarns.
   (d) What are the differences between woolen and worsted yarns?
3. (a) To what types of yarn is the word "spun" applicable?
   (b) For what purposes are spun nylon yarns used?
   (c) What are some advantages and drawbacks of stretch yarns in woven fabrics?
4. (a) In what ways does twist affect the yarn?
   (b) Of what value is it to know the number of turns to the inch?
   (c) What is meant by a S twist? a Z twist?
   (d) Of what value is it to know direction of twist?
5. Explain the terms
   (a) count of yarn.
   (b) denier.
   (c) monofilament yarn.
   (d) multifilament yarn.
6. Which is finer yarn, 30 denier or 15 denier? Explain your answer.
7. Which is finer, 100s cotton yarn or 150s cotton yarn? Why?
8. (a) What are novelty yarns?
   (b) What effect have they on the finished cloth?
   (c) How are metallic yarns made?
9. What are the differences between thread and yarn?
10. How is stretch applied to textile fabrics?

EXPERIMENT

Using the technique for identification of yarns given in this chapter, take yarns from the following fabrics:

(a) Dress satin
(b) Brocade
(c) Shantung
(d) Donegal tweed
(e) Tropical worsted
(f) Stretch corduroy or stretch denim
(g) Silk organza
(h) Fiberglas marquisette
(i) Sailcloth
(j) Linen crash

Answer the following for each yarn:
(a) Regular or novelty yarn?
(b) If regular, indicate
  (1) single or ply.
  (2) carded or combed, hackled.
  (3) spun or filament, reeled.
(c) If novelty, indicate
  (1) name of yarn.
  (2) how made.

GLOSSARY

Air-bulked yarn A textured yarn that is made by subjecting the filaments to air jets, which blow loops both on the surface of the yarn and in the *yarn bundle.*

Blended yarn A strand of fibers produced from two or more constituent fibers that have been thoroughly mixed (blended) before spinning.

Bouclé yarn A novelty yarn characterized by tight loops projecting from the body of the yarn at fairly regular intervals.

Bulky yarn A yarn that has been textured to give it bulk without increasing weight.

Cable cord The result of twisting singles together in various directions of twist, such as S/Z/S or Z/S/Z. See *S twist* and *Z twist.*

Carding An operation in yarn making that separates the fibers and puts them in a filmy sheet and then funnels them into a soft mass called a sliver.

Chenille yarn A soft, lofty yarn, somewhat rough in texture. See page 63 for details.

Combination yarn A ply yarn composed of two or more single yarns of the same or different fibers or twists.

Combing An operation in yarn making that makes the fibers parallel in the sliver and removes the shorter fibers.

Continuous filament See *filament yarns.*

Cop A package of yarn wound on a tapered tube.

Cord The result of twisting together ply yarns in a third twisting operation.

Count of yarn Size of yarn as distinguished by its weight and fineness. This term is applied to cotton, wool, and spun yarns.

Crimped yarn A textured yarn made from man-made fibers that have been crimped to resemble wool.

Curled yarn A textured yarn made by a heated blade that "curls" the filaments.

Denier Size of silk and filament man-made yarns.

Direct spinning A method of making yarn from man-made tow by breaking it into uneven lengths by stretching; the resultant sliver is twisted and wound.

Double and twist yarn A two-ply made from single yarns of different colors. A mottled effect is produced.

Durable press   A measure of garment performance. Features include shape of retention; durable pleats and pressed creases; durably smooth seams; machine washability and dryability; wrinkle resistance; and fresh appearance without ironing.

Filament yarns   Made of long continuous man-made fibers.

Fingering yarns   Light, medium-weight, two- or three-ply yarns for hand knitting.

Frill or spiral yarns   A corkscrew effect produced by twisting together a fine and a coarse yarn.

Garnetting   A process similar to carding applied to textile waste, clippings, and rags to restore them to fiber form.

Hackling   The process by which flax is prepared for yarn.

Hand   The feel of a fabric. See *texture.*

Hawser cord   The result of twisting together singles with various directions of twists.

Lea   Size of linen yarn. See *count of yarn* and *denier.*

Line yarn   A slack-twisted strand that is twisted to form loops or curls. This strand is held in place by one or two binder yarns.

Metallic yarn   Metal foil either wrapped around natural or synthetic yarn or coated on both sides with plain or plastic-covered film cut into strips.

Monofilament yarn   A yarn made of one filament (as in nylon hosiery).

Mule spinning frame   An early mechanism for spinning wool and cotton into yarn.

Multifilament yarn   A yarn made of man-made fibers consisting of a number of filaments.

Open-end spinning   A mechanical process of spinning yarn directly from strands of fiber that are carried around a rotating disk where centrifugal force twists the fibers into yarn.

Paper yarn   A strand made of paper that is slit and twisted in web form.

Permanent press   See *durable press.*

Plastic-coated yarns   Yarns made of natural or synthetic fibers that have been dipped into a coating of plastic.

Ply yarn   A yarn composed of two or more single yarns twisted together.

Raw silk   Reeled silk wound directly from several cocoons with only a slight twist.

Reeling   Winding of silk filaments directly from cocoons.

Ring spinning frame   A mechanical device used for spinning yarn, which feeds the roving to a ring around which it is spun rapidly to form a yarn that is immediately wound onto a revolving spindle.

Roving   Intermediate stage in yarn manufacture between sliver and yarn. A single strand of fibers having very little twist.

S twist   A left-hand twisted yarn.

Seed yarn   A very small nub, often made of dyed man-made fibers, applied to a dyed or natural-base yarn.

Sheath-core yarn   A very bulky yarn of synthetic fibers consisting of a core of fine-denier fibers with considerable shrinkage and a cover or wrapping of coarse-denier relaxed fibers.

Single yarn   One strand of fibers or filaments grouped or twisted together.

Sizing (of yarn)   Treating yarn with stiffening materials (such as starch or wax).

Slashing   Sizing yarn in an aqueous solution and then drying it to remove the water.

Sliver   A strand of fibers made from a filmy sheet of fibers resulting from carding. See *carding.*

Slub   An elongated nub. Slub yarn is identified by its elongated nubs.

Solution dye   Dyestuffs are put into the viscous solution before fibers are hardened.

Space-dyed yarns   Those yarns that have been dipped in dye or spotted in various places along the yarn.

Spinning   The process of drawing and twisting fibers together into yarns or thread.

Spinning jenny   The earliest mechanical device for spinning yarn.

Spiral   See *frill yarns.*

Splash yarn   An elongated nub yarn that has been tightly twisted about a base yarn.

Spun yarn   A yarn twisted by spinning; also yarn composed of man-made staple fibers.

Stretch yarn   A textured yarn that has good stretch and recovery. It may also refer to yarns made of fibers that have elastic properties or to those yarns whose elastic properties are obtained by alterations of the basic fiber.

Texture   The surface effect of a fabric; that is, stiffness, roughness, smoothness, softness, fineness, dullness, and luster. See *hand.*

Textured yarn   Any filament yarn that has been geometrically modified or otherwse altered to change its basic characteristics.

Thick and thin yarn   Yarn produced by varying the diameters of man-made fibers.

Thread   A special type of tightly twisted ply yarn used for sewing.

Throwing   The combining and twisting of strands of reeled silk into tightly twisted yarn.

Throwster   The operator who twists and manipulates strands of reeled silk into tightly twisted yarns.

Tow   Poorly hackled, uneven linen yarn made of short fibers. It also refers to strands of continuous man-made filaments to be cut in lengths for spun yarn.

Turns   See *twist.*

Twist   The number of times (turns) 1 inch of yarn is twisted.

Woolen yarn   A carded yarn made of relatively short wool fibers of varying lengths.

Worsted yarn   A combed yarn made of long-staple wool fibers.

Yarn   A strand of textile fiber in a form suitable for weaving, knitting, braiding, felting, webbing, or otherwise fabricating into a fabric.

Yarn-dyed   Yarn that is colored (dyed) before it is woven into cloth.

Z twist   A right-hand twisted yarn.

Chapter 4

THE LOOM AND BASIC WEAVES: PLAIN, TWILL, AND SATIN

Weaving and knitting are the two most common processes of making cloth. *Weaving* is the process of interlacing two sets of yarns at right angles. This operation is done either on a hand or a power loom. If one set of yarns forms loops—one loop caught into another and one row of loops hanging on the one below—the cloth is made by *knitting*. Of these two processes, weaving is the most common method, although new and improved knitting machines make cloth quickly, satisfactorily, and with attractive patterns. (See Chapter 6.)

DEVELOPMENT OF WEAVING

The principles of weaving were known to primitive man. He knew how to make baskets and mats by interlacing twigs, reeds, and grasses. But these fibers were long and required no spinning into yarn. Man learned later how to twist together short fibers, such as wool and cotton, to form yarn; and woven cloths for clothing and home use were made on a *loom*.

The Hand Loom

The first hand loom was crude. It is chronicled that *warp* yarns—the lengthwise yarns in a fabric—were suspended from a limb of a tree and held in tension by stone weights at the ends near the ground. The loom of the American Navajo Indian shows warp yarns tied between two sticks. In less primitive looms a wooden frame was made to hold the warps; when strung parallel in this frame, they resembled the slats of a bed.

Figure 4.1 Four-harness hand loom. (Photo by Dick Blick.)

In early looms the crosswise yarns, or *fillings*, were carried over and under each of the warp yarns (as is done in darning). A sharpened stick was used for this purpose. Greater speed in weaving was attained when the *harness* (composed of *heddles*) was developed. It was found that the filling yarn could be interlaced with the warps much more quickly if each warp yarn could be raised and lowered automatically so that the fillings could be shot through. This separation is done by the harness, and the operation is called *shedding*.

The hand loom in Fig. 4.1, equipped with four harnesses, is designed to weave a variety of articles, such as neckties, collars, cuffs, belts, scarfs, table mats, and shopping bags. It has an extremely simple mechanism and can be operated by an amateur.

This loom is constructed like an inverted letter "T." The *bottom frame* corresponds to the crossing of the "T." The *main upright frame* is placed at the middle of the bottom frame and perpendicular to it. There are four harnesses (four frames suspended from the main upright frame). These frames hold a series of wires, called heddles, each of which has an eye like that of a needle. (See Fig. 4.2.)

The cylindrical spool, called a *warp beam*, at the back of the loom holds warp yarns. To prepare the loom for weaving, the warp yarns are passed (1) up over the *breast beam* (the bar just above the spool of warp), (2) through the eyes of the heddles, (3) through the *reed* or swinging frame in front of the heddles, (4) over a breast beam in front of the loom, and (5) around a cylinder, called a *cloth beam* or *merchandise beam*, to which they are attached. When a portion of material

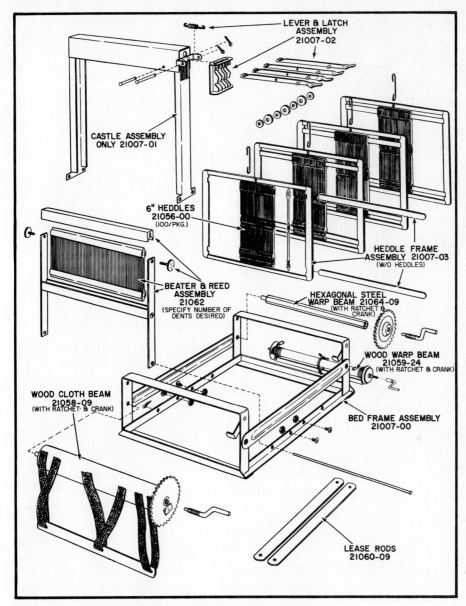

Figure 4.2 Parts of the hand loom. (Courtesy of Dick Blick.)

has been woven, it is wound on the cloth beam. If a cloth is several yards long, the entire yardage of warp yarns cannot be in tension on the loom at once; accordingly, the rest of the warp is wound on the warp beam, which unwinds at the speed the cloth is woven.

Just below the nameplate in Fig. 4.1 are four hooks, each suspended from

Figure 4.3 Professor oversees student in college weaving lab. (Photo courtesy of Winthrop College, South Carolina.)

an arm of a lever at the upper right of the main upright frame. Each hook is attached to the upper bar of one of the heddle frames or harnesses. Each heddle, or flattened wire, suspended between the upper and lower bars of the harness, controls the warp yarn that is threaded through its eye. The purpose of the harness is to raise groups of warps to form a shed so that the shuttle can be passed through the separate warps. Figure 4.1 shows the *shed*.

To make the plain weave, a two-harness loom is sufficient. The weaving method, if a two-harness loom is used, is as follows: warps 1, 3, 5, 7, 9, and so on are threaded through the heddles of one harness, and warps 2, 4, 6, 8, 10, and so on are threaded through the heddles of the other harness.

The reed frame located directly in front of the harness swings forward to beat the last filling inserted against the previous fillings to make a compact construction.

A two-harness loom can make only a plain weave or its variations. Looms with more heddle frames are necessary for more elaborate weaves in which more than two combinations of warp yarns must be raised. A simple twill weave may be made with a four-harness loom. Some looms have 19 to 25 harnesses.

Figure 4.3 shows a college student operating a hand loom.

The Power Loom and Its Operation

All woven cloth is made on some sort of loom. For most of the production, power looms have replaced hand looms, taking weaving from the home to the factory. Intricate designs, once considered masterpieces of handwork, are now copied quickly and inexpensively by machine. The first power loom was invented in England in 1784 by an Edmund Cartwright. Improvements have been taking place ever since.

The four steps in weaving, performed by the power loom as well as in hand weaving, are as follows:

1. After the warp yarns, up and down threads (called ends), have been strung into the frame of the loom, the warp yarns are separated by the motion of the harnesses.[1] This is the first operation; it is called *shedding.*
2. The filling is carried through the shed by one of various means. This operation is called *picking.* The term probably originated before the invention of the shuttle and the heddles, when every other warp yarn had to be picked up, as in darning, so that the filling could be passed over and under the warps. Each time the filling is carried across the cloth, one pick is made. A pick is synonymous with a filling; an end is synonymous with a warp.
3. Each filling yarn or pick is pushed up against the previous filling by the reed frame. This process is called *battening.*
4. The warp is released from the warp beam, and the finished cloth is taken up on the *merchandise beam.* This operation is called *letting off and taking up.*

These operations are repeated over and over again until the cloth is the desired length.

The shuttle in many looms that carries the yarn through the shed of warps in machine weaving is a wooden boatlike container about a foot long that carries a bobbin, called a pirn or quill, onto which filling yarn is wound. The shuttle is propelled through the shed formed by the warps raised by the heddles, thus carrying the filling yarn across the width of the material, as it unwinds from the bobbin. As soon as the shuttle reaches the other side of the material, the new filling yarn is battened down automatically, the heddles change the shed, and the shuttle is propelled back to provide another filling for the fabric. When the yarn in the bobbin is used up, the mechanism removes the bobbin from the shuttle, inserts a new filled shuttle, and continues the operation automatically, without interruption. In case a yarn breaks, the loom stops for repair.

Modern technology has led to many improvements in the shuttle loom. For example, one such loom (the TCP machine of Pignone) has seventeen shuttles that simultaneously insert picks (filling yarns) into separately formed sheds across a rotating reed and yet avoid undue tension on the filling yarns.

The Shuttleless Loom

The heavy shuttle in the conventional loom takes a great deal of power, is relatively slow in operation, is noisy, and is not usually satisfactory for the production of wide fabrics. This has led to the development of a variety of looms that carry the yarn through the shed without the use of a shuttle. The yarn is carried directly from a large cone of yarn located outside of the loom. There are a number of ways in which to propel the filling yarn. One is illustrated in Fig. 4.4. A small light projectile (gripper) grabs the end of the yarn from the cone and by

---

[1] For elaborate weave constructions, the harnesses are replaced by perforated card controls or electronic tapes that manipulate each warp separately.

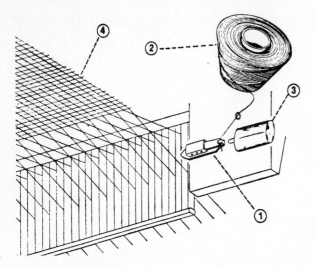

Figure 4.4 The shuttleless loom. Projectile (1) takes yarn from cone (2) and is shot by means of a pressure chamber (3) into the fabric in the loom (4).

means of a pressure cartridge projects the gripper pulling the yarn behind it to make a pick. The gripper is then returned by a conveyor to its original position near the cone of yarn. There it grabs more yarn and repeats the performance. This is repeated again and again at lightning speed.

The Rapier Loom

Instead of the projectile, a rapierlike rod or steel tape is used in some shuttleless looms to carry the filling yarns from the cone through the shed. The rod is quickly withdrawn, leaving the filling in place. More commonly, two rods are used: one carries the yarn halfway where the end of the yarn it carried is transferred to a rod propelled from the other side that pulls the yarn the rest of the way, while the first rod retracts; this speeds up the operation.

The MAV looms from France and the Dornier looms from West Germany employ the two rapiers that meet in the center of the loom and transfer the ends of the yarn at that point. The Iwer loom employs a single rapier that crosses the width of the loom and then returns back to grip the next pick. Currently, in the early 1980s, the rapier loom handles a greater variety of "problematic" yarns than does the air jet, described below.

Rapier looms, which are 54 and 71 inches wide, are used for dress goods, velours, men's dinner jackets, cummerbunds and neckties, upholstery, and ultramodern draperies. However, because of the high speed at which the filling yarn streaks through the tension devices, heat and friction occur. A replacement of the rapierlike needle ends that hold the end of the filling is required at times. Other looms make six widths: 40, 44, 50, 64, 82, and 90 inches.

In addition to the United States, Canada, and Japan, most of the countries in Europe are now making use of the shuttleless loom.

The textile industry's progress in the newer shuttleless looms continues as new looms are installed and improvements in loom motions and parts are made.

Figure 4.5 This shuttleless air-jet weaving machine is electronically controlled with weft insertion rate as high as 1200 a minute. It is a product of PICAÑOL, a leading Belgian loom manufacturer. (Photo courtesy of Weefautomaten PICAÑOL, Ieper, Belgium.)

An important advantage of these looms is their speed, which increases production and hence profits. Greater profits can, in turn, mean higher wages. Also, weavers prefer to work in the quieter weave rooms.

There are other variations of the loom. Some use either jets of air or water to carry the yarn. The latter is not suitable for fibers that lose strength when wet. The air-jet type is discussed more fully in the paragraphs that follow.

The Air-Jet Loom

The air-jet loom is becoming one of the most important types, rapidly replacing the conventional shuttle loom (see Fig. 4.5). In 1980, eight companies were marketing these in the United States (double the number two years before), and by late 1982, U.S. mills had bought over 6,500 of these looms.

Air-jet looms weave faster and have a lower noise level and little vibration. They require 10 to 15 standard cubic feet of air per minute at pressures of 45 to 115 pounds per square inch, depending on the loom type and the width and type of fabric. This dependence on compressed air has made its availability as important as water and electricity.[2]

In the late 1970s, Burlington established an ultramodern textile weaving mill in Burlington, North Carolina. It is equipped with Nissan air-jet looms made in Japan and costing some $36,000 each. To control the warp yarns, it uses

[2]*America's Textiles* (R/B edition), September 1980, p. 45; October 1981, p. 39.

Staubil machinery from Switzerland in conjunction with the weaving machinery. A labor force of eight hundred employees turns out four times as much output as did the same number of employees before the present plant was constructed. Despite the evidence today of the importance of technology in production, most of the modern machinery is coming from abroad.[3]

The Selvages

In yard goods, the outer edges are constructed so they will not ravel. These finished edges are called the selvages (self-edges) and are often made with heavier and more closely spaced warp yarns than are used in the rest of the fabric. Tape selvages, often in twill weave, are firmer and wider than plain selvages. For towels, sheets, and drapery and curtain fabrics, tape selvages give added strength to the edges. Selvages vary in width from one-quarter to three-eights of an inch. The warp yarns always run parallel to the selvages. Proper use of the selvages can also prevent the bowing and bias conditions that occur in some fabrics.

With the shuttleless loom, the ends of the filling yarns are cut and not carried back by a shuttle for the reverse pick to make a selvage. To avoid fraying, the shuttleless loom has a device to tuck in the ends of the filling yarns to the warps near the edge to form a selvage.

Count of Cloth

The yarns used for warp and filling are frequently not of the same diameter. Usually, there are more warp yarns than filling yarns to the inch, because the strain on a fabric that is being used comes primarily on the warp. Some cloths, like ginghams, are closely woven; others, like voile, are loosely woven. If the cloth is held to the light, the porosity of the fabric or the closeness of the weave can be discerned. Ordinarily, a closely woven fabric keeps its shape better, shrinks less, slips less at the seams, and wears longer than does a loosely woven cloth of similar texture and weight.

The closeness or looseness of the weave is measured by the count of the cloth. This is determined by the number of picks and ends (filling and warps) to the square inch. A small pocket magnifying glass, called a pick glass or linen tester, is used for this purpose. Several warp yarns and several fillings are removed from the cloth, thus creating a shredded edge. If the fabric is light in color, a piece of black material is put under it, or vice versa. The linen tester is then set against the shredded edge. Since the usual opening in the tester is one-fourth inch square, the yarns are counted in this space (first the number of warps, then of fillings). Then the number of the yarns that run each way is multiplied by four to give the count per inch. A pin sometimes helps in separating yarns for counting.

[3]*The New York Times*, May 10, 1981, Sec. 3, pp. 1, 22.

The textile weaving mill does its count of cloth at the loom. An electric-impulse mechanism counts the picks for each of ten looms on each of three shifts of personnel, plus the total picks per loom. Counters (actual counting mechanisms) remote from the loom are now set in a panel with a glass door. These count data are easy to read, encourage competition between shifts, and keep production high. In older mills, each loom has its own pick clock or counter.

If the count of the cloth is 80 warps (ends) and 80 fillings (picks) to the inch, the count is expressed as 80 × 80, or 80 square. If there are 60 warps and 50 fillings to the inch, the count is expressed as 60 × 50. This count is found in a plain gingham of medium quality. The count of surgical gauze is approximately 28 × 24. In comparison of the two counts, a 96 × 88 cloth is considered the higher-count cloth because it has more ends and picks (warps and fillings) to the square inch than has surgical gauze. There are, then, high-count and low-count cloths.

Since the yarns are closer together in high-count cloths than they are in low-count cloths, there is less danger of the yarns slipping out of place and causing a shreddy effect. Low-count cloths may be woven with only a few yarns to the inch, either to make the fabric lightweight and porous or to cheapen it.

The consumer can test the strength of a weave by gripping two edges of the cloth, and, with thumbs close together, pressing the thumbs downward on the cloth as hard as possible, and turning the cloth over as pressure continues. If the fabric gives way when hard pressure is exerted, the cloth will not be durable. Any slipping of yarns will also show weakness in the construction of the fabric and will make an unsightly, weak seam.

Balance of Cloth

The proportion of warp yarns to filling yarns (picks) is called the *balance* of a cloth. If the number of warps and the number of fillings to the inch are nearly the same (not more than ten yarns difference), a cloth is said to have good balance. The gingham whose count is 60 × 50 would be considered a fair-balanced cloth. Gauze with a count of 28 × 24 also has a good balance. A sheeting with 61 warp ends and 40 picks (61 × 40) has poor balance because there are too many ends and too few picks. Even though the sheeting is woven in the plain weave, ordinarily a strong construction, there are so few picks that the ends will slip over them very easily, causing a shredded effect. If this cloth were held to the light, the yarns would seem to run all one way—lengthwise. The cloth count is substandard for a sheeting and is not durable.

Good balance is very important in cloths that have to stand hard wear and many washings. Sheets, pillow slips, and towels for glasses and dishes, for instance, should have good balance. A cloth is not always durable, however, just because it has a balanced count. The count of a cloth may be 58 × 50, which looks like a splendid balance, but the cloth may not prove durable if the warps are only half as coarse and half as strong as the fillings. On the other hand, a cotton broadcloth may have an off-balance count, say, 144 × 76 (about twice as many warps as fillings). In this fabric, the fillings are larger than the warps to give a crosswise ridged effect; hence, there are fewer fillings than warps to the inch. Better grades of broadcloth have ply warps and single fillings (2 × 1) to make up in tensile strength for the fine warp yarns used. Best grades have both warps and fillings plied (2 × 2). A buyer, then, must consider both the comparative sizes and the tensile strengths of warp and filling yarns. The warp should be the stronger and usually the more tightly twisted.

The count of cloth and the count of yarn should not be confused. The former denotes the number of picks and ends to the square inch; the latter indicates the weight and diameter of the yarn.

CLASSIFICATION OF WEAVES

The ways in which the filling yarns are interlaced with the warps change the appearance of the fabric and produce many intricate designs that are woven into the cloth. Weaves are named according to the system or design followed in interlacing warp and filling yarns.

The different weaves are named as follows (each weave will be discussed in this and the following chapter in the order given):

1. plain
2. twill
3. satin
4. pile
5. double cloth
6. Jacquard
7. dobby

8. leno or gauze
9. triaxial
10. ornamental embroidered effects
    a. clipped spot
    b. swivel
    c. lappet
    d. schiffli embroidery

PLAIN WEAVE

In this, the simplest weave, the filling is passed over one warp yarn and under the next, alternating in this manner once across the cloth. The second time across, the filling passes over the warp yarns it went under, and under the

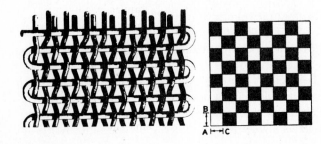

Figure 4.6 Left: Plain weave, showing interlacement of warp and filling yarns. Right: Point-paper design for the same construction.

Figure 4.7   Plain weave. (Photo by Jack Pitkin.)

warps it went over on the previous row. The third time across is a repetition of the first, the fourth repeats the second, and so on. (See Figs. 4.6 and 4.7.)

Point-Paper Design

Each weave can be presented in a squared paper design. For intricate woven-in patterns, designers use the point-paper pattern. Those who do not know how to use it often find their designs impractical from the weaver's standpoint. Figure 4.6 illustrates the pattern for plain weave. White squares are filling on the face—warp on the back. The warp runs lengthwise of the paper, and the fillings run crosswise. The diameter of filling yarns are the same size. The diameter of the filling yarn is represented by AB. AC represents the diameter of a warp yarn.

Cloths Made in the Plain Weave

The plain weave is sometimes called cotton, taffeta, or tabby weave. Some of the most durable fabrics are made in this construction. The weaving process is comparatively inexpensive because the design is so simple. Plain-weave cloths can be cleaned easily, and when firm and closely woven, they wear well.

A partial list of plain-weave fabrics follows:

1. *Cottons.* Gingham, percale, voile, plissé crepe, batiste, calico, chambray, cheese-cloth, chintz, crash, cretonne, muslin sheeting, cambric, lawn, organdy, shantung, unbleached muslin, scrim, crinoline, bunting, buckram, canvas, flannelette.
2. *Linens.* Handkerchief linen, art linen, crash toweling, cambric, dress linen.
3. *Nylons and other man-made fibered fabrics.* Organdy, lingerie crepe, shantung, taffeta, shirting (many of these constructions are also made in blends with natural yarns and with other man-made fibered yarns).
4. *Rayons and/or acetates.* Taffeta, georgette, flat crepe, seersucker, ninon, organdy, voile, rough crepe, chiffon, challis.
5. *Silks.* Taffeta, organza, voile, Canton crepe, crepe de Chine, flat crepe, chiffon, pongee, shantung, silk shirting, broadcloth, habutai, China silk.

6. *Wools.* Homespun, challis, crepe, batiste, some tweeds, voile.
7. *Blends and mixtures of the various fibers.*

Variations in the Plain Weave to Produce Different Effects

Variations in the plain weave are accomplished by using yarns of different fibers, sizes, twists, and/or colors. If the changes in yarn occur in the warp, the warp is strung up accordingly before weaving. If the changes are in the filling, it is necessary to have a separate shuttle or yarn-feeding mechanism for each variation. Provision is made for two, four, and six such variations in what are called *box looms*, with each variation in the yarn in its own ''box.'' The mechanical controls are set to activate the particular shuttle required for the pattern at the exact time it is needed in the filling. Similar adjustments are made in the case of the other basic weaves discussed in this chapter.

Rib Variation

The plain weave without any variation, as is found in sheeting and unbleached muslin, does not make a particularly interesting fabric. Several methods can be used to make a plain-weave fabric more attractive. The first is to produce a ribbed or corded effect by using fillings much heavier than warps, as in poplin, or by using warps much heavier than fillings, as in dimity. The former method is the most common. Bengaline and faille have regular fillingwise ribs; cotton broadcloth has a fine, irregular, broken fillingwise rib.

A striped effect is produced by alternation of fine and heavy warps at regular intervals, as in striped dimity or corded madras shirting. (See Figs. 4.8 and 4.9.) In addition, fine and heavy fillings may be alternated to produce a crossbar effect. Examples of this are crossbar dimity and tissue gingham.

The durability of fabrics in the rib variation of the plain weave may be questionable if the rib yarns are so heavy that they slip over or cut adjacent finer yarns. Such might be the case in striped dimity. The rib must be completely covered by many finer yarns, and the difference in weight between the rib yarn and other yarns should not be too great if wearing quality is to be assured. In heavily corded fabrics, like ottoman and bengaline, good coverage of the ribs is vital because abrasive wear occurs first on top of the ribs.

Figure 4.8 Point-paper design for striped dimity.

Figure 4.9 Rib-weave striped dimity.

Basket Variation

The basket variation of the plain weave is interesting from the design point of view, but it is not so durable as the average rib variation. One or more filling yarns are passed alternately over and under two or more warp yarns. If one filling yarn passes alternately over and under two warp yarns, the weave is called 2 × 1 basket. This weave is common in oxford shirting. The fabric is sometimes made in 3 × 2 (two fillings pass over and under three warps). A 3 × 2 oxford makes an interesting woman's blouse when made of colored warp yarns and white fillings.

In Fig. 4.10 the 2 × 1 basket weave shows one large filling yarn used for every two warp yarns. If a filling is exactly twice the size of a warp, the interlacing of one filling and two warps forms a design of a perfect square; if either set of yarns is not in this proportion, the interlacing of one filling and two warps makes a design in the form of an oblong.

In Fig. 4.11 two fillings pass alternately over two warps. Warps and filling yarns are the same size. A 4 × 4 or 8 × 8 basket weave is found in monk's cloth.

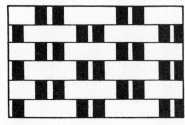

Figure 4.10 2 × 1 basket weave.

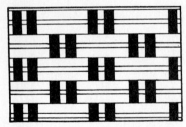 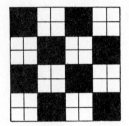

Figure 4.11 2 × 2 basket weave.

The basket weave is a decorative weave, but it is loose; therefore it permits slippage of yarns and stretches, and it may shrink easily in washing. Monk's cloth frays badly unless it is bound on the cut edges.

Visual Design or Effect

In both the rib and basket variations of the plain weave, there are structural changes in the point-paper designs. (See Figs. 4.8 through 4.11.) But the following ways of varying the plain weave may be employed, without structural changes, to give a visual effect (design) that is quite different from the usual appearance of the plain weave. Textural and new color effects can be produced by

1. *Varying the size of yarns.* When uneven yarns are used at irregular intervals (hit or miss), a roughened, bumpy texture is the result. Crash, shantung, and pongee illustrate this use of different sizes of yarns at irregular intervals. Modern drapery fabrics employ such visual effects. (See Chapter 21.)

Another rough texture can be produced with different sizes of ply yarn, as in ratiné and bouclé. Each ply yarn may be made up of different sizes of single yarns with varying amounts of twist.

2. *Varying the number of warp and filling yarns.* The count of cloth is dependent on the number of warps and fillings to the inch; the more yarns to the inch, the closer the weave and the higher the count, and vice versa. The fewer the warp and filling yarns to the inch, the more porous and open the cloth, providing the yarns are fine. Cheesecloth, gauze, voile, and theatrical gauze are low-count cloths. Batiste, lawn, organdy, and cotton broadcloth are considered high-count cloths.

3. *Variations made by use of different degrees of twist in yarns.* If the warp or the filling is twisted so hard that it crepes or crinkles, the appearance of the cloth is textured. Crinkled bedspreads of seersucker are made from yarns with different degrees of twist and tension in the loom. Creping, such as is found in flat crepe, Canton crepe, rough crepe, and crepe de Chine, is made with tightly twisted fillings, alternating right-hand and left-hand twisted yarns (S and Z twists). (See Chapter 3.)

Another variation is made with one set of yarns twisted tightly, but not enough to crepe or crinkle, and fillings twisted so loosely that a nap can be raised in the finishing process. Flannelette is an example.

4. *Combinations of different textile raw materials.* Some cloths are made more attractive by the use of yarns of different textiles or blends of different raw materials. A novel visual effect is produced by the use of a black cotton warp and orange jute filling. A metallic yarn put in here and there in a wool crepe is very attractive because the metallic yarn is so much more lustrous than wool that it shows up to advantage. Alpaca and romain crepes are made of acetate and viscose yarns plied together to form an abraded yarn. The shiny viscose ply and the dull acetate ply give varied luster and sparkle. Metallic yarns may be introduced in any weave for effect. (See Chapter 3.) Matelassé, a fabric with acetate face and rayon back, is a good example of high-shrink rayon and low-shrink acetate yarns.

5. *Variations made by use of fibers or yarns dyed in different colors.* A cloth with a colored warp and a white filling gives a grayed effect. Cotton chambray has this appearance. End-to-end madras, a men's shirting, is quite similar to chambray, the greatest difference being that in the former dyed and white yarns alternate in the warp. This cloth has less depth of color than chambray because there are more white yarns in it. Yarn-dyed stripes are common in madras shirting.

Plaid gingham is made with a series of colored yarns and a series of white yarns used alternately in both warp and filling. This alternation makes the plaid effect. Linen crash may be made with the insertion of large, irregular fillings dyed a different color from the rest of the yarns. Wool tweeds and homespuns use yarns of different colors. Fibers dyed different colors when in raw stock produce cloth with a mottled effect. Gray flannel with a mottled appearance is made in this way.

6. *Variations in dyeing and finishing.* Printing, piece-dyeing, and various finishes will vary the appearance not only of plain-weave fabrics but also of all other weaves. Variations due to different fiber combinations, kinds of yarn, and methods of dyeing, printing, and finishing vary the appearance of the cloth but do *not* affect the *structural* design (the weave).

TWILL WEAVE

Twill is the most durable of all weaves. In this weave the filling yarns are interlaced with the warps in such a way as to form diagonal ridges across the fabric. These diagonals, called *wales,* may run from upper left to lower right (Fig. 4.12(a)), from upper right to lower left (Fig. 4.12(b)), or both ways in the same cloth (Fig. 4.13). If the wales run from upper right to lower left, the weave is called a *right-hand twill;* if the wales run from upper left to lower right, the weave is called a *left-hand twill;* if the wales run both ways, the weave is a *herringbone.*

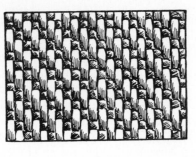

(a)

1 2 3 4 5 6 7 8 9 10 11   1 2 3 4 5 6 7 8 9 10 11

(b)   (c)

Figure 4.12 (a) Interlacement of yarns in uneven twill weave; wales run from upper left to lower right in this illustration. (b) Even twill weave; wales run from upper right to lower left in this illustration. (c) Uneven twill weave; wales run in the same direction as in (a).

The twill weave may also be called the serge or diagonal weave. In a piece of coarse serge, the filling yarn passes over two and under two warp yarns, alternating across the cloth. This is the first pick. For the second pick, or second time across, the filling passes over two and under two warps, but it laps back on the ground on the previous row, thus forming a stair pattern. In serge, the twill runs in the same direction as the twist in the yarns. Point-paper designs for two types of twills appear in Figs. 4.12(b) and (c).

In the even twill (Fig. 4.12(b)), the filling passes over the same number or warps as it passes under. The wale on the right side of the cloth is represented by the black squares. In this weave the wales and the valleys between them are the same width. On the wrong side of the cloth, the wales run from upper left to lower right.

The uneven twill (Fig. 4.12(c)) shows diagonals in black squares on the right side of the cloth. The filling passes under more yarns than it passes over

Figure 4.13   Herringbone weave. Left: point-paper design. Right: cloth. (Photo by Jack Pitkin.)

(under 2 and over 1). A twill pattern might also require the filling to pass over 1 and under 3, 4, 5, 6, or over 2 and under 1, 3, 4. To recognize even and uneven twills, compare the width of a wale with the width of a valley between two wales. If the wales and the valley are the same widths, the twill is even; if they are of unequal widths, the twill is uneven. If the valleys are narrower than the wales, the wales stand out predominantly.

The following is an outline of the shedding that forms the even twill in Fig. 4.12(b). Beginning at the right, the warps are lifted in the following combinations to allow the shuttle to pass under:

First row (top)	Warps 1, 4, 5, 8, 9, etc.
Second row	Warps 11, 8, 7, 4, 3, etc.
Third row	Warps 2, 3, 6, 7, 10, 11, etc.
Fourth row	Warps 10, 9, 6, 5, 2, 1, etc.
Fifth row	Repeat first row

In Fig. 4.12(b), it takes four picks (rows) to complete a design; four series of warps must be lifted and four harnesses must be used. This twill construction is called a *four-shaft* twill. A quick method to determine the number of shafts required is to add together the number of warp yarns the filling goes over and under. In this case, over 2 under 2. Therefore, 2 + 2 = 4 shafts. It is known as 2/2 twill or 2 X 2 twill.

The outline of shedding for the construction in Fig. 4.12(c) is as follows (the method is the same as already mentioned):

First row (top)	Warps 1, 2, 4, 5, 7, 8, 10, 11, etc.
Second row	Warps 11, 9, 8, 6, 5, 3, 2, etc.
Third row	Warps 1, 3, 4, 6, 7, 9, 10, etc.
Fourth row	Repeat first row

Another four-shaft twill is the 3/1 twill or 1/3 twill. Since it takes three picks or rows to complete a design and three series of warps must be lifted, this weave is called a *three-shaft* twill. Using the quick method: the filling goes under 2 and over 1 (2 + 1 = 3 shafts required) for 2/1 twill. This system automatically tells the number of shafts by simple addition.

Variations of the Twill Weave

The most common variation of the twill weave is the *herringbone*. In this weave the diagonal runs in one direction for a few rows and then reverses and runs in the opposite direction. The effect resembles the backbone of a herring, as the name implies. Figure 4.13 shows a point-paper design of a herringbone weave. Either the even or the uneven twills can make a herringbone, but in either case, there must be a variation in the weave at the apex of each pyramid to reverse the wales.

Other variations of the twill may be made to form diamond patterns, as demonstrated by some worsted cheviots. Passing the filling over a large number of warps at a time produces a heavy, corded wale, common in whipcord. The wales may be broken at intervals or may curve or wave for a more unusual effect. If the twist of the yarns runs opposite to the pattern, a rough twill is made.

Variations in the use of fiber blends and yarns of different sizes, qualities, colors, and finishes makes possible many visual effects in the twill weave, as in the case of plain weaves.

Advantages and Disadvantages of Twill Weaves

Twill weaves usually make fabrics closer in texture, heavier, and stronger than do plain weaves. This is why twills are so suitable for men's clothing fabrics. Also, it is possible to produce more fancy designs in twills than in plain weaves. As has been seen in the illustrations, more elaborate shedding is needed for the twill than for the plain weave. Therefore twill cloths may cost more. Twills do not show dirt so quickly as plain weaves, but once they are dirty, they are harder to clean.

Cloths in Twill Weave

Cloths made in twill weave may be classified as follows (it will be noticed that the twill is frequently used for cottons and wools):

1. *Cottons.* Jean, ticking, drill, Canton flannel, denim, gabardine, covert cloth, khaki, serge.
2. *Linens.* Ticking and table and towel drills.
3. *Silks.* Twill foulard, serge, surah.
4. *Wools.* Serge, worsted cheviot, gabardine, covert, flannel (twill or plain), tweed (twill or plain), unfinished worsted, broadcloth, sharkskin.
5. *Rayons, acetates, and blends.* Garbardine, surah, foulard, flannel.
6. *Polyester.* Suitings such as serge and gabardine.

SATIN WEAVES

Why do satins have sheen? In what way are they different from the dull-finished silks?

Any consumer may have asked these questions. The answer to both questions is that the type of cloth construction called the *satin weave* gives great sheen to a fabric and reflects the light better than dull-finished fabrics in plain or twill weave do.

The consumer should notice that whenever she feels a silk, polyester, or rayon dress satin, the hand slips more easily lengthwise than crosswise of the fabric (the right or shiny side should be felt). The reason is that more warps than fillings are exposed on the right side. If the fabric is turned over, more fillings than warps are visible. The sheen of the fabric runs warpwise on the right side. Dressmakers must be sure that dresses are cut so that the sheen runs lengthwise of the dress.

Cotton, if highly mercerized, may be woven in the satin weave and is knows as sateen.

Satin uses the principle of the twill. In fact, some authorities call this weave *rearranged* or *skipping* twill. In this discussion, however, the twill and the satin are considered separately. In satin, there is a semblance of a broken diagonal, but the interlacings of the warp and filling are placed as far apart as possible to avoid the forming of a wale. In the satin construction the warp may not interlace with the filling for four to twelve yarns. Thus, varying lengths of warp are left exposed on the surface of the cloth. When a warp skips seven fillings before it interlaces, the weave is called an eight-float satin; if the warp skips five yarns, the weave is a six-float satin. If the filling skips four yarns before interlacing with a warp, the weave is a five-float satin weave, and so on. Point-paper designs of the satin weave appear in Figs. 4.14 and 4.15.

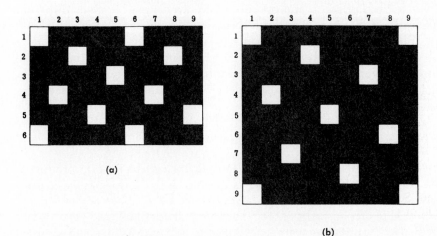

(a)

(b)

Figure 4.14 Left: Four-float satin weave. Right: Seven-float satin weave.

Figure 4.15 Short-float satin weave.

Figure 4.14 illustrates a long-float satin weave. The warp floats over eleven filling yarns. The blackened portion represents warp yarns brought to the face of the fabric. A predominance of blackened squares denotes a predominance of floating warps. Figure 4.15 illustrates a short-float satin weave.

Advantages and Disadvantages of Satin Weave

These constructions produce smooth, lustrous, rich-looking fabrics that give reasonably good service if they are not subjected to excessive hard wear. Short-float fabrics are more durable than long-float fabrics, for the former have less exposed yarn to catch on rough objects; long floats, although they increase the sheen of a fabric, snag and pull if there are any protrusions or splinters on furniture.

When style calls for luxurious fabrics for formal wear, satin is often chosen. It is an especially suitable fabric for coat linings because its smooth surface allows coats to be slipped on and off very easily. In general, it sheds dirt well, but a bright rayon in a long-float satin weave will often have a metallic sheen that may appear greasy after continuous wear.

The satin weave usually requires more shafts in the weaving than do the plain or twill weaves, thereby increasing the cost of production. For instance, in the design in Fig. 4.15, the filling passes over one and under four warps, so five shafts are required $(4 + 1 = 5)$.

Variations in the Satin Weave

Warp yarns may be twisted loosely, and long floats may be used to produce a high sheen. When a softer, lower luster is desired, warp yarns may be twisted more tightly and the floats may be shortened.

By the use of creped yarns of reeled or spun silk for filling and very loosely twisted reeled silk for floating warps, a warp satin face with a creped back can be made; the lustrous, smooth reeled-silk warps are thrown to the face of the fabric in warp floats, while the tightly twisted, dull, creped filling yarns are kept on the back. The fabric is reversible and is called satin crepe. Likewise, cotton or spun-silk yarns may be used for the filling. Since the warp made of lustrous reeled silk covers the face of the fabric, the cotton or spun silk can be carefully concealed. Since rayons, acetates, and nylons are woven in the same satin construction as are silks, their appearance can be changed in a similar manner.

The finishing processes and the amount of twist in the yarn affect the feel of the fabric. For example, a cloth may feel soft after the weaving; but if stiffened in finishing, the fabric will feel more crisp, less soft, and less elastic.

The satin weave may be varied. If highly mercerized cotton yarns are used, the sheen of sateen will be increased.

Cloths Made in Satin Weave

Materials that are made in the satin weave include antique satin (millions of yards per year), bridal satin, charmeuse, cotton satin, dress satin, satin bengaline, satin crepe, satin faille, slipper satin, and Venetian satin.

IDENTIFICATION OF WARP AND FILLING

The plain, twill, and satin weaves are the three fundamental weaves. Before studying more complicated ones, the reader should learn how to distinguish warp from filling in these weaves and how to choose between them for various uses.

With a large piece of goods sold by the yard it is easy to tell warp from filling, for the selvages, or finished edges, run parallel to the warp. But if there are no selvages and the consumer has only a sample of cloth of mail-order size, other methods to distinguish warp or filling must be used.

In Plain Weave

The count in plain-weave cloths is usually the determining factor. There are generally more warps than fillings to the inch. In a square-count cloth, 80 X 80, the way to identify warp is first to break a yarn in each direction to compare breaking strengths. The greater breaking strength is usually the warp because the warps are generally twisted more tightly—with the exception of the creped cloths such as flat crepe and satin crepe, in which the filling is the more tightly twisted yarn. In rib variations of the plain weave, the ribs of cotton broadcloth, cotton poplin, bengaline, grosgrain, and faille run fillingwise, but the rib in Bedford cord runs warpwise. In 2 X 2 and 4 X 4 basket weaves, the warps can be recognized by their twist or by their greater strength. In 2 X 1 basket weave, there is usually one large filling to two close, parallel warps. The uneven bumpy yarns in pongee and shantung run fillingwise.

RIGHT AND WRONG SIDES OF A FABRIC

To tell the right side from the wrong side of a plain-weave cloth is often difficult unless it is on a bolt, in which case the cloth may be folded with the right side inside to keep it clean. If one side of a fabric is more lustrous than the other side, the shinier side is the right side. A printed fabric design usually shows more clearly on the right side. In ribbed fabrics, the rib is often more distinct on the right side. Slub-yarn fabrics often show the slub more predominantly on the right side. Napped cloths are softer and fuzzier on the right side.

In Twill Weave

The side on which the wale shows up more clearly is the right side—unless the fabric is napped, in which case the side with more napping is the right side. With the right side to the observer, the fabrics should be turned until the wales run from the upper right corner to the lower left corner, or vice versa. When the sample is held in this position, the warp should run up and down and the filling crosswise. Warps are usually stronger and more tightly twisted than fillings. Sometimes warp yarns can be distinguished from filling yarns by the amount of wave or kink in them. Fillings are likely to be more wavy, because they are not held in tension in the loom as they go over and under the warps.

In Satin Weave

If the fabric is extremely lustrous and smooth, the consumer may suspect it is a satin construction. First, the finger should be run over the cloth to determine in which way the floats lie. The way the finger slips more easily is the way the floats run. If the fabric is silk, rayon, acetate, or a synthetic mixture, or a blend of these fibers, the warp floats, and the weave is satin. Silk and cotton mixtures, rayon and cotton, and acetate and cotton also have warp floats. If the fabric is all-cotton, the float is usually fillingwise and the fabric is also known as sateen. But the cotton satin that is used for coat linings—called farmer's satin—has a warp float.

INSPECTION OF WOVEN GOODS

As goods come from the weaving room, they must be inspected for defects.[4] In the past, and to a considerable extent today, the detection of defects was done manually, but recently a laser beam system has been devised by Springs Industries that speeds up the inspection process over 80 percent with no deterioration in quality. The new system also reduces operator fatigue, provides quicker feedback to correct deficient loom and yarn operations, reduces the cost of inspection, leads to no increase in seconds (goods with excessive flaws), and frees up space for the newer, larger looms.

[4]*America's Textiles* (R/B edition), August 1980, p. 31.

The cloth from the loom is passed under a scanner while moving at the rate of 250 yards a minute. A laser beam is projected on the cloth that scans both the warps and the fillings and is reflected onto mirrors both above and below the cloth. These identify the points at which flaws in the construction exist, and the types of flaws are determined:

1. Light reflected from the surface of the fabric reveals oil spots and colored threads.
2. Light reflected below the fabric identifies slubs, spun-in waste, and coarse filling yarn.
3. Light that passes through the fabric undisturbed indicates the presence of thin spots, fine yarns, and missing threads.

A marking system records these defects, and the cloth is passed to an inspection station where a manual operator analyzes the automatic findings and determines the adjustments required.

While currently used only for greige goods (see the glossary in this chapter), ultimately the system may be refined to scan for flaws in coloring as well. (See Chapter 7 for the inspection of finished goods.)

Figure 4.16 shows the inspection system layout. Rolls of cloth from the loom are sewn together, and several rolls are accumulated in a *scray*. This allows

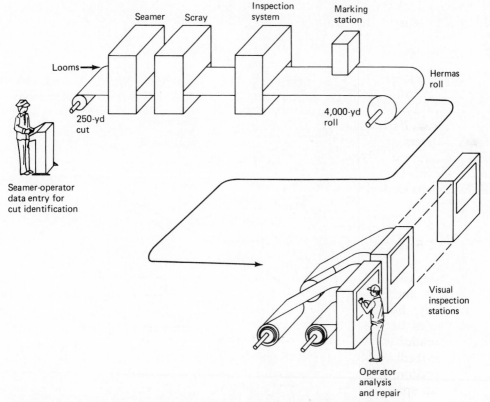

Figure 4.16 Inspection system implementation. (Courtesy of Springs Industries, Inc.)

a continuous flow of fabric through the laser inspection system and the marker, which sprays a removable ink mark near the defects. The large rolls of cloth then move on to the visual inspector, where the mark on the cloth reaches the inspector first, alerting him or her that the defect will follow within one yard of the mark. The information is then analyzed, and repair and/or adjustment decisions are made.

Figure 4.17 depicts the operation of the laser scanning system where the only moving parts are the rotating multifaceted mirror and the cloth itself.

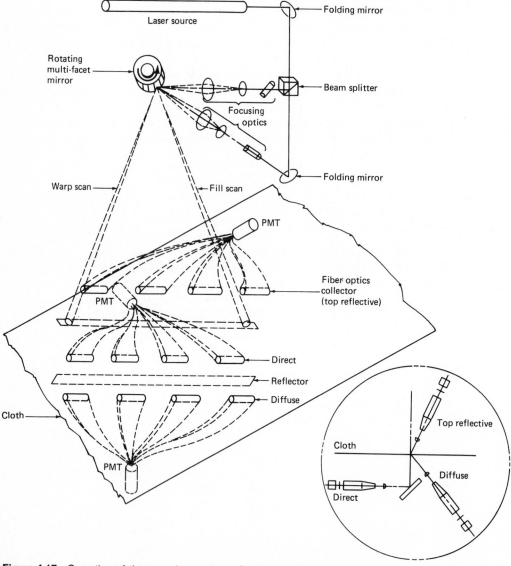

Figure 4.17 Operation of the scanning system. (Courtesy of Springs Industries, Inc.)

GUIDES TO CONSUMERS IN CHOOSING WEAVES

The consumer should know, first, the factors that enable one to choose suitable fabrics from the standpoint of type of fibers and yarn and should consider, second, the fabrics from the standpoint of construction or weave. In this chapter the three basic weaves—plain, twill, and satin—have been discussed.

If suitability is a factor of major consideration, the consumer should carefully consider the purpose for which the fabric is to be used. The plain weave is probably the most serviceable of all weaves. It is easy to dry-clean and to launder, wears well, is becoming to the majority of people, is comfortable, is usually in style in one cloth or another, and is comparatively inexpensive. However, loose weaves (the basket in particular) are more likely to shrink than are close weaves. The more the yarns slip or give, the more danger there is of their shrinking. A twill in wool keeps its press and shape well when used for suitings. For daily business wear, a plain-weave wool or silk crepe requires little pressing and is always becoming. For infants' wear, plain or twill cloths are best. Twill weaves do not show dirt so quickly as plain weaves, but more effort is required to clean them. For boys' wear, the twilled worsted is a durable suiting. For girls, a plain weave or a twill are both good. Many mothers prefer plain weaves for fabrics requiring frequent laundering and twills for wool goods.

Satins are impractical for active sports and for hard daily wear. There is the danger not only that they will snag, but also that in time they will look greasy. If style calls for a lustrous sheen for women's evening wear, the consumer should choose satin—provided she is not too stout—for satins tend to make one look larger. Style and becomingness go hand in hand. If wearing quality is a factor in selecting satin, a short float should be chosen. Beauty, appearance, and style usually govern the choice of satin. Since the satin weave requires more complicated machinery than do the plain or twill weaves, it is relatively more expensive.

SUMMARY

Plain, twill, and satin weaves with their variations are considered the three basic weaves in the construction of textile fabrics. The weaves are arranged according to the simplicity of their manufacture (with the plain weave as the simplest) and according to the frequency of use.

The plain weave is made from all types of textile yarns, but it is most common in cottons. Twill, the strongest weave, is used mainly when durability is the prime requisite. The satin weave is beautiful but may not be durable. The satin weave is most common in silks, rayons, acetates, and synthetics, where beauty depends upon richness of sheen. Sateen, a cotton fabric in the satin weave, may also appear in elaborate woven-in patterns. Fancy weaves are discussed in the next chapter.

REVIEW QUESTIONS

1. (a) What is weaving?
   (b) What is a loom?
   (c) How is the loom prepared for weaving?
   (d) Describe the action of the loom.
   (e) Can weaving be done without a shuttle? How?
2. (a) How is the plain weave made?
   (b) Draw a point-paper design to illustrate the plain weave.
3. In what ways may the plain weave be varied:
   (a) in actual construction?
   (b) in visual design or effect?
4. (a) What are the advantages of the plain weave?
   (b) What are its disadvantages?
5. Draw a point-paper design to illustrate (a) a rib weave, (b) a 2 X 2 basekt weave, (c) a 2 X 1 basket weave.
6. (a) What is meant by the count of cloth?
   (b) How does count of cloth differ from count of yarn?
   (c) Why is the count of cloth important to a buyer of cottons or linens?
7. (a) Explain the contruction of a twill weave.
   (b) Draw a point-paper design to illustrate a four-shaft twill, a three-shaft twill.
8. (a) What are the advantages of a cloth made in twill weave?
   (b) What are its disadvantages?
9. (a) In what respect does the satin weave differ from the twill weave?
   (b) What is sateen?
   (c) Draw a point-paper design illustrating a five-shaft warp satin weave.
   (d) Draw a point-paper design illustrating a five-shaft filling satin weave.
10. Which of the three standard weaves is
    (a) the most durable? Why?
    (b) the most beautiful? Why?
    (c) the most serviceable? Why?
11. List ten fabrics made in (a) plain weave, (b) twill weave, (c) satin weave.
12. Define float, four-shaft twill, point-paper design, warp, heddle, pick, shuttle, end, selvage, filling, balance of a cloth, letting out and taking up, merchandise beam, wale, herringbone, shedding, high-count cloth, crepe, pick glass.

EXPERIMENTS

1. *Identification of warp and filling.* Examine a number of swatches. Be sure you have the right side, the more lustrous side, toward you. Note whether or not there is a selvage to indicate which dimension is the warp. If there is no selvage, unravel a yarn either way. Which yarn is stronger? Which yarn has the tighter twist? Which yarn was in tension on the loom? Which yarn has the more kink in it? Which yarn, then, is the warp?
2. *Identification of weave.* Mount each sample on a sheet of paper with the warp running lengthwise of the paper. With the aid of a pin or a pick glass, look at the filling and count the number of warps it goes over and under. Write down the system of shedding used for each row. When does the design repeat? Are there wales in the fabric? Are there floats? Are there ribs? Is the design like the plaiting of a splint

basket? What is the name of the weave? Draw a point-paper design to illustrate the weave.

3. *Count of cloth.* Unravel a number of yarns both ways to make wide, frayed edges. If the fabric is of a light color, put it against something black, and vice versa. With the aid of a magnifying glass, or better, a pick glass, count the number of yarns to the ¼ inch, first one way of the cloth and then the other way. Express the count of the cloth by giving the number of picks and ends to the inch. Does the cloth have good balance? Why? Will the cloth wear well? Why?

4. *Test for durability of the weave.* Grip opposite edges of the cloth tightly. Put your thumbs together and press down hard on the fabric. Does the cloth tear? Does the weave become badly distorted? Is the weave durable?

PROJECTS

1. Construct a cigar-box loom, using yarn strung as warp yarns the length of the box and held in place with thumb tacks. Insert filling yarns by hand so as to construct one or more of the basic weaves.

2. Use strips of paper about one-quarter inch wide. Two colors are preferable—one for warp and one for filling. Interlace these strips of paper to form a paper mat of plain weave. Then make the twill and satin weaves. These mats should be kept in the textile notebook or manual.

GLOSSARY

Balance of cloth Proportion of warp yarns to filling yarns.

Balance of count Number of warps and fillings to the inch are nearly the same.

Basket weave Variation of the plain weave in which two or more filling yarns are passed alternately over and under two or more warp yarns.

Battening Pushing each filling (or pick) against the previous filling. See *reed.*

Box loom A loom with two or more shuttles used for weaving fabrics containing filling yarns that vary in fiber, content, size, twist, or color; the appropriate shuttle is activated at the point needed in the pattern.

Charmeuse A medium-weight satin fabric of silk or man-made fibers with a very high luster on the surface and a dull back of crepe yarns.

Cloth beam See *merchandise beam.*

Count of cloth Number of picks and ends to the square inch.

Crepe A fabric with a crimped effect.

Crowfoot weave A variation of the twill: three up, one down warp, or one up, three down filling.

Drill A strong cotton fabric in an uneven twill weave.

End A warp yarn.

Even twill Filling passes over the same number of warps it passes under.

Filling Crosswise yarn in woven cloth.

Float In a satin weave, the number of fillings a warp skips over before interlacement or the number of warps a filling skips over before interlacement.

Frame See *harness.*

Greige (or gray) goods Woven and knitted fabrics in an unfinished state, before finishing, dyeing, and printing.

Harness   The frame holding warp yarns, which are threaded through the eyes of its heddles. See *heddles*.

Heddles   Series of wires held by the frame or harness. Each wire has an eye like that of a needle through which a warp yarn is threaded. Heddles are raised to form the *shed*. See *shedding*.

Herringbone weave   Variation of the twill in which the wale runs in one direction for a few rows and then reverses.

Letting off   Releasing warp yarns from the warp beam as the weaving operation proceeds

Linen tester   See *pick glass*.

Loom   A machine for weaving cloth. It is operated either by hand or by machine.

Merchandise beam   Cylinder in the loom on which finished cloth is wound (taken up). It is synonymous with *cloth beam*.

Oxford weave   A 2 × 1 basket weave.

Pick   See *filling*.

Pick glass   A magnifying glass for counting cloth, also called a *linen tester* or *pick counter*.

Picking   Carrying the filling through the shed.

Plain weave   Each filling yarn passes successively over and under each warp yarn, alternating each row. A synonym is *tabby weave*.

Point-paper design   Squared paper pattern to represent a certain weave.

Reed   This frame, located directly in front of the harnesses, separates the warps and swings forward to batten the last filling inserted against previous fillings. See *battening*.

Rib weave   A variation of the plain weave made by using fillings heavier than the warps or vice versa

Sateen   Cotton fabric in a satin weave.

Satin weave   Characterized by a smooth surface caused by floats running warpwise or fillingwise.

Selvage   See the glossary in Chapter 2.

Shedding   The raising and lowering of the warp ends by means of the harness and heddles to form the shed (passage) for the filling yarn to pass through from one side of the loom to the other.

Shuttle   A boatlike device that carries a supply of filling yarn through the shed across the width of the fabric.

Shuttleless loom   A machine that carries the filling yarns through the shed by the use of air or water jets, projectiles, or "rapiers."

Structural design   A woven-in design, as opposed to a printed one, on a fabric.

Tabby weave   See *plain weave*.

Taking up   Winding up finished cloth on the merchandise beam as weaving proceeds.

Twill weave   Filling yarns are interlaced with the warps in such a way that diagonal ridges are formed in the fabric.

Uneven twill weave   The filling passes under more yarns than it passes over.

Wales   Diagonal ridges characteristic of the twill weave.

Warp beam   Cylindrical spool at the back of the loom on which warp yarns are wound.

Weaving   A process of making cloth by interlacing two sets of yarns at right angles.

Weft   See *filling*.

Chapter 5

FANCY WEAVES: PILE, PATTERN WEAVES, LENO, AND TRIAXIAL

Luxurious velvets with downlike textures, elaborate brocades with intricate woven-in designs, small geometrical patterns, and cobwebby lace effects are quite impossible to make on the plain harness loom described in Chapter 4. These fancy effects call for either special looms or attachments for the regular harness loom; the actual weaving is usually slower than standard weaving; and the price of these elaborate effects is higher than that of the plain weaves. Nevertheless, these fabrics are in demand; they are attractive and often are used in high style fashion goods.

PILE WEAVES

Cloths with soft, downy textures are velvets, velours, and plushes. All three of these fabrics are made in pile weave. The right side of these cloths consists of soft, clipped yarns, called *pile.* The wrong side of the fabric is smooth, with no pile and with the weave showing distinctly.

Pile weave is not an entirely new construction, for it uses the plain or twill weave as its base. Twill is the stronger of the bases. The back of the fabric indicates the basic weave. But the soft pile made from extra yarns is the novelty. The extra set of yarn may be warp or filling. There are four methods of weaving pile fabrics. These are discussed below.

The Wire Method

Good-quality velvets, plushes, and Wilton and Axminster rugs are made with extra warp to form the pile. One set of warps interlaces with the filling to form the plain- or twill-weave ground of the fabric; the other set of warps forms the pile. When a row of pile is made, the warp yarns to form the pile are first raised by the harness to form the shed. Then a wire is inserted through the shed, much as filling yarn is shot through. The size of this wire is determined by the size of the pile to be made. When the set of warps to form the pile is lowered, it loops over the wire and is held in place by the next filling. The wire is then withdrawn. As this is done, a small, sharp knife attached to the end of the wire cuts the pile warp loops. The ground is then woven for a certain number of picks; then the wire is again inserted to form the pile. If the pile has not been cut evenly by the wires, the fabric is sheared again with a device like a lawn mower. (See Fig. 5.1.)

Sometimes the pile is left uncut: a wire with no knife is used, or a number of filling threads are substituted for the wire and are then withdrawn. Friezé used for upholstery is usually made with uncut loops.

The Terry Weave or Slack-Tension Pile Method

A less expensive method of pile weaving omits the wire. Groups of warps are held in tension for the groundwork of the fabric. The warps that form the pile have their tension released at intervals and are thus shoved forward. The tension is restored, and the battening up of the filling causes these warps to appear in loops. The easiest way to make this construction is to use four

Figure 5.1 A carpet in a pile weave by the wire method (uncut pile).

Figure 5.2 The three-pick system in a Martex terry towel.
(Photo courtesy of Wellington Sears Co., Inc.)

harnesses, two for the slack pile warps and two for the tight ground warps. On the first shed, pile warps are raised; two fillings are shot through this shed, but are not battened by the reed. The pile warps are lowered, and a third filling is shot through to interlace with the ground warps. Then all three fillings are battened back. Because the tension on the pile warps is loose when the fillings are battened, the pile warps appear in loops. This is known as a three-pick terry cloth because two picks go under the looped pile and one pick goes between two rows of pile. Figure 5.2 shows the ground of terry with pile removed.

The pile is usually on both sides of the fabric (pile yarns alternate in forming loops on the face and the back of the cloth). However, the pile may be made only on one side to form stripes or designs. Turkish towels are woven in this manner. Instead of "pile weave," the name "terry weave" should be used when referring to turkish toweling.

Terry weave is used to make Turkish towels, terry cloth, some friezes, and shagbark gingham. There is no nap to terry weave fabric due to the fabric structure. Uncut loops make the surface absorbent. Sheared terry is less absorbent.

The Filling Pile Method

To make corduroy, velveteen, and some plushes, extra fillings are floated over four or five warps. (See Fig. 5.3.) The floats are cut after weaving, and then the cut ends are brushed up to form the pile. These floats require precision cutting in the center of the float by a special device equipped with knives. In corduroy, characterized by a pile stripe or wale alternating with a plain wale (no pile), a separate cutting knife is necessary for cutting the floats of each wale. If there are five wales to the inch in a wide-wale corduroy 40 inches wide, then twenty cutting knives would be required. A wide-wale cloth can have all the wales cut in one operation. Very narrow wale, called *pinwale*, would have sixteen to

Figure 5.3 Left: Gray goods with wire inserted. Right: Finished corduroy. (Courtesy of Crampton-Richmond Company. Photos by Jack Pitkin.)

twenty-three wales to the inch. Pinwales are fed through the cutting machine twice. Velveteen and filling plush have an all-over pile construction. This is achieved by random floats over the face of the fabric rather than floats placed in rows as in corduroy. A twill-back velveteen is more durable than a plain back. Another point in durability is the way in which the pile is held to the ground. If a pile loop is pulled from the fabric, its shape will be a *V* or a *W*. A *V* reveals that the pile filling has interlaced with only one warp yarn, whereas a *W* reveals an interlacement with three warps. *W* is more durable because it is held to the ground by three warps instead of one.

The Double-Weave Method

Many average-grade millinery and transparent velvets are woven double; that is, two cloths are woven at the same time, face to face. Two sets of warps and two sets of fillings are used, and an extra set of warps binds the two cloths together. The plain, rib, twill, or satin weave may be used as the ground. The effect is not unlike a sandwich, with the extra set of binding warps corresponding to the jam inside. When the cloth is woven, a knife in the loom cuts the binding yarns, making two separate fabrics with sheared pile surfaces. Velvet, velour, plush and fake fur may be woven and cut apart.

Other Methods of Achieving Pile Construction

A pile fabric may be achieved by methods other than weaving. Pile can be structured in a fabric by hooking or tufting into an already structured fabric, flocking onto an already structured fabric as a finishing process, or produced by the use of pile yarns such as chenille. These methods are discussed in later chapters.

Labeling Pile Fabrics of Fur Fibers and Man-Made Fibers

Real fur, fur blended with cellulose, nylon, acrylic, or modacrylic imitation fur may be used as pile. The back may be the same fiber content as the pile or a different fiber content. According to the TFPIA, the fiber content of pile fabrics, excluding rugs, must be labeled in percentages of fibers as they appear in the fabric by weight. Or, if desired, the pile may be stated separately, and the ratio between the pile and the back or base must be stated. (See Chapter 1 for the identification of fur fibers under the TFPIA.) In the finishing process, the pile can be printed to resemble leopard, for instance; or it can be processed to look like broadtail or ermine; or it can be sheared to resemble other furs. Sometimes the pile is curled to resemble Persian lamb. But the TFPIA has specified that textile fiber products may not employ any name directly or indirectly of fur-bearing animals, such as mink, mutation, and broadtail.

Identification of Warp and Filling

Velvets have extra warps for forming the pile. Velvet was originally made of the filament fiber, silk, and subsequently of other filament fibers such as rayon and nylon. Some upholstery velvets are made of cotton and linen.

To identify warp and filling, fold the fabrics first one way and then the other. The direction that shows distinct rows of pile is the filling direction. To check for accuracy, a yarn can be unraveled in each direction. One yarn looks like a caterpillar because the pile is clinging to it. Since extra warps make the pile in the fabrics mentioned, the filling yarn holds the pile and resembles the caterpillar. The pile does not adhere to the warp yarns.

In cotton velvet, velveteen, and some plushes, extra fillings make the pile. When yarns are unraveled both ways, one yarn holds the pile; this caterpillarlike yarn is the warp. The filling yarn will be smooth. Folding the fabrics shows distinct rows of pile lengthwise because extra fillings form the pile. No folding is required to identify the warp of corduroy. The wales run warpwise.

In terry weave with uncut pile, the best way to identify the warp is to pull a loop. Notice the direction from which it pulls. Since extra warps form the loop pile, the direction from which the loop pulls is the warp. A selvage always eliminates any complicated methods of identifying warp and filling.

Guides to the Buyer of Pile Fabrics

If pile construction is used for silk, man-made fibers, or fur, these textiles are presented to the consumer in their richest, most luxurious textures. Pile fabrics feel soft and downy. Silk pile takes a rich, deep color, especially when one looks directly into the pile. If the pile is pressed down, the fabric takes on a silvery, satin cast.

Pile fabrics are warm and hence are best used for fall and winter wear. Transparent velvet with a long pile and loosely woven back is not so warm as a fabric with a short pile and a tightly woven back. An all-silk velvet is warmer than a silk with a cotton back or rayon pile. Nylon pile is very resilient, resists waterborne stains, and is easily maintained.

For velvet dresses, dressmakers usually cut the fabric so that the pile runs up. The wearer then can appreciate the richness of the fabric by looking into the pile. Another reason for having the pile run up is that the pile is less likely to mat from friction. Velvet drapes well, especially when it is all silk, and looks effective in both tailored and feminine lines. Cotton velvet is stiffer and because of its bulkiness is generally more appropriate for sportswear than for lightweight dresses. Velvets and corduroys can be made spot-resistant and of durable press. Corduroys are frequently made water-repellent for raincoats. And there are some washable velvets.

In upholstery, pile fabrics look soft, cushiony, and inviting. Pile upholstery is warm-looking in summer and so may be covered with lighter fabric covers.

The Care of Pile Fabrics

Upholstery pile fabrics should be brushed frequently with a soft brush. Brushing first against the pile and then with the pile will usually remove matted spots.

It is best to steam velvets and velveteens to remove creases and matted spots. A good way is to hang the fabric near the shower bath. Very hot water, hot enough to make steam, should be run from the shower for about ten minutes, but at no time should the fabric get soaking wet. When it is removed from the steam, it should be shaken gently and hung over a line (with the pile out) or on a hanger to dry. A garment should not be worn until the pile is thoroughly dry. Water spots can usually be removed by steaming, but other stains can best be removed by a reliable dry cleaner. Velvet that has rayon pile can be steamed the same way as silk velvet, but care should be taken not to shake it while it is wet. Two kinds of finishes are used on velvets: spot- and stain-resistant and crush-resistant. No problems are evidenced on the former type of finish; the latter may reflect light differently when pile is distorted. A steam brushing may cause the pile to resume its original erect position.

Velvets and velveteens may be steamed by still another method. Stand a hot iron upright on the ironing stand; place a damp cotton cloth over the iron to generate steam; pass the velvet slowly over the damp cloth, with the pile away from the cloth. Velvets should never be ironed flat.

The terry weave generally appears in towels, bath mats, and bathrobes. The fibers are usually cotton. Since the pile is uncut cotton yarn, the fabric washes well and should be fluffed, not ironed. The more loops on the surface of the fabric, the more absorbent the cloth. Bathmats may have rayon pile and cotton groundwork. While these fabrics are most attractive, their laundering quality and durability are questionable.

Frieze, an upholstery and drapery fabric, may be made in wool, nylon, mohair, and cotton. It is a very durable, uncut-pile fabric that dry-cleans satisfactorily, but since the dirt settles between rows of pile, frequent brushings are essential.

Factors Determining the Wearing Quality of Pile Fabrics

The lashing of the pile to the back of velvets, fabrics of fur fibers, and plushes is an important factor in determining wearing quality. As has been stated, some pile yarns are passed around only one background yarn before showing a cut end again on the surface. One interlacing of the pile is not secure; the V-shaped pile pulls out easily and bare spots are likely to appear on the fabric. No one wants a bald velvet. If the fabric is a tight weave and the pile is close, the cloth is likely to wear better than a loosely constructed one.

Several factors must be considered in judging the wearing quality of a terry cloth: (1) Are the loops firmly held so that they will not pull out in laundering? (2) Will the ground warp yarns stand the strain of hard wear? (3) Will the selvage pull out? The first factor depends on the number of fillings used to interlace with the warp for every horizontal row of loops. If only one filling yarn interlaces with the warp for every horizontal row of looped pile, the cloth is termed *one-pick*. The construction is not durable, because one filling or pick is not enough to keep the pile warps from pulling out. A three-pick cloth is an average quality. Better grades may be four-, five-, or six-pick.

The weakness in ground warp is overcome if ply yarns or more ground warps and fewer pile warps are used. Although the resultant fabrics may have decreased absorptive qualities, their durability is increased.

Fabrics Made in Pile Weaves

Fabrics that can be made in pile weave are shown in Table 5.1.

Table 5.1 Pile Weave Fabrics

Cotton	Rayon	Silk	Wool	Man-Made Fibers and Blends with Natural and Man-Made Fibers
Velveteen	Transparent velvet	Plush	Velour	Plush
Velour	Chenille	Velvet	Frieze	Velvet
Terry cloth	Lyons-type	Velour	Corduroy	Chenille
Frieze	velvet	Chenille	Plush	Velour
Corduroy	Crush-resistant		Tuffed rugs	Rugs
Chenille	pile face		Wilton rugs	Frieze
Plush			Axminster rugs	
Rugs			Oriental rugs	

Figure 5.4 Double cloth. Fabric held open to show fifth yarn joining upper and lower cloths together. (Photo by Jonas Grushkin.)

DOUBLE-CLOTH WEAVE

Double cloth is not cut apart to produce pile as in the double-weave method sometimes used in making velvets. It has at least two sets of warps and two sets of filling yarns interlaced. There may or may not be a fifth or binder yarn. Five sets of yarn are used to construct a fabric called a *true* double cloth. When four sets of yarn are used, it is referred to simply as double cloth. A variation of the double weave that uses three sets of yarn is called double-faced or backed cloth. These may have two warps and only one filling or one warp and two filling yarns. (See Figs. 5.4 and 5.5.)

The double-cloth fabric may be reversible. It is pliable and warm. Five-yarn fabrics are used for coats, skirts, capes, and blankets. The four-yarn fabric is used for dress-weight and upholstery fabrics of matelassé and for brocatelle and coverlets.

Double-faced or-backed fabrics are used for some bathrobe fabrics, some blankets, reversible heavy satin ribbon, and some silence cloths.

Figure 5.5 Backed cloth. Upper cloth is black, lower cloth is white. Since there are only four yarns used, one cloth is part of the other cloth so they cannot be completely separated. Upper left shows amount cloth can be separated. (Photo by Jonas Grushkin.)

JACQUARD WEAVE

Up to this point, no explanation has been made of how beautiful floral designs or elaborate figures are woven into a cloth. How are shamrocks woven into linen tablecloths? What makes the basket of flowers in the upholstery damask? How is the wide border with the sailboat made in the Turkish towel? There are two methods of making all-over figured weaves: the *Jacquard* and the *dobby*.

The most elaborate designs are woven on an intricately constructed loom called the Jacquard loom, and the weave of these fabrics is called the Jacquard weave. (See Fig. 5.6.) The loom was invented by a Frenchman, Joseph Marie Jacquard, in 1801. Elaborate designs could not be made on the regular harness loom that makes the plain, satin, and twill weaves, because intricate designs require many variations in shedding. So it was necessary to find a means of controlling not a series of warps but individual warps. The Jacquard loom supplied the need.

This loom is very expensive and requires a room with a fairly high ceiling to house it. The standard operation (before the introduction of computer control, described later in this chapter) is as follows. Several weeks to three months are needed to prepare the loom for making a new complicated pattern, and the weaving operation is comparatively slow. Many, however, consider Jacquard-woven cloths to be the most beautiful and the most interesting of all. The price is

Figure 5.6a Punching the cards for a Jacquard pattern. (Photo courtesy of Bigelow-Sanford Carpet Co., Inc.) **Figure 5.6b** In many mills still, the fabric pattern is imposed on cardboard by a series of punch holes similar to those used on computer cards. The loom mechanism then manipulates the warp threads, raising or lowering them according to the punch tape design. (Photo courtesy of American Textile Manufacturers Institute.)

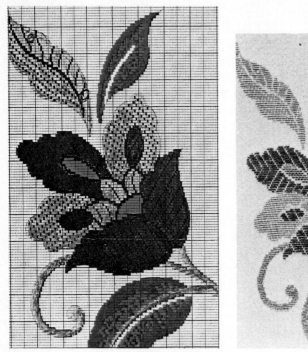

Figure 5.7 A point-paper design on the left (a) for a tapestry fabric for upholstery and on the right (b) a sample of the actual material woven on a Jacquard loom. (Courtesy of Roger Berkley, Weave Corp., Hackensack, N.J. Photo by Teri Leigh Stratford.)

correspondingly high. Since the Jacquard loom is extremely complicated, and a detailed explanation would be too lengthy, only an outline of its workings will be given here.

The design for the cloth is worked out in point-paper pattern first. (See Fig. 5.7.) Instead of harnesses, a series of oblong punched cards not unlike a large punched I.B.M. card control the raising of the warps. As many cards are made as there are picks in the design. In other words, if there are 4,000 picks or fillings to be shot across before the same design is repeated, 4,000 cards have to be made, which involves considerable labor and expense.[1] The cards are laced together in proper order and are rotated over an oblong cylinder on the upper part of the loom. From a frame hang long cords that hold fine steel wires, each with an eye through which a warp yarn is threaded. If the cloth is to have 4,500 warps, there will be 4,500 of these wires, one to control or lift each warp. It is quite evident that a great deal of effort and work are required to thread 4,500 warps through the eyes.

At the top of the loom each of these many cords is attached to a horizontal wire called a needle. These needles press forward against a card (or magnetic

[1]Compare with Jacquard-weave patterns for shuttleless looms, Chapter 4.

tape). The needles that go through the punched holes in the card pull on the cords that raise the warps to form the shed. The shuttle shoots through.[2] The card or portion of the tape just used is automatically passed on by a partial turn of the needles. Again and again, the principle of shedding is carried out until all the cards or tapes have been used once. The pattern is then repeated.

In view of the skill required to make the cards, the labor and time required to set up the loom, and the slow action of the loom, it is small wonder that Jacquard weaves were and still are expensive. Even though the use of the same cards again and again helps to decrease the price, the weaving is accomplished very slowly. To save expense, when one cloth is completed, new warps are tied to the old ones and are pulled through the loom, and another cloth is begun. Jacquard attachments are used on many types of looms and knitting machines.

The Jacquard weave is really a combination weave; two or more of the basic weaves are combined in the same cloth. For example, in table damask the design may be a satin weave with filling floats, and the background may be a satin weave with warp floats. (For the difference between single and double damask, see Chapter 19.) The sheen in the design runs in the opposite direction from that in the background, with the result that the design stands out clearly. Different colored yarns for warps and fillings make an even sharper contrast.

In a brocade, the background may be a warp satin and the design may be a fine twill or plain rib. Fiber combinations may also be used for variation in light reflectance. In borders of Turkish towels the design may be in pile weave and the background in plain or basket weave.

Computer-Aided Control in Jacquard Weaving

The speed of controlling Jacquard-woven designs can be aided by the computer. Since it takes a long time to produce a point-paper design (some two hundred hours for one design), the computer can scan the pattern very rapidly and, by means of an electronic unit, convert the warp and filling paths (the overs and unders) into a binary number form that can be "read" by the computer. A point-paper design is thrown on a television screen. At this point, the designer can change the pattern by drawing on the screen with a light sonic pen. Hence, the pattern is a row-by-row representation of the design. This information is used to control the mechanism in textile patterning machinery. (See Fig. 22.6.)

While direct control of the machinery by computer may prove too expensive, automation shortens the lead time between the design concept and the production of a sample. Fast sampling may be economical because styling approval can be given quickly. More than one version of a design can be made so there is more opportunity for experimentation in the designing process. Manual card cutting will be eliminated, for sampling as well as for large-scale production, because the computer can employ punched paper tape that is

---

[2]Magnetic and paper tape rather than cards are used with computer control as explained below.

standard for computer usage. Consequently, no special personnel need be trained and paid competitive wages for Jacquard card cutting. The magnetic tape required for making the final design can be stored in the computer for future use. Hence, in the computer-aided system, the information remains in the computer and can be used to control the design directly. (For computer control in knitting, see Chapter 6.)

Virtually all the Jacquard weaving and knitting machines currently marketed have computer controls, but the great majority in use still are the older card-controlled machines.

Identification of Warp and Filling in Jacquard Weave

If a combination of satin and sateen weaves is used, the warp usually floats in the background and the filling floats in the design when observed from the right side of the cloth. In fact, the warp is most easily distinguished if the background is observed first. If the background is plain or twill weave, the principles of identifying warp and filling in these constructions should be applied. (See Chapter 4.)

Factors Governing the Desirability of Jacquard Weave

As the satin construction appears frequently in either the background or the design of a Jacquard weave, the length of the float affects the wearing quality of the fabric. This principle is especially true in table damasks, which have to stand much friction and laundering. If long floats are used, the fabric shows a higher sheen, but durability is decreased. Cotton used in long floats is apt to lint as a result of friction. A loose weave in Jacquard construction is a great deal weaker than a tight, close weave. In selecting a cloth with a Jacquard weave, the purpose for which the fabric is intended and the kind of wear expected should be carefully considered.

Fabric Made in Jacquard Weave

Jacquard fabrics listed in Table 5.2 may be made in natural and/or man-made fibers. (See, also, Fig. 5.8.)

Table 5.2 Jacquard Fabrics

Cotton	Linen	Rayon	Silk	Wool
Damask	Damask	Damask	Damask	Damask
Terry cloth (with Jacquard designs or borders)	Borders of huck towels	Brocade	Brocade	Tapestry
Tapestry		Lamé	Tapestry	
			Lamé	

Figure 5.8 Jacquard loom products include fancy toweling and upholstery fabric. (Photo courtesy of American Textile Manufacturers Institute.)

DOBBY WEAVE

Small designs can be made inexpensively by the *dobby* attachment that is put on the plain harness loom. The dobby is an English invention. A chain of narrow strips of wood with pegs inserted in each indicates the pattern. These strips take the place of the cards of the Jacquard loom. Each strip of wood represents a pick in the design. The pegs raise the harness to form a shed. A second chain controls the shuttle. The dobby attachment may control as many as thirty-two harnesses, whereas the plain harness loom can control nineteen to twenty-five harnesses.

An American invention called the *head-motion attachment,* which is also connected to the plain harness loom, performs an operation similar to that performed by the dobby.

Simple, small geometrical figures in which the repeat in design appears often (every sixteen rows, possibly) can be satisfactorily made by these two devices. Since a woven-in design of this character was originally made only by the dobby attachment, the construction of these designs is still called dobby weave, even when the head-motion attachment rather than the dobby is used. Figure 5.9 shows a point-paper design for the dobby weave and the completed fabric.

Today, larger and fancier patterns are being made on the dobby, some simulating similar Jacquard effects, such as tulip and fleur-de-lis designs.

Small white satin float designs on a ribbed or plain white ground are called *white-on-white* or shirting madras. They are used for dress goods and men's shirts. The dobby is also used for men's ties with small geometric figures.

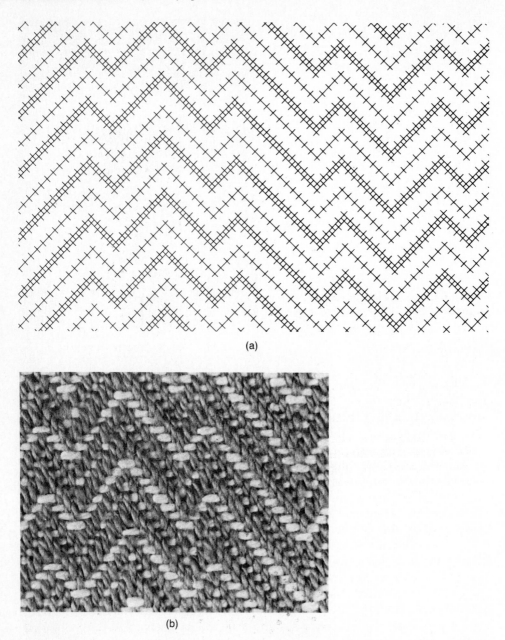

(a)

(b)

Figure 5.9 The point-paper design for a decorative fabric for upholstery on the top (a) and the completed fabric on the bottom (b) woven on a dobby loom. (Courtesy of David H. Lipkin, American Silk Mills Corporation, New York City. Photo by Teri Leigh Stratford.)

Bird's-Eye

Used for diapers, this is made in dobby weave and is characterized by small diamond-shaped figures with dots in the center. Nail-head or bird's-eye sharkskin men's suiting is made in dobby weave.

Huckaback or Huck Toweling

This is made of slack-twisted cotton or linen yarns in small geometrical designs. It is absorbent, slightly rough cloth used mostly for face towels.

Bird's-eye piqué and waffle cloth are made in a similar manner. The durability of huckaback depends on the balance of the count and the tensile strength of warp and filling; the closer the weave, the more durable the fabric. The dobby-weave design, when used for huckaback toweling, is sometimes called the honeycomb weave.

LENO WEAVE

Lacelike effects, such as those found in marquisette curtains, dishcloths, and some thermal blankets, are made by a *leno* attachment; consequently, the weave is called the *leno weave*. (See Fig. 5.10.) Leno weave comes in both curtain-weight and dress-weight fabrics, many of which are lacelike and diaphanous. In weaving, adjacent warp yarns are twisted around each other, usually in pairs. Both warps may be twisted like a figure eight, or one may be held in tension and the other twisted about it. The filling passes through the twisted warps. If one warp is in tension, and one warp twists, the weave may be called gauze. Surgical gauze is plain weave, however.

Sometimes the leno weave is combined with the plain or basket weaves to produce a lacy mesh called lace cloth. Again, a fabric of plain weave may have stripes of leno weave.

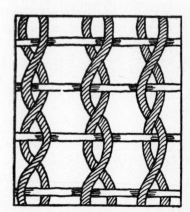

Figure 5.10 Leno weave.

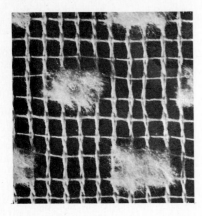

Figure 5.11 Figured marquisette, a fabric in leno weave.

Mosquito netting uses the leno construction. The fabric is made of loosely twisted yarns, and the weave is coarse compared with marquisette. After the fabric is woven, it is heavily starched to prevent dirt from sticking to it. Heavy warps and heavy fillings may be inserted at intervals to add strength.

Considering their open construction, fabrics of leno weave are durable. The figure-eight twist of the warp not only adds strength to that set of yarns, but it also prevents the filling from slipping. Leno is used in curtain marquisette. (See Fig. 5.11.) This weave is not an expensive one. Lenos are used extensively in coarse yarn drapery casement fabric, most recently with fire-retardant yarns or finishes.

TRIAXIAL WEAVE

This weave involves three sets of yarns that are interlaced so that two sets of yarn intersect a third, but at an angle other than 90°. There may be two intersecting yarns introduced from the warp direction at an angle to one filling or one warp with two filling yarns introduced at an angle to it. (See Fig. 5.12.)

Triaxial weaves give stability in all three fabric directions: warp, filling, and bias. So far, triaxial fabric structures have been used mainly in industrial and space projects.

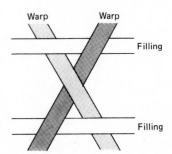

Figure 5.12 Triaxial weave.

ORNAMENTAL EMBROIDERED EFFECTS

Patterns similar to embroidery can be woven into cloth at the time the groundwork is woven. The difference between these patterns and Jacquard or dobby patterns is that embroidered effects can be pulled out by hand without injury to the rest of the cloth. Dobby or Jacquard patterns are such an integral part of the whole fabric that they cannot be removed. There are four types of these embroiderylike patterns.

Clipped-Spot Design

This is an ornamental woven effect most commonly used on cotton fabrics. An extra filling yarn generally of different size or color from the regular fillings is shot through at regular intervals in the weaving of the cloth. This extra filling is floated at points between the designs. After the cloth is woven, the floated yarns are raised so that the shearing knives may be run over these floats to cut them. The cutting is similar to that in corduroy. A single design consists of several parallel filling yarns. Swivel and clipped spot give the same effect. (See Fig. 5.13.)

Swivel Design

Extra bobbins called "swivels" carry extra filling yarns several times around a group of warp yarns to give an effect of being tied. The yarn is clipped at the end of a figure. The design, therefore, consists of one thread only. Imported dotted swiss made in Switzerland may be made in this manner. (See Fig. 5.13.) Most swivel patterns are woven into cotton fabrics. In this country the clipped-spot and flock-dotted designs have almost replaced swivel. Rayon yarns can be used for swivel designs, but rayon is too slippery to stay in well. To ascertain the wearing quality of a swivel design, pull out a cut end. If the yarn pulls out very easily, the design is not likely to be durable.

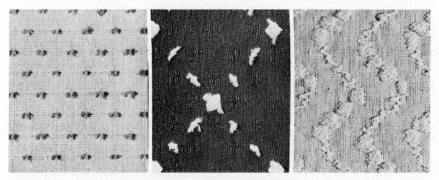

Figure 5.13 Left: Clipped spot (wrong side). Center: Swivel (wrong side). Right: Lappet (right side). (Courtesy of Stoffel & Co. Photos by Jack Pitkin.)

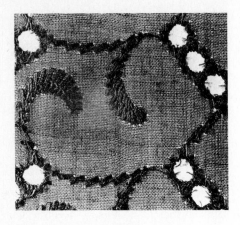

Figure 5.14 Eyelet embroidery done by the Schiffli machine. (Photo by Jonas Grushkin.)

Lappet Design

Still another pattern resembling embroidery is made by the lappet attachment. Needles threaded with yarns for the design are set upright in front of the reed, but the design yarns threaded through them do not pass through the reed. By moving the needles sideways, simple designs are woven over the regular filling yarns. A true lappet design thread is often carried in a zigzag line and is woven without being clipped. (See Fig. 5.13.)

The essential difference between a lappet design and a swivel is that in the swivel the design is done with extra *filling* yarns, which are cut off short at the end of each design. The lappet pattern appears only on the right side of the fabric, since the floats forming the pattern are fastened to the ground fabric only at their extremities. Lappet designs are made of one continuous yarn and are not clipped.

Lappet, swivel, and clipped spot are all woven fabrics; none is embroidered, although the effect is that of machine embroidery.

Schiffli Embroidery

Intricate machine embroidery on fabrics such as batiste, lawn, organdy, and piqué is generally done by the Swiss-patented Schiffli machine. (See Fig. 5.14.) The embroidery yarn may run in any direction, not just fillingwise as in clipped spot or zigzag as in lappet. Eyelets may be embroidered by the Schiffli machine.

GUIDES TO PROPER SELECTION OF WEAVES

A consumer should have a few general principles in mind when selecting a woven fabric. The purpose for which the fabric is to be used is very important. Some weaves are made for strength and durability; others are made for beauty, richness of texture, and design. In the former category are the plain and twill weaves; in the latter, satin, Jacquard, dobby, pile, and leno. To be sure, there are gradations of strength and durability in each classification. For example, a poorly balanced count in plain weave will not wear so well as a good balance. A rib weave may have ribs that are so large as to be out of proportion to other yarns in the fabric and consequently may cut the finer yarns. In pile weave, if the pile is lashed under only one background yarn, it will pull out more easily than will pile woven over and under three background yarns. If a fabric is suited to the purpose for which it is intended, it will give good service.

The consumer should determine the durability of the weave. Several factors influencing durability must be considered. First, the warp and filling yarns should be spaced evenly. Second, the weave should be straight, to ensure both strength and good appearance. Third, there should be no broken yarns or other defects in the weave. Fourth, the weave should be close, both to produce strength and to minimize shrinkage. Fifth and last, the selvages should be strong.

Do the style, novelty, beauty, and appearance of the fabric justify the price? Does the intricacy or elaborateness of the construction of the cloth justify the price? Are age and hand workmanship the chief factors? Do the raw materials and the weaving justify the price asked? The consumer should answer these questions independently and then come to a decision.

SUMMARY

Elaborate weaves, such as pile, Jacquard, dobby, and leno, should be purchased not so much for their wearing quality as for their beauty and appearance. The pile weave in velvets and in fabrics made to resemble fur has a richness of texture and a depth of coloring not found in other constructions. Terry weaves in Turkish towels have soft, absorbent surfaces and may have beautiful Jacquard and dobby designs. Leno weaves are purchased for their lacy, porous effects. In dress fabrics this weave is sheer and dainty. Jacquards are characterized by elaborate and intricate designs of remarkable beauty. Their price is correspondingly high. Dobby weaving makes simple geometric figures inexpensively. Embroidered effects produced by the lappet, clipped spot, and schiffli methods add to cloths interesting designs that are not integral parts of their construction.

REVIEW QUESTIONS

1. (a) Outline four methods of making pile weave.
   (b) Name a cloth that is woven by each method.
2. How is the durability of pile weave determined (a) in furlike fabrics? (b) in terry cloth?
3. (a) How is matted pile in a velvet dress restored to its original condition?
   (b) What instructions should the salesperson give a customer for cleaning and caring for pile fabrics used as upholstery?

4. (a) By what methods can fabrics be made to resemble fur?
   (b) Explain briefly the law for labeling and advertising such fabrics.
5. (a) Explain the action of the Jacquard loom.
   (b) How may the Jacquard loom be controlled by a computer?
   (c) Give the advantages of computer control.
6. How can the consumer tell whether the fabric is made on a Jacquard or a dobby loom?
7. What advantages has dobby weaving over Jacquard weaving? Explain fully.
8. What factors determine the wearing quality of a Jacquard weave?
9. (a) Explain the construction of the weave found in marquisette.
   (b) What are the purposes of this weave?
   (c) Is this weave usually durable? Why?
   (d) For what fabrics is this construction used?
10. (a) Describe a method of weaving the dots in dotted swiss.
    (b) How can the durability of these dots be determined?
11. (a) What is the difference between swivel and clipped-spot designs?
    (b) Which weave is more economical in the use of embroidery yarn?
    (c) How can one tell the difference among swivel, lappet, schiffli, Jacquard, and dobby patterns?
12. What factors determine the durability of any weave?
13. Define three-pick terry weave, ground warp, fake selvage, double-cloth weave, pile, velveteen, Jacquard cards, long float, huckaback, pile warp.

EXPERIMENTS

1. *Identifying fancy weaves.* Feel each fabric and look at it closely. Does the fabric have pile? Does it have a woven-in design? If so, is it small or large and intricate? Is the design an integral part of the cloth or can it be pulled out without injury to the fabric? Is the construction open and lacelike?
   (a) What is the name of each weave?
   (b) Which yarns are warp?
2. *Determining the wearing quality of fancy weaves.*
   (a) *Tearing test.* Tear a sample of material. If the fabric tears easily, the cloth will not wear well.
   (b) *Seam test.* Make a seam by pinning two edges of material together. Grip the fabric on either side of the seam. Pull the fabric. Does it show elasticity or does it split immediately? If the fabric splits easily, it will not wear well.
   (c) *Pulling test.* Grip the fabric at opposite edges; then pull slowly and evenly. Note how much strength it takes to split the fabric. Then pull the cloth with quick jerks. The fabric that will best stand quick, jerky pulling is the strongest.

GLOSSARY

Backed cloth A variety of double cloth that has two sets of fillings and one set of warps or two sets of warps and one set of fillings. See *double weave*.

Clipped-spot design Ornamental woven effect in which extra filling yarn is shot through at regular intervals in weaving of a cloth. The extra filling yarns are floated and later cut between designs. One design consists of several clipped parallel filling yarns.

Corduroy A pile fabric identified by warpwise pile wales alternating with plain wales. See *filling pile method*.

Dobby weave   A type of construction in which small geometrical figures are woven into the cloth.

Double weave   Two cloths are woven at the same time, face to face. Two sets of warps and two sets of fillings are used. One set of warps binds the two cloths together. The two cloths may or may not be cut apart. See *backed cloth*.

Filling pile method   Extra fillings are floated over four or five warps. The floats are cut after weaving and then the cut ends are brushed up to form the pile. See *corduroy*.

Flock-dotted   Designs of short fibrous materials printed in or onto the fabric with the aid of an adhesive. Electrostatic and lacquered applications of designs are two methods used. The former is durable in washing and dry cleaning; the latter may be nondurable.

Fur-fiber fabrics   Cloths woven of hair or fur fiber intended to resemble fur. For a manufacturer to use this term, the TFPIA states that the fiber content of a fabric must be hair, fur fibers, or any mixtures of animals (other than wool-producing animals) in excess of 5 percent of the total fiber weight of the textile fiber product. No direct or indirect reference to the animals' names is permitted.

Imitation velvet   A plain-weave fabric made to look like velvet by adding small tufts of fibers to the base fabric with an adhesive.

Jacquard cards   Oblong punched cards used to control the raising of warp yarns in a Jacquard loom.

Jacquard weave   A construction characterized by very intricate woven-in designs. A special Jacquard loom makes these designs by controlling each warp yarn.

Lappet   An ornamental embroidery woven into a cloth by a series of needles. The design, often in zigzag effect, is not clipped.

Leno weave   A lacelike construction made by twisting adjacent warps around each other like a figure eight. The filling passes through the twisted warps.

Pile   The cut or uncut loops composing the surface of a pile fabric.

Pile weave   A construction characterized by soft, looped yarns called *pile*. Pile may be on one or both sides and may be cut or uncut.

Pinwale   Pertaining to a cotton corduroy with very narrow wales (16 to 23 wales to the inch). See *wale*

Schiffli   Machine embroidery. The embroidery yarn is carried by a boat-shaped shuttle that can move in all directions to make intricate designs.

Swivel   Ornamental design woven in by extra filling yarns. Each design consists of one thread only, covering only the distance of one figure.

Terry cloth   Absorbent fabric made with uncut pile loops. See *terry-weave method* in the text.

Three-pick terry cloth   Two picks (fillings) go under the looped pile and one pick goes between two rows of pile.

Triaxial weave   A weave with three sets of yarn, two sets of warps and one of filling. The warps are set at 60° angles to the fillings. One set of warp yarns runs from upper right to lower left and one from upper left to lower right. The interlocking with the filling yarns results in a fabric that is stable and resists a sidewise pull.

Velvet   1. A cut pile fabric made of silk or man-made fibers in which extra warps usually form the pile by the wire method. The double-weave method may be used for average-grade transparent velvet. 2. The velvet weave. (See *Pile weave*.)

Velveteen   A cotton pile fabric usually made by the filling pile method and characterized by a plain weave or twill back.

Velour   A cut pile fabric heavier than velvet and characterized by a longer pile. The term is applied to cloths with a fine raised finish; to a cotton cut pile fabric with thicker pile than cotton velvet; to a woolen; and to knitted goods with the feeling of woven velour.

Chapter 6

KNITTING, NONWOVEN, AND OTHER CONSTRUCTIONS

"That which is or may be woven" is a definition of the noun "textile" in one standard dictionary. This definition is correct as far as it goes, but who would say that the fabrics used in the making of a sweater, a nylon hairnet, a felt hat, or a braided rug are not textile products? Yet none of these articles is woven; instead, they are all made into cloth by other methods, which include knitting, lace making, felting, braiding, and a variety of other nonwoven methods. Bonding and laminating should also be included.

KNITTING

Although weaving is the most common way of constructing cloth, knitting is the second most widely used method.

How are knitted cloths made? For knitted fabrics, a continuous yarn or set of yarns is used to form loops. For woven fabrics, two sets of yarns are necessary. The knitted cloth is composed of rows of loops with each row caught into the previous row and depending for its support on both the row below and the row above.

Knitted fabrics have invaded the woven apparel market owing to fashion changes, the demand for easy-care and comfortable clothing, the need for a diversity of constructions, and the variety of fibers and finishes available. But knitted goods have grown primarily because of the distinctive properties of knitted materials—their resistance to creasing and mussing, their easy launderability, and their ease in production as compared with woven cloth. Knitted cloth manufacture requires less lead time than does woven fabric construction; it can be switched readily from one structure to another; it provides a speedy way in which design can be incorporated.

History of Knitting

The knitting operation was supposedly invented in Scotland in the fifteenth century. The first stocking firms appeared in Nottinghamshire, England, in 1589. In 1758, a rib-knit apparatus was invented by Jebediah Strutt. But it was not until the middle of the nineteenth century that circular machinery produced tubular fabrics. Now the improved circular knitting machines are most common. Most types of hosiery, underwear, and outerwear are made in tubular form.

Kinds of Yarns and Fibers

Since an object of knitting is to construct an elastic, porous fabric, the yarns are more loosely twisted than they are for weaving. Since some knitted fabrics must have napped surfaces, slackly twisted yarn is preferable. Yarn types include flat and textured filament, spun, and blends of natural and man-made fibers.

The knitting industry's consumption of fibers and yarns has changed considerably over the years. Today, the principal raw material of the knitting industry is textured polyester yarn. It is used primarily in circular-knit (largely double-knit) fabrics and to a somewhat more modest extent in warp-knit (principally tricot) fabrics. For sweaters, the prime raw material is acrylic fiber, followed by wool. In knit sport shirts, the major fibers are cotton and polyester/cotton, with the latter gradually displacing the former because it shrinks less, is stronger, and resists abrasion. Acrylic fibers are also used in this product area, in 100 percent form as well as in blends. In the manufacture of tricot fabrics, the major raw materials are acetate, nylon, polyester, and rayon. Polyester is now an established yarn in that field and is used in either flat or textured form.

In the construction of fabrics (on the Raschel machine, to be explained later in the chapter), knitters employ a wide range of raw materials, both spun and filament, with the latter either flat or textured.[1] The chief raw material in the manufacture of fine-gauge women's hosiery is textured nylon. Spandex is also used, particularly in the manufacture of support stockings and pantyhose and in the newer, more popular contour-top pantyhose. In half-hose and other similar types of casual hosiery, virtually all the previously mentioned fibers are used, with man-made fibers significantly more important than either cotton or wool.

Hand Knitting

Hand knitting is a craft in which the knitter may show little or much creative ability. If the instructions are followed carefully, the knitter will doubtless turn out an article of a given size, shape, and texture. Should one elect to vary the

[1]For textured yarn, see Chapter 3.

instructions for choice of yarn, colors, or stitches, one will create a unique and/or artistic item.

Before a novice can make any article for personal or home use, the basic stitches in knitting must be learned.

Plain Stitch

Hand knitters call this stitch *plain knitting*. Rows of stitches, or components of the loops, run crosswise of the fabric on both sides. The first row of loops is

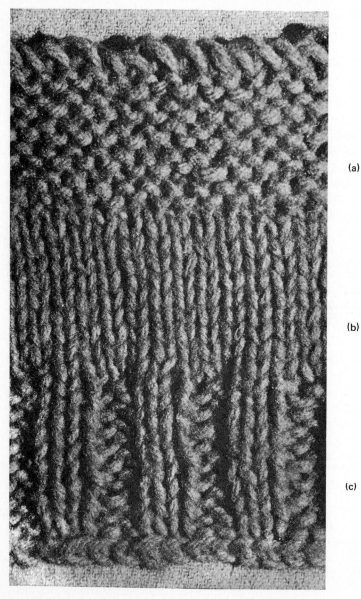

(a)

(b)

(c)

Figure 6.1 Hand knitting (right side). (a) plain stitch; (b) stockinette stitch; (c) rib stitch.

connected on the right side of the fabric, the second row is connected on the back, the third row is connected on the right side, and so on. These horizontal ridges are called courses. So, in the plain stitch, courses appear on both sides of the fabric. This stitch stretches more lengthwise than crosswise. Consequently it is not suitable for garments such as sweaters, hosiery, and underwear, in which the greater stretch must be crosswise. High-fashion sweaters, baby carriage covers, stoles, potholders, and dishcloths can be made with this stitch. (See Figs. 6.1 and 6.2.)

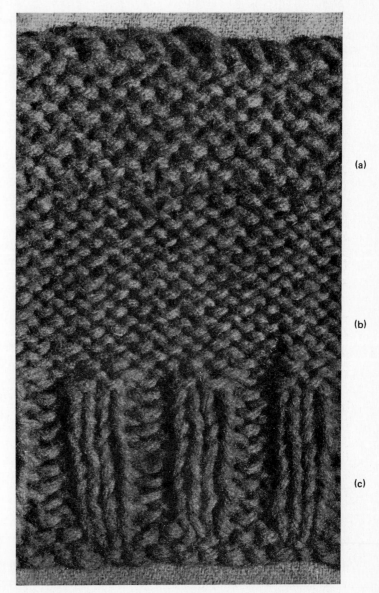

(a)

(b)

(c)

Figure 6.2 Hand knitting (wrong side). (a) Plain stitch; (b) stockinette stitch; (c) rib stitch.

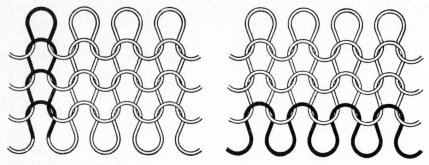

Figure 6.3 Left: A wale in a plain circular knit fabric. Right: A course in a plain circular knit fabric.

Stockinette or Jersey Stitch

In hand knitting, the plain stitch is often combined with the stockinette stitch by knitting the plain stitch in one row followed by the stockinette stitch in the next row, and so on, achieved by purling. (See *purl stitch* in the glossary.) The stockinette stitch is identified by vertical ridges on the face and horizontal courses on the back. (See Figs. 6.1 and 6.2) Since the stockinette stitch stretches more in width than in length, it is particularly suitable for hosiery, dress fabrics, underwear, sweaters, bathing suits, coats, gloves, caps, and mittens. The stockinette stitch is generally found in tubular goods, but it may be used in flat materials. Where a flat-surfaced fabric with a crosswise stretch is needed, the stockinette stitch is most common. Jersey is a fabric made in this stitch.

Rib Stitch

This is a stitch used often for boys' hosiery, for the ribbed cuffs on sleeves and legs of knitted union suits, and for garter belts on socks. Lengthwise wales appear on the right and wrong sides of the fabric. (See Fig. 6.3.) The hand-knit stitch is made by knitting two and purling two across the first row and then purling two above the two plain-knitted stitches and knitting above the two purled stitches on the second row. The result is called 2 × 2 rib. (See Fig. 6.4.) Each is two stitches wide, and each valley is two stitches wide.

Although this stitch is slower to make by machinery and requires more

Figure 6.4 2 × 2 rib knit (weft).

Figure 6.5 Warp knit. Left: Tricot (often identified as jersey). Right: Raschel (one of several types).

yarn than the plain stitch, it has an advantage in that it stretches in the width and generally returns to normal width after stretching.

There are many interesting effects possible by varying these three basic stitches to produce open work, tucks, cables, popcorn, and Jacquard patterns (argyle, for example). Hand-knit and crocheted sweaters with novelty yarns and novelty constructions have become high fashion and very expensive.

Machine Knitting

There are two basic types of machine-knitted cloth, namely, weft knitted and warp knitted. The weft-type method forms loops running crosswise on the fabric and links each loop into the one on the preceding row. Hand knitting is done in this way. (The technical name for this type of knitting is weft knitting.) Weft denotes crosswise loopings in knitting.

The second type is called warp knitted. It cannot be done by hand. The machine for this operation is called a warp-knitting machine that produces mostly open-width fabrics, but some warp-knitting machines can make tubular cloths. For warp knitting, parallel yarns must first be arranged in two tiers on the machine, with a needle for each warp yarn. Each needle makes a separate chain stitch, and the chains are tied together by the zigzag of the yarns from one needle to the other. The resultant fabric will not drop stitches, or "ladder," because loops interlock with one another both ways in the fabric.

Cut and Gauge

Gauge refers to the number of needles per 1½ or 2 inches of the needle bed in a warp-knitting machine or the number of needles involved on a 1- or 2-inch basis in the construction, respectively, of a tricot and a Raschel warp-knit cloth.[2]

Owing to the popularity of warp-knitted fabrics, mills design new constructions to increase the versatility of their products. Warp-knitted fabrics appear in intimate apparel, loungewear, dresswear, men's shirts, and women's blouses. (See Fig. 6.5.)

[2]See the glossary in this chapter.

Table 6.1 The Two Weft-Knit Fabrics: Double and Single Knits

Single Knit	Double Knit
Plain or patterned (Jacquard or striped) will curl at edges unless mechanically or chemically treated.	Plain, patterned, self-colored, or as many as four colors.
Generally lighter in weight.	Will not curl at edges.
Single-knit fabric categories: plain or stitch varied fabrics, striped fabrics, jersey, Jacquard or patterned fabrics, raised surface fabrics, plated fabrics, lay-in fabrics, fleece, velour (cut pile loops), terry (uncut loops), high pile, open work, or eyelet.	Generally heavier in weight.
	Double-knit fabric categories: interlock, narrow and broad ribs, non-Jacquard, double knit, intermediate Jacquard, and rib Jacquard double knit. Fleece, velour, and terry effects resembling those of single-knit construction can be made on double-knit machines with special attachments.

Weft-Knit Fabrics: Single and Double Knits

In weft knitting, loops are made in a continuous thread that runs crosswise to the fabric. There are two major categories of weft-knit fabrics: single knits and double knits. Fabrics made on a rotary machine with one set of needles around the cylinder are called *single knits*. Fabrics that are knitted on circular machines with two sets of cylindrically disposed needles, each set placed and operating at the right angle to the other, are designated as *double knits*. (See Table 6.1 for typical examples.)

Weft-knitted fabrics are produced in tubular form only when they come off a circular machine, but if they come off a flatbed machine (horizontal bed or V bed), they emerge in open width. Similarly, it is possible on a two-needle bar Raschel machine to produce a circular (tubular), as opposed to an open-width, fabric. For example, mesh stockings of several years ago were produced in tubular form on flatbed (double-needle or two-needle bar) Raschel machines.

Single Knits

In the jersey stitch, vertical components of the loops appear on the right side and horizontal components (courses) are seen on the wrong side. (See Fig. 6.6.) The face side of jersey usually has a softer hand than does the reverse side. Jersey Jacquard or patterned fabrics can be knitted in two or more colors, as can striped fabrics. There are many variations in patterns and stripes, such as

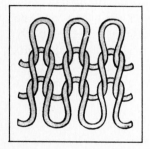

Figure 6.6 Weft knit. Left: Single knit (loops on one side of the fabric). Right: Double knit (loops on both sides of the fabric).

horizontal and vertical stripes, tartans, checks, Jacquard, eyelet, and printed patterns (design printed after knitting). Jersey fleece, velour, and terry fabrics all originate in loops protruding from the surface of the cloth. These loops are subsequently sheared and napped with the exception of terry, which is often left uncut. High-pile knitting is done by (1) sliver knit made by knitting of strands of individual fiber staple or (2) looptype made by cutting and whipping up the protruding cut ends to produce pile less deep than the former type. Plating is done by placing one yarn on the face and the other on the reverse side of a cloth. Laying-in is a technique done by placing a heavy or ornamental yarn between the loops of a fabric to make a lay-in cloth. Both plating and laying-in can be done in either a single-knit or double-knit construction.[3]

Fleecelike single-knit fabrics, commonly called fleece, are becoming a major development in modern knitting, succeeding double knit, terry, and velour (discussed earlier). It is knitted from soft spun yarn, such as cotton.

Fleece has grown steadily in demand and gives promise for a "rags-to-riches" story of old, traditional sweatsuit fabric becoming popular as a fashion item. Fleece's rise to prominence lies in its economic and creative possibilities. The knitter can produce fabric that is much lighter in weight and requires much less yarn than terry or velour does, yet gives a combination of the characteristics of terry and velour. Fleece has many creative possibilities and may show up in outerwear, evening wear, and sportswear.

Double Knits

An interlock fabric consists of two narrow ribs interknitted. It is usually a plain solid color. Stripes or small designs such as checks can vary this simple structure. Ribs range from narrow to broad widths. Non-Jacquard double-knit fabrics appear less riblike than do most double-knit fabrics. Variations of the non-Jacquard double knit are piqué, ottoman rib, Milano rib, and Ponte di Roma. Intermediate Jacquard and rib-Jacquard double-knit fabrics basically resemble in their composition non-Jacquard double-knit fabrics, except that they have an artistic design in two or more colors rather than a variation in the arrangement of fabric loops to create a stitch effect in self-color. Wide variation in width and depth of the knitted-in design is possible.

In knitting, different types of Jacquard constructions are not distinguished in the same way as in woven Jacquards. Knitters generally differentiate between full Jacquard and intermediate or mini-Jacquard. The former are patterns that are produced via a mechanical or electronic selecting mechanism for more than one complete revolution of the machine. The latter are patterns that are producible to the limit of one machine revolution and through the agency of a manually adjusted selecting means that cannot be changed unless a new pattern is required.

---

[3]"Facts About Knits: A Cutter's Guide to Basic Fabric Types," National Knitted Outerwear Association.

The rise and fall of double knits. Early in the 1960s, double knits of textured filament polyester, made on circular knitting machines in tubular form, enjoyed a rapid rise in production and in consumer demand. But this was followed by a sharp decline in the 1970s. In the 1960s, the cost of the basic material—petroleum—was reasonably low, the circular machine was easy and economical to operate, and the public was ready for the new, inexpensive product for dresses and separates. The initial success led many knitting concerns to expect a long-range period of growth. But the sharp rise in oil prices, engineered by OPEC, and the change of fashion acceptance, due in part to desire for seasonal changes in dresses and tops and for less weight in pants and skirts, caused demand to decline. Producers were slow in adjusting to the change, and many gave up the business. Close-out merchandise flooded the market with double-knit polyester clothing for several years.

Warp-Knit Fabrics

In warp knitting, the yarns that run lengthwise to the fabric, rather than across the fabric, are prepared on beams, with one or more yarns used for each needle. The resultant fabric has a flatter, closer, and less elastic knit than does that achieved with weft knitting.

Until recently, warp knitting was limited to lingerie and intimate apparel, but it has now achieved major fashion significance for outer clothing and home furnishings. A great variety of yarns and finishes may be employed.

Tricot, Raschel, Simplex, and Milanese

Of major interest in apparel are the four classes of warp knits: tricot, Raschel, simplex, and Milanese. The last two are of minor importance commercially.

Tricot. The name "tricot" comes from the French verb *tricoter*, meaning "to knit." The fabric has many surfaces: brushed, ridged, smooth, patterned, and printed. Tricot fabrics are usually designated by the number of sets of warps or lengthwise yarns that are used in their construction. The most common kind of tricot is two-bar tricot.[4] Two-bar tricot fabrics include tricot jersey, a fabric used most widely in lingerie, intimate apparel, printed outerwear, and the backing of bonded knits. It is also used in satin, sharkskin, tulle, and angel lace. Striped and patterned fabrics are included in this construction. Also produced are three- and four-bar tricots. The greater the number of bars used in making the tricot fabric, the more intricate the design. Tricot machines generally use a spring-beard needle, but compound needles are coming into use.

Raschel fabrics. These fabrics derive their name from the Raschel knit machine that produces them. This machine has a single or double alignment, horizontal-

---

[4]Bars guide the pattern in its production.

ly, of needles of the latch type. The varieties of Raschel fabrics are greater than tricot. They range from wispy netting, lace, and curtain fabrics to heavy plush and pile coating and carpet fabrics. Open work and crocheted effects come in this class of fabrics. Raschel can be single or double knitted, flat or tubular. A special device called a "chopper bar" can lay in heavier yarns to achieve a decorative surface effect. For men's suiting and trousers, it is possible to knit Raschel fabrics with similar patterns and stability of woven fabrics. Other types of Raschel fabrics include powernet for foundation garments and swimsuits; thermal cloth specially constructed for underwear; lace of weight and complexity of pattern similar to that made on Levers lace machines; and netting that ranges in structure from flimsy hairnets to deep-sea fishing or camouflage nettings. Lacey-patterned net stockings and patterned one-piece pantyhose in sheer and midsheer weights are possible. In short, Raschel is a most versatile fabric.

Simplex fabrics.   Simplex is a basic type of warp knit not used as extensively as tricot and Raschel in apparel. Actually a simplex fabric is nothing more than a double-knit tricot fabric. Simplex cloth is knitted with two sets of springbeard needles on a tricot-type machine. It looks and feels like weft-knit double jersey and is used for dress fabrics.

Milanese fabrics.   Another type of warp knit that is not too frequently used is Milanese, a name derived from the machine that makes the fabric. Its distinguishing characteristic is its diagonal, argyle-type pattern. Milanese is used as a lightweight dress fabric.

This discussion of weft and warp knits has not been exhaustive by any means. It is sufficient for the consumer and salesperson to have an appreciation of knitted cloths and their structures.

Knit Suedelike Fabric

Knitted fabric treated with a resin finish for abrasion resistance and to imitate suede has become important for outer clothing. One of the newest fabrics in this category is called *Suede 21*. It is a warp knit of 78 percent polyester and 32 percent nylon, with a coating of polyurethane. Others are made of various combinations of triacetate with nylon and polyester. Spandex may be included for extra stretch, or polyester may be used with no other fiber. (See Chapter 7 for a further discussion of suede and leatherlike finishes.)

Computer Control of Knitting Machines

Jacquard knitting machines are now controlled by computers that translate designs into a form that the computer can read or scan, and it can speedily control desired variations in design and colors.

At least seventeen companies have developed ingenious computerized Jacquard pattern preparation systems that translate designs into instructions for the machines and make it possible to produce quick modifications in patterns

Figure 6.7a A knitter places packages of yarn on a creel from which the yarn will be fed directly to a knitting machine like the other behind her. Fabrics from this machine are used for women's blouses and dresses.

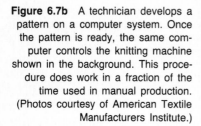

Figure 6.7b A technician develops a pattern on a computer system. Once the pattern is ready, the same computer controls the knitting machine shown in the background. This procedure does work in a fraction of the time used in manual production. (Photos courtesy of American Textile Manufacturers Institute.)

and instructions, including preparation for a wide variety of color combinations. (See Figs. 6.7(a) and (b).)

While the systems on the market vary in details, they do make it possible to express a design electronically in terms of the sequence of stitches. The design to be put into computer-readable form may be an original drawn by a designer, a print, a piece of knitted or woven cloth, or a piece of wallpaper. In many of the systems, a scanning unit scans the design very rapidly and, by means of a sonic pattern digitizer,[5] a point pattern of the stitch information is thrown onto a color television screen. There it can be modified in any way the designer wishes by

[5]An electronic unit that converts each tiny segment of a design into binary number form that can be "read" by the computer. The sequence of the electronic impulses produced controls the operation of the knitting machine and produces visual displays of the patterns.

drawing on the screen with a light sonic pen. In fact, a new design can be drawn directly on the screen and translated into a point pattern. When the pattern is judged satisfactory, a paper or magnetic tape or a disk pack is automatically prepared.

The data may be fed directly into the computer or stored on tapes or disks for future use. When ready for knitting, the master control in the computer processes the data into courses and relays. The output unit then presents the data to the knitting machine in a form that controls its operation. The number of stitches that the computer can handle varies from about 60,000 to as many as 500,000 in a large installation. Many existing knitting machines can be adapted for computer control.

However, mechanically controlled knitting machines still dominate production, although mechanical preparation for knitting is a long, arduous, and costly process with steel tapes, drums, or wheels controlling the pattern. Electronics, on the other hand, can provide the fabric maker with a sample in a few minutes and can greatly reduce time and costs involved in setting up, making changeovers, and correcting errors before the pattern is run on the machine. The electronic equipment, however, is very costly, a factor that retards quick introduction. At present, there is no evidence that electronic machines will be replacing mechanically controlled knitting machines in the near future. The electronically controlled knitting machines were formerly confined to making double-knit yard goods, but that concept is now applied to flat sweater-making machines.

Trade Standards for Knit Goods

There are no tradewide standards of quality for knitted fabrics under consideration at present. Knitted fabric technologists, under the direction of the Knitted Textile Association, have been developing specifications to describe the level of quality of knitted fabrics. They are attempting to group fabric performance factors into different classes, defining each class by different ratings. The group is also attempting to set up a uniform system to rate goods objectively for defects.

Care of Knitted Garments

Every woman knows how provoking it is to notice a dropped stitch or a run in her pantyhose. As each loop in knitting depends on other loops for its strength, a break in one loop affects all the loops below. Runs develop only in weft knitting. Hosiery can be made by regular warp knitting, but it is usually too heavy for the average consumer. If a consumer must have runproof underwear, she should buy a mesh. These fabrics have runs limited to only one direction. Runless, seamless nylon hosiery is a lock-stitch mesh.

To avoid runs in weft-knitted goods, it is advisable not to use pins, for they break the loops and start runs. When girdles are worn, fasten garters in the garter welt at the top of the stocking. This welt is of stronger construction than the boot or body of the stocking, and if a run should develop in the garter welt, it will not run below the run stop. All runs should be mended as soon as they are discovered to prevent them from running farther. Often the application of run-stop fluid, nail polish, or even water to the ends of the run may stop it temporarily.

The consumer should know a few points about the hand laundering of knitted goods. Because of their great elasticity and open construction, they may shrink or lose shape when they are washed. Care labels will specify hand laundering if required.

1. To remove dirt, use a neutral soap or mild detergent and the same cupping motion of the hands as is used for delicate fabrics. (See Chapter 16).
2. After rinsing, wrap cloth in a towel and squeeze out as much water as possible.
3. If possible, knitted fabrics should be dried flat, for the weight of water may pull a fabric out of shape and may break a loop and so cause a hole or run. If knitted fabrics must be hung, however, it is better to throw them over a line than to attach them with clothespins. When using clothespins, attach them only to the reinforcement of the toe or garter welt in hosiery. Sweaters and blouses containing wool should be washed with an all-temperature detergent in cold water, rinsed, and either drip dried or machine dried with a "cold" or "warm" setting. Garments of an all-polyester or blends should be washed in warm or cold water, drip dried, or machine dried at "warm" or "cold" setting. Laminated fabrics should be dry-cleaned only. In any case, save and follow the care label.

NONWOVEN FABRICS[6]

As used in the textile industry, this classification of fabrics is a misnomer. It does not include all fabrics that are not woven, such as knitting, felting, tufting, or the interlacing of yarns and threads. Rather, it is limited to fabrics constructed directly from a web of fibers rather than from yarns. These may be bonded together or entangled by various means. These fabrics are rapidly increasing in importance for both disposable and reusable goods.

Both natural and man-made fibers are used for the nonwovens, particularly cotton, rayon, acetate, polyester, and olefin. Combinations of fibers are also used.

Examples of nonwoven fabrics from cellulosic fibers are Webril, a cotton nonwoven made by the Kendall Company and used for wet towelettes, wipes, and headbands; Curamex and Millimex by Milyon S.A. (Mexico), both of rayon and used for medical/surgical and industrial purposes; and VAM, a cotton, rayon, and nylon blend by Pellon Corp., used for wipes and synthetic chamois. Others largely of polyester, nylon, and olefin are discussed in Chapters 14 and 15.

[6]The nonwoven fabric industry has its own association, the International Nonwoven and Disposables Association (INDA), with headquarters at 1700 Broadway, New York, New York 10019. It has published a useful *Guide to Nonwoven Fabrics.*

Construction

The construction of nonwoven fabrics begins with the formation of a carefully laid out web that is joined together by various means: application of an adhesive, heat, fusion, and entanglement. The following processes have been recognized by INDA, the association of nonwoven fabric manufacturers.

Dry Process

Compressed sheets of fiber are carded (a brushing action that smooths out the fibers), and textile wastes (such as rags and clippings) are garnetted by passing them between rollers with wire prongs. Another way of laying out the fibers to form a finished web is to suspend them in an air stream (the *air-laid* process) that forms them into a continuously moving web that is laid out more randomly than is the web produced by carding and garnetting.

The layer or layers of fibers are joined together and are compressed into a fabric that binds the fibers together by applying an adhesive or binder, such as a resin, and/or the application of heat. At this point, color is often added. The adhesive is often applied only as a pattern or on certain areas of the bat so that the other areas of the emerging fabric are not bonded. If this is done properly, a pliable fabric is achieved without unduly weakening the fabric. (See Figs. 6.8(a) and (b).)[7]

Wet Process

This is similar to the process of making paper. The fibers are suspended in water to achieve a uniform suspension. This flows over the moving screen. When the water filters out, the fibers remain in the form of a wet web. The remaining water is squeezed out and the fabric is dried. Further bonding may be achieved with rollers. Chemicals or adhesives may sometimes be applied. (See Fig. 6.8(c).)

Spunbonded Process

This method is used for man-made filament fibers that melt under heat, such as polyester. After these are extruded from a spinneret (see Chapter 14), they are laid out on a moving conveyor in such a way as to achieve the desired orientation of the fibers. This is accomplished by such means as rotating the spinneret, varying the speed of the conveyor, applying a controlled stream of air, and applying an electrical charge to make the fibers loop and crimp. The web of fibers is then fused by heat at the point at which the fibers cross one another. A chemical treatment may also be applied.

Two different types of fibers, for example, rayon and polyester, may be combined. The treatment fuses the thermoplastic fiber (polyester, in the

[7]Figures 6.8(a)–(g) show flow charts of processes for constructing nonwoven fabrics. They are reproduced courtesy of INDA, the association of the nonwoven fabrics industry in New York and excerpted from the association's *Guide to Nonwoven Fabrics*, 1978, with permission.

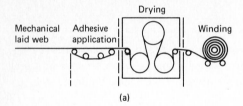

(a)

Figure 6.8a Dry process (carding or garnetting). The fibers are distributed mechanically into a uniform moving web. Adhesive or heat is then applied to convert the web into fabric.

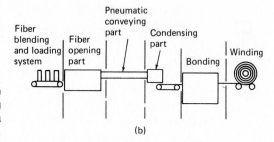

(b)

Figure 6.8b Dry process (air-laid). An air stream distributes the fibers into a continuously moving and randomly oriented web that is bonded into a fabric by the application of chemicals or heat.

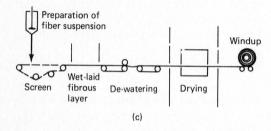

(c)

Figure 6.8c Wet process. Either natural or manmade fibers are suspended in water and are fed onto a moving screen where they form a fibrous layer. The water is then removed by squeezing and drying (a process similar to that of paper making).

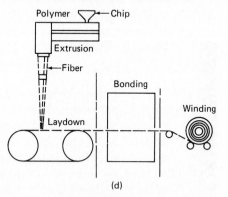

(d)

Figure 6.8d Spunbonded process. Man-made fibers are extruded through a spinneret and are laid down on a moving conveyor belt to form a continuous web that is bonded by chemical or thermal treatment.

Figure 6.8e Needlepunched process. A web of fibers is fed into a machine equipped with needles. These punch through the web intertwining the fibers so as to bind them together mechanically. Sometimes, a lightweight support fabric is also carried along with the web through the machine to provide extra strength and body.

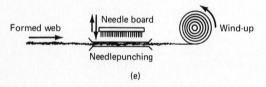

(e)

Figure 6.8f Spunlaced process. A web of fibers is entangled by means of high-velocity water jets that interlace the fibers so as to achieve mechanical bonding without adhesive or fusion.

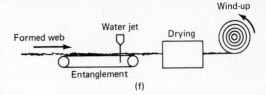

(f)

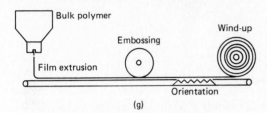

(g)

Figure 6.8g Film extrusion process. A polymer solvent is extruded, not as a fiber but, rather, as a sheet of film. This is embossed into a pattern and is then stretched and adjusted so as to open up the film into a network of fibers, thus forming a fabric.

example) to the rayon (which does not fuse) at their points of intersection. (See Figs. 6.8(d) and 6.9.)

Needlepunched Process

Instead of bonding by means of adhesion or fusion, the fibers may be joined together by entangling them. Needlepunching is one of the chief methods used to accomplish this. A needle loom is used that has a series of needles with barbed hooks that are punched through the bat of fibers that have been laid out by carding, garnetting, or air-laying. These needles force the fibers from layer to layer until they become entangled tightly together. (See Fig. 6.8(e).) A lightweight woven support material is sometimes used an as underlay in the punching process to add strength.

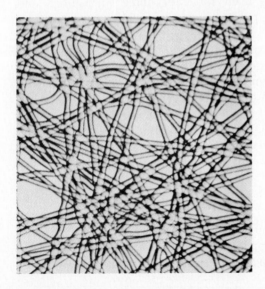

Figure 6.9 Magnification of spunbonded nylon. (Courtesy of Monsanto Co.)

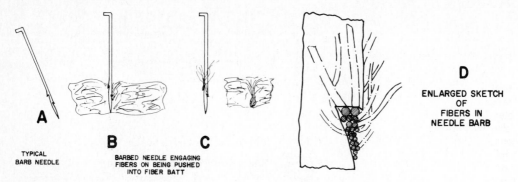

A TYPICAL BARB NEEDLE

B BARBED NEEDLE ENGAGING FIBERS ON BEING PUSHED INTO FIBER BATT

C

D ENLARGED SKETCH OF FIBERS IN NEEDLE BARB

Figure 6.10 Operation of the needles in the needlepunched process.

Variations. A somewhat similar process (with a Malivlies or Voltex machine) involves laying out long man-made filament fibers in one direction with short staple fibers placed crosswise. A machine stitches a series of loops from the long filaments to attach them to the staple fibers. As the loops are formed under tension, they interlock with the shorter yarns. The result is a stable fabric that may be piece dyed or printed. (See Figs. 6.8(e) and 6.10.)

Another process, which employs a Maliwatt or Archane machine, uses stitching thread to interlace and bind fibers together rather than stitching with the filament fibers in the bat.

Spunlaced Process

Another way in which to entangle fibers employs jets of water to entangle the fibers and hold them together by friction. No adhesive is used, and there is no fusion. Burlington makes a spunlaced polyester fabric, called Nexus, that is lightweight yet fairly strong. It is used for both home furnishings and institutional apparel. (See Fig. 6.8(f).)

Film Extrusion Process

There is another method of fabric construction that does not start with a fiber but with a plastic film. This film is extruded from a melted polymer (a chainlike structure from which man-made fibers can be derived) through a slotted die as a film rather than as fiber filaments. The film is embossed and then is stretched biaxially oriented, to the point where it opens into a netting of fibers. The form of the netting is controlled by the embossing pattern. Hercules Incorporated makes such a net fabric, which it calls Delnet. (See Figs. 6.8(g) and 6.11.)

Uses

The many uses of nonwovens may be classified as disposables, durable consumer goods, and industrial materials. All these areas are making increasing use of this kind of merchandise because of its low cost and its suitability for many needs.

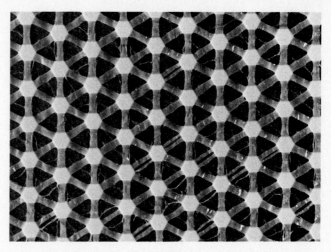

Figure 6.11 Delnet fabrics are based on either a filament or "Boss" design. The type of web produced is determined by the pattern of embossing. As embossing can be closely controlled, webs can be designed to have very specific dimensions and properties. Any one design of embossed film can produce a range of open webs according to the stretch imported to the web. (Courtesy of Hercules Incorporated. Photo by Teri Leigh Stratford.)

Disposables include medical, surgical, and sanitary goods; diapers; bibs; wipers; and even costumes for special events. They have recently become popular for lightweight "fun" clothes that can be washed a number of times.

Consumer durables include both household goods and clothing, draperies, towels, table cloths, blankets and carpet backing, linings and interlinings, and the reinforcement of other fabrics.

The many industrial uses include filters, packing materials, and road-building materials. (See Chapter 15.)

OTHER METHODS OF CONSTRUCTION

Net and Lace Making

Net is a geometrically shaped figured mesh fabric made of silk, cotton, nylon, polyester, rayon, or other man-made fiber. It comes in different sizes of mesh and in various weights. On the one hand, machine-made net is closely related to warp knitting because it is constructed on either a tricot or a Raschel warp-knitting machine; on the other hand, net is related to lace because many of the machine-made laces have geometrically shaped nets as their grounds. Bobbinet, made in a hexagonal-shaped mesh of rayon, nylon, silk, or cotton, is a popular fabric for evening dresses, veils, curtains, and trimmings. Like most nets and laces, bobbinet was originally made by hand on a pillow of the same width as the lace to be made. Small pegs or pins were stuck into the design. Thread was thrown around the pegs marking the design. When the lace was completed, the pillow was removed. (See *bobbin lace*, Chapter 19). A closely constructed, very fine silk or nylon net is called *tulle*. The first nets to be made by machine were the warp-knitted tricots that appeared about the middle of the eighteenth century. At the beginning of the nineteenth century, a bobbinet machine that could handle yarns in three directions was invented and patented by John Heathcote. Shortly after that, a patterned lace loom was devised.

Another type of net is the knotted-square mesh type with knots in four corners to form the mesh. Originally made by hand and used by fishermen, it is now made by machine. These modern fishnets of linen, cotton, or man-made fibers are used for glass curtaining in contemporary living rooms, sun porches, and dens. (See Chapter 21)

A lace is an open-work fabric made of threads usually formed into designs. (See the description of various laces, Chapter 19.) By hand, lace can be made with needles, bobbins, shuttle, or hooks. Handmade lace is called *real lace*. When needles are used, the lace is called *needlepoint;* when bobbins are used, the lace is called *bobbin* or *pillow;* when knotted with a shuttle, the lace is *tatting;* when made with a hook, it is called *crocheted.* Laces can also be made by hand with knitting or crochet needles.

Real lace was the only lace known until the invention of the lace machine in the early 1800s. This machine was later modified by several inventors, among them John Levers, whose name has come down to us via the Levers machine in use today.[8] Patterns of real laces can be reproduced on the modern lace looms, so we can now have their designs in quantity at a fraction of the cost of the handmade. Sometimes designs from various real laces will be combined in a single lace, which can be designated as *novelty lace.*

Braiding (or Plaiting)

This is a method of interlacing (plaiting) three or more yarns or bias-cut strips of cloth over and under one another to form a flat or tubular fabric. These braided textile bands, which are relatively narrow, can be used as belts, pull-cords for lights, trimming for uniforms and dresses, tapes for pajamas, and some shoelaces. Several widths of plastic or straw braiding can be sewn together to make hat shapes. Similarly, braids of fabrics or yarns may be sewn together to make braided rugs.

Tufting

Tufting is mostly used for making the pile on handmade hooked rugs and man-made tufted ones, as discussed in Chapter 20. They are used in making simulated fur pile fabrics. Instead of weaving or knitting the pile and the base cloth together in one operation, an inexpensive method is to use the Malipol machine that punches tiny tufts of pile yarn through a base cloth, commonly of cotton in plain-woven or knitted construction. The tufts on the face side appear as rows of chain stitching on the back. When laminated, the foam sticks to the stitching, not to the base fabric, so that in heavy use or dry cleaning, there may be some loss of pile. Long-pile fabrics so constructed are used for coatings, floor coverings, and blankets.

Short-pile fabrics are also made on the Malipol machine, with the pile tufts

---

[8]"Lace," *Fairchild's Dictionary of Textiles* (New York: Fairchild Publications, Inc., 1979), p. 339.

punched through scrim or sheeting and held in place with an adhesive. The front side is calendered to lay the pile in one direction so that the fabric looks like crushed velvet. This has a variety of uses in clothing.

A similar machine, called the Laropol, produces the pile on both sides of the cloth.

Felting

It is said that early peoples discovered what we know to be the felting process. By wearing the fur side of animal skins next to the body, these people discovered that the fur matted from the body's heat and perspiration and the pressure of the skin against the body. In our modern felting process, wool or fur fibers tend to mat or interlock when they are subjected to heat, moisture, and pressure. Hair of cows as well as hair of rabbits is used for woven felts and hair felts. Coarse hair of domestic cattle is used for inexpensive felted goods like insoles and underlays for rugs.[9] Fur felt hats are made from Australian, French, English, and Belgian rabbit fur.

Wool is probably most ideal for felting because the fibers swell in moisture, interlock, and remain in that condition when pressed and shrunk. When the fibers have been selected and, if necessary, blended with cotton or man-made fibers, they are carded into a flat sheet or bat. Bats are placed first one way and then the other in layers until the desired thickness is reached. Allowance has to be made for shrinkage, because steam and the pressure of heavy presses in the process of felting may increase the bats as much as 20 percent in thickness. To make the felt fabric stronger and more compact, the fabric is placed in warm soapy water, where it is pounded and twisted. For heavy felt, a weak acid is used instead of warm soapy water. (See *fulling*, Chapter 12.) The cloth is then ready for finishing processes, consisting of scouring, dyeing, possibly pressing or shearing, and treatment with special functional finishes to make it water-repellent, mothproof, and shrink-, crease-, and fire-resistant. Felt is made for men's and women's hats; women's skirts, vests, and slippers; and table covers, padding, and linings. Woven felts have their place primarily in the industrial field.

Laminating

Laminating, discussed briefly in Chapter 2, is the process of joining a fabric to a plastic foam backing or bonding two fabrics together. (See Figs. 6.12 and 6.13.)

There are two ways in which to laminate fabric to foam:

1. *Wet adhesive.* A water-based acrylic compound is applied to the fabric, followed by heat curing, which creates a permanent bond without affecting the draping quality of the face fabric or softness to hand.

[9]"What Is Felt?" *Ciba Review*, vol. 11 (November 1958), 2–3.

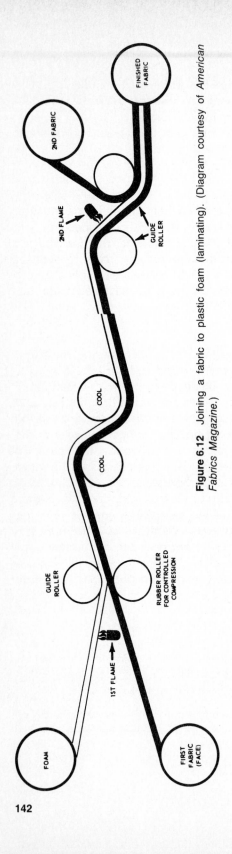

Figure 6.12 Joining a fabric to plastic foam (laminating). (Diagram courtesy of *American Fabrics Magazine*.)

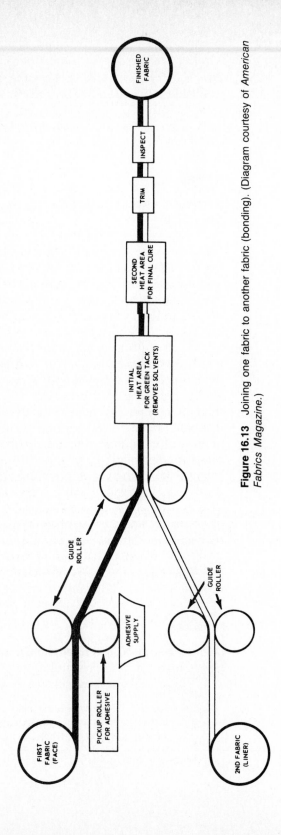

Figure 16.13 Joining one fabric to another fabric (bonding). (Diagram courtesy of *American Fabrics Magazine*.)

2. *Foam flame.* The foam is made sticky with a flame, and a small fraction of the foam's thickness is burned off. There are many uses of foam-backed fabrics, such as a stretch nylon seat cover with a foam backing that insulates to keep the rider cooler in summer and warmer in winter.

Laminating a layered fabric involves bonding two fabrics together with an adhesive, a bonding agent, or heat. An example of such a layered fabric is a pair of girls' denim jeans that have been lined at the cuffs with plaid flannelette. The flannelette has actually been laminated to the wrong side of the denim so that, when the pants are rolled up, the plaid shows. One of the fabrics used is often a nonwoven one.

Many consumers have occasion to use the same principle in mending or reinforcing clothing, sheets, or tablecloths with tape or patches by ironing the tape or patch treated with a binder against the cloth. When the proper amounts of heat and pressure are applied, the patch will adhere satisfactorily. Familiar brand names are Bondex and Irontex.

Problems of Serviceability of Laminated Fabrics

Layered fabrics sometimes come apart (become delaminated) by abrasion, because the adhesive cracks and the face fabric separates from the backing, or because in laundering one fabric shrinks more than the other due to poor stabilization. In dry cleaning, the fabric layers pull apart if the solvent solubilizes the adhesive. Designs formed by spot welding discolor or disappear—a common occurrence in simulated quilted fabrics. Mechanical action in dry cleaning might cause separation of the fabric and obliteration of the design. However, there has been a decided improvement in resistance to delamination.

Urethane backing can attract loose soil or dye particles during dry cleaning or use. This often occurrs with foam-backed placemats. The foam turns yellow or darkens owing to exposure to heat and atmospheric conditions. The outer layer of a garment can change color. Ripples and puckers might be caused by a shrinkage of one of the layers of the cloth. The spunbonded fabrics might have finishes that are not colorfast to light, washing, and perspiration. Again, the foam backing applied to upholstery may not be resistant to solvents in cleaning, even though the material itself is highly resistant. Testing with a dry-cleaning solvent will determine whether gentle washing should be substituted.

Malimo Stitch Through Construction

This is a relatively new variation of the plain weave. Instead of interlacing filling yarns through a shed of warp yarns, the filling yarns are laid out crosswise over a set of warp yarns. The warps and fillings are then sewn together with a third set of threads that stitch the warp and the filling yarns together. The stitching is done by what is known as the Malimo machine. Malimo fabrics can be constructed more rapidly and economically than they can under regular

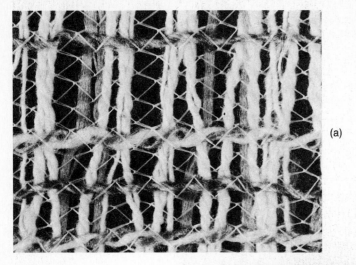

(a)

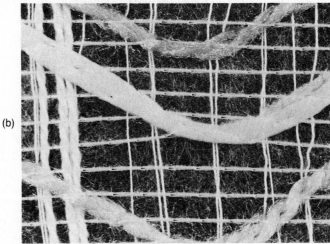

(b)

Figure 6.14 Malimo fabrics (with stitches that bind the warp and the filling yarns together). These drapery and curtain fabrics have a Malimo face. They are provided with a backing, such as acrylic foam or a thin nonwoven fabric applied during the construction. The backing acts as insulation to reduce heat loss; the application is inexpensive. The fabric at the left (a) shows the sewing threads that bind the warp and filling together. The fabric at the right (b), entirely of polyester, has binding threads that parallel the warp yarns until moved over to another warp yarn. This fabric has a tissue-thin backing of a nonwoven fabric. The decoration is sewn on by machine. (Courtesy of the Polylock Corporation, New York City. Photos by Teri Leigh Stratford.)

weaving, and less yarn is required. Whether this method will be a serious contender in the conventional weaving market is yet to be determined.

Figure 6.14 illustrates two drapery fabrics in which the Malimo construction has been used. The fabrics are insulated with a self-lined material to conserve heat. The process costs much less than lining the face fabric with a separate fabric.

Malimo fabrics are produced principally for industrial purposes of the following kinds: (1) coated and protective fabrics used for tarpaulins, belt conveyors, luggage, upholstery, and the like; (2) wiping cloths; (3) reinforced plastics; (4) bagging; (5) paper and tape reinforcement; (6) filtration; and (7) earth and ground containment—geotextiles.

SUMMARY

Knitted goods are especially suitable for garments requiring a snug fit, elasticity, and comfort. They are warm without feeling heavy, have good absorptive quality, and are hygienic. There are two methods of constructing knitted goods: weft and warp knitting. Although weft knitting has good elasticity, stitches may be dropped. On the other hand, stitches are not dropped in warp knitting. Also, in warp knitting the stretch is greater in the vertical direction.

Net making is closely allied to knitting because machine-made net can be made on a warp-knitting machine. Many laces have net grounds, and all have patterns.

To braid, three or more yarns are interlaced over and under to form a fabric. Braids are narrow goods, and several widths must be sewn together for shaped articles such as hats or rugs.

Felting is a nonwoven construction, although there is a woven felt. In felting, heat pressure and moisture cause the fibers to adhere. For bonding, a web of fibers is made and the fibers are held together by a binding agent. Felting is a much older process than is bonding, but the two processes are closely allied.

Laminating is a process of sticking a fabric to a plastic foam material or the bonding of a fabric to another fabric. Foam may be laminated to a knitted or woven fabric.

Of all the newer constructions, the nonwovens are the most important. Bonding fibers together by adhesive or fusion and by entangling them without the construction of yarn reduces costs and results in fabrics that have many uses, some disposable and some reusable. Such fabrics are well received and have a bright future.

REVIEW QUESTIONS

1. In what respects does the knitted construction differ from the woven? Consider the yarns and the knitting operation.
2. (a) What are the three principal stitches in weft knitting?
   (b) For what purposes is each used?
3. What advantages has the plain stitch over the ribbed stitch?
4. In hand knitting, contrast single and double knits.
5. (a) Describe warp knitting.
   (b) What advantages has warp knitting over weft knitting?
   (c) What fabrics are made by warp knitting?

6. (a) How do fabrics knitted in open width differ from circular- or tubular-knitted goods?
   (b) What are the advantages and the disadvantages of goods knitted by each method?
7. What instructions should salespeople give to customers on the care and laundering of knitted fabrics?
8. (a) Explain the methods of constructing nonwoven fabrics.
   (b) What are their major uses?
   (c) Differentiate among Malimo, Malipol and Maliwatt constructions.
9. Explain the following constructions:
   (a) Bobbinet
   (b) Tatting
   (c) Fishnet
   (d) Felting
10. What braided articles are used in apparel? in home furnishings?
11. (a) How are fabrics laminated?
    (b) Explain the merits and drawbacks of each method.
    (c) For what purposes are laminated fabrics used?

PROJECT

Visit the yard-goods and lace departments of your local store. List in separate columns all fabrics that are (a) woven, (b) knitted, (c) nonwoven, (d) net or lace, (e) felted, (f) braided, (g) laminated, (h) other construction. What percentage of the fabrics listed comes in each category? What conclusions can you draw?

EXPERIMENTS

1. *Determining the stitch used in knitting.* Unravel a yarn from a sample. Does it unravel back and forth from the fabric? In which direction does it stretch more? Is it weft or warp knitting? Look at the right and wrong sides of the fabric and answer the following questions:
   (a) Are there courses on both sides?
   (b) Are there wales on one side and courses on the other?
   (c) Are there wales on both sides?
   (d) Does the fabric have an open-work or mesh design?
   (e) Is the surface roughened or puckered in the knitting operation?
   (f) Has a pattern been knitted into the fabric?
   (g) What stitch or combination of stitches is used in this fabric?
2. *Determining the durability of the fabric.* Hold the fabric to the light. Answer the following questions:
   (a) Do you see thick and thin places in the yarn?
   (b) Is the knitting regular?
   (c) Is it a close construction?
   (d) Does the fabric spring back to its original shape after stretching?
   (e) Will the fabric be durable? Why?
   (f) Will a garment made from this cloth keep its shape? Why?
3. Collect examples of nonwoven fabrics. Determine fibers used and method of construction where observable.

GLOSSARY

Bobbinet See *net.*

Bonding See the glossary in Chapter 2.

Braiding See the glossary in Chapter 2.

Bulky knit A heavy or coarse stitch construction, with about 2½ to 6 stitches per inch. Used widely for sweaters.

Cable stitch A knit effect that looks like a twisted rope lengthwise of the fabric.

Circular knit Knitting in tubular form. Shaping is done by tightening or stretching stitches.

Cloqué A raised effect in Jacquard usually knitted from two colors.

Courses Horizontal ridges (components of the loops) in weft knitting.

Crochet A continuous series of loops of yarn made with a single hook. When these are connected to form patterns, the fabric is crocheted lace.

Curing The application of heat to a fabric or garment to impart properties such as dimensional stability, crease resistance, water repellency, and durable press.

Cut Number of needles per inch on the circular or flat bed of a weft-knitting machine.

Double knit Fabric knitted on circular machines with two sets of cylindrically disposed needles, each set placed and operating at a right angle to the other. See *single knit.*

Drop-stitch knit Open design made by removing certain needles at intervals.

Dry process (for nonwoven fabrics) A laying out of fibers by carding or garnetting or the application of a stream of air (air-laid process) and then applying an adhesive or heat.

Fashioning A shaping process of making flat-knitted fabrics by adding or subtracting stitches.

Felting See *fulling* in the glossary, Chapter 12.

Foam laminate A construction made by laminating a synthetic foam to a woven or knitted fabric.

Full-fashioned A term applied to sweaters and hosiery shaped by fashioning. See *fashioning.*

Gauge A term used to describe the number of needles per 1½ or 2 inches in a knitting machine, in single knits, double knits, and tricot fabrics.

Geotextiles Industrial fabrics used for earth and ground control.

Interlock knitting A process of making a compound fabric composed of two separate 1 × 1 rib fabrics interknitted to form one cloth—made on an interlock machine.

Jacquard patterns Fancy patterns knitted in articles made by a needle-selecting attachment on the knitting machine.

Jersey A knitted fabric of cotton, wool, nylon, acetate, polyester, rayon, or blends with man-made fibers. It is usually made in stockinette jersey stitch or two-bar tricot.

Knitted pile fabrics Extra yarn introduced and drawn out in loops to form the pile that may or may not be cut.

Knitting The process of constructing a cloth by interlocking a series of loops of one or more yarns. It may be done by hand or by machine.

Lace An open-work fabric made of threads usually formed into designs. It is made by hand or by machine.

Laminating The sticking of a fabric to a plastic foam or the bonding of a fabric to another fabric.

Lisle yarn   Yarn made of long-staple cotton of defined length in two or more ply and with a minimum twist for a given count specified by the FTC rules for hosiery.

Mesh   A knitted or woven fabric with an open texture. It can be made of any fiber, mixture, or blend.

Milanese   A kind of warp knitting with several sets of yarns. Characteristic is its diagonal argyle-type pattern.

Needlepunching (for nonwoven fabrics)   Laying out fibers and entangling them with barbed needles.

Net   A geometrically shaped, figured mesh fabric made in nylon, rayon, silk, or cotton. It has no pattern and is usually made on a warp-knitting machine.

Nonwoven fabrics   Webs of fibers held or bonded together with plastic, heat, pressure, or entanglement.

Open width   Fabrics that come off a flat bed machine (horizontal or V bed).

Open-work stitch   A construction of open spaces purposely made at regular intervals across the knitted cloth. It is a variation of a basic stitch.

Plain stitching   A knitting stitch that produces a series of wales on the face of the fabric and course (crosswise loops) on the back.

Plastic extrusion (for nonwoven fabrics)   Forming fibers from a plastic sheet extruded through a spinneret, embossed and stretched to create a fibrous material.

Plated goods   Knitted fabrics that have one kind of yarn on the right side of the fabric and another kind on the back.

Purl stitch   Generically, it is a knitting stitch. If by hand is made by inserting the right-hand needle into the front of the loop on the left needle from the right, catching the yarn with the right needle and bringing it through to form a new loop. Generally a weft knit in machine knitting.

Raschel knit   A warp-knitted fabric with intricate eyelet and open-work designs.

Real lace   Handmade lace. See *lace*.

Rib stitch   A weft knit identified by vertical ribs on both sides of the fabric—a very resilient stitch. When combined with the tuck stitch, it is called rib-and-tuck stitch.

Runless   A type of seamless nylon hosiery in a lock-stitch mesh.

Run-resistant   Knitted fabric constructed to make runs difficult.

Single knit   Fabric made on a rotary machine with one set of needles around the cylinder. See *double knit*.

Springbeard needle   A needle for a knitting machine with a long terminal hook (beard) that is flexed by an action called pressuring; the hook returns to its original position when it is removed.

Spunbonding (for nonwoven fabrics)   Laying out noncellulosic fibers by various mechanical means and then fusing them together at the points of intersection.

Spunlacing (for nonwoven fabrics)   Entangling the fibers with jets of water and joining them by means of friction with no fusing.

Stockinette stitch   In hand-weft knitting, characterized by vertical wales on the face and horizontal courses on the back of the fabric.

Thermal knit   A wafflelike knitted fabric that traps air between the yarns and thus acts as an insulator.

Tricot   From the French verb *tricoter*, meaning "to knit," a fabric made by a warp knitting (tricot) machine. See *two-bar tricot*.

Tubular knit   See *circular knit*.

Tuck stitch   A variation of a basic stitch in weft knitting to make a knobby, bumpy, knitted texture. Unknitted loops are slipped from one needle to another. On the following row, the unknitted loops are knitted as regular stitches.

Tufting   Attaching tufts of pile yarns to a backing fabric.

Two-bar (double-bar) tricot   A warp knit in which two sets of yarns are required, one knitted in one direction and the other in the opposite direction. A ribbed surface results. It is synonymous with double-warp tricot knit.

Wales (in knitting)   A series of loops in successive rows lying lengthwise on the fabric.

Warp knitting   A machine process with a needle for each warp yarn which makes a more dimensionally stable fabric than weft knitting. It is frequently run-resistant. Examples are tricot and Raschel.

Weft knitting   A process in which the thread runs back and forth crosswise in a fabric. See *warp knitting.*

Wet process (for nonwoven fabrics)   Laying out the fibers by suspending them in water and then drying; similar to paper making.

Chapter 7

FINISHES

A customer asks the salesperson, "If I buy these polyester/cotton slacks and the label says they are machine-washable, will I have to press them?" "No," replies the well-informed salesclerk. "They are durable press, which means they stay smooth after washing and drying."

A *finish* is a treatment applied to the fabric after construction. The stiffness of organdy, the smooth, silky feeling of batiste, the watered or moiré effect on acetate, and the whiteness of table damask are all results of finishing treatments to which the fabrics are subjected after they are made. A whole industry, called the *converting* industry, devotes itself to this finishing of cloth. The converter takes the fabrics from the mills and either treats them independently or has them treated to make them more attractive, more serviceable, and hence, more salable. Before goods are finished, they are said to be *in the gray* (or *greige*) *stage*, which does not necessarily mean gray in color.

There are the regular or basic finishes, such as napping, brushing, shearing, calendering, and the like, without which a fabric would not be suitable to sell. Basic finishes in some form have been applied to textile fabrics for centuries. Then there are the functional or special finishes that contribute a special feature to the merchandise. Permanent starchless, crease-resistant, and water-repellent are a few of the functional finishes. Finishing processes can be considered *mechanical* if they are done by copper plates, roller brushes, perforated cylinders, tenter frames, or any type of mechanical equipment. If fabrics are treated with alkalies, acids, bleaches, starches, resins, and the like, they are considered to have been subjected to *chemical* finishing processes. It is in the field of chemical finishes that the greatest developments have been made.

PERMANENT AND NONPERMANENT FINISHES: AN OVERVIEW

Permanent Finishes

Some fabrics must be so finished that friction will not harm the surface; others must be crease-resistant; and some must be unaffected by light, perspiration, washing, or water spotting. Fortunately for the manufacturer, fabrics do not have to be finished to withstand every hazard equally well; if they did, the finish would, of course, be considered permanent. But permanency of finish is not usually determined in this way. If a cloth has a finish that will withstand whatever affects it in its particular use, the finish is considered permanent. For example, an evening dress does not have to be fast to light or friction. A man's wool suit must be particularly fast to light and should be fast to friction, but it need not be fast to washing.

It is not wise to say that all types of any finish are permanent. For example, bleached silks may turn yellow sooner than bleached linens. One mercerized cotton broadcloth may lose its sheen in laundering sooner than another broadcloth. The mercerizing of the first piece may have treated only the surface of the fiber, whereas the mercerizing in the second piece may have penetrated to the core of the fiber. Permanency of finish is, of course, only a relative term.

Wash-and-wear finishes for cotton, first used in the late 1950s, have been improved considerably since their introduction. Consumers found that early wash-and-wear cottons did not all perform as the term indicated. Most of them required ironing to make them look fresh and smooth. The resin in the finishing caused the cottons to have a heavy, somewhat stiff hand. Many of the first wash-and-wear cottons turned yellow if a chlorine bleach was used on them.

Now, most of these finishes do not turn yellow. In fact, standards of quality have been set to ensure good performance of wash-and-wear finishes. Quality manufacturers asked the Sanforized Division of Cluett, Peabody & Company, Inc., to establish a standard, whereupon they developed an electronic instrument (the Electronic Smoothness Evaluator), which has an electric eye that sees—and counts—every crease and wrinkle. A fabric after washing must dry without too many wrinkles to measure up to this standard. It must resist wrinkling, not shrink out of fit, have good tensile strength, and have good tear strength. Wash-and-wear cottons that come up to all five of the Sanforized Division's specifications bear the label "Sanforized-Plus."[1] Merchandise so labeled gives the consumer insurance of satisfactory wash-and-wear performance. Such a finish would be considered permanent.

The term "permanent press" indicates a long life in durability. Hence the term *durable press* is being used in this text. "A permanent or durable press garment, or any other end use textile product such as sheets or drapery, does

---

[1]Sanforized-Plus is a trademark owned by Cluett, Peabody & Company, Inc., denoting a checked standard of wash-and-wear performance.

Figure 7.1 Fuzz on the yarns shows how napping raises short fibers in the yarns. (Photo by Jonas Grushkin.)

not require ironing for the use life of the product under normal usage conditions."[2] Manufacturers' quality-control standards call for a certain level of performance in use.[3]

Piece-dyed and printed fabrics may be fast to light, friction, and washing if their fibers have an affinity for the dyestuffs.

Beetling produces a comparatively permanent finish because the process flattens out the fibers themselves. Pressing tends to keep the fibers flat.

Nap wears off with friction but, if well made, does not wash off and is not affected by light. It is therefore generally considered a permanent finish. (See Fig. 7.1.)

Many fabrics are now treated with plastic resin. The resin is fixed in the fiber so that it becomes a part of it and cannot be felt or seen even under a microscope. The resin does not change the surface of the fabric, but it adds resilience and hence wrinkle resistance and reduces shrinkage in sponging and pressing. Flannels, light worsteds, and blankets so treated have better resistance to shrinkage. Oil-modified resins protect glass fibers. Cottons are often heat-set by applying resin first and then embossing. Wrinkle resistance and ease-of-care properties are given to cotton dress goods by using thermosetting resins, by using a catalyst, by curing at a high temperature, and preferably by washing afterward.

Glazed chintz and tarlatan my be treated with starch, glue, paraffin, or shellac and run through hot friction rollers to give the fabrics a high polish. These finishing materials are not permanent. However, plastic resins can be baked into the fabric to produce a permanent, washable finish. (See Fig. 7.2.) Everglaze is a trade name of such a finish.

[2]Definition given at the Sixth Annual Conference of the American Association of Textile Technology (AATT), 1966.

[3]Fabrics that have passed the test for performance standards of the Sanforized Division of Cluett, Peabody & Company, Inc., are labeled Sanforized-Plus for wash-and-wear and Sanforized-Plus-2 for permanent press.

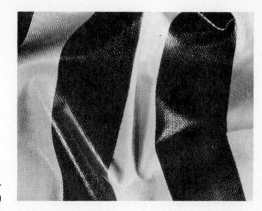

Figure 7.2 Chintz. Resin-finished glazing is permanent. (Photo by Jonas Grushkin.)

Permanent or durable press is obtained through chemical treatment applied to either a fabric or a garment for the purpose of creating permanent shape, permanent pleats, permanently pressed creases, durable smooth seams, wrinkle resistance, machine washability and dryability, and a fresh-pressed look without ironing. If care instructions are followed, durable-press finishes elminate the need for ironing after laundering. To be effective, many fabrics should be tumble dried. Trade names include Koratron, Dan-Press, Penn Prest, Coneprest, and many more. Durable press can also be added to stretch fabrics. The technology of durable press is discussed later in this chapter.

Nonpermanent Finishes

Surfaces that rub off when a cloth is brushed briskly are not permanent. Also, if the fabric loses its surface attractiveness or a good deal of its weight from cleaning or laundering, the finish is not permanent.

Sizing is a dressing that generally rubs off and washes out. With one or two exceptions, stiffening is not permanent. Cotton organdy, when heavily sized, is not permanent but, when given a starchless resin finish, will come back to its original stiffness when the fabric is ironed. Glazed chintz, which is sized first and then calendered, is not permanent, but it can be treated so that the cloth may be wiped with a damp rag in the same way as oilcloth is cleaned.

Weighting (adding material to give heaviness to a fabric) is applied to silk and wool and is not a permanent finish. (See Fig. 7.3.) If the finish washes out, the fabric becomes flimsy and shows its defects. As the chief constituents of "loading" in wool are a chemical and moisture, this finish is also easily removed. Flocking (steaming in extra fibers), which can be removed by brushing, is not a permanent finish. A table damask may be recognized as cotton if fuzz or lint appears after the cloth is washed.

Other finishes that are nonpermanent unless specially treated include calendering and pressing, embossing, moiréing, and creping. These finishes are discussed later in this chapter.

Figure 7.3 Left: Pure silk (no weighting). Reeled silk yarns in warp and filling. Note the beadlike residue where the silk taffeta was burned. Right: Weighted silk. Note the screenlike burned edge. (Photos by Jonas Grushkin.)

Some of the finishing processes discussed in detail here are mechanical in nature, including those that employ rollers, steam, brushing, napping, heat, and pressure. The rest of the finishing processes are chemical in nature and include weighting, mothproofing, and fireproofing; crease resistance, ease of care, and water-repellent finishes; and bleaching, dyeing, and printing. (Dyeing and printing are discussed in Chapter 8.)

The great improvements in finishing equipment and continuous finishing and dyeing operations have been primarily responsible for the wide variety of finished goods.

The consumer should be advised to consider, before a purchase is made, the purpose for which a fabric is to be used. Some finishes withstand laundering, sunlight, perspiration, and friction; others do not. The experiments at the close of this chapter should aid the consumer in making a decision.

PREPARATORY OPERATIONS

Before basic and functional finishes are applied to fabrics, certain preparatory steps must usually be taken. These include inspection of the goods while still in the greige, bleaching, scouring, degumming (of silk), immunizing, and occasionally mercerization (of cotton). Inspection takes place at the mill; the other processes take place at the finishing plant or at the mill.

Bleaching[4]

The object of this preparatory operation, of course, is to whiten the cloth, which may come from the loom grayish brown in color. Inexpensive cottons are often merely washed and pressed after coming from the looms and are sold as

[4]For bleaching of cotton, see Chapter 9; bleaching of linen, Chapter 10; silk, Chapter 11; wool, Chapter 12; rayon and acetate, Chapter 13.

unbleached goods. The natural tan color of flax makes bleaching one of the most important processes in finishing linen. Wild silks are usually bleached before they are dyed. If a silk cloth is to be a light color or pure white, it must be bleached. Wool is frequently bleached in the yarn, but it may be bleached after weaving or scouring.

Scouring

When scouring is done as a finish, it is called *piece scouring.* The purpose of the process is to remove any sizing, dirt, oils, or other substances that may have adhered to the fibers in the processing of the yarns or in the construction of the cloth. To avoid the formation of an insoluble soap film on the fabric, soft water is used for scouring.

Degumming

Before a silk fabric can be dyed or other finishes applied, it must be degummed, unless the yarns were degummed before weaving. Boiling silk fabrics in a mild soap solution followed by rinsing and drying will accomplish this purpose. As a result, the fabric will have a beautiful sheen and a soft hand.

Immunizing of Cotton Fabrics—A Chemical Modification of the Fibers[5]

Cellulose fibers, like viscose and cuprammonium rayons, take regular cotton dyestuffs; acetate fibers do not. (See Chapter 13.) Therefore, if cotton is treated with an agent such as acetic anhydride to change it from pure cellulose to an ester of cellulose (having the same chemical composition as acetate fiber), the cotton will be made immune to regular dyestuffs and will take the same dyes as the acetates. The result is a paler stain on the cotton than on the acetate, but a wider range of colors is possible. Cross-dyed effects may be obtained by weaving immunized cotton with regular cotton. (See *cross dyeing,* Chapter 8, page 204.)

Mercerization of Cotton

Although this process can be done in the skein of yarn, frequently mercerization is done after weaving. Any type of cotton, polyester/cotton, and polyester/rayon blend can be mercerized, but best results are obtained on long-staple cottons. (Newer rayon and cotton blends are now also being mercerized.) The process consists of holding the fabric in tension while treating it with a strong solution of sodium hydroxide at a uniform temperature of 70° to 80° F. Mercerization can be done before or after bleaching and occasionally after dyeing. In the last two instances, mercerization may be considered a basic finish. The purposes of mercerization are threefold: (1) to increase the fabric's luster, (2) to improve its

[5]"Immunizing," *Fairchild's Dictionary of Textiles* (New York: Fairchild Publications, Inc., 1979), p. 304.

strength, and (3) to give it greater affinity for dye. (Further treatment of this subject is given in Chapter 9.)

BASIC FINISHES

Finishes that enhance the beauty and attractiveness of a cloth and cover defects appeal to the eye. Finishes that add weight, body, or warmth to a cloth appeal to the sense of touch.

Finishes That Appeal to the Eye

An unbleached cotton muslin is not considered a beautiful fabric by most consumers, yet when the same fabric is bleached, singed, starched, printed, and calendered, it is thought by many to be attractive.

Unbleached muslin is commonly sold for household purposes, whereas a finished muslin print can be used for children's dresses, sportswear, and house dresses. Finishes that add attractiveness to a cloth are described in the paragraphs that follow. Dyeing and printing are reserved for Chapter 8.

Shearing

After a nap has been raised on a cloth, it is sheared to make the surface smooth and uniform. Shearing is also done to even the pile. To make carved effects, designs and ground can be cut in different lengths. In the case of hard-surfaced fabrics such as gabardine, shearing removes all surface fibers. The process also serves to cut off knots, ends, or other defects. The shearing device has revolving blades similar to a lawn mower. Shearing can be applied to any of the textile fibers or blends.

Singeing

Smooth-surfaced cloths are passed over either heated plates or gas flames to remove projecting fibers. The fabric must be passed rapidly over the gas flame so only these fibers are burned.

Brushing[6]

For smooth-surfaced fabrics, such as cotton dress percale, brushing with rollers covered with bristles removes short ends of fibers. In the case of wool fabrics, brushing frequently follows shearing, because in the shearing process cut fibers fall into the nap and must be removed. Two-brush cylinders lay the nap in one direction, and steam sets it. Brushing may be applied to any fabric.

Beetling

Linen damask has a glossy, hard, leathery feeling. To achieve this effect, linen fabrics and cotton fabrics made to resemble linen are pounded (beetled) with little hammers. (See Chapter 10.)

---

[6]See "Brushed Fabrics," *Fairchild's Dictionary of Textiles* (New York: Fairchild Publications, Inc., 1979), p. 86.

Figure 7.4 The tenter frame. After dyeing, the linen is dried to a uniform width. This picture shows the linen passing over hot air vents. (Photo courtesy of the Irish Linen Guild.)

Mercerization[7]

As indicated above, when mercerization is applied after bleaching or after dyeing, the process may be considered a basic finish.

Decating

Decating is a mechanical finish involving heat and pressure. It is applied to silk, rayon, and blends to set the luster, and in wool especially to develop a permanent luster. It softens the hand, reduces shine, helps to even the set and grain of the cloth, and delays the appearance of breaks and cracks. (See Chapter 12 on dry and wet decating of wool.)[8]

Tentering

To even fabrics in the width and to dry them, a tenter frame is employed. Pins or clips grip the fabric automatically by both selvages as the cloth is fed on the tenter frame. The distances between the two sides of the frame can be adjusted to the appropriate width of the fabric. Creases and wrinkles are pulled out, and the weave is made straight as the fabric is moved along the frame. The drying is done by machines, which either radiate heat from steam pipes or blow hot air through the fabric, or by drying cylinders. (See Fig. 7.4.)

Calendering

After all chemical and mechanical finishes have been applied, sometimes the cloth is pressed, or calendered, by passing it between hollow heated rollers. If the fabric is to receive a high polish, the cloth is usually stiffened with sizing or

[7]See *mercerizing,* Chapter 9.
[8]For finishes for wools, see *fulling, gigging, napping,* and *steaming,* Chapter 12.

resinated before it is calendered. Calendering, then, not only smooths out wrinkles but it also adds sheen to the fabric. One of the methods, called Schreinerizing, flattens the yarn to produce a soft look.

When one irons a fabric, one is really calendering it. In the making of velveteen, where flatness of surface is not desirable, the cloth is merely steamed while in tension, but it is not pressed. Calendering is an important finish for most cottons. It is used also for linen, silk, filament and spun rayons, and other man-made fibers when a smooth, flat surface is needed.

Variations of calendering operations include those producing moiréed, embossed, and glazed finishes.

Moiréing

One of the most interesting surfaces is the moiré finish. A cloth with a fillingwise rib weave is run between rollers engraved with many lines and is thus given a watered effect. On acetate cloths, this finish will remain in good condition after the fabrics are laundered. Rayons may be given resin treatment to set the design.

Pressing

Pressing accomplishes the same result for wool as calendering does for other fibers.

To press wool, the fabric is placed between heavy, electrically heated metal plates that steam and press the fabric. Sometimes the cloth is wound around a cylindrical unit that dampens the fabric and then presses it. This method can be used not only for woolens and worsteds, but also for rayons and silks.

Embossing

So that a design may be made to stand out from the background, the fabric is passed between heated rollers that imprint or emboss the design on the fabric. This design is less expensive than a woven-in design. Rayon pillows are embossed in this manner.

Cotton piqué may be made to look like dobby weave by an *embossing* process. Embossing is becoming more popular because a basic gray-goods construction can be used to obtain hundreds of pattern effects.

Creping

As a finishing process, creping may be accomplished by passing the cloth between hot rollers in the presence of steam. These rollers are filled with indentations, the counterparts of the waved and puckered areas to be produced. This method is inexpensive, but the crepe will iron out and wash out unless a heat-setting treatment is used. (See Fig. 7.5.)

A more permanent creping is done by the caustic soda method. The name of the fabric is *plissé*. Caustic soda paste is rolled onto the cloth in stripes or figures. The fabric is washed, and the parts to which the paste was applied

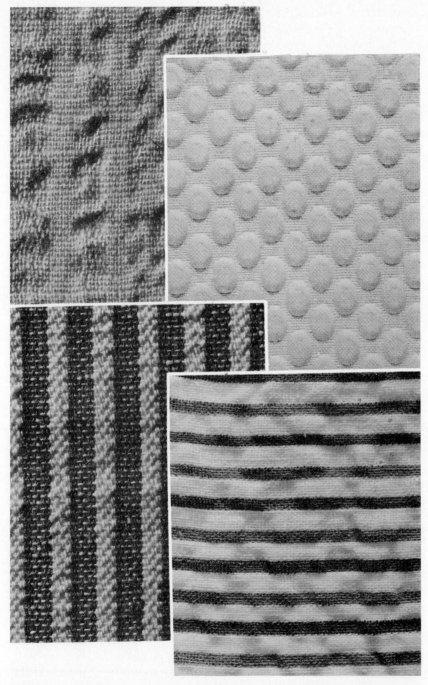

Figure 7.5 Top left: Crepes made by embossing. Top right: Crepes made by steam rolling. Bottom left: Crepes made by tension. Bottom right: Crepes made by caustic soda printing. (Photos by Jack Pitkin.)

shrink. The rest of the cloth does not shrink but appears puckered or creped. Sometimes a paste that resists the effect of caustic soda is put on the cloth in spots where the fabric is not to shrink. The whole cloth is then immersed in caustic soda; the untreated spots shrink, and the rest puckers or crepes. Crinkled bedspreads may be made in this manner. This method results in a more permanent crepe than does the first method. Creping can also be achieved by embossing.

Glazing

After fabrics are bleached, dyed, or printed, they may be given a stiff, polished, or glazed surface. Starch, glue, mucilage, shellac, or resin may be used to stiffen the fabric. Then, smooth, hot rollers that generate friction are applied. Chintz for upholstery and curtains is generally glazed.

Since the advent of resins in the finishing field, permanent-finish glaze can be applied to chintz and other muslins.

Polishing

Polished cotton or polyester blends may be mercerized first and then friction calendered. These fabrics, which look shiny and shed dirt very well, are softer than glazed chintz. Cottons that are commonly polished are *nainsook* and *sateen*. Silk and rayon fabrics may be treated with wax and calendered to produce a high polish that looks like patent leather. This is called *ciréing*.

Delusterizing

While some finishes, such as mercerizing, glazing, and polishing, add luster to a fabric, delustering is sometimes desirable. Special heat treatments are used that change the light reflection by softening the yarn and the surface of the cloth. Coating the surface of the fabric also has a delustering effect.

Optical Brightening[9]

Consumers may find that many fabrics lose their whiteness, brightness, and clearness during the wear life. To prevent this, optical brighteners have been employed. They are used as finishes and may be added to many home laundering agents. These brighteners become affixed to the fabric so that they appear to create brightness by the way they reflect light. Some optical brighteners are built into the product to ensure continued whiteness. The fluorescent material of the agent changes ultraviolet light wavelengths into visual wavelengths and remits them so as to give a fluorescent effect. Loss of energy of this fluorescent material through usage fails gradually to transform these light waves. Today, almost all soaps and detergents contain optical brightness additives to use with each laundering.

The effectiveness of optical brighteners, in large measure, is based on the

---

[9]Optical brighteners are also called ultraviolet brighteners (UV brighteners, fluorescent brighteners, and white dyes).

ultraviolet source of light, such as (1) natural sunlight, (2) fluorescent lighting, and (3) ultraviolet or "black" lamps. Regular household light bulbs have no ultraviolet light, so optical brighteners are of no value under this type of lighting.[10]

Pleating

Fabrics that are to be pleated for skirts, blouses, or by the yard are generally pleated not by the clothing manufacturer but by a specialized commercial pleater. If the fabric has been cut to the shape of the finished article, it is placed between molds of heavy pleated paper, hand pressed, put into a package that is steamed in an autoclave (a container that applies superheated steam under pressure), and then unrolled, inspected, and wrapped for delivery to the garment manufacturer. If the fabric has *not* been precut to shape, it is fed into a pleating machine with corrugated rollers that fold the fabric into the form selected by the manufacturer.

The permanency of a pleat depends upon (1) the fiber content (wool and man-made fibers that fuse, such as polyester, are preferable), (2) the construction (closely woven and knitted fabrics are better than loose ones), (3) the application of a permanent finish to the cloth and the proper use of the autoclave in the pleating process, and (4) the garment design (loosely fitting clothes are less likely to lose their pleats than are tightly fitting ones).

Finishes That Appeal to the Touch

Some finishes improve the softness of a fabric. For example, softeners and hand builders must be used on nearly all durable-press fabrics. Polyethylene emulsions improve abrasion resistance, sewability, and fabric hand. These emulsions have increased in use as softeners since the advent of durable press.

Other finishes give weight and body; still others give crispness; and still others give warmth.

Napping

The warmth and softness of a wool flannel or a brushed wool sweater is due in part to the fuzzy soft surface called *nap*. Napping, then, is a process of raising short fibers of cloth to the surface by means of revolving cylinders with metallic points. Cottons and synthetic fabrics of spun yarns may be napped to resemble wool in texture. (For the processes of napping woolens, see Chapter 12.)

Weighting and Flocking

Weighting in silk was intended to replace boiled-off gum. When weighting was excessive, it was employed to add body to an otherwise flimsy structure. The poor wearing quality of heavily weighted silks has been discovered by most

---

[10]J. J. Pizzuto, *Fabric Science*, rev. by A. Price and A. Cohen (New York: Fairchild Publications, Inc., 1974), p. 247.

consumers. Weighting was also accomplished in the finishing process, when the weighting substance is put in the dye. (The practice of weighting silk, now discontinued in the United States, is discussed more fully in Chapter 11.)

To make a firmer, more compact wool cloth, manufacturers steam fibers (obtained by shearing a cloth or recycled wool) into the back of a fabric. This is called *flocking*. Its presence can be detected by brushing the back of a cloth with a stiff brush to see whether short fibers come out.

Sizing or Stiffening and Starching

To increase weight, body crispness, stiffness, and luster, cottons or polyester blends are often stiffened. Substances such as starch, glue, wax, gelatin, casein, or clay are used. Sizing is not a permanent finish. (See Chapter 9 for a more thorough discussion of sizing cotton.) Very soft, limp rayons and linens are often improved by sizing.

Starchless Finish

To obviate the use of starch for a crisp finish that can be durable for repeated washings, cottons are treated with a resin (plastic). This starchless finish is permanent and does not dissolve in laundering. The fabric can be washed, and when ironed, presents its original crisp feel.

The permanent starchless finish is used on organdy, lawn, voile, and other sheet cottons. Fibers are sealed down by the starchless finish so that cotton fabrics stay clean longer. Heberlein is the original Swiss process for permanent crisp-finish organdy. In this process, chemicals fuse the cotton fibers, making the fabric smooth and lintless.

Permanent starchless finishes can also be used on curtains, draperies, bedspreads, and sheer cottons for apparel. Embossed or frosty-etched white patterns, formerly put in cloth by weaving, can now be applied in the finishing process at moderate cost. When applied to plissé crepe, greater permanency of crinkle is obtained.

Starchless finish can be used on cotton, linen, silk, and rayon fabrics to ensure permanent crispness without starch.

Leatherlike Finishes

A leatherlike finish appeals both to the sense of touch and that of appearance. This may be achieved by the application of a coating of polyurethane or of vinyl, such as polyvinyl chloride.

Urethane is an organic chemical or resin that liberates gas during reaction to form a foam. It is used not only for backing on carpets (see the discussion of lamination in Chapter 6) but also to provide a finish that makes the fabric look and feel like leather or suede. The coating, either clear or colored, is applied to a fabric backing of various fibers and constructions. It provides high luster, sheen, and a leatherlike ''hand'' and also makes the fabric water-repellent.

When a vinyl coating of polyvinyl chloride is applied to achieve a very similar effect, the fabric is commonly called PVC. It is used for jackets, handbags, and trimmings. If heavily coated, a somewhat similar vinyl coated fabric is used for upholstery.

While strong solvents may injure all such coatings, with proper care, they stand up well in use.

INSPECTION AND REPAIR

After the fabric is finished, visual examination to detect imperfections is required. The process may consist of throwing the fabric over a horizontal bar[11] for examination under a powerful lamp. Visual examination is a final step for the finisher. Goods are checked for proper finish, color, side-to-side shading, spots, streaks, and other imperfections. Technology has not yet devised a way to make use of laser inspection as described for greige goods in Chapter 4.

SHRINKAGE TREATMENTS

Nothing can prove more distressing to a customer than finding a garment that fit perfectly before laundering has shrunk a size afterward. The problem has been highlighted recently by the finding that some expensive designer blue jeans have not been preshrunk properly. The worst fabric offenders are cotton, linen, wool, and filament rayon. Acetate, silk, nylon, and the other synthetics are not subject to shrinkage, although the type of yarn used, the count of the cloth, and the type of finish are factors affecting this property of a fabric. For example, creped yarns and loosely constructed fabrics frequently shrink.

Causes of Shrinkage

There are three causes of shrinkage: relaxation, swelling of fibers and yarns, and felting.

Relaxation occurs in both laundering and dry cleaning if the fabric has not been preshrunk properly. During the weaving and finishing processes, the yarns are stretched and tend to return to their normal condition when cleaned. This is particularly true of cotton fabrics, but relaxation varies with construction. Percales may shrink 3 to 8 percent, whereas flannelettes may shrink 10 percent or even more.

Swelling of the fibers and yarns occurs in washing, not in dry cleaning. If the fabric is pressed by a hot iron while damp, at least some of this shrinkage may be removed.

Felting is peculiar to wool fabrics and is discussed in Chapter 12, on wool.

---

[11]See the discussions of perching, burling, and mending in Chapter 12 and of laser beam inspection in Chapter 4.

Preshrinking (Rulings on Shrinkage)

According to FTC rulings,[12] if the words "preshrunk" or "shrunk" are used on a cotton-goods label, the manufacturer must guarantee the maximum shrinkage: for example, "These goods have been shrunk (or preshrunk) to the extent that residual shrinkage will not exceed x percent when tested in accordance with the recognized and approved standards or tests." A test devised by the American Standards Association has been recognized as a standard test by the FTC. Another suggested form of label may read: "Preshrunk—residual shrinkage 1 percent, or 2 percent." Terms such as "full shrunk," "shrinkproof," and "nonshrinkable" are banned by this ruling if the goods so labeled have any further capacity to shrink.

In brief, if a manufacturer labels his or her goods as "preshrunk" or "shrunk," these goods must adhere to the FTC rules, but if the manufacturer does not label the goods as "shrunk" or "preshrunk," then he or she need not indicate the percentage of residual shrinkage.

Shrinkage can change a size 16 dress to a size 14 in bust, waist, and hips and to a size 12 in length. Even a 3 percent fabric shrinkage is undesirable. Should the collar of a man's shirt shrink 3 percent, a size 15 collar is reduced to a size 14½ and the sleeve length shrinks by a half an inch.

Cotton fabric shrinks because its yarns have been stretched during weaving and finishing. When the fabric is being laundered, the yarns relax and return to their normal position, thus causing shrinkage. Not all cottons shrink alike. Variations stem from type and construction.

In its advertising, Levi Strauss & Co. takes advantage of the shrinkage in its women's cotton denim blue jeans (style #501TM). When purchased new, these jeans measure considerably larger in waist and length than the size marked on the label, which is correct for use after washing. After a few washings, the jeans will shrink to a perfect fit and the fabric will become softer and lighter in color. (See Fig. 7.6.)

Shrinkage Controls

Almost everyone is familiar with the Sanforized label. (See Fig. 7.7.) Sanforized, as was mentioned earlier, is a trademark owned by Cluett, Peabody & Company, Inc., which permits its use only on fabrics that meet the company's rigid shrinkage requirements. Fabrics bearing the trademark Sanforized will not shrink more than 1 percent by the government's standard wash test. Sanforized is not the name of a shrinkage process; it does not denote a method of shrinking; it *does* denote a checked standard of shrinkage performance.[13] Therefore, when this Sanforized trademark is seen on a white broadcloth shirt, the consumer

---

[12]The ruling applies legally to goods sold in interstate commerce.

[13]"How to Use the 'Sanforized' Trademark," a leaflet prepared by the Sanforized Division, Cluett, Peabody & Company, Inc.

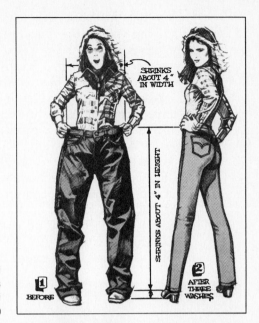

Figure 7.6 An advertisement for blue jeans (by Levi Strauss & Co.) that notes the shrinkage consumers can anticipate after three washings. (Courtesy of Levi Strauss & Co.)

Figure 7.7 Trademarks of the Sanforized Company, a division of Cluett, Peabody & Company, Inc. Fabric shrinkage of labeled merchandise will not exceed 1 percent by government's standard test. **Sanforized®:** The familiar trademark found on piece goods, clothing, home furnishings, and domestics means that the article will not shrink out of fit. **Sanforized plus®:** A trademark appearing on minimum-care merchandise. The item will not shrink out of fit. **Sanforized plus 2®:** A garment trademark found on durable-press garments. The article will not shrink out of fit regardless of how it is laundered. **Sanfor Knit®:** A trademark for knit garments. It ensures lasting comfort and fit of garments after repeated home washing and machine drying. Can only be used by a licensed garment manufacturer. **Sanfor Set®:** A new tumble-dry shrinkage standard; no-iron without shrink loss in cotton denims; ensures soft "hand" and smooth appearance and reduces edge abrasion. (Courtesy of the Sanforized Company, Cluett, Peabody & Company, Inc.)

knows that the fabric shrinkage will not exceed 1 percent despite repeated laundering. When the consumer sees the trademark Sanforized-Plus by the same company, he or she knows that the fabric has passed standard tests for proper performance of a wash-and-wear fabric. Similarly, Sanforized-Plus-2 refers to a fabric that has passed performance tests for durable press.

When a compressive shrinkage process is used on a fabric to eliminate customers' complaints of shrinkage, fabrics so treated gain in durability, because shrinkage increases the number of warp and filling yarns to the square inch (it raises the count of the cloth). The finish of the cloth is also improved, because the yarns are crinkled and are drawn closer, and the fabric is dried against a polished cylinder. These processes give smoothness, soft luster, and improved draping possibilities. The compressive shrinkage process adds a few cents a yard to the price the customer must pay. Practically every cotton can be so treated— even mixed fabrics made of cotton, silk, and wool. (See Fig. 7.8.)

Shrinkage control for wool felting is discussed in Chapter 12 and that for rayon is discussed in Chapter 13. The two leading man-made fibers, nylon and

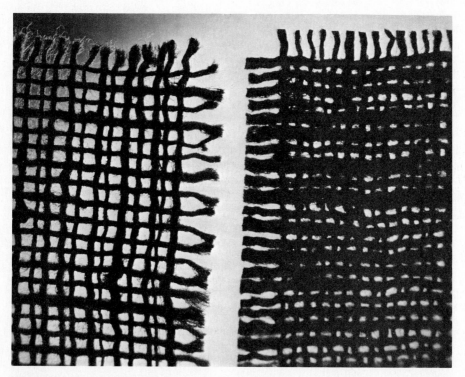

Figure 7.8 Photomicrograph of fabric showing how the compressive shrinkage process alters its construction. The process does not impair a fabric in any way. On the contrary, the fabric is improved since, after shrinking, there are more threads per inch in both the warp and filling. As a result, the shrunk fabrics have greater wearing qualities and improved hand. (Courtesy of the Sanforized Company, Cluett, Peabody & Company, Inc.)

Figure 7.9 Left: Linen with crease-resistant finish. Right: Linen without crease-resistant finish. Both fabrics were crushed in the hands. (Photos by Jonas Grushkin.)

polyester, are usually heat-set during the finishing process and are then not subject to shrinkage. Resin finishes also are a great aid in controlling the amount of shrinkage in fabrics.

FINISHES THAT MINIMIZE CARE

These important finishes have been and are a great boon to the consumer: wrinkle and crease resistance, durable press, and soil release.

Crease-Resistant Finishes (CRF)

A *crease* is a fold or deformation of a fabric intentionally formed by pressing; a *wrinkle* is formed unintentionally by washing and wearing. A wrinkle can usually be removed by pressing; a crease can generally not be removed. A durable-press article should have no wrinkles (See Fig. 7.9.)

Synthetic resins (melamine, epoxy, urea formaldehyde, or vinyl) can be used to give resiliency. In one process, cloth is immersed in a resin solution that has a molecule small enough to permeate the cotton fibers. The fabric is then pressed between rollers to squeeze out the excess fluid. The impregnated cloth is heated until the molecules swell inside the fibers so that the resin cannot be removed by normal use, dry cleaning, or washing. A resin may be applied during the dyeing process or immediately after the dyeing, when dyes have dried. Cottons so treated resist crushing, wrinkling, and creasing.

The Southern Regional Research Laboratory, Agricultural Research Service, U.S. Department of Agriculture, New Orleans, Louisiana, has developed several types of wrinkle-resistant finishes that cost only a few cents per square yard and can be easily applied with the usual equipment for resin finishing.[14]

[14]Crease-resistant finishes developed at the Southern Regional Research Laboratory include formic acid colloid of methylolmelamine resin and formaldehyde finish. A no-wrinkle process, employing liquid ammonia, is being used on denim by Erwin Mills, a division of Burlington Industries, Inc.

Other strides have been made in crease-resistance research. Modified starches, called oxidized starches, give crease-resistant finishes. Chemists have also discovered a compound that produces crease resistance as well as resistance to damage from chlorine after repeated washings.[15] The Electronic Smoothness Evaluator by Cluett, Peabody & Company, Inc. has already been described as the standard device for appraising the ability of a crease-resistant, wash-and-wear fabric to dry with a minimum of wrinkles after laundering. "Crease resistant" does not mean that the cotton so treated will not crease, crush, or wrinkle; rather, it means that, if and when wrinkles do appear, they can be shaken out and hung out in the air.

The crease-resistant finish has been a great boon to velvets and to linens, in which crushing and wrinkling are highly undesirable.

Wash-and-wear finish ensures minimum care of fabrics treated. (See *wash-and-wear*, page 151.) The wash-and-wear concept was built on the idea that such a finish would prevent both the removal of permanent-press creases (such as pleats) and the formation of wrinkles during wearing and washing. But durable press does more. It locks in the shape and locks out wrinkles for the life of a garment. Seams stay flat; ironing is not required. (See *durable press*, below.)

Wrinkle recovery of fabrics can be tested by the American Association of Textile Chemists and Colorists Method 128-1974. The object of the test is to determine the appearance of textile fabrics after induced wrinkling. Three test specimens are used, 6 inches × 11 inches, with the long dimension running in the warp direction of a woven fabric or the wale direction in a knit. A test specimen is wrinkled under standard atmospheric conditions in a standard wrinkling device under a predetermined load for a prescribed period of time. The specimen is then reconditioned in standard atmosphere for testing and is evaluated for appearance with three-dimensional reference standards.

Each of the three specimens is tested in turn. Then the observer, standing directly in front of the specimen 4 feet away from the board, assigns the number of the replica that most nearly matches the appearance of the test specimen. A number 1 rating is equivalent to WR1, the poorest appearance, whereas number 5 represents the smoothest appearance and best retention of original appearance.

Durable or Permanent Press

At the time of the fifth edition of this book (1964), durable press was a technical curiosity. In 1968, durable press became part of our household language; today it is taken for granted.

Durable press or permanent press is not a specific finish. The term is used to describe ready-made garments and domestics (such as table linens and bed sheets) that continue to maintain a smooth appearance after many launderings and wearings and require no ironing. Furthermore, durable press describes ready-made textile articles that retain or resist the removal of creases or pleats intentionally put into these articles.

[15]This is an almost unpronounceable compound: 1,3-dimethyl-4,5-dihydroxy-2-imidazolidinone. See *American Dyestuff Reporter*, July 24, 1961, pp. 27–30.

History of Durable Press

Prior to the development of durable press, certain cross-linking chemicals had been applied to cotton and rayon yard goods in the dyeing and finishing processes for the purpose of increasing wrinkle resistance and reducing shrinkage. Garments made of these chemically treated and cured (baked) fabrics were known as wash-and-wear. However, these garments often required touch-up ironing, and few garments retained their creases or pleats after repeated wearings and launderings. In short, these wash-and-wear fabrics were precured at the mill before the garment was constructed.

By adding two to three times as much resin as before to 100 percent cotton slacks and by *precuring* the flat fabric, excellent wrinkle resistance, crease retention, and dimensional stability were made possible. But reduced tensile strength and reduced edge abrasion became very noticeable. So the 100 percent cotton content of slacks was replaced by polyester/cotton and polyester/nylon blends. The cotton content gave required wrinkle resistance, and the man-made fibers provided improved edge and flat abrasion resistance. However, the precuring as a flat fabric presented a problem in some garments because, when the garment was constructed, the fabric had a "memory" for its flat state and tended to return to that condition. Particularly was this a problem in retention of sharp creases in slacks, pleats in dresses, and nonpuckering seams. Where the shape of a garment and its pleats and creases were factors, methods had to be found to give "memory" to the shape of the completed garment. One answer was to postcure the garment (after garment construction).

Methods of Producing Durable Press

Postcured or deferred cured. Polyester/cotton fabric is chemically treated at the mill or finishing plant, but it is not cured. The chemical component (a thermosetting resin) reacts with the cellulose fiber and is cured only when subjected to certain degrees of heat (325° F) for from 5 to 15 minutes. This is called post-, or deferred, curing because heat is applied after the garment has been constructed and pressed. Postcuring sets the pleats and the garment's shape permanently. The cotton content in the blend may have lost strength and abrasion resistance in curing, but the polyester compensates for the cotton's loss in strength. This method was first marketed in 1964. (See Fig. 7.10.)

Precured. A polyester/cotton blend is impregnated with resin and is cured at the mill or finishing plant. Hence the method is called precured. After curing, the fabric is sold to the sewn-goods manufacturer who cuts, sews, and presses it (with a hot-head press) to heat-set the thermoplastic (polyester) materials in the blend. Sewing with specially developed threads that are sewn in the seams and in a relaxed tension can prevent a seam from puckering. (See Fig. 7.10.)

Recured. As the fabric is being precured, a chemical is applied to it that breaks down the molecules of the resin being applied so that the fabric is temporarily uncured. Further application of heat both recures the resin and heat-sets the

THE POST-CURED PROCESS

THE PRE-CURED PROCESS

Figure 7.10 Flow diagrams of the postcured process (top) and the precured process (bottom). (Courtesy of Celanese Fibers Marketing Company.)

thermoplastic (polyester) fibers. Thus, the durable press is accomplished in two different ways at the same time.

No-cure. In this method, neither resin nor chemical is used. A special hot-head press is applied to the finished garment to heat-set the thermoplastic fibers, which should be at least 90 percent of the total fabric.

Cross linkage. Recently, it has been found that it is not essential to have polyester (or other man-made thermoplastic fiber) blended with cotton (or rayon) to produce a durable-press garment. A cross-linkage process has been perfected that modifies the molecular structure of the cellulose, particularly cotton, by treating it with a resin or chemical that reacts with the fiber, forming a chemical bond of the molecules. Heat treatment of a garment made from cross-linked fibers imparts crease and shape retention and wrinkle resistance. Thus, the fabric develops a "memory" of the form in which it has been heat treated, even after use and washing.

Some Problems of Durable Press

While durable press has been a great boon to the homemaker, it has had its problems. The following are some of the difficulties:

1. Frosting is a color change of a cotton/polyester-blended fabric that has been subjected to abrasion at certain wear points, for example, the crease of pants, collar, and elbows. Since cotton weakens when resin treatment is applied for durable press, the cotton wears away before the polyester does.
2. Repairs and alterations are difficult to make on durable-press garments; for example, it is difficult to lengthen the hems of dresses or slacks or to let out seams and still achieve a crease-free surface.
3. Seam puckering occurs in resin fabrics.
4. In laundering, wrinkles may occur unless durable-press garments are removed when the dryer stops because the heat of the dryer and the weight of the clothes in the dryer serve to introduce wrinkles.
5. Durable-press fabrics often possess an objectionable (fishy) odor caused by formaldehyde in the chemical treatment applied for curing. The odor may be removed by a second laundering, but the fact remains that some people are subject to an allergic rash from the chemical.

6. The poor moisture absorptive quality of durable press may make fabrics warm when hydrophobic plus plastic resins are used.

7. Durable press is prone to soil collection, especially collection of oily soils, in ordinary home laundering. For this reason, soil-release finishes have been developed.

Soil-Release Finishes

There are several types of soil-release finishes, and their chief purpose is the same, namely, to increase the absorbency of the fabric. In the previous discussion of problems encountered with durable press, it was noted that lack of absorbency of hydrophobic fibers plus the plastic resin used to achieve durable press were problems in stain removal. Hydrophobic fibers do not permit wetting thoroughly in laundering. (See Figs. 7.11 and 7.12.)

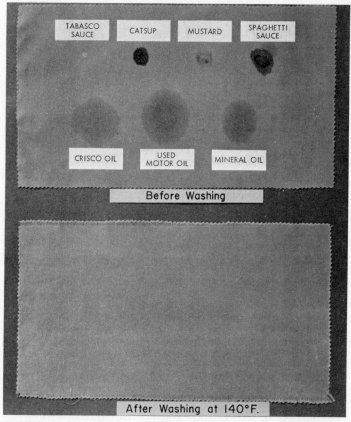

Figure 7.11 Acrylic polymer soil-release finishes are neither hydrophobic nor oleophobic but hold stains off the fiber. This soil-release product is based on fluorochemical technology developed by 3M. In the example above fabric treated for soil release is stained with the 7 materials named. It is then washed as indicated and all of the stains have been removed. (Courtesy of *Textile World*.)

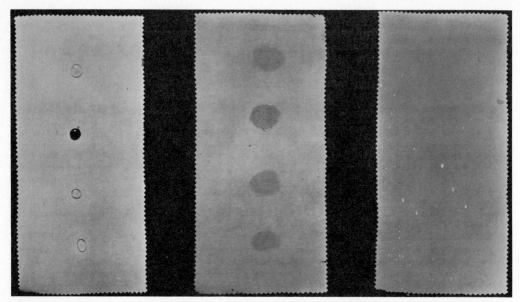

Figure 7.12 This soil-release finish is resistant to stains, rubbed in, and removed in one home laundering. The finish is chemical, using a modified fluorocarbon resin. The treated fabrics are stained at the left with 4 oily stains and at the middle with 4 waterborne stains. In washing all are removed. (Courtesy of *Textile World*.)

One type of soil release is said to have the following advantages:

1. Allowing the stain to leave the fabric more rapidly.
2. Enhancing wicking action for greater wear comfort.
3. Making the fabric dry-cleanable without appreciably affecting its soil-release properties.
4. Maintaining the brightness of the fabric through repeated launderings.

SPECIAL-PURPOSE FINISHES

Finishes that are applied to fabrics to make them better suited for specific uses come under this category. In general, these finishes are newer than the basic finishes, many of them having been perfected during World War II and later.

Abrasion Resistance

Abrasion resistance is a matter of the degree to which a fabric can withstand the friction of rubbing or chafing. The newer man-made fibers, such as nylon, acrylic, and polyester, have good abrasion resistance; the natural fibers lack this property. To overcome this drawback, fibers with high potential abrasion resistance can be blended with fibers of low abrasion resistance (not a finish).

The chief objection to the use of resins lies in the fact that these finishes may increase wet soiling of the fabrics.

In durable-press cottons, abrasion resistance is reduced to a third or less of untreated fiber. In the original concept of durable-press cotton, either the molecules were loaded with resin or the fiber structure was immobilized with cross links. This reaction made the fiber brittle as well as resilient. No amount of softeners would overcome this fault yet retain the resilient property. Considerable research has been done along these lines. By 1967, the Southern Regional Laboratory (New Orleans) reported that cotton fabrics and garments made of blends of cotton fibers—part of which have been impregnated with certain thermosetting and/or thermoplastic resins and untreated cottons—show excellent ability to resist damage by abrasion during laundering.[16] A number of treatments have aimed at keeping the cotton fiber slightly swollen while it is being cross linked. Then, there also have been improvements made in cross-linking agents. Finally, polyester blended with cotton compensates for loss of abrasion resistance and strength.

Absorbent Finishes

For such articles as towels, bed linens, diapers, and underwear, the absorption of moisture is important. A treatment with ammonium compounds causes cottons, linens, and rayons to absorb water more readily.

A chemical finish has been found that corrects the hardness and lack of water absorbency of nylon. The use of this finish has improved the appearance, comfort, and salability of finished nylon hosiery and piece goods.[17]

Air Conditioning

Short, fuzzy fibers are chemically sealed into the yarn. The fabric is thereby made more porous to permit circulation of air. Ventilation of the skin helps to make the fabric comfortable.

Slack Mercerization for Stretch

The purpose of this finish is not so much to achieve luster as it is to provide fabric elasticity. (See the discussion on page 155 for a description of regular mercerization.) In slack mercerization, the 100 percent cotton or cotton-blend fabric is immersed in a caustic soda (sodium hydroxide) bath without any filling tension, so that filling yarns in the fabric shrink or buckle. Stretch is evident when the fabric is pulled in the direction of the fillings to its unshrunken dimension. In this method, the amount of stretch and its durability are somewhat limited.

[16]*American Dyestuff Reporter*, February 1967, p. 23.
[17]Nylonex, by W. F. Fancourt Company, Greensboro, North Carolina.

Antibacterial Finishes

In a study of perspiration made by the chief bacteriologist of the United States Testing Company, it was found that sterile perspiration, which is odorless, has no effect on fabrics and fabric finishes. The finish, if soluble, may be dissolved by perspiration just as any other liquid, but sterile perspiration does not alter the chemical composition of the finish. Neither are the fibers weakened in tensile strength.

However, perspiration does not remain sterile. When perspiration is produced, it is immediately contaminated with various types of bacteria on the skin. Bacterial decomposition begins. It is this bacterial action that causes the odor of perspiration and has a deteriorating effect on the fabric. It may also change the color of the fabric or transfer the color to a lighter fabric.

Antiperspirants, applied under the arms, are commonly used to check perspiration, but they sometimes irritate the skin. To prevent the odor of perspiration, bacterial decomposition must be prevented. Frequent washing helps. Germicides can be applied on the skin or on the fabrics. If the latter is the case, the germicide has to be carefully chosen. It must be colorless, so as not to stain the fabric, and odorless; it should not affect the dyes or finishes of the fabric, should not irritate the skin, and should not be removed by the first few washings. A few compounds have been found to possess these qualities. Fabrics treated with these germicides-fungicides have been found to have semipermanent finishes (do not wash out in as many as forty washings) and to pass the sterility test of the U.S. Pharmacopeia. Fabrics treated with these compounds also sufficiently protect the wearer against the fungus that causes athlete's foot. This fabric treatment will prove effective for as many as twenty-five launderings.

Antibacterial finishes prevent bacteria-caused odors in textiles and/or reduction of the changes of bacterial infections resulting from contact with contaminated textiles. Sanitized is a trademarked finish that protects fabrics from deterioration and odor-causing effects of bacteria, mildew, and mold.

Antislip Finishes

Seam fraying and yarns shifting (slipping) in the fabrics are common annoyances to the consumer. Finishing agents such as resins—hard, waxy substances remaining after distillation of volatile turpentine—have been used, but they are not generally durable to washing. Other chemical treatments reduce surface slickness but are not durable. Urea and melamine formaldehyde resins are the most durable of the finishing agents used to reduce yarn slippage.

Antistatic Finishes

A chemical treatment applied to noncellulosic man-made fibers to eliminate static electricity is a boon to the customer. An annoyance to the wearer is a nylon slip that clings to the body or to an outer garment, or a crackling lining as a coat is taken off, or acrylic slacks that cling to the legs on a cold, windy day. Static charge or static electricity is controlled in natural fibers and in rayon by the introduction of humidity in the air and by employing some weaving lubricants in the processing of the fibers. The newer man-made fibers, such as nylon, polyester, and acrylics, are more difficult to process. Humidity is not the sole answer. Some type of coating must be used to carry away electrostatic charges built up on the fiber. For knit goods, Badische has developed an antistatic process that will last for the life of the garment.[18] Consumers can partially control the static by the use of softeners such as Sta Puf, Downy, and Negastat in the wash water. Permanent antistatic agents have been developed by the finishing industry.

Inflammability Finishes

The problem of flammability in textile fabrics came to the fore when some toddlers dressed in cowboy suits were fatally burned when they came too near a campfire. In another case, a woman wearing a sequin-trimmed gown accidentally came into contact with the lighted cigarette of a passerby and suddenly the woman's gown became a flaming torch. Such disasters as the Cocoanut Grove and Ringling Brothers fires exemplify the dangers of using flammable fabrics.

Regulations

California was the first state to legislate rules and regulations relating to the sale of flammable merchandise. The fire marshal was designated as the person to decide on the flammability of an article. For aid in this extremely difficult task, the marshal consulted with textile experts and performed experiments under laboratory conditions. The prolem of fire hazards stemming from flammable wearing apparel was nationwide; it was present in every American community. There was also the hazard of flammable wearing apparel being shipped in interstate commerce. This problem required federal legislation.

Accordingly, the 1953 Congress passed the Flammable Fabrics Act, which was amended in 1954. The purpose of the act was to eliminate from the marketplace easily ignitable (potentially dangerous) fabrics. In 1967 a new act was passed. Its purpose was to remove from the marketplace a wider range of articles of wearing apparel and interior furnishings that are so highly flammable as to be potentially dangerous when worn by consumers or used in the home. For a few years, the secretary of commerce, the secretary of health, education and welfare, and the FTC divided the responsibilities for enforcing this act. In 1972 the Consumer Product Safety Act was passed. This legislation created the U.S. Consumer Product Safety Commission, which has broad jurisdiction over product safety. The act also transferred responsibilities under the Flammable Fabrics Act to this commission.

The federal regulations cover general wearing apparel, carpets and rugs, mattresses and mattress covers, and children's sleepwear. (See Fig. 7.13.)

[18]*America's Textile Reporter/Bulletin,* April 1974, p. 43.

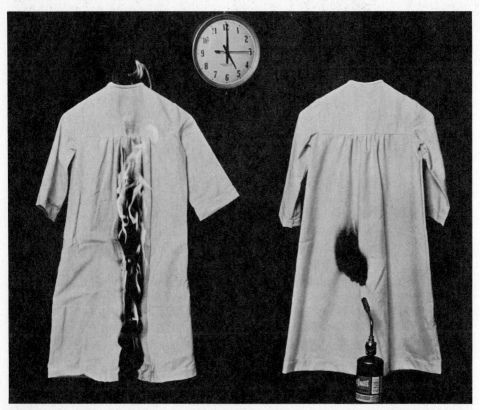

Figure 7.13 Self-extinguishing cotton flannel nightgown at right, treated with PROVATEX CP, a flame-retardant compound developed by CIBA Chemical & Dye Company, chars but puts itself out when exposed to flame from a Bunsen burner. However, the untreated flannel gown at the left, which was exposed to a lighted match at the same time, became engulfed in flame in 15 seconds. (Courtesy of CIBA Chemical & Dye Company.)

In 1972, for children's sleepwear, the most suitable flame-retardant chemical that met the federal flammability standards was TRIS, and it was in general usage by manufacturers. But the Consumer Products Safety Commission later found that its use was linked to cancer, and in 1977, it banned TRIS as a hazardous substance. This led to a tremendous inventory loss by sleepwear manufacturers, thirty-one of whom sued the commission in 1980 for its precipitous action without just compensation to them, since they had taken the steps approved at the time to meet the flammability requirements of the law.

The gist of the federal regulations appear in Appendix E.

Fireproof versus Flame-Resistant Finishes

There is a big difference between fabrics that are *fireproof* and those that are *flame-resistant*. An article is fireproof when, after exposure to fire, it is still useful for its original purpose. An article is flame-resistant when it may be consumed

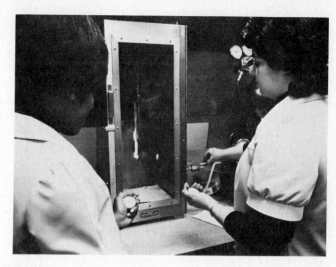

Figure 7.14 Testing for flammability.
(Photo courtesy of J. C. Penney Co.)

by the application of flame, but upon removal from the ignition source, no spreading of the flame occurs. If this characteristic is attained by treatment with a fire-retardant chemical, the fabric is said to be *flame-retardant*. Most are fabric finishes, but some can be added to the yarns, and, in the case of man-made chemical fibers, it is possible to add the material to the solution before the filament is formed.

There are several processes of rendering fabrics flame-resistant. One involves coating nylon or polyester fabrics with a new plastisol plus an adhesive bonding agent that will not fall off in molten drops when flame is applied to them. Three coats are given to each side of the fabric. The result is that there is no dripping under a gas flame and that burning stops when the flame is removed.

There also exists a flame-resistant finish for acetate, nylon, and acrylic fibers, but the process cannot be used on cotton or rayon. This fire retardant (for the earlier-mentioned man-mades) is an emulsified clear liquid that is applied by specific methods in the dye bath.[19] For cotton apparel, the retardant used most widely is called THPOH; for tents, it is PVC. While most flame-retardant finishes and treatments retain their properties after many launderings, some will lose their effectiveness when low-phosphate detergents or fabric softeners are introduced into the washing process.

Certificates or affidavits of flame resistance are required in most areas where local laws demand that such documents be issued by the processor. (See Fig. 7.14.)

The chief difficulty in using fire-retardant chemicals seems to be that, if, in overcoming combustibility, a large amount of chemical has to be applied to the cloth, it gives the fabric a different feeling and may damage fabric properties.

[19]This product is made by the Apex Chemical Co.

One principle of flame retarding is to create a finish that smothers a flame in the same manner as fire extinguishers do. Carbon tetrachloride or carbon dioxide has this effect: they cut off the supply of oxygen necessary to make a fire burn and fill the air about the flame with gases that do not induce burning.

Another principle is to treat the fabric with chemicals that, in the presence of heat, melt and cover the fabric with nonflammable film. Simultaneously, these chemicals give off a steam that, along with the film, accomplishes the fireproof effect. Treatment with various carbonates and ammonium salts results in the creation of noncombustible vapors.

Firegard, a finish suitable for styled fabrics, is produced by M. Lowenstein & Sons, Inc., which claims that it is nontoxic; that it does not support combustion once it is away from the flame; that it lasts through fifty washings; and that it does not affect the natural softness of cotton flannel.

How can flame-retardant finishes ensure protection? For a slightly extra cost (minimal in the case of small items), a treated flame-retardant fabric can save lives or prevent severe burns.

What fibers are comparatively flame-resistant without special treatment? Wool will ignite but will burn very slowly and will extinguish itself. Certain man-made fibers, including modacrylic, aramid, novoloid, vinyon, and fluorocarbon, are inherently flame-resistant. They do not support combustion when exposed to flame or heat. (See Chapter 15.) A high-temperature-resistant fiber called Nomex (by DuPont) does not support combustion. The FTC has given this fiber a generic classification called *aramid*. Nomex is used in spacesuits, military fabrics, and other protective clothing. Novoloid, another man-made fiber, is sold by Carborundum Co., Inc., under the trade name Kynol. Kynol chars without melting in high-temperature flames. DuPont's Teflon is a fluorocarbon fiber. Glass and asbestos fibers are flameproof for their entire wear lives.

Cotton and rayon burn rather quickly but can, with the exception of very sheer garments, be treated with chemicals as indicated earlier to make them flame-retardant.

Metallized Finishes

Woven fabric may be coated with synthetic resin containing a good percentage of finely ground aluminum bronze. Such fabrics have increased insulation and are therefore claimed to be warm. Another method is vaporization of a variety of metals onto fabrics in a high vacuum to produce a metal coating less than one-thousandth of a millimeter thick. Still another method impregnates the textile material or fabric with aluminum. This finish, which my be added to one or both sides of the fabric, makes the fabric heat-resistant up to temperatures of 2500° F. It is claimed by the United States Testing Company that the aluminum coating prevents 96 percent of the heat from penetrating the material. The coating has many consumer and industrial uses, among them barbecue mitts and curtains for industrial furnaces.

Draperies with metallized linings reflect sunlight and, hence, restrict heat penetration. When a room is being heated, the finish holds the heat in. Satins and taffetas respond well to metallized treatments. Trademarked names for fabrics so treated include Milium, Temp-Resisto, and Therm-O-Ray.

The Mobay Chemical Corporation has developed a fabric coated with metal that is permanently antistatic, heat-resistant, and able to reflect radar waves and to absorb microwaves. The coating is important in electrical, electronic, thermal, and safety applications. It will withstand heat up to 572° F, depending on the fabric used.

The coating, usually of nickel, reaches the individual filaments within a fabric that may be made of natural fibers or of synthetic ones. The coated fabrics can be washed repeatedly and are only slightly heavier than the uncoated ones.

In addition to industrial applications, the coated material is important in the laboratory and the operating room. It is likely to be used widely in the manufacture of heated clothing and blankets for cold-weather activities of many kinds.

Mildew- and Rot-Repellent Finishes

Mildew is a parasitic fungus that grows rapidly in warm humid weather. Fabrics of cotton, linen, rayon, and wool are particularly vulnerable to this fungus. Microorganisms present in the air and soil can grow on wet fibers. Consequently, if clothing is not completely dry before it is put away, it can mildew. If clothing is improperly rinsed, soap or oils adhere to the fibers and provide a field for the growth of mildew.

Prevention of mildew is possible by treating the fabrics with nontoxic, odorless germicides. Certain metallic salts have this effect. For cotton, one method is to modify the cotton fiber so that its surface is cellulose acetate, which is resistant to mildew. A resin impregnation of the cotton fiber, which prevents contact of the microorganism with the fiber, can also be used.

Permanent rotproofing of cotton is possible through a treatment with a condensation resin. A new technique overcomes the drawback of loss of strength of the cotton fiber that resulted from conventional methods of applying condensation resins. If a suitable organic mercury compound is added to the rotproofing finish, it is possible to protect cotton against surface mildew growth.[20]

The burying of treated and untreated specimens in soil rich in rot-producing fungi for a definite time is the test procedure for resistance of textiles

---

[20]Process by the CIBA-GEIGY Company, Basel, Switzerland.

to mildew and rot. When the specimens are removed from the earth, they are tested for breaking strength against controls.[21]

Moth-Repellent Treatments

To mothproof a fabric in the finishing process, colorless chemicals similar to dyestuffs are added to the dye bath. This treatment makes the fabric permanently moth-repellent. Although this method is effective, the high cost of the chemicals required may make its use prohibitive. Another way is to atomize the finished fabric with the mothproofing chemical, which is colorless, odorless, and harmless to humans. Fabrics so mothproofed are delivered to the garment manufacturer. The compound used in processing the fabric either poisons the moth or kills it upon contact.

Consumers and dry cleaners often make a fabric moth-repellent by spraying it thoroughly with a mothproofing chemical. This treatment is not a finishing process (see Chapter 21 for methods of mothproofing upholstery). Paradichlorobenzene crystals or naphthalene mothballs are recommended for the closet where wool garments are stored. A clean fabric does not attract moths as quickly as a soiled fabric does. Frequent exposure to sunlight is effective if the color is fast.

Wool or silk fabrics may be made moth-repellent. Cotton, linen, and the man-made fibers do not attract moths.

To test for insect resistance, a specified number of insects (black carpet beetles, furniture carpet beetles, webbing clothes moths, or other species of insect pests) are allowed to feed on a fabric for fourteen days under controlled conditions of temperature and humidity. Below a set tolerance limit, textiles are considered satisfactorily insect-resistant, and above this limit they are considered to be inadequately protected (AATCC Standard Test Method 24-1952).

Waterproofing and Water- and Stain-Repellent Finishes

The use for which a fabric is intended determines whether it should be waterproof, water-repellent, or stain-repellent. For umbrellas, galoshes, and raincoats, the fabrics should be waterproof. Waterproofing, done by several patented processes, closes the pores of the fabric. The most common processes consist of treatment with

1. Insoluble metallic compounds, such as aluminum soap, basic acetate of aluminum, mineral khaki, and cuprammonium.
2. Paraffin or mixed waxes.
3. Bituminous materials, such as asphaltum or tar.

---

[21] American Association of Textile Chemists and Colorists (AATCC) Standard Test Method 34-1952.

4. Linseed oil or other drying oils.
5. Combinations of methods 1, 2, 3, and 4.
6. Laminated film.

Treatment 1 (with cuprammonium) is often used to make cotton mildew-resistant. But this treatment cannot be applied at home. Formulas for waterproofing and mildewproofing are given in the *Farmer's Bulletin* No. 1454.[22]

A new development in waterproofing, called Gore-tex, consists of laminating a microporous film (see method 6 in the preceding list) to the outer surface of fabric or sandwiching it between two layers of fabric.[23] The film can be applied successfully to a great variety of fabrics and has been used in shell garments, insulated garments, active sportswear shoes, tents, and sleeping bags for backpacking, skiing, sailing, canoeing, bicycling, and mountain-climbing activities. This method might be classified as water-repellent, but the microporous nature of the film makes it virtually waterproof.

Water-repellent finishes do not close the pores of the fabric against air as does waterproofing. Hence, water-repellent fabrics are not so warm to wear as waterproofed fabrics are; on the other hand, the former fabrics are capable of "breathing." The fabrics are treated to resist the penetration of water. The degree of resistance varies from a spotproof or stain-repellent fabric to a showerproof cloth. To be showerproof, a cloth must resist penetration of water under considerable pressure.

Water repellents are surface finishes. Therefore, sizing, dirt, fats, and other foreign matter should be removed before finishing. Water-repellent fabrics are treated with wax and resin mixtures, aluminum salts, silicones, aluminum compounds, fluorocarbons, and others. Water-repellent finishes for polyester fabrics can be based on silicones or fluorochemicals. With proper preparation of polyester/cotton fabrics, water-repellent finishes can be applied in combination with cross-linking agents to give durable-press rainwear.

There are two classes of water repellents:

1. *Nondurable repellents.* On the one hand, these repellents have excellent water resistance, are inexpensive, and are easy to apply. On the other hand, this class is nonlaunderable and nondry-cleanable and does not resist oily liquids. These repellents are used for tarpaulins, tents, and awnings.
2. *Durable repellents.* Durable repellents are of several kinds. Some are developed for durability to dry cleaning only, others for durability to laundering only, while still others are durable to both dry cleaning and laundering. The fluorocarbon compounds are particularly resistant to oily stains. For instance, these fluorocarbon types used on wool resist oil as well as water.[24] Resistant to stains, they may be used on upholstery and table coverings.

[22]*Home and Garden Bulletin* No. 68, Consumer Service Department of the U.S. Department of Agriculture (Washington, D.C.: Government Printing Office, 1980).

[23]Developed by W. L. Gore and Associates, Inc., Elkton, Maryland.

[24]Scotchgard and Zepel.

There are several standard test methods developed by the AATCC[25] and the ASTM. These tests require special laboratory equipment. A simple consumer-type test is done by spreading the fabric on a flat table top to determine whether it is water-repellent. Sprinkle droplets of water on the surface of the fabric. Wait a few minutes to see if the cloth absorbs the water or if droplets of water will remain on the surface of the fabric. If droplets remain, the fabric is water-repellent.

The AATCC devised a method for predicting, by means of an air-porosity test before a fabric is treated, whether it is suitably constructed for a water-repellent finish and also the degree of protection that may be expected from this fabric when it has been treated.

The problem of water-repellent finishing is a difficult one because the fabric, to be comfortable, must be porous to allow circulation of air, and at the same time it must prevent water from leaking through. Consequently, the fibers and yarns must be water-resistant, and the construction must be well balanced and sufficiently close. In one test, two fabrics weighed the same number of ounces per square yard, the count of cloth was similar, the balance of the cloth was good, and it was adequate for the water-resistant finish; but the yarns in one sample were finer than the other, and the fabric with finer yarn showed leakage.

According to the results of this research, fabrics suitable for water-resistant finishing should have a combination of the following: (1) proper construction, (2) suitable permeability to air, and (3) satisfactory water resistance of fibers and yarns.

Generally, the label indicates whether the water-repellent finish can be dry-cleaned or laundered. Instructions on the label should be followed to ensure the maximum service from such finishes.

Fabric finishes vary in their effectiveness and durability. This means that the consumer who knows the difference between a water-repellent and waterproof garment will make a more appropriate selection of rainwear for a specific use. For example, for fishing or hunting in rainy weather, a waterproof raincoat would be essential because of the extensive length of time often spent in the rain. The informed consumer would choose a durable type of water-repellent coat for short exposure to rain or snow.

SUMMARY

The review in this chapter of the multitude of finishes that are now being applied to textiles points up the tremendous contribution to the field that has been made and is continuing to be made by the research chemists. These people are dedicating their expertise to creating fabrics that are ideally suited to the varying needs of the modern consumer.

Some of the finishing processes that have been discussed are of a mechanical nature; this group includes those that employ rollers, steam, and

---

[25]AATCC Standard Test Method 22-1952; ASTM 583-54.

pressure. The rest of the finishing processes are of a chemical nature; they include, among others, mothproof, flame-retardant, crease-resistant, water-repellent, and mildew-resistant finishes; wash-and-wear; durable press; and soil release, dyeing, and printing. These last two processes are discussed in the next chapter.

REVIEW QUESTIONS

1. List and describe the finishing processes generally used for cotton gray goods.
2. (a) What finishes give luster to a fabric?
   (b) Describe each finish.
3. (a) What is sizing?
   (b) Why is sizing used to finish cotton fabrics? linen fabrics? silk fabrics?
4. (a) How may permanent creped effects be produced?
   (b) How is permanent embossing possible?
5. (a) What is calendering?
   (b) What textile fabrics are calendered?
6. (a) What is a permanent finish? a nonpermanent finish?
   (b) Give examples of each type.
7. (a) What is weighting?
   (b) When would it be used?
8. Give the provisions of the FTC ruling for shrinkage.
9. Compare durable press and wash-and-wear.
   (a) Give the methods of producing each.
   (b) What are the merits and drawbacks of each?
10. What is the difference between waterproof and water-repellent finishes?

EXPERIMENT

Determining the permanency of finishing processes. Before undertaking any experiment, read the label or determine by any test previously outlined the kinds of fibers in the warp and filling of each sample:
A. If the fabric is cotton;
   (1) Rub your thumbnail over the cloth. Note whether little particles flake off the cloth. If so, the cloth is sized.
   (2) If the fabric is colored, rub a white handkerchief briskly against it. Note whether some color is transferred to the handkerchief. If so, the cloth is heavily sized.
   (3) Divide your sample in half. Take one half and tear it quickly. Note whether particles fly as the cloth is torn. If so, the cloth is sized.
   (4) Wash a portion of the sample with warm water and soap. Dry and iron the sample and compare the washed and unwashed portions as to weight of fabric and crispness of finish.
       (a) For each sample, indicate which test or tests removed the sizing or finishing.
       (b) Were any finishes so tested permanent? How do you know?
B. If the fabric is wool;
   (1) Brush the back of the cloth with a stiff brush. Note whether short fibers come out.

(2) Rub two pieces of the cloth briskly together. Note whether the surface shines more after friction is applied. Was any nap removed?

(3) Cut the sample in half. Wash one half with warm water and soap. Dry and iron it; then compare the washed with the unwashed portion as to size, color, and softness.

    (a) Was the sample flocked? If so, did the flocking affect the durability, weight, or warmth of the cloth?

    (b) Was the cloth tested fast to friction? Why?

    (c) Was the cloth fast to laundering? Why?

    (d) Would you consider the finish of a wool fabric permanent if it were fast to friction and to laundering? Explain.

GLOSSARY

Absorbent finish   Chemical treatment of fabrics to improve their absorptive qualities.

Antibacterial finishes   See *germ-resistant*.

Basic finishes   Regular processes (mechanical or chemical) applied in some form to a fabric after it has been constructed.

Beetling   A process of pounding linen or cotton to give a flat effect. Beetling gives a linenlike appearance to cotton.

Bleaching   A basic finishing process to whiten fabrics. Different chemicals are used for different fabrics. Sun, air, and moisture are good bleaches for some materials, although bleaching by this method is slower.

Boardy fabric   A fabric that is too stiff. May be due to excessive amounts or improper application of chemical finishing materials.

Brushing   Removing short, loose fibers from a cloth by means of cylinder rolls covered with bristles.

Burling   Removing of irregularities, such as knots or slubs, with a small pick.

Calendering   A finishing process for fabrics that produces a shiny, smooth surface by passing the cloth through hollow, heated cylinder rolls or by running the cloth through a friction or glazing calender, as for chintz.

Carbonizing   A chemical treatment of wool to burn out vegetable matter.

Chemical finishing processes   Treatments with alkalies, acids, bleaches, starches, resins, and the like.

Ciré   A material finished by means of a calendering process that produces a high polishlike patent leather look.

Crabbing   See Chapter 12, page 282.

Crease-resistant   A chemical finishing process to enable a fabric to resist and recover from wrinkling.

Creping   A chemical or embossing process that, when applied as a finish, gives a cloth a crinkled surface.

Decating   A process for setting the luster on wool, silk, spun silk, and rayons.

Degumming   A process for removing natural gum from silk by boiling it in a soap solution.

Dressing   See *sizing*.

Drip dry   To hang up without wringing and let the article drip and dry.

Durable press   See the glossary in Chapter 3.

Embossing   A finish produced by pressing a raised design into a fabric by passing the fabric through hot engraved rollers. Permanent when heat-set.

Finishes   Basic or functional processes applied to a cloth after it has been constructed.

Flame or fire-resistant   A fabric treated to prevent the spread of flame.

Flammable Fabrics Act   A law passed by the Eighty-third Congress and signed by President Eisenhower on June 30, 1953, prohibiting the introduction or movement in interstate commerce of clothing fabrics flammable enough to be dangerous when worn. Amended in 1967.

Flocking   Adding weight to woolens by steaming fibers into the back of the fabric or sticking short fibers to a fabric base with an adhesive or by electrolysis.

Fulling   A shrinking process to make wool fabrics more compact and thicker. See *felting* in the glossary in Chapter 2.

Functional finishes   Special finishes that contribute a specific attribute to the merchandise; for example, soil-release, crease-resistant, and water-repellent.

Germ-resistant   Fabrics treated with compounds to protect the wearer against fungi and germs.

Gigging   A process of raising fibers on the surface of a fabric to make it softer and to increase its warmth. It is done by teasels. See *napping.*

Glazing   A finishing process consisting of treating the fabric with glue, starch, paraffin, shellac, or resin and then moving it through hot friction rollers.

Gray goods   See the glossary in Chapter 1.

Limp fabric   A fabric that is too soft due to inadequate amounts or improper application of finishing materials.

Mechanical finishes   Those finishing processes done by copper plates, roller brushes, perforated cylinders, tenter frames, or any type of mechanical equipment.

Mercerization   A treatment of cotton with caustic soda to make it stronger, more lustrous, and more absorbent and to increase its affinity for dye.

Mildew-resistant   Fabrics treated with metallic compounds and certain organic compounds. Waterproofed fabrics will also resist mildew.

Milling   See *fulling.*

Moiréing   A finishing process that produces by engraved rollers a waved or watered effect on a textile fabric. Design is permanent when heat-set.

Moth-repellent   Fabrics treated with colorless chemicals, similar to dyestuffs, added to the dye bath. Another method atomizes the fabric with mothproofing chemicals.

Napping   The process of raising short fibers of a cloth to the surface by means of revolving cylinders with wire brushes.

Nonpermanent finish   A finish that is removed when subjected to such agents as friction, laundering, light, and heat.

Oleophobic   A fiber or finish that resists (does not absorb) oil.

Optical brightener   A finish that applies fluorescent material to reflect light.

Permanent finish   A finish that will withstand whatever affects it in its particular use.

Permanent starchless   A process that impregnates a cloth with compounds that are not dissolved in laundering. When ironed, the cloth returns to its original crispness.

Plastic-coated fabric   A plastic film supported by a woven or knitted cloth.

Preshrunk   Fabrics that have been given a shrinking process before being put on the market. The percentage of residual shrinkage must be declared.

Residual shrinkage The percentage of possible shrinkage remaining in a fabric after it has been preshrunk.

Schreinerizing A calendering method that flattens the yarn to produce a soft look.

Scray A device used in fabric inspection to accumulate fabric on a moving belt so as to allow time to sew on additional bolts of cloth and yet maintain a constant rate of feed of the fabric to the inspection point.

Shearing Cutting off excess surface fibers from a cloth.

Singeing Removing surface fibers and lint from a cloth with hot copper plates or gas flames.

Sizing A finishing process in which a vegetable or synthetic material, such as starch, wax, casein, or gelatin, is added to the cloth to give it additional stiffness, smoothness, or weight.

Soil release The ability of a fabric or a special finish to permit the removal of waterborne and/or oil stains by the usual laundering methods.

Special finishes See *functional finishes*.

Spot-resistant See *water-repellent*.

Stabilizing Treating a fabric so that it will not shrink or stretch more than a certain percentage; e.g., 2 percent.

Starching See *sizing*.

Tentering A basic finishing process done by means of a frame that makes the fabric even in width.

Wash-and-wear Garments that can be washed and reworn with little or no ironing.

Waterproofing Treatment of fabrics to close the pores of the cloth.

Water-repellent A chemical treatment of a fabric to reduce its affinity for water. Pores of the fabric are open, and the degree of repellency varies.

Weighting Finishing materials applied to a fabric to give increased weight.

Chapter 8

DYEING AND PRINTING

Mrs. Morris purchased a pair of bright red slacks at her favorite sportswear department. When she reached home she hurriedly read the care label, noting that it said, "This fabric is colorfast. That's good," she thought, and then cut off the label.[1] A few days later when the slacks needed laundering, she wondered if she should have them dry-cleaned or wash them in the washing machine. "Should I use hot or warm water, and what setting?" she thought. All these questions and more might have been answered on the label had Mrs. Morris left it sewn to the slacks.

COLORFASTNESS

A distinction should be made between the two coloring systems used in textiles: *dyeing* (internal pigmentation) and *painting*, which includes printing (external pigmentation). In dyeing and staining, the coloring material penetrates the fibers and becomes an integral part of their structures. In painting, the pigment is applied to the fiber surface with a polymer binder between the fiber and the pigment; this is also called the pigment emulsion method. In general, the internal method of coloring is more fast to color than the external one.

Suitability of Dyestuff

Perhaps if Mrs. Morris had carefully read the label on her slacks, she would have found not only instructions for laundering but also the information that the color was fast to sunlight—a characteristic so important in sportswear. The wise

---

[1]See permanent-care labeling, Chapter 1.

consumer considers, in addition to the qualities of the fibers, yarns, weaves, and finishing processes, the element of color—the suitability of dye to various uses. The buyer has a right to expect dyed fabrics to withstand the deteriorating elements or influences to which the finished cloth will be subjected, such as sunlight, perspiration, washing, and friction. Although most fabrics are not equally fast to all these destructive agents, they must be fast to those with which they will come in contact in their particular uses. For example, upholstery fabrics should withstand sunlight, but it is not so important that they withstand washing or perspiration. Summer furniture covers, on the other hand, must be fast to sunlight and to laundering. An evening dress should be fast to perspiration and to dry cleaning, but it does not have to be fast to sunlight. Fabrics for sportswear should be fast to sunlight, to washing, and generally to perspiration. Dyes that are fast for the purpose for which the fabric is intended are termed *fast dyes*.

Fastness to Sunlight

Commercial testing agencies frequently use standard tests for lightfastness. A specially designed powerful carbon arc lamp has the same effect as strong sunlight. Samples to be tested revolve around this lamp for a definite period of exposure.

Because consumers do not have access to standard laboratory equipment, some simple home tests are suggested here. For comparison, commercial tests are briefly outlined.

Home Tests

Exposure to outdoor light: A 3-inch square of colored fabric is cut in half. One half is placed under a glass outdoors in a spot where it will get the maximum of hours of sunlight. After one week's exposure, the exposed half is compared with the other half, which has been kept in a box. Any change of color is noted. The same fabric can be exposed similarly for two weeks, and then for three weeks. Any change of color can be noted each time. If there is an appreciable change of color, the color is not fast to sunlight.

Fading from exposure to direct sunlight occurs often on silk and wool garments in bright blues and greens dyed with impermanent dyes. If only two hours of exposure cause drastic fading, the customer is well advised to return the garment to the seller for an adjustment.

Commercial Tests

Sunlight method. Specimens are exposed against standards, on sunny days only, between the hours of 9 A.M. and 3 P.M.

Daylight method. Specimens are allowed to remain in a test cabinet for 24 hours a day. Specimens are also exposed to low-intensity radiation (before 9 A.M. and after 3 P.M.) and on cloudy days, during which time the specimen temperature

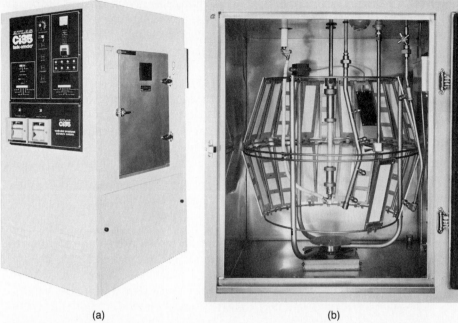

(a)   (b)

Figure 8.1 A new Fade-Ometer. The outside view (a) and the inside view (b). This machine has a xenon arc light source that gives a distribution of light very close to that of natural sunlight, much superior to the carbon arc lamp. The intensity of the source is always the same. (Photos courtesy of Altas Electric Devices Company, Chicago.)

may be low and the moisture content high. Since these tests may produce varying results, laboratories test a specimen under a variety of conditions simulating the performance of the fabric in a machine called a Weather-Ometer.

Fade-Ometer method.[2]   Colorfastness is rated in terms of number of "standard fading hours required to produce just appreciable fading" (change of color of any kind, when compared with unexposed samples). (See Fig. 8.1.)

Xenon Weather-Ometer.   For most fabrics not sensitive to low-intensity radiation and atmospheric contaminates, this xenon arc lamp method produces results comparable to the natural sunlight methods described previously.

Fastness to Perspiration

Light-colored silks, especially those used for evening wear, should be fast to perspiration. Most consumers rely on the salesperson's advice concerning the fastness of a fabric to perspiration. In fact, some large department stores have their own merchandise testing laboratories, to which buyers may send new

[2]AATCC, American Association of Textile Chemists and Colorists.

materials for testing fastness before instructions are given to the salespeople. Reliable manufacturers often provide the buyers with the same information. In buying yard goods, however, the consumer can usually obtain a sample of material, take it home, and test it before buying enough for his or her needs.

Home Test

It is best to subject the fabric to actual wear. A small piece of material may be worn in the sole of the shoe for a day. A quicker test is to sew a swatch of material to a white cloth of the same general texture, then immerse both for a moment in vinegar (not cider but synthetic vinegar), and let it dry. If stained, the sample is not fast to perspiration. Synthetic vinegar is used because it comes closest to perspiration; both contain acetic acid.

Commercial Test (AATCC 15)

Separate specimens are wetted out in alkaline and acid perspiration solutions. Fabrics are inserted in a perspiration tester, are subjected to a fixed mechanical pressure, and are allowed to dry slowly in an oven $100 \pm 2°$ F for at least six hours.

Bleeding, migration of color, or changes of dyed material are evaluated.

Fastness to Fumes and Ozone

When garments are exposed to the nitrogen oxide gases present in the atmosphere, color change often occurs. The change is gradual, showing up first in the most exposed part of the fabric and under the arms, where moisture accelerates the change. The problem can be observed more often in cities that support heavy industry. It is most commonly observed in acetate, as when a blue dyestuff turns reddish in color. The change is not reversible. However, if acetate and other man-made fibers such as nylon and polyester have the dye added to the spinning solution, fume fading is largely eliminated. Otherwise, fume-fading inhibitors should be applied in the dyeing or finishing stages.

Ozone fading is distinguished from fume fading, as the former is caused by nitrogen dioxide in the air and may occur even when the dye is fast to fume fading.

Home Tests

Home testing is not practicable, since the change takes place very slowly over an extended period of time.

Commercial Test (AATCC 23-1975)

This is a commercial test for burned gas fumes. A specimen of the fabric to be tested and a control fabric are placed in an exposure chamber with a lighted gas burner. In this way, they are exposed simultaneously to oxides of nitrogen from burned gas fumes until the control fabric shows a change in color that corresponds to a standard of fading established.[3] The change in the color of the fabric undergoing the test at the above point is measured by a "Standard Gray Scale" established for assessing the change in color.

Commercial Test (AATCC 109-1975)

This is a test for ozone in the atmosphere. A test specimen and a swatch of the control sample[4] are simultaneously exposed in a test chamber (called an Ozoniter) to ozone in the atmosphere under circulating room temperature and relative humidities not exceeding 65° F, until the control sample shows a color change corresponding to that of a standard of fading established. This exposure period constitutes one cycle. The cycles are repeated until the specimen shows a definite color change or for a prescribed number of cycles. The effect of color on the test specimen after any specific number of cycles is classified by reference to the Gray Scale for Color Change.

Fastness to Laundering

The best way in which to determine fastness to laundering is actually to launder a fabric. Ideally, the consumer should launder a small piece of material as many times as the fabric would be expected to resist laundering in actual use. Of course, this is too much to ask of the average consumer. Many testing laboratories do this very thing for the manufacturers and retail stores. For example, suppose that the specifications for a certain brand of sheet require that "the sheet must be fast to twenty washings in a reliable laundry and after these washings shall lose not more than 8 percent of its tensile-strength testing to make sure it is up to specifications."

Home Tests

Hand laundering. A 6-inch square of colored fabric should be cut into three equal parts. One of the parts is sewn to a 2-inch swatch of white cotton cloth of about the same weight and texture as the test cloth. It should be washed with warm water and strong soap, rinsed in clear water, and then dried. It should be ironed gently with little or no pressure, if necessary, to make it smooth. The color of the washed and unwashed samples is compared, and the white fabric is examined for any discoloration. One or two washings with strong soap generally give the same result as many washings with a mild soap.

Automatic washing. A 2-inch white swatch is basted to a colored fabric. These fabrics are subjected to a normal washing cycle in an automatic washer with

---

[3]The test control fabric is a secondary cellulose acetate satin dyed with 1 percent C.I. Dispersed Blue C (Celliton Blue FFRN). See *Bulletin FF296* (1981) of the International Fabricare Institute.

[4]The control sample is a tertiary shade of medium gray spun triacetate fabric. (The color change is mainly a loss of blue.)

Figure 8.2 Use of the Launder-O-Meter to test for colorfastness. (Photo courtesy of J. C. Penney Co.)

usual soap solution and water temperature. No chlorine is used. Washing of the test samples can be done with a regular load of colored clothes. If there is a change of color of the washed fabric or discoloration of the white fabric, the color is not fast to the test method used. (See Fig. 8.2.)

Commercial Test (AATCC 61)

In a 45-minute accelerated test, specimens are placed in stainless steel tubes or glass jars that revolve at a standard speed in a water bath that is thermostatically controlled. Metal balls are added to each tube to simulate washing action. (Table 8.1. reports a series of tests for the same fabric, with differences in temperature, soap solution, chlorine, and time of washing.)

Tested specimens are evaluated for alteration in color by comparing them with the International Geometric Scale. Color staining is evaluated by comparison with the AATCC chart for measuring transference of color or the Geometric Staining Scale.

Fastness to Dry Cleaning

Home Test

The procedure for dry cleaning should be followed explicitly as given in the directions on any standard brand of dry-cleaning fluid.

Table 8.1 Testing Methods in Laundering

Test Number	Temperature (°F)	Soap (percent)	Sodium Carbonate (percent)	Available Chlorine (percent)	Time (minutes)
1	105	40	0.5	None	30
2	120	49	0.5	None	30
3	160	71	0.5	0.2	45
4	182	83	0.5	0.2	45

Commercial Test (AATCC 132-69)

This is the standard test for commercial dry cleaning. While there are a number of solvents that may be used in dry cleaning, the one used almost universally in this country is perchloroethylene, which has the highest solvent power. Samples of the material are treated in a Launder-Ometer with a solvent and the tested specimen compared with the Gray Scale for Color Change. Problems are encountered when two or more pigments used to produce a color are differently affected. For example, a green may be produced by an application of blue and yellow pigments, but the yellow may be soluble in the dry-cleaning solution and the blue colorfast. Thus, the green may be changed to blue. See Chapter 16 for a discussion of dry-cleaning procedures.

Fastness to Pressing, Wet and Dry

Home Tests

To test fastness to pressing of cotton and linen fabrics, two samples, each 4 × 4 inches, are used. One sample is covered with a wet piece of bleached, unsized cloth.

The sample is ironed for 10 seconds at 350° F. The tested sample is placed in a dark room for about an hour to regain its natural moisture. The other test sample is ironed dry for 5 seconds at 425° F and is then placed in a dark room. Cotton and linen fabrics pressed wet that show no appreciable change in color and no appreciable staining of the white fabric are considered colorfast to wet pressing. Similarly, cotton and linen fabrics that show no change in color after dry pressing are colorfast to dry pressing.

For testing fabrics other than cotton and linen and other than woolens and worsteds, pieces of white wool, silk, desized cotton, rayon, and acetate cloths are sewn to one test sample. For wet pressing, the test sample is wetted, the surplus water is shaken off, and the sample is placed face down on the dry-test sample. Then the fabric is allowed to rest for one hour. Another sample is tested for ten seconds with a flat iron between 275° and 300° F. Fabrics that pass both tests are colorfast to wet and dry pressing.

Commercial Test (AATCC 117)

A piece of colored fabric is placed between two pieces of uncolored cloth (composite specimen). The fabrics are placed in a heating device or Scorch tester, German Precision Heating Press, or Molten Metal Bath for 30 seconds at one of the following test temperatures:

$$300° \pm 5° \text{ F}$$
$$325° \pm 5° \text{ F}$$
$$350° \pm 5° \text{ F}$$
$$375° \pm 5° \text{ F}$$
$$400° \pm 5° \text{ F}$$

The composite specimen is removed from the heating device and evaluated for each component by comparing with the Gray Scale for Color Change and the Gray Staining Scale.

Fastness to Crocking

Fabrics used for street and business dresses must withstand a great deal of friction; that is, the color should not rub off, or crock, even though the fabric is not intended to be washable. Dyestuffs that crock are very likely to bleed or run. This is usually due to dyestuffs left in the surface of the goods after processing because of improper afterwashing following the dyeing. In washable fabrics crocking may be an indication that the colors are not fast to laundering. Furthermore, if a dye crocks badly, it may discolor fabrics rubbed against it.

Home Tests

Dry crocking. A 2-inch square of colored fabric is rubbed against a piece of white sheeting. Any discoloration of the white cloth should be noted. If there is any discoloration of the fabric itself, the color is not fast to dry crocking.

Wet crocking. A piece of white sheeting should be dampened and rubbed against a piece of the untested colored fabric. Any discoloration of the white cloth should be noted. If this occurs, the color is not fast to crocking.

Commercial Tests (AATCC 8)

Dry crocking. A test specimen is fastened to the base of the Crockmeter. A standard crock cloth is attached to the rubbing finger of the machine. The finger is lowered onto the test specimen, and by turning the crank the finger is caused to slide back and forth twenty times.

Wet crocking. Fabric squares are wetted in distilled water and are then placed between two filter papers (like a sandwich). The "sandwich" is passed through a wringer. The transfer of color (both wet and dry) is evaluated by comparing with a chart for measuring transference of color or with the Geometric Staining Scale.

DYEING CLOTH

Fabrics in colors such as blue, yellow, red, green, and their combinations are made by impregnation of the cloth with certain color substances called *dyestuffs*. The fastness of these colors depends on the chemistry of the dyestuff, the affinity of the dyestuff for the fabric, and the method of dyeing the cloth. A fast dyestuff is minimally affected by sunlight, perspiration, washing, or friction.

Selection of the Proper Dyestuff

Until 1856, all dyestuffs were natural; that is, they were obtained from plants, shellfish, insects, and woods. Some of the most common natural dyestuffs are cochineal, made from the dried bodies of female insects found in Central America and Mexico, used to dye scarlet; logwood, taken from the brownish heart of a tree found in Central America; quercitron, which comes from the yellow inner bark of a large oak tree growing in the eastern part of this country; fustic, a light yellow dye coming from a tree growing in Mexico and the West Indies; and indigo, a blue dyestuff derived originally (by the Indians) from plants but now also made artifically.

Natural dyes were used in the early days of the Roman Empire–when so-called Tyrian purple was used for the clothing of the ruling family. The substance that first produced the color purple was derived from a kind of snail. Pliny tells us that the art of dyeing yellow, green, and black was brought from India to Greece by Alexander the Great. In the Middle Ages, northern Italians were most skilled in the art of dyeing. The early explorers who came to American brought back many dyestuffs. Certainly dyeing is one of the oldest arts.

In Oriental rug making a century ago, the modern commercial dyestuffs were unknown. Each family was skilled in making certain colors that would be fast to washing and sunlight. The secret formula for making a certain color from natural dyestuffs was handed down from one generation to another.

Obtaining natural dyestuffs and mixing them to obtain the desired color is a slow process compared with our present methods of commercial dyeing, in which all the dyes are synthetic or chemical. They are man-made by the mixing of certain chemicals whose bases are either salts or acids. At the present time synthetic dyes have practically replaced natural dyes.

The first synthetically made dyestuff was discovered by William Henry Perkin in 1856. He was experimenting with aniline, whose base is principally coal tar (a substance produced in the process of making coke), when he discovered the colored substance known as mauve. Later other coal tar colors followed. But the great development in chemical dyestuffs in this country has come since World War I. During the war years 1914–1918, the dyed fabrics in the United States were of poor quality and not fast. The United States had to do

Table 8.2 Degree of Fastness to . . .[b]

	Home Washing (AATCC #2)	Laundry (AATCC #3)	Light	Slasher Sizing	Chlorine	Cross-dyeing	Mercer-izing
1. Vat	Exc.	Exc.	Exc.	Exc.	Exc.	Exc.	Exc.
2. Napthol	Exc.	Exc.	Exc.	Exc.	Exc. to good	Exc.	Exc.
3. Bonded (fiber-reactive)	Exc.	Very good	Fair to good	Exc.	Most dyes poor	Good	Exc.
4. Developed	Good	Fair	Fair to poor	Exc.	Poor	Good	Good
5. Sulfur	Very good	Good	Good to fair	Exc.	Most dyes poor	Exc.	Exc.
6. Direct	Good in light shades of selected dyes	Fair in light shades	Exc. in selected dyes; others fair to poor	Good in light shades	Poor	Poor	Some good

[a]This table is only a generalization. If refers to the relative fastness of the different dyeing methods as a class. It should be borne in mind, however, that there are exceptions within each class. The numbers on the left indicate the price class, no. 1 being the highest priced, no. 2 next, and so on.

[b]Slasher sizing involves the application of sizing material to the warp yarns before the fabric is woven in order to smooth and strengthen them during the weaving process.

much experimenting before it knew the secret of making fast synthetic dyes. Before and during the war Germany held that secret.

Dyestuff chemists say that there are as many as four thousand different dyes or combinations of dyes being made and used today. They may be classified according to origin, chemical composition, nature of reaction necessary to produce color, and method of application to fiber or fabric.

The fastness to various treatments of some of the major types of dyes discussed in the following paragraphs appears in Table 8.2., as a generalization.

Acid Dyes

Acid dyes are essentially organic acids that are obtained by the dyer in the form of salts. They are applied to the fiber directly from solutions containing an acid, such as sulfuric, acetic, or formic acid. Acid dyes can be used on wool, modified acrylic, nylon, and Spandex and on certain selected polypropylene olefin fibers.

When wet-treated, bright acid colors may not be colorfast. Acid colors are only fairly or poorly fast to washing; they vary in degree of colorfastness to perspiration, but they exhibit good colorfastness to dry cleaning and to light.

Acid dyes are water-soluble and can be applied to silk, wool, and certain types of acrylic fiber using nylon without a mordant. Acid colors can be applied to Orlon 44 using conventional dyeing procedures. It is possible to obtain a larger range of dyes and better wetfastness than previously. Dynel modacrylic and the older Acrilan acrylic fibers can also be colored by acid dyes.

Mordant or Chrome Dyes

Although once of commercial importance, this method of dyeing is rarely used today, primarily due to environmental regulations and the availability of better dyestuffs. Chromium is used as a mordant to fix the dye on the cloth, as well as other metallic salts (iron, aluminum, and tin).

Basic or Cationic Dyes

These colors were the first synthetic dyestuffs to be discovered. Basic dyes are salts of colored organic bases. They may be called cationic because the colored portion of the dye molecule is positively charged (cationic).

Organic basic dyes are sometimes called aniline colors because the first few colors were made from aniline. Basic dyes can be applied to linen and silk for excellent color value and penetration as well as certain man-made fibers and modified polyester. Before the advent of synthetic fibers these dyes were not used frequently because of their poor lightfastness on cellulosic fibers. Selected basic dyes are now used extensively on some of the newer types of man-made acrylic fiber. These dyes are fast, very easy to apply, and require a very short dyeing time.

Basic dyes are seldom used on wool, because acid colors are generally more fast. For dyeing silk, basic dyes give brilliancy and depth of color.

Direct or Substantive Dyes

These dyestuffs, like acid dyes, are salts of color acids. They are applied directly to cotton, linen, and rayon, requiring no mordant. Shades so produced are duller than those colored by basic dyes, but they can be topped with basic dyes to brighten them. Direct dyes may be used for dyeing wool yarns used for knitting and weaving, for reused wool, and for casein fibers. These colors are generally not fast to washing. They are more fast to light when applied to wool than when used on cotton.

Direct colors may also be applied to silk, and shades so obtained are faster than they are on cotton. But these colors have normally been regarded as cotton dyes and have therefore not been used so frequently on silk and wool. When direct colors are used to dye nylon, the dye is usually applied from a bath set with either acetic or formic acid.

Direct dyes may be developed after application to the fabric. Naphtholic compounds are used as developers. A radical in the dye molecule reacts with the developer. Developed direct dyes may have excellent fastness to washing but a decreased lightfastness. (See *developed colors,* following.) Bright shades are obtained from both direct and developed direct dyes.

Developed Colors

These are dyestuffs that may be applied directly to the cloth and may change to a new color on the fabric when treated with nitrous acid and certain chemicals called *developers.* The intensity of the color and the fastness of the dyestuff may be changed by this treatment. A dye that is navy blue when applied directly to a cloth may become a fast black when developed. Cotton dyed with developed colors may be washed satisfactorily at home but should not be sent to a commercial laundry.

Developed dyes may also be used on rayon and other man-made fibers when developed from disperse-dye bases. (See *disperse dyes.*) Developed colors are sometimes used for discharge printing. (See page 207.)

Disperse Dyes

These dyes were formerly called acetate dyes because they were originally used to dye acetate fibers. They are now used for coloring acetate, polyester, acrylic, and nylon fibers. The molecules of these dyes are small, and the dye is slightly soluble in water but is easily *dispersed* throughout a solution. The fiber's dye sites are made more accessible by swelling the fiber with wetting agents, heat, or such. The small particles are "inserted," and the water medium is evaporated by heat. This seals in the dye molecule. Ratings for colorfastness to light, washing, and dry cleaning vary depending on the fiber used. Fume fading, said to be caused by exposure to nitrogen in the air, remains a problem when disperse dyes are used on acetate. This problem is minimal when these dyes are used on nylon or polyester.

Naphthol or Azoic Dyes

Naphthol dyes are commonly applied to cotton piece goods and are used extensively in cotton printing. The cotton is first impregnated with beta-naphthol that has been dissolved in caustic soda; then it is immersed in basic dye. Naphthol colors are fast to washing and to soaping when properly applied. The application of this type of dye requires a good knowledge of organic chemistry, and failure to follow directions for its application may result in poor colorfastness to crocking and washing. Fast bright scarlets and reds can be obtained at a fairly low cost. A naphthol dye can produce a green or blue-green shade on polyester fibers.

For the dyeing of acetate, certain of the insoluble compounds of azoic dyes are used. These compounds are treated with sulfonated oil or soap. By this treatment, a stable suspension for dyeing acetate is possible.

Azoic dyes can be applied to nylon by methods similar to those used for acetate; however, the colors are not as brilliant as on cottons. By first impregnating nylon with Naphthanil, then immersing in a second bath containing hydrochloric acid, and finally developing in a sodium-nitrite-acid liquor, strong, bright, well-penetrating colors with fastness to crocking are possible.

Vat Dyes

The name originated in the making of the old indigo dyes, when the dyestuff had to steep for some days in a vat before it could be used. There are two classes of vat dyes: (1) indigo, indigoids, indigosols, and algosols and (2) anthraquinoids.

Modern indigo is perhaps the most famous vat dye because of its fastness to light and washing. Increasingly important in this group are the indigosols (colorless dyestuffs), which are being used for dyeing wool. The wool or silk is saturated with dye, and color is later developed. The indigoids have a molecular structure similar to indigo.

The anthraquinoids are the fastest of the vat dyes. They are especially suitable for cotton and can be applied to acetate. In this category are the indanthrene dyes, which are extremely fast.

Probably the reason for the increased importance of the vat dye is that it possesses a higher degree of fastness to washing, light, bleaching, cross-dyeing, and mercerizing than do the other dyes. (See Table 8.2.) As a class, then, vat dyestuffs are particularly fast when applied to cotton. They are used to produce fast colors in cotton dress fabrics and in shirtings. Vat dyes can also be used for dyeing rayon.

Sulfur Dyes

Sulfur colors are used on cottons and other vegetable fibers. Although the colors are dull, they have good fastness to light, washing, and crocking and are relatively inexpensive. Sometimes sulfur black dye attacks and weakens the fiber, because oxidation of the sulfur gradually develops into a sulfuric acid.

Fiber-Reactive Dyestuffs (Bonded)

In general, all classes of dyestuffs are fixed to the fabric by means of physical absorption or mechanical retention of an insoluble pigment by the fiber. In both cases, the color appears to be a part of the fiber.

Fiber-reactive dyestuffs, however, couple the color to the fabric by a reaction with the hydroxide (OH) group of the cellulose molecule. In this reaction the dye molecule becomes an integral part of the cellulose. It is because of this chemical integrity that reactive dyes possess excellent washfastness and dry-cleaning properties.

Most reactive dyes are fixed to the fabric by a system that employs an alkali as a catalyst. This alkali promotes the transfer of electrons, which causes the color to be integrated with the cellulose. Of the many alkalies (electrolytes) used, the most common are sodium carbonate, sodium bicarbonate, and caustic soda.

In practice, the fabric would first be padded with the dye, then dried. The fabric would then undergo a second padding containing the alkali. Once this is completed, the fabric would be exposed to extreme heat, steam, or air.

Fabrics such as wool or silk can be dyed using either modified procedures or fiber reactive dyes designed for protein fibers. This system has obvious labor- and time-saving advantages. These are brought to light in a consideration of the time it takes to fix a dye in a system that fixes only when an exchange between dye and fabric comes to an equilibrium. An example of this is exhaust dyeing. The time element here may be from 10 minutes to several hours. Today, some reactive dyes can be fixed in 30 seconds.

Exhaust Dyeing

This is a process of dyeing from an aqueous solution, where nearly all the dye is absorbed by the material, thus "exhausting" the dye bath. The dye is diffused first onto the fiber surface followed by absorption into the fabric.

Exhaust dyeing is a relatively new process that provides fast, high-quality dyeing with minimal decomposition of the fiber. It is particularly suitable for dyeing wool, acrylic, polyester, or nylon fibers with basic dyes.

A *cationic retarder*[5] is used to saturate the fiber, the critical temperature range of exhaustion being determined by the type of fiber and dyestuff. The rate at which the dye is absorbed is obtained by a constant rate of increase within the critical temperature range. After sufficient dye bath exhaustion is obtained, a predetermined amount of dyeing time at a high temperature is necessary for the dye to penetrate sufficiently. This penetration time depends on temperature, fiber type, and diffusion speed of the dye, but not on dye concentration.

Benefits of this process include shorter dyeing cycles with better levelness of dyeing obtained without migration.

Metal Complex Dyes

The metal complex dyes are closely related to the mordant dyes. This class of dyestuffs is ionic and premetallized, thus eliminating the need for a mordant. Metal complex dyes are suitable for wool, silk, and polyamides. In addition to the salt formation of the dye with the amino groups found in these types of fibers, complex formation of the dyes with the substrate takes place. Wash- and lightfastness ratings are generally high for this class of dyestuffs.

---

[5] A chemical substance that retards or slows down the absorption rate of cationic dyes into dyeable fibers.

Oxidation Dyes

As with azoic dyes, oxidation dyes are formed in the fiber substrate. Their salts are water-soluble. They are applied to the fabric as an oxidation base in the form of water-soluble salts and thereafter oxidized to a pigment. A well-known example of this is the aniline black process, in which the aniline salt solution is applied to cotton in the presence of a catalyst and then is submitted to air oxidation, thus fixing the dye. Similar processes are used for dyeing animal fibers and human hair. Hydrogen peroxide is often used as the oxidizing agent.

Dyeing of Blends

The problem of dyeing textiles has never been an easy one if the selection of the dyestuff and its application is adequate to give the performance expected by consumers. With the advent of the newer synthetics, and with the increasing use of blends, the problem has become even more complex. For example, normal dyeing temperatures vary considerably, depending upon the particular process being used. Thermosol dyeing temperatures range from 380° to 425°F. Exhaust dyeing temperatures depend upon the fiber. Polyester fiber requires 240° to 275°F, whereas the normal temperature for nylon, acrylic, and cotton is 200° to 220°F and for cotton with fiber-reactive dyes 104° to 175°F.

CIBA-GEIGY Corp. (Basel, Switzerland) has developed a one-bath process for dyeing 50 percent wool/50 percent cotton blends. The process begins with an acid dye bath to which a wool-immunizing agent is added to keep direct color off the wool. Another ingredient is added to alkalinize the dye bath as the dyeing progresses. The fabrics are brought to a boil in 30 minutes and boil for 1 hour. A typical dye bath would consist of 100 units of fabric, 4,000 units of water, 6 units of 40 percent acetic acid, 40 units of Glauber's salt, and 13 units of immunizing agent. Color shades are made in the usual way, and excellent cross-dyes are possible.

These are only two of the many possible blends that a dyer may encounter. Percentages of each fiber as well as the kind of fibers and the number of different ones included in a blend are considerations in the proper selection and application of a dyestuff for a blend.

Figure 8.3 illustrates some of the methods of dyeing discussed in this section.

Points at Which the Dye Is Applied

When the proper type of dyestuff has been selected, the textile can be dyed by one of the following methods:

1. *Dyeing the raw stock.* This method is very common in dyeing wool. "Dyed in the wool" is a familiar expression; it means that the wool fibers were dyed before they were carded or spun. This method enables the dyestuff to penetrate the fibers thoroughly, so that the color is likely to be fast. Interesting

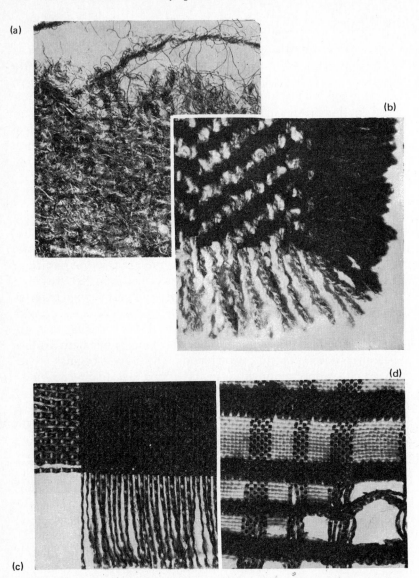

Figure 8.3 Methods of dyeing. (a) Dyed in raw stock (fibers in a given yarn are more than one color); (b) yarn-dyed; (c) piece-dyed; (d) cross-dyed. The cross-dyed sample at lower right consists of acetate, viscose rayon, and cotton. Some of the acetate yarns have been dissolved by acetone in a laboratory test. (Photos by Jack Pitkin.)

mixtures can be made by mixing two or more colors of raw stock. This method is more costly than other methods of dyeing textile fabrics. The favorite mottled gray flannel suiting is dyed in raw stock.

    2. *Dyeing the slub.* When the fibers have been carded and combed preparatory to spinning, they lie in the shape of a smooth slub, sliver, or rope.

This sliver can be printed with dye at the desired intervals. By drawing and spinning the yarn, interesting mixtures may be obtained. This method is also common for wool mixtures. The dyestuff penetrates the fibers easily, thus ensuring permanency of color.

3. *Solution dyeing.* Man-made fibers may be dyed while they are in the cellulosic or polymer stage before extrusion through a spinneret. The coloring solution used is usually a pigment rather than a true dyestuff. Such coloring is generally fast to destructive agents.

4. *Dyeing the yarn.* One of the best selling points a salesperson has for textile fabrics is the term "yarn-dyed." This means that the yarns were dyed before the fabric was woven. (See *space-dyed* yarns in the glossary.) In hosiery, the term *ingrain* is synonymous with yarn dyed.

Plaid ginghams, shepherd checks, and denims are yarn-dyed fabrics. An important method of dyeing yarn is called *package dyeing.* Yarn is wound around a cylinder known as a *package.* It is approximately 6 inches long by 5½ inches in diameter. Dye packages are placed in the dyeing machine—a stainless-steel cylinder (like a pressure cooker) with vertical spindles fastened to the bottom or to a removable carrier. The packages are placed on the spindles and the lid is closed. The dye is pumped through the packages from the inside out. (See Fig. 8.4.)

5. *Dyeing in the piece.* Although it is possible to make fast colors by piece-dyeing, the dyer must make sure that the cloth is covered evenly and that the dye has penetrated the fibers thoroughly. Piece-dyeing is done a great deal, for it

Figure 8.4 There are many methods of dyeing fabric. Shown here is dyed yarn being unloaded from an automatic dye machine after a process called package dyeing. (Photo courtesy of American Textile Manufacturers Institute.)

is economical for the manufacturer—especially in fabrics such as hosiery, whose style in colors changes rapidly. Another advantage is that any shade can be dyed on short notice. The knitting mills can make up a huge stock of undyed hosiery and wait until the demand comes for a definite amount in a certain color, dye that amount, and wait for another order. The same thing is done with other woven fabrics.

An important advance in the dyeing of hosiery is exemplified by the Milnor Rapid Dye Extractor. It consists of a rotary cylinder that provides in one basket the capability for scouring, dyeing, softening, and extracting moisture. It automatically controls filling, adding dyes and chemicals, raising and holding the temperature, coating, washing, draining, and extracting. The process reduces fuel consumption and water usage and labor costs—all of great importance today. It also provides for the saving of chemicals and dyestuffs. The dye cycle time is reduced greatly, a distinct advantage in handling rush orders for hosiery. It is also used for sweater bodies, T-shirts, throw rugs, and similar articles.[6]

6. *Cross-dyeing.* Since not all dyestuffs have an equal affinity for both vegetable and animal fibers, very interesting mixtures and frosted effects are produced by cross-dyeing. For example, when a cloth contains both vegetable and animal fibers, a dyestuff may be used that colors the animal but not the vegetable fibers.

Rayon and acetate mixtures can be dyed with a dyestuff that takes on the rayon but is resisted by the acetate. Blue wool suiting with a white cotton hairline stripe can be made by cross-dyeing. The dyestuff colors the wool blue but does not color the cotton stripe. Similarly, the acrylics Acrilan and Acrilan 1656 can be cross-dyed. If basic dyes are applied under strong acid conditions, Acrilan 1656 is dyed, whereas the older Acrilan resists the dye.

Years ago, when large quantities of yard goods were to be dyed, the operation was performed in comparatively small batches (lengths) of cloth. The operation had to be stopped when the fabric was transferred from one location to another. The slowdown was costly in time and money. Two DuPont inventions involving a continuous dyeing process have made large dyeing operations economically feasible with no distortion or stretching of lightly constructed fabrics.

Complexities of the Dyer's Problem

The preceding discussion suggests that dyeing is a highly technical process. The dyer must determine the right dyestuff, the right concentration, the right temperature, and the right time required to obtain complete penetration of the fiber or fabric under the following variable conditions:

1. The particular fiber or fabric to be dyed.
2. The exact color to be achieved.

[6]*America's Textiles* (K/A edition), September 1980, p. 36.

3. The particular end use of the final product in terms of exposure to deteriorating elements.

The dyer is limited by the equipment available and the need to keep costs at a minimum. Basic elements in cost are the dyestuff itself, the carrier (the solution that carries the dyestuff), the energy for heat and machine operation, and the time required to complete the operation. Clearly, a well-trained chemical engineer plays an important role in the high technology of the textile industry.

PRINTING CLOTH

Fabrics with colored figures stamped on them are known as printed cloths. The design in this case is not woven into the cloth but is printed on after the cloth has been woven. If the background of the fabric is to be white, the cloth is usually bleached before it is printed.

The printing of fabrics represents an important part of the textile industry. It is interesing to note that printed goods are often bought on impulse by the consumer because a particular pattern, design, or color combination in a dress, sport shirt, or sheet appeals to him or her. To retain this market, the print industry and those involved in the textile business face a major problem of meeting competition and maintaining price levels in the face of increasing raw material and labor costs. To alleviate this problem, chemists have developed new methods.

The Basic Process

First, the artists submit their textile designs to manufacturers. Out of an assortment of designs submitted, great numbers are rejected. The few accepted ones are then printed on samples of fabrics.

Dyestuffs used for printing are the same as those used for piece-dyeing or yarn-dyeing, except that dyestuffs may be thickened with starch, gum, or resin to prevent a color from bleeding or running outside the outline before it is dry. When they are dried, printed cloths are passed over hot rollers and then steamed so that the colors are set. Any excess dye is removed by a washing after the steaming. Colors carefully printed can be fast to both light and washing. It has been found that mercerization of the gray goods before printing results in a brighter, stronger colored print.

Kinds of Printing

There are many different ways of printing fabrics. The chief ones are as follows:

1. *Direct or roller printing.* The chosen designs are enlarged so that flaws may be detected and corrected. The design is "separated" into its individual colors, a roller being used for each color in the design. The actual printing is done as the cloth passes over a series of rollers that revolve in a vat of dye. Each

Figure 8.5   Fabric being roller (direct) printed. (Photo courtesy of Cranston Print Works Company.)

roller retains its particular color in the etched design and prints it on the fabric. (See Fig. 8.5.)

As many as sixteen colors can be printed at the rate of up to 200 yards a minute. Almost any textile fabric can be printed in this manner, including percale, dress linen, rayon and silk crepes, and wool challis.

A design may be printed on the warp yarns before the cloth is woven, When so printed, the fabric is called *warp printed*. The designs may appear grayed and their outlines may be hazy, because the filling yarns are usually a neutral shade—often white. *Vigoureux printing* is a variation of warp printing that is used on wool. Before the yarn is spun, color is applied to the wool tops or slubbing in the rope form. A variation of the roller method applies the colors in horizontal or cross-striped designs. When the wool is spun into yarn and woven into cloth, the stripes are broken into colored flecks. This type of printing is also called *mélange*.

(a)

(b)

Figure 8.6 Left: Roller (direct). Right: Discharge. Right sides are shown with wrong sides in the turned-up portions. (Photos by Jack Pitkin.)

2. *Discharge printing or dyeing.* When the design is to contain not more than two colors, the method called *discharge* is often used. The whole cloth is dyed a solid color first; then the design on the roller is covered with a chemical, which, when it is applied to the cloth, discharges (removes) the color from it in those portions that correspond to the design on the roller. The background is left colored and the design is white. The same depth of color appears on both sides, because the colored portion was piece-dyed first. Likewise, the color in the background can be discharged if the background is printed with chemical so that the design is left colored. Usually, however, the background is darker than the design. Polka dots and the figures in the foulards are often printed in this manner. (See Fig. 8.6.)

3. *Resist printing or dyeing.* In this method, the design is printed first with a chemical paste so constituted that when the cloth is dyed the parts covered by the paste resist the dye and retain their original color. Batik work is an excellent example of one type of resist dyeing. The portions of the fabric that are to resist the dye are covered with paraffin. The whole cloth is then dyed and, when dried, the paraffin is removed. At times the paraffin cracks during the dyeing, so that little runs of color appear in the resisted portions. Often the resisted portions are painted by hand in different colors.

Sometimes certain yarns are chemically treated to resist dye before they are woven. When the cloth is piece-dyed, the yarns so treated do not take the dye. Accordingly, stripes and checks appear in piece-dyed goods.

Another type of resist dyeing is called *tie-dyeing*, used in fabrics for scarfs and other accessories. Pieces of string are tied around bunches of cloth where the dye is to be resisted. The fabric is left tied in many little bunches while immersed in the dyestuffs. When the fabric is dry, the strings are removed, and very interesting sunburst designs appear. Parts of the fabric may be tied in different proportions and dipped in more than one color. It is possible to produce a varicolored design in this way. Still more complicated designs can be made by stitching the design areas rather than by tying. (See Fig. 8.7.)

Figure 8.7 Resist (done by tie-dyeing). (Photo by Jack Pitkin.)

Another type of resist dyeing is *stencil printing*, which is done by hand. Paper or metal is cut in the desired pattern and is placed over the fabric where the pattern is to be resisted. The parts that are covered do not take the dye.

4. *Hand block printing.* Before the method of direct roller printing was discovered, fabrics were printed by hand. The method is very similar to rubber stamping. A wooden block with a portion of the design carved on it is inked with dyestuff and stamped on the cloth by hand. The number of blocks used corresponds to the number of colors in the design. Great skill is required to stamp each portion of the design accurately so that all designs will be clear in outline and proportionate without a change in depth of color. Hand blocking gives a greater variety of designs and color effects, for the regular repetition of a pattern that is necessary in the roller method is not necessary in hand blocking. (See Fig. 8.8.)

Linen is used quite extensively for hand blocking because it has the proper texture and quality. As hand-blocked fabrics are generally expensive, it does not pay to do such handwork on a poor grade of cloth. Real India prints are produced by hand block printing.

One way of detecting hand blocking is to look along the selvage for the regularity of the repetition of the design. In roller printing, the design must be

Figure 8.8 Hand-blocked wool challis.

repeated at regular intervals. Not so with hand blocking. Another way of detecting hand blocking is to look at the edges of the designs. Almost invariably one color runs into another in at least a few places. Also, the quality of workmanship may be determined by the clearness of each color, the sharpness of outline, and the regularity of the design.

5. *Duplex printing.* When a fabric is intended to be reversible, it is printed on one side, turned over, and then printed again on the other side so that the outlines of the designs on each side coincide. There is a special machine called a *duplex printing machine* that prints both sides of a fabric simultaneously. This method, if done well, gives the impression that the design is woven in. (See Fig. 8.9.)

6. *Flock printing.* The application of short, dyed cotton, rayon, or wool fibers to fabric or to paper is called flock printing. There are two methods of application: (a) The flock fibers are pressed into the resin substance, which has already been printed on the fabric. (b) The flock is applied to the resin-printed fabric by electrolysis. The second method produces a velvety surface.

7. *Painted design.* Hand painting is most effective on silks. The design is outlined on the fabric with wax and is filled in later by hand brushwork. Usually the wax is mixed with dye so that the outline appears a different color and so stands out from the background. The dyes may be thickened, as is done for roller or block printing, or real oil paint may be used for the design. Most hand-

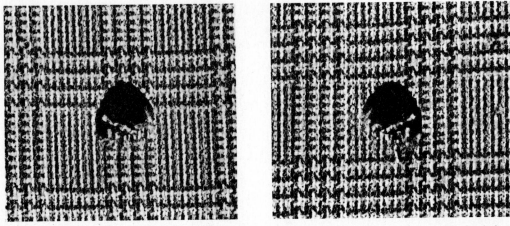

Figure 8.9 Duplex print. To determine a good quality duplex print, a pin may be used to pierce the fabric from the right side. The pin should appear at the same position in the design on the opposite side; in this example it does not. (Photos by Jonas Grushkin.)

painted fabrics are expensive because of the great amount of artistic labor involved.

Another method is painting the fabric with mordants rather than with color. When the dyebath is applied, each mordant reacts differently to the same dyebath. For more complicated designs, mordant printing can be combined with the wax-resist process. A modern version of mordant printing is called *madder* printing, so called because a dye prepared from the madder plant was formerly used for painting fabrics. This natural dyestuff has now been replaced by a synthetic dyestuff. Mordants are printed on the fabric first, and different colors are developed from a single dyebath.

8. *Screen printing.* When a design called for delicate shading, the process originally employed to produce the pattern was similar to that used for reproducing photographs in newspapers. Today a photochemical process reproduces the design exactly as it was painted. Elaborately shaded effects can be printed exactly like the original and reproduced many times. The fabric is first stretched on a padded table. A printing screen, made of silk, nylon, or metal stretched on a frame, is placed over the fabric. The parts of the pattern on the screen that are not to take the print are covered with enamel or certain paints to resist the printing paste. The printing paste is poured on the screen and pushed through the pattern portion with a wooden or rubber paddle called a *squeegee*. When one section of a pattern has been finished, the frame is moved to the next section, and so on until the entire length has been completed. (See Fig. 8.10.)

For screen printing, a continuous operation has now been mechanized, so that several yards can be printed every minute. The fabric moves along a table, and the automatic application of the screens is electrically controlled. An automatic squeegee operates electronically. Mechanized printing reduces costs

(a)

(b)

Figure 8.10   Above: Hand screen printing. Below: Automatic screen printing. (Photos courtesy of Cranston Print Works Company.)

appreciably for large batches. Whenever high-quality fashion prints on exclusive dress goods or intricate patterns and big repeats are requisites, screen printing is an important process.

Fabrics with large designs in limited quantities are frequently screen printed by hand. Rayon jerseys, crepes, and other dress fabrics, luncheon cloths, bedspreads, draperies, and shower curtains are often screen printed. Although screen printing is a slower and more expensive process than roller printing, the pattern repeats can be large—up to 80 inches. Pigment colors are sometimes put on in layers to give a look of handcraftsmanship.

9. *Rotary screen printing.*[7] Rotary screen printing is a combination of screen and roller printing. A perforated cylindrical screen produces the design rather than a flat screen. The color, in paste form, is fed into the inside of the screen and is forced through the "pores" in the screen into the fabric. New technological developments make it possible to produce fine line engravings. Intermittent patterns are being printed with extreme accuracy on sheetings and other household textiles. To handle repeat orders, changeover time has been reduced greatly as have faults in the prints that make it necessary to sell imperfect goods as "seconds" at much reduced prices. The newer machines have computer-guided electronic controls for each roller screen. (See Fig. 8.11.)

10. *Pigment printing.* Instead of applying dyestuffs that impregnate the fabric, color is produced by finely ground insoluble particles of color that remain on the surface and are not absorbed into the material. The pigment is dispersed in an emulsion of water and oil and a resin binder is stirred in that, with the application of heat, binds the pigment to the cloth. The pigment is usually applied by means of screen printing. Pigment printing is sometimes called pigment dyeing because the entire fabric is colored solid and not in patterns and a variety of colors.

This method is popular because it permits a wide range of colors to be applied to virtually all types of woven and knitted cloth, at a lower cost than dye printing. It may also be used in the chemical solution that is to be extruded into man-made filament fibers. But this method requires careful application of the proper binder to assure that the color will be fast to both laundering and dry cleaning and also to crocking.

11. *Photographic printing.* A design is photographed and the negative is covered with a screen plate to break up the solid areas of the design. A light is then projected through the screen plate onto another film to make a contact print. This film is placed on a copper roller treated with sensitizing solution. A powerful arc light focused on the film affects the sensitized roller by baking the coating where the light passes through. The roller is then washed to take away the solution from sections that the light did not reach. These portions of the roller are etched away to form the pattern. The roller is then treated to remove

[7]See "Printing Progress Unlimited," by S. M. Suchecki, in the July 1980 issue of *Textile Industries.*

Figure 8.11 Rotary screen printing is one of the fastest printing methods, combining a number of the advantages of the older screen and roller printing processes. This system utilizes a porous cylinder to hold the print design, much like a roller printer. The operator touches up details on the screen. Next the dye is forced through a pattern of holes in the cylinder and the cylinder is rolled over the cloth, leaving the colorful print. (Photo courtesy of American Textile Manufacturers Institute.)

the baked coating, and printing is done from the roller. This method provides fine designs for dress goods.

12. *Airbrushing*. Another method of producing shaded effects on fabrics employs a mechanized airbrush to blow color into the fabric. The hand guides the brush. This method is most effective on silk brocades and fabrics that are made in Jacquard or dobby designs.

13. *Heat-transfer printing*. In this technique the fabric is printed in nonpolluting color on large rolls of paper. The fabric in the greige and the printed paper are carried around a heated cylinder on a Nomex blanket.[8] The heat transfers the design to the cloth. Heat, speed of rotation, and blanket tension are adjusted to the requirements of the cloth to ensure that virtually all the dye in the pattern is exhausted. The paper is then discarded as trash. Almost any design can be printed by this process. (See Fig. 8.12.)

Costs of production are kept down by storing fabric in the greige until needed to fill orders. Only the printed paper needs to be stored until required, at a much lower cost than storing fabric.

This method is suitable for printing on fabrics of thermoplastic fibers, such as polyester, that melt at high temperature.

[8]DuPont's high-temperature-resistant fiber is aramid.

Figure 8.12 A heat-transfer printing machine. (Photo courtesy of David Gessner Company, Worcester, Mass.)

14. *Polychromatic printing or jet printing.* This is a process of applying (squirting) dye on a continuous width of fabric. The movement of the various jets controls the design. Patterns in stripes of many colors are possible with this technique. Jeans, shirts, scarfs, and bathroom mats can be printed in this way. This process is sometimes called polychromatic printing because the fabric shows a variety of colors.[9]

Electronic Laser Engraving[10]

This automated process is the newest development in roller end-plate printing. It uses both electronic and laser beam equipment to read artwork and to engrave directly rubber rollers or plates. It eliminates steps usually required to turn artwork into printable form. While a variety of different types exists, the most efficient, giving quick performance and fine detail, consists of four basic components: a low-power laser scanner, a high-power laser engraver, a computer system, and a modular mainframe. The artwork is engraved in dot form onto the printing roller. The helium-neon laser moves along a scanning platform, receiving optical information that it translates into an electronic signal for processing by the computer. The high-power laser then receives commands from the computer instructing it when to turn on and off to form the dots that make up the design.

[9]See Chapter 20 for jet printing of carpets using a chromotronic computer.

[10]For details, see "Electronic Laser Engraving," by Donald Bennett and Malcolm Webster, in the June 1979 issue of *Textile Asia*, pp. 88–94.

DISTINGUISHING DYEING AND PRINTING PROCESSES

Yarn-Dyed and Piece-Dyed Fabrics

Although raw stock and yarn dyeing usually produce the best color-fastness, depth of color, and luster, many piece-dyed fabrics are colorfast and equally attractive. Colorfastness depends on the degree to which the fibers have been penetrated by the dye. Since fibers and yarns are more easily penetrated before they are woven, a yarn-dyed cloth is more likely to be colorfast than is a piece-dyed cloth.

Of course, microscopic examination will reveal the degree of penetration of the fibers by dye, but the consumer does not usually have access to a microscope. A simple though not infallible test is to unravel yarns and untwist them. In piece-dyed cloths the core of the yarn may be white or a lighter color than the outer surface. This is especially true in piece-dyed linens and in cottons finished to resemble linens.

Printed and Woven Designs

Many consumers confuse a small, geometrical printed pattern with a dobby weave. But if the cloth is unraveled enough to include a portion of the design, an examination of the yarns may reveal a printed pattern. In a design printed on the cloth, the individual yarns will be in two or more colors where the design is present. For example, one yarn may contain white, yellow, and blue, and another yarn white and blue. Such a cloth is printed. In a woven-in pattern, individual yarns are the same color throughout their length. One yarn may be blue and another white, but from selvage to selvage a yarn is either all blue or all white.

COMPUTER PROCESSES IN SHADE MATCHING

In the dyeing industry, servicing both the dyeing and printing of fabrics, as in nearly every industry, there is an effort to computerize those processes that lend themselves to repetitive actions and inventory controls.

In short, what the computer does is to re-create a certain color by analyzing the information stored in the computer. The information is derived from machines that can break down the color constituents of a sample of fabric or liquid. This information is then put into terms of concentration of color, which colors are to be used, and the desired shade. In turn, all these earmarks of the specific color are translated into computer language to be stored and cross-referenced for later usage.

The most common devices used to find the *fingerprints* of a color are the spectrophotometer and the colorimeter. The spectrophotometer measures the amount of light reflected by a sample of colored material. The measurement derived is in the form of a graph that shows at what parts of the spectrum the sample reflects light, hence its color to the eye, and the intensity of this reflectance. Once it is known what colors the sample reflects—what it is made up of—it is known what it takes to make the color.

In digital systems, a computer has a great advantage—that of speed. Once the colorist decides on the dyes that he or she believes will make the shade, the colorist "plugs in" points in the color spectrum. The computer prints out the formula for the match. The computer's large storage capacity and rapid calculating speed allow it to make formula selections for any unknown combinations in the matching of shades. It will search through all possible combinations, along with their costs, and changes in shade from one source of light to another to arrive at the correct formula.

In general, it seems unlikely that the industry can ever be computerized in the same sense as those giant plants that need but a handful of personnel to run their computers. Indeed, the computer is a tool that narrows the field of dyestuff selection, checks over results, eliminates some of the trial-and-error methods, and keeps stock of what has been done. However, the matches that the computer makes can never really be perfect. Variables such as substrate, dyeing procedure, auxiliaries, and even the devices used to check the result must all be constant to ensure a precise match. In fact, the identical temperature and humidity on a particular day would help to provide better results.

The experience of the dyer and colorist are essential. Although it is possible to quantify many of these variables, experience is still the greatest asset. The substrate's preparation for dyeing, the action of the dyes themselves and their interaction, the differences in machinery, and the end use of the fabric all must be considered in making a match. A computer could probably store the information if the Herculean task of programming it were ever undertaken. Yet some of the factors that influence the dye match cannot be measured by machines. However, when two dyers get together, they know exactly what they are talking about.

SUMMARY

Consumers are becoming more conscious of the color of fabrics. Through the educational aid of intelligent salespeople and national advertising, consumers are learning what colors and their combinations best suit certain types and are becoming more particular in selecting colors for the home. Furthermore, consumers want fabrics to perform satisfactorily in their intended use. They have learned how to care for fine fabrics to preserve their original beauty. For these reasons manufacturers must produce a variety of beautiful, and at the same time fast, dyes.

Prints have become classic with Americans and are here to stay. To be sure, some years are more definitely print years than others. Most consumers like the novelty of printed apparel or perhaps a new printed sheet each year.

In conclusion, a fabric made from good raw stock, beautifully and strongly woven, can be enhanced manyfold by the application of the proper coloring. The reverse is also true—that good fibers and yarns, even if durably woven, can be ruined by the use of fugitive dyestuffs crudely applied.

REVIEW QUESTIONS

1. When is a dye considered fast? Explain fully.
2. Is there such a thing as an absolutely fast dye? Why?
3. Outline a method for testing the fastness of a color to light, perspiration, washing, friction, wash-and-wear.
4. When is a color considered absolutely fast to light? moderately fast? fugitive?
5. (a) What is meant by bleeding of colors?
   (b) What test can be used to determine whether or not colors will bleed?
6. (a) What is crocking?
   (b) What is a good test for crocking?
7. (a) Explain the difference between natural and synthetic dyestuffs.
   (b) Name some of the most important dyestuffs of each classification.
8. What are the advantages of synthetic dyestuffs over natural dyestuffs?
9. (a) What are basic dyes?
   (b) What are acid dyes?
   (c) To which fibers are basic dyes applied directly without prior chemical treatment?
10. (a) What is a mordant?
    (b) When is a mordant necessary?
11. (a) What are vat dyes?
    (b) Describe their method in application and use.
    (c) What are pigments?
    (d) When are they used?
    (e) What are some of the more recent developments in the dye industry? Explain.
12. (a) Explain fiber-reactive dyes, metal complex dyes, oxidation dyes.
    (b) How are they used?
13. (a) List the methods of dyeing cloth.
    (b) Explain each method.
14. (a) What kinds of cloth are made from dyed raw stock?
    (b) Name two fabrics that are usually yarn-dyed.
    (c) When is cross-dyeing advantageous?
    (d) List the different methods of printing cloth.
    (e) Explain each method.
15. Describe the procedure for transferring the design from the original to the copper roller.
16. (a) How does resist printing differ from discharge printing?
    (b) How is batik made?
17. (a) What are the selling points of a hand-blocked linen drapery?
    (b) How can hand block printing be distinguished from roller printing?

    (c) How can a duplex-printed fabric be distinguished from a woven cloth?

    (d) Describe jet printing and the heat-transfer technique.

18. What test is helpful in distinguishing yarn-dyed from piece-dyed fabrics?

19. At what point in dyeing and printing are computers now being used?

EXPERIMENTS

1. *Determining the permanency of dye.* Samples of five different materials should be tested for both permanency of dye and method of dyeing.

    (a) Fastness to light:

        Follow the instructions for home test (page 188).

        (1) When did the fabric fade slightly?

        (2) When did it fade appreciably?

        (3) Is the dye fast? moderately fast? fugitive?

    (b) Fastness to perspiration:

        Follow the instructions for home test (page 190).

        Is the dye fast to perspiration? Why?

    (c) Fastness to laundering:

        Follow the instructions for home test (page 191).

        Is the dye fast to washing? Why?

        (1) Baste half of the fabric to a piece of white silk. Wash and dry.

        (2) Compare the washed colored fabric with the unwashed piece. Note especially, after the two washed fabrics are separated, whether the white silk has been discolored.

            (a) Did the colors bleed?

            (b) Are the colors fast?

    (d) Fastness to crocking:

        Follow the instructions for home test (page 194).

        Is the dye fast to friction? Why?

2. *Determining the method of dyeing.*

    (a) If the fabric is solid colored,

        (1) Untwist several yarns in both warp and filling.

        (2) Note the evenness or unevenness of color penetration.

        Is the cloth piece-dyed or yarn-dyed? Why?

    (b) If the cloth is figured,

        (1) Unravel yarns in both warp and filling.

        (2) Note the color of individual yarns.

            (a) Are individual yarns the same color throughout their length or are they of more than one color?

            (b) Is the design printed or woven in?

    (c) If the cloth is printed,

        (1) Count the colors in the design.

        (2) Note the shape, regularity, and order of the patterns.

            (a) Are there more than two colors in the design?

            (b) Are the designs small and geometrical?

            (c) Are the designs placed at regular intervals with regular repetition of the patterns?

            (d) Are the outlines clear?

            (e) Does one color overlap another?

            (f) By what method is the cloth probably printed?

GLOSSARY

Acetate dye See *disperse dyes*.

Acid dye A type of dye used on protein fibers such as wool and silk and on nylon and modified acrylics such as Orlon 44 and Acrilan 1656.

Airbrushing Blowing color on a fabric with a mechanized airbrush.

Alizarin dye A vegetable dye originally obtained from the madder root, now produced synthetically. It is best used on wool but can be used on cotton, particularly in madder prints.

Aniline dye A term generally applied to any synthetic, organic dye. Originally from indigo, now from coal-tar products.

Azoic dye See *naphthol dye*.

Basic dye A type of dye used to dye acrylic fibers and certain modified polyester fibers such as Dacron 64. This dye is not used on wool today.

Batik A kind of resist dyeing in which parts of a fabric are coated with wax to resist the dye. It is usually done by hand but can be imitated by machine.

Catalyst A substance or agent that initiates a chemical reaction and makes possible for it to proceed under milder conditions than otherwise possible.

Cationic dye See *basic dye*.

Chrome dye See *mordant*.

Crocking Rubbing off a fabric's color.

Crock meter A standard device for testing a fabric's fastness to crocking.

Developed dye A type of dye in which one color may be changed by use of a developer. The intensity of the color and the fastness of the dyestuff may be changed by this treatment.

Dip dyeing A process of piece-dyeing hosiery or other knitted goods after construction.

Direct dye A type of dye with an affinity for cellulosic fibers. These dyes have moderate fastness properties.

Direct printing Application of color by passing the cloth over a series of rollers engraved with the designs. Developed direct dyes have good resistance to washing.

Discharge printing A method by which the cloth is piece-dyed first and then the color is discharged or bleached in spots, leaving white designs.

Disperse dyes Dispersions of colors or pigments in water. They were originally known as acetate dyes. At present these dyes are also used to color the newer synthetic fibers.

Dope-dyed See *solution-dyed*.

Duplex print Method of printing a fabric on the face and then on the back.

Dyed in raw stock See *raw-stock dyeing*.

Dyeing A process of coloring fibers, yarns, or fabrics with either natural or synthetic dyes.

Exhaust dyeing Dyeing from an aqueous solution where most of the dye is absorbed from the dye bath.

Fade-Ometer A standard laboratory device for testing a fabric's fastness to sunlight.

Fast dyes Those dyes that are fast for the purpose for which the fabric is intended.

Fiber dye See *raw-stock dyeing*.

Fugitive dye Those colors that are not fast to such elements as light, washing, perspiration, and crocking.

Hand-blocked print Fabrics printed by hand with blocks made of wood or linoleum.

Heat-transfer process See *sublistatic printing*.

Indigo A type of dyestuff originally obtained from the indigo plant, now produced synthetically. Blues are brilliant. It has good colorfastness to washing and to light.

Ingrain A knitted or woven fabric made of yarns dyed before knitting or weaving.

Jig dyeing Passing the cloth through a jig-dyeing machine (a large tub holding dye). It is used particularly for dark, direct dyes.

Laser engraving An automated process using electronic and laser beam equipment to "read" artwork and engrave rubber rollers and plates.

Launder-Ometer A standard laboratory device for testing a fabric's fastness to washing.

Madder See *alizarin dye*.

Metal complex dyes A class of dyestuffs that is ionic and premetallized (chemically coupled with nickel, copper, and cobalt salts to make the dye on the fiber).

Migration of dye The tendency of some dyes to spread from an intended point on a fabric to another.

Mordant A substance that acts as a binder for the dye. A mordant has an affinity for both the dyestuff and the fabric.

Naphthol dye Insoluble azoic dyes formed on the fiber by impregnating the cotton fabric with beta-naphthol that has been dissolved in caustic soda and then immersed in a naphthol salt.

Oxidation dyes A class of dyestuffs formed in the fiber substrate. These dyes are applied to the fabric as an oxidation base in the form of water-soluble salts and thereafter oxidized to a pigment.

Pad dyeing A process of first passing the cloth through a trough containing dye, then squeezing it between heavy rolls to remove excess dye.

Photographic printing Application of a photographic image to a fabric.

Piece-dyeing A fabric dyed after weaving, knitting, or other method of construction.

Pigment dyes Dye emulsion made with certain kinds of fine synthetic pigment in a solution of synthetic resins in an organic solvent; water is stirred in with a high-speed mixer. Often applied by pad dyeing and more recently by a printing process. Good colorfastness to light, washing, acids, and alkalies. When resin binder is ineffective, dye may crock or have poor resistance to washing.

Polychromatic printing or jet printing A process of applying (squirting) dye on a continuous width of fabric. The movement of the various jets controls the design.

Printing Methods of stamping colored figures on cloth.

Raw-stock dyeing Dyeing of fibers before spinning into yarn. It is synonymous with *fiber-dyed*.

Resist printing Application of substances to a cloth to resist dyeing; the cloth is immersed in dye, and the "resist" is then removed. See *batik*.

Roller printing See *direct printing*.

Screen printing Background of design painted on screen first. Dye is printed on exposed portions of fabric.

Slub-dyed Sliver-dyed or printed.

Solution-dyed Man-made fibers dyed in the spinning solution.

Space-dyed yarns Those yarns that have been dipped in dye or spotted in various places along the yarn.

Spun-dyed See *solution-dyed*.

Stencil printing   A type of resist printing in which portions of the design are covered with metal or wood so the covered parts do not take dye.

Sublistatic printing   A technique in which the design, printed on rolls of paper, is pressed against the fabric. When heat is applied, the design is transferred to the fabric.

Substrate   An underlying support or foundation, for example, fiber substrate prepared with a mordant before dyeing.

Sulfur dye   A dye derived from chemicals containing sulfur. It is used mostly for vegetable fibers. It has fair resistance to washing, poor resistance to sunlight.

Thermosol   Method of dyeing man-made fiber, especially polyester and other thermoplastic fibers, by padding fabric with disperse dyes or selected vat pigments. Dry heat (390° to 450° F or 198.9° to 232.2°C for about 1 minute) is used to make dyes migrate or "move" into and color fibers.

Tie-dyeing   A type of resist printing in which pieces of string are tied around bunches of cloth, or the fabric is stitched where dye is to be resisted.

Vat-dyed   This process uses an insoluble dye made soluble in its application. It is then put on the fiber and is oxidized to its original insoluble form. Excellent colorfastness to washing and sunlight.

Warp printing   Printing of warp yarns with the design before weaving. A hazy grayed effect is produced.

Weather-Ometer   A device that can simulate weather conditions, such as sunlight, heavy dew, rain, and thermal shock. The deteriorating effects of these conditions on fabrics are the objectives of tests in this device. These effects can be determined in a few days.

Chapter 9

COTTON
AND
THE CONSUMER

Do you know what consumers look for first in their choice of clothing? According to a national consumer study by Opinion Research Corporation, the consumer's first concern is *comfort*. In fact, 85 percent of those in the study chose comfort. Cotton is a desirable fabric because it is, indeed, comfortable. Being a hollowlike fiber, it breathes like a person does. This means that cotton remains porous no matter how it is woven or knitted. These pores permit body moisture vapor and air to pass constantly and invisibly through the cloth. Consequently, it is comfortable. Cotton fabrics feel good against the skin regardless of the temperature and humidity.[1]

Comfort is a buying point for the consumer and a selling point for the salesperson to emphasize in selling. The salesperson should have a knowledge of the qualities of each of the textile raw materials: the kind of fiber used, the type and quality of yarn, the construction, and the finish. Such knowledge helps the salesperson to assist a consumer in making a proper selection of fabrics for different uses.

From a knowledge of the qualities of the different textile raw materials, the salesperson should develop selling points.

This chapter considers the physical and chemical characteristics of cotton fibers and how these factors contribute to buying points. The type of yarn, construction, finishes, and coloring of cotton and their specific contributions to buying points will be discussed.

---

[1]See "Sew Something Beautiful with Cotton the Natural Fiber," a pamphlet offered by Cotton Incorporated.

Figure 9.1 Cotton bolls.

HISTORY OF COTTON

The history of cotton may go back seven thousand years. Even earlier than 2500 B.C., Egyptians were known to be wearing cotton as well as flax and wool. Through the ages cotton has clothed and sheltered man. In 1793 Eli Whitney's invention of the cotton gin revolutionized the processing of cotton and led to the Industrial Revolution.

Production processes that heretofore had been carried out in widespread locations were now centralized so that operations became more efficient. Upon the introduction of the power loom in 1884, cloth manufacturers could devote their energies to improving and varying the fabric itself.

CULTURE OF COTTON

Cotton is a white or yellow-white vegetable fiber grown in greatest amounts in the United States, the Soviet Union, China, and India, followed in descending order of importance in cotton production by Pakistan, Brazil, Turkey, Egypt, Mexico, Iran, and the Sudan. Over fifty-five other countries produce lesser amounts. In this group, the larger producers include Syria, Peru, Colombia, Greece, Nicaragua, Guatemala, and Argentina.[2]

Cotton fibers come from a plant, related to the hollyhock, that ranges in height from 2 to 20 feet, depending upon the variety. The plant requires a warm climate with about six months of summer weather for full development. It blossoms and produces bolls, or pods, of cotton fibers. (See Fig. 9.1.)

[2]Rankings prepared with the assistance of Cotton Incorporated.

In the United States, cotton is grown in the so-called Cotton Belt, which covers roughly the southern and western states from the Carolinas to California.

Production methods differ in various parts of the Cotton Belt, according to Cotton Incorporated. Such factors as types of soil, climate, moisture, growing conditions, and physical features of a locality determine the varieties of cotton to be planted, crop income, size of farms, and yield per acre.

The chief steps in cotton production are as follows:

Preparation of the Soil

Production of next year's crop generally starts right after the completion of harvesting in the fall. Old stalks are chopped and shredded by machine. The residue is plowed under, and the field is generally left rough until spring tillage.

Before planting, the soil is tilled to a depth of several inches. Smoothing and laying off in rows follows.

Planting

Machines plant cotton four, six, or eight rows at a time, usually with planters timed to drop about half a dozen seeds in a group the desired distance apart. In some areas, the seeds are planted in a thin, continuous row, but the practice of thinning by hand hoes has been discontinued except in rare cases.

Cultivating

A cotton grower has a wide choice of fertilizer, material, and equipment. Application of fertilizer may be made prior to, during, or after planting.

Pre-emergence weed control is carried out by applying a chemical herbicide to a 10- to 14-inch band over the drill area at the time of, or just after, planting. For a few weeks, this band is not disturbed. The chemical does not harm cotton seedlings, but it does kill germinating weed and grass seeds.

Postemergence weed control consists of spraying an area 6 to 8 inches wide on both sides of the plant. Weed and grass seedlings are killed without injury to the young cotton. Care must be taken not to kill the cotton by spraying chemicals on leaves or branches. Almost every acre of cotton is now treated at least once with weed control compounds, and most of the acreage is treated more than once.

Improved cultivators and rotary hoe attachments for cultivators also help keep weeds and grass under control. High-speed rotary hoes travel through the field at rates up to 7½ miles per hour.

Insect Control

Losses due to insects amount on the average to about one bale out of every five to six bales. The boll weevil and the boll worm account for most of this damage. Insecticides are applied at various intervals during heavy infestation—either by airplanes, which can cover up to 1,500 acres a day, or by tractor-mounted ground rigs, which can spray several rows of cotton at one time.

Maturation of the Cotton Boll

The cotton plant first buds, and about 21 days thereafter, creamy white to yellow flowers appear. These later turn red, and after about 3 days, wither and drop from the plant, leaving the ovary on the plant. When the ovary ripens, a large pod, known as the cotton boll, is formed. Moist fibers growing inside the boll expand it until it is about 1½ inches long and 1 inch in diameter. The boll opens approximately 1½ to 2 months after the flowering stage.

Preparation for Harvesting

So that the bolls will open quickly and uniformly, before the fall rains damage fibers and seed, cotton plants are treated chemically to make them shed their leaves. This process, called *defoliation* or *dessication*, is important if cotton is to be picked mechanically. Furthermore, it is a method of insect control. Cotton is then ready for picking.

Picking

Before the advent of the mechanical picker, cotton was picked by hand. The great labor shortage in the South was a major reason why mechanical pickers became so important. Smaller farms were consolidated into larger farms as mechanical pickers were perfected. (See Fig. 9.2.) In the United States machine harvesting jumped from 32 percent in 1957 to virtually 100 percent in the mid-1970s.

Figure 9.2 Two-row mechanical cotton picker. (Photo courtesy of Cotton Incorporated.)

To accompany this accelerated shift to mechanical harvesting, changes in ginning processes have taken place. An increasing number of gins are using multiple lint cleaners, and there is a marked increase in the use of stick- and green-leaf removing machines. Two types of machines harvest the cotton: the *picker* and the *stripper*. The picker has vertical drums equipped with spindles (barbed or smooth) that pull the cotton from the boll. This machine can harvest 5 to 15 acres a day depending on whether the machine does one or two rows at a time. The stripper pulls the bolls off when they enter the rollers of the machine. Some strippers have mechanical fingers to do the job. This type of tractor-mounted machine can harvest two rows at once and 10 to 15 acres a day. To compare hand and machine picking, a single stripper can harvest as much cotton as twenty-six laborers can hand-snapping the bolls.[3]

PROCESSING OF COTTON

Ginning

After the cotton has been picked, the fibers are separated from the seeds by a process called *ginning*. The ginning is done by circular saws revolving on a shaft. The grower normally takes the cotton to the gin and pays for ginning. After the ginning, the cotton is packaged in bales of about 500 pounds each. At this point, the seeds and the fibers go their separate ways.

Processing the Seeds

Seeds go to the crushing mill, where they are *delinted* (fuzz is removed mechanically). The short fuzzy fibers so removed, called *linters,* are used in mattresses and other cushioning and in the making of plastics, fine paper, and other products.

Hulls are next removed from the delinted seed. The hulls serve as cattle fodder or as the source of a chemical used in making synthetic rubber or plastics. Inside the seed is oil that can be pressed out in the crushing mill or removed by solvent extraction. This cottonseed oil is valuable in making cooking oil, shortening, salad dressings, and margarine. The meat of the cottonseed serves as feed for cattle.

A process developed by the U.S. Department of Agriculture makes it possible to extract high-purity protein concentrates from the seed. The concentrates are for human food, and the first commercial plant for extracting protein from cottonseed has an ultimate capacity of 25 tons per day. It may be used to fortify cereals or meats, as a flour in baked products, or as a protein supplement in soft drinks.

[3]Cotton Incorporated.

Baling and Classifying the Cotton

Cotton is baled after ginning, and then it is classified by (1) staple length (fiber length), (2) grade, and (3) fiber character. Fiber properties measured are fineness, color, length, uniformity, and strength.

A practical but unofficial basis of classifying by staple length is as follows:

1. *Extrashort-staple cotton* (not over ¾ inch). This length is not very suitable for spinning and is best used in batting and wadding.
2. *Short-staple cotton* (¾ inch to 1 inch). This type is spinnable and is used for coarser, inexpensive goods.
3. *Medium-staple cotton* (1 inch to 1⅛ inches). The United States produces the bulk of this variety for its own use and for export.
4. *Long-staple cotton* (1⅛ but less than 1⅜ inches). The United States produces the bulk of its own requirements. Imports are relatively small.
5. *Extralong-staple cotton* (1⅜ inches and longer). United States production is limited; we import from Egypt, Sudan, and Peru.

Of the cotton used for spinning, long staples account for 1 percent of the domestic crop. Group 3 accounts for 75 percent, and group 2 accounts for 24 percent.

Classification by Grade

In the trade, American cotton is classified not only according to length of fiber, but also according to the visual condition of the cotton, called *grade*. Grade is related to the color, leaf content, and preparation (smoothness). For instance, middling cotton is creamy white with only a few pieces of leaf and a very smooth appearance. The following grades and half grades are recognized:

1. Good middling
2. Strict middling
   Middling plus
3. Middling
   Strict low middling plus
4. Strict low middling
   Low middling plus
5. Low middling
   Strict good ordinary plus
6. Strict good ordinary
   Good ordinary plus
7. Good ordinary

Good middling—the best—has lustrous, silky, clean fibers, whereas good ordinary contains leaf particles, sticks, hulls, dirt, sand, gin cuts, and spots. To indicate the degree of whiteness of the cotton, five distinct color groups are used: white, spotted, tinged, yellow-stained, and gray. Practically all U.S. cotton falls below strict middling.

SPECIES OF AMERICAN COTTON

Classification of American cotton according to length of staple is probably more logical than a geographical classification, because the length of staple and fineness of fiber are criteria in judging the quality of cotton and the end products that can be manufactured from these.

Pima

That the importance of fine long-staple cotton is realized by American cotton growers can be seen from the fact that an American-Egyptian type is being grown here, chiefly in the irrigated lands of Arizona, New Mexico, and around El Paso, Texas. This pima has an extralong (1⅜ to 1⅝ inches) staple. Of the American cottons, pima ranks next to Sea Island (see glossary) in order of quality. It is used in sheer woven goods and in fine knitted fabrics.

Cotton farmers and the U.S. Department of Agriculture, in cross-breeding seeds of all kinds, were responsible for the producing of the silky, long-staple, lustrous, and strong *pima cotton.* They cooperated in development work and produced a superlative cotton fiber. Marketed under the trademark Supima, it is used in promoting garments and fabrics made from the pima variety. It is grown in Arizona, New Mexico, Texas, and California, where climate and soil are right for its growth. The staple is longer, finer, stronger than any other, takes colors well, and has a smooth silky hand. It can be woven from a sheer chiffon weight to a heavy broadcloth.

Upland (Gossypium hirsutum)

The term "upland" originally denoted cotton raised away from the sea coast on higher land, as distinguished from cotton grown on the lowlands, the coastal regions. Now upland cotton is produced at all altitudes, from the foothills of the Ozark and Blue Ridge mountains to the Mississippi Delta. Sheetings, carded broadcloths, twills, drills, print cloths, and carded yarns for knitting are commonly produced from fibers of this class. Upland cotton constitutes over 99 percent of the United States production. It produces fibers ranging from ¾ to 1½ inches in length.

New Varieties

Many new varieties have been and are continuously being developed and improved. Among these are Acala, Coker, Deltapine, Stoneville, and Tamcot. These new and improved varieties offer increased yields, better mechanical harvesting, and more desirable fiber qualities. Seed breeders are now providing growers with wider choices of the exact fiber properties, yields, and regional adaptation for best growth under the widest range of soil and weather conditions.

SPECIES OF FOREIGN COTTON

Egyptian (Gossypium barbadense)

Egyptian cotton, next to Sea Island cotton, has the longest fiber. It can be made to look almost like silk by mercerizing. This type of cotton is grown along the Nile Delta. It is a light tan or brown in color and therefore must usually be bleached. Hosiery, knit goods, and underwear are often made of Egyptian cotton. It is only slightly shorter in length than the Sea Island variety, the former averaging mostly 1½ inches or less. Other African production (except Egyptian) is in medium- and long-staple groups.

Tanguis (Gossypium barbadense)

Tanguis cotton has fibers averaging 1¼ inches in length. It comes from Peru. Most Tanguis cotton fibers have a rough, harsh, wiry, woolly feel, and a slight crimp. For this reason they are often mixed with short-staple wool. Such cotton-and-wool mixtures may be used for underwear, if knitted so that the cotton will be next to the skin and the harsher wool will be on the outside. Hosiery may be similarly made of this cotton.

Indian (Gossypium arboreum and Gossypium herbacium) and Other Varieties

India and Pakistan also grow the American upland type of cotton. The fiber length averages from 1 to 1½₂ inches. China also grows cotton, but it has a yellowish-brown fiber and is not often exported. Israel grows the American-type Acala and fine pima cotton and has one of the highest average yields per acre of cotton fiber in the world.

CHARACTERISTICS OF THE COTTON FIBER

Microscopic Appearance

When seen under the microscope, unmercerized cotton fibers resemble flat twisted ribbons. The unripe cotton fiber is a tubelike structure or canal (lumen). Within this tube is a cell protoplasm that either dries as the cotton ripens or shrinks back to the stalk of the plant. The disappearance of this substance causes the fiber to flatten and twist, so that under the microscope it appears like a twisted ribbon. The canal can be seen. (See Appendix A.) When cotton is mercerized by treatment with caustic soda, the twist comes out to some extent, depending on the degree of mercerization.

Length of Fiber

Cotton ranges in length of staple from ¾ to 1½ inches. Since the very short lengths are difficult to spin, they are not considered in the figures given here.

Yarns made of short staple are more apt to be linty and fuzzy than are those of longer staple. For combed yarn, a long staple is advisable.

Diameter of Fiber

The diameter of the cotton fiber ranges from 0.0005 to 0.0009 inch. The U.S. Department of Agriculture *Bulletin No. 33* places the range from 0.00064 (Sea Island) to .00844 (Indian) inch. Pima and Egyptian fibers have the smaller diameters and so can be spun into the finest yarns.

Luster

Untreated cotton has no pronounced luster. Therefore cotton fabrics that need to be lustrous to imitate silk must be mercerized to produce the desired result.

Strength

Tensile strength is obtained on a small bundle of fibers [ASTM (American Society for Testing and Materials) method D-1445]. A single cotton fiber will sustain a dead weight of 2 to 8 grams. Such a fiber is not very strong, but the finished cotton cloth can be made very strong if tightly twisted mercerized yarns are used in it. Mercerization adds both strength and luster. Through scientific breeding, cotton farmers are growing a better product—longer, finer, more lustrous, and stronger. With further developments in scientific breeding, there are even greater possibilities of improving the value of cotton for the end uses the consumer wants.

Elasticity

In a study of the hand of different textile fibers, it was found that cottons have more elasticity than linens but not so much as the animal fibers. The natural twist in cotton increases the elasticity and makes it easier to spin the fiber into yarn.

Hygroscopic Moisture

Hygroscopic moisture is not the water content of the raw material, but the moisture (water) held in the pores of the fiber and on its surface. It is not a part of the chemical constituents. Some scientists give raw cotton 5 to 8 percent of hygroscopic moisture, whereas others rate it as high as 7 to 10 percent. This is much higher than most thermoplastic fibers, which have little hygroscopic potential. If the moisture in the air is great, the moisture content in the fabric is increased.

Composition of Fiber

The chief constituent of cotton is cellulose (87 to 90 percent). Cellulose is a solid, inert substance that is a part of plants. The fact that it is the chief component of cotton fibers and is an inert substance explains cotton's characteristic feel. Water

(5 to 8 percent) and natural impurities (4 to 6 percent) are the other components of a cotton fiber. The cellulose can be modified by cross linking to give cotton the properties of wash-and-wear. (See Chapters 2 and 7.)

Hygienic Quality and Launderability

Cotton is the whitest and cleanest natural fiber. It can be laundered easily, for it withstands high temperatures well (boiling water does not hurt the fiber), and it can be ironed with a hot iron because it does not scorch easily. A chemical process, called partial acetylation, gives cotton fabrics additional heat resistance. Cottons so treated make excellent ironing-board covers. Weak alkalies, such as ammonia, borax, and silicate of soda, and cold dilute bleaching agents, such as hypochlorites or chlorine bleach, are not detrimental to the fiber. Bleaching agents must be used only under controlled conditions, since too high temperatures and concentrations destroy the fiber. Treatment of cotton fabrics with resins improves crease resistance and crease recovery after washing.

Action of Strong Acids

Concentrated acids, such as sulfuric, hydrochloric, hydrofluoric, and nitric, destroy cotton fibers if the fibers are "cooked" in these acids for a few minutes. Dilute solutions of the acids may weaken a cotton fabric and may destroy it if it is allowed to dry without being rinsed.

Action of Light

If cotton is continuously exposed to sunlight, it loses strength. This fact is particularly true of curtains, which may appear in perfect condition when hanging at the windows but when taken down may fall apart in spots where sunlight has reached them.

Affinity for Dyestuffs

Cotton takes dyes that are fast to washing and to sunlight. For a vegetable fiber, cotton has a fair affinity for dye. Vat dyes as a class are the fastest to all the following elements listed. Vegetable fibers do not take dye as readily as do animal fibers. (See Table 9.1.)

Mildew Damage

Cotton is subject to rotting caused by mildew, which is caused by fungi. Heat and dampness further the growth of mildew. Considerable research has revealed that a chemical compound produced by the fungi has the power of changing cellulose in the cotton to sugar. The fungi feed on the sugar. It was found that there is less rotting if the cotton is treated to make it fire-resistant and water-repellent. (See Chapter 7.) Hence, mildew can be prevented. Former attempts to protect cotton against mildew by treating it with fungicides proved ineffective under climatic conditions favorable to the growth of fungi. Cotton

Table 9.1 Fastness of Dyes of Different Classes on Cotton Goods[a]

Price Class:	1	2	3	4	5	6	7
Dye Type:	Vat	Naphthol	Developed	Sulfur	Basic	Direct	Fiber Reactive
Home washing	Exc.	Exc.	Good	Good	Poor	Good (light shades) Poor (heavy shades)	Exc.
Laundry	Exc.	Exc.	Poor	Poor	Poor	Poor	Good to Exc.
Light	Exc.	Very good	Poor	Good	Poor	Some very good	Good to Exc.
Bleaching (chlorine)	Exc.	Exc.	Bad	Bad	Bad	Bad	Very poor
Cross-dyeing	Exc.	Exc.	Good	Good	Bad	Fair	Good

[a]There are some exceptions to these general rules in each class.

Source: American Fabrics, Vol. 52 (Spring 1961), 74. Column 7 was added by the authors.

can be treated with a chemical called acrylonitrile. (See Chapter 7.) Such treatment makes cotton not only permanently resistant to mildew but also more resistant to wet and dry heat and gives it greater affinity for dyes.

Improvements in Cotton Quality

Early in 1981, the U.S. Department of Agriculture announced a number of patents designed to improve the quality of cotton fibers and the fabrics made from them. One is an apparatus that measures the color, length, and foreign matter content of fibers entering into production and also rids them of lint. Another is a process to coat fibers with a vinyl monomer (a simple form of compound) that improves resistance to abrasion, the ability to accept dyes, and durable-press properties. A somewhat similar process applies the vinyl to the fabric.[4]

COTTON YARNS

Preparing the Cotton

Figures 9.3(a)–(k) show the steps through which cotton passes at the mill. Cotton is unbaled and is then pulled out in small tufts and beaten to remove impurities. The tufts are compressed into a sheet called a *lap*. Several laps may be combined into one.

[4]*The New York Times*, March 7, 1981, p. 38.

Figure 9.3a Blending cotton from several bales in opening room. (Photo courtesy of Cotton Incorporated.)

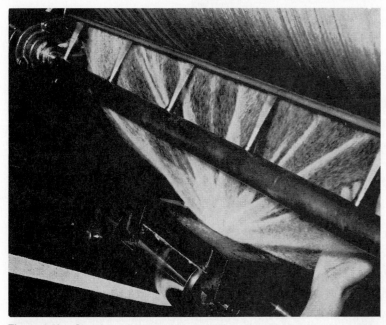

Figure 9.3b Cleaning and separating individual fibers takes place in carding machine. The web of fibers is formed into a ropelike strand or "sliver." (Photo courtesy of Cotton Incorporated.)

Figure 9.3c Lap, composed of slivers, is passed through comb which combs out short fibers. Output of comb is formed again into sliver. (Photo courtesy of Cotton Incorporated.)

Figure 9.3d Lapping. (Photo courtesy of Springs Industries.)

Figure 9.3e Finisher drawing. Strands of combed sliver are blended on finisher; drawing machines for still greater uniformity and paralleling of the cotton fibers. (Photo courtesy of Springs Industries.)

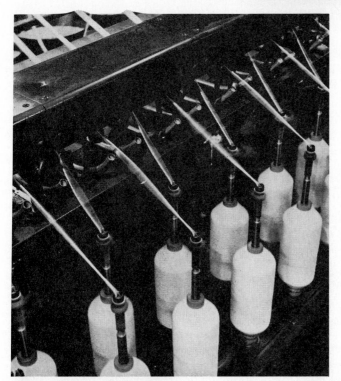

Figure 9.3f Slivers are fed into roving frame where cotton is twisted slightly and drawn into a smaller strand. (Photo courtesy of Springs Industries.)

Figure 9.3g Roving is fed to spinning frame where it is drawn out to final size, twisted into yarn, and wound on bobbins. (Photo courtesy of Cotton Incorporated.)

Figure 9.3h Several hundred warp yarns are rewound from cones or cheeses (see glossary) into large section beams. (Photo Courtesy of Cotton Incorporated.)

Figure 9.3i In slashing, threads are unwound from assembly of warper beams, immersed in sizing mixture, dried, and rewound on loom beams. (Photo courtesy of Cotton Incorporated.)

Figure 9.3j Weaving room. (Photo courtesy of Cotton Incorporated.)

Figure 9.3k Inspecting. (Photo courtesy of Cotton Incorporated.)

Carding

Cotton is not thoroughly clean until particles of leaf are removed. A machine called a *card* separates the matted fibers and removes leafy matter. In colonial times, carding was done by hand with a pair of *cards*–rectangular pieces of wood with wire teeth on one side of each card and with wooden handles. The teeth were placed together, and the cotton was pulled and straightened between the teeth. Now this process is done by machinery. The carded cotton in lap form is drawn through an aperture and comes out in rope form called a *card sliver*. The short fibers that fall to the floor or cling to the machinery during the carding are never wasted, but are often used to make fabrics in which evenness and strength of yarn are not requisites. (See Fig. 9.4.)

Drawing

If the yarn is to be fine enough for use in clothing, the diameter of the yarn must be reduced to a size appropriate to the particular fabric. Several card slivers may be fed between two pairs of rollers, the second of which revolves faster than the first. This operation draws out or stretches the sliver, thus decreasing its diameter. The sliver may be drawn three times and may be reduced further in size and given a slight twist by a process called *roving*. In this process, the sliver is passed through rollers and is wound onto bobbins set in spindles. Improved carding devices, together with new and faster machinery for drawing, and new roving frames have increased production and decreased labor costs.

Figure 9.4   Left: Carded cotton cloth. Right: Combed cotton cloth. (Photo by Jack Pitkin.)

Combing

This process is really a continuation and refinment of the carding process. Short fibers are eliminated from the sliver; fibers are laid more nearly parallel; and the filmy sheet of fibers is further attentuated. Cotton yarns for fabrics are carded, but not all are combed. On the other hand, some fabrics are made of yarns that have been combed several times. Combed yarns are even and free from extraneous material. Yarns that are merely carded are not so clean or so even as those that are given further treatment. Yarns can be made finer by combing; those used for fine-quality French voiles and batistes receive a good deal of combing. Yarns for coarse, unbleached muslins and unbleached duck are usually only carded. Even many good-quality fabrics are only carded.

Spinning

The spinning process puts in the twist. Some yarns are loosely or slackly twisted, whereas others are tightly twisted. The more twists or turns to the inch, the stronger the cotton yarn.

Winding

Yarns are wound on spools, on paper tubes, on double-headed bobbins, in skeins or hanks, in ball form, or on warp beams, ready for the weavers.

Single and Ply Cotton Yarns

Cotton yarns are made in singles or in plies. A tightly twisted cotton yarn may have a rayon yarn twisted loosely with it to form a two-ply yarn.

Ply yarns are ordinarily stronger than singles of the same diameter. Unique effects are produced in ply yarns by the use of singles with different degrees of twist. A ratiné or bouclé has a rough Turkish-towel effect made by ply yarns in different tension. Slack-twisted yarns make soft fabrics that drape gracefully. Tightly twisted yarns make strong, hard-feeling fabrics.

The finer the yarn count, the higher the price. Also, two-ply yarns cost more than single yarns, combed yarns cost more than carded yarns, and yarns ready for use as warp cost more than yarns on bobbins (used for filling). (See Fig. 9.5.)

Sizes of Cotton Yarns

Most sewing cotton is marked 60 or 80. These numbers, as we have already mentioned, denote the fineness of the thread—80 being finer than 60. Similar yarns used in fabrics are given numbers or counts to denote their weight and fineness. In size 10 yarn there are 10 × 840 or 8,400 yards to the pound. Size 10 in this case is the count of the yarn. A small "s" after the number means the yarn is single; that is, 10s, 20s, 30s. The notation 10/2 means that size or count 10 yarn is two-ply. Yarn spun in this country reaches as high as 160s; a medium count is 30s; Egyptian is 100; Brazilian, 40; Surat from India, 30; Peruvian, 30.

Figure 9.5   Top: Two-ply yarn. Bottom: Single yarn. (Photo by Jack Pitkin.)

COTTON THREAD

Americans have had cotton sewing thread only since 1840. This thread was first produced in 1812 in Paisley, Scotland (the small town where Paisley shawls were made), by James and Patrick Clark, who were searching for a new material for making the heddle eyes of the loom. The heddle eyes have to be smooth, for it is through these eyes that warp yarns are threaded into the loom. The Clark brothers perfected a cotton yarn smooth and strong enough to replace silk for this purpose. By chance, the yarn was found to be suitable for sewing. At first this yarn, called *thread,* was sold in hanks, but it was later wound on spools as it is today.

James Coats, who had also been associated with the manufacture of Paisley shawls, employed his knowledge of yarn-making and weaving when he built a factory to make high-grade cotton thread. His factory, later owned by his sons James and Peter (J. & P. Coats), competed with the Clarks.

In 1840 Andrew Coats, a brother of James and Peter, came to America as a selling agent for J. & P. Coats of Scotland. A factory was built in Pawtucket, Rhode Island, and in 1841, George and William Clark, sons of the third generation, came to the United States. Mills for making thread were built in Newark, New Jersey. The companies merged on Dec. 31, 1952.

The O.N.T. so commonly seen on Clark's spool cotton stands for "Our New Thread." This softer, stronger thread was composed of six strands of cotton twisted together, instead of the usual three.

Cotton thread comes in sizes ranging from coarse to fine: 8, 10, 12, 16, 20, 23, 30, 36, 40, 50, 60, 70, 80, 90, 100. (See Chapter 3 for the differences between thread and yarn.)

COTTON FABRICS

Woven

Plain Weaves

Cotton can be made in all weaves and variations. The cotton fabric called *muslin* traces its name to the French *mousseline,* which in turn derived its name from the town of Mosul in Mesopotamia. Muslin is the generic name of cotton fabrics in plain weave ranging from the sheerest batiste to the coarsest sheeting. The lower counts, 48 square to 80 square (finished), are called *print cloths,* the higher counts in sheer fabrics are *lawns,* and the higher counts in sheetings are *percales.*

Cottons in the basket weaves include oxford 2×1, 2×2, and 3×2 and monks cloth 4×4 and 8×8.

In rib variations of the plain weave, there is the poplin or popeline, first woven at Avignon, France, as a compliment to the reigning pope. Ribs are closely spaced next to each other fillingwise. Broadcloth is similar to poplin, with finer, closer ribs. Dimity is also a ribbed fabric, but the ribs are spaced at regular intervals either in warpwise strips or in crossbars. Numerous fabrics in plain weave are described in Part Two.

Twill Weaves

Denim (de Nimes), first woven in Nimes, France, and *jean*, first made in Italy, are typical twill weave fabrics. Another closely woven, wind-resistant cotton and rayon twill is used in ski suits, parkas, football and basketball uniforms, and rainwear. It is lustrous and durable.

Satin Weave

When the warp or filling floats in cotton, the fabric is called sateen. Sateen is often found in linings of men's clothing as well as in drapery linings.

Fancy Weaves

Damasks for both dresses and tablecloths are illustrations of cotton Jacquards. Dobby appears in bird's-eye diaper fabrics and in huck toweling. White-on-white broadcloth or madras shirtings are Jacquard or dobby.

Terry cloth and Turkish toweling are uncut looped pile. Velveteen is also pile weave.

Marquisette for curtains is made in leno. It may have embroidered effects. In fact, any cotton fabric may be embroidered or given an embroidered effect.

Laces

Cotton is currently used more than any other textile for laces. (See Chapter 19 for kinds of laces.)

Nonwoven

A web of cotton fibers held together by an adhesive is called a nonwoven cotton fabric. (See Chapter 6 for methods of construction.) Articles such as disposable napkins, wallpaper backing, bandages, polishing cloths, tea bags, dish and guest towels, and tablecloths can be made of nonwoven fabrics. One of the greatest potentials for the nonwoven goods industry is in hospital and medical supplies.

Knitted

A common weft-knitted cloth in stockinette stitch is cotton jersey, used in T-shirts and basque shirts. The tops of men's socks and the wrists of sweat shirts are commonly rib-knit. The purl stitch, called plain knitting by hand knitters, is used for scarfs, baby carriage covers, and pot holders.

The warp-knitted cotton fabrics in tricot and Milanese are frequently used in fabric gloves. A modified tricot knit of fine cotton yarns sueded on one side is manufactured into gloves and sports jackets.

DYEING, PRINTING, AND FINISHING

After cotton fabric is received in its unfinished state as greige or "gray" goods, some mills dye and finish fabric in addition to spinning and weaving.

There are varied and complex processes in dyeing and finishing cotton. In its simplest form, it consists of cleaning and preparing the cloth, finishing, and dyeing or printing.

Preparatory Process

Singeing

The first step in the finishing process includes singeing or gassing to remove lint and loose yarn. The fabric is drawn rapidly over hot plates or through gas flames at high heat, singeing both sides.

Continuous bleaching further removes foreign material, waxes, and sizing. Fabric is bleached and scoured at speeds of 200 yards a minute. Large J-boxes are used to store the fabric for the boiling solutions to act on the impurities and to remove the cotton's natural yellowish color.

Mercerizing

If a cotton fabric is to have a glossy surface, it is mercerized after it has been bleached. Sometimes the mercerizing is done in the yarn stage or possibly in the fiber stage, in which case the operation is not repeated in the finishing of the cloth.

The process of mercerizing was discovered by John Mercer about the middle of the nineteenth century. He happened upon it quite accidentally when he found he had left some cotton in a caustic soda solution and feared the treatment had been too long. Upon microscopic examination, he found that the fibers had lost their natural twist, appeared structureless like silk, were shiny, and had increased in tensile strength. For about thirty years the discovery was practically forgotten, because the process was too expensive to be used commercially. Then, in 1890, Lowe of England patented a process by which the cotton fiber was made lustrous if held in tension in caustics. Improvements have been made in the combined methods of Mercer and Lowe, and now mercerization is used on a large scale.

Formerly, few mercerized cotton fabrics were available. Now we have many, including sateen, batiste, cotton satin, better grades of cotton broadcloth, cotton poplin, and knitted underwear.

For mercerizing, cotton of long staple (long fiber) gives best results. The fibers are carefully combed, and the cloth is singed and bleached before it is mercerized. Since most cloths are mercerized in the piece, this process is generally considered a method of finishing.

Mercerization gives cotton fabrics definite advantages. It makes them stronger, more elastic and pliable, more lustrous, and more absorbent, and it gives them a greater affinity for dyestuffs.

Drying

Cotton cloth needs to be dried frequently during the finishing process. Several methods are used including a "dry can" around which the cloth is passed.

In "festoon" or "blower" dryers, the cloth is passed through heated chambers in a loosely plaited form. In "hot frame" or "tenter frames," damp cloth is run over a frame and is grasped on each side by tenter clips that hold it at the desired width while it is being dried. This evens the fabric, giving the cloth the proper width, "feel," and other fabric properties such as shrinkage control and seam slippage.

Application of Color and Pattern

Color is applied to textiles at any one of several stages: the loose fibers (raw stock) before spinning into yarn, spun yarns before weaving or knitting, and constructed fabrics after weaving or knitting. (See Chapter 8 on dyeing and printing.)

Colors may be printed on cotton cloth much like printing on paper. Pastes containing starch and resin that carry dye are used instead of inks. After printing, this starch-resin portion is washed out, leaving only the dye on the colored area.

Finishing

In some respects, it can be said that a fabric is produced twice; first it is constructed (woven or knitted), and then it is finished. Improved finishes for cotton have been responsible in large measure for cotton's popularity. Among them are the resin and nonresin finishes that give cottons the same easy- or minimum-care features that man-made fibers possess. Advances in antibacterial, mildew-resistant, and flame-resistant treatments have improved the effectiveness of the performance of cotton in various end uses. Since the regular and special finishes have been described in Chapter 7, only those finishes applied to cotton will be considered here.

Probably more special or functional finishes are applied to cotton than to any other fiber. Finishing processes determine the "feel" or "hand" of the fabric. They include setting of the color, softness of the fabric, firmness, crispness; crease, perspiration, mildew, flame, and stain resistance; waterproofing and water repellency, shrinkage control, permanent glazing, heat-setting, permanent starchless, absorbency, germ resistance, wash-and-wear, and durable press. With cotton/polyester durable-press blends it is the cotton that carries the durable-press treatment. The polyester is added to overcome the strength loss.

Mechanical Finishing[5]

Tentering (Hot Frame)

This process evens the fabric in the width.

Calendering

This process smooths the cloth by a series of rollers using great pressure and heat, not unlike the process of hand ironing a fabric to smooth out wrinkles.

A cotton fabric may be passed between calender rolls revolving at different speeds. This causes a frictional or rubbing effect on the side of the fabric in contact with the faster roll and results in "polished" cottons. Still other types of calenders may be used to emboss cotton fabrics with various textured effects. Raised designs of almost any description may be produced.

Napping

This is used to alter the final hand and appearance of fabrics by producing soft, fluffy surfaces such as those of blankets or flannels. The cloth is drawn through a series of rollers clothed with closely set wires much like a steel brush. These rapidly revolving roller brushes gently pull up fibers from the fabric surface to produce a "raised" finish.

Compressive Shrinkage

Fabric is compressed lengthwise while it is in a damp and softened state. By this means, shrinkage can be reduced to any desired amount. Compressively shrunk fabrics have been popularized under the trademark, Sanforized.

Chemical Finishing

Formerly, most wet-finishing treatments for cotton involved adding substances such as clay or starch. These affected the hand and appearance of the fabric but washed out after the first few launderings.

Now, through chemical finishing, a finishing agent becomes a durable part of the fabric. This is the result of chemical reaction with the fiber. Synthetic preservatives such as acrylic, glyoxal, and melanine resins are used to give cottons the same easy-care features that man-made fibers possess.

Durable Press

After a generation of research by the cotton industry, new no-iron, 100 percent cotton, lightweight and heavyweight fabrics are appearing on the retail market. Recent advances enable mills to produce commercially acceptable

[5]Information on mechanical finishing was supplied by "Cotton from Field to Fabric," a pamphlet of Cotton Incorporated.

lightweight shirtings, dress weights, and bed sheeting that retain cotton's natural advantages wth the addition of no-iron convenience.

The all-cotton, no-iron fabric is attempting to expand its share of two of cotton's largest markets—shirts and bed sheets. Previously, the percentage of 100 percent cotton had been marginal, representing only 5 percent in men's shirts and 3 percent in sheets. Industry sources estimate a 25 percent and even higher market share as introductory prices come down and additional mills produce the new goods. Such growth will challenge the dominance of mostly polyester blends in lightweight fabrics suited for apparel use.

Another recent development in durable-press cotton is all-cotton woven stretch fabrics. Stretch is ideally suited to one of the most rapidly growing markets in apparel: active sportswear, especially blue jeans.

The family of new wovens with both stretch and no-iron features is achieved without the addition of synthetic stretch fibers. Unique yarn and fabric engineering plus Sanfor-Set treatment is used by the Joshua L. Baily Co. to deliver both stretch and no-iron features.[6] The cotton fibers are treated with liquid ammonia that makes them shape retentive. Arrow's "Cotton Ease" shirts are made from a fabric so treated as are Van Heusen brand shirts.

CONSUMER DEMAND FOR COTTON

Cotton is plentiful and economical to produce, although the use of petroleum-based fertilizers has contributed to higher-priced products. Cotton has inherent comfort characteristics that consumers want. According to *Textile Organon*, the world output of basic textile fibers (cotton, wool, and man-made fibers) was 68,287 million pounds in 1981. Of the total output, cotton accounted for over 49 percent, wool for 5 percent, and man-made fibers for 45 percent. Silk was a nominal percentage of the total.[7] (See Chapter 15 for additional data.)

Cotton is currently meeting the competition of the man-made fibers that began to invade the market during the 1930s. Man-made fibers still present cotton and other natural fibers with a challenge.

Man-made fiber and yarn companies have spent huge sums of money on basic research, development, and promotion of their products. Despite increases in cotton's research and promotion expenditures in recent years, its total outlay in these areas is still much less than expenditures by man-made fiber producers. Their promotional efforts have been instrumental in capturing part of cotton's share of the fiber market, but in 1981 cotton remained the largest-volume fiber consumed by U.S. textile mills, accounting for 24.6 percent of total pounds used. The remaining 75.4 percent was shared by a host of other natural and man-made fibers. Data from the *Textile Organon* indicate that cotton accounted for 34.8

---

[6]Cotton Incorporated, 1979 annual report.
[7]*Textile Organon*, June 1982, p. 147.

Table 9.2 Consumers' Rankings of Fabric Characteristics[a]

	Men	Women	Teens
Comfort	1	1	1
Value	2	2	2
Durability	3	6	7
Shape retention	4	4	4
No shrinking	5	3	3
Feel of fabric next to skin	6	7	6
Ease of cleaning/washing	7	5	NM
Wrinkle free	8	8	NM

[a]Ratings are in order of importance, from 1 (highest) through 8. The number 7 indicates that teenagers named durability as their seventh most important consideration, and they ranked fashion fifth.

NM – Not meaningful.

percent of all fiber consumption in apparel, 21.9 percent in home furnishings, and 11.8 percent of all fibers consumed in industrial textile markets[8]

The cotton industry is making every effort through improvement of processing machinery, reduction of labor costs, and improvement and promotion of functional finishes for cotton fabrics to impart permanent press, flame retardance, and other desirable properties. Cotton growers finance much of this effort through contributions of approximately $2.50 per bale into Cotton Incorporated, which carries out an intensive program of research and promotion.

What will happen? Eventually, there will probably be a balance between the use of natural and man-made fibers. Blends will maximize the advantages and minimize the disadvantages of each. Each fiber must continue to improve its quality, beauty, and suitability while remaining competitively priced. None can remain static.

BUYING POINTS OF COTTON FABRICS

Table 9.2 presents consumers' rankings of fabric characteristics when buying apparel for themselves,[9] referred to at the beginning of this chapter.

Those are the buying points that consumers consider in buying apparel. Let us review those points in relation to cotton.

Comfort

Cotton conducts moisture away from the body and allows the cooler temperatures outside to reach the body, so it is a cool material for summer or tropical wear. But, since short cotton fibers nap easily, cotton fabrics can also be made

[8]*Textile Organon*, November 1982, p. 214.
[9]National consumer study by Opinion Research Corporation.

warm when necessary. Knitted cotton underwear absorbs perspiration and keeps the wearer comfortable.

In the study cited, better than half of the women and almost 60 percent of the men preferred cotton, in terms of the *feel of the fabric next to the skin*, over polyester and rayon.

Value

By *value* is meant providing good quality for the money. Value was ranked second in consumer preference for apparel. In short, the consumer wants his or her money's worth.

In considering the price of cotton garments, the following factors are involved: (1) quality of fibers, (2) quality of yarn, (3) construction, (4) finishes, (5) style, and (6) workmanship.

Durability

Durability refers to the length of time that a fabric will wear. Workmanship indicates the skill and care that is given to a fabric when it is manufactured. Cotton fibers are comparatively short; therefore, one would expect them to produce a yarn that is fairly weak in tensile strength. However, a cotton fiber, because of its natural twist, spins so well that it can be twisted very tightly; hence, since tightly twisted yarns are more durable than those that are slackly twisted, cotton yarns are strong and fabrics made from them are durable.

Two-ply yarns are more durable than single yarns of the same diameter; so a turkish towel made of two-ply yarn will be stronger and more absorbent than will one constructed from a single yarn. It is also important to remember that yarns of even and regular texture are usually stronger than irregular yarns of the same average diameter. Also, since cottons are temporarily stronger when wet than when dry, there is no need to worry about their breaking when they are in the wash.

Cotton yarns, then, can be given considerable tensile strength, and the cloth made from these yarns can be durable. It is the quality of the yarn, (in addition, of course, to weave and finish) that primarily determines the durability of the cloth.

There is little need for the consumer to fear that a guaranteed colorfast cotton fabric will fade if hung as a widow drapery. It is not likely that the hand laundry or the household automatic washer will remove color from table damasks, dresses, or colored domestic cotton. There is still some danger that an unreliable commercial laundry will use bleaches under poorly controlled conditions and consequently cause fading of color. Any good detergent may be used. Cottons resist the alkali of which some soaps are made.

Cotton can be pressed with a hot iron; its scorching point is high. Since cotton fiber is fairly inelastic, most cotton fabrics wrinkle easily and, hence, unless they are finished for crease resistance, need frequent pressing. Unless they are treated for mildew resistance, they should not be folded and kept on shelves where there is dampness. Moths, however, will not attack cotton.

Shape Retention

As explained, an innovation in fabric finishing provided durable-press cotton clothing. The resin finish, called Koratron, imparts permanent crease and shape to a garment. After cutting, the fabric is heat-cured to "bake in" the resin. Fabrics so finished are wrinkle- and crease-resistant and should not require ironing. The shape of the garment is thus retained permenently.[10]

Resistance to Shrinkage

One of the chief objections to cotton was its danger of shrinkage. A generation ago, consumers allowed a whole size for shrinkage of a shirt after laundering. Shrinkage-control treatments can now be applied to cottons so that not more than 1 percent residual shrinkage remains to be taken into account. (See Chapter 7.)

Feel or Hand

This characteristic is related to how the cotton fabric feels next to the skin. In the consumer survey, almost 60 percent of the men associated cotton specifically with comfort and *feel of the fabric next to the skin.* Cotton ranked over polyester by more than 2 to 1.

Cotton fibers feel cool, smooth, and soft. When cotton is processed into fabric, the feel or hand can be changed by the type of yarns, construction, and finish applied.

Ease of Cleaning/Washing (Care)

The factors of light, laundering, ironing, and perspiration are the common considerations in colorfastness of cottons. Possibly dry cleaning should be added, but inasmuch as cotton per se is considered washable, it would be assumed that it is dry-cleanable if colorfast. Some consumers will not purchase a cotton fabric if the label reads "Dry clean only."

In the discussion of physical characteristics of cotton, it was stated that cotton takes dyes that are fast to washing and to sunlight. Standard Fade-Ometer tests appropriate to the fabric's end use can be made to determine the degree of colorfastness.

In resistance to fading by perspiration, cotton is considered good.

The fact that cotton fabrics with durable-press finish can be washed, dried, and appear wrinkle-free with no ironing required is an important reason for buying cotton articles.

[10]"Cotton Its Properties and Uses," a pamphlet by the Canadian Cotton Council.

Fashion Rightness[11]

The couturiers of New York and Paris have considered cottons glamourous enough for inclusion in their collections. Probably the special finishes have been largely responsible for the fashion rightness of cotton today. Then, too, the textured effects obtained by blending cotton with other fibers in nubby, bouclé, and novelty yarns have glamorized cotton. Fabrics such as cotton brocades, tweeds, shantungs, and suitings have appeared. Staple fabrics, such as chambray, denim, corduroy, and jersey, have been restyled for the casual mode.

Cotton Incorporated, formerly the National Cotton Council of America, is the marketing and research company of the American cotton producer and, as such, has worked diligently to improve cotton products and to introduce new cotton products as they evolve. For example, through sales marketing efforts, the first all-cotton durable-press shirt and sheets were launched. Its work also is reflected in an array of other developments that have increased cotton's value to consumers.

Versatility

Cotton can serve for food (cottonseed products), for clothing, and for shelter. Cotton clothing can be worn around the clock. A single cotton fabric, piqué, can be used for a house dress, a sports dress, a summer business dress, a bathing suit, or a beach bag. It is particularly adapted to children's dresses. Cotton, then, is appropriate for wearing apparel, home furnishings, industrial uses, and military supplies.

Improvements in Finishes

The improvements in finishes have given newer and better uses to cotton. Other than the basic finishes, there are treatments for resistance to stains, water, flame, mildew, and germs; also functional finishes for permanent stiffness, crease resistance, crease retention, wash-and-wear, durable press, and embossed or heat-set patterns. (See Chapter 7 for a discussion of each process.)

COTTON DUST—MYTH OR REALITY?

A potentially serious threat to cotton production is the respiratory ailment known as byssinosis that may affect some cotton mill workers. Theories about the possible causes of this disease are being tested. Yet many questions remain. There are two different views on the causes and solutions of the disease:

Cotton Dust Update[12]

A major problem in the processing of cotton, especially in the spinning of yarn and weaving of cloth, is cotton dust that tends to permeate the atmosphere of the workplace. It gets into the lungs of factory workers, causing a serious disease called

---

[11]As already indicated, fashion ranked fifth by teenagers in a survey by the Opinion Research Corporation.

[12]From *American Textile Fabrics*, November 1980.

technically "byssinosis" and colloquially "brown lung." It is estimated that approximately a quarter of the workers in the textile manufacturing industry are in an area where there is possible significant exposure to cotton dust. Of these, those contracting "brown lung" are estimated by the industry at 1–2%, but other investigators set the incidence much higher.

The cotton industry has been taking many steps to eliminate the problem, including:

Harvesting the cotton before the boll opens
Washing the raw cotton (helps but may negatively affect the quality of yarn)
Enclosing the lines that feed in the cotton for carding
Using a carding process that separates the lint from other short fibers
Handling automatically the production process that separates the lint from other short fibers
Handling other production processes automatically
Installing air filtering systems
Requiring that workers wear respiratory masks
Transferring workers who develop any symptoms to other locations in the plant

The Federal Occupational Safety and Health Administration has set such high standards for the removal of cotton dust in the work place as to be almost unattainable without incurring costs that tend to destroy the industry. The industry has already spent over $2 billion in attempting to solve the problem and is planning to spend much more. The very high cost involved may put a serious damper on the competitive position of cotton in spite of growing consumer interest in cotton clothing. It may be difficult for cotton to compete with the low prices of man-made fibers, especially polyester.

Byssinosis—Physicians Group Explodes Disease Myths[13]

Several myths surround the textile-related disease known as byssinosis, including its cause, disease symptoms, and its solution.

The cause of the disease is not known, nor is the causal agent. One thing is clear: the cause of the disease is neither cotton fibers nor lint; the causal agent is found in the invisible respirable dust brought into the mill with the raw cotton. There is good evidence that the offending agent is contained within the bracts of the cotton plant and that the cotton becomes contaminated with it.

Since the visible dust in a mill is primarily lint, statements referring to the dustiness of a work area may have little or no bearing on the presence of the agent that causes byssinosis.

It is recognized that a certain number of workers who have been exposed to significant dust levels over a long period of time will develop chronic bronchitis. Although many have speculated that the acute symptoms progress into the chronic phase, this has never been clearly established.

It is difficult to make a definitive diagnosis of chronic obstructive pulmonary disease due to byssinosis. There are no characteristic findings on physical examination, chest x-ray, pulmonary function studies or even lung biopsy which are specific for the diagnosis of byssinosis.

Autopsy studies have revealed no increased pigmentation of the lungs in textile workers. Therefore the use of the term "brown lung" is questionable.

Recent mortality studies have not shown an increased death rate in workers in cotton textile mills as opposed to other workers in the general population. Textile workers die from heart disease, cancer and other causes.

[13]From *The Springs Bulletin*, September 1980.

More often than not, individuals who claim disability from byssinosis have multiple other problems which produce similar symptoms. It is not easy to separate the degree of impairment due to cotton dust exposure from the impairment resulting from other causes of injury, primarily cigarette smoking.

At this writing, the jury on byssinosis is still out. Students should determine the current status of the problem.

SUMMARY

Mistakes are frequently made by both the consumer and the salesperson because each fails to appreciate the inherent qualities of a fabric. The consumer will make a better buyer if he or she knows the *characteristics* of cotton and their *effect* on the finished fabric. Salespeople will improve their selling efficiency if they increase their technical knowledge of how cotton will best serve the customer; and they will be better equipped to answer customers' questions, such as, "Will the fabric wash well?" "Will the material be suitable for an evening dress?"

Satisfied customers are those who buy the fabrics best suited to their needs. These customers are assets to any store.

REVIEW QUESTIONS

1. (a) Of what value to the salesperson is a knowledge of the qualities of cotton?
    (b) Of what value is such knowledge to the consumer?
2. (a) In what countries is cotton raised?
    (b) Which species of cotton has the longest fibers? Which cottons have the finest fibers?
    (c) Which kind of cotton is best for use in hosiery and knit goods? Which for mixing with wool?
3. (a) What advantages has the mechanical cotton picker?
    (b) What are its disadvantages?
4. Explain the classification of upland cotton.
5. What effect have the fineness of the fiber and the length of the fiber had on the finished cotton fabric?
6. Define tensile strength, mercerization, hygroscopic moisture, cellulose, carding, count of yarn, ply yarn, combing, spinning.
7. (a) What effect on cotton have weak alkalies, such as borax, ammonia, phosphate of soda, and soap?
    (b) How will this knowledge help the consumer in laundering cottons?
    (c) What is the effect on cotton of strong, concentrated mineral acids such as sulfuric acid, nitric acid, and hydrochloric acid?
8. (a) Under what conditions does cotton mildew?
    (b) How may mildew be prevented?
9. Describe the process of making cotton yarn.

10. Describe the effect of the following types of yarn on the finished cloth:
    (a) slack-twisted yarns   (f) coarse yarns
    (b) tight-twisted yarns   (g) fine yarns
    (c) irregular yarns   (h) carded yarns
    (d) even yarns   (i) combed yarns
    (e) ply yarns   (j) low-count yarns
11. (a) In what woven constructions are cotton-fabrics made? Give fabric illustrations in each construction.
    (b) In what knitted constructions? Give fabric illustrations in each knitted stitch.
12. In what ways have finishes improved cotton fabrics?
13. What is meant by *versatility?* Illustrate the versatility of cotton.
14. (a) What qualities in the cotton fibers and yarns make cotton fabrics durable?
    (b) Why does cotton launder easily?
15. Forecast and defend the use of cotton in consumer goods.

EXPERIMENTS

(Tests to determine the effects of chemicals on cotton)

1. *The alkali test.* Ordinary lye, which can be bought in the grocery store, may be used for this experiment. Boil several pieces of cotton cloth for 5 minutes in a 5 percent solution of lye. Remove from the fire and place what remains on a blotting paper. Describe the residue left after boiling. What was the effect of the lye on the cotton yarns? Boiling the test fabrics for 5 minutes in a 10 percent solution of sodium hydroxide is equally effective.

2. *The acid test.* An ounce of concentrated sulfuric acid will suffice for this experiment. Place the liquid in a beaker or a heavy, shallow/glass dish. Drop several cotton yarns into the acid, but do not boil them. Let the yarns remain in the acid for 5 to 10 minutes. Note any changes that take place during that time. Remove any residue and describe the result of this test. A 25 percent solution of aluminum chloride may be used instead of concentrated sulfuric acid. In this case, saturate the fabric thoroughly, then press the cloth with a very hot iron. Vegetable fibers scorch and pulverize when abraded between the fingers.

3. *The microscopic test.* This test is the most accurate of all for distinguishing one textile fiber from another. Consumers will have difficulty in obtaining a microscope, but college students can arrange to use the biology laboratory if they have no microscope in the textile laboratory. Unravel a cotton yarn and pull out one or two of the fibers. Put a small drop of water or glycerin on the glass slide. Place one or two fibers in the drop of water and cover all with a cover glass. Use the lower power first and note the general appearance of the fiber. Then, without moving the slide, switch to the higher power. In your textile notebook draw the cotton fiber as seen through the microscope.

GLOSSARY

Acrylonitrile   A chemical used for treating cotton to make it permanently resistant to mildew and to give it greater affinity for dyes.

Apparel fabrics (cotton)   See listings in the glossary in Chapter 17.

Bird's eye   A woven-in dobby design used in cotton diapers, piqué, and wool sharkskin.

Brown lung disease See *byssinosis.*

Byssinosis A serious lung ailment thought to be caused by cotton lint or dust, especially in the spinning section of the cotton mill.

Carded yarn See *carding* (glossary, Chapter 3).

Chambray A cotton print cloth made of yarn-dyed yarns. Staple chambray has colored warps and white fillings.

Cheese A cylindrical package of yarn wound on a paper or wooden tube.

Classed Classification of cotton by staple length, grade, and character.

Combed yarn See *combing* (glossary, Chapter 3).

Conditioning A finishing process of sizing a fabric after dyeing to give it a hand.

Cotton A white or yellowish white vegetable fiber coming from a plant related to the hollyhock, grown in the United States, the Soviet Union, China, India, and other countries.

Cultivating Controlling weeds in cotton fields by mechanical means.

Defoliation Chemical treatment of cotton plants to make them shed their leaves.

Delinting Mechanically removing short fuzzing fibers from cotton seeds.

Dimity A cotton ribbed fabric with ribs spaced at regular intervals either in crosswise stripes or in crossbars.

Durable press See the glossary in Chapter 3.

Egyptian cotton A species grown along the Nile Delta. It averages more than 1½ inches in length.

Extralong-staple cotton Fibers 1⅜ inches and longer.

Ginning A process of separating fibers from the seeds.

Good middling The best grade of cotton—lustrous, silky, clean fibers.

Good ordinary The poorest grade of cotton. Contains leaf particles, sticks, hulls, dirt, sand, and the like.

Hill dropping A method of planting cotton seeds by dropping them in hills.

Home furnishings fabrics (cotton) See the glossaries in Chapters 20 and 21.

Linters Short fuzzy fibers removed from the cotton seeds.

Lumen The open structure or canal from which the protoplasm has disappeared.

Marquisette A cotton, silk, rayon, or other man-made fibered fabric in leno weave. May have clip-spot design.

Mechanical picker See *picker* and *stripper.*

Medium-staple cotton Fibers 1 to 1⅛ inches long.

Mercerization See Chapter 7.

Muslin Generic name of cotton fabrics in plain weave, ranging from the sheerest batiste to the coarsest sheeting.

Nonwoven cotton fabrics See *nonwoven fabrics,* Chapter 6 and the glossary.

Oxford A cotton fabric or blend with man-made fibers, in basket weave 4 × 4 and 8 × 8.

Picker A mechanical device with vertical drums equipped with spindles that remove the cotton from the boll.

Pima American cotton grown chiefly in the irrigated lands of Arizona, New Mexico, and El Paso, Texas. Extralong staple averaging 1⅜ to 1⅝ inches.

Poplin A cotton, acetate, rayon, wool, or silk fabric in the rib variation of the plain weave. Ribs are closely spaced fillingwise. Broadcloth has finer ribs.

Print cloths Cotton muslin fabrics ranging in counts from 48 square to 80 square (finished).

Rugs   See *cotton rugs*, Chapter 20.

Sanforized   Trade name of a process for shrinkage control. Residual shrinkage of not over 1 percent guaranteed.

Sateen   Mercerized cotton fabric in satin weave.

Sea Island cotton   A species of American cotton once produced off the coast of the Carolinas. Has the longest staple, averaging about 2 inches. Now produced on the Lesser Antilles—Montserrat, St. Kitts, Nevis, and St. Vincent.

Short-staple cotton   Fibers ¼ to ¹⁵⁄₁₆ inch long.

Stripper   A mechanical device that pulls the bolls off when they enter the rollers of the machine.

Tanguis   A species of cotton averaging 1¼ inches in length. Grown in Peru, which also grows other types of cotton, including pima and Egyptian.

Terry cloth   A cotton fabric with uncut looped pile, used in Turkish toweling.

Thread   See the glossary in Chapter 3.

Upland   Cottons of the species *Gossypium hirsutum*. They usually produce staples from ¾ to 1½ inches.

Velveteen   A cotton pile-weave fabric in filling pile construction, with either a twill- or a plain-weave back.

Wash-and-wear   See the glossary in Chapter 7.

Chapter 10

LINEN
AND
THE CONSUMER

The use of linen, or *flaxen cloth*, dates back to the European Neolithic people who lived before the appearance of metals—probably about ten thousand years ago. These people dressed in skins, but they made coarse cloth and fishnets from flax. Fragments of the cloth and nets have been discovered in parts of Switzerland, the home of the Neolithic Lake Dwellers.[1]

Fine linens have been the burial shrouds of the Egyptian pharaohs, the textile of Bible times, a fashionable and regal fabric of the Middle Ages, and the pride of the modern hostess.

Probably the most famous antique linen now extant is the Holy Shroud of Turin, safeguarded in a chapel in the Italian city, Turin. It is a cloth 14 feet long and 3 feet 7 inches wide, with the imprint of a human figure. It is estimated to be about two thousand years old and is believed by many investigators to be the shroud in which Christ's body was wrapped after he was taken from the cross. The linen had been dresed with cornstarch, causing the apparent blood stains to turn magenta rather than dark brown.

Linen, then, has served man as a textile for thousands of years. It has been more important in the past than it is today. Flax lost much of its importance when the cotton gin was developed. More recently the emphasis on quality, high-fashion linen fabrics and blends for apparel and for the home has satisfied a traditional respect for and interest in linens. Even so, world production of flax fiber is only 1 percent of all fibers produced.

[1]H. G. Wells, *The Outline of History* (New York: Macmillan Publishing Co., Inc., 1921).

FLAX PRODUCTION

Flax for Fiber

Flax is a vegetable fiber plant. When grown to full height, it resembles golden-colored straw. The fibers for spinning are obtained from the outside of the stem. These fibers are a type of bast fiber. Others in this group are discussed later in this chapter.

Belgium, France, Holland, and the Soviet Union and its satellites are the principal flax producers. (Ireland, England, Germany, Sweden, and Italy reduced production after World War II.) Belgium produces the tallest, best grade of flax; the Soviet Union produces the greatest acreage—several million acres of shorter length. The United States raises low-growing flax for seed. The Oregon flax industry partially attributes its growth to newer and better methods of harvesting. The cost of labor for cultivating, harvesting, and preparation of the fiber, added to a lack of suitable climatic conditions, has prevented flax production from becoming important in the United States.

Flax for Seed

Flax for seed to be processed into linseed oil for paints and finishes is raised in Michigan, Minnesota, and the Dakotas. Flax plants raised for seed do not produce good fibers for spinning. Stalks of the straw are used as fodder for cattle. The best portion of the flax may be used for fibers, for twine, and for rope. Quality tow and line fibers[2] are used to back upholstery and rugs, depending on the weave. Linen fibers used as backings include those used for damask, velvet, satin, twill and plain weaves, and pile for woven rugs.

Argentina and Brazil rank high in flaxseed production in the southern hemisphere. India, Canada, Morocco, Lithuania, and Latvia produce flaxseed and hempseed.

Flax Culture

A consistently moist but mild climate is necessary for the growing of flax for fiber. It requires more care than cotton before it can be made into cloth. A considerable amount of the labor in foreign countries is performed by hand—selecting, sorting, and grading. If climatic conditions are right, large quantities of flax for fiber can be produced. Great progress has been made in mechanizing the flax industry. Specially designed machines have now replaced many of the laborious hand operations. (See Fig. 10.1.) In northern countries, flax is sown in the spring, like wheat and rye. The flax plant has an erect stem about 3 feet in height, toward the top of which are branches that carry blue or white flowers and later bolls of linseed. Flax fibers surround the pithy center of the stem. Little

[2]Short flax fibers are called tow and long flax fibers are called line.

Figure 10.1 Early in spring, flaxseed is planted and grows to maturity about 3 feet high. Large machines harvest the plants by pulling; they are never cut. The stalks are bundled and threshing machines remove the seeds used for linseed oil. (Photo courtesy of the Belgian Linen Association.)

care is needed until harvesting time, which comes in late July or August. Large harvesting machines pull up flax plants by the roots when the stalks begin to turn yellow at the base and when the seeds are turning green to pale brown. This ensures long, unbroken fibers that can be spun into yarn easily, and at the same time clears the field for the next rotation of crops.

DRESSING THE FLAX

Rippling

Rippling is a process of removing the seeds. Today it is done by threshing machines that strip the seeds before tank retting is undertaken. Bundles of flax are piled into wigwams in the fields to dry.

Retting

Retting or soaking loosens the flax fiber from its inside straw. It is done by the following methods, either in natural water or chemicals. (See Figs. 10.2 and 10.3.)

1. *Tank retting.* The best grades of Belgian flax are retted in water from the River Lys. Bundles of flax are placed in huge concrete tanks with river water that is heated to 75° F and is gradually increased to 90° F. It requires 24 to 25 days and produces strong, lustrous, highest-quality flax.

Figure 10.2 Here men are loading the bundles of flax into retting tanks filled with heated water from the River Lys. The soaking action loosens the outside flax fibers from the woody center stalk. (Photo courtesy of the Belgian Linen Association.)

Figure 10.3 Chapels of flax out to dry after soaking in retting tanks of heated water that separates outside fibers from the straw. (Photo courtesy of the Belgian Linen Association.)

2. *Dew retting.* The object of this process is to let the dew loosen the fiber from the stalk. If the flax is dew-retted, the harvesting machine lays out small bundles of uprooted plants in orderly rows. The seeds are extracted by a special machine (rippling process). The bundles of flax are turned by a mechanical tender to ensure retting of the upper and lower layers. A great deal of flaxseed is often wasted. Although dependent upon the weather, dew retting is the most common method in use today and the most economical process. However it is difficult to control the quality uniformly. This process is used extensively in France, Belgium, and the Soviet Union.

3. *Chemical retting.* Many processes have been tested, but the use of this method is limited.

Scutching

After the flax has been thoroughly dried, it is run through a machine that breaks the wooden stalk by crumbling or crushing it. The flax is now ready for *scutching*—the removal of the fibers from the woody stalks. A machine with a series of fluted rollers beats the fibers free.

Hackling

This process, sometimes called *combing,* corresponds to the carding and combing of cottons. (See Fig. 10.4.) The object is to prepare the fibers for spinning by laying them parallel with one another. On large machines a series of combs with

Figure 10.4 Emerging from the combing process, these long wisps of fiber have passed over the series of graduated metal pins of the combing machine. A man gathers the glossy flax that now resembles switches of human hair. (Photo courtesy of the Belgian Linen Association.)

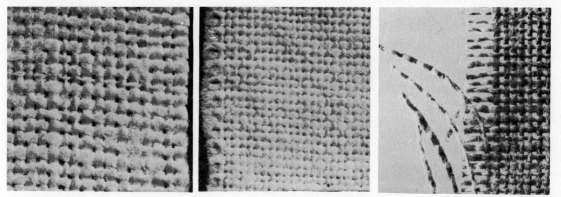

Figure 10.5   Left: Tow Linen. Middle: Line linen. Right: A poorly hackled tow linen. (Photos by Jack Pitkin.)

iron teeth ranging from very coarse to very fine are used. The scutched fibers are pulled through each comb, beginning with the coarsest one. Some short fibers adhere to the teeth of the comb, become entangled, or drop to the floor. These short fibers, called *tow,* are used in yarns designed for draperies and upholstery, and in artistic effects found in table linens and dish towels. (See Fig. 10.5.) Such fabrics are called tow linens. The long, regular, even fibers, laid parallel in the hackling, are called *line;* they are used in fine tablecloths, handkerchiefs, and decorative dress fabrics. Tow is separated from line. Cotton or polyester may be blended with tow linen.

CHARACTERISTICS OF THE LINEN FIBER

Microscopic Appearance

Linen fibers are round and at intervals have cross markings (nodes or joints) that give the fibers the appearance of bamboo poles. There is evidence of a central canal, but it is not continuous like that of cotton. The nodes keep the fiber from collapsing. These round, jointed structures make linen harder to spin than cotton. The longer fibers are more resistant to discipline and for that reason tend to create a curly or wavy effect.

Length of Fiber

Linen fibers are longer than cotton fibers. In fact, linen fibers used in fine yarns average 18 to 20 inches in length. Consequently, it is not so necessary to spin linen fibers tightly to hold the ends of the fibers in the yarn as it is with cotton.

Diameter of Fiber

Linen fibers range from 0.0047 to 0.0098 inch in diameter—the average breadth being greater than that of cotton. All cotton fibers are finer than the finest flax fibers.

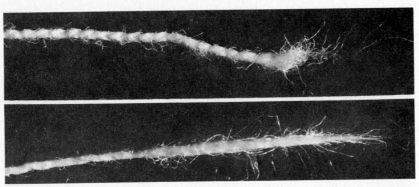

Figure 10.6 The breaking test, showing broken ends of two yarns. (a) Cotton is brushlike; (b) linen is pointed. This is a nontechnical test that may be made by removing a yarn from a fabric and pulling it until it breaks. An all-linen yarn is more difficult to break than is an all-cotton yarn. (Photo by Jack Pitkin.)

Luster

Linen fibers have a characteristic silky luster, much more pronounced than that of untreated cottons. Linens are rarely mercerized. The natural look, cool hand, and textured appearance give it a unique quality.

Strength

Linen is stronger than cotton, and its tensile strength increases when the fiber is wet. Overretting weakens the fiber appreciably. (See Fig. 10.6.)

Heat Conductivity

Linen is better than cotton as a conductor of heat. It carries heat away from the body faster. Hence, garments made of linen feel cooler than do those of comparable weight in cotton.

Hygroscopic Moisture

Flax fibers have about the same amount of hygroscopic moisture as cotton— between 6 and 8 percent. Linen fabrics, unless beetle-finished, absorb moisture quickly and dry faster than does cotton. Linen dish towels will dry more dishes than cotton before feeling damp.

Composition of Fiber

As is true for cotton, linen is composed chiefly of cellulose, but it has 15 to 30 percent more natural impurities. The chemical constituents are pure cellulose (65–70 percent), pectic substances–plant cells (20–25 percent), woody and cuticular tissue (4–5 percent), and ash (1 percent).

Launderability

Linen fiber is smooth; dirt and germs do not collect on it easily. Linen launders easily, but not so easily as does cotton. However, since it tends to return to a natural twist with dampness, it either must be pressed when evenly damp or controlled with a blend of polyester that makes it no-iron.

Action of Strong Acids and Alkalies

Linens, like cottons, are vegetable fibers; hence, acids have the same effect on linens as on cottons. Concentrated mineral acids, such as sulfuric, hydrochloric, hydrofluoric, and nitric acids, destroy linen fibers that are soaked in them for a few minutes. Dilute acids also affect linen and cotton similarly; they tend to weaken the fabric, but do not destroy it if it is not allowed to dry.

The flax fiber is attacked more readily by alkalies than cotton is. It is more difficult to bleach linen than cotton because of the natural impurities in its fibers. Weak alkalies, such as borax, ammonia, or phosphate of soda, do not injure linen.

Action of Light

Linens are much more resistant to the ultraviolet rays of the sun than are man-made fibers.

Figure 10.7 A vast amount of research has gone into the production of fast dyes. This picture shows the Moygashel fabrics going through the machine in the warm, damp atmosphere of the dyehouse. (Photo courtesy of the Irish Linen Guild.)

Affinity for Dyestuffs

Linen requires special dyes because of the hardness and less penetrability of the fiber. Its cells are held together with tissue that is broken down only under processing. Linen yarns often being of uneven thickness will dye somewhat unevenly and this fact gives linen its natural look of quality. (See Fig. 10.7.)

MAKING LINEN YARN

Preparation

After the flax fibers have been sufficiently hackled or combed, the fibers go to the *preparing room*. The first machine, called the *spread board*, lays wisps of flax fibers parallel on traveling bands in continuous lines, with the ends of the wisps overlapping. These lines of fiber are then passed through sets of rollers that draw one fiber away from the other to produce a ribbon of fibers (sliver). Ribbons of sliver are drawn out longer and thinner until the last machine, the *roving frame,* puts in a loose twist. It is wound on large wooden bobbins that are mounted on the top of the spinning frame.

Wet Spinning

The roving on the bobbins is immersed in hot water, dried, and put on rapidly revolving spindles (2,000 to 3,000 revolutions per minute) that put in the twist. The twist or spin of the spindles is the operation of spinning the flax fibers into linen yarns.

Weaving

Essentially the preparation and weaving of linen is not very different from that of wool, cotton, silk, and other textile yarns.

The manufacturer runs the cones directly onto the warp beam; several of these beams then go to the weaver's beam. The warps are set up in the loom, the filling shuttles are prepared with yarn, and weaving begins.

Plain Weave

A few years ago few linens were used for ready-to-wear, but they are now coming back into popular demand, mostly in plain weave and knits, as discussed later in this chapter.

A sheer linen in plain weave for handkerchiefs or fine blouses is called handkerchief linen, but in most cases it is superseded by man-made fibers of similar weave. Some slightly heavier linens for dresses or sportswear may be embroidered.

The greatest variety of weaves are created for home furnishings, although plain weaves of many weights are designed for colorful prints and are dyed very effectively. Schiffli embroidery is applied to the lighter weight for draperies and the heavier weaves for upholstery.

Plain weaves of different weight are widely distributed for embroidery of pictures and crewel pillows or other novelties. Basic weaves are also in demand as luggage and briefcase linings.

Novelty Weaves

The Belgians, who have produced fine linens for over a thousand years, create the most unusual weaves. From the sheer casements for large contemporary windows to drapery, slipcover, and upholstery weaves, the linen yarns are skillfully designed so that nubs will repeat to create the desired effect. It is the thick and thin look, spaces, or twisted yarns that make the difference. This craft is so specialized that few others attempt it.

Twill Weave

Linen fabrics are far more numerous in plain weave than in twill. Twill weaves are sometimes seen in drapery and upholstery linens. Fine twills are used for crewel work, especially copying antique pieces, which revived in popularity in the 1970s.

Jacquard and Dobby Weaves

A limited amount of linen is at its most beautiful when woven in Jacquard as a table damask and in novelty dobby designs, giving a three-dimensional look: on the right side, the warp floats in a satin weave ground and the filling floats in the design.

Velvet (Pile) Weaves

Luxurious linen-faced velvets are an important item, made of a pile construction. They include not only plain and antique velvets, but also crushed and printed colorings. Belgium is the main producer for the U.S. market. Velvet weaves are made in many colors, with the less expensive low pile and most expensive highest pile. The backing is cotton or man-made fibers.

FINISHING LINEN FABRICS

Bleaching

In the past, the snowy whiteness of linen was obtained by the centuries-old practice of *grass bleaching*. Grass bleaching produced beautiful color and did not injure the strength of the fiber. But since this process required weeks or even months, much capital and land are necessary.

In today's modern bleaching processes, chemicals are used under carefully controlled conditions so that an even whiteness is achieved for dyeing light colors or printing. Important processes clean the fibers of impurities in large boiling tanks and only at the end of the process is the linen fully bleached.

Regular and Special Finishes

Regular finishes for linens have been discussed in Chapter 7 and may be referred to at this point.

There has been much discussion about flameproofing linens for contract use, about durable finishes, and about effects on the fiber after a period of time. A number of processes now used are successfully applied to linens. Flameproofing has the following additional features: (1) it may shrink fabric to the same degree as plain water; (2) it does not accelerate fading; and (3) water-repellent fabrics may be flameproofed with the durable types of flameproofing.[3]

Many cities and states have their own flameproofing regulations for fabrics used in public buildings—regulations that surpass the federal regulations.

Among the more recent functional finishes are permanent-press soil-release finishes for table linens. To make a table linen no-iron, permanent-press, soil-release, it is necessary to have a ratio of 65 percent linen and 35 percent polyester in which the polyester controls the curl of the linen yarns and gives space for the finishing chemicals.

FIBER IDENTIFICATION OF LINEN

Linen is a generic fiber name recognized by the FTC under the Textile Fiber Products Identification Act. Consequently, fabrics made of linen must be labeled with this generic fiber name and with percentages (over 5 percent) in order of predominance by weight of the constituent fibers in the textile fiber product, exclusive of ornamentation[4]; for example, 60 percent linen/40 percent cotton. The act states that "Fiber or fibers in an amount of 5 percent or less must appear last and be designated as 'other fiber' or 'other fibers,' as the case may be." A label might read, for example, 60 percent linen/36 percent cotton/4 percent other fibers. If the article is all linen, it may be identified by those words or by "100 percent linen."

In advertising, the percentages of the fiber need not be stated but simply listed in order of predominance by weight. The rule for fibers in an amount of 5 percent or less is the same as for labeling.[5]

Under the TFPIA, a retailer who imports linen products directly must

---

[3]"A Guide to Fabric Finishing, Flameproofing, and Service," a pamphlet from the Perma-Dry Division, Kiesling-Hess Finishing Co., Inc., New York, Philadelphia, and Los Angeles.

[4]*Ornamentation* is defined as "any fibers or yarns imparting a visibly discernible pattern or design to a yarn or fabric."

[5]See Chapter 1 for a discussion of the TFPIA.

assume full responsibility for the correct labeling of his or her product. Should the retailer purchase an imported linen article from any person residing in the United States, he or she should obtain a guarantee issued in good faith by such a person. This rule applies to all imported textile fiber products.

SOURCES OF LINEN FABRICS

Belgium, Ireland, and Scotland are the principal exporters of linen fabrics to the United States. Smaller amounts are imported from other European countries and from Argentina, Brazil, and Japan.

The difference between the linen produced in Northern Ireland and Belgium is mostly a matter of specialization. Both produce the weaves they are most skilled at manufacturing, and each produces some of the same items as the other country—for example, oyster and plain linens used for table linen—in comparable quality. However, sheer handkerchief weaves, hemstitched linen, and damasks are mainly Irish, whereas the novelty weaves—textured and drapery weaves—are mainly Belgian. There has been a decline in sales of damask to the United States, owing to competition from Japan's rayon/cotton damask and the demand for no-iron tablecloths.

In table linens, Ireland produces more finished goods, whereas the greater part of Belgian linen enters the United States as gray goods, which are dyed, printed, trimmed, and finished here. Ireland and Belgium ship to Portugal and the Azores for hand-embroidered cloths, mats, napkins, and novelties.

In 1955 a New York center for the Belgian Linen Association was opened. Its activities include publicity, sales promotion, public relations, advertising, and education. Its blue and white shield is well known as it appears on tablecloths and drapery fabrics. The Linen Trade Association was organized by linen importers.

Trade Names of Linens

Over the years, even for several generations, certain names on labels have spelled quality of linen fabrics to consumers. One such name is Moygashel, from an old Gaelic castle in Dungannon, Ireland. The making of linen fabrics at Moygashel goes back fifteen hundred years.

In 1953 Moygashel Ltd. was formed and became a public corporation, incorporating the interests of Stevenson & Sons Ltd. and twenty-two other firms. In the spring of 1969, Moygashel Ltd. became a subsidiary of Courtaulds Ltd.

Many of the old Irish firms have gone out of business. Belgian firms flourish from the sale of no-iron colored and embroidered tablecloths and high-priced and exclusive decorative fabrics.

CONSUMER DEMAND FOR LINEN

At a time when there are copies of almost any weave or texture, it is interesting to speculate on why many consumers search for the natural linens woven of yarns spun from real flax. It is not so much the appearance, which is unique, as the way in which the light reflects from the more distinct fibers of its surface. The way in which linens take dyes or prints is another prime reason for their choice. For clothing, linen has regained some of its one-time popularity, partly because of improved laundry methods and partly because of crease-resistant finishes that are now often applied. It also makes up into an interesting blend. Because it is cool and smooth to the touch, linen outerwear is often chosen for spring- and summertime clothing. For sweaters, knits of linen yarn or blends of linen and cotton are proving popular for both men and women.

Many households have inherited fine table linens, damasks, or hand embroideries that have been handed down from mothers, grandmothers, or even great-grandmothers. For centuries—in fact, since the Egyptian, Greek, and Roman periods—linens have been cherished. Today, due to the faster pace of living, linens that are no-iron, soil-release are used for every day, while others become part of special occasion settings.

Linens for home furnishings are a different matter. Department stores and decorating shops sell thousands of yards of printed fabrics for draperies, slipcovers, and upholstery that may contain no linen, but that, although cotton or a man-made fiber, are in demand because they have linen's textured look. It is easy enough to tell the fabrics that are 100 percent linen or have a high percentage of it. The hand is cool and the fabrics have a crisper look. For the most part, linens for home decoration are ordered through interior designers; since such specialized work goes into them prices are necessarily higher.

Of the many countries that have produced linens over the years, both by hand weaving and by highly mechanized machines, the Belgians have been famous for intricate weaves since the eighth century. Today, these are mainly expressed in sheer casements. As they hang at the windows, open warp stripes, tied and knotted threads, colored yarns, and heavy nubby yarns contrasting with smooth light threads give a very special style. Other countries are now in this market, both in Europe and South America. One of the best things about such linens is that they are resistant to deterioration by the sun, as may not be the case with some fabrics of man-made fibers.

In recent years velvets woven in Belgium have a linen pile and cotton back. Even strong dyes have a deep, not shiny, look of an almost antique patina. They are available in a wide spectrum of colors.

Above all, the natural undyed linens are in demand, from sheer fine weaves, to close weaves, to heavy nubby weaves. Most of them also come in bleached white, which is effective for contemporary rooms. In other markets, closely woven natural linen is made into shoes and handbags with leather trim.

Highly prized are sets of luggage with linen on the outside, and briefcases with linen on the inside.

BUYING POINTS FOR LINEN FABRICS

In aiding the customer to buy linen, the salesperson should stress the following features, in addition to its coolness for summer wear, already mentioned.

Durability and Workmanship

The durability of the cloth depends on the fibers and yarns of which it is made. Care in growth, harvesting, and dressing of flax affects the quality of the fiber. If flax is allowed to overripen, the fiber becomes too brittle to make good cloth. If fibers are overretted, they become too tender. If care is not taken in scutching and hackling, good-quality fibers may be broken or wasted. Consequently, the durability of linen cloth depends upon the degree of skilled workmanship. Since the linen fiber is longer and stronger than cotton of the same diameter, linen should be more durable than cotton, considering fibers alone. Linens and cottons are stronger when wet than when dry, so that washing does not weaken them. Weaving them together creates a durable fabric.

The strength of linen yarn does not increase with the number of twists or turns to the inch, as does the strength of cotton. The linen fibers are sufficiently long and strong to require little twisting.

Absorbency

Linen is absorbent because the flax fiber is hollow through the center, like bamboo. Since linen dish towels will dry more dishes than cotton before feeling damp, fewer dish towels are required. The consumer may not appreciate the absorbency of linen until after it has been laundered, for frequently linen's leathery beetle finish restricts absorbency.

Since linen absorbs moisture readily, dries quickly, and does not "perspire" or mold, it is well suited for drapery use in humid climates. Also, the absorptive nature of linen yarns contributes to sound deadening. This feature partially explains the increased use of linen for wall coverings. Belgian linen in particular is also well suited for draperies and upholsteries. Of all the natural fibers, linen is the least elastic. It also repels dust and does not attract it. The fiber has excellent tensile strength. (See Fig. 10.8.)

Ease in Care

Because flax fiber is inelastic, linen fabrics require frequent pressing to remove wrinkles, unless the fabric has been treated for crease resistance. It is best to sprinkle the fabric and to iron it while damp.

Figure 10.8 A paper-backed, 100 percent Belgian linen wallcovering. Some of the characteristics of linen for this purpose include dimensional stability, antistatic power, solidarity of color, and acoustical properties. (Photo courtesy of the Belgian Linen Association.)

Linen does not get soiled as quickly as cotton because the fibers are longer, harder, and smoother. Hot water and soap will not injure the fiber, but care should be taken not to starch linens heavily (especially damasks), for there is danger of breaking the fibers under a heavy iron.

Washability of linen is a strong buying motive for any consumer. Household linen, handkerchiefs, and linen apparel (but be sure to check the label, since many articles require dry cleaning) all wash easily week after week, year after year, and get softer with use. Linen is a clean, sanitary textile. White linens should be dried in the sun if they are to keep their whiteness. (For care of specific articles, see Chapter 16.)

Generally speaking, dry cleaning is the recommended method for drapery and upholstery linens. Decorative linens should not be washed, unless labeled washable and preshrunk. Since linen does not have static properties, dust particles are not attracted and do not cling to the fabric, and therefore it may require less cleaning. The permanent-press, soil-release finishes are now used effectively on 65 percent linen/35 percent polyester tablecloths, napkins, and mats.

MINOR NATURAL VEGETABLE FIBERS

Ramie

Ramie, or rhea, is a bast fiber that has often been sold as a substitute for flax. The fiber comes from within the upright 5- to 6-foot stems of a nettlelike East Indian shrub. It is also produced in Europe, China, and Egypt.

The first ramie plants were brought to the United States in 1855. Ramie grows best in a semitropical climate with abundant rainfall. The stems must be cut at maturity, because immature plants yield coarse, brittle fibers. The plants send up a new growth after each cutting. Hence three to five crops a year are possible.

Research on ramie by the U.S. Department of Agriculture has led to the growth of ramie in Florida. E. B. Elliot, president of his own outdoor advertising firm, is credited, on the basis of his personally financed research, with finding a method of recovering and refining ramie fibers on a large commercial scale. Experimental plantings of ramie in Savannah and New Brunswick, Georgia, southern Mississippi, Louisiana, Alabama, and Texas augured success. But it has not been possible for promoters to develop a process commercially.

The fiber ranges from 2½ to 18 inches in length and from 0.002 to 0.003 inch in diameter (finer than flax), and it is very strong. One authority states that ramie is seven times stronger than wool and twice as strong as flax. Ramie is claimed to be stronger than flax when wet. Its smooth, lustrous appearance seems to improve with washing. Ramie fabrics keep their shape and do not shrink. They resist mildew, absorb more moisture than linen, and dry quickly. They dye easily, but fibers are brittle and have low twisting and bending strength. In the United States, processors experienced difficulty in spinning methods. Ramie is spun here on the worsted system, but to do so, fibers must be cut into staple lengths. The shortened fibers produce coarser fabrics. Finer fabrics would require the use of the full, lengthy ramie fibers. The countries of Europe find it practical to spin ramie on the silk system. By so doing, the whole length of fiber can be used. Ramie is also blended with wool and rayon in carpets.

Jute

Jute is a bast fiber that comes chiefly from India, because the plant grows well in rich land, especially along tidal basins. India, through improved methods, financial aid, and greater acreage, has increased its production. There has been some attempt to raise jute along the Gulf of Mexico, but the cost of labor has been too high to warrant its cultivation.

The jute plant grows to a height of about 12 feet. It is cut off close to the ground when it is in flower. Like flax, it is stripped of its branches and leaves and is put through a retting process to loosen the fibers from the stalk. After they are separated from the outer bark, the fibers are dried and cleaned.

Jute fibers are weaker than those of linen. The fibers are very short, but lustrous and smooth. Because jute is affected by chemical bleaches, it can never be made pure white. It is not very durable and is very much weakened by dampness. It is attacked by sunlight. Since alkalies used in the laundry weaken jute, neutral soaps containing no free alkali should be used. Jute can be distinguished from linen or cotton if the fibers are stained with iodine and then concentrated sulfuric acid and glycerin are applied. Jute fibers remain yellow; cotton and linen turn blue.

Jute is used chiefly for gunny sacks, burlap bags, cordage, and binding and backing threads for rugs and carpets. One company[6] finishes burlap with a flame-resistant finish for uses on walls of bowling alleys and night clubs with modern décor. The company also makes a rotproof finish that permits nurserymen to bury shrubs wrapped in burlap in the soil.

Hemp

The Philippine variety is white; the outer fiber is used for cordage, and the inner fibers can be woven into webbing and gauzes. The Central American variety is not so strong as Philippine hemp and is used mainly in cordage. The Indian product is not so strong as Central American and Philippine varieties, but it can be used in cables and canvas. Hemp is stronger than flax, jute, or cotton. It is dark brown in color and cannot be bleached without an appreciable loss of strength. It is less elastic and harsher than linen and so cannot be used extensively in woven cloth.

Hemp fiber has the microscopic nodes and joints of linen, but the central canal is wider. If the same test (sulfuric acid, iodine, glycerin) is applied to hemp, jute, linen, and cotton, hemp turns bluish green; jute, yellow; and cotton and linen, blue.

Manila hemp is not actually hemp but is used for similar purposes including Manila hats. It comes from the leaf stems forming the abaca plant native to the Philippine Islands and Central America.

SUMMARY

Linen is a competitor of cotton and the man-made fibers for household use. But although it may be suited to almost as many uses as cotton, the cost of producing and manufacturing linen keeps the price of good, durable qualities higher. Now that a chemical treatment has been found to give linen and polyester tablecloths a no-iron, soil-release finish, a wider market has opened up.

It is highly improbable that the United States will ever be able to compete with Belgium in the production of fine linen fabrics. Since we have to import most of our linen, the cost will doubtless exceed that of cotton. Although the initial investment in a linen article is high, its beauty and durability make the purchase economical in the long run.

REVIEW QUESTIONS

1. What are the chief physical and chemical characteristics of flax fibers?
2. Compare each of the characteristics just listed with the corresponding characteristic of cotton.

[6]Jonell Corporation, Bridgeton, Rhode Island.

3. Describe flax production and culture.
4. (a) What are the different methods of retting flax?
   (b) Give the advantages of each method.
5. (a) How are linen yarns made?
   (b) How does this method differ from that for making cotton yarns?
6. Why does linen require more care in bleaching than cotton?
7. What is the law on labeling textile fiber products made of linen?
8. Write a label for a fabric that contains 20 percent cotton, 15 percent rayon, 65 percent linen.
9. Why do consumers buy linen fabrics?
10. (a) Why is linen suitable for dish towels?
    (b) Why is linen suitable for table coverings?
11. (a) For what purpose is jute used?
    (b) What are the advantages of hemp for use in cordage?

EXPERIMENTS

1. *Alkali test.* Use the procedure outlined for cotton, Chapter 9.
2. *Acid test.* Use the procedure outlined for cotton, Chapter 9.
3. *Microscopic test.*
   (a) Look at linen fibers through the microscope. Draw and describe their microscopic appearance.
   (b) Perform the same experiment on jute, hemp, and ramie. Describe the results of your tests.
4. *Test to determine the durability of yarns.*
   (a) Use yarns from three linen and two cotton fabrics.
   (b) Untwist each yarn and note
       (1) Whether yarn is linen or cotton.
       (2) Amount of twist.
       (3) Evenness of yarn.
       (4) Construction (single or ply).
       (5) Amount of hackling or combing.
       (6) Length of fibers.
   (c) Judging from the preceding factors, is the yarn durable?
5. Determine the construction and count of the fabric.
6. List the finishes applied to the fabric.

GLOSSARY

Art linen   An ecru, white, or unbleached linen fabric in plain weave. It is used for embroidery, dresses, uniforms, and table linens.

Bast fiber   Fibers between the pithy center of the stem and the skin. Flax, jute, hemp, and ramie are the chief bast fibers.

Beetle finish   See *beetling* (glossary, Chapter 7).

Bouclé yarn   Linen yarn often plied with yarns of other fibers for textural interest. (See glossary, Chapter 3).

Butcher linen A variety of plain-woven crash originally used for butchers' aprons. All-rayon or rayon and acetate blend in crash is often erroneously called butcher linen.

Crash A coarse linen fabric made of thick, uneven yarns and having a rough, irregular surface. It may also be cotton, spun rayon, or blends. It is used for dresses, draperies, and table linens.

Damask A glossy linen, cotton, rayon, silk, or mixed fabric. Patterns are flat and reversible. Linen and cotton damask are used for table coverings.

Dress linen See *crash*.

Embroidery linen See *art linen*.

Flax Fibers of the flax plant, which are spun into linen yarns and woven into linen cloth.

Friction towel A terrycloth made with linen pile. It may be made into a mitt used to develop friction against the skin after bathing.

Grass bleaching Whitening fabrics by laying them on the grass in the sun.

Hackling A process that prepares the flax fibers for spinning by laying them parallel. It may be done by hand or by machine and corresponds to the carding and combing of cottons.

Handkerchief linen A well-hackled sheer linen fabric in plain weave that is used for handkerchiefs, blouses, summer dreses. It is synonymous with *lawn*.

Hemp A plant grown in the Philippines, Mexico, Central America, the West Indies, and India. Outer fibers are used for cordage, inner fibers for cables and canvas.

Huck or huckaback A honeycombed dobby face towel. It may be linen or cotton or mixtures with rayon.

Irish linen Linen products that come from Ireland, mainly Belfast in northern Ireland.

Jute A bast fiber, chiefly from India, used mostly for gunny sacks, bags, cordage, and binding threads of rugs and carpets.

Lawn A light, well-hackled linen fabric first made in Laon, France. Linen lawn is synonymous with handkerchief linen. Cotton lawn is a similar type of fabric. It can be white, solid colored, or printed.

Line Longest flax fibers, used for fine, even linen yarns. Shortest flax fibers are called *tow*.

Linen A vegetable fiber obtained from the inside of the woody stalk of the flax plant.

Moygashel A trade name representing excellent quality in imported Irish linen.

Ramie or rhea A bast fiber from a nettlelike East Indian shrub, also produced in China, Egypt, and the United States. It is used for shirts, suitings, automobile seat covers, table covers, and, in blends with wool, for carpets.

Retting A process for loosening the flax fiber from the woody stalk. This may be done by several methods: pool, dew, tank, and chemical.

Rippling Threshing of flax to strip the seeds or bolls from the plant. This process may be done by hand or by machine.

Roving frame A machine that puts a loose twist in the drawn-out sliver.

Scutching Removing the flax fibers from the woody stalk by a series of fluted rollers.

Sisal A variety of hemp grown chiefly in Kenya, East Africa. It is used primarily for cordage but may also be used for millinery.

Spinning The operation of putting the twist into linen yarn.

Spread board A machine that lays wisps of flax fibers parallel on traveling bands in continuous lines, with the ends of the wisps overlapping.

Spun linen　Finest hand-woven linen fabric, used for handkerchiefs, women's collars, and so on.

Suiting　A heavy, fairly coarse linen fabric in plain, twill, or herringbone weaves, used for women's and men's suitings. It is also made in cotton, spun rayon, or acetate.

Tow　Short flax fibers, separated by hackling (combing) from the longer fibers.

Tow linen　Fabric made of uneven, irregular yarns composed of the very short fibers.

Chapter 11

SILK AND THE CONSUMER

In this chapter we discover why silk, throughout many centuries, has been the premier fiber for outerwear, underwear, and home furnishings, even though its sales volume is now relatively quite small, due to the fiber's scarcity and high price.

Silk clothing is no longer limited to women's wear and men's suits; sportswear, shirts, and slacks are now being made from silk or silk blends, reflecting the growing Chinese influence on fashion.

If a consumer has a garment that may include silk, he or she can make a simple test to determine silk's presence: pull out a yarn from the seam and light a match to it. If it is silk, the fiber will smell like burnt feathers, and the embers will crush easily between the fingers.

SERICULTURE

History of Silk Culture

Silk was used by the ancients. History records the Chinese as the first people who knew how to raise and manufacture it. About 1725 B.C. silk culture, sponsored by the wife of the emperor, was begun in China. Until the time of the Chinese People's Republic of 1958, the Chinese empress paid homage to the "Goddess of the Silkworms" on a special day each year by feeding the insects.

About 1765 B.C. the mulberry tree was cultivated to provide food for the silkworm. The secret of the cultivation of these worms and of the manufacture of their fibers into cloth was carefully guarded for about three thousand years. Eventually, according to one story, two monks sent to China by the Byzantine

Emperor Justinian stole mulberry seeds and silkworms' eggs. At the risk of their lives, they brought them back to Byzantium in their walking staffs. From these monks, Justinian learned of the Chinese sericulture. From this knowledge a large silk industry grew up in the Byzantine Empire. Rich fabrics woven of silk on imperial looms are still in existence there.

With the rise and spread of Islam, silk culture spread to Sicily and Spain with the Moslem conquests. After the Moslems withdrew from conquered soil, the art of silk weaving remained.

By the twelfth and thirteenth centuries A.D., Italy had become the silk center of the West. The art of weaving ecclesiastical and ducal silk fabrics was unexcelled. For over five hundred years, Italy was the leader in silk production. But by the seventeenth century, the French city of Lyons was vying with Italy for excellence and beauty in weaving silk.[1]

Parts of Japan had been raising silkworms as early as A.D. 300, when the Japanese had learned the secret of sericulture from four Chinese girls they had kidnapped. Still later, India learned this secret when a Chinese princess came to India to marry an Indian prince.[2] Today, Japan is the chief producer and exporter of quality silk.

England began to weave silk in the fifteenth century, when Flemish weavers fled to England from the Low Countries. In the sixteenth century Huguenot weavers settled in the vicinity of Spitalfields. The English climate was not suitable for sericulture, but silk weaving was extensive.

England showed interest in the silk industry and sponsored its introduction to the American colonies in 1623. The colonial government allotted land grants to Virginia settlers on condition that they plant 10 mulberry trees on every one hundred acres. In the 1760s, Connecticut became a productive silk-raising section.[3] The Carolinas also raised silk in the nineteenth century. These experiments have long since been abandoned as the cost of labor needed for silk cultivation excluded the United States as a silk-raising country, even though it is an important importer. Nevertheless, the U.S. mill consumption of silk is less than one-fifth of what it was some thirty years ago before the wide availability of synthetic substitutes. The quality, however, is high, with some of the most beautiful fabrics in the world being woven on American looms.

Life of the Silkworm

Silk is an animal fiber. It is the product of the silkworm, of which there are two varieties: the wild and the cultivated. The fibers of the wild silkworm are yellowish brown, instead of yellow to gray, and have a coarse, hard texture. This worm feeds on the scrub oak instead of the mulberry leaf. It grows in India, China, and Japan.

[1]*Silk,* a pamphlet of the International Silk Association.

[2]*The History of Silk and Sericluture,* a pamphlet by John Kent Tilton, formerly Director, Scalamandre Museum of Textiles.

[3]George E. Linton, "8000 Years of Textiles," part 2, *American Fabrics Magazine,* Winter 1955–1956, pp. 93–100.

The cultivated silkworm requires a great deal of care. Quiet and sanitation are necessary. A whole scientific industry, that of raising mulberry trees for food for the worms, has grown up. The best mulberry leaves seem to come from plants that are the result of a combination of the tall mulberry tree and the dwarf or shrub mulberry tree.

Silkworms live a very short time—only about 2 months. During that period they pass through four stages of development: (1) egg, (2) worm, (3) chrysalis (pupa) or cocoon, and (4) moth. (See Fig. 11.1.)

For commercial purposes, life is measured from the moment the egg is hatched and the worm is killed by heat after spinning the cocoon. The worms spinning the largest and heaviest cocoons are permitted to live and continue the next cycle. (See Figs. 11.2 and 11.3.)

The industry differentiates between nonhibernating and hibernating eggs (those that are in the process of development and those that are dormant). Nonhibernating eggs hatch in about 10 days after they are laid. In the hibernating egg, development of the embryo is retarded through seasonal temperature conditions or in modern sericulture, through cold storage at 2.5°C. Hatching of cold-storage eggs is induced by warming the eggs to room temperature (about 25°C) and soaking them in hydrochloric acid. The eggs will hatch in about 10 days after this acid treatment.

A tiny white worm about one-fourth inch long is hatched from each tiny egg. These worms are very delicate and require the utmost care. They are placed on bamboo trays covered with straw mats on which selected mulberry leaves are laid. The worms are very greedy; it is estimated that each worm eats about 30,000 times its initial weight and grows tremendously. During this stage the silkworm molts (sheds its skin) four times. At the end of about 30 days, the worm ceases to eat, attaches itself to a piece of straw, and begins to spin its cocoon.

Two filaments are ejected from the mouth—one an almost invisible silk filament and the other a glutinous substance. The filaments merge and harden when exposed to the air. The worm covers itself with these filaments, completing the cocoon in about 3 days. The worm is then transformed into a moth in about 8 days. One manufacturer estimates that 2,500 to 3,000 cocoons are necessary to make 1 yard of silk fabric. The color of the cocoon is either white or yellow, depending on the species. The color is not dependent on its feeding, and there is no difference in the quality of silk produced. However, the white cocoon silk does not have to be bleached.

If the moth is permitted to emerge from the cocoon, the silk filament is broken into many short pieces. Therefore the chrysalis (unless it is selected for breeding) is steamed or is subjected to hot air to kill the larva inside the cocoon. Long, thin fibers can be reeled from the unpierced cocoons.

The moths that are reserved for breeding purposes emerge from cocoons creamy white. Three days after they have hatched, they mate, lay eggs, and die. Their cycle of life is complete.

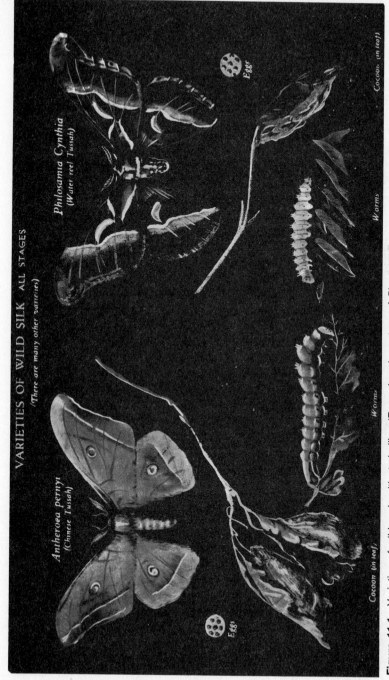

Figure 11.1 Varieties of wild and cultivated silks. (Reproduced courtesy of Cheyney Brothers, Inc.)

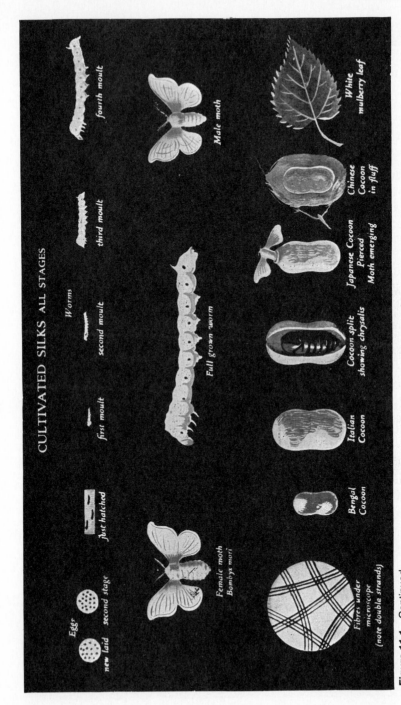

Figure 11.1 Continued.

Figure 11.2 When the silkworms are ready to spin their cocoons, the farmers put them in a *mabushi,* or bed of straw. In three days the worms will have spun their cocoons, which are then ready to be treated in the next stage of silk making. The beds shown here are old-fashioned, but they are used by 20 percent of the Japanese silkworm-farming households. (Photo courtesy of the International Silk Association.)

Sorting

Cocoons most suitable for propagation of the species are separated from those to be used for weaving. For propagation, it has been found that cocoons with a "waist" are preferable. Elliptical or nearly round cocoons are used for reeling

Figure 11.3 An up-to-date cocooning frame, an "apartment house" for cocoons. Separate living quarters ensure a finer gloss and more uniformity in the finished silk. (Photo courtesy of the International Silk Association.)

into yarn. The former type is sorted by sex. Cocoons pass along a belt that allows the heavier ones (males) to drop down into a container and the lighter cocoons (females) to continue on the belt.

Reeling

The unpierced cocoons, whose larvae have been killed, are used for reeling (the unwinding of the silk from the cocoons onto a winding frame). Once done by hand, today automatic reeling machines reel raw silk in the desired denier size directly off the required number of cocoons. For instance, to produce 20/22 denier raw silk, the machine will in one step combine the (approximately 3 denier) filaments of seven or more cocoons, more likely more because the denier drops as the cocoon is used up. Six to eight of these strands are attached to revolving reels that twist them into a stronger strand. The resultant yarn is the product of about forty-eight cocoons. This yarn is now ready for winding into skeins and packing into bales. In this condition, the thread is too thin and weak to be used without further twisting (throwing) and doubling into strands of varying thicknesses. Throwing increases the strength of a yarn. However, a silk thread need not necessarily be thrown to make a yarn for weaving, thus differing from wool and cotton, which must be spun and twisted.[4]

Yarns made of reeled-silk threads twisted together are called *thrown silk*. These yarns are wound on spools or in skeins, ready for the weavers. To facilitate handling, oils may be added to the gum weight by the throwster. Up to this point, silk is lusterless and harsh to the touch. This is because the gum is still in it. Silk in the gum is called *raw silk*. To make it soft and lustrous, it is boiled in soap and water until the gum is removed.

CHARACTERISTICS OF THE SILK

Microscopic Appearance

Under the microscope, cultivated silk fibers in the gum appear rough, like sticks of wood. Sometimes two fibers are held together by silk gum. After degumming, the fibers are structureless, transparent, and rodlike. The unevenness in diameter of the fibers distinguishes them from rayon. (See Appendix A.) Wild silk fibers are very irregular and resemble flattened, wavy ribbons with fine lines running lengthwise.

Length

The silk fiber ranges from 800 to 1,300 yards in length. This characteristic—great length—aids the manufacturer because he can easily combine a number of the filaments, which require little twist to give them strength. Also, long fibers make more lustrous yarns than do short fibers.

[4]*What Is Silk?*, a pamphlet of the International Silk Association.

Diameter

It is estimated that the diameter of silk fibers ranges from 0.00059 to 0.00118 inch. Finer fibers can be spun into finer yarns, and the resultant fabrics are sheer. Furthermore, many fibers can be combined in a fine yarn. The silkworm's fiber varies in diameter throughout its length, but the combination of several fibers to form a yarn equalizes the natural unevenness of the individual fibers.

Color of Fiber

Cultivated silks are yellow to grayish white in color. The color of the wild silk fiber is usually yellowish brown. The brown color is in the fiber itself, but the color of cultivated varieties is in the gum and so can be removed by washing.

Luster

Silk in the gum does not possess high luster, but after the gum has been removed silk has a soft, fine luster. This fact is important in the manufacture of satins, the beauty of which lies in unbroken sheen. Yarns of long reeled-silk fibers lie flat, lengthwise on the right side of the cloth, with only occasional interlacing with the filling or crosswise yarns.

Strength

Silk is one of the strongest of the textile fibers—that is, of fibers of the same diameter. Silk is often compared with iron wire of the same diameter. Although it has only about one-third the strength of good-quality iron wire, these fine fibers are very strong. Silk is weaker when wet than when dry, but like rayon, its original strength returns when it dries.

A silk fiber can sustain a dead weight of 5 to 28 grams before breaking. One silk filament is so strong that it will support the weight of a cocoon. However, hosiery made of silk snags if it is given a sudden, sharp pull. But silk will withstand even pulling better than it will a sudden, severe strain.

Elasticity

Silk is very elastic—more so than linen, rayon, or cotton. In fact, silk will stretch one-seventh to one-fifth of its length before breaking. Rayon and other man-made fibers will elongate, but they may not return to their original length. Therefore, silk weavers prefer all-silk warp yarn to a synthetic warp in Jacquard weaving, for in this weave warp yarns are subjected to stretching due to the pull exerted on the yarn. Silk, then, is resilient (elastic); synthetics elongate. Silk's elasticity means that no loose threads will be evident on the finished fabric. One of the first questions a silk weaver asks the synthetic yarn manufacturer is, "How much will the synthetic yarn elongate?" On the basis of elongation, a silk weaver can determine whether he can use the synthetic for warps. Garments made of silk keep their shape and do not wrinkle badly.

Hygroscopic Moisture

Silk absorbs about 10 percent of moisture. It has a higher average for absorptive quality than do cotton, linen, or rayon. The strange and important fact is that silk can absorb a great deal of moisture and still feel comparatively dry. Silk absorbs perspiration and oil from the skin, but it sheds dirt easily.

Composition

The chief constituents of silk are fibroin, the silk fiber, and sericin, the silk gum. Cultivated silk also contains small percentages of fats, waxes or resins, and mineral matter. The chemical constituents of fibroin are carbon (48.3 percent), hydrogen (6.5 percent), nitrogen (19.2 percent), and oxygen (26.0 percent).[5]

Effect of Light

Laboratory tests show that silk is not so resistant to strong light as cotton. There is a tendency for bright light to weaken silk. Accordingly, fabrics should be stored in a cool, dark place and should not be selected for curtains that are to have considerable light exposure. And yet, when damask draperies made of a combination of silk and cotton were removed from the White House in 1953, the silk was in about the same stage of deterioration as the cotton. In this instance, silk and cotton had about the same degree of resistance to light. Heavily weighted silks are less resistant to light than are pure silks.

Mildew

Mildew is seldom found on silk. It is relatively resistant to other bacteria and fungi. Rot-producing conditions will decompose silk.

Effect of Heat

White silks turn yellow after 15 minutes in an oven at 231°F. Cottons would not be affected at this temperature. Silk fabrics may turn yellow wth the use of too hot an iron. Silk scorches if heat exceeds 300°F. This factor is important to the tailor who uses a steam press and to the consumer when ironing.

Effect of Acids

Acids, such as sulfuric, hydrochloric, and nitric, do not injure silks if they are dilute. Silk is more resistant to acids than are the vegetable fibers, but concentrated acids destroy silk if it is soaked in them or if the acids are allowed to remain on the silk any length of time.

Formic acid and acetic acid (found in vinegar) have no injurious effect on

---

[5]George H. Johnson, *Textile Fabrics* (New York: Harper & Row Publishers, 1927), p. 64.

silks. Oxalic, tartaric, and citric acids are not injurious if they are removed promptly.

Effect of Alkalies

Concentrated solutions of alkali, such as caustic soda or caustic potash, dissolve silks if the solutions are hot.

Weak alkalies, such as ammonia, phosphate of soda, borax, and soap, attack silk more quickly than they attack cotton or linen. It is therefore advisable to use a mild soap with no alkalies for washing fine silk fabrics.

Action of Bleaches

Chlorine or hypochlorites are not used on silk, because of their deteriorating effect. Hydrogen peroxide and perborate bleaches are used when silk requires bleaching. Care should be taken to control bleaching conditions. Many popularly priced printed silks develop holes because acid bleaches are too strong.

Chloride salts in perspiration, in conjunction with deodorants, are one of the major causes of deterioration and destruction of dress silks, especially under the arms. (Underarm pads should be worn. A similar type of damage can result from spillage of foodstuffs or beverages that contain chloride salts. Remove staining as soon as possible; the longer the salts remain in the fabric, the greater the probability of severe weakening of the fabric.

Affinity for Dyestuffs

Silk has a natural affinity for dye. Probably the chief reason is that silk fiber has good penetrability. Basic, acid, and direct dyestuffs are all used on silks. But water-soluble dyes should be avoided in the selection of silk fabrics that may become wet with water or perspiration. Some dyes on silk bleed and even lose color with the application of any solution containing alcohol, such as perfume. The fabric should be dried before pressing. (For a description of these dyestuffs, see Chapter 8.) Cotton and linen do not have as good an affinity for dye as silk.

KINDS OF SILK YARNS

Reeled Silk[6]

Thrown Silk

This is a single yarn made of several strands of reeled silk twisted together.

Organzine

This is a ply yarn of raw silk used for warp where strength is required, as in upholstery, drapery fabric, or sheeting. The twist of the ply is in the reverse

[6]See page 282.

direction to that of the singles, to give additional strength and hold in the twist. Organzine yarn is made from the center section of the yardage reeled from the cocoon (500 to 1,000 yards).

Tram

This is also a ply yarn of raw silk generally used for filling. The twist of the singles and the final twist are in the same direction. This yarn has a higher luster because it has a slacker final twist than the organzine (about two and a half turns to the inch for tram and four and a half turns for organzine).

Douppion

Derived from the Italian word *doppione,* it means double. Two silkworms (regardless of sex) have an affinity for each other and want to stay together, so together they spin one cocoon. It is difficult to reel filaments evenly from these cocoons, so that a knotted yarn results. This textured yarn is particularly suited to fabrics such as shantung and some of the contemporary draperies and upholsteries. Douppion can also be made into spun-silk yarns.

Tussah

This is wild silk reeled from cocoons of uncultivated worms that have fed on oak leaves. These rough, yellowish brown fibers are made into tussah silk yarns.

Spun Silk

Before silk can be reeled from the cocoon, long, tangled ends must be removed so that an end can be found with which to start the reeling process. The tangled ends, called *floss,* are put aside because they cannot be reeled. Likewise, when most of the fiber has been reeled from a cocoon, there may be short lengths. Only about half the silk of a cocoon is fit to be reeled, but the rest cannot be wasted; it is made into spun silk. All floss and silk from pierced and defective cocoons appear in spun-silk yarns. Spun silk requires more twisting than does reeled silk, to hold in all the short fibers. Twisting decreases luster, so that spun silk appears less lustrous than reeled silk. It also has less tensile strength, less elasticity, and a rather linty, cottony feeling.

Spun silk is less expensive than reeled silk and is suitable for the crosswise or filling threads in a cloth. These threads do not have to be as strong as warp yarns. Plush, velvet, satin, lace, flat crepe, and silk broadcloth may have spun-silk yarns.

The silk to be used for this purpose is scoured, the gum is boiled off, and the fibers are dried. Then the fibers are combed to separate, straighten, and make them lie parallel. The filmy sheets of fibers are then drawn out between rollers several times. A slight twist is put in—called *roving.* A spinning frame, which winds and rewinds the yarn on spindles, puts in the twist. A tighter twist than that used for thrown silk is necessary.

Noil Silk

In the procesing of spun-silk yarn, there is a certain amount of waste called *silk noil*. According to the FTC Trade Practice Rules for the Silk Industry, such waste shall be labeled "silk noil," "noil silk," "silk waste," or "waste silk." Silk noil is used extensively for powder bags in artillery units. It can also be used in modern textured draperies and upholstery. Noil silk is dull, rough, and lifeless.

Identification of Reeled, Spun, and Noil Silk

Long fibers of reeled silk lie parallel and are only slackly twisted together. The yarns are lustrous, and the fibers shred apart. If the fibers are short and of uneven length, generally in dull yarns, the yarns are spun silk. If the yarns are coarse and very dull and if the fibers are very short and very uneven, the yarns are noil silk.

Chiffon crepes look dull and sometimes cottony, but that does not necessarily mean that yarns are of spun silk; rather, the tightness of the twist—made tight to produce fine crepe—has decreased the luster.

Weighted and Pure Silk

When yarns are prepared for weaving, the skeins of yarn are boiled in a soap solution to remove the natural silk gum, or sericin. The silk may lose 20 to 30 percent of its original weight as a result of boiling. Since silk has a great affinity for metallic salts, such as those of tin and iron, the lost weight used to be replaced through the absorption of metals or of tannin.

The burning test may be used to identify pure and weighted silk. If the yarns char but do not burn, they are weighted; if they burn slowly and leave a residue in the form of a gummy ball, they are pure silk.

Heavily weighted silk has been found to have disadvantages:

1. It does not wear as long as pure unweighted silk because sunlight and perspiration weaken and even destroy the fiber. Also, the long treatment of silk in the weighting process may have a weakening effect.
2. Heavily weighted silk causes the material to crack.
3. Silk can be weighted only about 1 percent at each application of weighting material; this makes the process costly.

Accordingly, the practice of weighting has virtually been discontinued. None is thought to be done in the United States, and little is believed to be done abroad. Nevertheless, the FTC has established rules for weighting that are still on the books, even though not of present concern.

A weighted silk must be labeled "weighted," with the amount of weighting indicated. A variation of five points from the stated percentage is tolerated to allow for unavoidable variations in processing, but not to allow for a lack of "reasonable effort to state the percentage of proportion accurately." For example, a weighted silk label may appear as "Silk, weighted 5 percent" or "Silk (weighted 25 percent) and rayon." The percentage of weighting may be disclosed as not over a certain percentage or as ranging from a certain minimum to a maximum figure.

Silk containing no metallic weighting may be called "pure silk," according to the FTC rules. The terms "all silk" or "pure dye silk" may also be used for fabrics whose fiber content is silk exclusively, with no metallic weighting. The rules for labeling and advertising as specified under the Textile Fiber Products Identification Act are required for silk textile fiber products. (See Chapters 2 and 10.) The FTC rules allow the finisher or the dyer to use special finishing materials, other than metallic weighting, that will make the fabric more useful— water-repellent finishes, for instance. The maximum percentage of the finishes present must be disclosed if such special finishing materials exceed 10 percent on colored fabrics and 15 percent on blacks.

Size of Silk Yarn

Sizes or counts of reeled-silk yarns, like rayon counts, are expressed in terms of denier.[7] There are several methods of computing denier, all differing slightly from that used for rayon. The International Denier method uses 500 meters of silk yarn, weighted with a 0.05-gram weight. If 500 meters weigh 0.05 gram, the yarn is #1 denier. If 500 meters weigh 1 gram, the denier is $1 \div 0.05$, or # 20.[8]

Spun-silk sizes are computed in two ways: by the English and French systems. The English system sets 840 yards as equal to 1 pound (the same as with cotton). The yarns are designated as 20/1 or 20/2, meaning 20 single- or 20 two-ply. In a pound size of 20/2 there are 840 yards times 20 or 16,800 yards. The French system uses as its base the number of 1,000-meter skeins weighing a kilogram.

WEAVING AND KNITTING SILK FABRICS

Plain Weave

No matter in what construction silk is used, the fabric appears attractive. In plain weave, silk apparel dress fabrics include habutai, shantung, flat crepe, crepe de Chine, taffeta, pongee, ninon, organza, chiffon, and broadcloth. For men's wear, there are silk broadcloth and habutai (shirtings). In ribbed variations, there are several fabrics for both men and women: faille, moiré faille, grosgrain, bengaline, rep, poplin, and ottoman. (See the glossary in Chapter 17.) For home furnishings, there are taffeta (pillow covers, bedspreads, and curtains); voile and ninon (glass curtains); and China silk, flat crepe, and pongee (lampshades).

---

[7]Legal denier: When the weight of 450 meters is 0.5 gram, the denier is #1.
[8]See "Tex" system, Chapter 3.

Twill Weave

There are not as many silk twills as there are satins or plain weaves, but the following twills are most common: silk serge, piqué, foulard, and surah. These fabrics can be used in dresses and in men's ties.

Satin Weave

Probably this is the most beautiful of the basic weaves to which silk is adapted. All varieties of satin, including dress, slipper, bridal, and upholstery satins, are made in this construction. Slipper and upholstery satins may have cotton backs. Antique satin has become very popular for draperies and upholsteries. Although this fabric is not always made of silk, some of the most beautiful and high-priced draperies are silk.

Fancy Weaves

Silk, because of its natural beauty, is particularly suited to the fancy constructions. Jacquards, such as brocades and damasks, make luxurious draperies for formal traditional living rooms. (See Chapter 21.) Lamé and brocade make exquisite evening gowns. Small dobby designs are found in silk scarfs, linings, and men's tie fabrics. In pile construction, silk velvet, velour, and brocaded velvet are always considered luxury fabrics. Silk pile rugs are museum pieces. The pile should never be ironed, to avoid flattening and damaging it.

Knitted Construction

Silk knitted jersey and bouclé are excellent fabrics for traveling because they are attractive and do not wrinkle when worn.

FINISHES OF SILK FABRICS

Some of the regular finishes applied to silk include the usual tentering and calendering (particularly for polished surfaces), dry decating to set the luster permanently, napping of spun silk to raise the fibers, shearing when needed to cut the surface fibers, and steaming to shrink and condition certain spun silks.

Silk fabrics may be treated for fire resistance to comply with the Flammable Fabrics Act. They may also be given germ-resistant, moth-resistant, permanent starchless, and water-repellent finishes.

Quick removal of stains is important as it avoids permanent yellowing, but stain removal should never be accomplished by rubbing. Blotting, followed by dry cleaning, is recommended.

BUYING POINTS OF SILK FABRICS

Beauty

No fabric is so luxurious in appearance as silk. It has a natural deep luster that makes it an aristocrat among textiles. Compare a Louis the Fifteenth chair covered in silk damask (woven in floral design) with a similar chair covered with wool damask in the same design. The silk covering has a regal look; the wool has a utilitarian look.

A silk dress, whether it is a shantung for sport or an organza for evening, looks dressy. Similarly, silk draperies are more luxurious than the average cotton, linen, or wool. Cotton draperies are particularly suited to informal rooms, whereas silks in varied textures are appropriate in any room except possibly the kitchen and the bathroom.

Since silk fiber has a good affinity for dye, the colors found in silks are innumerable.

Fabrics of wild silk and douppion silk appear rougher, often gummier, and less lustrous than the cultivated or mulberry silks. Crepes made with tight-twisted yarns are less lustrous than are satins made with loose-twisted yarns. Spun silks are soft, but are less lustrous than thrown silks.

Durability

Diametrically, silk is the strongest natural fiber. Thus, silk fabrics can be made durable. If silks are pure and unweighted, they will last for years, as is evidenced by the perfect preservation of many silks worn generations ago.

At present, weighted dress silks are not found in retailers' stocks in the United States. Spun silk has a lower tensile strength and lacks the elasticity of reeled silk. It has short fibers, which, although twisted tightly, may work themselves loose and make a fuzzy, rough, uneven surface. Noil silk is inferior to reeled or spun silk, but it has textural interest when used for draperies.

Comfort

Silk, like other animal fibers, is warmer than rayon, cotton, or linen of comparable weights. Because silk is very absorptive, silk fabrics, when they become drenched with perspiration, do not feel so damp and clammy as do fabrics made entirely of hydrophobic fibers. Hence, underwear and blouses are appropriately made of silk.

Silks can be woven of very fine yarns in open weaves, a fact that makes silk fabrics feel cool in summer. Organza, georgette, net, and chiffon are illustrations of sheer silk fabrics. Silk is lightweight, a factor in traveling comfort. (See Fig. 11.4.)

Because of its elasticity, silk can be made up into accordion pleats that hold creases. One designer of exclusive misses' dresses who has used a pleated skirt

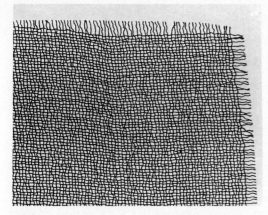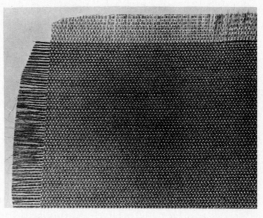

Figure 11.4 Left: Silk pongee, made from wild silk. Right: Silk chiffon, made from pure cultivated silk. (Photos by Jonas Grushkin.)

successfully found that, by starting the skirt's fullness below the hips, by pressing each pleat individually, and by stitching the pleats properly, the creases stayed. This same designer preferred silk and natural fibers for her line because they held their shape better. Pure silk ties also retain their shape better than do rayon or acetate ties. Silk dresses are very serviceable for traveling. They can be packed in a small space; in dark colors they do not show dirt; and wrinkles in silk crepes will hang out especially well.

Silk mixes easily with rayon, adding the elasticity that rayon lacks. It also mixes with nylon and with Orlon acrylic in shantung.

Suitability

The purposes for which silks are intended determine in a large measure the methods used in their manufacture. For example, long, reeled-silk fibers are used in fine silk yard goods, such as satins, crepe satin, and ribbons. Fine sewing thread is also made of reeled silk.

Silk thread comes in more than three hundred colors, so that fabrics can be matched easily. For sewing lustrous fabrics, silk thread should be chosen to match the luster of the fabric. All-silk or all-wool materials should be sewn with silk thread because silk and wool are animal fibers and so react similarly to laundering or dry cleaning. Silk threads make smooth, flat seams. Spun silk is suitable for knit goods, such as sweaters, hosiery, and underwear; for embroidery silk, braids, bindings, laces, crochet silk, and crepes; and for the pile of plushes, velvets, and velours.

Some yarns are twisted more tightly than others, according to the type of fabric in which they are to be used. Creped yarns used crosswise of the fabric are twisted forty to eighty turns to the inch. Silk creped fabrics include, among others, flat crepe, satin crepe, chiffon, and crepe faille.

Warp yarns—those running lengthwise—should have a very slack twist, so that fibers lie on the surface of the fabric and do not break the sheen. Dress satin, satin crepe, and satin linings are made this way.

Fabrics that have rather rough, bumpy surfaces, dull luster, and a gummy feeling may be made of wild silk. Shantung and pongee are examples.

Since wild silk cannot be made a snowy white and since it is rougher than cultivated varieties, its uses are limited more to sports fabrics, underwear, and draperies. For the latter use, it is desirable to line silk with silk or cotton material, because a lined drapery hangs better. The lining should be placed next to the glass.

Pongee and shantung may also be made of douppion silk. The fibers are very irregular and cannot be reeled in long, even filaments, but the irregularities of the fiber and resultant yarn make an interesting fabric quite suitable for modern textured draperies and for shantung. Douppion can be reeled or spun yarn.

Silk fabrics lend themselves to any style changes that may occur. At one time the mode for evening dresses may demand a firm fabric that can be tailored easily. In another season, evening dresses may be fluffy, ruffly creations. Silk faille, broadcloth, and shantung will suit the tailored mode, for these fabrics are dull, strongly constructed materials of plain weave. Chiffon and marquisette give the soft, fluffy, feminine effect. Organza gives a bouffant effect.

Since silk fits into the mode for both tailored garments and the more feminine frills, the consumer should select silk fabric with the purpose clearly in mind.

Silk has a wide variety of uses, especially in the apparel, drapery, and upholstery fields. There is not an hour of the day when a silk dress is not appropriate. A blended fabric, if predominantly silk, must be handled as carefully as a pure silk.

Sentiment

Silk, like linen, is sometimes purchased for reasons of sentiment. An old silk prayer rug may be bought because of associations it brings to mind or because of its rarity. Old silk damask hangings or silk laces may be bought for similar reasons. Works of art made of silk are bought by museums, collectors, and those who appreciate rare things. A living room may be furnished chiefly in silk damasks, satins, and brocades because its owner likes the elegance and luxury that silk reflects.

Price

If raw silk is selling at approximately $16 a pound and rayon yarn at 42 cents, one can see there is a tremendous difference between the price of a finished silk article compared with a finished rayon article. Thus, high price may be a buying point for the affluent.

While silk is more expensive than any other fiber, it can be used in less expensive ways if

1. Spun silk can be used in the filling of the fabric; reeled silk in the warp or vice versa.
2. Spun silk can be used entirely, instead of thrown silk.
3. Wild silk can be used instead of mulberry silk.
4. Rayon may be used one dimension of the fabric and silk the other.
5. Mercerized cotton can be used one dimension of the fabric and silk the other.
6. Spun douppion silk may be used one or both dimensions of the fabric.

Care of Silk Fabrics

Dry cleaning is generally to be preferred, since in laundering, detergents and dyes in other clothes may adversely affect the appearance of the silk. For goods with care labels attached, follow the instructions carefully. For certain small items without lining or other material attached, careful hand washing is permissible (with mild soap and lukewarm water). Chlorine bleach should never be used.

For long-time storage, silk should be sealed against light, air, and insects.

SUMMARY

Silk, as an animal fiber, is the product of two distinct varieties of silkworms: wild and cultivated. Wild silks, often called tussah silks, are gummy in feeling, dull in luster, and have rough, uneven yarns. From the cultivated silkworm's cocoon a fine, even, long fiber can be reeled.

There are several terms applying to raw or reeled silk that should be borne in mind. Raw silk is the fiber reeled in the gum from the unpierced cocoon.

Several strands of reeled silk are twisted together into a yarn called thrown silk. Two kinds of ply are made from the same yarn: a yarn for warps called organzine and a yarn for fillings called tram. Douppion silk comes from one cocoon spun by two silkworms. Yarns of douppion silk can be reeled or spun.

Spun-silk yarns are made from silk waste—the tangled fibers removed from the outside of the cocoon before the reeling, the short lengths of fibers from the inside of the cocoon, and the short fibers from the pierced cocoon. These fibers are usually twisted into yarn. They are duller in luster than reeled silk and weaker in tensile strength. Noil silk is the waste from spun-silk yarn manufacturing.

REVIEW QUESTIONS

1. What is the effect of the degumming process on the silk yarn?
2. (a) Explain the meanings of pure silk and weighted silk.
   (b) What effect has weighting on durability, versatility, launderability, comfort, and price?

    (c)   What is the FTC ruling on weighted silk?

    (d)   According to the TFPIA, how should an all-silk with no weighting be labeled?

3.   Describe the life cycle of the cultivated silkworm.

4.   What are the chief advantages of spun silk? the chief disadvantages? its principal uses?

5.   In what ways do the length and the fineness of silk fiber affect the appearance of the finished fabric?

6.   (a)   What are the chief characteristics of wild silk?

    (b)   What are the uses of wild silk?

7.   In what ways does the elasticity of silk fiber affect the finished cloth?

8.   (a)   What is the TFPIA regulation on labeling silk mixtures and blends?

    (b)   What is the FTC ruling on special finishing materials?

9.   Outline instructions for laundering a pure silk flat crepe.

10.   (a)   What texture in silk fabrics may become the matron with a mature figure?

    (b)   What texture in silks may the young high school girl with a slender figure wear?

11.   (a)   What factors should be considered in determining whether or not silk yarn is durable?

    (b)   How are sizes of silk yarns computed?

12.   By what methods can the cost of a silk fabric be lowered?

13.   Define the following: reeled silk, thrown silk, spun silk, wild silk, douppion silk, mulberry silk, weighted silk, tussah, chrysalis, noil silk, resilient silk, degummed silk, organzine, tram, raw silk.

EXPERIMENTS

1.   *Yarn tests.*

    (a)   Unravel silk yarns from each of five samples of silk material and place a few fibers of each under the microscope. Draw the fibers as you see them. Are the fibers mulberry silk or wild silk, silk in the gum or degummed silk? Give reasons for your answer.

    (b)   Burn yarns from each sample. Note the speed with which each yarn burns and describe the residue. Are the yarns weighted or pure silk? Give reasons for your answer.

    (c)   Unravel yarns from each sample. Do the fibers seem about the same length? Are they long and parallel, or are they of different lengths and not parallel? Are the yarns reeled or spun silk? Why?

2.   *Alkali test.* Prepare an alkaline solution of 10 percent sodium hydroxide. Boil a small piece of silk in this solution for 25 minutes. Note the results of strong alkali on silk.

3.   *Acid test.* Dip a few yarns or a piece of silk in concentrated sulfuric acid for 1 or 2 minutes. Wash the residue with water and dry it on a clean blotter. Note the results of concentrated acid on silk. What is the effect of acid on an animal fiber? What is the effect of acid on a vegetable fiber?

GLOSSARY

Antique satin   See the glossary in Chapter 21.

Antique taffeta   A taffeta often woven of douppion silk (see *shantung*) to resemble beautiful fabrics of the eighteenth century. It may be yarn-dyed with two colors to make an iridescent effect.

Canton crepe A fabric heavier than crepe de Chine with a slightly ribbed crepe filling. It was originally made of silk in Canton, China. It is also made of the man-made fibers.

Chiffon An extremely sheer, airy, soft silk fabric with a soft plain or rippled finish that is used for evening dresses and scarfs. It is made also in rayon and other man-made fibers.

Chiffon velvet A lightweight, soft, usually silk fabric with a dense pile.

Chrysalis The dormant silk larva within the cocoon.

Cocoon A covering of silk filaments extruded by the silkworm.

Crepe de Chine A very light, sheer flat crepe as now made. It was originally a pebbly, washable silk fabric, degummed after weaving.

Cultivated silk Fibers from a silkworm that has had scientific care.

Damask See the glossary in Chapter 10.

Douppion Silk from two silkworms that have spun one cocoon together.

Faille A soft, finely ribbed, glossy silk fabric. It may also be made in cotton or man-made fibers.

Flat crepe A firm silk crepe with a soft, almost imperceptible crinkle. See *crepe de Chine*. It may also be made of man-made fibers.

Floss silk Tangled silk waste. Floss is also a twisted silk yarn, used in art needlework.

Foulard A fine, soft twill-weave silk fabric, often printed—used for neckties and dresses. It may be made in mercerized cotton, rayon, acetate, or thin worsted.

Gauze A thin, sheer fabric in plain-weave silk, rayon, or other man-made fibers. It is used for curtains and trimmings of dresses. In cotton, gauze is used for surgical dressings.

Georgette A soft, sheer, dull-textured silk fabric with a crepy surface, obtained by alternating right-hand and left-hand twisted yarns.

Honan The best grade of Chinese silk; a finer weave but similar to pongee.

Lyons velvet A stiff, thick pile velvet; may be silk pile and cotton or rayon back. Lyons-type velvet may be 100 percent of man-made fibers.

Mousseline de soie (silk organdy) A very sheer, crisp silk fabric.

Noil silk Short fibers of waste silk produced in the manufacture of spun silk.

Organza A lightweight transparent fabric in plain weave of silk, rayon, nylon, or polyester with a crisp feel. Silk organza gains its crispness not by a finish but from the natural gum of the silk fiber left on the filament yarns.

Peau de soie (skin of silk) A reversible silk fabric in a variation of the satin weave with riblike fillings.

Piqué A silk, rayon, or cotton fabric with raised cords or wales. In true piqué the cords run crosswise, but most of the piqués are now made like Bedford cord with warpwise wales.

Pongee A light- or medium-weight Chinese silk fabric made from wild silk. See *tussah*.

Pupa See *chrysalis*.

Pure silk Silk containing no metallic weighting. It is synonymous with pure-dye silk. See *weighted silk*.

Raw silk Reeled silk wound directly from several cocoons with only a slight twist.

Reeling The process of unwinding silk from the cocoon onto silk reels.

Satin brocade A satin with a raised woven-in design. It resembles a fine embroidered pattern.

Satin fabric A shiny, smooth cloth in warp satin weave. It may be made of acetate, rayon, or synthetic blends or mixtures.

Scroop   The rustle of crisp silk. See *taffeta*.

Serge   Twilled silk or rayon commonly used for linings. It is also made of worsted.

Sericin   Silk gum extruded by the silkworm; it holds fibers together.

Sericulture   See *silk culture*.

Shantung   A silk fabric with a nubby surface similar to but heavier than pongee. It was originally woven of wild silk in Shantung, China. Now made of almost any fiber, blend, or mixture.

Silk   The natural fiber that a silkworm spins for its cocoon.

Silk broadcloth   A soft spun-silk fabric in plain weave, used for shirts, blouses, and sports dresses.

Silk culture   The care of the worm that produces silk fibers, from the egg to the moth.

Silk illusion   A net similar to tulle but even finer in mesh, used primarily for bridal veils.

Spun silk   Either yarn or fabric made from short silk fibers that cannot be reeled.

Surah   A soft fabric, usually in a variation of a twill with a flat top wale (sometimes described as a satin-faced twill). It is used for neckties, mufflers, dresses, and blouses, is made in plaids, stripes, or prints, and is also made of man-made fibers.

Taffeta   A fine yarn-dyed, plain-weave fabric (closely woven) with a crisp feel. The rustle of silk taffeta is called *scroop*. It is also made in rayon and other man-made fibers.

Throwing   See the glossary in Chapter 3.

Tissue taffeta   A crisp, lightweight taffeta.

Tulle   A very soft, fine, transparent silk net used for evening dresses and veiling. It may also be made of nylon or rayon.

Tussah silk   Fibers from the wild silkworm. Tussah is strong but coarse and uneven. Its tan color is difficult to bleach. Used in shantung and pongee.

Weighted silk   Fabric in which metallic salts have been added in the dyeing and finishing to increase its weight and to give a heavier hand. FTC ruling requires weighted silk to be marked and the amount of weighting indicated.

Wild silk   See *tussah silk*.

Chapter 12

WOOL AND THE CONSUMER

HISTORY OF WOOLEN CLOTH

The herding of flocks of sheep was one of the earliest stages of man's cultural development between barbarism and civilization. In the Old Testament of the Bible, we read of sheep wandering "through all the mountains and upon every high hill." History records that in the fourth century B.C., when Alexander the Great conducted an expedition to India, he found that natives were wearing wool cloth. In A.D. 50, an Italian took sheep from Italy to Spain to be crossbred with the Spanish variety—the *Merino*. In the thirteenth century, Spain was producing fine wool cloth. Later, France, Saxony, Germany, England, Austria, South America, South Africa, and New Zealand imported the Spanish Merino for breeding. Beginning in 1810, Australia showed the best results in raising this variety of sheep. England was the only country that was unsuccessful; English sheep were primarily raised for mutton, and crossbreeding for the fleece-wool variety was not satisfactory. The United States imported Spanish sheep about 1810. They were first raised along the Atlantic seaboard. Later, sheep raising spread westward. In the Ohio Valley, the Merinos were crossbred with native sheep, with good results. The wool produced is called Ohio Delaine, and the fibers are the best quality of merino wools produced in this country.

WOOL PRODUCTION

Merino wools come from Australia, South Africa, and South America. The best come from Australia (the world's largest wool producer), because better care is given the sheep there than in other places. The Australians use what is known as the *paddock system*, where the sheep are allowed to graze in large enclosed areas called paddocks.

Merino wool has shorter fibers than does wool from native English sheep. Lincolnshire and Leicestershire raise the longest wool fiber. Carpet or braid wools are very coarse; they come from Turkey and Argentina.

The wool produced in the United States is classified according to the region in which the sheep are raised: (1) *domestic* wools, from the eastern and middle western states; (2) *territory* wools, from the Rocky Mountain Plateau states; and (3) *southwestern* wools, from Texas, New Mexico, Arizona, and southern California.

The domestic wools are softer and finer than the territory wools. The southwestern states mentioned are great sheep-raising states but, since they usually shear their sheep twice a year, their wools are not classified as domestic or territory wools, which are usually clipped once a year. Texas wools have become finer and are more nearly like the Merino. Boston is the largest wool port in this country and, along with Philadelphia and New York, is a big wool marketing center. Since we cannot supply enough wool to meet domestic demands, we must import large quantities from abroad. In fact, all our carpet wool is imported.

Sheep raising in the United States has declined more than 60 percent between 1960 and 1981 for the following reasons:[1]

1. Man-made fibers are replacing wool for both clothing and carpeting.
2. The cost of sheep raising in this country is high in comparison with costs in competing foreign countries. This is due not only to wages; it also includes competing for what was once grazing land and the loss of young sheep to predators, especially coyotes. It is estimated by the U.S. Department of Agriculture that coyotes kill 8 to 10 percent of the sheep population. The use of poison, the most effective way of reducing the coyote population, has been banned, and other methods have not been successful.

As Table 12.1 indicates, the world production of wool has changed little. Since population is growing rapidly and costs of production increasing, it is not surprising that wool is in relatively scarce supply.

The largest producing countries are Australia and New Zealand, which together account for nearly 40 percent of the world's production; the Soviet Union with about 18 percent; followed by China with 7 percent. About 76 percent of the entire production goes into the apparel market, with the rest to carpeting and other household and industrial products.

While for many years Great Britain has not been a major producer of wool, it has a large woolen and worsted weaving industry, making the finest materials in the world for suitings and overcoats, such as Huddersfield worsteds. Sales to the United States have been curtailed by a 50 percent duty, but one of the largest British producers—Illingworth, Morris—is opening a mill in the United States.

---

[1]See "Coyotes," *The New York Times*, March 28, 1982, p. 20.

Table 12.1 World Production of Raw Wool, 1960–1982p
(million kg)

	1960/61	1970/71	1976/77	1977/78	1978/79	1979/80	1980/81	1981/82p
Greasy basis								
Argentina	195	200	182	175	173	166	163	165
Australia	737	891	703	677	706	713	700	711
Brazil	23	32	25	24	25	29	30	30
Bulgaria	21	29	34	34	35	35	36	36
Chile	22	22	19	19	19	20	21	22
China	. .	. .	130	132	136	153	176	189
France	26	20	22	22	23	24	24	24
Greece	11	8	9	9	9	9	10	10
India	35	33	35	35	35	35	35	35
Iran	31	37	30	30	30	30	30	30
Iraq	13	16	18	18	18	18	18	18
Irish Republic	11	10	9	9	9	8	8	8
Italy	15	12	12	12	12	12	13	13
Lesotho	3	4	2	3	2	2	3	3
Morocco	15	18	21	21	21	21	22	22
New Zealand	267	334	303	311	321	357	381	375
Pakistan	20	20	31	33	36	39	43	46
Peru	10	13	11	11	11	11	11	11
Portugal	11	14	10	10	9	9	9	9
Romania	22	30	32	35	36	37	38	39
South Africa	144	123	111	114	109	111	112	116
Soviet Union	352	419	436	459	467	472	462	454
Spain	38	34	29	28	29	29	28	29
Turkey	47	47	54	55	57	59	60	61
United Kingdom	55	46	48	46	49	48	52	51
United States	147	85	53	51	47	48	49	51
Uruguay	82	78	64	62	64	72	75	72
Yugoslavia	14	12	10	10	10	10	10	10
Other	189	221	220	224	237	241	247	246
Total	2,556	2,808	2,663	2,669	2,735	2,818	2,866	2,886
Clean basis								
Merino	560	610	619	621	626	628	619	621
Crossbred (mainly apparel)	627	714	473	474	498	529	546	551
Other (mainly carpet type)	293	298	402	403	414	430	449	453
Total	1,480	1,622	1,494	1,498	1,538	1,587	1,614	1,625

Source: the Wool Bureau, Inc.

Grading for Marketing

For marketing purposes, wool is classified as Merino (full-blood) and crossbreed. The latter are graded as three-fourths blood, one-half blood, three-eighths blood, and one-fourth blood, depending upon the proportion of Merino blood in the sheep producing the wool. To provide a more exact measure, there are also grades of fineness from under 40 for coarse wool to as high as 80 for very fine wool. The standard for full-blood is 64, with crossbreed lower. For example, three-eighths blood is graded from 50 to 58.

Sheepshearing

Most sheep are shorn in the spring in the northern hemisphere and in our fall in the southern hemisphere. Formerly, wool was clipped from the sheep's body by hand, but now as many as two hundred sheep can be clipped in one day by machinery. In the United States, the fleeces clipped from sheep are usually all one piece. In Australia, separate fleeces are taken from the same animal—that is, fleece from the belly is kept separate from fleece from the sides. The Australian method is the better, because different grades of wool come from the same sheep. The fleece of the head, belly, and breech is inferior to fleece from the shoulders and sides of the sheep.

Fleece Wool versus Pulled Wool

The wool shorn from the live sheep is termed *fleece wool*. It is usually marketed to wool buyers before washing or scouring. Some sheep die from disease or are slaughtered. Their skins are wetted, treated with lime paste, and then "sweated." The fibers can then be pulled easily from the skin. This class of wool is called *pulled wool*. It is not so good a grade as fleece wool, but pulled wool can be blended with noils (short fibers separated from the long by combing) and with recycled wool used in inexpensive suitings and blankets.

Sorting and Grading

Wool is graded by individuals who have developed an extremely keen sense of touch; they grade wool according to the fineness of the individual fibers. Each fleece is graded according to what the grader believes the majority of the fibers to be. The sorter shakes out each fleece and separates fibers from different parts of the body. The wool is then ready for the worsted or woolen goods manufacturer.

Australian wool is delivered to manufacturers sorted and graded. Actually, Australia uses some five thousand classifications for grading. This practice lowers conversion costs.

The U.S. Department of Agriculture, in cooperation with experiment stations, is promoting the sorting and grading of our domestic wool before it is delivered to the manufacturer. It is felt that this will help the wool growers to get a better price for their product. The department has set up standards for grading wool by fineness of diameters of wool fiber and "wool tops" (long combed slivers). The method followed is that prescribed by the American Society for Testing Materials (ASTM Designation D472-50T, issued 1947, revised 1950). Effort is being made to grade wool in the grease (before it is scoured) by this method.

A SUMMARY OF THE WOOL PRODUCTS LABELING ACT

The Federal Trade Commission's regulations (amended as of 1980), based on the Federal Wool Products Labeling Act (effective in 1941), specify that any wool product made either wholly or partly of wool that is entering, or is likely to enter, interstate commerce must carry a label[2] that displays the type of wool in the product and the percentage of the type of wool to the entire weight of the product. Two types of wool are recognized: new wool and recycled wool. (See Fig. 12.1.)

Wool (also called new wool, virgin wool, all wool, or 100 percent wool) is a fleece shorn from a sheep or lamb and also includes mohair (hair of the Angora goat), cashmere from the Kashmir goat, and the hairs of the following: camel, alpaca, llama, and vicuña that are being used for the first time in the manufacture of a wool or of a part-wool product. The names of the specialty fibers given above may be used in lieu of the term "wool," provided that the percentages by weight of each of the named specialty fibers present are displayed.

Recycled wool consists of the subtypes that need not appear on the label: *reprocessed* wool and *reused* wool.

Reprocessed wool has been previously made into woven or felted fabric and then reclaimed into fibrous form but has never been used by the ultimate consumer. Cuttings from garment manufacturers' workrooms are a major source. *Reused wool* is the resultant fiber when wool has been woven, knitted, or felted into a wool product that has been used by the ultimate consumer and subsequently reclaimed into a fibrous state. The process of conversion to fiber includes cleaning the used article and putting it through a garnetting machine that passes the material through rollers with wires that break up the material into fiber form.[3]

---

[2]The TFPIA specifies that any product composed in whole or in part of wool or furs must be labeled by reference to the respective regulations on wool and furs issued under the Wool Products Labeling Act or the Fur Products Labeling Act, respectively.

[3]There is an odd anomaly in the definitions of reprocessed and reused wool. Reprocessed wool covers only the woven and felted material but reused wool covers knitted goods also. Thus, knitted goods and yarn that have never been used by the ultimate consumer and are then reclaimed into a fibrous state may be classified as wool rather than recycled wool.

PURE WOOL

Figure 12.1 The woolmark label is your assurance of quality-tested products made of the world's best . . . Pure Wool. (Reproduced courtesy of the Wool Bureau.)

The percentage of wool or recycled wool must always appear on the label, but less than 5 percent of other fibers present in a product may normally be labeled as "Other Fibers." The regulations of the FTC under both the Wool Products Labeling Act and the Textile Fiber Products Identification Act also contain special regulations involving wool products such as labeling unknown fibers used in production and fabrics with different fibers in various parts of a garment such as in linings, padding and stiffening, and in the pile. If a fabric has fiber ornamentation (stripe or woven figure, for instance) not exceeding 5 percent of the total fiber weight of the product, a phase such as "exclusive of ornamentation" must follow the statement of the fiber content. Should the fiber ornamentation exceed 5 percent the percentage must be included in the percentage statement of the fiber content. A label might read: "50% wool/25% rayon/25% cotton (exclusive of ornamentation)." (See Fig. 12.2.)

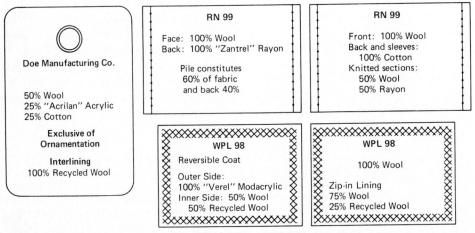

Figure 12.2 Examples of wool labels approved by the FTC.

In addition to the required fiber information on the label, the name of the manufacturer, the distributor, or the registered number of the manufacturer or distributor must appear; also the country of origin if imported. The retailer may substitute his own label, revealing, instead of the manufacturer's name, the name under which he does business. He may employ a word or trademark or housemark for this purpose if it has been registered with the U.S. Patent Office and if, prior to use, the FTC is furnished a copy of the registration. The retailer can secure a guarantee from the manufacturer that a specific wool product is not misbranded under the provisions of the act, or the retailer may secure a continuing guarantee filed with the Federal Trade Commission that will be applicable to all wool products handled by a guarantor. These guarantees must conform to the rules and regulations of the Commission. Such guarantees between manufacturer and retailer must be made in good faith.

Since the wool labeling law pertains to sales of wool products in interstate commerce, every retailer must actively and intelligently comply with its requirements. Manufacturers, wholesalers, retailers, and consumers have a common interest in maintaining truthful merchandising practices.

The improper use of the term "virgin wool" on tags and labels and in advertising of fabrics represents a deception of the consumer and therefore, under provisions of the Wool Products Labeling Act, constitutes an offense subject to corrective measures.

The consumer should bear in mind that this act is intended to inform him of the exact fiber content of a fabric containing wool from which garments are made. The consumer must also realize that the presence of recycled wools does not necessarily make a fabric inferior in quality. The grade of the fabric depends upon the *quality* of the recycled wool. Sometimes a mixture of new wool with recycled wool is like a metal alloy—particularly strong and durable for the purpose for which it was made. In other cases, the use of recycled wool does not have the effect of a strengthening agent, but makes it possible for a manufacturer to sell a garment at a price that would be impossible if first-grade new wool were used. The fact that a garment is labeled recycled wool doesn't mean that the consumer is not getting service commensurate with what he pays for the garment. Labels are merely a guarantee as to the history of the fiber content, not the quality of the fabric.

CHARACTERISTICS OF THE WOOL FIBER

Microscopic Appearance

Under the microscope, a wool fiber resembles a worm with horny scales. Wool fiber consists of three parts: (1) the medullary, (2) the cortex, and (3) the outside scales. (See Figs. 12.3 (a) and (b).) The medullary is a honeycombed cellular section found in medium and coarse wools. Not all wool fibers have a medulla, and it is not necessary to the growth of the fiber. Its chief function seems to be

. . . encasing imbricated (overlapping) outer layer

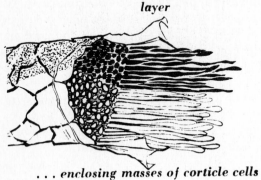

. . . enclosing masses of corticle cells

Figure 12.3a Top: Outerlayer of wool fiber; microscopic view. Bottom: Enclosing masses of corticle cells. (Courtesy of the Wool Bureau.)

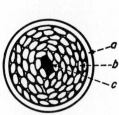

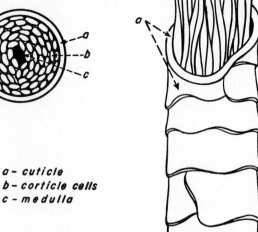

a – cuticle
b – corticle cells
c – medulla

Figure 12.3b Elements of the wool fiber. (Courtesy of the Wool Bureau.)

"to increase the protective properties of the fiber by adding internal air spaces."[4] The cortex consists of cortical cells that are really bundles of fibrils.[5] The outside scales have a protecting membrane called the *cuticle*. The scales overlap, and their free ends point toward the tip of the fiber. Hence, the scales are partially responsible for the wool fiber's slipping and sliding more easily toward the root of the fiber. On the other hand, materials coming in contact with the fiber slip more easily toward the tip of the fiber. This difference in friction on a sheep's back causes burrs and dust particles to work their way out of the wool. This same frictional difference is a factor in giving wool its felting quality. When wool is wet, the fibers move and entangle as the wet cloth is manipulated mechanically (chemicals may or may not be used to cause felting). Excessive shrinkage occurs when felting is not controlled. See *shrinkage control of wool*, pp. 319–20, and Chapter 7, *Finishes*.

Length of Fiber

Wool fibers range from 1 to 14 inches in length, depending on the kind of sheep and the part of the sheep from which the wool is taken. Wool is a comparatively short natural fiber and is surpassed in length by silk and linen. The shorter fibers are used chiefly in woolens, and the longer ones are used primarily in worsteds. Fibers used for worsteds average 3 to 8 inches in length, whereas those used for woolens are 1 to 3 inches (usually 2 inches or less).

Diameter

The average wool fiber is coarser than rayon, silk, linen, or cotton fibers. The approximate diameter of wool fiber is 0.0005 to 0.0015 inch. Therefore, wool yarns are ordinarily not so fine as other textiles.

Color of Fiber

Wool fibers range in color from whitish to gray, brown, and sometimes black. The color pigment is distributed through cells in the cortex and medulla. As in the case of human hair, it is easy to dye the scales and the cortex, but the dye rarely penetrates the medulla. Bleaching has a similar effect, although for all practical purposes, bleaching with peroxide is permanent. Black sheep's wool cannot be bleached white.

Luster

Luster of wool will vary according to the origin and breed of the sheep and with climate. The luster is higher in poor-quality wools than in good grades. A poor-grade serge suit is more shiny when purchased and will show a greasy shine

[4]Werner Von Bergen and Herbert Mauersberger, *American Wool Handbook,* 2nd ed. (New York: Textile Book Publishers, Inc.), pp. 133–34.

[5]The nucleus at the center of each cortical cell is a granular structure. The electron microscope reveals still finer filaments than fibrils, called microfibrils; ibid., p. 130.

more quickly than will a better-grade serge. Although luster is temporarily removed by a sponging with an ammonia solution, the shine will return. Dull wools are better buys in the long run with one exception—broadcloth, which is purposely steam-lustered in the finishing process to increase the luster and lay the nap.

Strength

A single wool fiber can sustain a dead weight of 15 to 30 grams. A silk fiber will break at 5 to 28 grams. But although wool fiber seems stronger than silk according to these figures, the diameters of the two fibers are usually quite different. Wool fiber is coarser than silk, so it is logical to expect greater tensile strength from wool; but if five of the major fibers of equal diameter are compared, nylon ranks first, silk second, wool third, and then rayon and cotton. There are so many different grades of each fiber that it is difficult to generalize.

Wool is stronger dry than wet. Vegetable fibers, with the exception of rayon, are stronger when wet. Rayon's wet strength has been improved appreciably through improved manufacturing techniques utilizing modern processing technology.

Elasticity or Resilience

Wool is the most elastic of the natural fibers. It stretches 25 to 35 percent of its length before breaking.

Wool fiber possesses crimp or wave, the amount of crimp varying with the fineness of the fibers from almost no crimp to 22 to 30 crimps per inch.[6] The finer fibers have a pronounced crimp. This characteristic crimp causes wool fibers to repel each other when in fabrics. When a wool fiber is stretched, the crimp comes out, but when the fiber is released, the crimp returns—the fiber springs back. If masses of wool fibers are pressed together, they spring apart as soon as pressure is released. This quality is called resilience or elasticity. It is very important in wrinkle resistance and insulation of wool. Resilience is also a factor in tailoring. Wool tailors easily because it is a "live" fiber. Furthermore, it is easily shaped and steamed while parts of the garment are being put together.

Insulation Value

Heat conductivity and insulation are not the same, although the terms are related. The insulation value of a fabric depends on the amount of air enmeshed within the fabric and on its surface. The actual heat conductivity of the enmeshed or trapped air is important, rather than that of the fibers themselves. Trapped air is a nonconductor of heat. In wool fabrics, because of their porosity and the fact that by nature wool fibers stay apart (repel each other), about 80

---

[6]Giles E. Hopkins, *Wool as an Apparel Fiber* (New York: Holt, Rinehart and Winston, 1953), p. 9.

percent of the entire fabric volume is air.[7] The air held closely against the fiber surfaces prevents heat loss by the body, thus keeping the body warm. Even when the wool is wet, its resilience remains, so its insulating trapped air remains. Hence, the wearer of wet wool garments does not chill suddenly.

Furthermore, a loosely twisted woolen yarn with varied lengths of nonparallel fibers can enmesh more still air than can a worsted yarn with its long parallel fibers held in the yarn by twist. A porous plain weave would also serve to create air pockets. Woolen yarns, with their resilient fibers of varied lengths, lend themselves to napping, and napped fibers of varied lengths create more air pockets. Not only the repellence of fiber to fiber and resilience of the fiber, but also the type of yarn, weave, and finish are factors in heat conductivity.

Microscopic Moisture

Wool has a high absorptive quality, but it absorbs moisture in the form of water vapor very slowly. Observation of liquid spilled on wool garments shows that, if the surface is slanted, the liquid runs off, but if horizontal, the liquid is absorbed very slowly. Wool is naturally water-repellent, because the membrane protecting the scales is nonprotein, so that liquid water is not attracted to the fiber's surface. However, water vapor can penetrate the fiber's interior, which has a strong affinity for moisture. This quality of wool explains why wool garments can absorb body moisture in the form of water vapor without feeling damp. This moisture from the body is then released to the atmosphere slowly, so that the body is not chilled.

Although wool can absorb a great deal of moisture, it does so slowly, and it dries more slowly than does silk or linen. Wool can absorb much moisture before it feels damp.

Composition of Fiber

Wool is the only fiber containing sulfur. Its chemical composition is carbon, hydrogen, nitrogen, oxygen, and sulfur. The wool fiber is composed of animal tissues, which are classed as a protein called *keratin*.

Effect of Light

Laboratory tests show that raw wool is about as resistant to light as cotton or jute. Dyed wool, used in woolen suits and hats, does not seem to lose as much strength in the same test.

Mildew

Wool is attacked by mildew only if the fabric has remained damp for some time. Mildew-resistant processes may be applied in finishing wool goods.

[7]Ibid., p. 67.

Effect of Acids

Dilute acids, even if boiling, do not injure wool. Highly concentrated acids, such as sulfuric, hydrochloric, and nitric, will destroy wool if the fabric is soaked in them for more than a few minutes or if the acid is allowed to dry in the fabric. Often raw wool is treated with dilute sulfuric acid to remove any vegetable matter, such as burrs, from the fibers. Formic and acetic acids are not detrimental to wool. Oxalic, tartaric, and citric acids are not injurious if the acid is not allowed to dry on the cloth. In fact, formic, acetic, oxalic, tartaric, and citric acids are less injurious than dilute sulfuric, hydrochloric, or nitric acids, given equal concentration.

Effect of Alkalies

Weak alkalies such as ammonia, borax, phosphate of soda, and soap are not injurious to wool if care is taken to keep the temperature below 68° F. But boiling in a 5 percent solution of caustic soda (lye) for 5 minutes will completely disintegrate wool. Wool is sensitive to alkalies; therefore, the use of neutral soaps with no free alkali is advised.

Effect of Bleaches

Chlorine bleach is ordinarily harmful to wool. The use, in the past, of a form of chlorine to shrinkproof or feltproof wool was very unsatisfactory, because it caused loss of strength and elasticity. Furthermore, fabrics so treated would still felt, and they did not have the durability of untreated wool. Now, however, the use of a chlorinating agent can be satisfactorily controlled so that shrinkage is prevented.

Potassium permanganate, sodium peroxide, and hydrogen peroxide are used for bleaching and removing some kinds of stains.

Affinity for Dyestuffs

Wool has a good affinity for dyestuffs. Its chemical structure enables the fiber to unite chemically with a wide variety of dyestuffs. Acid or basic dyes, chromes, indigo, and even vat types can be used for wool. Selected basic dyes can be used for dyeing wool and acrylic fiber blends and mixtures, but the cationic dyes, developed especially for acrylics, are better.[8] Deep rich colors and pale pastels are possible because of the wool fiber's affinity for dye.

Moth Damage to Wool

The larva of the clothes moth feeds on wool. The female moth lays eggs in a dark spot such as the nap of a wool sweater, blanket, or rug. The moth larvae first eat the nap and then the ground yarns in a fabric.[9] Washing will kill moths and

---

[8]*Textile World*, Vol. 112 (April 4, 1962), p. 82.
[9]*Fabric Care*, International Fabricare Institute, October 1982, pp. 1–2.

eggs. A reinfestation may be prevented by sealing the washed article in paper or cellophane. Mothproofing techniques are described in Chapter 7.

MANUFACTURE OF WORSTED YARNS

Wool fibers can be manufactured into two kinds of cloth: worsteds and woolens. (See Figs. 12.4 and 12.5.) Worsteds are characterized by smooth surfaces, and they are harder to the touch than woolens. The weave or pattern is clearly visible in worsteds, and for this reason they are described as *clear finished*.

Worsteds are made from long wool fibers, usually 2 to 8 inches in length. The English-type wools are often imported for worsted manufacture.

Sorting

When wool reaches the mill it is sorted; this process has been described earlier in the chapter.

Opening

After sorting, the wool is put through a machine, called an *opener* or *breaker*, containing a tooth cylinder, the purpose of which is to remove all loose dirt and sand and to separate the whole fleece into small sections.

Scouring

Since wool contains grease, dirt, and other substances, the fibers must be washed or scoured. A mild alkaline solution of soap or soda ash is the more common method of removing grease and swint (perspiration). Other methods include *swint washing* (wool is steeped in water, and the swint liquor, after removal of sand and dirt, is used for scouring); solvent scouring (with white spirit and chlorinated hydrocarbons) followed by water; refrigeration processing (wool grease is frozen and removed as powder by treatment in a dusting machine); and scouring by using soda ash to remove free fatty acid oils and an emulsifier and synthetic detergent to remove mineral oils.

Wool Drying

The wet scoured wool is dried in a machine that provides a gentle flow of air and heat.

Carding

The carding of wool is similar to the carding of cotton. Large revolving cylinders with wire teeth all running at different speeds lay the fibers in a filmy sheet that is condensed into a large round, open rope or sliver. Carding partially straightens the wool fibers and lays them in one direction. The carded wool sliver is then made even.

Figure 12.4 The worsted process. "Bradford" yarn has largely been replaced in the United States by "American ring system" which is faster and abbreviated over the "Bradford system." "French yarn" is also declining in use in favor of the "American." (Reproduced courtesy of Industrial By-Products & Research Corp.)

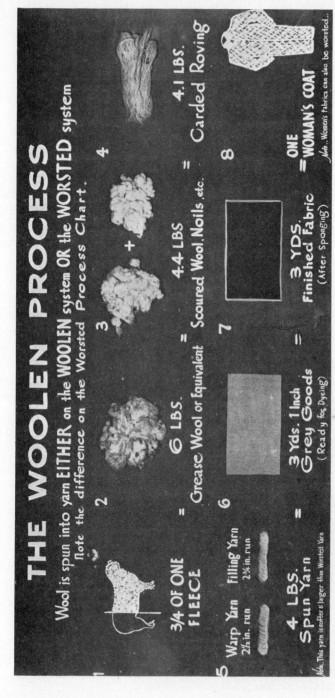

Figure 12.5 The woolen process. Even though it takes the fleece of more than one sheep to produce a man's worsted suit, with the woolen process, it requires the fleece of only three-fourths of a sheep to produce one women's coat. (Reproduced courtesy of Industrial By-Products & Research Corp.)

Combing

Worsted cloths show the woven pattern clearly, so that any unevenness in the yarn is noticeable in the finished cloth. The carded slivers are run through a combing operation to (1) remove the short fibers from the sliver, (2) straighten the remaining fibers and make them parallel, and (3) remove any foreign matter, such as straw, burrs, or dirt. Combing adds to cost but is essential if felting is not desired.

The short fibers are called *noils*—corresponding with *tow* in linen. The long fibers lying parallel in the sliver are called *tops*. (See specifications and methods of test for determining fineness of wool tops, page 301.)

Slivers of tops are combed and drawn out. This drawing process is called *drafting*. Slivers are drawn out narrower and narrower until the desired thickness is reached. A sufficient twist is put in to prevent further drafting (*drawing*). The combed top can now be dyed, because the color can penetrate through the fibers at this point in the process better than it can after the cloth is woven.

Spinning

Spinning puts in the required twist. Spools holding slivers are arranged horizontally to revolve on a frame. From these spools the slivers are carried to another series of spools, arranged vertically on another frame. The speed and tension of winding are so regulated as to twist the yarn as it is wound from one spool to the other. Worsted yarns are usually more tightly twisted than woolen yarns. (See Fig. 12.6.) The yarns are sold to the weavers on these spools, or in skeins or hanks.

Figure 12.6 Photomicrograph of woolen (bottom) and worsted (top) yarns. (Photo courtesy of the Wool Bureau.)

Twisting

Twisting is spinning two, three, or four yarns together (plies). Two-ply yarns are generally used for weaving and machine knitting, and three- and four-ply yarns are sold for hand knitting.

Reeling

Worsted yarns are then reeled into skeins.

Inspection

Inspecting the skeins and putting them into bundles of about 40 pounds each completes worsted yarn manufacture.

Sizes or Count of Worsted Yarns

The size of worsted yarns is determined by the number of hanks of 560 yards weighing 1 pound. If one 560-yard hank weighs 1 pound, the count or size is #1. If 5,600 yards weigh 1 pound, the count is #10, and so on. Yarns numbered 5s to 10s are very coarse and are used for heavy sweaters; 10s to 30s are medium; 40s to 60s are fine. Worsted yarns are two-ply, three-ply, and four-ply as well as single. (See the "Tex" system, Chapter 3.)

Quality of Worsted Yarn

The quality of worsted yarn depends on the grade of the fibers used, the amount of carding and combing, the skill applied to these operations, and the regularity of the spinning.

Fabrics made of worsted yarn include tropical worsted, unfinished worsted, worsted flannel, worsted cheviot, worsted covert, sharkskin, and gabardine.

MANUFACTURE OF WOOLEN YARNS

Selecting the Fiber

Fibers averaging less than 2 inches in length are customarily selected for woolen yarns. Short-fiber Merino wool is especially good. Since the beauty of a woolen lies in its softness and warmth, this type of cloth lends itself more to adulteration than does worsted. The woven pattern is usually indistinct and often obliterated. The felting, or shrinking, of wool goods after they are woven makes it possible to conceal many varieties of fibers.

For woolen yarns, then, short fibers of new or virgin wool can be used; if any recycled wool is used, the percentage by weight must appear on the label.

Processes Preliminary to Carding

The processes of preparing wool for carding are similar to those used in preparing wool to make worsted yarn.

Carding

The purpose of carding woolen yarn is to make it fuzzy enough to allow a nap to be raised later. The process is more violent than that used for worsteds; rollers with wire teeth revolve in opposite directions, whereas for worsteds they revolve in the same direction. Woolen yarn may be carded several times, but it is not combed since felting is desired. Short fibers are not taken out of the sliver as they are for worsted yarn. Like worsted yarn, it is drawn out and twisted. Woolen yarn has a slacker twist than worsted yarn. (See Fig. 12.6.) It is then wound on bobbins and rewound on spools or made into skeins. Woolen yarn may be dyed before it is woven, and when that is done the cloth is said to be yarn-dyed. Sometimes the wool stock is dyed before carding. In this way it is possible to produce heather and melange effects.

Size or Count of Woolen Yarns

There are two methods of computing sizes of woolen yarn: one method, the American *run count*, is discussed here. If 1,600 yards weigh 1 pound, the count or size is #1. This yarn is very coarse and is used for overcoats and blankets; #3 and #4 yarns are medium; and #6½ to #10 yarns are fine. (See "Tex" system, Chapter 3.)

Fabrics made of woolen yarn include homespun, tweed, wool flannel, wool cheviot, wool covert, wool shetland, and wool broadcloth.

WOOL BLENDS

Wool fibers are often mixed, or blended, with other natural or man-made fibers. This may have two advantages: (1) the second fiber is usually less expensive than wool, thus reducing the price of the fabric. (2) Blending may provide advantages that wool does not, such as the strength of polyester. But if the customer wants wool for warmth, a very low percentage count of wool in the blend should be avoided.

Blending can be done before the fibers are carded, during the carding process, or even during the drawing-out process. Care is taken to maintain the same proportion of wool as the other fiber or fibers used.

As indicated in Chapter 2, a blend should not be confused with a mixture. In the mixture, one type of fiber is used in each yarn, but yarns each of a different fiber are used in the construction process in weaving, usually one for the warp and another for the filling.

WEAVING, KNITTING, AND FELTING FABRICS

Weaving

Plain

Although more men's suitings are made in twill than in plain weave, the plain weave is popular where porosity, softness, and sponginess are factors. Men's and women's suitings and coatings in this construction include home-spun, Donegal tweed, and tropical worsted. Women's dress fabrics include wool crepe, batiste, nun's veiling, poplin, faille, and some flannels and tweeds.

Twill

The twill is a durable construction and therefore particularly suited to suitings and coatings. Kersey (heavy felted overcoating), cheviots, coverts, tweed, broadcloth, flannel, whipcord, and serge are made in twill for men's wear. Women wear most of the fabrics listed, but the weight is lighter and the finish usually softer.

Pile

Many fabrics are made in pile construction to imitate fur. Some fleeces, double-cloth coatings, velours, velvets, friezes, and plushes are made in this manner. Velour, velvet, and plush are upholstery fabrics in pile weave. Rugs with wool pile include Wilton, Axminster, tufted, and velvet. (See Chapter 20 for construction of rugs.)

Dobby

The very durable elastique and cavalry twill, originally used for uniforms for the armed forces, is dobby weave and is particularly appropriate in civilian jackets and trousers when durability is a major factor.

Knitted Construction

Jersey blouses, wool basque or polo shirts, some fleeces, and bouclé dresses are knitted. The familiar sweater and wool sock are of this construction. Wool's resilience, bulk, and ease in handling make it most appropriate in knitted goods. (See Chapter 6.)

Felting

Because of the scales in wool that entangle and interlock when subjected to heat, moisture, and pressure, a felt fabric may be made that is neither woven nor knitted. A layer of fibers is treated mechanically or sometimes chemically. The resultant compact fabric, felt, is widely used for hats, floor and table coverings, paddings, and industrial purposes.

FINISHES FOR WORSTED AND WOOLEN FABRICS

Worsteds look more ready for sale than do woolens when they come from the loom because their attractiveness depends on their even yarns and structural design, whereas much of the attractiveness, softness, and often the warmth of the woolen depends on its finish. Usually woolens are more heavily felted than worsteds. Woolen and worsted fabrics are given one of two finishes: (1) clear or hard finish or (2) face finish.

The clear-finished fabric, which includes most of the worsteds, has a smooth, even surface with the weave clearly visible. For clear finishes very little, if any, fulling is done. (See page 318.) A slight fulling of a worsted would produce a good, firm hand.

The face finish has either a pile or a nap on the surface, which almost, if not entirely, obliterates the weave. Considerable fulling is done, and a nap is raised. The nap may be pressed in one direction, as in broadcloth. Sometimes the finisher produces a fuzz or nap on a worsted, called *unfinished worsted*. Then again the finisher may make one side of the fabric *clear finished* and the back *face finished* with a nap.

Perching or Inspecting

All fabrics must be subjected to this visual examination. (See *inspection*, Chapter 7.) Inspection is done both before and after finishes have been applied.

Burling[10]

For inspection, the cloth is laid over a smooth, sloping table. The inspector or burler first examines the back of the cloth to detect and remove snarls, slubs, and straws. All thick warp and filling yarns are opened with a pick called a *burling iron*. The burler next examines the face of the cloth for irregularities. All imperfections are pushed through to the back of the cloth so that the right side of the fabric will be smooth.

Mending

This is a finishing process in which weaving imperfections, broken yarns, or tears are repaired before further finishing.

Bleaching and Whitening

Wool is frequently bleached in the yarn, but it can also be bleached after weaving and scouring.

Natural wool fibers are slightly yellowish, black, or brown. The yellowish

---

[10]Von Bergen and Mauersberger, *Wool Handbook*, pp. 809–10.

color predominates. As the amount of deeply colored wool is small, these wools are rarely bleached. The yellowish tinted wool can be whitened by (1) tinting, (2) sulfur dioxide, or (3) hydrogen peroxide.[11]

Tinting consists of a dyeing (not bleaching) of the wool with violet or blue to neutralize the cast of the natural pigment and change the tint to gray. There is no destruction of the natural pigment, and the gray tint is so slight that the eye perceives the wool as white.

The sulfur dioxide bleach is an older method of bleaching, but it is less permanent than the hydrogen peroxide bleach. In the sulfur dioxide method the cloth is subjected either to a sulfur dioxide gas or to an acidified solution of bisulphite.

In the third method of whitening, the well-scoured fabric is saturated and steeped for about 12 hours in a bath of hydrogen peroxide made slightly alkaline with sodium silicate or ammonia. A thorough rinsing in dilute acetic acid removes bleaching chemicals. To cheapen the bleaching process and to provide a milder bleach, stabilized hydrosulfite compounds are used. Frequently, this method is combined with the peroxide method.

Scouring and Carbonizing

Both these processes are preliminary cleaning processes. Scouring removes oil, dirt, and sizing from wool, cotton, linen, and rayon fabrics. Carbonizing frees wool of burrs and vegetable matter by use of an acid solution and heat. A rinse is an alkali that neutralizes the acid. When the wool is dry, the carbonized matter "dusts off."[12] This process can be done in the fiber stage, but the purpose is the same when done as a finishing process.

Brushing and Singeing

These processes, described in Chapter 7, remove short, loose fibers and lint from wool.

Shearing

To cut off excess surface fibers and to even the pile in length, wool fabrics may be sheared.

Crabbing[13]

This operation is a permanent setting of the weave to prevent uneven shrinkage, which may develop in crimps, creases, or cockles when the fabric is fulled. The process consists in passing the fabric in full width around a series of rollers and

[11]Ibid., pp. 791–94.

[12]*Dan River's Dictionary of Textile Terms*, 10th ed. (Danville, Va.: Dan River Mills, Inc., 1973), p. 17.

[13]Von Bergen and Mauersberger, *Wool Handbook*, pp. 813–14.

immersing the cloth in a number of tanks. Each tank is equipped with steam pipes and cross sprays. At the end of the machine, there are two rollers that squeeze water from the fabric. This equipment is used not only for worsteds but also for wool and rayon blends.

Decating (Dry and Wet)

Wool is dry decated to set the luster and wet decated to add luster.

1. Dry *decating* (often called semidecating).[14] The operation consists of applying hot steam to a dry cloth wound under tension on a perforated roller. The roller is not really sealed, but merely contains the steam and allows the steam to escape through the perforations and hence through the fabric.

    Then the process is reversed by forcing steam through the cloth from the outside to the inside. The cloth is then removed from the tank and is cooled by air.
2. *Wet decating.*[15] If the finished wool fabric must have luster and a more permanent setting of the fibers, the fabric is wet decated. For this process, heat, moisture, and tension are needed. The cloth is wound in tension around a perforated metal cylinder that is placed in a trough of water 140° to 212° F. The 5- to 10-minute treatment consists in circulating the water from the tank through the fabric into the cylinder, and vice versa. Hot water plus steam will make the process more effective. The fabric is then cooled with cold water or cold air.

Fulling

If wool is to be made more compact and thicker, the fabric is placed in warm soapy water or a weak acid solution, where it is pounded and twisted until it has shrunk a desired amount—10 to 25 percent. This process may last 2 to 18 hours and is called *fulling, felting,* or *milling.* The secret of fulling lies in the structure of the wool fiber. The scales of the fiber swell in the warm water, and the pounding and twisting cause them to entangle or interlock with one another. When the fabric is dried, the fibers stay massed together—they are felted. Worsteds are fulled to close the weave and to soften the cloth. Slight fulling of a woolen will give it compactness and softness.

Gigging

The raising of a nap on a wool fabric may be done with teasels—burrlike plants 1½ inches to 2 inches in length.[16] The teasels are set in rows in frames mounted on revolving drums. As the cloth comes in contact with the teasels, the fibers are untangled and lifted. It is wise to use worn teasels first so that fibers will not be torn out. New teasels are sharper and are best introduced gradually until the desired nap is raised. Gigging is also used for spun silk and spun rayon.

[14]Ibid., pp. 860–61.
[15]Ibid., pp. 837–38.
[16]Ibid., p. 839.

Napping

Those woolen fabrics that are to have a fuzzy surface are fulled a great deal more than the others, because the more the short fibers of wool are massed together the thicker will be the nap. After they are fulled, woolens are washed, dried, and tentered (evened in their width). The cloth is then passed over cylinders whose surfaces are covered with wire bristles. When teasels are used, the process is called gigging. The teasels make a more natural nap and are not so rough on the cloth as the wire bristles. But where fibers have formed a felted surface, napping is necessary to untangle them. The nap is then sheared to a certain length.

Steaming[17]

This operation, when applied after drying, partially shrinks and conditions the fabric. After the cloth has been decated, steaming takes off unsightly glaze. The fabric is run over a steam box with a perforated copper cover, and the steam is passed through it. While this process is not essentially for shrinkage, it does have that effect. Silk and spun rayons may also be steamed.

Weighting of Woolens

To make a firmer, more compact cloth, manufacturers steam fibers (obtained by shearing a cloth) into the back of a fabric. Recycled wool may also be used for this purpose. Men may have discovered little rolls of wool in the pockets of their overcoats. This is *flocking*. Its presence can be detected if the back of the cloth is brushed with a stiff brush to see whether short fibers come out. If the manufacturer uses a good quality of wool fiber for flocking and does not use it merely to cover defects in weaving, the practice is considered legitimate.

    Unscrupulous manufacturers may take advantage of the absorptive qualities of wool and treat fabrics with magnesium chloride so that the cloth may absorb more moisture than it naturally would. This practice is called *loading*. It gives the buyer a good percentage of water with his purchase.

Shrinkage Control

Great strides have been made in overcoming objectionable shrinkage of wools. Although such finishes as steaming, fulling, and decating help to lessen wool shrinkage in use, these finishes do not ensure fabrics against progressive shrinkage in washing.

    It is estimated that there are hundreds of shrinkage-control processes for wool. Five of the methods in current use in this country are (1) chlorination (either dry or in neutral or acid solutions), (2) resin treatment, (3) a combination of alkaline hypochlorite and permanganate, (4) a combination of very mild chlorination plus a resin addition, and (5) blending wool with nylon in the yarn.

[17]Ibid., p. 870.

The chemical methods cause the wool to resist felting and hence to resist shrinkage. Chlorination consists in subjecting wool tops, yard goods, or garments to a chlorine agent. The chlorination process modifies the fiber structure of wool. Under the microscope the scales of treated fibers may appear less clear or may disappear substantially. Since the treatment prevents felting shrinkage, directional frictional effect (discussed earlier as fiber slippage from tip to root to tip) is diminished, and that reduces resilience. It has been found that chlorination may reduce washfastness of the dyes.

Application of melamine formaldehyde resin masks the scale structure but does not modify that structure. Essentially, the process deposits resin on the surface of the fabric. One scientist compares resin's action with spot welding of the fibers—an action preventing movement of the scales and hence preventing felting. This method, although it is effective in preventing shrinkage, causes fabrics to lose woollike hand because of fiber-bonding and increase in fabric weight.

Acrylic resins stabilize wool and avoid the undesirable effects on secondary fabric properties from which other commercial treatments suffer.[18]

The third method has enjoyed considerable commercial success. When applied to gray goods, decreased affinity for dyes and uneven dyeing have been drawbacks. Also, there have been few dyes that maintain their shade and fastness if applied before this treatment.

The fourth method uses a much reduced level of chlorination in which virtually no fiber scales are damaged or removed. Following this mild treatment, resins of the nylon and polyester type are found to spread and adhere permanently in an ultrathin layer on each individual fiber in the treated structure. Dyeing is not impaired, and the hand is not changed. However, the nylon treatment tends toward yarn slippage, limiting its use to the plain weave. Polyester reduces slippage in twills and other weaves, but it does not control shrinkage as well as the use of nylon does.

The fifth method, in wide use today in the manufacture of children's wear and popularly priced clothing, is blending wool with about 15 percent nylon fiber. The nylon tends to keep the wool from felting.

Present industrial shrink-resistance treatments are capable of preventing any wool fabric from felting in any washing machine. However, there may be disadvantageous side effects, such as loss of strength and woollike hand, change in appearance, and possible stretching of the treated fabric when given a mild laundering. (For brand names of finishes for shrinkage control, see Chapter 7.)

Wash-and-Wear

Wool, by nature, is elastic and therefore wrinkle-resistant, and wrinkles tend to hang out. The major problem in making wool fabrics wash-and-wear are those of shrinkage, felting, and fuzzing in laundering. The shrink-resistant finishes

---

[18]Trade names for this technology are Dylan GRB and Superwash.

are being improved to the point where wash-and-wear wools are becoming commonplace.

Heat-set treatments have become a boon to the man-made fibers and to cottons in permanent pleating of fabrics. A process for improving the permanence of pleating in wools was developed by Unilever Ltd. of Great Britain. In this pretreatment process, the salt linkages in the keratin are partly broken, after which the fabric is steam-pressed.

Tentering

Evening a wool fabric in its width is especially important. (For a description of the tentering process, see page 157.)

Pressing

Pressing accomplishes the same result for wool that calendering does for other fibers. Calendering is also a pressing process, but the term is not applied to wool.

To press wool, the fabric is placed between heavy, electrically heated metal plates that steam and press the fabric. Another method is to wind the fabric around a cylindrical unit that dampens the fabric and then presses it. The latter method can be used not only for woolens and worsteds but also for spun rayons and silks.

Fire-Resistant Finish

Some fire insurance companies recommend wool blankets for smothering fires. Why? Laboratories have found that wool absorbs about twice as much moisture as cotton and that moisure absorption is a factor in reducing flammability. The chemical nature of wool also contributes to its natural flame resistance. Even when forced to ignite, wool has a very low temperature of burning; thus there is reduced hazard of flash burning. Another factor involved in flammability is the construction of a cloth. A flame must have sufficient heat concentration and new fibers to consume, plus enough oxygen to keep burning. If a flame is applied to an all-wool fabric, it is slow in ignition, and if the material is dense enough, the fire will often go out when the flame is removed. If may be deduced that flammability is not a problem in 100 percent wool fabrics. However, blends, depending on the nature and percentage of other fabrics, may create a flammability problem. Also, if flammable finishing materials are used in sufficient amounts, flammability must be reckoned with under the Flammable Fabrics Act.

Other Functional Finishes for Wool Fabrics

Wool is not subject to mildew unless it is allowed to remain damp for some time; however, wool may be given a mildew-resistant finish. (See Chapter 7.)

The attack on wool by moths is always a worry to a consumer. Again, a proper moth-repellent finish done by the finisher or by the consumer can be adequate to prevent eating by moths. 'See page 180 for chemicals used in this finish.

Wool fabrics for rainwear are treated for water repellency. The degree of repellency and the length of time the treatment will last after dry or wet cleaning depends on the nature of the finish. Trade names of water-repellent finishes for wool include Cravenette, Neva-Wet, Rainfoe, Zelan, and Zepel (spot- and stain-repellent).

BUYING POINTS OF WOOL FABRICS

Appearance

The attractive appearance of a wool fabric lies partly in its natural low luster for good-grade wools or in its steam-lustered finish for fabrics like wool broadcloth. Colors can be soft and muted or high in intensity, with depth and permanence. The depth and softness of a woolen pile, the nap of a woolen, and the intricacies of weave in a worsted have an eye appeal. A fabric that drapes and fits well helps to present a good appearance.

Ease in Care

Wool's elasticity is responsible for its wrinkle-resistant quality, a particularly important factor in suits and coats that have almost daily wear. The ability of worsteds to take and hold a crease is also important, particularly in men's slacks. Wools are slow to show soil because of the fiber's resilence. Since moisture is absorbed slowly, many liquids can be sponged from the fabric before it dries, thereby taking the soil particles with the liquid. As explained, the covering of the scales makes the fiber naturally water-repellent; hence, liquid will run off the fabric if it is slanted. Wool's low static quality is also a factor in resisting soil. Once soil becomes embedded in the fabric, it can generally be removed by washing or dry cleaning. Improvements in shrinkage control and resistance to felting will make laundering of wool easier. (See Chapter 16 for general rules to follow in the care of fabric.)

The Wool Bureau, Inc., has been instrumental in perfecting and introducing to the trade a permanent creasing (and pleating) process for all-wool garments. Known as the WB-4 process, it is a chemical add-on that imparts a "memory" to the wool fiber, helping it to keep its crease throughout the life of the garment.

Hand

The soft, springy, warm feel (hand) or wool is pleasing to the buyer of wool fabrics. To be sure, the softness or stiffness of a fabric is controlled not only by the choice of fibers but also by the kind of manufacturing processing they receive. In general, large-diameter fibers produce a stiffer hand than do fine fibers. Large slub or nubbed yarns present a more bumpy surface texture than do smooth, even yarns. A woolen usually has a more hairy surface then does a worsted, which has had the short fibers removed from the yarn. Therefore, woolen feels warmer, generally softer, less firm, and less smooth than a worsted does. The amount of other fibers mixed or blended with wool may affect the hand.

Comfort and Protection

Why wool is warm and therefore comfortable, particularly in cold weather, has been explained. The same principle of trapped air is applicable to napped wool blankets. And yet wool fabrics can be woven or knitted so that they are so loose and porous that air transmission is good. The wearer is protected from sudden chill by the wool fabric's natural water repellency and slow absorptive quality. The fact that wool is slow to ignite protects the user of wool pile rugs and wool blankets.

Suitability

Wool fabrics are made in many weights, from the filmiest sheer veiling to the heaviest overcoating.

Sheer fabrics, such as wool georgette, voile, featherweight tweeds, lightweight crepes, and some sheer wool meshes, can be used for clothing requiring softness and draping, such as women's dresses and blouses.

Certain fabrics, such as checked or plain tweeds, are adapted to sports clothes, depending on the climate. Smooth, luxurious flannels and broadcloths are suitable for dress wear for men. Men's suitings (some in lighter weight) are being used extensively for women's suits. Wool or blends with wool make warm, comfortable sweaters.

The hard-finished worsteds are good for tailored styles, because these fabrics tailor easily, hold their shape, and press better than woolens. A woolen in men's suiting requires frequent pressing, since creases do not stay long in the cloth. As a class, worsteds are more durable than woolens, and they are generally more expensive. (For a more complete discussion of men's suitings, see Chapter 18.)

MINOR HAIR (SPECIALTY) FIBERS

Hair fibers classed with wool as specialty fibers by the FTC include various breeds of goats and camels. In addition, less used hairs from the cow and horse, fur from rabbits, and feathers from the duck, goose, and ostrich are not to be overlooked. (See the requirements of the Wool Products Labeling Act, page 301.)

Microscopically, the medullas show in hair fibers and differ from sheep's

Table 12.2 Hair Fibers and Their Common Uses

Fiber	Animal	Major Source	Uses (alone and in blends)
Mohair	Angora goat	Asia Minor (Turkey) and the Cape Colony, Texas	Upholsteries, draperies, spreads, linings, braids, men's suits, riding habits, brushed-wool sweaters, gloves, mittens, socks, imitation astrakhan, plush
Alpaca	Camellike ruminants	South America (Peru)	Men's coat linings, women's furlike fabrics, dress goods, linings
Llama	"	South America	Dress goods, sweaters
Vicuña	"	South America	Sweaters, fleece fabrics, coats (very rare)
Cashmere	Kashmir goat	Himalaya Mountains, Tibet, Kashmir	Shawls, sweaters, coats
Camel's hair	Camel	Asia, Africa, China, Russia	Oriental rugs, sweaters, blankets, coats, gloves, piece goods
Horsehair	Horse	South America	Braid, upholsteries, fur
Rabbit hair	Angora rabbit	Turkey	Felt, knitted garments

wool. (See Appendix A.) In some, hair scales are faintly visible; in others they are not.

A list of hair fibers and their most common uses appears in Table 12.2.

Mohair

Mohair is obtained from the Angora goat, which is raised in the southwestern United States, South Africa, and Turkey. The United States is producing good grades domestically.

Mohair comes in different grades. Adult and kid hairs are the broad classifications. Kid hair, clipped twice a year, is the finest grade; adult hair, very strong and resilient, is the lowest grade. While the top grade is very expensive, it is one of the softest and most luxurious of the wool and hair fibers widely used.

The fiber, which ranges from 6 to 12 inches for a full year's growth, is smooth and lustrous, because the scales scarcely overlap.[19] Since mohair has fewer surface scales and less crimp than sheep's wool, it is more lustrous, smooth, and dust-resistant. The bundles of fibrils in the cortex are similar to wool, and the cells in the medulla are few in a good-grade fiber. Chemical properties are similar to those of wool.

Mohair can be used alone or blended with sheep's wool and other fibers. It is desirable for men's suitings, women's dresses, coats, and sweaters, net and braid trimmings, the pile of rugs, automobile and furniture upholstery, draperies, lap robes, and stuffing around the springs in furniture.[20]

[19]Von Bergen and Mauersberger, *Wool Handbook*, p.221.

[20]"Mohair, Distinguished Fiber of Unlimited Uses," a pamphlet by the American Wool Council, Inc.

Cashmere

Those who have worn a cashmere sweater or coat appreciate its warmth and lightness. The fleece is grown on the Kashmir goat, a small, short-legged animal that resides in the high plateaus of central Asia in Chinese Mongolia, Soviet Outer Monglia, Iran, and Afghanistan.[21] The finest and most expensive fibers come from the Mongolian regions. These fibers are used mostly in sweaters. The coarser fibers from Iran and Afghanistan are used in woven cloth for coats and sports jackets.

We read of Kashmir shawls worn by the Roman Caesars, woven of cashmere from the Vale of Kashmir. Actually, very little cashmere now comes from the state of Kashmir, India.

Cashmere is naturally gray, brown, or white (white is very rare). Fleece of the animal is never shorn but is plucked or combed out by hand. When the animal molts, it rubs itself against the shrubs to relieve itself of itching. The fibers adhering to shrubs are picked off and used.[22] In handpicking, much long hair from the animal's outer coat is mixed with the soft inner fibers. These coarse outer fibers can be removed by special machinery.

Fibers range from 1¼ to 3½ inches long. The scales are hardly visible under the microscope. The diagonal edges of the scales are more or less sharply bent. The cortical layer is striated and filled with color pigment. Some medullas are continuous. Chemical properties of cashmere are similar to those of wool.

The amount of fibers from a single animal is very small: a male produces about 4 ounces and a female about 2 ounces per year. It is estimated that fleece of from four to six animals would be needed for a sweater.[23] Small wonder, then, that articles of 100 percent cashmere must be high priced.

Camel's Hair

There are two types of camels: the dromedary, which is not heavy enough to produce usable fiber for cloth manufacture, and the Bactrian, the heavier, two-humped, pack-carrying species whose hair is suitable for cloth. This animal lives in all parts of Asia, from the Arabian Sea to Siberia, Turkestan, Tibet, Mongolia, Manchuria, and to all parts of China.[24]

The camel has a fleece with an outer layer of coarse hair and an inner layer of finer hair like a cashmere goat. The inner fibers, called *down*, run 1 to 5 inches, whereas the outer fibers range up to 15 inches. Down is used for clothing. The camel is never sheared or clipped like sheep. At certain seasons, when the warmth of the body expands the skin, the animal sheds its hair. The hair is gathered from the ground. Only when soft underfibers or down is desired must

---

[21]*The New York Times*, February 2, 1973, p. 3.

[22]*Cashmere* (New York: Bernhard Ulmann Co.), p. 24.

[23]Ibid.

[24]*The Story of Camel Hair* (New York: S. Stroock & Co., Inc., 1936), p. 3.

the camel be plucked.[25] A combing process separates the down from the hair. Wool is often added to camel's hair to give it strength in spinning into yarn. However, the more wool added, the coarser the fabric becomes. Polo cloth, by the Worumbo Manufacturing Company, is an illustration of a fine camel's hair and wool blend. Also, the camel's natural pale tan hair is sometimes blended with clear white cashmere, llama, or some of the fine, rare wools for the purpose of obtaining light-colored fabrics. Camel's hair can also be blended with cheaper grades of fibers to bring down the cost. One of the most common uses of camel's hair is in men's and women's coats, because it has a high insulation quality and wears satisfactorily. It may also be found in Oriental rugs, blankets, and sweaters.

The Llama Family

This family is large and may be called "the camel of South America." A few members of this family are the alpaca (the closest relative to the llama), the huarizo and misti (hybrids of the llama and alpaca), and the guanaco and vicuña. The family inhabits the heights of the Andes Mountains. These animals have some of the characteristics of the camel, yet there is no real proof that the camel and llama have the same origin.

The llama and the alpaca are domesticated members of the family; the guanaco and vicuña are the wild members. Most scientists believe the llama and alpaca to be direct descendants of the guanaco and the vicuña to be a distinct species.[26] Until shearing time, alpacas roam the range during the day and return to primitive corrals at night. November and December, the spring in llamaland, is shearing time. This is done by hand, half a fleece at a time. Sorting and baling follow. Fleeces of llamas are fine and lustrous but not curly, and the fiber is strong in relation to its diameter. Scales of the fiber are only partly visible and, like the camel's hair, the fiber has a medulla down the center.

The alpaca fibers are white to black in color and are 8, 12, 16, or even 30 inches in length. Llama fibers are black to brown, the guanaco is reddish brown, and the vicuña cinnamon brown (generally used in natural color because of its resistance to dye). Since the vicuña has only recently been breeded, in small numbers and under government control, production of the fiber is limited. These animals live at great heights and are found in Peru, Chile, and Bolivia.[27] The vicuña, which produces the world's most valuable specialty fiber known, is protected by law. Only the most opulent consumer can buy a coat of vicuña. Knitting yarns and knit goods are possible uses.

Llama fabrics are used in women's coats, suits, and dresses and men's summer suits, topcoats, and overcoats.

[25]Ibid., p. 11.

[26]*Llamas and Llamaland* (New York: S. Stroock & Co., Inc., 1937), p. 6.

[27]*Vicuna, The World's Finest Fabric* (New York: S. Stroock & Co., Inc. 1946).

Musk Ox

The federal government is protecting a herd of musk ox, similar to the bison, which is being raised in Alaska. One domesticated breed, the white-faced, has soft, fine, grayish-colored fleece similar to cashmere.

Miscellaneous Hair Fibers

Cow hair, obtained from our own slaughtered animals and from Japan, England, Canada, and Spain, is used for rug cushions, felts, and coarse rugs.

We import *horsehair* from Argentina and Canada. Horsehair is used principally in interlining for men's suits and coats and as filling for upholstered furniture.

The *Angora rabbit's fur* has proved very popular for knitting. It can also be blended with wool for filling yarn of a fabric. Such a cloth will feel soft and luxurious. The United States, England, the Netherlands, and Belgium raise the Angora rabbit.

Common rabbit's hair is used for felt hats. The most desirable is the white-faced rabbit, found on this continent and in Europe, parts of China, and Japan. The cheaper gray, wild rabbit's fur, from New Zealand, Australia, and Great Britain, is also used.

Feathers and Down

Goose and duck feathers and down have always had considerable use for filling pillows, comforters, and upholstery. Sometimes down is blended with wool to produce a luxurious effect in fabrics. They are also used widely today for warm yet light overcoat filling, as well as other active sportswear apparel.

SUMMARY

The consumer who selects a wool fabric should be willing to pay for wearing quality, if that is the major factor governing the decision. A good-quality wool is not cheap, and prices are tending to rise. A good grade of recycled wool, however, is sometimes superior to a poor grade of new wool. Blends of wool with man-made and natural fibers have grown in importance. The consumer should read the percentages of each fiber and any selling points on the label. His or her own judgment and that of the salesperson will help to decide whether the particular blend will satisfy his or her needs.

REVIEW QUESTIONS

1. (a) What is the definition of wool as given in the Wool Products Labeling Act?
   (b) What are "specialty fibers"?
2. (a) What is the difference between *domestic* wool and *territory* wool?

(b) In what respects is Australian wool superior to wool grown in the United States?

(c) What is the difference between Australian Merino wool and English Lincolnshire or Leicestershire wool? For what purposes is each used?

3. (a) Tell the differences between new wool and recycled wool.
   (b) Define recycled wool.

4. What factors determine the grade or quality of wool fiber?

5. (a) How do worsteds differ from woolens in manufacture?
   (b) What are the chief characteristics of worsteds?
   (c) What are the chief characteristics of woolens?

6. (a) Name five fabrics made of woolen yarn.
   (b) Name five fabrics made of worsted yarn.

7. In what ways do the length, diameter, and strength of the wool fiber affect the final cloth?

8. What part do the scales on the fiber play in the manufacture of wool goods?

9. What factors should be considered in judging the durability of wool yarn?

10. (a) For what purposes is recycled wool important?
    (b) If a label reads "all wool," what should the consumer infer?

11. Why are wool fabrics comfortable?

12. What laundering instructions should a salesperson be able to give a purchaser of a wool fabric?

13. Define mohair, alpaca, cashmere, fleece wool, pulled wool, merino wool, noils, scouring, tops, yarn dye.

PROJECT

Make a tabular presentation comparing the physical and chemical properties of the four major natural textile fibers. Use the following form:

Physical Characteristics	Cotton	Linen	Silk	Wool
Microscopic appearance				
Length of fiber				
Diameter				
Color				
Luster				
Strength				
Elasticity				
Heat conductivity				
Hygroscopic moisture				

EXPERIMENTS

1. Examine a wool fiber under the microscope. Draw the fiber as you see it.

2. Boil several wool yarns or a sample of wool fabric in a 10 percent solution of sodium hydroxide for 5 minutes. Describe the result.

3. Boil a wool-and-cotton fabric for 5 minutes in a 10 percent solution of sodium hydroxide. Describe the result.
4. Place several wool yarns in concentrated sulfuric acid for 5 minutes. Note the result.
5. Unravel yarns both ways from a wool fabric. Is the yarn loosely or tightly twisted? Are the fibers parallel, or do they run in every direction? Are the fibers less than 2 inches or more than 2 inches in length? Are the fibers all about the same length? Is the yarn a worsted or a woolen?

GLOSSARY

Alpaca   Domesticated member of the llama family, species of "South American camel."

Breaker   A machine containing a tooth cylinder used to remove all loose dirt, sand, and the like, and to separate the whole fleece into small sections.

Burling   The process of removing knots, loose threads, burrs, etc., from a fabric, generally of wool.

Camel's hair   Fibers from the Bactrian, a two-humped, pack-carrying species.

Carding   A process of opening and cleaning the fibers and putting them in a sliver or web preparatory to spinning.

Carpet or braid wool   Very coarse wool from Turkey, Siberia, China, and South America, primarily used in carpets; not suited for clothing.

Cashmere   Fleece from the Kashmir goat of Tibet, Mongolia, China, Iran, India, and Iraq.

Cheviot   A woolen or worsted fabric in twill weave originally made of wool from sheep of the Cheviot Hills along the English-Scottish border. It has a slightly rough, napped surface and is used for men's and women's coats and suits.

Chlorinated wool   Woolens chemically treated to decrease shrinkage and to increase affinity for dyes.

Clips of knitted fabric   New wool; never used or worn in any way.

Combing   Removing short wool fibers from the sliver and making the fibers parallel.

Cortex   Cortical cells in the wool fiber consisting of bundles of fibrils.

Covert   A woolen or worsted coating or suiting in twill weave made with two-ply yarns. One of the yarns in the ply may be white and the other colored. This gives a flecked appearance. Covert has recently been made in solid color. It is very durable and is also made in cotton fabrics for work clothes.

Crimp   Natural wave of a wool fiber.

Domestic wools   From the eastern and middle-western states.

Donegal tweed   Originally, a thick woolen homespun tweed woven by hand by Irish peasants. Now it refers to a tweed in plain weave characterized by colorful slubs woven into the fabric.

Drawing   Attenuating a sliver till it becomes narrower and narrower. Drawing is synonymous with *drafting.*

Dry decating   A process of setting the luster of a wool fabric.

Felt   A fabric made from wool or hair fibers where the scales in a layer of fibers are locked together by heat, moisture, and pressure to form a compact fabric.

Finished worsted   Fabric with a softened finish. It is synonymous with *semifinished.*

Flannel   An all-wool fabric of woolen or of worsted yarns, finished with a soft nap that practically obliterates the weave. It is also made in cotton.

Fleece wool   Wool shorn from the live sheep. It is superior to *pulled wool.*

Fulling   A finishing process for woolens and worsteds where the fabric is shrunk into a smooth, tight surface.

Gabardine   A tightly woven twilled worsted with a raised diagonal wale on the right side. It can also be of cotton, rayon, and blends or mixtures.

Garnetting   Shredding wool fabrics into a fibrous state, prior to remanufacture into woolen yarn.

Gigging   Raising nap by means of teasels.

Grading   Determining by touch the fineness of the diameters of individual fibers. *Wool tops* are graded in this fashion. Efforts are now being made to grade wool in the grease by this method.

Grease   Natural grease adhering to the wool fiber, which must be removed by scouring.

Guanaco   A wild animal of the llama family. See *llama family*.

Hard-finished   A term applied to woolen, worsted, and cotton fabrics that are finished without a nap. Synonym: *clear-finished*.

Homespun   A coarse, nubby woolen in plain weave.

Horsehair   Fibers for the most part from Canadian and Argentine horses.

Jersey   A wool fabric, usually in stockinette stitch, used for blouses, dresses, and basque shirts. See the glossary in Chapter 6.

Kemp   Short-fibered, harsh wool, used principally in carpets.

Keratin   A protein substance that is the chief constituent of the wool fiber.

Lamb's wool   Soft, resilient wool from lambs seven to eight months old. It is used in fine-grade woolen fabrics.

Llama family   A large family of "South American camels." It includes the llama, alpaca, huarizo and misti, guanaco, and vicuña.

Medulla   Honeycombed cellular section found in medium and coarse wools.

Merino wools   From Merino sheep of Australia, South Africa, and South America.

Mohair   Hair fibers from the Angora goat.

Napping   Raising nap by means of wire bristles.

New wool   Wool not previously woven or felted into a wool product.

Noils   Short wool fibers separated from the long fibers by combing.

Opener   See *breaker*.

Paddock   A large enclosed area for sheep grazing. The paddock system is common in Australia.

Perching   Visual inspection of wool fabrics.

Polo cloth   Trade name for a fine camel's hair and wool blend by the Worumbo Manufacturing Company.

Pulled wool   Wool removed from pelts of dead animals by means of chemicals.

Rabbit hair   Fur from the Angora rabbit.

Recycled wool   Reprocessed or reused wool. Both types must use this name for all label information.

Reprocessed wool   Includes scraps and clips of woven and felted fabrics made of previously unused wool. It must be labeled "Recycled wool."

Reused wool   Old wool that has been made into a wool product and used by consumers, then cleaned, garnetted, and remade into merchandise. It must be labeled "Recycled wool."

Scales   Protective covering of the wool fiber.

Scouring   The process of freeing wool from dirt, grease, and swint.

Serge Worsted fabric in even twill with the wale showing on both sides. It is piece-dyed to a solid color. It may be cotton, rayon, or silk.

Sharkskin A wool fabric in twill weave, originally made of yarns of two colors; it is so-called because of its resemblance to sharkskin leather. Used for men's and women's suitings and slacks, it comes in a clear or semifinished worsted. Patterns include plaids, stripes, nailheads, and bird's eye. It is made also of man-made fibers and blends.

Sheared wool See *fleece wool*.

Shoddy See *reused wool*.

Sorting Separating wool fibers by touch according to fineness of fibers.

Southwestern wools From Texas, New Mexico, Arizona, and southern California.

Specialty fibers Hair fibers from various breeds of goats and camels. Also included are cow hair and horsehair, fur from rabbits, and feathers of the duck, goose, and ostrich.

Swint Perspiration on the wool fiber.

Territory wools From the Rocky Mountain plateau states.

Tops Long wool fibers in the combed sliver.

Tropical worsted A lightweight, plain-weave suiting for men's and women's summer wear. To be labeled "tropical worsted," it must be all-wool worsted. It is made in a variety of fiber blends and mixtures.

Unfinished worsted A worsted fabric finished with a nap.

Vicuña Wild member of the llama family. It produces the world's most valuable specialty fiber.

Virgin wool New wool to be used for the first time. A term applicable to wool fabrics or products that contain no recycled wool or wastes from preliminary processing of new wool.

Wash-and-wear A wool fabric that is shrink-resistant, will not felt or fuzz in washing, has good wrinkle resistance and recovery, and has good tensile strength. See *wash-and-wear*, Chapter 7.

Wet decating A finishing process to add luster to wool fabrics.

Whipcord A twill-weave worsted fabric with a pronounced diagonal wale on the right side, more pronounced than in gabardine. It may also be made in cotton. It is used for riding habits and outdoor wear.

Wool Fibers from lambs, sheep, and certain other animals. "Wool" refers to fleece wool used for the first time in the complete manufacture of a wool product.

Wool Products Labeling Act A law requiring that all wool products moving in "commerce" shall be labeled. Carpets, rugs, and upholstery fabrics containing wool come under the TFPIA.

Wool rugs A wool floor covering made of carded yarn.

Woolen A class of wool fabrics made of short-staple carded yarns.

Worsted A wool fabric made of long-staple combed yarn.

Chapter 13

RAYON AND ACETATE AND THE CONSUMER

The fibers to be discussed in this chapter and the two that follow are called *man-mades*, fibers that are produced chemically (or mechanically) from materials found in nature. Fifty years ago, they accounted for hardly 3 percent of the world's textile fiber output. Today, they are about equal to the world output of natural fibers, and it is estimated that by 1990 the demand for synthetics will soar to about two-thirds of the total market.

Figure 13.1 shows how man-mades have moved ahead of natural fiber production in U.S. mill consumption since 1940.

RAYON

History and Production of Rayon

Rayon, the first of the man-made fibers, is a generic name coined in 1924 at the National Retail Dry Goods Association (now the National Retail Merchants Association) to replace the names "artificial silk," "fiber silk," and "glos." These terms had been applied to the man-made fiber since its discovery in 1884 by Count Hilaire de Chardonnet, who dissolved nitrocellulose in alcohol and ether in the hope of producing silk. He made a vegetable fiber, not an animal fiber as is silk. But his discovery led to the making of a fiber by the nitrocellulose process, one that is no longer used in the United States. The fibers were highly flammable and especially weak when wet. By 1924 there were other methods of making this man-made fiber, but the term "rayon" was intended to apply to all methods then used. For making each type of rayon, cellulose, the fibrous substance of all forms of plant life, was the basic ingredient. The cellulose was derived from

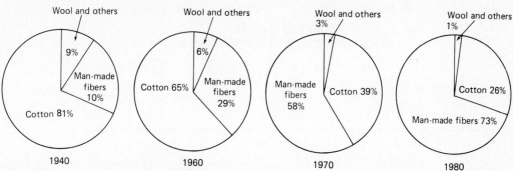

Figure 13.1 The trend toward man-made versus natural fibers in U.S. mill consumption, 1940–1980. (Courtesy Man-Made Fiber Producers Association; 1980 figures are from the American Textile Manufacturers Institute.)

either cottonseed after the long fibers were removed by ginning or from spruce and other soft woods. Today the cellulose used comes almost entirely from the latter source.

The Viscose Process of Making Rayon

Three English chemists, Cross, Bevan, and Beadle, discovered this process in 1892, but commercial production did not begin until 1910, after the turn of the century. The process is illustrated in Fig. 13.2, and the steps in the process are explained in Table 13.1.

In step 7 in the illustration, the fibers are regenerated and stretched to (1) orient the cellulose chain molecules in a more orderly fashion, (2) control the crystal size of the cellulose, and (3) achieve the desired fiber tenacity and elongation properties. The fibers are then fed into a spinning box that revolves, with the centrifugal force throwing the filaments to the side of the box and putting in a twist at the same time. The yarn emerges from the box in a form resembling an angel cake.

The term "viscose process" is derived from the syrupy, honeylike viscous solution that is extruded through the spinneret. (See Fig. 13.3.) Modifications and improvements have been made and will be discussed later in this chapter. Most rayon is made by the viscose process.

The Cuprammonium Process of Making Rayon

Louis Henri Despaisses developed this process in France in 1890, and the process was later improved. The following steps are necessary:

1. The purified cellulose is dissolved in a solution of copper oxide and aqueous ammonia.
2. The dark blue solution is forced through spinnerets.
3. Filaments (fibers) are hardened in mild sulfuric acid.
4. They are stretched as in the case of viscose.

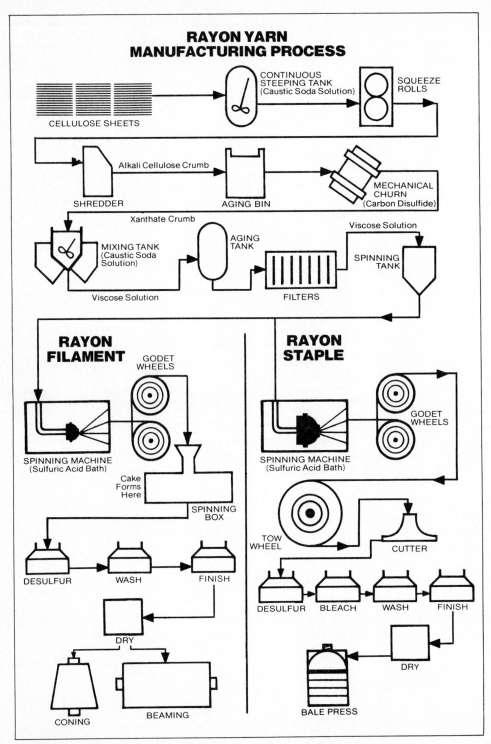

Figure 13.2 Rayon yarn manufacturing process. (Courtesy of Avtex Fibers, Inc.)

Figure 13.3 A spinneret extruding fiber to be hardened. (Photo courtesy of Man-Made Fiber Producers Association.)

     5. a. For filament yarn, most of the cuprammonium rayon is twisted into yarn by the continuous spinning method. Several filaments passing through the spinneret are grouped together, the number depending on the size of the yarn required. These grouped filaments are wound on spools and then rewound on other spools as they are being twisted. They are then wound onto bobbins for weaving.

          b. Tow and staple fiber are produced as in the case of viscose.

Table 13.1 Explanation of Steps in Rayon Yarn Manufacturing Process

1. Viscose rayon production begins with cellulosic sheets made usually from wood pulp that dissolves readily.
2. The sheets are steeped in caustic soda.
3. After a given period of time, the excess caustic soda solution is pressed out, and the sheets are shredded into fine crumbs. After the crumbs have aged, they are chuted to tumbling barrels where carbon disulfide is added and a chemical reaction takes place. This is called the xanthation process.
4. The xanthate crumbs are then fed into viscose dissolvers where they are mixed with weak caustic soda and stirred to form a viscose solution.
5. The viscose solution is filtered.
6. It is then pumped to a spinneret emerging from the holes as bundles of smooth, soft filaments that are extruded into a sulfuric acid bath that coagulates and regenerates the cellulose into continuous filaments, a process called wet spinning.

Rayon Filament	*Rayon Staple*
7. From the spinneret or spinning machine, the rayon filament is stretched and guided over rollers (Godet wheels) into a spinning box.	7. The filaments are assembled into large ropelike groups, called tow.
8. The filament is desulfured, bleached, washed, and dried.	8. These are carried to a cutter where they are cut into short lengths, called staple.
9. It is then stored in cone or beam form ready for marketing or weaving.	9. These are then desulfured, bleached, washed, dried, and baled, ready to be spun into various types of yarn by the same processes that are used for natural fibers.

Viscose and cuprammonium rayons are regenerated rayons because their basic material is cellulose and the final product is a cellulosic fiber. In other words, the reconversion of the soluble compound to cellulose causes rayon to be referred to as a regenerated cellulose fiber. The Federal Trade Commission uses the term "regenerated cellulose" in its definition of rayon: "Rayon is a manufactured fiber composed of regenerated cellulose as well as manufactured fibers composed of regenerated cellulose in which substituents have replaced not more than 15 percent of the hydrogens of the hydroxyl groups." This definition of the generic fiber rayon conforms to the authority given the FTC by the Textile Fiber Products Identification Act.

Rayon fibers—both viscose and cuprammonium—are *wet-spun;* that is, the filaments extruded from the spinneret pass directly into chemical baths for solidifying or regeneration rather than being solidified in the air. (See Fig. 13.4.)

Some of the trade names under which regular rayon is marketed include Aviloc (Avtex Fibers), Briglo (American Enka), Coloray (Courtaulds), and Enkrome (American Enka).

Modified Rayons

Basic technical developments in the field of cellulosic fibers have caused rayon to achieve renewed importance to the consumer. These developments include high-tenacity rayon, which has increased its durability in apparel; high-wet-modulus rayon for less shrinkage; rayon fibers with permanent crimp, which are adaptable to fabrics of a bulky texture and cellulosic-based fibers with a basic inner structure similar to the natural cellulosic fibers; and dry spinning, which results in a fiber that has an extremely high tensile and wet strength.

High-Tenacity Rayon

Rayon, while in the plastic (viscous) state, is modified with regeneration-retarding chemicals to produce a filament that is stronger than regular rayon and that can be stretched to higher levels.

High-Wet Strength Rayon

This type of modified rayon has been commercially available since 1961. In a study of the natural cellulosic fibers, it was found that these fibers are characterized by a very fine fibril structure and that the molecular orientation is very regular. Scientists know that natural cellulosic fibers such as cotton have increased tensile strength when wet, a low swelling factor, and good dimensional stability. So they directed their efforts to develop man-made cellulosic fibers whose structure would be similar to the natural cellulosics. On the other hand, a study of the properties of man-made cellulosic fibers has contributed to the improvement of the natural cellulosic types.

This type of fiber—referred to as a high-wet modulus rayon—is sold under various trade names, including Avril (Avtex), Zantrel (American Enka), and Xena (Beaunit).

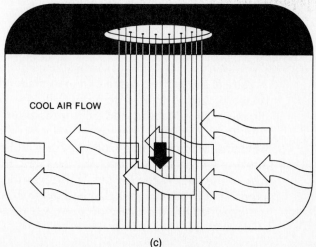

Figure 13.4 Filament extrusion: wet spinning, dry spinning, and melt spinning. (a) The fibers may be hardened by extruding the filaments through the spinneret into chemical baths that convert or "regenerate" the soluble compound into the insoluble substance that will constitute the fiber. This is called wet spinning and is used for rayon.

(a)

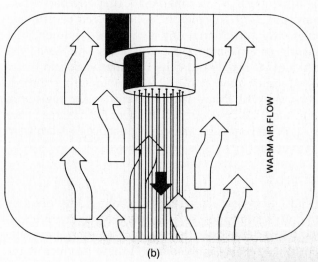

WARM AIR FLOW

(b)

(b) When a derivative to be spun is dissolved in a solvent that can be evaporated, leaving the desired filament to be hardened by drying in warm air, the process is called dry spinning. It is used for acetates and triacetates.

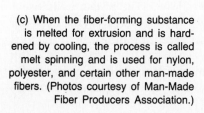

COOL AIR FLOW

(c) When the fiber-forming substance is melted for extrusion and is hardened by cooling, the process is called melt spinning and is used for nylon, polyester, and certain other man-made fibers. (Photos courtesy of Man-Made Fiber Producers Association.)

(c)

A 50/50 blend of high-wet strength rayon and carded cotton produces a fabric with the aesthetic quality, hand, and appearance of 100 percent combed cotton, normally at a lower price. Style can be added to a cotton fabric, and at the same time, carded cotton can be upgraded to the combed category. Furthermore, to enhance their beauty, some of these fabrics can be mercerized, because they are more resistant to caustic soda than is regular rayon. Fabrics can be stabilized by compressive shrinkage (as is the case with cotton) and treated with resins for minimum care.

Crimped-Fibered Rayon

Crimped (viscose process) rayon is achieved by utilizing one of several different processes, each of which modifies the internal molecular structure of the fiber. In one method, the crimp is due to the asymmetry in the molecular structure of the fiber. The crimp is permanent because it is an integral part of the fiber itself. Crimped Fibro (Courtaulds) is produced by this method. Crimped fibers when used in dress goods are warm and soft and may be solid colored or printed.

Change in the molecular structure of rayon by a chemical treatment that cross-links the molecules—as in cotton—makes it possible also to "cure" the resultant clothing so as to retain its shape and thus become wash-and-wear. High-tenacity and high-wet strength rayon staple fiber, permanently crimped, is produced by Avtex Fibers as Avril Prima rayon. Prima is the registered trademark of ITT Rayonniere, Inc., the developer of the fiber, and Avtex is the manufacturer and marketer. J. P. Stevens is the major producer of the yarn from this fiber; it enjoys wide use in the bulky hosiery business.

Acid-Dyeable Filament and Staple

The acid-dyeable filament and staple rayon products, Encrome, developed by American Enka, have all the physical properties of regular rayon. In addition, they can be dyed with acid and premetalized dyes as well as those generally used on regular rayon. Probably the greatest advantage of these products is the possibility for new styling.

ACETATE AND TRIACETATE

Acetate is the generic name of a man-made fiber whose basic ingredient is also cellulose that is treated to form cellulose acetate. The acetate solution was discovered by Maudin and Schutzenburger in 1869, but it was not used for spinning commercial fibers until 1924, after World War I. The British Cellulose & Chemical Manufacturing Company had utilized this method to make dope for airplane wings. Dope prevented the fabric from deteriorating in the ultraviolet rays of the sun. A coating of varnish was the necessary weatherproofing. After World War I, the factories that had made this material would have closed had it not been for the discovery of a method of making yarn by a similar process.

Production Process

Briefly, the steps are as follows:

1. Wood or cotton linters are treated with a solution of acetate anhydride in glacial acetic acid to form cellulose acetate.
2. The ripened product is plunged into cold water, where the cellulose acetate separates into white flakes.
3. The flakes are washed and dried.
4. They are then dissolved in acetone into a liquid solution and mixed.
5. The syrupy solution, either colorless or dope-dyed, is forced through the holes of a spinneret and hardened by the evaporation of the acetone in warm gas (dry spinning) to form a vegetable and chemical fiber.
6. a. The hairlike filaments are then stretched and twisted into filament yarn and wound on a bobbin by means of the continuous spinning method (used for cuprammonium rayon).
   b. Instead of twisting the continuous filaments into yarn, they may be assembled as tow and cut into controlled lengths of staple fiber. (See Fig. 13.5 for details.)

Acetate and triacetate, described below, are dry spun, not wet spun as is rayon. This means that the liquefied solution forced through the spinneret is passed through a current of warm gas that evaporates the liquefying material and hardens the fiber. With acetate, it is the acetone that is removed, and with triacetate, it is the mixture of methyline chloride and methanol. These solvents that are removed are recycled.

Since both filament yarns and staple yarns can be produced in any desired weight, size, length, and color, they have a uniformity not found in cotton, wool, and flax.

Filament yarns are used to make sleek, smooth textures such as satins, chiffons, taffetas, and moirés. Staple fibers are used to produce spun yarns for fabrics such as gabardines, challis, and crash in clothing and for a variety of fabrics used for upholstery, draperies, and bedspreads. Staple fiber cut in short lengths produces a fabric that looks like cotton, whereas in long lengths the fabric looks like worsted. (See Fig. 13.6.)

Variations

Acetate can be modified to give the fibers special characteristics. They can be treated to become high-tenacity rayon. They can also be crimped by fusing with heat. A permanent crimping process has been developed that can be used in blends with wool in cotton skirts, dresses, and shirtings. They can also be made flame retardant. (See Chapter 7.)

Producers

Acetate fibers were first produced commercially in the United States in 1924 by the Celanese Corporation. Celanese now markets acetate under a variety of trade names, including the well-known Arnel. Other products are manufactured by Eastman, with the trade names Estron, Chromspun, Ariloft, and others, and by Avtex Fibers, with its trademarked Sayfr.

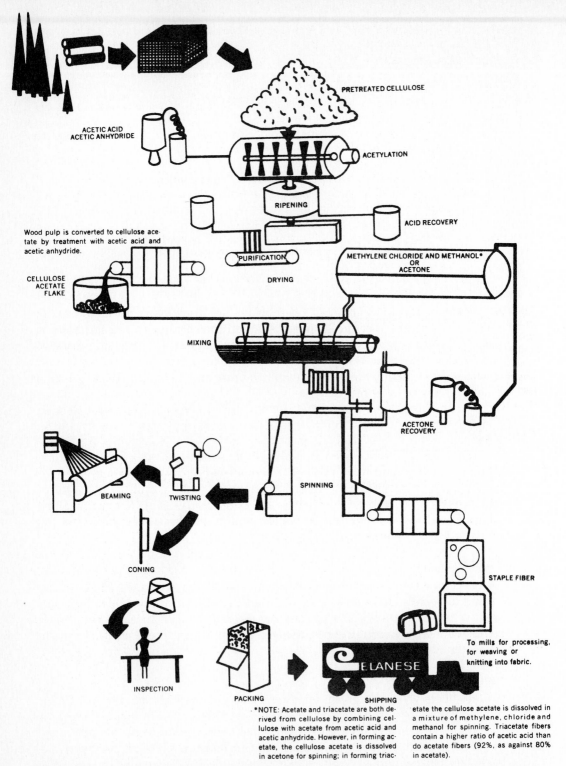

PRETREATED CELLULOSE

ACETIC ACID
ACETIC ANHYDRIDE

ACETYLATION

RIPENING

ACID RECOVERY

Wood pulp is converted to cellulose acetate by treatment with acetic acid and acetic anhydride.

CELLULOSE
ACETATE
FLAKE

PURIFICATION

DRYING

METHYLENE CHLORIDE AND METHANOL*
OR
ACETONE

MIXING

ACETONE
RECOVERY

BEAMING

TWISTING

SPINNING

CONING

STAPLE FIBER

INSPECTION

PACKING

SHIPPING

To mills for processing, for weaving or knitting into fabric.

*NOTE: Acetate and triacetate are both derived from cellulose by combining cellulose with acetate from acetic acid and acetic anhydride. However, in forming acetate, the cellulose acetate is dissolved in acetone for spinning; in forming triacetate the cellulose acetate is dissolved in a mixture of methylene, chloride and methanol for spinning. Triacetate fibers contain a higher ratio of acetic acid than do acetate fibers (92%, as against 80% in acetate).

Figure 13.5 Acetate and triacetate manufacturing process. (Courtesy of Celanese Fibers Marketing Co.)

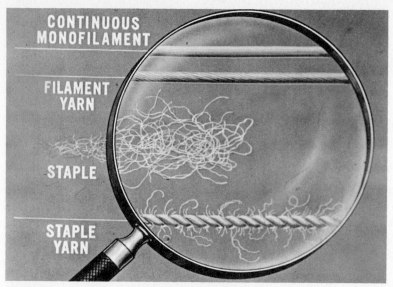

Figure 13.6 Forms in which fibers are utilized, in varying deniers, are (a) continuous monofilament: single filament; (b) filament yarn: continuous strands of two or more monofilaments that have been twisted together; (c) staple: discontinuous lengths of fibers that have been cut or broken from large bundles of continuous monofilaments; and (d) spun staple yarn: staple fiber that has been aligned, combined, and twisted into continuous lengths. About half the man-made fibers used in the United States are in the form of continuous monofilaments or filament yarns; the remaining half are used in the form of staple. (As in the case of yarn spun from staple, continuous monofilaments and filament yarns are utilized in weaving and knitting fabrics.) (Courtesy of the Man-Made Fiber Producers Association.)

Triacetate

One of the consumer's objections to acetate was that it fuses when pressed with a hot iron. Triacetate was the answer to that problem. It was first produced by the Celanese Corporation in the United States in 1954.

As is true for acetate, triacetate is derived from cellulose by combining cellulose with acetate from acetic acid and acetic anhydride. Then the cellulose acetate is dissolved in a mixture of methylene chloride and methano (for spinning). The solution is extruded from the spinneret and the solvent is evaporated in warm air (dry spinning). Triacetate fibers contain a higher ratio of acetate to cellulose than do acetate fibers. Once classed as a modified acetate, now the FTC permits the use of triacetate as a generic name of the fiber provided "not less than 92 percent of the hydroxyl groups are acetylated." This means that triacetate is a thermoplastic material that contains three acetate components.

We are all familiar with Celanese Arnel triacetate jersey—its minimum-care characteristics, its good colorfastness to light and washing, its basic stability in washing, its relatively low cost, its ability to be pressed at a much higher temperature than regular acetate, and its permanency in holding pleats. Yet even Arnel is not perfect in all respects. It has relatively limited abrasion resistance and tensile strength. But it is the modified rayons and acetates that have helped rayon and acetate to compete with other man-made and natural fibers.

CHARACTERISTICS OF RAYON, ACETATE, AND TRIACETATE FIBERS

Microscopic Appearance

Under the microscope, viscose rayon has even, rodlike fibers. Small, lengthwise striations, like shadows, are distinguishing features of bright or lustrous viscose. In viscose rayon that is made dull, the fibers become specked as with pepper.

Under the microscope, acetate fibers also appear even and rodlike. In cross section, the fiber is similar to the clover leaf. The lustrous type does not seem as glossy as do the regenerated rayons. There are heavy grooves or line marks running the length of the fiber. (See Appendix A.) Arnel's lengthwise microscopic view is much like regular acetate, but its cross-sectional view has less distinct cloverleaf configurations.

Cuprammonium rayon fibers are even in diameter and rodlike, but with no lengthwise markings. When delustered, the surface of the fiber is covered with fine pigment. Under the microscope the fiber looks peppered. (See Appendix A.)

The modified rayons Avril and Zantrel are cylindrical in cross section. Other characteristics of rayon and acetate appear in Table 13.2.

All man-made fibers, including rayon and the acetates, can be extruded in different diameters, since the holes in the spinneret can be made in different sizes.

RAYON, ACETATE, AND TRIACETATE YARNS

Kinds

The kinds of yarn can be classified as follows:

1. Filament rayon and acetate yarns are made of continuous filaments grouped together to lie parallel. Because they are all long, only a very slight twist is needed to hold the fibers together.

Thick and thin slub yarns vary in thickness because they are made of continuous filaments that vary in diameter.[1] Such yarns are novelty yarns. Another type of novelty yarn is made by flattening the yarn so that it has high luster. Other novelty yarns include textured and spiral yarns.

2. Filament high-strength yarn is made of a continuous filament chemically or mechanically treated while in the viscous state. These yarns may be used in hosiery, sports clothes, shirtings, toweling, sailcloth, draperies, filter cloths, football uniforms, belts, tire-cord fabrics, and coverings for elastic yarns. (See page 336.)

[1] Spun yarns may also be made thick and thin and slubbed.

Table 13.2 Characteristics of Man-Made Cellulosic Fibers

Length of fiber	In filament form, continuous; in staple form, cut to any length desired.
Luster	Normally bright, but may be delustered by adding mineral oil or insoluble white pigment to the spinning solution.
Strength	Fairly strong, but not as strong as many of the noncellulosic fibers. Normally stronger dry than wet (opposite of cotton and linen). Rayon may be made in four degrees of tenacity: regular, medium, high, and high-wet modulus. All are stronger than acetate and triacetate.
Resistance to	
Mildew	Fair; acetate more than rayon.
Heat	Viscose rayon more resistant to heat than cuprammonium or acetate; may be ironed at 300°F or higher with certain types; rayon does not melt but burns readily. Acetate shines when pressed at about 270°F and sticks at about 350°F; it softens at about 400°F and melts at 500°F; burns relatively slowly. Triacetate, before special treatment, sticks at about 465°F and melts at 575°F.
Acids	Tend to weaken and concentrated acids to destroy, but formic and acetic acids, while injuring acetate, do not injure rayon.
Alkalies	Potassium permanganate bleach weakens rayon, and ammonia, borax and phosphate of soda deaden luster of acetates.
Light	Rayon much the same as cotton; acetate more resistant; triacetate still more resistant.
Gas fading	Acetate, when dyed in the spinning solution is resistant to atmospheric fumes. Otherwise, fading inhibitors must be added in the dyeing or finishing process.
Moisture absorption	Rayon somewhat greater than cotton; acetate somewhat less; triacetate very little.
Affinity for dyestuffs	Rayon very good, with the same dyes used for cotton; acetates require other types of dye.

3. The high-wet strength modified rayons are good blenders (with cotton in particular). Minimum-care finishes employ resins in these rayons much the same as in all-cotton.

4. Spun yarn is spun from staple fibers, combined with one or more of the natural or newer synthetic fibers. This mass of short fibers bundled together is straightened before being twisted into yarn. Spun yarns are tightly twisted to hold the short fibers together. The ends of the fibers project from the yarn to make a fabric with a fuzzy surface.

5. Combination yarns can be made with rayon and acetate yarns combined in ply form (often in different degrees of twist) or with rayon yarns combined with yarns of another fiber. It should be remembered that filament or spun yarns can be composed of fiber blends.

6. Textured and novelty rayon yarns include bulky types that are used in pile fabrics. Skyloft is a bulked continuous-filament rayon yarn by Enka; Loftura is a slub voluminized filament acetate yarn by Eastman.

See Figs. 13.7 through 13.13 for the construction of rayon and acetate yarns.

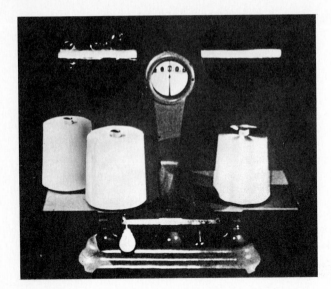

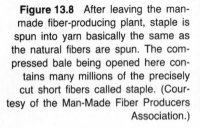

Figure 13.7 The two cones of bulk-textured filament yarn on the left side of the scale are the same weight as only one cone of nontextured filament yarn on the right. (Courtesy of the Man-Made Fiber Producers Association.)

Figure 13.8 After leaving the man-made fiber-producing plant, staple is spun into yarn basically the same as the natural fibers are spun. The compressed bale being opened here contains many millions of the precisely cut short fibers called staple. (Courtesy of the Man-Made Fiber Producers Association.)

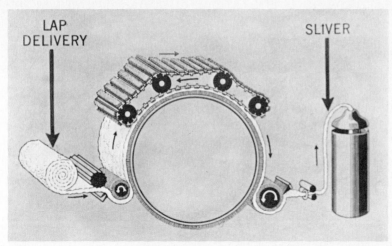

Figure 13.9 The staple fibers are formed into a compact roll called a lap. The lap is delivered into a carding machine where the fibers are straightened and assembled into a ropelike strand called a "card sliver" ("slyver"). (Courtesy of the Man-Made Fiber Producers Association.)

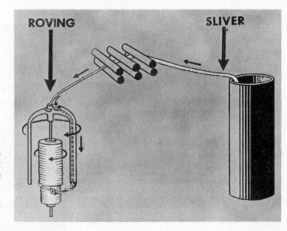

Figure 13.10 A blended sliver is fed into a roving frame that draws it down in size and at the same time gives it a small amount of twist. The strand is now called "roving." (Courtesy of the Man-Made Fiber Producers Association.)

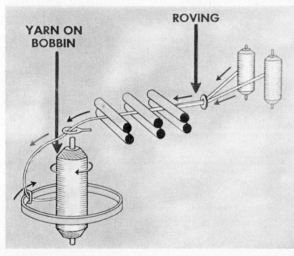

Figure 13.11 The spinning operation is the final step in spun-yarn production. Two packages of roving are feeding into a spinning frame that draws the material down still farther and completes the twisting of the finished yarn. A winding machine will rewind the yarn onto packages that meet the requirements of manufacturers of fabrics and other articles. (Courtesy of the Man-Made Fiber Producers Association.)

Figure 13.12 Blended yarn is made by combining two or more types of staple fibers, either natural or man-made. Here are acetate staple, rayon staple, and the yarn made from them. (Courtesy of the Man-Made Fiber Producers Association.)

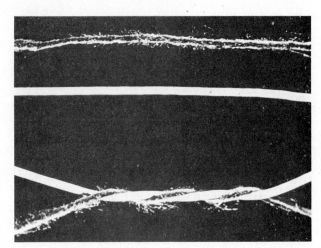

Figure 13.13 A combination yarn is formed by twisting or plying together a staple yarn (shown at top) and a continuous monofilament or a filament yarn. (Courtesy of the Man-Made Fiber Producers Association.)

Size of Rayon, Acetate, and Triacetate Yarns[2]

The size of filament rayon and acetate yarn is computed on the denier basis. (See Chapter 3.) Rayon yarns average between 100 and 200 denier, with 150 the usual. The coarsest yarn is 2,200 denier. Fifteen denier would be considered a fine yarn.

[2]These measurements are used for the other man-made fibers as well, except in the case of glass fibers.

Avtex PARA staple rayon fiber is available in a range of 1 to 15 denier, making possible very fine and soft fabrics. Such fine rayon fibers can also be used in blends with pima and Egyptian cotton, fine wools, and silks. Acetate yarns have similar deniers.

The sizes of spun-rayon yarns may be computed on the same basis as cotton (840 yards to the pound for count #1), but the woolen (1,600 yards to the pound) and the worsted (560 yards to the pound) bases are also used, depending on the spinning system employed. Single rayon yarns range approximately from a coarse yarn of #10 to a fine yarn of #80, with an average of #30 on the cotton system of spinning. The same sizing system is also used for the noncellulosic fibers discussed in the following chapters.

CONSTRUCTION OF RAYON, ACETATE, AND TRIACETATE FABRICS

Since rayon, acetate, and triacetate can be made to resemble cotton, linen, silk, or wool textures, the choice of fiber (staple or filament), type of yarn (filament, spun, combination, or novelty), construction, and finish will be determined by the appearance and the desired use of the resultant fabric.

The fabric constructions considered here have application also to the noncellulosic fibers discussed in the next two chapters, so much of this information will not be repeated.

In Plain Weave or Its Variations

In the cottonlike textures, rayon and/or acetate may be made in gingham, seersucker, poplin, and sharkskin (for blouses). A cotton and rayon blend may be used in ottoman for dresses and suits. One of the most popular textures, made to resemble linen, is rayon and/or acetate butcher, used in sportswear. To resemble wool, there are challis, some flannels, some bouclés, and crepe, used in clothing. A few of the silklike textures in plain weave are rayon or acetate shantung, faille, taffeta, moiré, flat crepe, chiffon, and bengaline used in dresses, and ninon or voile in curtains, and shantung in draperies.

In Twill Weave or Its Variations

A good rayon twill may be used for linings in mens' and womens' coats. Serge in polyester and Avril rayon are suitable for sportswear. Many tweeds, most flannels and gabardine, and many sharkskins (suiting) are twills. In silklike textures, there are foulard and surah.

In Satin Weave

Satin in dress, bridal, slipper, or drapery weights is frequently made of these fibers and resembles silk in construction.

In Jacquard and Dobby

Rayon and/or acetate necktie fabrics in Jacquard or dobby are silklike in texture. Brocades, damasks, and tapestries for draperies, upholsteries, and other home furnishings may be made in part or entirely of rayon or acetate.

In Pile Weave

Probably the best known pile fabric in these fibers is transparent velvet. Brocaded velvets frequently are made with the pile designs of rayon for evening gowns and upholstery. Furlike fabrics made to simulate broadtail, beaver, mink, and Persian lamb may be partially of rayon, for winter coats. There are a few novelty terry cloths made with rayon pile, for robes and towels.

In Leno Weave

Marquisette for glass curtains and dress fabrics is always made in leno weave, no matter what fiber is used.

In Knitting

The webbing of foundation garments may be knitted acetate. Tricots for dresses and blouses are often made of triacetate. Ready-made knitted slipcovers have the advantage of stretching to fit a chair, for example. Pleated knitted garments are wrinkle-resistant and hold their pleats when made of triacetate. Machine-made laces, produced on a tricot or Raschel knit machine, can be of rayon or acetate.

In Nonweaving

Rayon staple, as distinct from filament, has been the chief fiber used for nonwoven fabrics, but the use of polyester has increased rapidly in the past few years to nearly an equal amount. These two fibers have accounted for about 90 percent of the nonwoven use, with olefin and vinyon accounting for most of the rest.

A special type of highly absorbent rayon has been developed for nonwoven use in the medical, surgical, and sanitary goods markets. American Enka has a fast-wicking rayon, called Absorbit; Avtex Fibers produces thirty varieties of rayon for the nonwoven industry, varying from "cottonlike" to "woollike."

RAYON, ACETATE, AND TRIACETATE FABRICS: REGULAR FINISHES

Bleaching

Finishers may bleach rayon fabrics. To do so, they use sodium hydroxide, sodium perborate, and hydrogen peroxide. Sodium hypochlorite is used for acetate cloth. A wool-and-acetate blend is generally bleached with hydrogen peroxide.

Singeing and Shearing

Both processes may be needed to remove surface fibers and lint. Even though a fabric has been singed, fibers may become raised as the cloth passes through various finishing processes and may have to be sheared. Pile is shortened by shearing.

Scouring

This process is applied to most fabrics to remove oil, sizing, and dirt.

Sizing

Sizing material, such as gelatin or starch, is applied to the warp yarns to assist in weaving.

Shrinking

Shrinkage of rayon in width and in length can now be controlled—stabilized to repeated launderings. (See Chapter 7 for shrinkage-control finishes.) When the fabric is resin-treated, the stability is good. The new modified rayons have greatly improved stability over the regular type. Cotton and rayon blends are stabilized with mechanical compressive shrinkage procedures similar to those used on all-cotton fabrics. There is less loss of strength in the new modified rayon than in the cotton component. Acetates normally have good dimensional stability and have fair stability after repeated launderings.

    The serviceability of rayon fabrics is reduced if the manufacturer has failed to preshrink them or has applied sizing and dyestuffs that are water-soluble. In wet cleaning, these fabrics tend to shrink excessively, and rings are likely to develop that are difficult to remove. In the case of draperies, unless a water-repellent finish has been applied, the length varies with the humidity. In damp weather, the absorption of moisture causes them to draw up, lengthening somewhat in dry weather. This is true of all cellulosic fabrics, including cotton.[3]

[3]*Fabricare News*, November 1981, pp. 1–2.

Inspecting, Tentering, and Calendering

All fabrics must be inspected visually and then tentered to even them in width. The calendering finish smooths, glazes, moirés, or embosses. On acetate and triacetate, a slight fusion by heat embosses or moirés a fabric permanently.

RAYON, ACETATE, AND TRIACETATE FABRICS: FUNCTIONAL FINISHES

Absorbent

Since foundation garments and underwear should absorb moisture, an absorbent finish is sometimes used for triacetate fabrics. Rayon needs no finish to enhance absorption. Synthetic resins give additional resiliency. Resin, normally used for cotton, works well with rayon to produce fine wash-and-wear and durable-press fabrics.

Flame-Resistant

Vegetable fibers, such as cotton and rayon, burn much more rapidly than does wool. The speed of burning depends not only on the fibers but also on the twist of yarn, construction, and finish. Napped or so-called "brushed" rayon is highly flammable unless treated for fire resistance. (See Chapter 7.) Trademark finishes in this field include Pyroset (American Cyanamid) and Sando flame (Sandos).

Germ-Resistant

Fabrics to be made germ-resistant, such as linings in slippers, are treated with germicides-fungicides.

Starchless

Bobbinets, glass curtainings, and organdies are fabrics in which stiffness and crispness are characteristics. There are several durable, washable finishes that may be applied in manufacture. They are used particularly for curtains to keep them crisp.

Minimum Care

Since modified rayons can be treated for crease resistance, can be shrinkage controlled, and have good tensile strength when wet, these rayons are used particularly in blends with cottons, polyesters, and acrylics. A successful durable-press item is a polyester/rayon blend that is chemically treated and cured.

Water-Repellent

Most consumers are familiar with the permanent Zepel finish by DuPont for rayon, acetate, cotton, and blends. (For water repellency treatment, see page 180.) The Cravenette Company has several water-repellent finishes: (1) a nondurable wax finish, (2) a semidurable wax finish called Long Life, and (3) a durable Super Silicone finish. These finishes are used on apparel, slipcovers, draperies, and curtains. Impregnole, by Warwick Chemical Company, Inc., is made in both nondurable and semidurable types. A professional cleaner will use another nondurable type to reapply to cleaned articles. Permel Plus, made by American Cyanamid, is a durable water-repellent finish, as is Hydro-pruf, by the Arkansas Company.

ALGINATE FIBER

There is another man-made cellulosic fiber that is manufactured in England, from a seaweed base. The extract is treated chemically to form algenic acid that is neutralized with caustic soda to form sodium alginate. This is extruded like rayon through a spinneret and is coagulated in a wet solution. The resultant filament may be cut into staple. The fiber is fireproof, but it dissolves in soapy water; however, it can be dry-cleaned. It may be used for theater curtains. When woven with wool yarns, the alginate yarn is often dissolved by laundering, leaving a lacelike effect in the fabric. Lacelike embroidery is also made in this way.

DESIRABILITY OF THE CELLULOSIC MAN-MADE FIBERS

Rayon, acetate, and triacetate quickly appealed to consumers because they incorporated many desirable characteristics. They were (1) *economical*, especially when compared with wool and silk; (2) *attractive*, with permanent luster in bright, semibright, and dull shades; (3) *versatile*, suitable for most types of clothing and many home furnishings (also for tires); (4) *comfortable*, absorbing moisture readily (hydrophilic), except for triacetate, and feeling cool in summer; (5) *durable*, especially if made from high-tenacity and high-wet modulus fibers, but tending to slip at the seams unless substantial allowance is made and the tension and length of the stitches are regulated properly; and (6) *easy to iron* if heat controlled properly. Rayon can withstand higher temperatures than acetate can. (See Table 13.2.)

Over the past several years, demand for acetate and triacetate filament yarns has been stimulated by the development of a wide variety of knitted surface-finished fabrics. Through the means of sanding, sueding, brushing, and napping, knitters have introduced velours, fleeces, chenilles, suedes, terries, and other types of fabrics using triacetate for such applications as robes, loungewear, sports jackets, tops, sports shorts, and jumpsuits. Some of these fabrics are also made in combinations with either polyester or nylon yarns. This has been a significant market trend, and it coincides with the demand for active sportswear as the American consumer has become more concerned with physical fitness.

FIBER PRODUCERS' CONCERN FOR CONSUMER SATISFACTION

Typically those fiber producers who sell fibers under their own registered trademarks advertise that the fabrics and the garments and home furnishings made from them meet standards of performance that will assure consumer satisfaction. This requires licensing agreements between the fiber producer and the product manufacturer.

For example, Celanese Corporation, in connection with its registered Arnel trademark for its triacetate fiber, enters into licensing agreements with manufacturers that use Arnel, requiring that the fabrics meet established fiber content and fabric performance that will ensure customer satisfaction with the finished product. Tests are required depending on the intended end use. These cover such qualities as colorfastness, launderability, and shrinkage, durability, stretch, and puckering and slippage resistance.[4]

TRENDS IN THE OUTPUT OF THE CELLULOSIC FIBERS

Historically, rayon and acetate are very important, representing a breakthrough in technology that until then had depended on the natural fibers for textile products. But they are no longer keeping pace because of the broad acceptance of the noncellulosic man-made fibers. In the United States, until the early 1960s the mill consumption of the cellulosics exceeded the noncellulosics, since the latter were in their infancy. Since the comparison has been reversed, the consumption of the cellulosics has dropped about 50 percent to about 800 million pounds in 1979, whereas the noncellulosics have more than quadrupled to about 8.7 billion pounds. However, the consumption of the noncellulosics has remained nearly stationary since 1975.

Rayon production is about two-thirds more than that of acetate when both filament yarns and tow are included. But the production of acetate filament yarns exceeds that of rayon filament. Most of the tow yarn is rayon; in fact, very

---

[4]*Fabric Performance Standards for Trademark Licensing,* Celanese Fibers Marketing Co., March 1981.

little tow acetate yarn is produced in this country. The demand for a silklike luster and hand coupled with greater stability (than rayon) probably accounts for the importance of acetate filament yarns.

SUMMARY

Of all the man-made fibers, rayon is the oldest. Although its original creators were trying to make silk artificially, they actually discovered a new and distinct fiber more versatile than any natural one. Rayon can be made to imitate cotton, wool, silk, and even linen, and it can produce effects not possible with these natural fabrics. The availability of the raw materials from which rayon is made (a renewable resource, made from trees) assures the consumer an ample supply at moderate prices. Acetate, another of the older manmade fibers, has properties different from rayon. These properties must be considered in the end uses for acetate and in its care. (For the care of fabrics, see Chapter 16.)

However, the pre-eminence of rayon and acetate has been challenged by nylon and the other new synthetics. Each of these fibers has properties peculiar to itself, and all possess certain properties in common. There is a place for all these fibers in consumer goods. The problem lies in the proper selection of fibers to give the best service in end uses.

REVIEW QUESTIONS

1. (a) Who was the father of the rayon industry?
   (b) What method did he use to make artificial textile fibers? What was its chief disadvantage?
   (c) Is that method used today?
2. When was the name *rayon* coined?
3. (a) What is the present federal law on labeling and advertising of rayon and acetate fibers?
   (b) How does this law protect the consumer?
   (c) Is the present TFPIA adequate? Explain.
4. (a) Outline briefly the most important steps in the making of rayon by the viscose and cuprammonium processes.
   (b) Explain the differences between rayon and acetate fibers.
5. (a) How are dull rayon yarns made?
   (b) How would you identify filament rayon yarn, spun-rayon yarn, and combination yarns?
   (c) How is high-strength rayon yarn made? Give its uses.
   (d) How does high-tenacity rayon yarn differ from high-wet strength yarn? Give the selling points of the latter.
6. (a) Which type of acetate fiber has the strongest tensile strength?
   (b) Which is the strongest when wet: cotton, regular rayon, regular acetate, or linen?

7. For each of the following brand names indicate (1) the name of the producer or sponsor, and (2) the type of man-made cellulosic fiber used:
   (a) Ariloft
   (b) Arnel
   (c) Aviloc
   (d) Avril
   (e) Avril Prima
   (f) Briglo
   (g) Chromspun
   (h) Encrome
   (i) Estron
   (j) Sayfr
   (k) Xena
   (l) Zantrel

8. In what ways do the following characteristics of rayon and acetate affect consumer demand?
   (a) Length of fiber
   (b) Microscopic appearance
   (c) Strength of fiber
   (d) Elasticity
   (e) Hygroscopic moisture
   (f) Effect of light
   (g) Composition of fiber
   (h) Heat
   (i) Effect of acid and alkali
   (j) Affinity for dyestuffs

9. Describe briefly the differences between the continuous spinning and the box methods of spinning rayon yarn.

10. (a) How are the sizes of rayon and acetate filament yarns computed?
    (b) What is the range of denier in rayon yarn?
    (c) Give the denier number of a coarse yarn; of a fine yarn.

11. (a) List the uses for rayon
    (b) List the uses for acetate
    (c) In what constructions are rayons and acetates made? Name a fabric to illustrate each construction.

12. (a) List the finishes that would be applied to a rayon blanket.
    (b) When would a water-repellent finish be considered durable? Give two trade names of durable water-repellent finishes.

13. How can the use of alginate fibers in woven fabrics result in a lacelike product?

EXPERIMENTS

1. *Alkali test.*
   (a) Boil some rayon yarns for about 5 minutes in a concentrated solution of caustic soda (lye). Describe the effect of strong alkali on rayon.
   (b) Make the same test with acetate yarns. Describe the effect of strong alkali on acetate.

2. *Acid test.*
   (a) Place a few rayon yarns in concentrated sulfuric acid for 5 or 10 minutes. Describe the effect of strong acid on rayon.
   (b) Make the same test on acetate yarns. Describe the effect of strong acid on acetate.

3. *Microscopic test.* Examine a rayon fiber under the microscope. Draw the fiber as you see it. How does its appearance differ from that of cotton and linen? Examine and draw an acetate fiber.

GLOSSARY

Abraded yarn A two-ply combination filament yarn, generally of rayon or acetate, cut or roughed up at intervals to produce a hairy appearance.

Acetate Man-made fibers or yarns formed by a compound of cellulose and acetic acid that has been extruded and hardened.

Arnel See *triacetate.*

Bright yarns Made with rayon or acetate fibers of high luster.

Brushed rayon A rayon fabric that has been heavily napped. This type of fabric is highly flammable and must be treated for fire resistance.

Chardonnet, Count Hilaire de Inventor of the first synthetic fiber through dissolving nitrocellulose in alcohol and ether.

Combination yarn A ply yarn in which each ply is composed of a different fiber; for example, one-ply acetate, one-ply rayon.

Cross-linked cellulose See the glossary in Chapter 9.

Cuprammonium Type of regenerated rayon fiber or yarn made by dissolving cellulose in ammoniacal copper oxide, extruding the solution, and hardening.

Delustered fibers Those permanently dulled by incorporating mineral oil or microscopic solids in the spinning solution. When delustered, fibers are said to be pigmented; for example, pigment taffeta.

Dimensional stability Ability of a fabric to keep its shape and size.

Dope-dyed See *solution-dyed.*

Dry spinning A derivative to be spun is dissolved in a solvent that can be evaporated, leaving the desired filament to be hardened by drying in warm air or gas.

Filament A fiber of indefinite length (continuous). This term is applied to the continuous synthetic fibers.

Filament yarn Yarns made of continuous filaments.

Gas fading Change of color of some acetates when exposed to nitrogen in the air.

Groove markings Rather heavy line markings running lengthwise of the acetate fiber; a mark of identification.

High tenacity See *modified rayon* and *modified acetate fibers.*

Hydrophilic A fiber that has a high affinity for water.

Hydrophobic A fiber that lacks affinity for water.

Jersey Weft-knitted rayon, acetate, or two-bar tricot-knitted rayon or acetate used for slips, gowns, and blouses. Jersey is also made of wool, cotton, silk, nylon, or blends with the newer synthetics.

Linters Very short fibers that cover the cotton seeds after the long fibers have been removed by ginning. Linters are a source of cellulose for rayon and acetate.

Marquisette A sheer fabric in leno weave used for glass curtains. It is made of cotton, rayon, acetate, nylon, polyester, acrylic, glass, silk, or mixtures.

Modified acetate fibers Acetate fibers modified to give special characteristics by stretching the fibers and then treating them with alkali.

Modified rayon fibers Rayon fibers modified by chemical treatment while fibers are in the plastic state to give them high tenacity (high strength) and wrinkle resistance. Changes in the molecular structure of the fiber have been made.

Nitrocellulose rayon The first type of synthetic fiber discovered—no longer made in the United States. This type of rayon is made of a solution of nitrated cellulose solidified into filaments.

Pigmented fibers White or colored pigments added to a fiber-forming substance before spinning.

Rayon A manufactured fiber composed of regenerated cellulose.

Solution-dyed Dyestuff is put into the spinning solution, and the color is "locked in" as the fiber is coagulated. Synonymous with *spun-dyed* and *dope-dyed.*

Spinneret A jet or nozzle containing very fine holes through which the spinning solution is forced (extruded).

Spun-dyed   See *solution-dyed*.

Spun yarn   Yarn made of staple fiber.

Staple (man-made fiber)   Man-made filament fibers that have been cut into definite lengths for spinning into yarn. The term is best prefaced by the generic name of the fiber involved.

Striations   The many fine microscopic lines extending lengthwise on the viscose rayon fiber; a mark of identification.

Synthetic fibers   Man-made textile fibers derived from natural bases; the term is often limited to exclude the cellulosic-based fibers.

Thick and thin yarns   Yarns made of fibers of varying diameters.

Tow   Continuous-filament man-made fibers, grouped without twisting and ready to cut into staple form. See *staple*.

Transparent velvet   A sheer cut pile velvet usually all rayon or with rayon pile, suitable for evening dresses, wraps, and millinery.

Triacetate   The generic name for a cellulosic and thermoplastic man-made fiber that has a higher ratio of acetate to cellulose than does acetate. It does not dissolve in acetone, and it can be ironed with the heat set for linen.

Viscose process   A method of making rayon fibers from purified cellulose.

Wash-and-wear   See the glossary in Chapter 7.

Wet spinning (as applied to rayon)   A system of making the man-made fiber by immersing the spinneret in a liquid to coagulate the filaments that are extruded.

Chapter 14

GENERAL-PURPOSE NONCELLULOSIC FIBERS AND THE CONSUMER

Consumers may be satisfied that they are acquainted with rayon, acetate, and polyester. They may think they know how fabrics of these fibers will perform and how to care for them. But do they? As stated in the previous chapter, improvements in rayon and acetate may change a consumer's image of these fibers if he or she purchases a newly manufactured rayon or acetate article. The noncellulosic fibers such as nylon, polyester, acrylic, and modacrylic are also undergoing improvements to meet the needs of consumers.

Before the midtwentieth century, chemists made a great discovery. To get textile fibers, it was not necessary to depend on natural fibers or on man-made fibers derived from plants or animal protein. Chemists discovered that materials from the mineral world could be subjected to chemical synthesis and could produce fibers with desirable characteristics not found in the natural ones or in those with a cellulosic or protein base.

Thus, the great noncellulosic man-made industry was born, one that included a wide variety of chemicals and fibers, each with varying use characteristics.

With a plethora of brand names attached to these newly created fibers, the Federal Trade Commission was authorized under the Textile Fiber Products Identification Act to set up generic names for the varying types, so that the consumer could come to know the characteristics of each class. Classes were based on the different chemical compositions of each. Starting with generic classes for noncellulosic man-made fibers, the commission now recognizes the seventeen listed in Table 14.1. It also recognizes acetate, including triacetate, and rayon as man-made fibers of the cellulosic type.

Table 14.1   Generic Names of Noncellulosic Fibers

acrylic	metallic	polyester
anidex	modacrylic	rubber (includes lastrile[a])
aramid	novoloid[a]	saran
azlon[a]	nylon	spandex
glass	nytril[a]	vinal[a]
	olefin	vinyon

[a]Not currently produced in the United States.

In this chapter, we discuss the composition and the advantages and drawbacks in performance of the four general-purpose generic fiber classifications. The remaining thirteen may be thought of as special-purpose fibers and are considered in the next chapter. Within a classification, of course, there may be certain brands of fibers and yarns that vary slightly in their plus or minus qualities from characteristics of the generic classifications. But discussion will necessarily be limited to the general classification.

NYLON

Some of the registered brand names (trademarks) under which nylon fiber and yarn of various types are marketed for consumer use include

> Allied Chemical's Caprolan (type 6), Anso (for carpets).
> American Enka's Crepeset (knitting yarn), Enka Nylon (type 6, carpets), Enkasheer (hosiery).
> Badische's Zeflon (type 6), Vinana, Rovana, and Pluscious.
> Celanese's many numbered types.
> Courtaulds's North America's Courtaulds Nylon.
> DuPont's Antron (many numbered types), Cordura, Qiana (high quality, silklike), and many other numbered types.
> Firestone's Nytelle (filament yarns).
> Monsanto's Ultron, Blue "C" (many type varieties, also used for polyester), Cadon, and Cumuloft (for carpets).

According to the Federal Trade Commission rules, as indicated in Chapter 2, such brand names may not be used *alone* on labels and in advertising but only in close conjunction with nylon and in no larger or more prominent type.

Production of Nylon

While it is popularly said that nylon is made from coal, air, and water, the major contributors of raw materials have been the carbon obtained from petrochemicals and natural gas, also nitrogen and oxygen and water (hydrogen). While hydrocarbons can be obtained from coal, costs have been considerably lower when they have been derived from petroleum or natural gas, but the situation

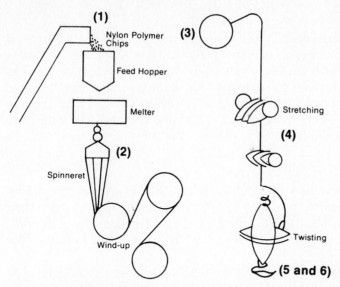

(1) Nylon Polymer Chips

Feed Hopper

Melter

(2) Spinneret

Wind-up

(3)

Stretching

(4)

Twisting

(5 and 6)

1. The production of nylon fibers begins with hard white fragments called nylon polymer chips.

2. The chips are melted and the fluid is pumped to a spinneret where it is extruded and solidified to form continuous mono-filaments.

3. Assembled continuous monofilaments are taken up on a bobbin.

4. The bobbin is transported to another area where the nylon is stretched. Stretching allows molecules within the continuous monofilaments to be arranged in a more orderly pattern.

5. The assembled continuous monofilaments are twisted into yarn.

6. The yarn is then wound onto bobbins and is ready for shipment.

Figure 14.1 Nylon production. (Courtesy of the Man-Made Fiber Producers Association.)

may change. Much of the energy needed for chemical synthesis has been derived from the same sources. There are two major types of nylon that vary slightly in the chemical composition of the ingredients: nylon 66 and nylon 6. The first was created by DuPont in 1938 and is now also made by others in the United States and by many others abroad. It involves treating hydrocarbons to yield the compounds adipic acid and hexamethylene diamine. When these are treated under pressure, the acid molecules hook up with the diamine molecules to form new larger molecules in a molecular chain clled a *polymer*. The polymer in the viscous state leaves the reaction vessel through a slot at the bottom and is poured over a rotating wheel, where water hardens it into a translucent, ivory-colored ribbon. A rotary cutter processes the solid into chips or flakes. These are processed as described in the paragraphs that follow and in Fig. 14.1.

Type 6 nylon was first produced in America by Allied Chemical, Badische, and American Enka (1954). Now made by others as well, it accounts for about one-third of the nylon produced in this country. It is made from caprolactam, which in turn is derived from cyclohexanone or hydroxylamine.[1] The manufacturing process is very similar to that of type 66. The Badische Corporation is the largest producer of caprolactam in this country.

Type 66 melts at a higher temperature than does type 6. Type 6 dyes at a more rapid rate, has a softer hand, and is slightly more elastic than nylon 66. Both have a wide variety of uses.

[1]The reactive groups of the lactam are at opposite ends of the carbon chain; a ring of six carbon and one nitrogen unit is opened up and polymerized into nylon 6.

The Nylon Filament

The flakes or chips are created by the chemical reaction and are melted and extruded through a spinneret, a perforated plate with tiny holes, and are cooled by air flow into nylon filament fiber. This method is called melt spinning. The extruded strands of nylon can be stretched to three or four times their original length. This stretching improves strength and elasticity. Nylon is made both in filament and in staple fibers. Single filaments (monofilaments) are made into such items as sheer hosiery, blouses, gowns, and veils.

Characteristics of Nylon Filaments

Under the microscope, nylon filaments appear either bright or dull. Bright filaments closely resemble the filaments of cuprammonium rayon. Their diameters are even and the surfaces smooth and structureless, like glass rods. There are no crenulations (fine notches) such as there are in most rayons. (See Appendix A.)

The dull nylon filaments show pigmentation of titanium oxide, similar to that of medium-dull rayon, but the pigmentation of nylon is more sparse.

Nylon is a chemical compound that reacts to strong mineral acids by losing strength or even by dissolving. Because nylon may be destroyed by acids, an accepted test to separate nylon from wool and vegetable fibers, for fiber identification, is to immerse a yarn or fabric in a solution of one part concentrated hydrochloric acid to one part distilled water for 60 minutes at room temperature. The nylon is dissolved. Nylons can be bleached with an oxygenated bleach, available in some stores. Chlorine bleach may be used, but it tends to yellow nylon ultimately.

Table 14.2 presents the characteristics of nylon important to the consumer and the fabric manufacturer.

Types of Nylon

Within the definition of the chemical construction that constitutes nylon, the leading manufacturers have developed a wide variety of types of fiber that differ in many respects from one another, such as affinity for different dyestuffs, difference in breaking strength, denier, luster, resilience, melting point, and elongation. Some are given nonstatic or fire-resistant properties. And some represent continuous filaments and some tow or staple fibers in varying lengths. Such proliferation makes one type better than the others for specific uses. DuPont has about 150 different types of nylon and Monsanto has about 20.[2]

Certain premium types of nylon provide special qualities. For example, a silklike quality is now available from several companies. One, called Ultron, is produced by Monsanto. It is antistatic and has good moisture transport

---

[2]Similar breakdowns of generic fibers into types occur in polyester, acrylic, and modacrylic discussed in this chapter and in olefin, spandex, and aramid in the next. For example, Fiber Industries has about forty-five different types of polyester, under the trade name of Fortrel.

Table 14.2 Characteristics of Nylon

Tensile strength	Strongest of the textile fibers, except for a high-tenacity type of aramid. Wet strength only 15 percent less than dry strength. (See Fig. 14.2.)
Luster	Bright and smooth, but may be modified for dullness by adding pigments to the polymer solution.
Affinity for dye	Can be dyed in a broad range of colors and be colorfast. But in the solution, the yarn or the fabric dyeing of blends that contain nylon may prove difficult.
Blending	Staple nylon blends well with wool, since the nylon contributes strength, abrasion resistance, and dimensional stability in washing.
Crimping	Staple nylon fiber crimps well, a factor important in spinning for use in sweaters, socks, flannels, rugs, and blankets.
Resistance to	
Abrasion	High, many times that of wool.
Heat	Safe to iron at 300° to 350°F. Nylon 66 sticks at 445°F and melts at 500°F; nylon 6 melts at between 414° and 428°F.
Sunlight	As in the case of cotton, may be injured by strong or long sun exposure, but virtually all commercial nylons are now treated with a sun-resistant agent.
Soil	Does not soil easily since filaments are smooth and nonporous.
Insects	Not vulnerable to moths, silverfish, mildew, and fungi.
Chemicals	Resists damage from alkalies and oil.
Absorption of perspiration	Tends to slow water absorption. Dries quickly.
Dimensional stability	Excellent stability to repeated laundering and holds its shape if heat-setting has been done properly.
Elasticity	High. When a filament stretches 20 percent, recovery after the first stretch is 95 percent and thereafter 93 percent. Also returns to original form after compression.

properties for use in sleepwear, lingerie, and other intimate apparel. Another is DuPont's Qiana, which also has silklike properties combined with ease in care. Another DuPont fiber, trilobal in cross section, provides a delustered yarn called Antron, used for women's jersey blouses. A special type of Antron has antistatic properties, while still another contains a microscopic structure specifically for use in carpets.

A more recent nylon fiber modification is the development of different dye levels that produce various color effects in a single dye bath. Through the chemical modification of the fiber, striking two- and three-color patterns can be achieved without the cost of yarn dyeing. Cross-dyeable nylon yarns and cross-dyed garments are now widely marketed by major producers.

Several producers have developed a continuous-filament cross-dyeable yarn for heather effects. Before introduction, nylon yarns for heather effects were generally spun from blends of dissimilar dyeing nylon staple fibers. Unfortunately, the differential-dyeing nylons did not always have the required matched physical properties, and the staple yarns did not fare too well in the tortuous piece-dyeing step. The finished garments were also plagued with pilling (the formation of little balls of fiber on the surface of the fabric) and other assorted ills associated with high-strength staple yarn products. Filament nylon provides high-performance pill-resistant heather products at moderate cost.

Yarn Making

After the nylon fibers have been extruded from the spinneret, they are hardened, grouped together in a strand, and wound into a "cake" or spinning bobbin preparatory to stretching (called drawing by the industry). A series of rollers revolving at different speeds stretch the fibers. The operation aligns the molecules adding both strength and elasticity to the yarn.

Nylon is made in both multifilament yarn and monofilaments (single filament types). (See Chapter 3.) Throwsters twist the multifilament yarn to give it tensile strength, snag resistance, and durability, and spinners spin or twist nylon staple into yarn, much as cotton and wool are spun. (Fig. 14.3.) Most nylon yarns are made in the multifilament type and are used in dresses, hosiery, blouses, lingerie, upholstery, and carpets. Monofilaments are used in such items as sheer hosiery and various net fabrics.

The sizes of filament nylon yarns are figured on the denier basis, similar to rayon. Spun nylon yarns are on a count basis, like spun rayon.

Spun yarn is made of either 100 percent nylon or of blends of staples. Nylon staple is cut in different lengths, 1½ to 8 inches, depending upon the spinning system being used—cotton, woolen, worsted, silk, or other. Spun yarn

Figure 14.2 The grab tester illustrated here is being used to determine the degree of stretch before the breaking point of nylon is reached. (Courtesy of the J. C. Penney Co.)

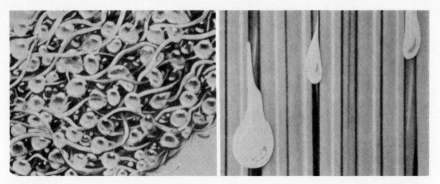

Figure 14.3 Left: Garment woven of spun yarn does not dry rapidly because each of the air spaces fills with water. Right: Garment woven of continuous-filament nylon has practically no air spaces in which to trap moisture. (Reproduced courtesy of E. I. DuPont de Nemours & Company, Inc.)

is light, soft, and springy and is very popular in woollike textures and blends, especially in socks and sweaters.

The making of bulky yarns was described in Chapter 3. By combining different deniers and plies of looped, curled, and crimped varieties of yarn, it is possible to obtain a great many new textures from continuous-filament nylon. Stretch yarns were also discussed in Chapter 3. Improvements in the luster of yarn have occurred, as evidenced by DuPont's Sparkling Nylon in 1959 and a nylon jersey of Antron trilobal multifilament yarn in 1960.

Texturing Nylon Yarns

The comfort factor in nylon clothing can be improved by texturing. (See Chapter 3.)

Textured yarns achieve the following:

1. Combine the high abrasion resistance, strength, toughness, and ease-of-care properties of nylon or polyester with stretch, bulk, superb hand, and more rapid wicking of perspiration for greater wearing comfort.
2. Permit simulation of some of the better characteristics of fabrics made from spun yarns while permitting new and novel approaches to styling and fashion.
3. Have better drape and greater cover and opacity.
4. Have texture and hand that can be varied at will depending on the method and conditions under which the yarn is textured.
5. In many cases, enable garment manufacturers to produce stretch-to-fit items in a smaller number of sizes that span the complete size requirements.

Because it is thermoplastic, nylon yarn, like some other noncellulosics, can be textured to impart loft, bulk, stretch, and a drier hand than "flat," or nontextured, filament yarns. In texturing, the yarns are coiled, crimped, or the filaments are entangled by a number of different processes. (See Chapter 3.) Textured nylon yarns are widely used for carpets and to a lesser degree for clothing.

Nylon 66 was essentially concentrated on fashion uses in intimate apparel, both in knitting and weaving. Continuous-filament nylon is important for basic knit construction in foundation garments, lingerie, and women's and men's hosiery. In 1957 DuPont introduced Tissue Tricot, and in 1960 Tricot Satinette. These constructions of warp knitting were achieved through the use of fine-denier nylon yarns combined with a special calendered fabric finishing process.

Nylon 66 is also used to make a spun-combed (nonwoven) fabric, called Cerex by Monsanto. It is resistant to high temperature, alkali, and most solvents. It has a slip surface that permits, for example, autoseat covers to be slipped over foam seat forms.

American Enka produces physically modified crepeset monofilament yarns that can be knitted on tricot machines to obtain fabrics with a definite, permanent crepe effect for lingerie and blouses. (See warp knitting, Chapter 6). Stretch fabrics can be both knitted and woven. Bulky-knit sweaters, either hand- or machine-made, are popular for sports and casual wear. Special types of nylon and other noncellulosic fibers may be molded. Bras are often made by this process. A molded bra is comfortable because it has no seams; it keeps its size and shape permanently after machine washing and drying; it is durable; and it has an aesthetic appeal.

A nylon monofilament straw, made by a process developed in Switzerland, is sold under the name of Yuva. It can be woven or knitted into shoes, belts, hats, handbags, lampshades, curtaining, and automobile fabrics.

Any type of weave—plain, twill, satin, or fancy—can be made in 100 percent nylon or in blends or mixtures. The principal constructions are hosiery, tricot slips, gowns, shirts, and blouses. Nylon fleeces, furlike pile fabrics, and rugs are popular, as are laces and nets.

Finishing for Nylon Fabrics

Nylon fabrics can usually be bleached safely with sodium chloride without risk of tendering. All nylon fabrics are subjected to heat-setting conditions that must be controlled with care. All parts of the fabric must be subjected to heat-setting to make them dimensionally stable (given permanent shape). Excessive time at high temperatures must be avoided. Setting of nylon fabrics is an essential step, since an unset finished cloth would not be stabilized; it would not be smooth; and it would wrinkle easily.

To make a durable stiff finish, a melamine resin is used that does not penetrate but polymerizes on the surface. Nylon taffeta petticoats are finished in this fashion. Nonslip finishes do not penetrate the fabric either, but they bond the warp and filling yarns to make a firm hand. A resin polyethylene oxide is claimed to eliminate fiber static. Some fabrics are calendered. (See Chapter 7.)

Table 14.3 Why Customers Buy Nylon Fabrics

Durability	From a consumer's point of view, nylon provides the following advantages: exceptional strength and recovery from small stretching forces. Coupled with lightness in weight, it makes very desirable sheer fabrics.
Suitability	The resilience and strength of nylon make it suitable for hosiery and underwear. Panty-hose do not become baggy at the knee, and in pile velvets, the pile is not deformed when crushed.
Ease in care	Heat-setting makes embossing of fabrics permanent and sets permanent pleats. Heat-setting also prevents shrinking or sagging. Nylon fabrics are easy to wash, many of them drip dry, and need no ironing. Nylon dries very quickly. Nylon is mothproof and not adversely affected by water, perspiration, or dry-cleaning agents. However, mildew may discolor nylon.
Versatility	The versatility of nylon seems limitless, particularly in blends with other fibers. With rayon, nylon adds strength, abrasion resistance, and stability in washing and wearing. A nylon/rayon blend makes a fine-count, strong yarn for lightweight washable fabrics. When nylon and cotton are blended, nylon again contributes its strength, abrasion resistance, and dimensional stability, as well as better resistance to perspiration, a softer hand, better elasticity, and quick drying qualities. Nylon combined with acetate or acrylic fiber adds strength and wearing quality.
	Nylon staple is particularly suitable for reinforcing socks, anklets, swimsuits, under-shirts, denim, upholstery, industrial fabrics, and sewing and darning threads and is frequently used in 100 percent form in lingerie. Some of these same properties make nylon an excellent material for woven and tufted carpets and upholstery used in homes, institutions (schools and hospitals), and commercial enterprises (restaurants and air-ports). It is also used for tents, ropes, cordage, liners, tarpaulins, tire cord, and filtration fabrics. It also has nontextile uses such as bristles and films, which are characterized by toughness, elasticity, and strength. (See Fig. 14.4.)

Piece-dyeing is a method of coloring nylon fabrics after construction. (See Chapter 8.)

Why Customers Buy Nylon Fabrics

Customers buy nylon for durability, suitability, ease of care, and versatility, as explained in Table 14.3.

Overcoming Some Limitations of Nylon

Research has been responsible for the great strides in the uses for nylon. Early consumer objections to faults such as pilling, development of static electricity, graying of white nylon, and clamminess of 100 percent filament nylon have all been alleviated to varying degrees by active research programs.

Both Enka and DuPont produce antistatic nylon for women's lingerie. These yarns are chemically modified so that the antistatic properties are inherent and last for the life of the garment.

Some fabrics may always retain one or more objectionable features. There is no one perfect fiber for all purposes. If the fiber possesses all the minimum

Figure 14.4 Use of nylon for tents. (Courtesy of Monsanto Textiles Company.)

requirements needed to perform satisfactorily in a given end use, there should be no customer objections. However, to meet price competition, certain treatments necessary for satisfactory performance may be omitted by the fabric manufacturer. As a result, the consumer may have legitimate grounds for dissatisfaction with a fiber.

THE POLYESTERS

Polyester,[3] a chemically created fiber with properties differing from those of other man-made fibers, has shown the greatest growth potential of all man-made fibers. It has been often believed that polyester may ultimately become the world's most important fiber. Consumption in the United States was estimated at 3.7 billion pounds in 1979, exceeding that of any other fiber, man-made or natural. This figure accounts for over half of all yarns consumed—spun and filament—in men's, women's, and children's tailored and knitted outer-

---

[3]Polyester is defined by the Federal Trade Commission as a manufactured fiber in which the fiber-forming substance is any long-chain synthetic polymer composed at least 85 percent by weight of an ester of a substituted aromatic carboxylic acid, including but not restricted to substituted terephthalate units and para-substituted hydroxybenzoate units.

wear. Textured woven fabrics of polyester, both rigid and stretch, have a significant position in the apparel market. Polyester filament textured and untextured yarns (and in combination with spun yarns) are well received. Over two-thirds of its usage is in apparel, about 6 percent is in home furnishings, and about one-fourth goes to industry. But the domestic use of polyester filament has not increased much since 1973, and the future trend is somewhat uncertain.[4]

Development

Some years ago, British chemists developed polyester and called it Terylene. Their work was based on research by DuPont that resulted in nylon. DuPont and the British group effected a licensing agreement that permitted each company to pursue parallel commercial development programs. Thus, in 1953, DuPont opened its first polyester plant (in Kinston, North Carolina) and became the first commercial producer.

DuPont named its fiber Dacron (pronounced day-cron), and it quickly achieved wide consumer acceptance. Today, a score of other companies are producing polyester in America. The product is made available in bright, semibright, and dull lusters and in varying tenacities (strengths). Many companies produce other variants for special uses. As in the case of nylon, selection of the appropriate type for an intended use is important.

DuPont has recently produced a special type of Dacron called Matte Dacron of 70-denier fine-filament polyester that is soft and glitter-free and is especially suited for dresses, shirts, and blousewear.

The well-publicized brand names under which polyester is available, in addition to Dacron, are the following:

Avlin (Avtex Fibers)
Blue "C" (Monsanto), also applied to nylon
Caprolan (Allied Technologies)
Crepesort (American Enka)
Encron (American Enka)
Fortrel (Fiber Industries)
Kodofill (Eastman Chemical), a fiberfill
Spectran (Monsanto)
Strialine (American Enka)
Trevira (Hoechst)
Zetran (Badische)

Production of the Fiber and the Yarn

The process of producing polyester fiber is an intricate one. Basically, the raw materials are petroleum or natural gas and air and water. There are two different combinations of chemicals that produce virtually identical fibers. One is a

[4]*America's Textiles* (R/B edition), September 1980, p. 86.

combination of dimethyl terephthalate and ethylene glycol, "cooked" at high temperatures. The other combines terephthalic acid and ethylene glycol. The result of both chemical processes is solid, hard, porcelainlike chips that are melt-spun into a honeylike liquid and extruded through a spinneret and solidified to form continuous filaments. These are taken up on a winding tube and then stretched to many times their original lengths and twisted to add strength and elasticity. The number of filaments and the amount of twist determines the size and texture of the yarns.

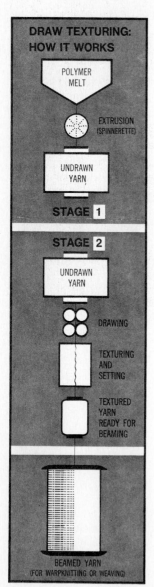

DRAW TEXTURING:
HOW IT WORKS

POLYMER
MELT

EXTRUSION
(SPINNERETTE)

UNDRAWN
YARN

STAGE 1

STAGE 2

UNDRAWN
YARN

DRAWING

TEXTURING
AND
SETTING

TEXTURED
YARN
READY FOR
BEAMING

BEAMED YARN
(FOR WARPKNITTING OR WEAVING)

Figure 14.5 Draw-texturing polyester yarn. The conventional process for texturing filament yarns has two stages: (1) yarn is extruded through a spinneret and is wound; then (2) it is unwound, drawn through heated stretchers, and is processed through a texturing machine. The textured yarn is wound on wide beams for warp knitting or to serve as warp in woven fabrics. (Courtesy of FMC Corporation, now Avtex Fibers.)

To eliminate the steps in the production process that produces chips and melts them, a continuous process may be used. The chemicals are combined in a continuous polymerizer (pressure cooker) that permits the polymer to be extruded directly through the spinneret.

There are many types of polyester. For staple yarns, filaments are crimped and cut into desired lengths. Smooth filament yarns are used for taffetas, sheer curtains, satin, and lightweight apparel fabrics for both men and women.

Textured polyester filament yarns (see Fig. 14.5), made today by the false-twist method, are used extensively both in men's and women's knitted slacks and suits and in stretch woven fabrics. At least 70 percent of polyester filament yarns used in apparel fabrics are of the textured variety to provide bulk and nonslick aesthetics. Fabrics of these textured yarns are the major output of Burlington's North Carolina mill in Burlingham, referred to in Chapter 4.

Spun yarns are used in fabrics whose texture is cotton- or woollike, since they produce soft, hairy yarns. Fillings of staple polyester for pillows, comforters, sleeping bags, upholstered furniture, mattresses, and auto cushions do not mat and are lightweight, comfortable, and nonallergenic.

Modifications in polyester fiber types and yarns are continually being made to produce products more suitable for specific end uses. For example, DuPont produces a yarn of Dacron in which the filaments have a cross section. Textured wovens and double knits of this yarn do not glitter in sunlight, an advantage in men's wear. American Enka produces a thick and thin yarn called Strialine that gives a linenlike appearance with a differential dyeing look to knitted and woven fabrics. This company produces another filament yarn used to make fabrics that have a silky touch and improved drapability. Hoechst Fibers Industries makes a polyester fiber, Trevira, used in carpets and a variation for apparel. (See Fig. 14.6.)

Polyester filament yarns enjoyed a boom in the early 1970s since they were used mainly in the production of double-knit fabrics and apparel that were, at that time, in tremendous popular demand. But the zeal for double knits dropped sharply in about the middle of the decade because the fabrics proved to be heavy, warm in hot weather, and expensive, requiring extra yarn to produce. This has led to a sharp cutback in polyester filament, even though polyester staple fibers continue to increase in production and use. Nevertheless, some textile producers believe that polyester filament yarns will return to long-term profitability.

Blends of the Yarn

Polyester staple fibers are especially appropriate for blends. Blends of 50 to 65 percent polyester with cotton have become popular in minimum-care men's shirtings, women's blouses, dresses, slacks, knitted T-shirts, sportswear, and many home furnishings items, particularly bedsheets. A polyester and acrylic blend (50 percent each) is used for slacks, sportswear, and dresses. Combination fabrics of polyester blend yarns and polyester filament yarns are used in fabrics for men's and women's apparel and home furnishings.

Figure 14.6 This Oscar de la Renta design is made of Trevira® and wool from a J. P. Stevens machine-washable woolens line. (Photo courtesy of Hoechst Fibers Industries. Trevira is a registered trademark of Hoechst AG.)

Blends of polyester and worsted (normally 55 percent polyester and 45 percent worsted) are used for men's regular suitings, and increasingly also for women's apparel. This fabric holds its press and resists wrinkles, and the wrinkles hang out readily. It is lighter in weight than is 100 percent worsted and tailors beautifully. Nevertheless, the high cost of wool has led to a great increase in all-polyester suitings. Another satisfactory blend is polyester and rayon, either 65/35 or 50/50 for slacks and dresses.

Polyester/cotton blends are finished differently from 100 percent cotton. The cloth is singed before scouring and heat-set after finishing to obtain dimensional stability. Polyester/rayon blends are treated with resins for shrinkage control. However, the polyester/modified rayon blends do not require resin treatment.

A careful study reported in 1979 of a blend of a 65 percent polyester and 35 percent cotton shirt against an all-cotton shirt reports that the cost of energy in washing, drying, and ironing the blend was only half as much as laundering the all-cotton shirt and that it had a 50 percent longer life.[5] A person who attempts to dry a cotton and a polyester/cotton shirt will probably find that the former is still damp when the latter is dry.

Characteristics of Polyester

Polyester has established itself as an all-purpose fiber, suitable for a great many uses—for apparel, in the home, and in industry. (See Fig. 14.7.) It blends well with many other fibers and yarns, which makes a variety of effects possible.

---

[5]"Those New No-Iron Cotton Shirts," *Good Housekeeping Magazine,* June 1979, pp. 26–28.

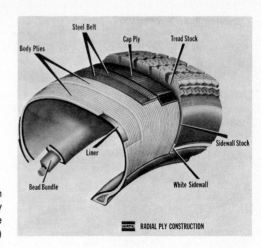

Steel Belt
Cap Ply
Tread Stock
Body Plies
Sidewall Stock
Liner
Bead Bundle
White Sidewall

RADIAL PLY CONSTRUCTION

Figure 14.7 An important use of polyester and nylon is in the construction of truck tires. In this radial-ply construction, the body ply and the cap ply are made of polyester or nylon. (Courtesy of Uniroyal, Inc.)

From the consumer's point of view, polyester is prized for its ease in care, reflected in its wrinkle resistance, its stability in repeated washings, its requirement for little or no ironing, and its affinity to permanent heat-setting to control shrinkage and sagging and to retain pleats. It is resistant to most outside elements, such as sunlight, acids in the air, bleaches, and dry-cleaning solvents. Originally high in price, volume production has made its price moderate, even lower than that of cotton at times.

The standard commodity product has some limitations in dyeability and printability because carriers are generally required for coloration. Serious pilling problems in staple constructions are largely overcome by the use of special low-pilling grades or by the use of filament polyester, which is generally also textured for comfort. Stains, particularly oily stains, frequently cannot be removed satisfactorily, and resoiling is often a problem. Difficulties with static electricity have resulted in the development of a wide variety of industrial home finishes, which generally are only partially successful.

Table 14.4 provides an overview of polyester's properties.

Improved Polyester Yarns

Polyester yarns have been produced now that improve upon the standard product. An example is Spectran by Monsanto. It is similar to conventional polyester in its round cross section; it has disperse dyeability and excellent strength, but in other qualities it is quite different from conventional polyesters. It offers a warm soft hand, greater bulk, and supple drape.

It can be dyed with disperse dyes without carrier at atmospheric pressure. With pollution problems mounting, dyeing polyester without carrier is certain to become more important. Printing yields good results on fabrics of Spectran polyester, both woven and knitted. It can be used in 100 percent form or in blends with acrylic and wool fibers in jersey constructions.

Stain-release properties of Spectran are superior to those of regular

Table 14.4 Characteristics of Polyesters

Tensile strength	Very strong, but not as strong as nylon or aramid; also very durable.
Luster	Bright to dull, depending upon whether a delusterant is used.
Affinity for dyes	Easy to dye fast colors with basic and dispersed dyes in the presence of a swelling agent.
Blending and crimping	May be combined with other fibers and yarns, especially with woolens for suitings and cottons for shirtings.
Resistance to Abrasion	Tends to pill.
Heat	Can be ironed at 300° to 400°F, but may stick or soften at temperatures above 400°F and will melt at 480° to 550°F.
Sunlight	Equal to nylon but better for curtains since window glass screens out wavelengths harmful to polyester.
Insects	Moths do not consume it.
Chemicals and fungi	Not affected by dilute acids, cleaning solvents, and microorganisms.
Soil and stains	Readily removed except for oil-based stains; tends to gray; picks up soil from the skin ("ring around the collar"). Newer types are overcoming this problem.
Effect of perspiration	As with nylon and acrylic, it is hydrophobic, resisting the absorption of water; it regains moisture more slowly than nylon does.
Dimensional stability	Resists shrinkage, stretching, and wrinkling. Easy to wash with little or no ironing; keeps shape and can be heat-set for permanent press; does not mat.
Elasticity	Superb hand, resilient.

polyesters. In particular, release of oil-based stains, such as motor oil, butter, mayonnaise, hand cream, and mineral oil, is improved over that of regular polyesters in normal laundering.

Regular polyester fabrics have a persistent tendency to gray upon repeated laundering because they tend to act as scavengers for oils, grease, and particulate matter in the wash water. In contrast, fabrics of Spectran, because of their inherent resistance to soil redeposition, launder better and retain a satisfactory appearance longer.

Likewise, Spectran polyester/wool blend fabrics have been developed. The hand of these styles is soft—almost cashmerelike—and pleasantly different from the somewhat harsh, unyielding hand of regular polyester/wool blend constructions.

Polyester is also used in a leatherlike fabric, called UltraSuede, by Springs Industries. It consists of 60 percent polyester fiber and 40 percent nonfibrous polyurethane. Another variety is made from ultrafine nylon fibers of 0.001 to 0.01 denier. It has the feel of leather but is much lighter in weight; these costly fabrics are used for dresses, coats, and some accessories.

Trevira, the polyester fiber manufactured by Hoechst Fibers, has also achieved an important advance. A flame-retardant modifier is applied, not to the fabric as a finishing process, but to the polymer from which the polyester fiber is extruded. The fabrics constructed from both staple and filament fibers and yarns so treated stand up well in washing and retain a soft, comfortable touch. When constructed properly, their inherent flame resistance makes them well suited for both clothing and home furnishing uses, where there may be a potential fire hazard.

Nonwoven Fabrics of Polyester and Nylon

Polyester and nylon are used widely not only for woven and knitted fabrics but also for nonwoven constructions, as was explained in Chapter 6. Except for rayon, polyester is the most widely used of the man-made fibers for this purpose. Table 14.5 gives some of the major trade names recently on the market

Table 14.5 Trademarks of Some Nonwoven Fabrics of Polyester, Nylon, and Blends

Trademark	Producer	Fiber	Construction[a]	Major Uses
Bidim[b]	Monsanto	Polyester	Needlepunched	Road construction, track bed repair, drainage.
Cerex	Monsanto	Nylon 6.6	Spunbonded	Upholstery stabilization, fill in quilts, lamination with fragile tissue for surgical use.
Confil	International Paper	Polyester glass fiber and cellulose	Wet formed	Interlinings, wall coverings, filters, engineering products.
Keybak	Chicopee Mills	Polyester, rayon	Wet and dry formed	Wipes, facings, diaper linings, medical and surgical products.
Enkamat[c]	American Enka	Nylon	Melt bonded	Matting replacement for asphalt and concrete to avoid soil erosion and to encourage grass growth.
Nexus	Burlington[d]	Polyester	Spunlaced	Substrate for luggage, shoe, and automotive products, diapers, bedspreads, filters, medical, and institutional apparel.
Pellon	Pellon Corp.	Polyester, nylon, acetate, and rayon blends	Dry formed	Apparel, interlinings, and interfacings.
Reema	DuPont	Polyester	Spunbonded	Interlinings, carpet backings, permanent-care labels.
Sontara	Dupont	Polyester	Spunlaced	Drapes, bedspreads, mattress pads, table linens, medical gowns and dressings, decorative felts.
Stabilenka	American Enka	Polyester (some with acrylic binders)	Needlepunched	Filter medium for erosion control.

[a]See Chapter 6 for the various constructions.
[b]Monsanto discontinued this product in 1981.
[c]See Figure 14.14.
[d]Nexus is made by DuPont as Sontara with special finishing, processing, and marketing by Burlington.

and some chief facts about these fabrics. They are mainly for industrial and institutional use.

THE ACRYLICS

Production

Acrylic fibers are made from a chemical compound called *acrylo*nitrile (the italicized letters of the compound indicate the derivation of acrylic fiber).[6] It is derived from chemicals taken from coal, petroleum, or natural gas and from air, water, and limestone. After a series of complicated chemical reactions (often combined with other chemicals to improve dye absorption), the solution formed is extruded through a spinneret. The extruded filaments are dried and stretched to improve the strength and elasticity of the fiber. (See Fig. 14.8.) The fiber may be either wet-spun or dry-spun. (See Chapter 13.) Acrylic fibers are produced only in staple/tow fiber form in this country. Although used primarily in 100 percent form, they are found blended with natural fibers, especially wool, and other synthetics in a variety of knit and woven apparel. In solution form, acrylic is important in the manufacture of paint, a nontextile.

Bicomponent acrylics (see Chapter 15), an important subclass of acrylics, available from several companies, are permanent-crimped fibers. The shape of the crimp is comparable to the spiral of a corkscrew. The fiber is not a conventional type but is made of two components, each of which differs from the other in molecular structure. Because of this unique structure, the fiber develops a three-dimensional spiral crimp when the fabric is processed. This fiber has been responsible for new style developments in knitwear because of its aesthetic appearance and woollike resilience. Bicomponent acrylics, such as Orlon types 4, 21, 24, and 78 by DuPont, Acrilan types 57, B-94, and B-96 by Monsanto, and Creslan 68 by American Cyanamid are widely used in sweaters and other outerwear, hand-knitting yarns, and carpets.

Uses

The major uses for acrylics, where they represent more than half of all fibers consumed are sweaters, socks, hand-knitting craft yarns, pile fabrics, and blankets. Other significant markets include carpets, circular knit fabrics, and in Europe, home upholstery. Woven apparel fabrics and several minor industrial applications complete the list of end uses. In solution form, acrylic is important in the manufacture of paints.

Acrylics are readily and inexpensively dyed to almost any color, from subtle earth shades to bright hues. Colorfastness is good in all but fluorescent shades.

---

[6]Acrylic is defined by the Federal Trade Commission as a manufactured fiber in which the fiber-forming substance is any long-chain synthetic polymer composed of at least 85 percent by weight of acrylonitrile units.

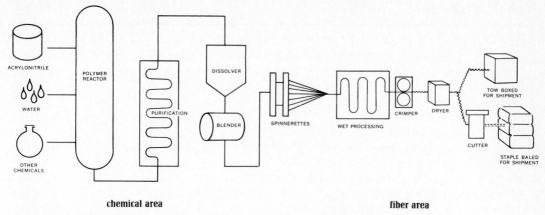

chemical area   fiber area

Figure 14.8 How Creslan acrylic fiber is made. (From Creslan pamphlet, American Cyanimid Co., center spread.)

Development

The first major acrylic fiber was Orlon. Preliminary work on it was started in the pioneering Research Division of DuPont's Textile Fibers Department as early as 1940, but the fiber was not available commercially until 1948. Others entered the field and now there are several brands of acrylic fiber in addition to Orlon, among them

Acrilan and Bi-Loft (Monsanto)
Creslan (American Cyanamid)
Zefran (Badische)

They are made in a variety of types.

Characteristics of Acrylic Fibers

The acrylics are soft, since virtually all in the United States are made in staple form, and although they are bulky, they are light in weight. Acrylics are not as strong or as resistant to abrasion as nylon. Excellent resistance to sunlight, to pressed-crease retention, and to moths is important to the consumer. Finishing acrylics presents no particular problem. Acrylics have moderate to good resistance to pilling. They are subject to the same problem of static electricity as other noncellulosic man-made fibers, but this is generally overcome by application of selected antistatic finishes.

The chief characteristics that knowledgeable consumers have in mind when selecting acrylics in 100 percent form or in blends depend upon end use. For outer clothing, this fiber holds its shape well, resists abrasion, washes easily, dries quickly, and needs little or no ironing. It avoids crushing and mussing in travel. For coats it is fluffy and light. For carpeting, acrylics provide a luxurious texture and ease in cleaning.

Table 14.6 summarizes the characteristics of this fiber.

Table 14.6 Characteristics of Acrylics

Tensile strength	Fair in spun form but durable.
Weight	Light and soft, fluffy and bulky in fabric form.
Affinity to dyeing	Many types can be dyed in bright colors. If solution-dyed, fast to perspiration (as well as to sunlight).
Blending	Adds above characteristics to blends.
Resistance to	
Abrasion	Good, but only moderate to pilling.
Heat	Holds heat, warm, sticks at 450° to 497°F depending on retention type.
Sunlight	Colorfast if solution-dyed.
Soil	Easy to wash, quick to dry.
Insects	Moth-resistant.
Chemicals and microorganisms	Excellent resistance.
Absorption and perspiration	Poor; hydrophobic, like nylon and polyesters.
Dimensional stability	Excellent crease retention, resistance to wrinkling, sagging, shrinking, and stretching; withstands repeated laundering (wash-and-wear).

THE MODACRYLICS

The modacrylics, which have been in the marketplace for many years, were once simply called "acrylics," a term used to describe almost any fiber containing acrylonitrile. Under the Textile Fiber Products Identification Act of 1960, acrylics are officially described as containing at least 85 percent acrylonitrile. Fibers containing 35 to 84 percent acrylonitrile are described as "modacrylic" fibers. (See Fig. 14.9.) These chemicals are derived from elements in natural air, salt, and water. True, these modacrylics rendered excellent service in industrial and certain apparel and home furnishings end uses, but they could be described more realistically as polyvinyl chloride fibers, and their properties mirrored their makeup. Other modacrylics did have acrylonitrile as a major component by a narrow margin, but they had serious deficiencies that limited their use.

As more emphasis was placed on flame resistance and other built-in pluses mentioned shortly, the fraction of additives in premium acrylics rose steadily until the 15 percent limit of other chemicals was exceeded and these precisely engineered fibers became modacrylics. Fabrics of these acryliclike modacrylics are a growing segment of the textile market, as their use, in many instances, meets regulatory requirements for flame resistance without sacrificing the superb aesthetic properties of acrylics. Moreover, these modacrylics are engineered to perform well in both wet and dry processing, and specific products are tailored to meet the precise needs of each market.

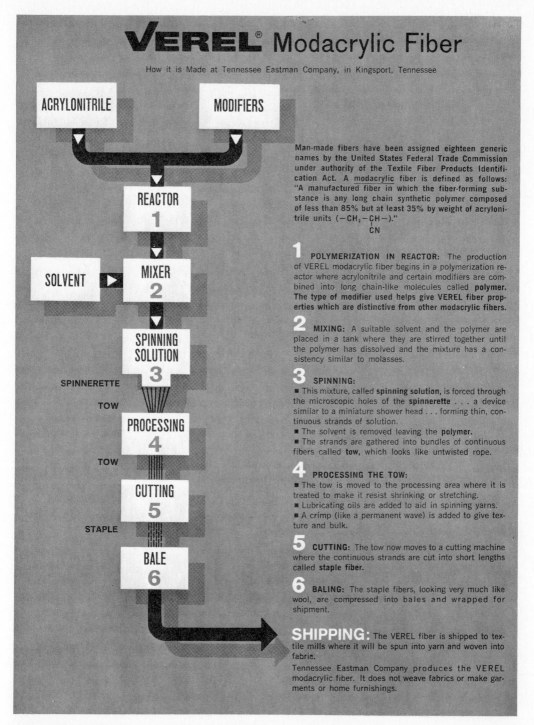

VEREL® Modacrylic Fiber

How it is Made at Tennessee Eastman Company, in Kingsport, Tennessee

ACRYLONITRILE

MODIFIERS

REACTOR 1

SOLVENT

MIXER 2

SPINNING SOLUTION 3

SPINNERETTE

TOW

PROCESSING 4

TOW

CUTTING 5

STAPLE

BALE 6

Man-made fibers have been assigned eighteen generic names by the United States Federal Trade Commission under authority of the Textile Fiber Products Identification Act. A modacrylic fiber is defined as follows: "A manufactured fiber in which the fiber-forming substance is any long chain synthetic polymer composed of less than 85% but at least 35% by weight of acrylonitrile units $(-CH_2-CH-)$."
$$CN$$

1 POLYMERIZATION IN REACTOR: The production of VEREL modacrylic fiber begins in a polymerization reactor where acrylonitrile and certain modifiers are combined into long chain-like molecules called **polymer.** The type of modifier used helps give VEREL fiber properties which are distinctive from other modacrylic fibers.

2 MIXING: A suitable solvent and the polymer are placed in a tank where they are stirred together until the polymer has dissolved and the mixture has a consistency similar to molasses.

3 SPINNING:
■ This mixture, called **spinning solution,** is forced through the microscopic holes of the **spinnerette** . . . a device similar to a miniature shower head . . . forming thin, continuous strands of solution.
■ The solvent is removed leaving the **polymer.**
■ The strands are gathered into bundles of continuous fibers called **tow,** which looks like untwisted rope.

4 PROCESSING THE TOW:
■ The tow is moved to the processing area where it is treated to make it resist shrinking or stretching.
■ Lubricating oils are added to aid in spinning yarns.
■ A crimp (like a permanent wave) is added to give texture and bulk.

5 CUTTING: The tow now moves to a cutting machine where the continuous strands are cut into short lengths called **staple fiber.**

6 BALING: The staple fibers, looking very much like wool, are compressed into bales and wrapped for shipment.

SHIPPING: The VEREL fiber is shipped to textile mills where it will be spun into yarn and woven into fabric.

Tennessee Eastman Company produces the VEREL modacrylic fiber. It does not weave fabrics or make garments or home furnishings.

Figure 14.9 Production of modacrylic fibers. (Courtesy of the Tennessee Eastman Company, now Eastman Chemical Products, Inc.)

Major Characteristics

Compared with the acrylics, the major advantage of modacrylics is its high flame resistance. Fabrics of modacrylic are difficult to ignite when exposed to flame and are self-extinguishing. But they have a lower melting point and will soften at a lower temperature and shrink at 250°F. This feature makes it possible to mix fibers that shrink in different amounts in the surface of a pile fabric. When applied to heat, the surface takes on the appearance of natural fur, with both long and under hairs.

Modacrylics also have a specially soft resilient texture and a warm and luxurious hand. Since hydrophobic, drops of water on a coat can be shaken off, leaving the coat dry.

As with the acrylics, modacrylics resist acids well and have a good resistance to abrasion. They can be dyed in a wide range of colors and, if solution-dyed, are colorfast and resistant to sunlight, perspiration, and wetness. They may be heat-set for shape resistance and shrinkage control.

Brands and Their Special Characteristics

One of the earliest modacrylic fibers was Dynel, produced by Union Carbide from vinyl chloride and acrylonitrile. It has since been discontinued. Another early modacrylic fiber, Verel, produced by Eastman Chemical Products, is still on the market. (See Fig. 14.10.) It is resistant to chemicals, resilient, and nonflammable. It has excellent abrasion resistance. It is used primarily for furlike fabrics, apparel, draperies, and carpets. It is available only in staple, not filament, form.

Figure 14.10 The Collins & Aikman pile fabric of Verel modacrylic and acrylic provides lightweight warmth. (Photo courtesy of Eastman Chemical Products, Inc.)

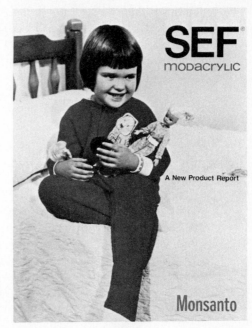

Figure 14.11 Properly constructed and finished children's sleepers of SEF modacrylic meet U.S. Department of Commerce Standard DOC FF3-71 for flammability of children's sleepwear, combining the fine aesthetic and performance properties of Acrilan acrylic with the flame retardancy of modacrylics. (Photo courtesy of Monsanto Company.)

Verel can be dyed in a variety of shades and cross-dye effects. The neutral-dyeing premetallized dyes are usually best for fastness to light and washing. For most purposes, Verel does not require bleaching, because it is unusually white. Should bleaching be desired, sodium chlorite and formic acid are used.

A series of acryliclike modacrylic fibers are being marketed today primarily to meet needs for reduced flammability. One Japanese product, used to make Kanekalon wigs, combines many of the aesthetic and performance characteristics of human hair with certain advantages of man-made fibers—good resistance to flammability and to damage from heat. (Some wigs frizz when hit with a wave of heat from opening an oven door.)

Modacrylic for Kaneka America's wigs is producer-colored in carefully selected wig shades. The different deniers available permit control of wig softness.[7]

Another acryliclike modacrylic fiber produced by Monsanto is SEF. It has a semidull luster and can be dyed in a variety of colors. Properly constructed and finished apparel fabrics of SEF modacrylic fiber will extinguish when the source of ignition is removed, and they meet or exceed recognized standards, such as the Consumer Products Safety Commission's Standard FF3-71 for the flammability of children's sleepwear. (See Fig. 14.11.)

Several companies have marketed various types of children's sleepwear made from SEF fabrics. Woven and knit fabrics, including warp knits, are used

[7]A similar product by Monsanto is no longer on the market.

to make flame-retardant garments in virtually all the favorite styles, including the popular fleece types. Other sleepwear, institutional garments, and dresses with SEF are also marketed. As important as the safety and comfort features are soil-release factors and the resistance to shrinkage.

Flame-retardant blankets, draperies and casement fabrics, and bathmats and sets made of SEF modacrylic fiber and its blends are being marketed by many companies. These fibers are also well suited for bedspreads and upholstery.

SUMMARY

Consumers are more aware of the fiber content of their garments since the TFPIA has required that all fibers be labeled by generic names as specified by the FTC. Previous to the enactment of this law, a few consumers had become familiar with trade names such as Orlon, Dacron, and Acrilan.

But with the newer generic names such as acrylic, modacrylic, and polyester, the consumer not only has to learn what these terms mean but also has to learn the characteristics of each of these new classes of fibers and how to care for them. If informative labels are adequate, learning is relatively easy. Also, if the consumer associates a trade name with the generic class to which it belongs, he or she will be able to differentiate these generic names. For example, if consumers remember the phrases Orlon acrylic fiber, Acrilan acrylic fiber, Dacron polyester, and Fortrel polyester, they will probably remember the characteristics of each generic classification.

By and large, the man-made fibers with noncellulosic bases—nylon, polyester, acrylic, and modacrylic—have the following plus qualities (unless the structure of the fiber is modified):

1. Dimensional stability (when properly heat-set).
2. Strength and durability (long wear).
3. Ease of care (ease in washing, quick drying, little or no ironing, durable pleats and creases).
4. Resiliency (wrinkle resistance).
5. Elasticity (comfort and fit).
6. Resistance to moths and mildew.

Although pilling and static electricity may still exist, ways have been found to overcome or to lessen these objectionable features.

REVIEW QUESTIONS

1. (a) What is the major difference between rayon and the noncellulosics?
   (b) What is the major difference between acrylic fibers and nylon?
   (c) What is the major difference between polyester fibers and nylon?

2. Define the following:
   (a) Polymerization
   (b) Melt spinning
   (c) Stretch spinning
   (d) Curing
   (e) Pigmentation
3. (a) Name two solvents for nylon.
   (b) How can nylon be identified chemically?
4. (a) List the important physical properties of nylon.
   (b) List the important chemical properties of nylon.
5. (a) Give ten specific uses of nylon.
   (b) Why do consumers buy nylon?
6. (a) What is meant by a bicomponent acrylic fiber?
   (b) How does Verel differ from Orlon chemically?
   (c) What specific advantages does Orlon have over Verel?
7. (a) For what purpose is SEF modacrylic suited?
   (b) What is an advantage of Orlon acrylic over nylon for a girl's sweater?
8. How does Dacron polyester differ physically and chemically from Orlon acrylic?
9. (a) What can be done to overcome static electricity?
   (b) What can be done to prevent pilling?
10. (a) Why do consumers like Dacron polyester?
    (b) For what uses is Spectran polyester most popular?

EXPERIMENTS

1. *Alkali test.* Take yarns or small pieces of fabric constructed from the four fibers discussed in this chapter. Boil for 5 minutes in a 10 percent solution of sodium hydroxide. Describe the effect of a strong alkali on each.
2. *Acid test.* Place as many of the yarns from these fabrics as possible in concentrated sulfuric acid for 5 to 10 minutes. Describe the effect of strong acid on each fiber.
3. *Microscopic test.* Examine the nylon fiber under the microscope. Draw the fiber as you see it. Examine and draw as many of the newer general-purpose synthetics as possible. Note the similarities between some of these fibers and the difficulty in identifying them by microscope.

PROJECT

Fabrics of what man-made fiber would you advise for the different articles in a wardrobe for a two-week winter cruise to Puerto Rico and the Virgin Islands, a trip on which there will be limited laundry facilities?

GLOSSARY (See Chapter 15)

Chapter 15

SPECIAL-PURPOSE NONCELLULOSIC FIBERS AND THE CONSUMER

In addition to the four main classes of man-made noncellulosic textile fibers—nylon, polyester, acrylic, and modacrylic—that can be thought of as all-purpose fibers, others excel in filling special purposes and needs. They may be grouped as follows:

> To reduce flammability: glass, aramid, and novoloid.
> To resist wetness and sunlight: olefin and saran.
> To stretch and provide permanent stretch: spandex, rubber (including lastrile), and anidex.
> To achieve an aesthetic effect: metallic.
> To bond and provide fire resistance: vinyon.

All the fibers listed are chemically derived except for natural rubber, glass, and metallic, which are derived from nonfibrous sources.

These special-purpose fibers are discussed in the order indicated. Four other special-purpose fibers—azlon, novoloid, nytril, and vinal—are not produced in the United States and are of little importance in American consumption.

GLASS FIBERS

The generic name "glass" is defined by the FTC as a "manufactured fiber in which the fiber-forming substance is glass." Its mill consumption in pounds is the largest of the special-purpose fibers discussed in this chapter. The process of

Figure 15.1 Hallway entrance to the Metropolitan Opera's executive office area. Window draperies are made of a medium-weight, open-weave fabric of Fiberglas, "Fresco." (Photo courtesy of Owens-Corning Fiberglas Corporation.)

making glass into fiber was discovered by research engineers of Owens-Illinois Glass Company at Newark, Ohio. The product, called Fiberglas, was first produced commercially by Owens-Corning Fiberglas Corporation in 1936. Thus it is the first of the noncellulosic fibers produced, but not the first made by chemical synthesis—that was nylon in 1939. These fibers have had a phenomenal development, and their future looks bright. Other producers of glass fibers are PPG Industries, Inc. (formerly the Pittsburgh Plate Glass Co.) and Ferro Corporation. There are others. (See Fig. 15.1.)

Production

Glass marbles five-eighths of an inch in diameter are melted in an electrically heated furnace that has a V-shaped bushing made of a metal with a higher melting point than glass. Molten glass enters the top of the bushing and is drawn downward by gravity. It emerges through orifices at the bottom of the bushing. Each hole makes a long continuous filament, and these filaments are combined to make one strand. Then the strands are wound on spools that put in the twist. The winder revolves faster than the molten glass flows, and the resulting tension draws out the filaments. The yarns and cords are then processed on standard textile machinery.

The diameter of the fiber can be controlled by regulating (1) the viscosity of the molten mass through temperature control, (2) the size of the holes through which the glass flows, and (3) the rate of speed at which fibers are drawn.

To make staple fiber, jets of compressed air are used to draw the molten glass. The molten glass flows through orifices at the base of the furnace. Compressed air, or steam jets, break up the filaments into lengths varying from 8 to 15 inches. The staples so made are drawn upon a revolving drum in the form of a cobwebby ribbon. This web of fibers is gathered into a sliver and wound in such a way that the fibers lie parallel lengthwise. These slivers can be made smaller in diameter and then twisted or plied into yarns by the same type of machinery used to process other long-staple fibers.

Two general types of finishes are employed on Fiberglas, depending upon its end use as an industrial fiber or as a decorative fabric. We are concerned here with the decorative type, with such fabrics as marquisettes and casement cloth, and fabrics that are to be screen-printed. A basic finishing process subjects the fabric to high temperatures to release the stress developed in the yarns during twisting and weaving. This treatment gives fabrics principally a good hand, wrinkle resistance, and durability. Then fabrics are treated to relubricate the filaments. Color can be applied, and a protective agent may be administered to improve abrasion resistance. Coronizing, a finish of Owens-Corning, is a combination of (1) heat-setting to relax the fibers, to crimp the yarn permanently, and to set the weave and (2) finishing with resins to produce resistance to abrasion, color retention, water repellency, and launderability. It has been found that a Coronized glass fabric treated with a special chemical solution improves the hand and its dyeability.

Fiberglass can be yarn-dyed or printed, with good resistance to crocking. Pigmented resins are applied in the same manner as in the pigment printing or dyeing of cottons and rayons.

Characteristics

The outstanding characteristic of glass fiber is that it is fireproof. Glass fiber will not burn and will not melt below 1500° F. It has very great tensile and bursting strength and resistance to microorganisms, moisture, and sunlight; and it provides electrical insulation. But glass fiber is attacked by hydrofluoric and phosphoric acids and by hot solutions of weak alkalies as well as cold solutions of strong alkalies. The fiber will not shrink, stretch, or sag.

The fibers, which under the microscope resemble translucent rods, will not absorb moisture, and a wet surface of the fabric will dry quickly without affecting the strength. While glass fabrics will not crock when dyed, they do not resist abrasion. Another shortcoming is that, in spite of their high longitudinal strength, they are brittle and cannot tolerate twisting or bending.

Major Uses

The fire-resistant quality of glass fiber and its resistance to sunlight deterioration make it admirably suited for curtains and draperies in the home, theater lobby, public commercial building, and also for fireproof and waterproof wallpaper. Since glass fibers will not shrink, stretch, or sag, accurate measurements for curtains and draperies are possible. Glass is also used for reinforcements for molded plastics in boats and airplane parts and as batting for insulation in buildings, boats, and railway cars.

Fiberglas is well suited for nonallergic pillow filling, ironing board covers, and interlinings for women's and men's wear. Fiberglas yarns suitable for wearing apparel are being developed by Owens-Corning.

Some homemakers who have had trouble sewing glass-fibered fabrics might avoid future difficulties by the following procedures:

1. Use a good-quality, fine cotton mercerized thread.
2. Use a longer stitch.
3. Use looser tension top and bottom threads.
4. Lighten pressure of the pressure foot.
5. Use a sharp needle.

Furthermore, the sewing machine should be guided rather than pushed or tugged. Only washable drapery heading should be used with Fiberglas, and Fiberglas ought not to be lined.

Glass fibers can be easily washed by hand and drip-dried. Cloths of glass fibers should not be ironed. They are not machine-washable or dry-cleanable. Because glass fibers are easily abraded, they should not be allowed to blow in the wind at open windows, where they could be badly damaged.

Optic Fibers

An imminent use of glass fibers of major importance is not for consumer goods but rather for industry. Fibers of pure glass as fine as a hair are starting to replace the much heavier copper wires now largely depended on to carry messages and pictures. They are activated by very rapid laser beam pulses of light rather than electricity. A pair of these fibers can carry simultaneously 1300 phone calls compared with only 24 through a pair of copper wires. This optic fiber device is free of electrical interference and wire tapping is very difficult.[1]

[1]*The New York Times*, February 11, 1983, p. D1.

ARAMID

Aramid is the name given by the Federal Trade Commission in 1974 to a class of aromatic polyamide fibers, distinctly different in properties from the more conventional aliphatic polyamides, or nylons. On an equal-weight basis, the high-tenacity aramid fibers have greater strength than does any other fiber, although nylon is as high as other aramid types. The aramids perform well at highly elevated temperatures and can be made with a high "modulus," or resistance to stretch, that makes them especially well suited for industrial applications.

There are two commercial aramids, both products of DuPont. One is Nomex, a high-temperature-resistant fiber used in protective clothing for fire fighters; race car drivers; industrial workers exposed to heat, flames, and corrosive chemicals; and the military. Under most circumstances Nomex does not support a flame but merely chars at temperatures in the range of 1800° to 1850°F. (See Fig. 15.2(a).)

The other newer aramid is Kevlar, whose major use is for tire reinforcement where its great strength (five times that of steel on a weight basis) and resistance to stretch is most valuable to tire performance. There are two other types of Kevlar in use.

Kevlar 49 is the high-modulus fiber used as a reinforcement for plastic

Figure 15.2a Firefighter wearing turnout coat of DuPont Nomex aramid fiber. (Photo courtesy of E. I. DuPont de Nemours & Company, Inc.)

Figure 15.2b Top U.S. racer, *Kaama*, driven by Betty Cook, won the U.S. Offshore Campionship in 1978 and was the world offshore champion the year before. The racer is reinforced with Kevlar 49 aramid fiber to help withstand the pounding it takes on the 200-mile-long ocean courses. (Photo courtesy of E. I. DuPont de Nemours & Company, Inc.)

composites in aircraft, high-pressure vessels, sporting goods, and boat hulls. (See Fig. 15.2(b).) Kevlar 29 is used in cables and ropes. Fabric of Kevlar 29 serves as soft armor to protect police officers from bullets and knives and, when resin impregnated, is used to armor Navy ships and armored cars. Aramid is fast becoming an important substitute for asbestos in many applications, including clutch linings and pump packing.

OLEFIN

The generic name "olefin" denotes fibers with paraffin bases and is defined as a manufactured fiber. At least 85 percent of the fiber-forming substance must be a long-chain synthetic polymer composed of at least 85 percent by weight of ethylene, propylene, or other olefin units.

There are two varieties: polyethylene and polypropylene. Polyethylene is a resin that is formed as a result of polymerization of ethylene under heat and pressure. This resin is melted, extruded, and cooled in continuous-monofilament form. The polyethylene fibers have a waxy hand, low heat resistance, a fair-to-good average strength (depending on the type), fair abrasion resistance, and floating ability. Such characteristics appear to render these fibers unsuitable for use in apparel. But because of their good resistance to sunlight, they have found uses in drapery and upholstery fabrics. Since these fibers have excellent resistance to chemicals, they can be used in filter cloths, braids, cords, ropes, and webbings. Considerable research and development may bring new uses for them.

DuPont's product, Vexar plastic netting, is made by extruding a thermo-plastic polymer directly into net form, having the appearance of open mesh fabrics available in various weights. Plastic netting may be produced from polyethylene, polypropylene, nylon, or other extrudable plastics. The Vexar netting will have the characteristics of the base resin, and the most frequently used is polyethylene resin having flexibility and resistance to moisture, chemicals, rot, and mildew.

Polypropylene, based on propylene gas, was first produced for textiles in Italy by Montecatini in 1951. Today it is produced by several U.S. companies as well as firms in Europe and Japan. It is a paraffin-based fiber and therefore is classed under the generic name of olefin. Propylene's advantages over ethylene are that it is lighter, stronger, and less sensitive to heat and that it does not have the undesirable waxy hand.[2] It is also quite inexpensive and has excellent resistance to chemicals, excellent strength, good resistance to sunlight (in special light-stabilized grades), and very good abrasion resistance. Its chief drawbacks

---

[2]See Appendix E for the effect of heat on the major man-made fibers, including olefin.

have been its low melting point (325° to 335°F). Montecatini has developed the first commercial polypropylene fiber that is dyeable. It is a chemically modified type that can be dyed in raw stock, yarn, or piece, alone or in blends. Acid, premetallized, chrome, vat, and reactive dyestuffs may be used.

Fiber producers have used various means to add a dye receptor to the fiber by incorporating nickel or aluminum salts to provide dye sites for metallized disperse dyes. An acid-dyeable polypropylene fiber has been developed.

Significant developments in dyeability of fibers that previously resisted available dyes are accelerating the use of olefin in apparel and home fashions. Both solution-dyed and dyeable forms are offered commercially.

Hercules, under the brand Herculon, produces some twenty different types of polyethylene. Other important trade names are Vectra and Polyloom (Chevron Chemical, Fibers Division), Marquesa and Patton (Amoco Fabrics), and Marvess (Phillips Fiber).

Major Uses

The largest single application of polypropylene is in carpeting. Carpets made from olefin are used in homes and in nonresidential installations (hotels, schools, offices, and stores). In addition to conventional carpet pile, polypropy-

Figure 15.3 Oriental-design area rugs power-woven with polypropylene yarns are attractive, durable, and economical. (Photo courtesy of Phillips Petroleum Company.)

lene olefin is used in nonwoven felts for outdoor purposes. The durability of polypropylene has made it a dominant fiber for indoor-outdoor carpeting, where weather resistance, good cleanability, strength, and resistance to moisture, mildew, and rot are important factors. Oriental-design area rugs made with polypropylene-bulked continuous-multifilament yarns feature striking designs and ease of care. (See Fig. 15.3.) They are premium products, comparable to wool but at more attractive price points. Upholstery fabrics are another important polypropylene product. The fabrics are generally plaids and stripes, but subdued colorations are also being offered.

Automotive construction component and interior fabrics are being made with needlepunched polypropylene staple, which is lightweight, durable, and economical. Indoor-outdoor rugs in attractive designs are also made of polypropylene. (See Fig. 15.4)

Figure 15.4 Hatchback interiors—one of the many automotive applications of needlepunched olefin staple fiber. (Photo courtesy of Phillips Petroleum Company.)

Olefin fibers, both the woven and nonwoven forms, are used extensively in industry for filter and ground-control fabrics, industrial felts, laundry bags and dye nets, rope and cordage, sewing thread, and sandbags. This fiber has a dominant position in backing fabrics for tufted carpets, replacing jute.

Nonwoven Fabrics of Olefin

Specialized nonwoven fabrics made with polypropylene or polyethylene have widespread applications, including furniture and bedding construction, vinyl laminate fabric backings, and civil engineering applications such as road reinforcement membranes and soil stabilization separation and drainage components. (See Fig. 15.5.) Table 15.1 presents a listing of representative nonwoven fabrics of olefin.

Figure 15.5 Civil engineering fabric such as Petromat (Reg. TM, Phillips Petroleum Company) is economical and helps to prolong the life of roads. (Photo courtesy of Phillips Petroleum Company.)

Table 15.1 Representative Nonwoven Fabrics of Olefin—Mostly Industrial and Institutional Usage

Trademark	Distributor or Producer	Construction[a]	Major Uses
Delnet	Hercules	Film extrusion mostly of polyethylene	Bonding other fabrics together, retaining breathability; upholstery backing, nonstick coverings for disposable medical/surgical pads.
Delweve	Hercules	Two Delnet nettings laminated at right angles	Same as above but stronger in both dimensions.
Duon	Phillips Fibers	Needlebonded	Furniture, bedding, and auto construction, replacing heavier fabrics, upholstery lamination.
Fibretex	Crown Zellerbach	Spunbonded	Upholstery, bedding, medical, and personal hygiene products.
Mirafi 126 and 140	Celanese Marketing	Thermalbonded	Drainage and soil-erosion control.
Petromat	Phillips Fibers	Needlebonded	Protective paving for roadways and airstrips.
Supac	Phillips Fibers	Needlebonded	Drainage and soil stabilization.
Typar	DuPont	Spunbonded (polypropylene)	Bagging, carpet backing, filtration, coating substrate.
Tyvek	DuPont	Spunbonded	Wall coverings, packaging, signs, disposable medical apparel.
Vexar	DuPont	Film extrusion (both polypropylene and polyethylene)	Industrial purposes, commercial and medical sheeting, packaging where ventilation is important, textile reinforcement.

[a]See Chapter 6 for an explanation of construction methods.

SARAN

Saran is the generic name for vinylidene chloride and vinyl chloride (at least 80 percent by weight) copolymer resin and yarns extruded from it.[3] It was first introduced as a fiber in 1939 by the Dow Chemical Company; it is now manufactured in the United States by Amtech, Inc.

Like nylon, polyester, and other fibers made from synthetic polymers, saran is thermoplastic. Its basic raw materials are petroleum and salt. Ethylene is made from the petroleum and chlorine from the salt. These two chemicals combine to form another, which is converted into vinylidene chloride. The chemical is easily polymerized. Resin is supplied to the manufacturer in powdered form. The powder is heated to form a fluid, which is forced through a spinneret. The filaments are hardened in water, stretched, and wound on spools.

Major Uses

Saran is used for trolling lines, fishing leaders, tennis racket strings, laundry nets, and suspenders. Originally made in monofilament yarn for outdoor furniture, seat covers for automobiles and buses, and upholstery, it is now also used for drapery fabrics, sheer curtains, rugs, and doll's hair, often in combination with modacrylics. Saran is appropriately used where colorfastness (color is "built in"), easy cleaning, quick drying, and resistance to mildew, moths, soil, grease, chemicals, and abrasion are requisites.

VINYON

The basis for the generic class of fibers called "vinyon" is polyvinyl chloride whose basic materials are found in salt water and petroleum. To be classified generically as vinyon, the FTC has specified that the fiber be composed of not less than 85 percent of polyvinyl chloride.[4]

Vinyon was first produced commercially in the United States in 1939 by the American Viscose Corporation, now part of Avtex Fibers, Inc., and marketed as "Vinyon of Avtex."

Vinyon has poor tensile strength, shrinks at 150°F and melts at 260°F, but it is fire-resistant. It also has good resistance to chemicals, bacteria, and moths. It can also be dyed with dispersed acetate dyes.

Vinyon is used widely for industrial purposes as a bonding agent for nonwoven fabrics, but it also has important consumer uses. When combined

---

[3] Defined by the FTC under the TFPIA.

[4] While the monomer vinyl chloride is a dangerous toxic, this is not true of the polymer made from it, since the latter does not degrade during spinning.

with polyvinyl acetate (85 percent polyvinyl chloride and 15 percent acetate) as a biconstituent fiber, its major use is for tea bags.

A vinyon drapery and blanket fabric from Italy is being marketed under the name of Leavin. The fiber is spun and is dyed in the solution stage. In purchasing, allowance should be made for shrinkage. To avoid yellowing, it should be dried and ironed at a low temperature.

A blend of vinyon and acrylic fibers, called thermolactyl, which is imported from abroad, is being marketed successfully in this country as thermal underwear by Damart, a Portsmouth, New Hampshire, mail-order house. Even though lighter in weight, it retains body heat better than does wool or cotton and retains little or no moisture from perspiration, thus keeping the body dry and comfortable. It must be washed in cold or lukewarm water, never in hot, to avoid excessive shrinkage.

Japan manufactures a biconstituent fiber, 50 percent vinyon and 50 percent vinyl (polyvinyl alcohol) called Cordelan, which is distributed in the United States. It is fire-resistant and abrasion-resistant. It is used for clothing and for such home furnishings as draperies and blankets, where fire resistance is of importance. This fabric should be dried and pressed at low heat.

The term PVC is sometimes applied to a fabric treated with polyvinyl chloride in resin form to look and feel something like kid leather but at a much lower cost. It is being used for jackets and handbags. It is water-resistant and is cleaned readily with soap and water.

ELASTOMERIC FIBERS AND YARNS

A number of generic fibers in yarn form can be stretched repeatedly at room temperature to at least twice their original length and return to approximately their original length when the force is removed. These are spandex, rubber, and anidex.

Spandex

Spandex is the generic name for synthetic fibers of a segmented polyurethane composition (which must comprise at least 85 percent of the long-chain synthetic polymer). A segmented polymer is a block copolymer in which blocks of distinctly different character alternate. These different blocks or segments in spandex fibers consist of rubbery and hard polymers, called soft and hard segments, with urethane linkages. Two classes of compounds are used for the rubbery soft segment, namely, polyesters and polyethers.

Spandex fiber threads are man-made elastic threads with properties better than those of natural rubber. The general structure is typical for elastomers in that flexible chains are held together in a network that will resist permanent orientation and crystallizes only temporarily when held under stretch. The presence of hard segments in spandex fibers, however, provides a completely different structure from that found in conventional rubbers, which has important consequences. First, spandex can be broken reversibly by high mechanical stress, by heat, and by strong solvents. Second, the spandex fibers are spaced more regularly than in a randomly vulcanized rubber.

Spandex fiber and rubber have significantly different properties. Spandex is an all-round superior type of elastic thread with higher strength and about twice the retractive force of rubber of equal denier. Spandex fibers also provide better resistance to degradation by sunlight, heat (over 300°F), chemicals, oils, and perspiration. It provides better whiteness and offers good dyeability with several classes of dyestuffs with acceptable light and washfastness. Spandex also is cleaner, and mill handling is more efficient and more consistent. Further, spandex can be provided in practical, fine-denier yarns that make possible the modern, lightweight, comfortable elastic fabrics available today.

White fabrics containing spandex fiber may discolor in atmospheric exposure depending on the nature and concentration of pollutants present.

The balance of properties of spandex fibers has led not only to replacement of conventional rubber thread in many of its established uses, but has led also to the development in many new stretch fabric applications.

Major Uses

Major uses for spandex fiber include women's sheer hosiery, intimate apparel, swimwear, leotards, narrow elastic webbing or trim (waist and leg bands, bra straps, athletic applications, elastic bandages, shoes, sheeting tape), and miscellaneous active sportswear. Consumers like spandex because of its lightweight elasticity, wear comfort, and easy home-care features.

Two manufacturers currently produce spandex fibers in the USA: Lycra spandex fiber is produced by E. I. DuPont de Nemours & Company, Inc., and Glospan and Clearspan spandex fibers are produced by Globe Manufacturing Company.

Rubber

Rubber is the generic name of man-made fibers in which the fiber-forming substance is comprised of natural or synthetic rubber.

Fibers from Natural Rubber

The core of fibers is made with natural rubber. (Natural rubber is made of a milky fluid called latex, which is tapped from the bark of the Para rubber tree.) The latex fluid is forced through tiny holes the diameter of the thread desired and is hardened in a solidifying bath. Then the thread is vulcanized, and ammonia is added to preserve it. Round threads retain their elasticity longer than do strips cut from sheets, because round threads can have their surface completely vulcanized, whereas strips cut from sheets necessarily have two unvulcanized edges. This latex elastic rubber fiber is covered with cotton, silk, wool, or rayon to form a yarn that can be woven or knitted into cloth for clothing.

Lastex is a trademark for a combination yarn originally produced by UniRoyal, Inc., and now by Tel-elastic Company of High Point, North Carolina. The core of the yarn is covered with cotton, silk, wool, rayon, or nylon to make a yarn that can be woven or knitted into cloth or webbing. As webbing, it is used for foundation garments, shoes, garters, suspenders, tops of shorts and briefs, wristlets and anklets, tops of hosiery, shoelaces, and surgical bandages. In cloth, it is used for riding breeches, bathing suits, nets, and laces. Lastex yarns can be used for gathering the tops of blouses and to stabilize the ribbing of nylon sweaters.

The chief advantage of Lastex is enduring elasticity. Lastex garments shape themselves to the figure of the wearer and hence fit well. The Lastex garment should be laundered frequently with lukewarm suds for best service.

Fibers from Synthetic Rubber

Chemists have succeeded in creating synthetic rubber that has much the same qualities as natural rubber. It has both textile and nontextile uses. For consumer goods, it is used for a variety of knitted and woven fabrics, either covered or uncovered, where stretch is important.

There are actually three varieties that differ in their chemical composition. One is made from chemicals that produce hydrocarbons that are chemically very similar to natural rubber. Another is a polymer of acrylonitrile and butadiene units. This type may properly be called "lastrile" as a generic name, but it is not manufactured in the United States. The third is a chemical composition that contains at least 35 percent chloroprene as the fiber-producing substance.

Anidex

Anidex is the generic name of a man-made fiber in which the fiber-forming substance is any long-chain synthetic polymer composed of at least 80 percent by weight of one or more esters of a monohydric alcohol and acrylic acid.[5]

The fiber was first produced in 1969 by Rohm and Haas Co., under the trademark Anim/8. Anidex is neither spandex nor rubber but is a monofilament elastomeric acrylate fiber. The fiber can be used in the ways that spandex yarns are used, for example, uncovered, wrapped, and core-spun forms.

Characteristics

Permanent stretch and recovery are the most important characteristics of anidex. While Anim/8 can be dyed with both disperse dyes and basic dyes, fastness to light is not as good when dyed with basic dyes as with disperse dyes. Foundation garments and hosiery made with anidex have improved fit, comfort, and appearance. Since this fiber has resistance to gas fading, oxidation,

---

[5]Definition by Federal Trade Commission.

sunlight, oils, and chlorine bleach, it can be used in sportswear, athletic wear, career apparel, and upholstery.

METALLIC FIBERS

The FTC defines the generic term "metallic" as "a manufactured fiber composed of metal, plastic-coated metal, metal-coated plastic, or a core completely covered by metal."

Real gold and silver are seldom used for textile yarns, but their effect can be duplicated by the use of aluminum in combination with man-made substances which produces a pleasing esthetic effect.

A common process for producing metallic filaments is to coat one or both sides of aluminum foil with adhesive to which coloring matter has been added. To each side of the adhesive coated foil a sheet of transparent plastic film is applied. The resultant product is then slit into narrow widths.

The Mobay Chemical Corporation coats fabrics of both natural and man-made fibers with metal, usually nickel, to produce antistatic garments and heated clothing. The coated fabrics have important industrial uses in today's space age activities.

The advantages of coated metallic filaments are that they are nontarnishable, can be dry-cleaned or washed, and can be ironed at a low setting. But they do require considerable care in use and in cleaning. Color may change from perspiration and from rubbing against objects and in removing spots and stains.

Metallic yarns in clothing fabrics have become a major fashion in the 1980s, especially for pants, skirts, sweaters, belts, shoes, fashion fabrics by the yard, and knitting and crocheting yarns. They are also frequently used for draperies, placemats, and table cloths. Steel yarns are used in making tires.

A few of the trade names for metallic yarns are Chromeflex and Lurex, both produced by Metal Fibers, Feltmetal produced by Brunswick, and Melton offered by Melton.

FLUOROCARBON FIBERS

The two fibers discussed in this section—fluorocarbon and carbon—are not used as consumer goods, but rather for special industrial purposes where resistance to heat and to changes in heat are important. A brief description of ceramic fibers also is included.

Fluorocarbon Fibers

These fibers are based on a compound of carbon and fluorine that is extruded through a spinneret. DuPont manufactures them as Teflon. While this resin in plastic form is used as a nonstick coating for cooking utensils, it is also extruded as a fiber. DuPont makes two types of fluorocarbon fibers: Teflon TFE-

Figure 15.6 These flight coveralls are made from 100 percent Teflon TFE-Fluorocarbon fiber (shown here in a mock-up *Apollo* capsule). The fiber is self-extinguishing in a 100 percent oxygen atmosphere, is comfortable to wear, and is resistant to abrasion. (Photo courtesy of E. I. DuPont de Nemours & Company, Inc.)

Fluorocarbon fiber[6] and Teflon FEP-Fluorocarbon fiber. The former, naturally dark brown, may be bleached to a pure white. It is made available in multifilament form for construction into woven, knitted, braided, or felted fabrics. It is highly resistant to heat and is the most resistant to chemicals of any fiber known. It has low moisture regain, which results in poor dyeability. It is used for a variety of industrial operations, including pump and valve packing, filters, and clothing that is protective against fire and corrosives. (See Fig. 15.6.)

Teflon FEP-Fluorocarbon fiber has a somewhat different molecular structure and a lower melting point. It is made available in monofilament form and is manufactured into filter cloth and liquid mist eliminators in processes where streams or gas exist.

Another producer of fluorocarbon fiber is the W. L. Gore Co. under the trademark Gore-Tex.

Carbon Fibers

Carbon fibers, also called graphite fibers, were first developed some twenty years ago, but they are just now coming into prominence. They are made from graphite, a form of carbon derived from coal and also by chemical synthesis. Fibers from this material are often bound together with a gluelike substance: they look like black strands of yarn. Materials made from these fibers are stronger than steel and lighter than aluminum. These attributes make them especially important in the aerospace industry that is expected to account for two-thirds of the growing production. They are also used in the making of sporting goods, especially tennis rackets, golf clubs, and fishing rods. Other industrial uses exist as well.

[6]Made by combining molecules of tetrafluoroethylene and nexafluoropropylene to form a long-chain molecule.

Wings of some airplanes are made of plastic material that first is covered with layers of tapes made of the carbon fiber. The covered wires are then "cooked" to form a single lightweight material of great strength. In making rackets and golf clubs, the plastic and the carbon fiber may be molded together.[7]

The chief producers of carbon fibers are Hercules Incorporated and Union Carbide Corporation.

The chief advantages of carbon fiber are

1. Great specific strength relative to weight; about seven times as strong as most metals.
2. Great tensile strength relative to weight; about five times as strong as most metals.
3. Only slight expansion and contraction under a wide range of temperatures.
4. Higher resistance to "fatigue" (when subjected to extended strain) than either steel or aluminum.

Because of these attributes, carbon fibers in both molded and fabric form are used for

1. Aerospace equipment, especially where point (3) above is of great importance.
2. Sports equipment, such as fishing poles, golf clubs, and tennis racquets.
3. Industrial applications, including molded parts and high-speed rotating equipment.
4. Automotive equipment, where the current emphasis is to combine light weight with strength.

The major producing countries are the United States and Japan.

Ceramic Fibers

The 3M Company has recently introduced Nextel, a high-temperature, flexible, and continuous ceramic fiber that can be treated as a textile, replacing asbestos and silica. It withstands prolonged exposure to temperatures up to 2600°F and to short-term exposures up to 3000°F. It is destined to be important in the construction of the space shuttle and for use in gaskets, seals, and other industrial uses involving high temperatures.

OTHER MAN-MADE NONCELLULOSIC FIBERS PRODUCED ABROAD

Except for vinylon fibers, discussed in this section, the others described here have been defined as generic by the Federal Trade Commission.

Azlon

Azlon as defined by the FTC is "a manufactured fiber in which the fiber-forming substance is composed of any regenerated naturally occurring proteins."[8] Azlon, then, includes fibers derived from plant and animal proteins. Natural

---

[7]"Carbon Fiber Market Brighter," *The New York Times*, August 24, 1982, pp. D1, 8.
[8]Not currently produced in the United States.

sources of raw materials (for these fibers are proteins) are milk curd (casein), peanuts, cottonseed, cornmeal (zein), egg white, soybeans, and chicken feathers. Azlon has been blended with wool for suits, coats, and knitted outerwear.

Novoloid

Novoloid is the generic name for a noncellulosic man-made fiber derived from phenol, a chemical compound of carbon, hydrogen, and oxygen. It is highly flame-resistant. It is also lightweight, resilient, and unaffected by many acids. It is used for felting, batting, and flame-resistant clothing. It is not currently produced in the United States, but it is being imported under the name Kynol.

Nytril

Nytril is a man-made fiber composed largely of a complex chemical substance known as vinylidene dinitrile (where the vinylidene dinitrile content is no less than every other unit in the polymer chain),[9] derived from ammonia and natural gas.

This fiber, marketed under the trade name Darvan, was developed by the B. F. Goodrich Chemical Company in the late 1950s. They sold the patent rights to Celanese Fiber Company who, early in 1962, reached an agreement with Farbwerke Hoechst of Germany to build a jointly owned plant in Europe for the production and marketing of Darvan. (In Europe, the fiber is known as Travis.) Its uses include sweaters, suits, and coats. The United States has not produced nytril since 1961.

Nytril's properties resemble those of the acrylic fibers, although it is weaker, harder to dye, and slightly more sensitive to heat than either the Orlon or Acrilan acrylics. Nytril fibers are suitable for articles that need no pressing, such as pile fabrics and blends with wool. Nytril can be permanently pleated and has excellent sunlight resistance, good stability after repeated launderings, fair tensile strength, and fair resistance to pilling.

Available in staple form, its uses are in sweaters, suits, coats, and a variety of other products.

Vinal

Vinal is the generic name for man-made fibers in which the fiber-forming substance is any long-chain synthetic polymer composed of at least 50 percent by weight of vinyl alcohol units and in which the total of the various acetal units is at least 85 percent by weight of the fiber. This class of fibers was developed in Japan.

Vinal is claimed to have very good strength and abrasion resistance but does not match nylon in these qualities. Vinal fibers soften at low temperatures

[9]Generic name recognized by the FTC.

but have good chemical resistance. Colorfastness can be achieved in vinal with vat dyes. For apparel uses, its poor dry-wrinkle resistance is a drawback. It is made in filament, staple, and water-soluble forms. There are two types of vinal. One type is made by a system that approximates rayon technology in its sequential stages of coagulation, drawing, heat treatment, and formalization to develop and harden the fiber structure. With certain modifications, this fiber has been the chief commercial type. Its high strength and its abrasion and weather resistance have made it useful in products in which cotton is traditionally used. The second type of vinal, used for tire cord, is a highly crystalline form of pure polyvinyl alcohol.

Vinylon

Not to be confused with vinyon, vinylon is a form of vinal fiber manufactured in Japan of polyvinyl alcohol. It is strong and has good stretch and recovery. Available in both staple and filament form, it is used for women's apparel, such as underwear and linings, and for industrial purposes. Under the trade name Mewlon, of the Dai Nippon Spinning Co. Ltd., it is sold largely for ropes, fishnets, and filter cloths.

BICOMPONENT AND BICONSTITUENT FIBERS

Man-made noncellulosic fibers of different types and of different generic classes are often combined with success in the spinning solution before extrusion through a spinneret. This achieves a single fiber that has the advantages of the types or classes combined.

Bicomponent or conjugate fiber is produced by extruding side by side or one around the other the molten polymers or solutions of polymers of different types of the fibers that are usually in the same generic class.[10] (See Fig. 15.7.) For example, DuPont's Cantrece for hosiery combines two different types of nylon that differ in degree of shrinkage. Because the bicomponent is accordingly self-crimping, it gives the hosiery fit, retention, and comfort. Bicomponents are also constructed from different types of classes other than nylon.

Biconstituent fiber is produced by extruding through the spinneret the polymers of different generic classes that are homogeneously mixed together. This gives the new fiber the advantages of both classes. An example is Fortran of Fiber Industries, which is a nylon/polyester biconstituent.

Another is Monvelle of Monsanto, a biconstituent of nylon/spandex. The spandex adds stretch to the strength and sheerness of nylon. The two components are so dissimilar that drawing develops an intense crimp. This causes the fiber to coil like a spring. A tight crimp is caused by the rubberband nature of spandex, which causes it to "try" to return to its original length but is

[10]As reported in *Knitting Times*, November 5, 1973.

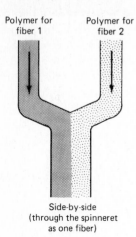

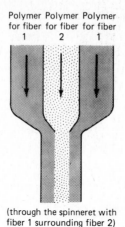

Polymer for fiber 1   Polymer for fiber 2   Polymer Polymer Polymer for fiber for fiber for fiber 1   2   1

Side-by-side (through the spinneret as one fiber)

(through the spinneret with fiber 1 surrounding fiber 2)

Figure 15.7 Two ways to form a bicomponent fiber.

restrained by the nylon. With one part of the fiber contracting and the other not, crimping force is built into the fiber.

The combination of an elastomer (spandex) and a thermoplastic (nylon) leads to several properties that are important to the consumer as well as to the manufacturer. First, it provides comfortable support to pantyhose and hosiery. Second, fabrics of Monvelle, with its snug cling and high denier per filament, tend to prevent formation of loops and loose filaments that would cause snagging, pulling, and running. Third, because of the acid-resistant urethane content of spandex, garments do not fail as quickly as would nylon alone in acid-polluted atmospheres.[11]

According to FTC regulations, fabrics made of those biconstituent fibers in which two or more generic classes are involved must carry labels that reveal the fibers in the biconstituent and the percentages of each by weight. Bicomponents that consist of conjugate fibers of the same generic class but of different types of that class do not have to be so labeled.

CURRENT STATUS AND TRENDS IN MAN-MADE FIBERS

Table 15.2 illustrates how the man-mades are dominating many markets, especially those involved in consumer goods.

The trend for the future is somewhat uncertain. As indicated in Chapter 9,

[11]When the polymer solutions are extruded one around the other, different generic classes can be used, since, when one is "wrapped" around the other, they do not separate in subsequent manufacturing processes as they might when extruded side by side. This is not true of different types of the same class.

Table 15.2 U.S. Mill Consumption, Selected Years 1965–1981 Est.
(millions of pounds)

	1965		1973		1979		1981 Est.	
Natural fibers[a]		4,910		3,835		3,201		2,860
Man-mades								
Cellulosic[b]	1,593		1,389		831		680	
Noncellulosic[c]	1,677		6,103		6,927		6,260	
Other[d]	367	3,627	1,256	8,748	1,973	9,731	1,800	8,740
Total fibers		8,537		12,573		12,932		11,600
% Natural		57.5%		30.4		24.8		24.7
% Man-made		42.5		69.6		75.2		75.3
Cellulosic		18.7		11.1		6.4		5.8
Noncellulosic		19.5		48.5		53.6		54.0
Other		4.3		10.0		15.2		15.5

[a]Excludes silk, linen, and hard fibers (sisal, jute, etc.). Cotton constituted about 3.0 billion pounds and wool about 135 million pounds in 1979.

[b]Rayon, acetate, triacetate—filament, staple, and tow.

[c]Nylon, polyester, acrylic—filament, staple, and tow.

[d]Textile glass, spandex, olefin, spunbonded products, minor noncellulosics (vinyon, saran, etc.). Excludes rubber thread and spunbonded polyethylene.

Source: Textile Economics Bureau, Inc.

cotton is making something of a comeback. Its price per pound in late 1982 was approximately 25 percent lower than that of polyester. Higher prices for crude oil will probably increase further the price of the major man-made fibers, but the price of cotton goods is dependent partly on the price of raw cotton, which is dependent on weather conditions in the South and the Southwest and on costs of harvesting.

Table 15.3 provides additional details on the distribution of fiber consumption according to end use.

World Production

Table 15.4 reports a different picture—that of world production of major textile fibers from 1976 through 1981—which indicates that cotton is still king. Olefin, glass fiber, and the minor natural fibers have been omitted, since adequate worldwide data are not available. The natural fibers have remained at between 54 and 55 percent of the world total, while man-made fiber production has been at the 45 to 46 percent level of total world production.

While annual cotton production alone continues to exceed that of man-made fibers, man-mades are moving up because of the growing demand for the noncellulosics, which have enjoyed an increase of over 4½ billion pounds since 1976.

Table 15.3 The Dominant Position of Man-Made Fibers in 1980

	Man-made Fibers	Natural Fibers
65% of all fibers used in apparel are man-made:		
Pantyhose	100%	—
Women's dresses	78	22%
Sweaters	89	11
Lingerie	77	23
Men's and boys' shirts	80	20
Women's blouses and shirts	65	35
Men's suits, slacks, and coats	47	53
Women's suits, slacks, and coats	60	40
75% of all fibers used in home furnishings are man-made:		
Bedspreads and comforters	62	38
Blankets	90	10
Carpeting (face yarns)	99	1
Curtains	92	8
Draperies and casements	74	26
Mattress ticking	93	7
Sheets and pillowcases	51	49
Upholstery	75	25
80% of all fibers used in industrial textiles are man-made:		
Textile tire cord	100	—[a]
Industrial hose	83	17
Textile fiber filters	86	14
Medical, surgical, and sanitary supplies	68	32
Transportation fabrics	63	37

[a]Cotton.

Source: Textile Economics Bureau, Inc.

COST RELATIONSHIP BETWEEN THAT OF THE FIBER AND THE RETAIL PRICE OF APPAREL

The cost of the man-made fibers used in apparel is a very small part of the retail price of clothing into which they are made, as Fig. 15.8 indicates. While all the prices given in the illustration may continue to rise, the percentage of the fibers to the final retail prices may drop, since the increase in the cost of the man-made fibers since 1973 has been slower than that of apparel and is much slower than that of most other commodities.

At the end of 1979, the price advantage of polyester over cotton was about 9 cents a pound, but it was reversed by late 1982 (68 cents for cotton to 77 cents for polyester). However, a poor crop yield and huge expenditures for reducing cotton dust in the manufacture of cotton could reverse the price again, unless it

Table 15.4 World Production of Certain Textile Fibers, 1976–1981[a]
(millions of pounds)

Type of Fiber	1976	1977	1978	1979	1980	1981
Rayon-acetate fibers						
Yarn and monofilaments	2,619	2,584	2,542	2,593	2,560	2,432
Staple and tow	4,457	4,649	4,742	4,837	4,588	4,605
Total	7,076	7,233	7,314	7,430	7,148	7,037
Noncellulosic fibers[b]						
Yarn and monofilaments	9,101	9,508	10,148	10,799	10,461	10,599
Staple and tow	9,862	10,663	11,973	12,588	12,670	13,056
Total	18,963	20,171	22,121	23,387	23,131	23,655
Total man-made	26,039	27,404	29,435	30,817	30,279	30,692
% of world total	46	45	48	47	46	45
Natural fibers						
Raw cotton	27,513	30,690	28,600	31,460	31,451	33,922
Raw wool	3,278	3,280	3,369	3,468	3,486	3,547
Raw silk	106	108	112	121	123	126
Total	30,897	34,078	32,081	35,049	35,060	37,595
% of world total	54	55	52	53	54	55
World total	56,936	61,482	61,516	65,866	65,339	68,287

[a]Silk and man-made fiber data are on a calendar-year basis; figures for cotton and wool are on a seasonal basis.
[b]Except olefin.
Source: Textile Organon, July 1982, p. 147

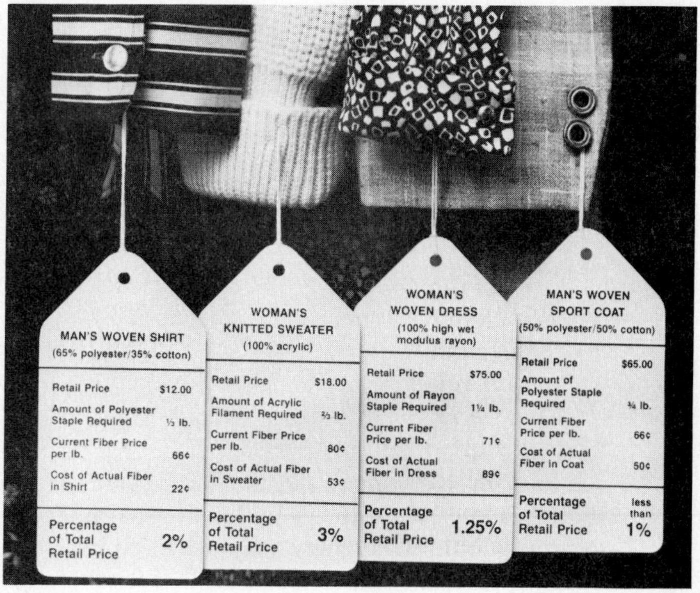

Figure 15.8 Comparisons of 1980 retail prices with the cost of fiber components. (Photo courtesy of Man-Made Fiber Producers Association.)

is offset further by the rise in the price of oil, the key ingredient in creating the polyester polymer.

TRENDS IN TECHNOLOGY

Most technologists believe that it is unlikely that the next few years will see the emergence of a "new" generic fiber—at least not by today's definition of what constitutes a new generic. What we probably will see are fiber variants, many of them of sufficient magnitude to seek separate generic status. Basically, the variants will fall into the following broad classifications known as second- and third-generation fibers.

The second generation of man-made fibers evidenced modifications made to alter the fibers' physical appearance and aesthetic properties to suit a particular end use or need. Variations occur in fiber cross sections, luster, crimp, strength, dyeability, and flame resistance.

The third generation of man-made fibers is characterized by the engineering of a group of more sophisticated and custom-tailored items, such as bicomponent and biconstituent fibers and textured filament yarns for specific markets in response to consumer desires.

The future of blends also seems limitless. Any fiber is a potential contributor to a blended fabric. Testing goes on constantly to find out what the best fiber blends are and what percentages are best adapted to certain uses. The results of tests so far show that no fiber can be ignored as a tool in a blend. But to get the maximum of one quality, such as abrasion resistance, another quality may be sacrificed. If the sacrificed quality is not important in the fabric's use, it will not be missed. All fibers may be complementary and supplementary to one another.

Second- and third-generation fibers that meet special requirements without blending are already on the market. Antron nylon, Spectran polyester, various flame-retardant fibers, and many similar advanced products offer properties significantly different from the conventional generic fiber, and even more revolutionary variations are virtually certain to come into the marketplace at a greater and greater rate.

None of these man-made fibers is an all-purpose fiber. Technical changes are continually taking place, so it is not possible to associate any particular advantages for long periods with any particular fiber.

New Fiber Experiments

In spite of the many fibers now on the market, the end of fiber development is not in sight. New fibers are likely to be created in university laboratories where the research is subsidized by leading manufacturers of man-made fibers. For example, Yale University has entered into a contract with the Celanese Corporation that will subsidize basic research to determine if naturally recurring

Figure 15.9 Specialty fabrics open the door to a new era in textiles. This space shuttle ejection escape suit is made of *polybenzimidazole* (better known as PBI). It resists temperatures above 1000°F for short periods of time and 400°F for longer periods. (Photo courtesy of the National Aeronautics and Space Administration.)

enzymes can be used in the construction of fibers that would replace chemicals that are often pollutants.[12]

Figure 15.9 shows the use of another new specialty fiber that resists very high temperatures.

REVIEW QUESTIONS

1. (a) Describe the manufacture of glass fibers.
   (b) What are the chief advantages of glass fibers?
   (c) What are this fiber's limitations?
   (d) For what purposes are glass fibers used?
2. What are the techniques and uses of the flame-resistant fibers, aramid and novoloid?
3. (a) Name the olefin fibers.
   (b) In what ways is polyethylene similar to polypropylene?
   (c) In what ways are they different?
4. (a) List the chief uses of natural rubber yarn.
   (b) How does Lastex differ from Helanca yarn?
   (c) What is spandex?
   (d) How does spandex differ from natural rubber fibers?

[12]*The New York Times*, February 18, 1982, p. B1.

5. (a) What is the chemical composition of metallic yarns?
   (b) List the uses of metallic yarns.
6. (a) What is vinyon?
   (b) What are its advantages?
   (c) For what purposes is vinyon used?
7. (a) How do azlon fibers differ from nylon, polyester, and acrylic fibers?
   (b) Where is azlon used?
   (c) What are the advantages and weaknesses of these fibers?
8. (a) What is nytril?
   (b) For what purpose may it be used?

EXPERIMENTS

1. Obtain as many samples as you can of fabrics made of the following: glass fiber, anidex, novoloid, and olefin.
2. Try to ignite each piece with a match or lighter. Report on your results in detail.
3. Wet and rub dirt into each fabric and then dry. Wash or rinse out in cold water. Compare your results.
4. From these tests, can you come to any conclusions as to the best end uses for the different materials? Explain.

PROJECTS

1. Collect magazine advertisements featuring glass fiber, olefin, saran, spandex, rubber, and possibly other special-purpose fibers. Obtain a sample of each and classify it by group origin. Indicate its most appropriate uses (give reasons for your choice). Check the veracity of advertisement claims by your own original test or tests and look for any new third-generation fibers.
2. (a) What advice would you, as a salesperson, give a consumer on the choice of fabric for automobile seat covers?
   (b) How would you advise a consumer to choose fabric for an outdoor American flag? carpeting for a patio? lawn chair? Support hose? webbing for belts? trimming on an evening jacket? draperies?

GLOSSARY

Acetate See the glossary in Chapter 13.

Acrylic fibers The generic name of fibers made from acrylonitrile.

Acrylic resins Thermoplastic in nature, of synthetic type. These resins are polymerized from acrylic and methacrylic acid.

Acrylonitrile A chemical compound from which acrylic fiber is made. This compound is made by the reaction of ethylene oxide and hydrocyanic acid.

Alginate A man-made cellulosic fiber from a seaweed base.

Anidex A generic name for an elastomeric fiber made of monohydric alcohol and acrylic acid.

Antistatic finish A chemical treatment applied to noncellulosic synthetic fibers to eliminate static electricity.

Aramid   Generic name for a noncellulosic man-made fiber. A class of aromatic polyamide fibers differing from nylon's polyamide fiber by having at least 85 percent of the amide.

Ardil   A fiber derived from protein in peanuts; it is made in England. A type of azlon.

Autoclave   A vessel similar to a pressure cooker in which a chemical solution is heated under pressure.

Azlon   A generic name for man-made textile fibers made from protein, such as casein, zein, soybean, and peanut.

Bicomponent or conjugate fiber   A man-made fiber produced by extruding, side by side or one around the other, molten polymers or solutions of polymers. For the side-by-side configuration, different types of one generic class of polymer are used; in the circular configuration, two generic classes of polymer may be used.

Biconstituent fiber   A man-made fiber produced by the extrusion of two molten polymers or solutions of polymers in which the polymers are of different generic types. The extrusion is such that the polymers are homogeneously mixed together.

Blend   See the glossary in Chapter 2.

Bright yarn   A high-luster yarn.

Caprolactam   The raw material for nylon 6.

Carbon fiber   An acrylic fiber made from polyacrylonitrile of great specific and tensile strength in relation to weight and dimensional stability under changes in temperature. Synonymous with graphite fiber.

Carrier   An agent that swells fibers to improve the diffusion rate of disperse dyes into the fiber. Widely used in the dyeing of conventional polyester.

Casein   A protein compound found especially in milk. Synthetic fibers can be derived from this protein.

Ceramic fiber   A man-made fiber based on clay.

Coronizing   A finish for Fiberglas that heat-sets the fibers, crimps the yarn, wets the weave, and produces abrasion resistance, color retention, water repellency, and launderability.

Count   Size of a spun synthetic yarn. See the glossary in Chapter 3.

Denier   Size of a nylon or any other synthetic filament yarn. See the glossary in Chapter 3.

Dimensional stability   See the glossary in Chapter 13.

Dye carrier   See *carrier.*

Ester   A technical chemical term for a compound formed by substituting a hydrocarbon radical for the hydrogen of an acid.

Filament yarn   See the glossary in Chapter 13.

Fleece   Furlike pile fabrics made of Orlon acrylic, nylon, Verel modacrylic, Dynel modacrylic, Dacron polyester, or other synthetic pile.

Fluorocarbon fibers   Man-made noncellulosic fibers extruded from a compound of carbon and fluorine.

Glass fiber   A man-made fiber made from glass.

Heat-set finish   The stabilization of synthetic fabrics to ensure no change in size or shape. Methods of setting fabrics of nylon and polyester fibers, for example, include treatment of fabrics at boiling or near boiling temperatures one-half hour to one hour; treatment with saturated steam; and application of dry heat. Heat-setting also secures maximum dimensional stability of acrylic fibers.

Hexamethylene-diammonium-adipate   A solution of a salt that is polymerized and hardened into a solid and cut into flakes, then melted and extruded into nylon fibers.

Hydrophilic fiber An absorptive fiber, with a great affinity for water.

Hydrophobic fiber A nonabsorptive fiber, with no affinity for water.

Lastrile The generic name for a man-made type of rubber from copolymer of 10 to 50 percent acrylonitrile units and a diene such as butadiene.

Metallic The generic name of a man-made fiber composed of metal, plastic-coated metal, metal-coated plastic, or a core completely covered by metal.

Mixture See the glossary in Chapter 2.

Modacrylic fibers The generic name of man-made fibers composed of less than 85 percent but as least 35 percent by weight of acrylonitrile units.

Monofilament A single filament.

Monomer A simple form of chemical compound from which a polymer can be made.

Multifilament yarn Continuous strands of two or more monofilaments that have been twisted together.

Novoloid A generic name for a noncellulosic man-made fiber made from a cross-linked polymer derived from carbon, hydrogen, and oxygen.

Nylon A man-made polyamide fiber derived largely from petroleum, chemically combined with air and water.

Nytril A generic name for noncellulosic man-made fibers made from a polymer of vinylidene dinitrile derived from ammonia and natural gas.

Olefin The generic name for a man-made fiber derived from polyethylene or polypropylene.

Pigmented fibers and yarns Delustered or, occasionally, producer-colored with pigment to a desired hue. See the glossary in Chapter 13.

Pilling Fibers of certain synthetic spun yarns form little balls or pills on the surface of the cloth.

Polyamide A chemical rearrangement of atoms to form a molecule of greater weight. A resin made by condensation. Nylon is a polyamide.

Polyester fiber The generic name for a man-made fiber made from a chemical composition usually of glycol and terephthalic acid.

Polymer A large molecule produced by linking together many molecules of monometric substances from which man-made fibers are made.

Polymerization The way in which certain small molecules are combined into long-chain fiber-forming molecules.

Rubber The generic name of man-made fibers in which the fiber-forming substance is natural or synthetic rubber.

Saran The generic name of vinylidene chloride fibers.

Soybean A small herb of the bean family of India and China; source of protein for certain man-made fibers.

Spandex The generic name of man-made fibers derived from a chemical substance called segmented polyurethane.

Spinneret See the glossary in Chapter 13.

Spun yarn See the glossary in Chapter 13.

Static electricity Stationary electric charges caused by rubbing an article or exposing it to abrasion. Static electricity attracts small particles to the object.

Synthetic fiber A man-made fiber produced by chemical synthesis.

Thermolactyl Yarn and fabric made from a blend of 85 percent vinyon and 15 percent acrylic fibers.

Thermoplastic   A fiber that has the property of softening or fusing when heated and of hardening again when cooled.

Vinal   The generic name for a man-made fiber derived from a polymer consisting of at least 50 percent polyvinyl alcohol units.

Vinylon   A form of vinal, manufactured in Japan.

Vinyon   The generic name of a man-made fiber made from polyvinyl chloride, derived from natural salt, water, and petroleum.

Zein   Cornmeal from which protein is derived for the construction of man-made fibers.

Chapter 16

THE CARE OF TEXTILE FABRICS

The proper care of garments and home furnishings are, from the viewpoint of the consumer, as important as having the right fiber, fabric, finish, color, and design. An article given intelligent care will last longer, perform better, and look better than will one that is neglected. Care includes three activities that the consumer can usually perform at home: cleaning (washing, drying, and pressing), refreshening, and storage. These activities can, of course, also be performed by a commercial laundry or dry-cleaning establishment.

CLEANING OF TEXTILE PRODUCTS

Cleaning is a more complicated process than is either refreshening or storage. It involves both overall cleaning and spot removal. There are two overall cleaning methods: washing and dry cleaning. For either process, there are variations in the required temperature, the nature of the detergent, soap or solvent used, the use of bleach, the length of cleaning time, including the speed and agitation time, the method of moisture or solvent removal, and the method and amount of pressing required.

Hand Laundering

General Procedure for Hand Laundering

Although most of today's fabrics are either machine-washable or dry-cleanable, hand washing continues to be important, not only for small washes but also for certain materials. In general, silks, antique and sheer fabrics, knitted woolens, and curtains of glass fibers should be washed by hand. Fabrics in which the fastness of color is uncertain may also be washed by hand but can be washed separately in a washer.

Some Guides for Hand Laundering

1. Launder fabrics before they become too soiled.
2. Examine the fabric thoroughly for spots, stains, soil, small tears or holes and mend before laundering.
3. Remove any accessories that are not washable.
4. If dye fastness is unknown, wash an inconspicuous part of the fabric first. A small piece of fabric can be clipped from one of the seams. Dry it and compare the washed with the unwashed part. If there is fading or streaking, the cloth should be dry-cleaned.
5. For delicate and lightly soiled fabrics, use a mild soap. In hard-water areas, use a light-duty detergent. In lukewarm water gently press the solution through the fabric. Very dirty spots may require additional soapings. Follow with several rinses.
6. Roll the fabric in a terry towel and gently squeeze out excess moisture. Gently pull the fabric to shape and spread it over a line.
7. For knitted fabrics, especially wool or rayon, measure the dimensions before washing or draw them on a sheet of paper. After washing, squeeze out excess water and lay the garment on a flat surface and ease (work) it to the proper shape and size; then dry. Do not hang on a line where it is likely to dry in a longer and narrower shape than before.

Washing by Machine

The Automatic Washer

The majority of U.S. households own or use an automatic washer and wash very little by hand. (See Fig. 16.1.) Most standard-sized washers can handle as much as 16 pounds of mixed laundry items and are loaded from the

Figure 16.1 Electronic controls are used in this laundry pair from Whirlpool Corporation. (Photo courtesy of Whirlpool Corporation.)

top. Portable washers can handle approximately 7 pounds of laundry, but they are a boon to those with limited space.

Standard top-loading machines are programmed to move the wash through four cycles:

1. Filling the tub (many with soak cycle).
2. Washing by means of an agitator or pulsator.
3. Rinsing, an operation repeated two or three times.
4. Spinnng the inner tub to remove water.

To conserve energy, standard temperatures may be reduced. Some detergent manufacturers have recommended cold water for most washing. While cold and warm temperatures conserve energy, their general use may result in a degree of cleanliness not acceptable to the consumer. However, warm water, rather than hot, may be used for whites and colorfast fabrics, if they are not heavily soiled. Cold water, rather than warm water, is to be recommended in the rinse cycle, particularly for permanent press. The sequence of steps for achieving effective wash results appears in Figure 16.2.

Determining Colorfastness

If colorfastness is unknown, fabrics should be put aside to wash separately or subjected to a wash test.

To determine the colorfastness of a textile fabric being examined in the store, make a simple crock test. Moisten a white handkerchief and rub it over a small section of the material to see if the color rubs off. This is more likely to happen on printed material than on yarn-dyed material.

Sorting the Laundry

Heavily soiled clothes should be separated from lightly soiled articles to help eliminate the latter picking up dirt from the former. Polyester and its blends tend to pick up oily soil from oily clothes in the same wash. Heavily soiled laundry should be prewashed for five minutes. Infants' clothing and articles from a sick room should be washed separatedly and bleached with chlorine bleach as a disinfectant.

Fabrics of large size may be mixed with small ones in the same water (that is, sheets may be mixed with undershirts). A load of sheets alone interferes with free movement in the water. However, single heavy items such as bedspreads and cotton rugs should be washed separately.

Washing Durable Press

Instructions for durable-press washing are especially important and should approximate the following:

1. Use the wash-and-wear or durable-press setting with cold rinse to avoid wrinkling.
2. Use regular laundry detergent.

How to do the laundry

Sort Clothes

By color:

WHITE **COLORFAST** **NONCOLORFAST**

If colors bleed dye, wash these items alone or with the same colors.

By type of fabric and construction:

COTTONS & LINENS **WASHABLE WOOLS** **DELICATES** **PERMANENT PRESS & MAN-MADE FIBERS**

By amount and kind of soil:

HEAVY **NORMAL** **LIGHT**

By size:
Heavy, bulky items – blanket, bedspread or slipcover – should be washed alone.

Check Clothes
Close zippers, fasten hooks.

Empty and brush out pockets.

Take off pins, ornaments, heavy buckles. Mend rips, tears.

Remove spots and stains (see stain removal chart).

Loosen ground-in dirt by making a paste of detergent or soap and a little water or use a liquid laundry detergent or bar soap.

Dampen the soiled area and gently rub in the solution. Use on collars and cuffs, feet of socks and knees of pants.

Measure and Add Washing Products
Read and follow package directions.

Size of the washing machine.

Kind of water. If water is hard, use more detergent. Soft water may require less, depending on amount and type of soil.

Put Clothes in Washer
Mix small and large pieces together.

Don't overload the machine.

Set Washer
Turn on both hot and cold water faucets.

Select wash and rinse temperatures.
   Different kinds of clothes require different water temperatures.

Set water level control if there is one.

Select the cycle for the correct wash action.

Start Washer

KNOW YOUR WASHER AND HOW TO USE IT.

WASHER CONTROLS DIFFER SO READ AND FOLLOW THE DIRECTIONS IN YOUR WASHER MANUAL.

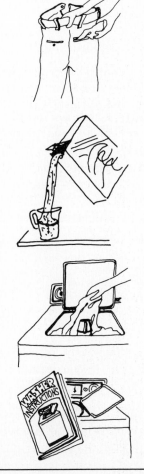

Figure 16.2 How to wash by automatic washer. (Courtesy of *Housekeeping Directions—A Simplified Guide*, Soap and Detergent Association.)

3. Do not overcrowd the washer; make up several smaller loads.
4. Tumble dry and remove from the dryer as soon as it stops.
5. Hang dried clothing on hangers (of the nonrusting variety) immediately after drying. Slacks should be hung on spring-clip hangers.
6. If touch-up ironing is desired, use a steam iron on a "low" setting.
7. Wash durable-press garments frequently, as heavy stains are difficult to remove.

The Pilling Problem

Loosely woven knitted and woven cloth made from short fibers tend to *pill;* that is, balls of tangled fibers work loose from the fabric and remain attached to the surface. This occurs where there is a rubbing action, either in laundering or in use. Stopping the washer's agitator while draining and filling may reduce the problem. If the fabric is made of one of the stronger man-made fibers, the pills can be cut off without injury; otherwise, the fabric may be weakened.

A similar problem, called *snagging,* is more likely to occur with fabrics of filament yarn. These long fibers are often partially pulled out of loosely constructed materials when they catch onto another surface.

Drying the Clothes

The old-fashioned method of drying was to remove excess water by hand wringing followed by laying the goods flat in the sun or hanging them on a line. Later, the wringer, consisting of two rubber cylinders, with a handle to turn them, replaced much hand wringing. Today most households are equipped with automatic drying machines. All the standard-sized machines have a drum that revolves in a cabinet, a heating unit, a screen to catch the lint, a safety door switch (to turn off the power when the door is opened during operation), and a control panel. The heat source may be electric or gas. Controls permit the selection of three or more cycles that regulate the heat:

Regular (normal)	For most laundered items.
Delicate	For sheers, lingerie, and many synthetics.
Air (no heat)	For fluffing items such as pillows and rugs and removing wrinkles and odors..
Heat drying followed by a cool-down period may be combined with the delicate cycle	For permanent press, knits, and man-made fibers.

Pressing and Ironing

Before the advent of durable press, most articles needed some pressing after laundering to restore them to their original appearance. It should be observed that fibers are affected differently by heat and steam. Therefore, it is important to know if ironing is required. The seller's care instructions are the best guide. Even if the laundered article is labeled "durable press," it may need a certain amount of ironing, a little "touching up," to improve its appearance.

REFRESHENING

Some garments, particularly those of wool fiber, require frequent refreshening to maintain their appearance and pleasant odor. These should be brushed at frequent intervals, especially before wearing them. Since wool absorbs oil from the skin, any dirt attracted to these fabrics mixes with the oil and a greasy stain is the result.

Blankets, bedspreads, and woolen clothing should also be refreshed by an occasional airing. Hang in the fresh air—in sunlight, if possible.

With velvets, corduroy, and other pile fabrics, wrinkles are best removed by hanging the garments over either a bathtub filled with steaming hot water or a steam-filled shower stall.

STORAGE

Ideally an outer garment should be brushed lightly and promptly hung on a hanger after wearing. Good ventilation should be provided to remove dampness, perspiration, and odors. If woolen goods are to be stored for some time, mothballs should be put in the storage bag, or a similar naphtha preparation should be sprinkled or sprayed on the garments to avoid damage by the moth larvae. If the storage space is subject to dampness, goods should be sprayed with a compound to prevent mildew. Bathing suits should be rinsed in fresh water and thoroughly dried before storage.

Contrary to general opinion, recent research findings indicate that synthetic fabrics can be damaged by insects. As with moths, it is the larvae of the insect that attack fabrics in areas stained or spotted by food. Cottons, linens, and other cellulosics are also subject to insect damage, especially by roaches, silverfish, and termites. To avoid such damage, it is important to clean all fabrics of food stains before storage, since insects will attack noncellulosic fabrics also where they are stained.[1]

Knitwear, underclothing, domestics, and curtains and draperies should be stored flat since light deteriorates some fibers. Hanging of knitwear is not recommended. Nearby steam radiators and hot-water pipes also should be avoided, particularly in the storage of silks, wools, and acetates. Fiberglass does not need to be stored, since it is resistant to light, moths, moisture, fire, and fumes.

[1]*Fabric Care*, International Fabricare Institute, October 1982, pp. 1–2.

Some homemakers roll linen fabrics in colorfast blue paper before storage to prevent yellowing. It is also desirable to wash new linen before storage, for the starch or dressing plus dampness may promote mildew.

DRY CLEANING[2]

In general, any article of clothing or household use not specifically launderable must be cared for by dry-cleaning methods. Dry cleaning, which uses solvents as the cleaning elements, minimizes shrinkage, fabric distortion, and seam puckering and is safe for water-soluble dyes and finishes. Unless the label warns against dry cleaning, all washable articles are considered dry-cleanable under the 1972 FTC Permanent Care Labeling Regulation Rule for Wearing Apparel and under revision of the two national, recommended practice labeling standards in support of the regulation.[3]

Dry cleaning may be done professionally as a full-service treatment, or it may be carried out in coin-operated, self-service machines. The machines used in both types of service are engineered to recover and keep solvent clean and to protect against fumes. But some cleaners have been plagued by dirty solvent, containing a high level of color and soluble soil, that causes graying of fabrics. By far the most common solvent worldwide is nonflammable perchlorethylene, a completely manufactured chlorinated hydrocarbon. Refined petroleum solvents are still common, but only where flammable solvents are permitted. An example of a more recent competing solvent is Valclene, a DuPont product based on fluorocarbon 113.

Dry cleaning at home (except localized spot removal) requires extreme caution because of possible flammability or toxicity of solvents. Instructions on the container should be followed carefully.

The International Fabricare Institute tests articles for serviceability. The item is run for three or more cycles, after which it is measured for dimensional change (shrinkage or stretch), change of appearance (color, pilling), and change of hand (softness or stiffness).[4]

The FTC labeling rule makes desirable the use of these test and perfor-

---

[2]Prepared especially for the seventh edition of this book by Albert E. Johnson, formerly Seal and Trade Relations Director, International Fabricare Institute, with revisions for this, the eighth edition.

[3]These standards are D3136–1972, American Society for Testing and Materials, and 128.1, American National Standards Institute.

[4]Standard laboratory tests include American Association for Textile Chemists and Colorists Test #132–1973 for colorfastness using a Launder-Ometer and AATCC Test #86, Durability of Applied Designs and Finishes. American National Standard L22 (transferred to subcommittee D1356 of the American Society for Testing and Materials) specifies minimum performance requirements for essential properties of consumer-type textiles, including dry cleaning. ANS L24, sponsored by the American Hotel and Motel Association, covers institutional textiles. ASTM Test #D3135–1972 specifies requirements for launderability and dry-cleanability of bonded fabrics. All dry-cleaning test methods specify perchlorethylene because any material that withstands this solvent is dry-cleanable in the other solvents, whereas the reverse may not be true.

Table 16.1   Responsibility in Dry Cleaning

Responsibility of	Number of Garments	% of Total Garments Handled
Consumer	9,455	39.8%
Dry cleaner	4,089	17.1
Manufacturer	10,241	43.9
Total	23,785	100.0%

mance standards for determining correctness of dry-cleaning instructions on apparel.

Stain Removal in Dry Cleaning

Ninety percent of all stains (food oils, wet paints except lacquers, greases, beverages) respond to either proprietary cleaning fluids or to water and should be applied in that order. All chemical stains (perfumes, dried paints, lipstick, inks, polishes) are best treated by professional dry cleaners. "Rings" form easily on smooth, light-colored fabrics and are difficult to prevent without the special equipment used by dry cleaners. Solvent-formed rings come out in regular dry cleaning. Water-formed rings must be "feathered" out with a steam gun.

In dry cleaning, the consumer should point out to the cleaner any food, beverage, or perfume that has been spilled on the garment, even though the stain may not be noticeable. Cleaning with solvent without preliminary spot removal is likely to result in discoloration.

Standard Cleaning Procedures

The International Fair Claims Guide for Consumer Textile Products of the International Fabricare Institute is the standard reference used by dry cleaners, Better Business Bureaus, and others for settling questions of responsibility for damage claims, definitions of terms related to fabric care, and adjustment values.

Types of Problems Facing Dry Cleaners[5]

In 1980, the Garment Analysis Department of the International Fabricare Institute handled 23,785 problems related to items that had been dry cleaned. These were grouped as shown in Table 16.1

Of the 9,455 items where the customer was deemed responsible, the chief seven causes, accounting for about two-thirds of the total, were, in order,

Acid and bleach damage
Color change: sun, acid, alkali, etc.
Mechanical damage and wear

[5]*Fabricare News*, March 1981, pp. 2–3.

Local color loss: bleach

Shrinkage

Household stains: ink, adhesive, etc.

Beverage and sugar stains

It seems evident, according to these figures, that the consumer should exercise particular care in handling acids and bleach and in avoiding spills.

Mandatory Care Labels as Guides to Dry Cleaning

As was explained in Chapter 1, the Federal Trade Commission requires that care labels be attached permanently to most items of apparel, piece goods intended for the home sewing of apparel, draperies, towels, and bedding. The gist of the regulation itself is given in Appendix D. The required information is generally limited to washing and cleaning. (See Table 16.2.)

Table 16.2 Care Labeling

Care Labeling:
Consumer Rights and Responsibilities

When they shop:	Observe warning to professional dry-clean only.
Use CARE LABELS to determine performance and cost of upkeep in choosing which items to buy.	Expect commercial dry cleaners to observe CARE LABELS.
Expect salespersons at fabrics counters to provide CARE LABELS suitable for application to each finished garment.	*In speaking up:*
	Share with FTC ideas to improve care labeling.
When they sew:	Complain to store managers if rule appears to be violated. Obtain name of manufacturer and complain in writing.
Attach CARE LABELS to garments.	
In washing, ironing, and dry cleaning:	Complain to manufacturers if care instructions are confusing or appear to result in damage to garments.
Follow CARE LABEL instructions.	
Observe solvent warnings when using coin-operated cleaning equipment.	

Industry Responsibilities

The person or organization that directed or controlled the manufacture of the finished article is responsible for care labeling of apparel. In most cases, this will be the finished product manufacturer. However, in some situations responsibility may rest with jobbers or retailers.

The manufacturer of piece goods is responsible for supplying retailers with enough labels to satisfy individual consumers. Retailers are responsible for making such labels available at point of sale.

The importer is responsible for seeing that imported items are properly labeled before they are sold in commerce.

Source: FTC, *Fact Sheet, Care Labeling Rules,* Vol. 1.1.

PRODUCTS USED IN CLEANING

Soaps

Soap is the result of the reaction of fat with an alkali. The fats used are generally tallow (animal fat) and coconut oil. The alkali is sodium hydroxide or potassium hydroxide. Historians report that thousands of years ago when the Romans sacrificed animals the fat mixed with ash and rain carried the mixture through the clay soil. Ancient launderers soon found that using soapy clay made it easier to wash clothes in the streams. As time passed, many refinements were made in the basic process.

Today there are two kinds of laundry soaps: light duty and all purpose. The chief difficulty with all soap is that it tends to form an insoluble residue, called soap curd, that picks up soil from the water and sticks it to whatever surface it contacts, such as the clothes in the wash. However, soap with builders may be satisfactory in parts of the country where the water supply is generally soft, such as the Pacific Northwest.

Detergents

In many parts of the country, the water is at least seasonally hard, containing relatively large amounts of calcium and magnesium. This makes the dirt difficult to remove. As clothes dry, dissolved solids form a precipitate on them making them stiff and sometimes discolored, in addition to leaving curds if soap is used. Hard water prevails in the Great Plains area, and in other parts of the country, hardness occurs in many places and at different seasons. It even varies block by block in the same community.

These problems have led to the development of detergents, which are cleansing agents, synthesized from a variety of raw materials, that contain a surface active ingredient that wets and penetrates the material more thoroughly and quickly, loosening the soil and removing it more readily. Detergents often contain other agents such as whiteners, builders to counter water hardness, suds controllers, and ingredients to prevent soil from resettling on the clothes.

Kinds of Detergents

There are both light- and heavy-duty detergents. The former are suitable for delicate fabrics and those slightly soiled. In liquid form, these are frequently used for dish washing. Heavy-duty offerings are all-purpose detergents that contain builders, chemical materials that increase cleaning ability, emulsifying greasy soil and softening fabrics. Heavy-duty detergents are well suited for the general wash and heavily soiled items by permitting the use of cold and warm water rather than hot. (See Fig. 16.3.)

Detergents containing phosphates, usually in the form of STPP (sodium tripolyphosphate), are superior in water softening and in avoiding fabric stiffness. They hold minerals in solution so that they do not form insoluble

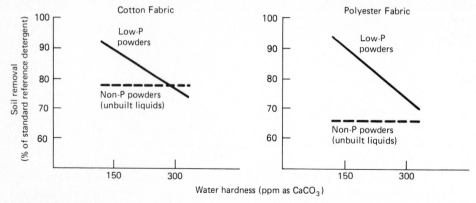

Figure 16.3 Heavy-duty laundry detergents and the effects of water hardness on soil removal. According to the illustration, for cotton and polyester fabrics, the harder the water, the smaller the percentage of soil removed, even with heavy-duty detergent. (Courtesy of *Detergents in Depth, '78*, Soap and Detergent Association.)

deposits. But they have been banned in some localities as a cause of contamination of the environment. They are blamed for the aging of lakes and ponds, as they become rich in dissolving nutrients that promote the rapid growth of algae.

To replace STPP, detergent manufacturers have done a great deal of research since the late 1960s and have developed three sodium compounds that are now widely used: silicate, sulfate, and carbonate. (See Fig. 16.4.) Others are

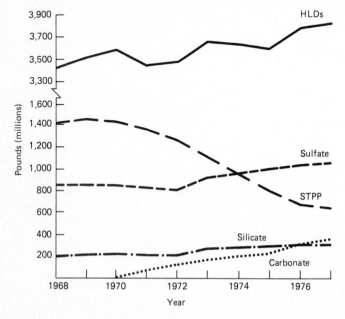

Figure 16.4 Usage of product varieties in the U.S. home laundry detergent market, 1968–1977. (Courtesy of *Detergents in Depth, '78*, Soap and Detergent Association.)

Table 16.3 Specialized Laundry Products

Product	Purpose
Water softeners	To remove water-hardness material from the wash water. (May be done mechanically in the water line.)
Bleaches, including bluing	To whiten fabrics and remove yellowing and graying. A chlorine-based material is generally used.
Disinfectants	To destroy harmful bacteria. A liquid chlorine bleach may be used for this purpose.
Starches	To make fabrics stiffer, crisper, and shinier.
Fabric softeners	To make fabrics softer, fluffier, and less subject to wrinkles.

being researched and developed. They are not believed to be harmful to the environment, but some have a caustic substance that tends to shorten the life of clothing and injure the porcelain finish of the washer, where the water is hard. They may also be hazardous to children. Consumers should read labels carefully to note directions and cautions.

Presoak Products

Presoak products are not complete detergents but are very effective for use with the detergent to provide an additional cleaning agent for stubborn soils. The presoak products contain enzymes and are used in a presoak wash. Chlorine should never be used with enzyme presoak products since chlorine destroys the enzymes. Examples of presoak products include Axion, Biz, and Trizyme.

Additional Products to Use in the Laundry

Table 16.3 lists additional products that may be used in the laundry process and their purposes. Some of these products are included in various brands of detergents on the market. Space does not permit a detailed description and evaluation here.

SPOT AND STAIN REMOVAL

Prompt and proper treatment of spots and stains will save a great deal in dry-cleaning bills. Fortunately, some clothing today is treated with a finish that repels stains. The consumer should look for such a finish when buying garments made from hydrophobic fibers, such as polyester. A process called Scotchgard, used on raincoats, men's and women's suitings, upholstery fabrics, and tablecloths, makes the fabric resistant to both water and oil stains, through many launderings.

The chances of successful spot removal are best with washable fabrics and rough-finished dry-cleanable ones. The first rule is prompt treatment before the

Table 16.4 Treatments for Removing Common Stains from Washable Fabrics

Type of Stain	Treatment
Blood[a]	Soak in warm water and an enzyme presoak product for half an hour. Launder as usual. A few drops of ammonia may help.
Chewing gum	Put ice on gum to harden it. Take gum off fabric with a dull knife. Place fabric face down on paper towels and sponge with a dry-cleaning solvent. Launder.
Coffee or tea[a]	Soak in enzyme presoak product or oxygen bleach. Rinse and wash. If stain remains, launder in hot water; use chlorine bleach if safe for the fabric.
Cosmetics	Dampen stain. Rub with bar soap. Then rinse and wash, using chlorine bleach if safe.
Deodorants, antiperspirants	Rub liquid detergent on light stain and wash in hottest water safe for the fabric. For heavy stains, place garment facedown on paper towels and sponge back of stain with dry-cleaning solvent; rinse. Rub with liquid detergent and rinse. Launder in hottest water safe for fabric.
Fabric softener	Dampen stain and rub with bar soap. Rinse and repeat if necessary. Then wash.
Grass	Soak in enzyme presoak product. Then wash in hot water. If still stained, use chlorine bleach if safe for fabric, and launder.
Greasy stains (car grease or oil, butter, margarine, lard, salad dressings, cooking oils)	Apply absorbent powder or place stain face down on paper towels. Put dry-cleaning solvent on back side of stain. Brush from center of stain to outer edges with a clean white cloth. Dampen stain with water and rub with bar soap or liquid detergent. Rinse and launder.
Ink, ballpoint	Place stain face down on paper towels. Sponge back of stain with dry-cleaning solvent or rubbing alcohol. If some ink still remains, try oily-type paint remover. Avoid water until stain is removed; rinse and wash.
Lipstick	Place stain face down on paper towels. Sponge back of stain with dry-cleaning solvent. Move fabric to clean area of towel frequently to take out more of the color. See *ink, ballpoint.*
Mildew	Wash with detergent and chlorine bleach if the fabric can be bleached. If not, soak in an oxygen bleach or sponge with hydrogen peroxide; then wash.
Milk, cream, ice cream[a]	Soak in cold water with an enzyme presoak product. Wash in hot water with chlorine bleach; rinse.
Paint, water-base	Rinse fabrics in warm water while stains are still wet. Then launder. Once paint is dried, it cannot be removed.
Oil-base paint, varnish	Use the solvent recommended on the paint can as a thinner; if not available, use turpentine. Rinse and rub with bar soap. Rinse and wash.
Perspiration[a]	Dampen stain and rub with bar soap. Soak in an enzyme presoak product. Launder in hot water and chlorine bleach if safe for fabric. If color of fabric has changed, use ammonia for fresh stains and vinegar for oil. Rinse and launder in hottest water safe for color.
Rust	A few spots can be removed with a rust stain remover dissolved in cold water. Rinse and wash in hot water. If a full load of white items shows rust, use a fabric color remover. Launder.
Scorch	Soak in an enzyme presoak product or oxygen bleach. Then launder. If stain remains, use chlorine bleach if safe for fabric and launder again using hottest water safe for fabric. Severe scorch is not removable.

Table 16.4 (cont'd)

Type of Stain	Treatment
Shoe polish[b]	Remove excess polish. Sponge with liquid detergent followed by cleaning fluid. Rubbing alcohol, diluted, is often effective.
Urine, vomit, mucous[b]	Soak in an enzyme presoak product. Launder using a chlorine bleach if safe for the fabric or an oxygen bleach. If color changed, sponge with ammonia.
Wine, soft drinks[a b]	Soak in cold water in an enzyme presoak product, bleach using hottest water safe for fabric. If stain remains, use a detergent; launder in hot water, using chlorine bleach if safe for the fabric.

[a]The IFI reports that a few drops of mild 3 percent hydrogen peroxide will remove fixed stains such as blood, foods, beverages, and perspiration. But on colored material, it may not prove safe. Since peroxide acts slowly, the application may have to be repeated. Flushing with water after the application is essential. See *Fabricare News*, May 1981.

[b]Added by the authors.

Source: See *Housekeeping Directions*, pp. 53–54; minor additions have been made by the authors. Soap and Detergent Association.

stain "sets." Cool water is generally the best treatment for nongreasy stains, and particularly for dye stains such as one might get from colored paper napkins. Some fresh grease stains can be removed by absorbent powder such as talcum or cornstarch or by an absorbent powder mixture. On a dark article, however, this method may lead to the additional problem of removing the white powder. Cleaning fluid will remove grease from colored washables and dry-cleanable fabrics.

If the fabric is washable and colorfast, soaking of a stain in a detergent is helpful in many types of stain removal. Soaking in an enzyme product for 30 minutes (or overnight if necessary) will break down or digest by chemical means the various kinds of organic matter, protein, and starch into very small particles. This is a technique of soil release for polyester/cotton blends with durable-press finishes. (See Chapter 7.)

Table 16.4 shows some treatments for removing common stains from washable fabrics.[6] Success of stain removal depends on following the procedures, but some stains cannot be removed. When using any stain-removal material, read and follow instructions carefully. Some products may be flammable or toxic. Follow all safety suggestions. Work where there is plenty of fresh air.

CONSUMER CLAIMS FOR UNSERVICEABLE OR LOST TEXTILE ARTICLES

When a consumer believes that he or she has purchased unsatisfactory merchandise or service, it is first necessary to determine who is at fault: the seller, the manufacturer, the dry cleaner, the commercial laundry, or

[6]A more detailed guide in wall chart form is available from the Home Economics Department of the Maytag Company, Newton, Iowa.

the consumer. If the product is at fault, the consumer will seek redress from the retailer who in turn looks to the manufacturer or wholesaler involved. If the dry cleaner or commercial laundry seems to be at fault, these organizations will be contacted directly.

Determination of an acceptable value for the loss may be made from standard tables that report the normal life expectancy of the particular classification of the article, the current age of the article, its replacement value, and its condition before the damage or loss.

For example, a high-fashion evening dress with a replacement value of $300 may be damaged in dry cleaning. It was in good condition when taken for cleaning after a year of purchase. The life expectancy for this class of evening dress is reported in the table as being three years. After a year from purchase has passed, the table reports that the dress is worth 60 percent of replacement cost, or $180.

These tables may be used not only for claims but for determining the fair market value of used garments donated to charitable organizations as well. Tables are also available for men's and boys' wear and for household textiles. (See the *International Fair Claims Guide for Consumer Textile Products,* issued by the IFI in 1981.)

For instructions in the care of draperies and curtains, see Chapter 21; for instructions in the care of soft floor coverings, see Chapter 20.

SUMMARY

The manufacturer's informative label is the consumer's best guide for the care of fabrics, especially with blends. If, however, there is no label giving instructions for care, then the consumer should clean the blend according to the method required for the fiber that needs the most special care.

Fiber content is one criterion for the kind of care that should be given a fabric to ensure proper satisfaction in use. The type of yarn, closeness and firmness of construction, the nature and permanency of finish, and colorfastness are also important factors in determining the proper care for a fabric. But the best criterion is the mandatory care label permanently attached to or printed on the apparel.

REVIEW QUESTIONS

1. To ensure proper care of textile fabrics, what three elements must be considered? Explain.
2. (a) What fabrics are best washed by hand?
   (b) Explain the procedure for hand washing a wool scarf.
3. Under what conditions should one use hot, warm, or cold water in the wash?

4. (a) What is wrong with each of the following brief statements, sometimes found on garment care labels: machine wash, hand wash, dry clean, no bleach, never needs ironing?
   (b) Study the detailed permanent-care regulations in Appendix D. In view of the trend toward less regulation by government, are they too specific, going beyond what the typical consumer needs to be told? Discuss with others.
5. Describe the method of removing ballpoint ink stains from (a) white cotton and (b) colored linen.
6. In view of the information in Chapter 11 on silk, why should alkalies in the wash and high heat in ironing be avoided?
7. In view of the information in Chapter 12 on wool, what cleaning recommendations would you make?
8. How can a sound evaluation be made of a used garment ruined in dry cleaning?

EXPERIMENTS

Select as many of the following fabrics as possible for this experiment: white nylon tricot jersey, pure silk shantung, colored dress linen, colored cotton broadcloth, white polyester/cotton shirting, 100 percent polyester, or polyester/cotton crepe.
   (a) Follow the instructions for either home automatic washing or the durable-press instructions. Analyze the results of each test.
   (b) Evaluate the results of the test by stating the purpose for which the fabric is best used. Give reasons for your decision. What instructions should the consumer be given for laundering the fabric.?

PROJECT

Write a manual of instructions for the consumer on one of the following topics:
   (a) Care of men's suits, shirts, sweaters, or hosiery.
   (b) Care of women's pantsuits, sweaters, or hosiery.
   (c) Care of household textiles (rugs or draperies and curtains).

GLOSSARY

Bluing   A liquid, bead, or flake-type tint that makes clothes look whiter but has no real whitening or cleansing action; used mostly on cotton or linen.

Builder   An ingredient in a detergent that reduces hardness in wash water, provides the proper alkalinity, and helps to keep the soil from being redeposited on clothing.

Built soap   Soap that has a builder, such as phosphate, added.

Chlorine   A liquid-type bleach and disinfectant.

Cold-water detergent   An agent that cleans and germproofs in cold water.

Completely washable fabric   A fabric washable by machine in water hot enough to clean the fabric efficiently (160° F in the tub).

Detergent   A cleansing agent, synthesized for a variety of raw materials, that contains a surface active ingredient that lowers the surface tension of the water so that it penetrates the clothes more quickly and thoroughly. It often contains other special-purpose ingredients.

Dressing   See *starch.*

Drip dry   A method of drying a fabric without wringing or squeezing it. After a garment has been cleansed and rinsed, it is hung directly on a hanger. Every care is taken not to wrinkle it so that it will drip and dry with no wrinkles, thus reducing ironing to only a touch-up.

Dry cleaning   The removal of soil from fabrics by means of a solvent.

Durable press   See the glossary in Chapter 3.

Enzyme   Organic catalyst used to speed soil removal from a fabric, as in presoaking, and to speed decomposition of starch especially during desizing of fabric preparatory to dyeing or finishing.

Fabric softeners   Chemicals added to the wash, final rinse, or dryer to improve the hand of fabrics, especially terry cloth and infants' wear.

Fine fabric   A fabric that usually requires hand washing or dry cleaning.

Heavy-duty soap   A pure, mild soap that has special alkalies added to improve its cleaning power.

Heavy-duty synthetic detergent   One that has a builder for improved cleaning power. A suds-making ingredient is added primarily for automatic washers. A low-sudsing detergent is often recommended for the front-loading type of automatic washer.

Hydrophilic fibers   Fibers that absorb water readily, take longer to dry, and require more ironing. See *hydrophobic fiber* (in the glossary in Chapter 15).

Informative label   Factual information about the goods. See Chapter 1.

Laundry soap   A heavy-duty soap with special alkalies added to improve its cleaning power.

Load   The number of garments or pounds that can be put into an automatic washer at one time.

Nep   An entangled ball of fibers spun into the yarn that breaks loose.

Neutral soap   A mild soap that has little alkali.

Pill   A ball-like tangle of fibers on the surface of a fabric.

Presoak product   A product, generally containing enzymes, that is used before the wash to treat stubborn stains and soil that tend to resist the detergent used.

Soap   A cleansing agent produced by the action of alkali and fat.

Sodium perborate   A bleach in the form of powder (an oxygen bleach).

Soil release   See the glossary in Chapter 7.

Sorting   Separating articles to be washed by color, type of fabric, degree of dirt, and size, to assure that the articles in the load should be washed together.

Sour   The commercial use of an acid in the rinse bath to neutralize the residue of alkaline products to prevent yellowing.

Spin dry   Partial removal of water by spinning in the washer.

Starch   A white, odorless, dry or liquid vegetable compound used for stiffening fabrics. Plastic starch is made of resin (plastic) that can permanently stiffen cloth.

Tumble cold   Drying in a tumble dryer with the heat off.

Tumble dry   Drying in a heated tumble dryer, with heat to 180°F.

Unwashable fabric   A fabric that should not be washed by hand or by machine. Such fabrics are usually labeled "Dry Clean Only."

Washable fabric   A fabric that can be washed. The method of washing (by hand or machine) may not be designated.

Wash-and-wear   See the glossary in Chapter 7.

Washing Cleaning textile products with water.

  Hand wash Washing carefully by hand.

  Hot wash Laundering in hot water, up to 160°F, with a built soap.

  Medium washing Laundering with water not to exceed 120°F.

  Mildly washable Laundering in water no more than 105°F with a reduced rate of agitation.

Wash test A trial washing of an inconspicuous part of a garment to determine if the color is fast to washing.

Water softener A chemical compound added to the rinse water or to both the wash and the rinse water if the water is very hard. Its purpose is to prevent the formation of film and deposits that tend to gray or spot the fabric.

Wet cleaning A process similar to hand washing, carried out by a professional dry cleaner.

Chapter 17

WOMEN'S AND GIRLS' WEAR

Planning and selection of clothing by the typical woman is one of the most creative activities in which she is engaged. Nearly every woman attempts to express her personality and her sense of becomingness as reflected in her various moods.

How often do we hear the word "relax"? Most of us hear it frequently. We want to go home to relax after a hard day's work at the office; we want to relax as we sunbathe by the pool; we want to relax after a strenuous game of tennis. What article of clothing could feel more relaxing than a loose flowing caftan, a chemise, or a knitted dress or pants with stretch that moves with the body.

When speaking of "relaxed styles" in dress, we mean that women are wearing many types of garments in a variety of combinations for the same occasion. For example, for a cocktail party in the winter, a long velvet skirt with a blouse of sheer crepe, a velvet suit with pants or skirt, a crepe de Chine dress, or a long matte jersey dress with a metallic knitted sweater would be appropriate. The combinations are almost limitless, and there is no longer any one type of garment that is worn for a given occasion. Therefore, the salesperson can help the customer by showing her the various combinations possible.

Just as there is no longer one acceptable style for a particular occasion, there is no longer one fabric that surpasses all others for that occasion. (Compare Figs. 17.1 through 17.5.) In fact, many men's wear fabrics have become popular for women's wear. For example, a Harris tweed coat is suitable for both sexes. Home furnishing fabrics have also entered the women's wear field. Chintz, especially popular for slipcovers and curtains, is now frequently found in

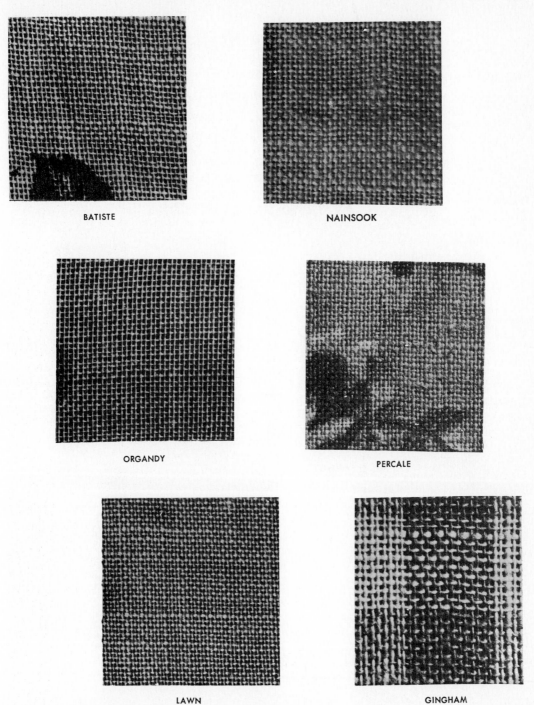

Figure 17.1a   Dress fabrics in plain weaves. (Photos by Jack Pitkin.)

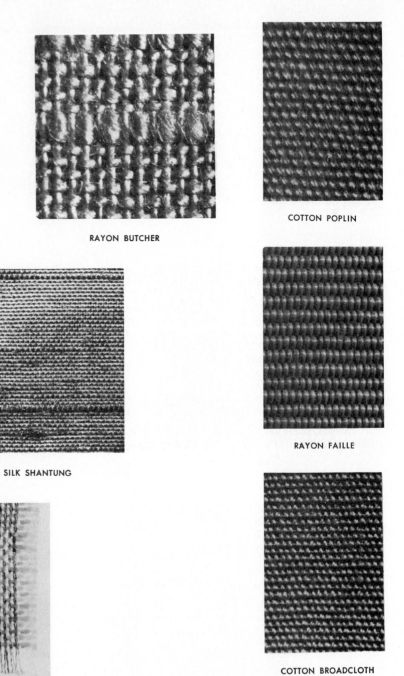

RAYON BUTCHER

COTTON POPLIN

SILK SHANTUNG

RAYON FAILLE

2 x 1 BASKET (OXFORD)

COTTON BROADCLOTH

Figure 17.1b Dress fabrics in plain weaves. The butcher and shantung have slub (uneven) yarns; others are ribbed except for the oxford. (Photos by Jack Pitkin.)

COTTON GABARDINE RAYON TWILL

2 x 1 TWILL DENIM RAYON SURAH WOOL FLANNEL

Figure 17.2 Dress fabrics in twill weaves. (Photos by Jack Pitkin.)

women's summer dresses, skirts, and aprons. In short, certain fabrics are no longer exclusively confined to women's, men's, or home furnishing categories.

Of course, differences in weight automatically limit some fabrics to particular seasons and uses. In summer, the weather calls for thin materials, such as voile, eyelet batiste, sheer crepes, and chiffons; in winter, for heavier materials, such as wool tweeds, homespuns, velveteen, velvet, corduroy, and furlike fabrics. Some stiff fabrics look better when a crisp appearance is required; soft and clinging fabrics are appropriate when a slinky, draped effect is desired; rich and luxurious fabrics look best in the evening; washable fabrics appear to advantage and are suitable for wear at work, at leisure, or for active or spectator sports at home.

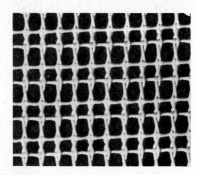

RAYON MARQUISETTE

BROCADE (SILK WITH METAL THREADS)

Figure 17.3 Dress fabrics in fancy weaves. (Photos by Jack Pitkin.)

STYLES AND FABRICS IN WOMEN'S AND GIRLS' OUTER APPAREL

It is estimated that more than 45 million women in the United States are sewing at home.[1] With home sewing so popular, the problem of selecting the proper fabric for the particular purpose required has become a major one. Therefore, the first part of this chapter will assist the home sewer in selecting the appropriate style and fabric for construction of a garment. Fabrics for outerwear may be grouped under the following classification of occasions for which they are worn: (1) day wear, (2) active sportswear, and (3) evening wear.

[1]Information provided by the National Home Sewers Association, New York, N.Y., Dec., 1982.

RAYON MATELASSÉ

RAYON ROUGH CREPE

RAYON ALPACA

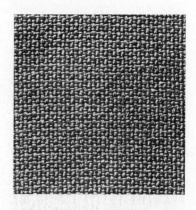

RAYON CREPE ROMAINE

FLAT CREPE

CHIFFON

Figure 17.4 Crepes. (Photos by Jack Pitkin.)

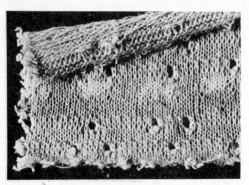 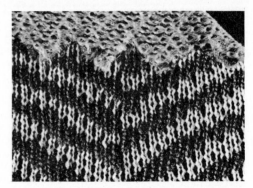

Figure 17.5 Left: A cotton open-work jersey, single knit. Right: Double knit with herringbone design. (Photos by Jonas Grushkin.)

Styles and Fabrics for Daytime Wear

The 1970s initiated the "pants era." No longer are pants confined to the young living in suburbia. Women of all ages, in town and country, wear pants for street and business, classes in schools and colleges, housework, baby tending, gardening, food marketing, and parties. Pants became suitable for any and all daytime activities and for many evening activities. They continue to be very popular in the eighties.

Pants are made in many styles: high waisted and natural waisted. They may fit snuggly or loosely. Pant legs may be straight, tapered, flared, or baggy and may end at any length from shorts to floor length.

Skirts are alternatives to pants in A-line, pleated, gored, wrap-around, and straight styles of various lengths.

Tops for both pants and skirts include shirts (woven and knitted), vests, blouses, sweaters, and suit-type jackets to match the pants—an ensemble called a pants set.

For spring, summer, and early fall, cotton, man-made fibers, and blends are important. For skirts, pants, and dresses, woven cotton fabrics such as denim, gingham, gabardine, and sailcloth are popular. Heavier fabrics, such as melton fleece flannel, double knits, velveteen, and corduroy are suitable for fall and winter.

Both woven goods and knits are used for tops. Woven fabrics include crepes, triacetates, acetate polyesters, and blends and are found in blouses, shirts, and jackets. Sweaters and vests are usually knitted of acrylic or man-made-fibered yarns and wool blends.

Tops, pants, and skirts (called "separates" because each article is sold separately) are made of all-wool melton, wool/nylon, polyester/wool, wool/rayon, and 100 percent acrylic. The familiar jeans are made of 100 percent cotton or polyester/cotton denim for fall and winter weights.[2]

---

[2]For definitions of fabrics used in women's wear, see the glossary at the end of this chapter.

Dresses

In spite of the current emphasis on separates and coordinates for women's and children's outer apparel, the dress continues to hold a dominant position in the fashion market. In fact, before the depression of the 1930s, the dress accounted for most of the outerwear volume in the United States. And until World War I, most dresses were made either at home or by a professional dressmaker. The fabric was purchased from yard-goods stores or department stores. The heavier fabrics were sold, in a "domestic" section, for housework (often done by servants). The lighterweight fabrics were sold in the dress section. This distinction no longer holds because of the great variety of yarns, of both natural and man-made fibers, that makes it possible to finish most basic constructions, such as denim, to make them suitable for a wide variety of uses.

Today, dresses are usually classified by body build and by occasion of use: street and business wear, utility (house dresses), bridal and formal, and maternity. The street dress classification is broken down further into body types and sizes: junior, junior petite, misses, women's, and half-sizes. The standard measurement of each of these classifications, with "young juniors" added, appears in Table 17.1.

The major classifications of dresses are subdivided further as one-piece street or business, two or more piece and ensembles, and "after 5" and evening dresses. Within these groupings, assortments available may be grouped by color and by price lines.

One-piece dresses are available in many styles, including shifts, chemises, coats, and shirtwaists, with straight, gored, and gathered skirts. (See Fig. 17.6.)

Historically, the silhouette of the dress has passed through three cycles that repeat: straight or tubular, bell-shaped or bouffant, and bustle or full-backed. The third type is now out of style, and the bouffant is expressed not with hoop skirts but with variations in the flair of the skirt.

For spring and summer wear, the cotton jersey T-shirt dress is much in demand. Once used only for underwear, cotton jersey is now dyed and printed and given a stylish treatment. It is cool in hot weather, since cotton conducts moisture away from the body. It tends to wrinkle, since cotton is not elastic, but the weft knit retards this tendency. Also, the garment may be ironed with a hot iron. A preshrunk garment is preferable.

Suits

Suits are worn the year round, with darker colors worn in the fall and winter in colder climates. Among many other fabrics, they may be made of tweed-textured or solid fabrics in the fall and winter and of shantung, lightweight flannel, or ribbed fabrics in the spring and summer.

Suits may be classified as soft or tailored. (See Fig. 17.7.) The soft suit is unstructured. The tailored suit fits the figure as a man's suit does.

A good fit in a coat or suit means that the style is cut full enough so that the arms can be raised above the head without pulling at the seams. This fit requires

Table 17.1 Body Measurement Chart as Established by the Pattern Fashion Industry

Misses'
Misses' patterns are designed for a well-proportioned and developed figure; about 5'5".

Size	6 In.	6 Cm	8 In.	8 Cm	10 In.	10 Cm	12 In.	12 Cm	14 In.	14 Cm	16 In.	16 Cm	18 In.	18 Cm	20 In.	20 Cm
Bust	30½	78	31½	80	32½	82.6	34	87	36	92	38	97	40	102	42	107
Waist	23	58	24	61	25	64	26½	67	28	71	30	76	32	81	34	87
Hip	32½	83	33½	85	34½	88	36	92	38	97	40	102	42	107	44	112
Back waist length	15½	39.5	15¾	40	16	40.5	16¼	41.5	16½	42	16¾	42.5	17	43	17¼	44

Junior
Junior patterns are designed for a well-proportioned and shorter-waisted figure; about 5'4" (1.63 m) to 5'5" (1.65 m) without shoes.

Size	5 In.	5 Cm	7 In.	7 Cm	9 In.	9 Cm	11 In.	11 Cm	13 In.	13 Cm	15 In.	15 Cm
Bust	30	76	31	79	32	81	33½	85	35	89	37	94
Waist	22½	57	23½	60	24½	62	25½	65	27	69	29	74
Hips	32	81	33	84	34	87	35½	90	37	94	39	99
Back waist length	15	38	15¼	39	15½	39.5	15¾	40	16	40.5	16¼	41.5

Young Junior/Teen
This size range is designed for the developing preteen figure and teen figure; about 5'1" (1.55 m) to 5'3" (1.6 m) without shoes.

Size	5/6 In.	5/6 Cm	7/8 In.	7/8 Cm	9/10 In.	9/10 Cm	11/12 In.	11/12 Cm	13/14 In.	13/14 Cm	15/16 In.	15/16 Cm
Bust	28	71	29	74	30½	78	32	81	33½	85	35	89
Waist	22	56	23	58	24	61	25	64	26	66	27	69
Hips	31	79	32	81	33½	85	35	89	36½	93	38	97
Back waist length	13½	34.5	14	35.5	14½	37	15	38	15⅜	39	15¾	40

Women

Women's patterns are designed for the larger, more fully matured figure; about 5'5" (1.65 m) to 5'6" (1.68 m) without shoes.

Size	38		40		42		44		46		48		50	
	In.	Cm	In.	Cm	In.	Cm	In.	Cm	In.	Cm	In.	Cm	In.	Cm
Bust	42	107	44	112	46	117	48	122	50	127	52	132	54	137
Waist	35	89	37	94	39	99	41½	105	44	112	46½	118	49	124
Hips	44	112	46	117	48	122	50	127	52	132	54	137	56	142.2
Back waist length	17¼	44	17⅜	44	17½	44.5	17⅝	45	17¾	45	17⅞	45.5	18	46

Half-Sizes

Half-size patterns are designed for the fully developed figure with a short back waist length; about 5'2" (1.57 m) to 5'3" (1.6 m) without shoes. Waist and hips are larger in proportion to bust than in other figure types.

Size	10½		12½		14½		16½		18½		20½		22½		24½	
	In.	Cm	In.	Cm	In.	Cm	In.	Cm	In.	Cm	In.	Cm	In.	Cm	In.	Cm
Bust	33	84	35	89	37	94	39	99	41	104	43	109	45	114	47	119
Waist	27	69	29	74	31	79	33	84	35	89	37½	96	40	102	42½	108
Hips	35	89	37	94	39	99	41	104	43	109	45½	116	48	122	50½	128
Back waist length	15	38	15¼	39	15½	39.5	15¾	40	15⅞	40.5	16	40.5	16⅛	41	16¼	41.5

Junior Petite

Junior petite patterns are designed for a well-proportioned, petite figure; about 5' (1.52 m) to 5'1" (1.55 m) without shoes.

Size	Small				Medium				Large			
	3JP		5JP		7JP		9JP		11JP		13JP	
	In.	Cm	In.	Cm	In.	Cm	In.	Cm	In.	Cm	In.	Cm
Bust	30	76	31	79	32	81	33	84	34	87	35	89
Waist	22	56	23	58	24	61	25	64	26	66	27	69
Hips	31	79	32	81	33	84	34	87	35	89	36	92
Back waist length	14	35.5	14¼	36	14½	37	14¾	37.5	15	38	15¼	39

Figure 17.6 This dress proved to be an outstanding seller in the spring season of 1982. It was offered to the public by a leading mail-order firm. It is of textured polyester in Raschel knit. The suitability of fiber, construction, and style account for its big success. (Photo courtesy of New Process Company.)

large armholes and curved underarms. The fabric in the body and sleeves should be cut with the grain of the fabric, and the bottom of the coat or suit should hang evenly. An outer garment should have smooth shoulders that are the right width. Seams should be adequately wide, even, and pliable so that they will not pull out. Reinforcements should be found at points of strain, buttons should be sewn firmly, and buttonholes or loops should be made evenly and strongly sewn.

If the coat has a collar, it should fit the neck snugly. Lapels should be the same width and should roll back smoothly. A belt ought to be stitched firmly at the sides of the coat or be run through three loop carriers.

Styles and Fabrics for Active Sportswear

The nature of the sport generally governs the type of garment to be worn. For spectator sports, any garment style suitable for daytime wear is appropriate. Inasmuch as space will not permit a discussion of all types of active sports,

Figure 17.7 Lightweight pure wool ensemble from Jones of New York in a classic business suit. (Photo courtesy of the Wool Bureau.)

tennis, swimming, skiing, and golf will serve as examples. (See Figs. 17.8 (a) and (b).)

For tennis, women usually wear a one-piece dress consisting of a bodice and very short skirt over panties. (See Fig. 17.8 (a).) Some dresses are tailored; others may be fancier. Many styles originate from the personal preferences of

Figure 17.8a A Bill Blass tennis dress made of Kodel polyester and cotton. (Photo courtesy of Eastman Chemical Products, Inc.)

Figure 17.8b Active sportswear. A running outfit of Trevira® polyester/cotton blend. (Photo courtesy of Hoechst Fibers Industries. Trevira is a registered trademark of Hoechst AG.)

celebrity tennis stars and other sports personalities, who also may license the use of their names on sports apparel.

For swimming, a suit that fits the body snugly but does not constrict its movements is desirable. A knitted stretch nylon and spandex is recommended because it has the desired features and dries quickly. A lightweight suit is preferable—one whose colors and finishes are not affected by salt water or chlorine in the swimming pool. The crotch of the panty should be lined for health reasons. The one-piece tank suit worn by competitive swimmers is generally plain, whereas most one-piece swimsuits are pull-on styles with stretch straps and elasticized legs for comfort. Other styles may have skirts or cut-out sections. The two-piece bikini consists of a bra with adjustable straps and an abbreviated panty of the pull-on type. After a swim, a terry cloth beach robe or shirt with or without attached hood may be worn. A stretch polyester or terry knit is also serviceable for this purpose.

Skiing is a very popular winter sport. One should be dressed warmly but in lightweight clothing that acts as a windbreaker and is water-repellent. A nylon taffeta jacket and pants with quilted polyester or nylon insulation will suffice. A knitted acrylic cap or nylon hood with quilted lining will also meet the clothing requirements for ski wear because all these articles are lightweight, warm, strong, water-repellent, and quick drying. A wool shirt or sweater worn underneath the jacket adds another layer of clothing to trap warm air of the body, keeping the cold air out.

The golfer prefers casual attire that may consist of slacks, shorts, or skirts, of cotton or cotton/polyester gabardine, twills, cords, denim, seersucker, or double knit in solid colors, plaids, or stripes. A knitted or woven sport shirt or a sleeveless V-neck acrylic knitted top may be worn sometimes with a white or colored Jacquard-textured blazer with double rows of stitching, or a crocheted sweater or knitted cardigan. The traditional unlined nylon taffeta or polyester zippered golf jacket is usually a part of the golfer's clothing for cool weather.

One garment that became very popular during the 1970s and continues to enjoy acceptance in the 1980s is the warm-up suit. These casual suits are worn before, during, or after active participation in many sports. Warm-up suits, also called sweat suits, are also worn for relaxation by people who are not actively engaged in athletics. The suits are made in knit construction and therefore offer considerable flexibility and comfort; they are worn by men, women, and children. (See Figs. 17.9 and 17.10 for two styles of today's active sportswear offerings.)

Styles and Fabrics for Evening Wear

Women wear trousers to cocktail parties, dinners, the theater, nightclubs, and dances. However, the fabrics used in nighttime trousers or long skirts are more luxurious than are those used for daytime wear. Velvet, velveteen, metallic

Figure 17.9 Active sportswear. Sweatpants made of Trevira® polyester and cotton. (Photo courtesy of Hoechst Fibers Industries, Man-Made Fiber Producers Association. Trevira is a registered trademark of Hoechst AG.)

Figure 17.10   Girls' fashion coordinates in swimwear. (Photo courtesy of Catalina.)

knits, matte jersey, brocade, and satin are all suitable. For tops to the costume, a blouse or jacket may be made of the same fabric as the trousers or skirt, or a more sheer fabric, such as chiffon, voile, or crepe de Chine, may be used. Metallic cloths (woven or knitted), satin, velvet, taffeta, and lace make exquisite formal evening gowns. For summer formals, sheer fabrics such as chiffon, organza, voile, and tulle may be worn.

Coats and Jackets

Coats and jackets are worn over dresses, skirts, and pants with tops. There are two kinds: dressy and casual.

Dressy Coats and Jackets

The dressy coat usually covers the long or short dressy dress or long skirt and blouse. Usually a dressy coat has a smooth or shiny texture. Hence, it can be made of wool broadcloth, polyester/wool blends, furlike fabrics of acrylic or modacrylic fibers, and suede. Often cloth coats are trimmed with furlike fabrics to give a dressy, dramatic effect. In mild weather a velveteen or metallic cloth jacket or sweater can also serve as a wrap.

For formal evening wear, long coats or capes with or without hoods are appropriate. Wool flannel or wool blended with polyester or nylon, transparent velvet, crushed velvet, or velveteen are suitable. In mild climates a silk or velvet jacket may be worn over a ball gown. (See Fig. 17.11.)

Figure 17.11 Elegance in evening wear is achieved with this rich black wool flannel designed by Evan Picone. (Photo courtesy of the Wool Bureau.)

Casual Coats and Jackets

Casual clothes are garments with easy, fluid, flowing lines that present an uncluttered, fresh, relaxed appearance. Such coats may be made of camel's hair. These garments may be made of machine-washable polyester-blend pile with vinyl trim, cotton suede, cotton-backed rayon, or acrylic fleece or plush, cotton corduroy, polyester woven tapestry, or loden cloth. Some jackets and coats consist of a polyester or polyester/cotton shell with a down filling or a polyester fiberfill to provide extra warmth. Pea jackets that are styled like the sailor's short coat are usually made of wool melton. Double knits of acrylic or polyester are found in shirt and sweater jackets and also in sweater coats. Sports jackets and blazers are made of wool flannel or wool-blend flannel, 100 percent polyester with a worsted texture, and polyester knits and wovens. (See Figs. 17.12 and 17.13.)

For some time now, the quilted coat with down, feather, or man-made fiber filling has proven very popular in winter because it is both warm and light.

All-Weather Coats for Women and Girls

When women buy coats they look for style, color, fabric, fit, comfort, and price. To one woman, color and style may be most important; to another, comfort and price are paramount. And to still another, fabric, color, and fit may be the major considerations.

Figure 17.12 A classic wrap coat from Fleurette of California is 100 percent Merino extrafine wool. The ascot-necked pure wool dress from Jerry Silverman creates a dramatic contrast. (Photo courtesy of the Wool Bureau.)

Because style in coats changes more or less from season to season, it would be inadvisable to stress current styles in this book. But there are styles—basic ones that do not change except for minor details—that are known as staple or classic styles. For example, in dresses we think of the shirtwaist as a classic style, because buyers must always have some in stock to satisfy customer demand.

There are classic styles in coats as well, in both fur and cloth. Since real fur is not a textile, only cloth coats will be discussed here. The following terms for cloth coats are general categories, whether intended for winter, spring, or fall:

Polo coat: A coat made of camel's hair or wool; generally double-breasted with tailored patch pockets and a tailored collar, with or without belt.

Princess coat: A coat fitted closely through the waist, with darts, and gored skirt that flares at the hem.

Box coat: A straight-lined, full-length coat with a collar.

Reefer: A short or long double-breasted box coat.

Balmacaan: A loosely flaring coat with raglan sleeves and small collar.

Chesterfield: A single-breasted smooth wool coat cut straight or slightly fitted. Usually dark color or black, with a velvet collar.

Officer's, coachman's, or guardsman's coat: A heavy, fitted double-breasted coat buttoned up high on the chest. May have wide revers and big collar, a half-belt, and back pleat or flared skirt.

Tuxedo coat: An unfitted coat with a turned-back flat collar that forms a band down the front to the hem. When it has no front fastenings, it may be called a *clutch coat.*

Figure 17.13 Informality is appropriate for some business calls. This casual suit, designed by Ellen Tracy, is made of a pure wool-loden green fleece jacket and pure wool gabardine trousers. (Photo courtesy of the Wool Bureau.)

Trench coat: A double-breasted wool, cotton gabardine, or covert, belted all around. It may have a lining.

Sport coats and jackets, although they come in all lengths, are usually worn to the hips or just below. The car coat typifies these lines, although it may be belted. Raincoats, which may be either straight or fitted, are waterproof or water-repellent and are sometimes reversible.

The popular all-weather coat, which may be tailored in balmacaan style with raglan sleeves, is commonly made of 65 percent polyester and 35 percent cotton in a permanent-press poplin that is completely machine-washable and dryable. A Scotchgard finish repels rain and stains. With a warm acrylic pile zip-out lining, such a coat can be comfortable in all kinds of weather.

Linings should be cut to fit the outer garment smoothly and should not strain at the armhole when the garment is put on. Seams should be stitched firmly and should not pucker. The linings in coats of good workmanship have loose stitching at the bottom, so that the lining will not show below the exterior of the garment.

Sizes in Outerwear

Formerly there were only five size ranges in women's outer apparel. A young junior/teen replaces the former preteen and teen types. The long-established

Table 17.2 Sizes in Outerwear for Women and
Teenagers

Misses	6–20
Women's	38–50
Half-size	10½–24½
Junior	5–15
Junior petite	3–13
Young junior/teen[a]	5/6, 7/8, 9/10, 11/12, 13/14

[a]Vogue does not use this size range.

ranges were found to be inadequate for pattern sizes because of (1) the great variation in body height that in the past made shortening, lengthening, and waist adjustment so often necessary, (2) the increasing demand for exact fit without alteration, and (3) the necessary catering to those with special needs, such as the very tall woman or the teenager.

The four major pattern companies (Butterick, McCall's, Simplicity, and Vogue) have cooperated toward a revision of size standards for patterns. They studied the size standards of the federal government and of the popularly priced ready-to-wear and mail-order garment industries. The object was to establish new standard body measurements for the pattern industry, to enable the home sewer to buy a dress, coat, suit, or sportswear pattern of the same size as specified for ready-to-wear.

These standards (see the chart of sizes) took effect in January 1968.[3] Now the consumer is actually buying one size smaller by the revised size standard. Formerly, a size 34 bust (misses) required a size 14 pattern. In this standard, it calls for a size 12 pattern.

To determine the correct size, the figure type must first be determined. (See Table 17.2.) The correct pattern size should be based on the measurement of the bust, waist, hips, and back neck-to-waist length.

In ready-to-wear there are no size standards, for ready-made dresses are not as exact as those for the pattern industry.

In response to these consumer demands, the wholesale ready-to-wear market has both broadened the size ranges and has added new ranges. Whereas misses' sizes used to run 10 to 20, they are now available in sizes 6 to 22; and juniors, once 7 to 15, are now available in sizes 3 to 17. To accommodate the short misses and junior figure, petite misses' sizes and petite junior sizes have been introduced. And for the tall miss, 5 feet 7 inches (1.7 m) and over, a special tall size has been created. Similarly, to take care of the woman who is under 5 feet 3 inches (1.6 m), a short half-size has been added. With the regular half-size and the short half-size, it may not be necessary to offer regular women's sizes.

[3]See body measurement chart, Table 17.1.

BUYING YARD GOODS AND HOME SEWING

Planning Your Shopping Trip

Before you go to your favorite store for yard goods or an article of apparel, make a checklist of the following:

1. Items of apparel you need most in your wardrobe.
2. Items of apparel you will wear together.
3. List of colors that will become you and your wardrobe needs.
4. Your skill as a seamstress. (If you are a novice, choose a simple pattern and a fabric that is easy to handle.)
5. How much care you want to give a garment and the cost involved in its upkeep. (Dry cleaning bills can cut into the budget.)
6. The price you wish to pay for the finished garment.

Selection of Pattern and Fabric

The home sewer can consult pattern books readily available in any store that sells yard goods to select the style and size of the garment. However, she will want a pattern that will require as few adjustments and alterations as possible. To determine one's figure type and size, have someone take measurements of the bust, waist, hips, and back (from the base of the neck to the waist). When taking measurements, be sure the home sewer wears the same foundation garment she will wear under the outer garment she will make. At the pattern counter, the sewer should compare her measurements with those in the pattern catalog. The correct bust measurement is the most important for all garments except skirts and slacks, so she should select the pattern that has this correct measurement and if necessary alter the pattern in the waist or hip dimensions. The correct hip measurement should be selected for skirts and slacks. Alterations of waist size may be made if necessary.

With a knowledge of fibers, yarns, constructions, and finishes that are desirable in that use, fabric selection should be made easier. In any case, the customer should look at tags that give instructions for care. Usually a tag marked "machine washable" will ensure ease of care. She should be sure that the basic fabric lining and interfacing materials, tape, and/or decorative trim are compatible. For example, the lining of a jacket might shrink more than the outer fabric, resulting in an ill-fitting garment after washing.

A final decision should be made only after a thorough examination of the cloth. The customer should look for loose threads, misweaves, overaccentuated slubs, uneven selvages, and poor dyeing. For example, friction in wear will make slubs weaker and often unsightly.

The home sewer should have the necessary sewing aids, such as thread, needles (rounded for sewing tricot and lightweight knits), tracing wheel or chalk for marking, sharp shears, dressmaker's pins, and pin cushion. It is assumed that she has a smooth table or cutting board and a sewing machine in good condition with a machine needle of correct size—10 for lingerie, 11 or 14 for double knits.

Cutting, Sewing, and Pressing[4]

Before the fabric is cut, it should be washed or dry-cleaned to preshrink it. The lining, zipper, and tape should also be preshrunk.

1. Press out the fold line in the yard goods.

2. Lay out the pattern on the fabric, following instructions.

3. The grain of the cloth should follow the line of dress design. Good fit is ensured if the grain of the cloth (the warp) is straight vertically at the center of the bodice. An exception, of course, would be bias-cut blouses or dresses. For straight skirts, the side seams should be cut with the grain of the goods, leaving a slightly biased center seam. Since bias-cut skirts tend to sag, an allowance for sagging should be made in the pattern. Some dressmakers find that, if the garment is allowed to hang for a few hours before it is completed, the sag can be adjusted.

Similarly, the lengthwise grain of the cloth (warp) should run straight from the shoulder seam to the back of the wristbone. The crosswise grain of the sleeves should then run similar to the crosswise grain of the blouse. The shoulder line will be smooth if the sleeve is eased into the blouse, rather than the blouse into the sleeve. Armholes, to fit well, should not be cut too low.

4. Seam and hem allowances should be adequate and workmanship should be neat.

5. Cut the fabric with sharp shears. Take long, keen strokes with the shears.

6. Edge-finish all pieces by overcasting, multiple zigzag, serpentine, or straight stitching (⅛ inch from cut edge) before beginning to assemble the garment. Handle man-made fibered fabrics as little as possible, and finish cut edges as soon as possible. Stitch length should be adjusted to 6 to 10 stitches per inch for heavy woven fabric, 10 to 14 for lightweight cloth. Probably 10 to 15 stitches per inch or per 2.5 cm will be adequate for knitted fabrics. The machine instruction manual will tell how to adjust the tension so that the stitches look the same on both sides.

7. A trial seam should be made and then checked for smoothness. Seams will be flatter if pressed immediately after stitching.

8. Garments to be backed with any type of material should have each garment piece pinned to backing not more than 2½ inches or 6.3 cm apart (pins perpendicular to cut edge).

[4]Adapted from pamphlet "Sew On and Sew Forth," by Celanese Fibers Marketing Co.

9. Stitch the backed pieces of the garment (backing on top of garment) as described in step 6. Plain-stitch center of darts before assembling.

GENERAL REQUIREMENTS FOR
SERVICEABILITY OF OUTER APPAREL

Whether the consumer is buying ready-to-wear or yard goods to sew at home, the requirements for garment serviceability are similar.

In workmanship, the consumer should look for

1. Colorfast, strong thread darker than the fabric.
2. Smooth seams.
3. Pinked seams for firm fabrics.
4. Overcast seams for pliable fabrics.
5. Seam binding for hem without showing stitches on right side of hem.

Dressmaking details should meet these standards:

1. Fitted darts should be straight and smooth, inside and outside the garment.
2. Placket closing should be one continuous, lengthwise seam.
3. Front facing should be turned over the hem. Bias facings should be cut on a true bias.
4. Pleats are usually made on the lengthwise grain of the fabric, and the underfold of the pleat should be deep. Pleats should be pressed straight.
5. Pockets should be sewn onto the garment to appear either functional or decorative. Pockets should be reinforced by tape stitching at points of strain.

POINTS IN SELECTING WOMEN'S AND GIRLS'
READY-TO-WEAR

In the previous section, emphasis was placed on pattern and fabric selection and tips for the home sewer. Now we consider the important points when buying ready-made dresses, tops (sweaters, vests, shirts, and blouses), bottoms (pants, slacks, and skirts), and sportswear.

Dresses

1. Make sure the dress style and color fit into the needs of your wardrobe. (It was previously suggested that you preplan a shopping trip.)
2. Always try on the dress before you decide to buy it.
3. Check the fit of the dress while you have it on by noting whether[5]
   a. Wrinkles appear in front of the shoulder seam or crosswise on the front of the bodice along the armhole. If so, the inset-sleeve shoulder is too loose.

[5]*The Custom Look*, one of the series of illustrated books, *The Art of Sewing* (New York: Time-Life Books, 1973).

b. Crosswise wrinkles appear below the shoulder dart in a raglan-sleeve shoulder near the arm. If so, the shoulder is loose.

c. Crosswise wrinkles appear below the shoulder seam in a kimono sleeve. If so, the kimono-sleeve shoulder is loose.

d. In an inset-sleeve shoulder, the shoulder seam feels too snug. If so, wrinkles appear just below the shoulder near the armhole.

e. In raglan-sleeve shoulder, the dart feels taut. If so, vertical wrinkles appear below the shoulder dart near the arm.

f. In a kimono sleeve, if the fabric binds the shoulder near the upper arm and if vertical wrinkles appear below the shoulder point, the kimono-sleeve shoulder is tight.

g. The neck seam lies away from the base of the neck—the neckline is too loose. If the neck is tight in front, back, or both, the fabric bunches, and small crosswise wrinkles appear below the neck seam line, the neckline is too tight.

h. The back of the bodice feels snug over the shoulder and stands away from the back of the neck and wrinkles radiate from the upper back toward the armholes. If so, the upper back is too tight.

i. Wrinkles appear across the top of the sleeve along the armhole seam. If so, the sleeve top is loose in the inset sleeve. In the raglan sleeve, the wrinkles appear at the top of the arm. In the kimono style, the sleeve droops from the shoulder over the arm and wrinkles appear at the top of the arm. If the inset-sleeve top is tight, the top feels tight around the upper arm and wrinkles radiate from the armhole on both the sleeve top and the shoulder. A too tight raglan sleeve will bind over the shoulder and down the top of the arm. The kimono style will have wrinkles radiating from the natural shoulder point.

j. A high, narrow bustline needs adjustment. If so, the underbust dart angles inward and ends less than an inch below the forward point of the bust.

k. A low, wide bustline needs adjustment. If so, the underbust dart angles outward and ends more than an inch below the forward point of the bust.

l. A too rounded bustline is present. If so, diagonal wrinkles form in the fabric below the side-bust dart and radiate down from the armhole toward the center of the bodice.

m. The bustline is too flat. If so, diagonal wrinkles form below the forward point of the bust and radiate down toward the side seams.

n. The skirt front is tight if the skirt feels snug across the abdomen and wrinkles radiate from the abdomen toward the side seams.

o. Crooked side seams are present if the side seam fails to run vertically from armhole to hem. It may be curved in one or more places, or it may veer diagonally forward or backward.

p. Consider the length of the skirt and sleeves. Should adjustment be needed, can it be done at home?

4. Consider the cost of alterations as estimated by the fitter. The cost may bring the price of the dress above your budget.

5. If possible, ask the advice of a third party (other than the salesperson) before you buy the dress.

6. Read the care label carefully to see how much the maintenance of the dress will cost in light of the amount of service it should give.

Apparel Tops

When pants or trousers became suitable for all occasions, a change in women's and girls' outerwear occurred. This change emphasized the importance of "tops," including sweaters and vests, shirts and blouses.

Women's and Girls' Sweaters and Vests

The sweater, a knitted garment for the upper part of the body, has long been a staple for both casual and dressy wear. There are two main or classic types: the pullover or slip-on and the cardigan. (See Fig. 17.14.) Either type may have long or short sleeves, and either type may be in a classic or contemporary style. The classic sweater, not usually bulky, has a round neck without a collar.

A variation of the sleeveless pullover sweater is the knitted vest. It is worn over a shirt or under a long-sleeved cardigan. The vest goes well with either pants or skirts. In some instances, the sleeveless vest may be lengthened and buttoned down the front with patch or flap pockets. When worn with a skirt or pants it makes an attractive ensemble.

Until the development of the noncellulosic man-made fibers, wool was the major fiber used for sweaters, with cotton an important fiber for children's wear. But today the acrylics are in first place, with blends second and wool third. The reason for the great popularity of the man-made fibers is that they can be washed in the home laundry machine at the setting for fine or delicate fabrics, and they need no reshaping. Wool sweaters, unless labeled "machine washable," should be hand washed in cold-water detergent, reshaped, and dried most carefully. Also man-made fibers are usually less expensive than comparable wool products and are better than wool in resistance to abrasion. The degree of softness of sweaters made from man-made fibers depends on the fiber denier (weight and fineness)—the finer the denier, the softer the fabric.

Figure 17.14 Women's wear lambswool pullover and matching cardigan from J. L. Sport. (Photo courtesy of the Wool Bureau.)

The acrylics can provide a woollike bulkiness that resembles wool fibers. Thus they provide more warmth than nylon. Nylon is less bulky and has a smoother texture and a slightly shiny surface. It is more readily distinguishable from wool than is acrylic fiber.

Acrylic fiber pills more than nylon does in laundering and more particularly in rubbing against other garments or furniture. On the other hand, nylon is more easily snagged by sharp objects and fingernails. Sweaters are also made of 100 percent polyester.

Sweaters are made from many varieties of wool (particularly Shetland), wool and nylon, and mohair blended with wool and polyester. The finer sweaters are cashmere, noted for great softness and lightness. As indicated in Chapter 10, sweaters of linen yarn or of a blend of linen and cotton are proving popular for spring and summer wear.

Some suggestions for evaluating sweater construction are the following:

1. For good fit, look for full fashioning where panels are individually knit and where lines of knitting at the seams are turned parallel.
2. Examine seams and buttonholes for finishing; avoid buttons snagged in buttonholes and ribbed neckbands with crooked or uneven seams.
3. Make sure that buttons and buttonhole tabs are securely attached.
4. If possible, try on the garment to note the set of the shoulders.
5. If the sweater is long sleeved, be sure that there is a long-ribbed cuff, well finished on the reverse side to allow turning up.
6. Where trying on is not possible, buy a size larger than dress size. Women's sweaters run from size 32 to 42; larger sizes, 44 to 48. A woman wearing a size 18 dress would be well advised to buy a size 40 sweater. Children's sizes run 2 to 10, and a four-year-old would probably wear a 6.

Shirts and Blouses

A shirt is a tailored garment with or without sleeves that covers the torso from the neck to below the hips. A long shirt that extends to and fits the crotch with elasticized leg openings is called a body shirt. Shirts often have pointed collars. They may be worn inside or outside pants or skirts and may be woven or knitted. They may be worn inside a vest or sweater or may be covered by a blazer or shirt jacket with pointed collar, drawstring waistline, buttoned front closing, and buttoned cuffs.

Blouses are tops that usually have a less tailored appearance than shirts. For example, a neckline may be scooped, ruffled, or lace trimmed. The waistline and wrists may be elasticized. Cuffs may consist of ruffles edged with lace or embroidery. Also, in general, shirts are made of less luxurious fabrics than are blouses, such as broadcloth, knits, poplin, and heavy crepe. Blouses may be made of chiffon, satin, tricot metallic cloth, velvet, or lace.

Durable-press shirts and blouses are important in any woman's wardrobe. Fabrics that resist wrinkling are those made of the acrylics, polyesters, triacetates, blends of cotton and man-made fibers, and the new durable-press 100 percent cotton.

When you select a blouse or shirt,

1. Try it on to be sure that it fits your figure.
2. Look at the facing of the collar. Be sure that the facing is smooth and even, with medium to fine stitches.
3. See if the seams are smooth, even, and adequate in width.
4. Look at the buttons to see if they are smooth, of uniform thickness, and well fastened. Buttons with plastic tops or bottoms may fuse or drop off in cleaning.
5. Examine buttonholes for loose threads and insecure stitching. Buttonholes should be cut on the grain of the goods.

Sizes of women's blouses are not standardized. Misses' sizes are usually less full through the bust, waist, and hips than are women's sizes. Women who wear half-sizes, juniors, or talls may have a problem in fit because blouses are not sized to particular figure types.

Apparel Bottoms

Pants and Slacks

Probably the most popular of garments worn as bottoms of a costume are jeans. Jeans are trousers worn not only for work, play, and sport, but also for casual wear and even for some more dressy occasions by both sexes and all ages. They are made of the classic fabric jean, denim, twills, and double knits in solid colors, plaids, and stripes. (See Fig. 17.15.)

Figure 17.15 One of today's most popular fashions—flare-leg jeans—is nearly a century old. "Spring bottom" pants, as Levi Strauss dubbed this well-received new style in the 1880s, were designed to fit over boots. (Photo courtesy of Levi Strauss & Co.)

Jean, the fabric, may be all-cotton cloth, made of carded yarns in a 2×1 twill construction with colored warp (and generally blue) and white filling, or the fabric may be made of cotton and man-made fibers such as nylon and/or polyester. This combination of fibers adds resistance to wear, and durable press ensures abrasion resistance and no ironing as well. In fact, an entry describing this blended fabric in a mail-order catalog stated that the fabric jean is so rugged that it was used for the mat of a child's trampoline.

Slacks are trousers that may be dressy, tailored, or casual, fitted or elasticized at the waist, cuffed or uncuffed. Styles are similar to men's and boys' constructions. (For guides to fit, see Table 18.4.) Slacks are often worn with sports jackets or blazers.

Skirts

Women's skirts are cut on the straight, the bias, or circularly from the same fabrics that are used for dresses and suits. The fit or, more particularly, the hang of a skirt is important. A skirt should not wrinkle below the waistband and should be even at the hem. The aspects of garment construction (cuffing, sewing, and pressing) should be checked by the consumer. Sizes for juniors are 5 to 15; misses, 8 to 18; women, 34 to 44. Size may be stated by waist measurement.

The principles for selection of appropriate outer garments for adults are essentially the same for girls.

Pleats in both skirts and dresses are often sold as "permanently pressed," but unless the pleats are sewn in, this is not literally true. Pleats in fabrics of natural fibers have very limited pleat retention unless blended with a high percentage of man-made fibers. Special finishes help, but pleats in soft, loosely woven wool, sheer rayon, or silk tend to open up with wear and contact with moisture. Also, if sheer fabrics are cut on the bias, pleats have a tendency to distort and become uneven in wear.[6]

The principles for selection of appropriate outer garments for adults are essentially the same for girls.

Sportswear

Sportswear is designed as separate pieces in a wardrobe with suitability as an important factor in selection. Fabrics that are attractive and stylish yet require minimum care are most serviceable. Spot-resistant, crease-resistant, and water-repellent finishes and durable press are a great boon to the sportswear business.

Active sportswear can be classified as garments for summer sports and garments for winter sports. Some of the styles and fabrics for active sportswear were discussed earlier in this chapter. Styles and fabrics in coats and jackets were also discussed earlier.

---

[6]Data from a poster prepared by the International Fabricare Institute.

POINTS IN SELECTING UNDERWEAR, SLEEPWEAR, LOUNGEWEAR, AND INTIMATE APPAREL

Underwear

Styles and Fabrics

Styles in the cut of undergarments vary, as do the types of materials used. Nylon underwear is important because it is soft and lightweight, comes in attractive colors, is easily laundered by hand or machine, is quick drying, and needs no ironing. Other underwear fibers are cotton, acetate, rayon, silk, and blends of cotton and polyester.

Underwear garments include slips and half-slips, camisoles, panties, briefs, and body suits. Peignoirs, robes, loungewear, and bed jackets may also be included in the underwear classification. Bras are discussed under *Intimate Apparel*.

Slips

Slips are either one-piece dress-length undergarments with shoulder straps or half-slips (garments extending from the waist to slightly above the hemline of the dress). In many instances, slips are trimmed with nylon lace, embroidery, or appliqué. (See *embroidery and lace,* Chapter 19.) The amount, type, and quality of the trimming accounts for some of the differences in the prices of slips.

Slips may be knitted or woven. Knitted constructions predominate because they cost less to produce; they are elastic, porous, resilient, crush-resistant, and easy to launder; and they require no ironing as compared with woven fabrics.

The TFPIA requires the fiber identification of fabrics used. But there are other considerations in the selection of a slip besides fiber, yarn, construction, and finish of the fabric. The following points should receive attention:

1. Garment construction. Seams should be overcast to protect the cut edge of the fabric if knitted (pinked if woven).
2. Close, firm stitching. Lace should be attached firmly with close, zigzag stitches, and straps or elastic waistbands should be firmly attached.
3. Residual shrinkage in percentage stated on the label.
4. Garment measurement. The garment should be measured against the customer or tried on in the store to be sure it fits.
5. Laundering instructions. Instructions for laundering should be stated on the label.

Regular slip sizes run according to bust measure: 32, 34, 36, 38, and so on. Extra sizes are 46, 48, 50, 52. A person who wears a size 10/12 dress should select a size 34 slip; one who wears a size 12/14 dress, a size 36 slip; a size 14/16 dress, a size 38 slip. The Commodity Standards Division of the U.S. Department of Commerce suggests that half-slips are mostly made for younger figures.

Table 17.3 Sizes in Tights and Body Suits

Children's		Women's		
Size	Underwear Size	Size	Height	Metric Height
Small	4–6	A	5'–5'4"	(1.52–1.55 m)
Medium	7–10	B	5'5"–5'8"	(1.65–1.72 m)
Large	12–14	C	5'8"–6'	(1.72–1.83 m)

Therefore, misses' standard sizes are more prevalent than women's sizes, 34, 36, 38, and so on.

Panties and Briefs

A panty is a garment with legs cut longer than a brief. It may have straight or flared legs. Briefs are very short, close-fitting, waist-height garments with elasticized waist and leg openings. Some leg openings are made with bands and crotch linings and are usually cotton for health reasons.

The sizes of panties are governed by hip measurements. For example, a hip size of 33 to 34 inches or 83.8 to 86.3 cm, would require a size 4 panty, 35 to 36 inches or 88.9 to 91.4 cm, would take a size 5, and so on up to a 49 to 52 inches or 124.4 to 132 cm for size 11.

Tights and Body Suits

Tights are snug-fitting garments usually knitted of stretch nylon, in black, white, and colors. They are often sold in either the underwear or hoisery departments. The size ranges are shown in Table 17.3.

Body suits are one-piece garments that cover the torso and have elasticized leg openings and a snap crotch. They are often made of nylon or polyester rib knit, short or long sleeves, ribbed neck or turtleneck. The body suit is often worn with jeans. It is a versatile garment because it can serve as outerwear or underwear;[7] it moves with the body and is therefore comfortable.

Sleepwear and Loungewear—Styles and Fabrics

Sleepwear includes nightgowns, pajamas, and sleep sets (consisting of a coat and gown, tunic pajamas, or sleeveless nightgown and coat with elbow-length sleeves—a peignoir set). The lines, designs, and colors vary with fashion. Some common fabrics for gowns and pajamas are fleece, nylon tricot, flannelette, batiste, stretch nylon, terry cloth, brushed nylon knit, chiffon, and challis. Dainty gowns may be trimmed with lace, embroidery, appliqué, or contrasting bindings. (See *embroidery and lace,* Chapter 19.)

Sizes of gowns and pajamas are determined by bust measure. The length of these garments depends upon the style.

[7]See body shirt in section on apparel tops.

Garments related to the sleepwear category, and the fabrics in which they are made, are the following:

Robes and lounge wear: Wool flannel and blends, all-cotton blanket-type robing, velour, fleece, brushed knits, quilted fabrics, chenille, terry, corduroy; also cotton crepe, cotton broadcloth, and chiffon (for summer).

Bed jackets: Knitted wool or acrylic, quilted cotton or man-made fibers, brushed textured fabrics, and cotton, rayon or wool challis.

Peignoirs and travel sets (coat-and-gown or coat-and-pajamas): Spun rayon, acetate or nylon crepe, tricot, brushed knits, all-over lace, trimmings of satin ribbon, lace,fur, metal threads, embroidery, and self-bindings.

How to Select Underwear, Sleepwear, and Loungewear

In buying these garments, the customer wants apparel that is comfortable—soft and lightweight—and will conform to body lines yet not constrain bodily movements. The garment should neither irritate the skin nor cling to outer garments.

The garment should require a minimum of care. This means fibers that can be washed by machine, dry quickly, and require no ironing, or merely touch-up ironing. Velour and velvet usually should be dry-cleaned.

Underwear and loungewear come in solid colors or prints, and some articles are trimmed with lace or embroidery. Trimming should be of good quality and should be sewn on evenly. Seams and hems should be even, narrow, and smooth. These are marks of good workmanship. In addition, buttonhole bindings should cover all cut edges. No threads should trail from any part of the garment.

Intimate Apparel

This classification includes bras, girdles, corsets, panty girdles, and garter belts. There are various styles in each of these articles.

Women are conscious of the lines and fit of their outer apparel, and many realize that the fit of a dress can be improved by a perfect-fitting foundation garment. The items of apparel that control and support the figure are specially classed as foundation garments. A girdle of webbing made of spandex or rubber yarns gives a limited amount of support. With additional heavy woven fabric over the abdomen and buttocks, the garments gives improved support and figure control, and with varied amounts and weights of boning, the figure can be well controlled. A professional corsetiere should be consulted in the fitting of a corset. It is advisable to try on girdles, particularly the boned ones, to ensure proper fit and the desired support and control.

Garments that are intended for support are made with at least a portion of webbing of rubber or spandex. Some girdles are made entirely of spandex or power net (nylon or acetate and spandex). Girdles with legs are called *panty girdles*. A girdle with bra attached may be termed *all-in-one*. Fabrics used for foundation garments include nylon and spandex power net, panels of brocade or satin elastic (acetate, cotton, polyester, or spandex), trimmings of elasticized lace, and nylon tricot for panel linings and crotches. Abdominal support belts have light boning at the front, sides, and back. They may be made of knitted elastic (cotton, rayon, rubber). Panty girdles come in small, medium, large, and extra-large sizes. A small size should fit a size 12 or under; medium, a size 14; large, a size 16; and extra large, a size 18.

Bras, styled for various figure types in length, size of bust, and features for control and slimming, are either separate items of apparel or part of a corset. They are made with or without adjustable shoulder straps of corded or satin ribbon of cotton, acetate, or nylon, or they may be elastic. Bust measurement in inches denotes the size, and cups are designated as A, small; B, medium; C, large; and D and DD for extra-large sizes.

The frame and cups may be made of power net, nylon lace, tricot, embroidered nylon, or polyester/cotton. Linings may be cotton or taffeta tricot; padding may be spun polyester or polyurethane. (See Fig. 17.16.)

Garter belts, designed to hold up stockings, may gently firm and control a more youthful figure. Sizes are small, medium, and large.

HOSIERY AND PANTY HOSE

While cotton hosiery (especially lisle) and wool hosiery are worn for sports, children's and men's wear, the great majority of women today wear nylon most of the time mainly in panty hose form.

Figure 17.16 The Running Bra™, which took two years to perfect, is designed to eliminate bounce, skin irritation, and collagen tissue breakdown that can result in sagging. Among its features are Enka nylon cups lined in pure, absorbent cotton, a stay-put leotard back, and plush lined straps. (Photo courtesy of Formfit Rogers.)

Cotton, acrylic and stretch nylon, cotton and spandex, and 100 percent stretch nylon are used for women's and girls' socks and for boys' and men's socks as well.

Leggings, a hosiery accessory, have become a popular fashion item in the eighties. Probably the increasing consumer interest in active sportswear accounts for this appeal, particularly for skiing and other winter sports. Yarns used in the knitting of leggings are principally high-bulked acrylic and wool fibers. The style depends upon the intended use, but is usually footless and extends from the ankle to over or under the knee to provide maximum warmth.

Stretch Yarn

To an increasing extent, nylon hosiery and panty hose are being made from stretch textured yarns that are fluffy and have great permanent elasticity. This nylon is made from a continuous-filament fiber and should not be confused with spun nylon made from short lengths of fiber. Because of their stretching property, stretch nylons will adjust themselves to the size of the foot. Thus, three sizes are all a store need carry: small, fits sizes 8 to 9; medium, 9½ to 10½; and large, 11 to 12.

One of the principal advantages of stretch nylon socks for children is that youngsters do not outgrow a pair so fast. Mothers with several small children can buy the same socks for all and keep them together in one drawer. This hoisery has been found to fit snugly and to be fast-drying and comfortable. However, some wearers object to a tight fit at the tip of the toes. In addition, if the sock is too snug, it may develop a hole. Stretch nylon yarn has been modified to create a leg with elastic-support properties; one such garment is marketed under the name of Supp-hose. The manufacturer claims that these stockings alleviate "tired legs," and it is implied that they take the place of surgical rubber stockings used for varicose veins. Although the support stocking probably is not an adequate substitute for the surgical rubber type, they afford more support than hosiery and panty hose without these modified yarns. Support stockings are now made of a combination of nylon and spandex.

Types of Hosiery

There are two types of hosiery: full-fashion knit and circular knit. Full-fashioned hose are knitted flat. Stitches are taken off (two stitches are knit as one to decrease the number) so that the fabric is narrowed at the ankle. The two edges of the fabric are sewn together, which provides a real seam from toe to heel and up the back. Two machines may make full-fashioned hosiery: one, called the *legger*, makes the leg; another, called the *footer*, makes the foot. There are also single-unit machines. On either side of the back seam, over the calf, small dots are visible. These dots, really double loops, are the points where stitches are decreased to make the hosiery narrower. They are called *fashion marks*. They are also visible on either side of the seam under the arch of the foot.

Circular-knit hosiery is commonly called *seamless,* because no back seam is present. In this type, the tension of needles is tightened at the time of knitting to shape the stocking below the calf of the leg. Thus, there are the same number of wales at the ankle as farther up the leg. In circular-knit hosiery a seam appears about an inch from the tip of the toe rather than at the toe as it does in full-fashioned hosiery.

Full-fashioned hosiery, a better fitting fabric than circular knit, retains its shape bettter during wear and after washing. However, the overwhelming majority of women today wear seamless stockings. They eliminate the problem of crooked seams and fit smoothly on the foot. In a recent price list of six offerings by a mail-order house, five were for seamless and only one for those with seams.

Panty Hose

Until the advent of the mini skirt, the standard length of women's regular nonstretch knit hosiery was 30 inches or 76 cm from the heel to the top of the garter belt. With the much shorter skirts, longer lengths of hosiery were required. Thus, thigh top and a hip length with opaque panels that hook to an elasticized waistband were made to meet consumer demand, leading quickly to the development of the panty hose which combines the panty and stocking. Panty hose had immediate market acceptance, and sales now far exceed those of conventional hosiery, including socks and knee-high varieties. This change has been a major one, for hosiery sales have declined and panty hose has taken its place.

The consumer is assured of a smooth, snug-fitting garment from toe to waist. The stocking section can be patterned in variegated-size mesh, polka dot, point d'esprit, rib, cable, lacy, and crochetlike textures. Panty hose can also give mild support if the panty is knitted of nylon and spandex.

Standards and Specifications for Hosiery and Panty Hose

Grades

Hosiery and panty hose are classified first quality, irregulars, seconds, and thirds. A stocking may be marked "irregular" if there are irregularities in dimensions, size, color, or knit, without the presence in the hose of any mends, runs, tears, or breaks in the fabric or any substantial damage to the yarn or fabric itself. Seconds and thirds include hosiery that contains runs, obvious mends, irregularities, substantial imperfections, or defects in material, construction, or finish. Irregulars can be marked seconds or thirds if they have runs, mends, defects, and the like, but seconds and thirds cannot be marked irregulars according to government standards.

Table 17.4 Stocking Chart

If shoe size is	3	3½–4	4½–5½	6–6½	7–7½	8–9	9½–10	10½–11	Over 11
Hose size is	8	8½	9	9½	10	10½	11	11½	12

Foot Size

Except for stretch socks, the foot size of hosiery is measured in terms of inches. For instance, a size 9½ stocking should fit an average foot 9½ inches long or 24.3 cm. The standard size scale is 8½ to 11 inches or 21.8 to 28 cm in ½ inch or 1.3 cm intervals. The relation to shoe size is given in Table 17.4.

To facilitate fitting, most salesclerks have access to a foot size chart that shows the stocking size needed. As already indicated, if stretch yarn is used, three sizes may prove adequate for most customers, greatly simplifying stock problems.

Length

Hosiery is available in four lengths—ankle or calf, knee-high, over-the-knee, and thigh-high, in addition, of course, to panty hose. Spandex knitted into the top band commonly holds the garment in place.[8]

Mesh knit, as compared with plain knit, has such great stretch that a single foot size will fit most women from 5'2" to 5'8" tall or 1.6 to 1.7 m, but two or three length variations are provided. Better hosiery may be length-sized to shape.

Gauge

This term refers to the degree of closeness of knitting, especially in full-fashioned hosiery. The closer the knitting, the higher the gauge number, the stronger the fabric, and the greater the snag resistance. Gauge is determined by the number of wales to an inch or the number of stitches to an inch and a half. The number of needles per inch is two-thirds the gauge number. For example, in a 45-gauge knitting machine, there are 30 needles to the inch or 2.5 cm. This 45-gauge machine knits a fabric 14 inches or 35.5 cm wide, so this machine would use 30 × 14, or 420 needles.

In seamless (circular-knit) stockings and panty hose, the term *needle count* rather than gauge is often used. In the example above the needle count is 420. Sometimes the manufacturer does not put into operation all the needles on the machine. In the example given, the manufacturer may not use all the 420 needles and erroneously call the product 45 gauge.

Denier

Hosiery and panty hose are often classified as sheer, semisheer, and service weight, with most today in the sheer and semisheer classes. The degree

[8]Over-the-knee hose and thigh-high hose are commonly called *stockings* as distinct from socks.

of sheerness is determined partly by the gauge but primarily by the denier. This is the weight of the yarn as indicated by a standard numbering system. (See Chapters 11 and 13.) In the wholesale trade, nylons are classified by denier. The designation 30s and 40s means 30 and 40 denier. The higher the denier number, the coarser, heavier, and stronger the yarn. For instance, 30 denier is twice as heavy and twice as strong as sheer 15 denier. Today the consumer may have a choice of several deniers, 10 to 50.

While panty hose may be made entirely of sheer 15-denier yarn, they may also be made of two denier sizes—a sheerer denier for the stocking and a coarser one for the panty. For example, regular-knit hose may be 28 denier knitted into a 40-denier panty; a sheer seamless 21 denier (three threads of 7 denier twisted together for strength) may be knitted onto a 50-denier opaque panty.

Through the years, hosiery has become more and more sheer. Before World War II, 30 denier was the sheerest; today we have 10, 12, and 15 denier. And then consumers ask, "Why don't my nylons wear the way they used to?" Obviously, since they are much more sheer, they are not so strong.

When an advertisement refers to nylon stockings or panty hose as 12/.66s, it means that the stockings are made of 12-denier nylon yarn with 66 stitches to 1½ inches or 3.8 cm of fabric measured around the stocking.

Reinforcements

Reinforcements, by means of extra yarns, are commonly placed in the toe, heel, sole, and crotch in the case of panty hose, in direct proportion to the weight and style of the stocking. Nylon is so sturdy that it will stand a lot of abrasion, so some sheer hosiery styles are not reinforced. Frequently nylon yarns are used as reinforcements in wool and cotton socks.

Splicing styles (reinforcements above the heel) change from season to season. One style may call for a short, wide splicing; another may require a narrow, high splicing; another may feature a triangular effect. Whatever form splicing may take, it should be symmetrical for each stocking. Nylon seamless stockings do not necessarily have splicing above the heel.

Stretch

The stretch crosswise at the top of the garter welt in women's medium-length hosiery should be 12 to 13 inches or 30.5 to 33 cm when measured flat. Less than 12 inches is not sufficient stretch for comfort. If more than 13 inches, there is danger that the fabric will lose its elasticity and will not spring back to its original width. Such a fabric does not give the trim, snug fit desired. The elasticized waist and hips of panty hose should stretch to nearly double their unstretched measurement.

The stocking should stretch to 7 or 7¼ inches or 18 cm at the instep. To determine this measurement, grip the fabric at the instep and the point opposite on the sole and stretch the cloth. The attempt to make narrow heels may cause some manufacturers to narrow the width of the reinforcement on the sole. Then, when the stocking is worn, too much strain is put on the fabric at the instep.

Holes may consequently appear at the point where splicing and sole reinforcement meet.

Color

Hosiery is dyed in the yarn before it is knitted or in the piece after it is knitted. Hosiery that is dyed in the yarn is called *ingrain* hosiery, whereas that dyed in the piece is called *dip-dyed* hosiery. The former has a more even, richer, deeper brilliance than the latter.

From the standpoint of economy, manufacturers prefer to dip-dye their hosiery. They can knit a supply in natural color and dye the fabrics later as the style demand arises. An overstock of ingrain hosiery in an unpopular color may prove difficult to sell to the retailer.

Suggestions for Hosiery Selection

Many women who have worn the patterned mesh hosiery seem to enjoy not only its attractive appearance but also its serviceability.

The shorter the skirt length, the greater the focus on hosiery. A variety of fashion colors have appeared, and interesting patterns have been knitted into the stockings. Hosiery has become a fashion item.

Some suggestions for hosiery selection follow:

1. If durability is important, avoid very sheer, low-denier hosiery.
2. If you buy panty hose, be sure to consider your shoe size, your height and weight, and your leg contour. A stocking may fit perfectly, but the panty section may not fit ill-proportioned hips.
3. For children, buy cotton lisle, cotton mixtures, or stretch nylon.
4. Buy wool hosiery a size larger than normal, unless drying forms are used or the label is marked "preshrunk, residual shrinkage less than 3 percent."
5. For durability, look for a reinforced heel and toe, a special toe guard, a wide garter welt, and a run-stop below the garter welt.
6. Ingrain hosiery is normally to be preferred to dip-dyed; it is likely to retain its color better.

SELECTION OF CLOTHING ACCESSORIES

In addition to underwear and negligees, which are sometimes classed under accessories, there are many small items of clothing or personal adornment that are made of textiles.

Neckwear, Scarfs, and Ties

Neckwear may include collars, cuffs, and stoles. Since these pieces, with the exception of stoles (made of wool or acrylic knitted goods and furlike fabrics), are made of the same materials as dresses, they need no further description. The same is true of scarfs and ties. They are commonly made of silk, rayon, acetate, acrylic, nylon, polyester, wool, cotton, or mixtures of these materials. Typical fabrics include twills, satins, foulard, crepes, and knitted goods. Scarfs may be square, 23 × 23 inches (58.5 × 58.5 cm) or 27 × 27 inches (68.5 ≤ 68.5 cm); oblong, 11 × 36 inches (28 × 91.5 cm), 15 × 44 inches (38 × 112 cm), or 14 × 64 inches (35.5 × 162.5 cm); or cravat shaped. Ties may be in several styles: string ties, bow ties, menswear-type or lariat-style ties. The neckwear department often carries small capes and short jackets as well.

Artificial Flowers

Many artificial flowers are made of nontextiles such as paper, glass, plastic, and wax, but flowers are also made of velvet, velveteen, taffeta, satin, lace, chiffon, and organdy. Very often flowers on coats and dresses are made of the same material as the coat or dress.

Handkerchiefs

There are different types of women's handkerchiefs for different occasions. They are made of handkerchief linen, batiste, lawn, and washable silk. A silk, nylon, or polyester handkerchief may be used to tie around the neck to ornament a sweater or jersey blouse. Chiffon and lace are common materials used for evening.

When buying a handkerchief, consider the following points:

1. General appearance
2. Wearing quality or durability
   a. Grade of fabric
   b. Workmanship
   c. Quality of trimming, embroidery, and design
3. Purpose or suitability for its use
4. Price

With respect to durability, the buyer should know that a good grade of linen will outwear the average cotton. White linen will appear fresher and more lustrous after laundering. Thin silks, nylons, polyesters, and rayons appear to advantage for evening or occasional wear if frequent laundering is not essential.

Hems rolled and sewed by hand are considered better than those that are machine-stitched, because they do not pucker and the stitching is not so noticeable. The firmness and quality of the hemstitching or other embroidery are important. If lace or other trimming is used, the sewing that attaches it to the handkerchief should be firm, even, and fine.

Millinery

Styles

In the decade of the seventies, one woman said to a friend who was considering wearing a hat to a luncheon, "You are dated if you wear that hat. Only old women wear hats. This is a hatless era." There has been a strong trend to hatlessness, but the trend appears to be reversing itself in the early eighties. Many women buy several kinds of hats to protect the head from winter's cold and summer's sun, to add height if needed, or to flatter the face.

The trend toward hatlessness has caused manufacturers to exert efforts to create new colors, lines, and sizes of hats. Hatlessness has also spurred the trend of hair ornaments, which has taken the place of the hat in many instances. Materials and styles change season to season.

Fabrics

Felts are made of either fur or wool. The former is more luxurious, softer, and more expensive than the latter. A velour is a fur felt with a long silky pile. In a discussion of felting, it was stated that pounding and steaming locks the wool fibers together. Staple polyester fibers can be felted by heat setting.

Both natural and synthetic straw is used for hats. Natural straws are made from grasses, rice shoots, stems, and leaves. Synthetic straws are made from nylon, modacrylic, rayon and cellophane.

Steps in the manufacture of natural straw include

1. Bleaching to make the straw white or cream colored.
2. Weaving into a rough form; for example, panama, baku, leghorn, toyo; or braided into narrow strips sewn together into a desired shape.
3. Blocking by steaming and drying on a form.

Synthetic straws are made in different widths and colors. Their prices range from inexpensive to moderate.

Fabric hats are made of nylon and polyester velvet, cotton, acrylic, or modacrylic furlike fabrics. These materials are often draped over a frame of buckram. Real fur and leather are also used, but these materials are nontextiles and so are not discussed here.

Trim

Hats and hair ornaments are often trimmed with ribbon, flowers made from textile fabrics, feathers, felt, or leather and novelty ornaments such as buckles, stones, and beads. One of the common ribbon fabrics is grosgrain, a heavy fillingwise-ribbed rayon, acetate, or nylon material. The ribs may have a cotton core. There is quite a bit of body to the material and it wears well. Taffeta, moiré, velvet, velveteen, satin (both single-faced and double-faced), metal cloth, and novelty weaves are other common ribbon materials. Acetate moiré taffeta has become popular for ribbons because the fabric can be woven wide and cut into ribbon width, and the cut edges can be fused by heat. This method makes the ribbon inexpensive. Velvet ribbons with cut instead of woven edges can also be used for inexpensive trimmings for millinery. The velvet with cut edges ravels easily and, hence, is not too satisfactory.

In selecting the style, suitability, shape-retaining quality, colorfastness, and finish are the important factors in head gear.

Gloves

Although formerly most gloves were made of leather, many are now made of knitted and woven goods. Fabric gloves may be made of cotton, wool, cashmere, acrylic, rayon or nylon tricot mesh, crocheted cotton, and woven goods such as lace and dress fabrics. Mittens are also popular for some kinds of sporstwear and are made from the same fabrics and in similar construction.

Handbags

Due to economics, handbags are becoming more important in fabric in addition to leather or a substitute. Faille, tapestry, double-woven stretch nylon, furlike fabrics, and fabrics may be used for everyday. For evening, metallic fabric on acetate backing, peau de soie, cotton, velveteen, satin, and brocade are appropriate. For summer handbags, the fabrics used include linen crash, homespun, canvas, the fabric of the dress being worn, straw, and nylon knits or crocheted materials. Linings include rayon and nylon satin, rayon faille, crepe, and printed cottons. Large beach bags for swimsuits or for knitting may be made of homespun, string, canvas, sailcloth, cotton tapestry, or synthetics. They may even be waterproofed.

Women's and Children's Shoes

Most shoes are made of leather or simulated leather, but fabric shoes have become popular for many occasions: for beachwear and sports, casual shoes made of webbing, canvas, cotton crash, or cretonne; for street wear, canvas or crash; for evening, brocades, metal cloth, satin, faille, moiré, or taffeta.

For active sportswear, the uppers of sneakers are textiles made of polyester/cotton poplin, cotton army duck, cotton canvas, or denim. Slippers for summer can be corduroy, terry, or nylon tricot; for winter, cotton velour with nylon or acrylic lining, rayon or acetate plush, quilted cotton, acrylic pile on cotton knit, acrylic and modacrylic blends, and cotton knit backed with polyurethane foam.

INFANTS' WEAR

Certain articles, such as sacques, bootees, dresses, shirts, blankets, diapers, and bonnets, are always essential for infants. The styles in length, type of yoke, and trimming of babies' wearing apparel may change slightly, but the general silhouette does not alter. Infants' clothing is sized according to age: 6, 12, 18, 24 months.

Toddlers' sizes 1 to 4 are designed for tots whose figures still retain the rounded contours of infancy. Coat and dress lengths are short; legs and seats are cut full to accommodate diapers. Height of the child is most important in determining size. For the child who is losing the roundness of infancy, a more fitted style is appropriate (sizes 2 to 6x). Again, height is a most important factor in determining size.

Materials for babies' clothing are, generally speaking, cotton and man-made fibers alone or in blends. A 50 percent cotton/30 percent polyester/20 percent nylon blend has the softness and absorbency of cotton and the strength and durability of nylon; therefore, it is well suited for underwear. It is also machine washable and dryable.

The department or specialty store salesclerk can recommend a choice of layette. In some instances, stores have made up suitable lists of layettes at various prices.

Diapers

Two of the most important items in a layette are diapers and pads. Should the mother decide to use a diaper service or disposable diapers, she may not need to buy any diapers, although a few for emergency are desirable. For traveling, the throwaway, nonwoven type are convenient. Diapers are made of gauze, flannelette, knitted, and bird's-eye in rectangular or fitted types. Gauze, which allows air to circulate, is comfortable and easy to wash and dry. Flannelette is soft but bulky. Pinked edges are more comfortable than hemmed ones. Cotton bibs, pads, and diapers that are double woven allow air to circulate between the layers to dry the material much faster and make it more comfortable.

The double-woven pads are more absorbent than quilted pads. As soon as the moisture hits the absorbent pad it spreads out as if it were on a blotter. On the quilted pads the water stays in one spot and then slowly spreads out. Plastic-coated and rubber pads are waterproof but are hotter in summer because they lack porosity.

ADULT DIAPERS[9]

Diapers are also used in the hospital for adult care. These diapers generally consist of a rubberized fabric, a cotton backing, and an absorbent filler between. These present certain problems in laundering: (1) high temperatures in both laundering and in drying make the rubberized material tacky, sticking together when the diapers are folded. Flat storage is to be recommended. (2) Unless a high water level and a short spin cycle are used, the filler tends to separate from the fabric and become lumpy. (3) If bleaching is required, the cotton in the backing is likely to be damaged, unless *all* the bleach has been removed in the wash.

[9]See International Fabricare Institute, *Capsule News*, January 1982.

SUMMARY

This chapter shows the possibilities that a person faces in choosing clothing fabrics for different uses and sets forth the points for selection of yard goods and ready-made apparel for women and girls. No one becomes expert in judging fabrics until he or she is willing to study their characteristics thoroughly, a pursuit that requires patience, time, and practice. To this end, the glossary for this chapter describes fabrics used in women's and girls' clothing. Definitions of some items of apparel are also included.

PROJECTS

1. From the articles of apparel listed here, select one garment for study: nightgown, robe, shorts, slacks, baby's bonnet, child's pajamas, head scarf, raincoat, pants suit, body suit, furlike fabric coat. Write up the information in the form of a merchandise manual to include
   - (a) Where found in a store.
   - (b) Fabrics of which it is made.
   - (c) Size range.
   - (d) Selling points.
   - (e) Instructions for care.
   - (f) Retail price range.

   Where size ranges available are small, medium, large, and sometimes extra-large, are these ranges adequate from the consumer point of view?

2. Develop a research project to answer the following: Are blue jeans appropriate for office and other white-collar wear? Interview at least five young working women, an office or personnel manager, and one manager of a business enterprise. If you do not live or study in a large metropolitan community, is the practice there different? Write a report of your findings.

3. Until recently working women moving up the business ladder tended to wear masculine-like apparel. Now some observers report a trend in the opposite direction. Investigate and report on the current situation in your area.

GLOSSARY[10]

Batiste A very sheer, combed, mercerized muslin identified by streaks lengthwise. Better grades are highly mercerized. It is also made in spun rayon, wool, or silk and is used for summer dresses, blouses, lingerie, infants' dresses and bonnets, and handkerchiefs.

Bengaline A warp faced heavy fabric with a coarse filling yarn, used largely in women's apparel.

Bias cut A fabric cut diagonally across the warp and filling yarns. A true bias is cut on a 45° angle from the lower left to the upper right of a cloth.

Bouclé See the glossary in Chapter 3.

Brassiere or bra An undergarment that covers and supports the bust and may extend to the waistline.

Brief A short panty. See *panty*.

Broadcloth A plain-weave cotton fabric, with fillingwise rib finer than poplin. Best grades

[10]Since all apparel fabrics cannot be defined in a glossary, for those omitted see *Calloway Textile Dictionary* (Calloway Mills, La Grange, Georgia), *Dan River's Textile Dictionary* (Dan River Mills, New York), or *Fairchild's Dictionary of Textiles* (Fairchild Publications, Inc., New York).

are made of combed pima or Egyptian cotton. It is used for women's blouses, tailored summer dresses, men's shirts. It can also be made of silk and polyester and cotton blends. See *wool broadcloth* (Glossary, Chapter 18).

Brocade   Fabric with slightly raised Jacquard designs that may have gold or silver threads. It is used for formal dresses, blouses, evening wraps, and bags. See the glossary in Chapter 21.

Brocatelle   See the glossary in Chapter 21.

Butcher   A coarse rayon or rayon and acetate blend made to resemble the original butcher linen used for the butcher's apron.

Cambric   A muslin that is lightweight, sized. Very low-count, heavily sized glazed cambric is used for costuming.

Canton crepe   Thick, slightly ribbed crepe, heavier than crepe de Chine. It may be silk, rayon, or acetate and is used for business and afternoon dresses.

Challis   A very lightweight plain-weave wool, spun rayon, or mixed fabric usually printed with small floral designs that is used for dresses, blouses, scarfs, and infants' sacques.

Chambray   A plain-weave cotton fabric with colored warp and white filling that may have woven-in stripes. It is used for women's and children's summer dresses and blouses and men's shirts.

Chenille   A fabric woven from fuzzy caterpillarlike yarns. Usually the filling is the chenille yarn and the warp a regular textile yarn.

Chesterfield   Coat style adapted from that of Lord Chesterfield.

Cheviot   See the glossary in Chapter 18.

Chiffon   A sheer plain-weave crepe fabric in silk, rayon, or nylon with either soft or stiff finish. It is used for formal dresses, scarfs, and evening handkerchiefs.

Chinchilla   Heavy twill-weave coating that may be all wool or mixed with cotton. Little nubs or tufts of nap make the characteristic surface to resemble chinchilla fur. It is used for coats and jackets.

Corduroy   Heavy cotton or rayon pile fabric. The cut pile forms wales warpwise. It is used for dresses, coats, sports jackets, slacks, draperies, upholstery, and other home furnishings items.

Corselet   A type of girdle, with a boned front, that extends from above the bust to below the buttocks. Bras may hook onto girdle.

Corset   A heavily boned foundation garment for the torso.

Covert   See the glossary in Chapter 18.

Crash   A coarse linen, cotton, or rayon fabric with uneven yarns woven in plain weave. It is used for dresses, suitings, table linens, and draperies.

Crepe   A fabric with a crinkled surface that may be made by several methods.

Crepe de Chine   Originally made in silk with the fabric degummed to produce crinkle. As made now, it is a sheer flat crepe in silk or man-made fibers. It is used for lingerie, dresses, and blouses.

Damask   A reversible Jacquard fabric. The designs are not raised as in brocade. It is made of almost any fiber or blends. It is used for afternoon and evening dresses, table covers in linen, draperies and upholsteries in heavier fabrics. See the glossary in Chapter 21.

Dart   A tapering fold that is stitched in a garment to improve its fit.

Denim   A heavy, strong twill-weave cotton fabric woven with colored warps and white fillings. Originally blue or brown, denims are now also made in stripes and figures. They are used for jeans, work clothes, overalls, draperies and bedspreads.

Dimity A sheer cotton with corded stripes or checks, used for children's summer dresses, bedspreads, curtains, and blouses.

Donegal tweed See the glossary in Chapter 18.

Dotted swiss Sheer, crisp, plain-weave cotton fabric with either clipped spot or swivel dots, colored or white. It is used for children's party dresses, women's summer dresses, lingerie, and curtains.

Dress linen See *crash.*

Embroidery Ornamental needlework done on the fabric itself.

End use Intended use by the consumer.

Faille A flat, crosswise, ribbed fabric with more ribs to the inch than bengaline. It is made or rayon, acetate, cotton, wool, or mixtures and is used for tailored dresses, coats, suits, and draperies. Tissue faille is a lightweight faille.

Faille crepe A silk, rayon, acetate, or other man-made-fibered dress fabric with a decided wavy (crepe) cord fillingwise. It is used for negligees, blouses, daytime and evening dresses, handbags, and trimmings.

Flannel Originally an all-wool fabric of woolen or worsted yarn with a soft napped finish. Now often a rayon or cotton fabric slightly napped on both sides to resemble woolen or worsted. It may be twill or plain weave and is used for coats, suits, and dresses. Viyella flannel is a Williams, Hollins and Company trade name for a cotton and wool flannel made in England.

Flannelette A lightweight cotton flannel napped on one or both sides, which may be printed. It is used for sleeping garments, sport shirts, and sheets.

Flat crepe A medium-weight crepe with creped fillings alternating with two S and two Z twists. The surface is fairly flat. It is used for dresses, negligees, and blouses.

Fleece A fabric with a deep, thick-napped surface that may be of wool, cotton, acrylic, nylon, or other man-made fibers.

Foulard A lightweight, soft, twill-weave silk, cotton, or rayon fabric that is often printed with small figures on light or dark grounds. It is used for spring and summer dresses, scarfs, robes, and neckties.

Fur-fiber fabrics See the glossary in Chapter 5.

Gabardine A tightly woven, steep twill with rounded wales and a flat back. Made in wool, cotton, rayon, polyester, or mixtures. It is used for suits, coats, tailored dresses, and slacks.

Garter belt A fabric belt to which garters are attached.

Garter welt A reinforcement with extra stretch at the top of the stocking to permit attachment to a garter belt.

Gauze A sheer, open plain-weave cotton fabric used for diapers and surgical dressings. It can also be made of silk or man-made fibers for use in curtains.

Georgette crepe A sheer, dull crepe. The texture is obtained by alternating right- and left-twist yarns in warp and filling. It is used for summer and evening dresses.

Gingham A yarn-dyed plain-weave cotton fabric with woven-in plaids, checks, or stripes. It is used for women's and children's dresses and blouses and men's sport shirts.

Girdle A foundation garment extending from the waist or bust to below the buttocks. It has all-elastic webbing or inserts of webbing and fabric, with or without bones.

Gros de Londres Ribbed or corded fabric. The flat, fillingwise cords alternate wide and narrow. It is used for dresses and millinery.

Grosgrain   A heavy ribbed fabric in ribbon width, made in silk or rayon warp with cotton cords. The cords are round and firm. It is really a bengaline in narrow goods and is used for ribbons, neckties, and lapel facings.

Honan   A heavy silk pongee, originally the product of wild silkworms of Honan, China. Honan has slub yarns in both warp and filling and may be made with synthetic fibers.

Jean   A solid-colored or striped twill-weave cotton fabric, softer and finer than denim, but sometimes used interchangeably with denim. It is used for work shirts, girls' and women's and men's pants and shorts, and children's overalls.

Jeans   Pants worn for work, casual, and even dress wear made from the fabric *jean* or from denim, twill, or double cloth in solids, plaids, or stripes.

Jersey   See the glossary in Chapter 13.

Lace   An open-work fabric made by looping interlacing or twisting thread. (For kinds of laces, see Chapter 19.)

Lamé   Brocade, damask, or brocatelle in which flat metallic yarns are woven in warp and filling for a luxurious effect. Metallic yarns may be used in the main construction. Also a trademark term for a nontarnishable metallic yarn. It is used for evening dresses, blouses, and trimmings.

Lawn   A cotton muslin fabric generally more sheer and with a higher count than nainsook. It may not be sized.

Lingerie crepe   Formerly called French crepe because it was originally made in France. The creped surface was made by embossing (pressing cloth over a fleece blanket). Since it is no longer pressed, it is not a crepe. It is used for lingerie and spring and summer dresses.

Loden cloth   A fleecy coating woven of coarser grade of wool in the Austrian and German Tyrol. Since the wool has some grease, it is naturally water-repellent. Generally a soft wood green.

Marquisette   See the glossary in Chapter 13.

Matelassé crepe   A double cloth with quilted or blistered appearance that is used for afternoon, dinner, and evening dresses and for trimmings.

Melton   A heavy woolen with clipped surface nap; somewhat feltlike in feeling; lustrous like a dull broadcloth.

Mesh   Any woven or knitted fabric with an open mesh texture. It is used for foundation garments and hosiery.

Moiré   A fabric with a wavy watered pattern embossed on it.

Moss crepe   A type of crepe woven and finished to have a mossy look.

Muslin   Any plain-weave cotton cloth ranging in weight from the sheerest batiste to the coarsest sheeting. Muslins include such fabrics as voile, nainsook, lawn, and percale.

Nainsook   A cotton muslin fabric heavier and coarser than lawn. In better grades it may be polished on one side. When well-polished, it is sold as polished cotton.

Negligee   A loose, robe-type garment, worn in the boudoir, made of sheer fabric and often lace or fur trimmed.

Net   A silk, rayon, nylon, or cotton mesh fabric. The size of the mesh varies as well as the weight of the net. It is used for veils, evening dresses, and trimmings.

Ninon   A voile with warp yarns grouped in pairs. It is made of rayon, acetate, silk, or man-made fibers and is used for dresses and curtains.

Nun's veiling   A sheer, worsted, silk or mixed fabric that is dyed black or brown for religious garb and dyed in colors for dresses.

100-denier crepe   A 100-denier viscose rayon yarn made in a flat crepe construction.

Organdy   A thin, stiff transparent cotton muslin used for summer dresses, neckwear, and trimmings. Permanent starchless finishes do not lose their crispness in laundering.

Organza   A thin, stiff, plain-weave silk or rayon fabric used for formal dresses, trimmings, and collars and cuffs. See *organdy.*

Ottoman   A heavily corded silk or rayon fabric. The cords are heavier than bengaline and are widely spaced. The cords usually are cotton or wool.

Oxford   A basket-weave cotton fabric (2 × 1, 2 × 2, or 3 × 2) used for sport dresses, blouses, and shirts.

Pants suits   A two-piece garment consisting of jacket and long pants.

Panty   A woman's or girl's undergarment, with an elastic waistband, that is bound, scalloped, or lace-trimmed at the bottom. A panty girdle is an elasticized, form-fitting panty.

Panty girdle   A foundation garment with legs attached. See *girdle.*

Panty hose   Stockings and panty knitted as one garment.

Peau de soie   A soft silk fabric ("skin of silk").

Pebble crepe   Usually woven of abraded yarns (rayon and acetate) warp and filling. It is a plain weave with skips of warp over two fillings and two fillings over two warps at intervals, to give pebbled surface.

Peignoir   A loose robe worn in the boudoir or a coat worn over a bathing suit at the beach. It is often made of terry cloth to absorb water after bathing.

Percale   A medium-weight muslin similar to cambric but dull in finish. It is generally printed for apparel. Heavy grades in higher counts are used for sheeting. Dress percale runs 80 square or 160 yarns to the inch, whereas percale sheeting is 180 or 200 yarns to the inch.

Piqué   A fabric with warpwise wales made in cotton, rayon, or other man-made fibers. In honeycomb design it is called waffle piqué; in diamond pattern, bird's-eye piqué. It is used for dresses, collars, cuffs, and shirts.

Placket closing   A narrow piece of material used to finish an opening made in a fabric to enable the wearer to put on the garment with ease.

Plissé or crinkle crepe   A crinkled, striped, or blistered pattern produced on a cotton, rayon, or acetate fabric by treating parts of the fabric with caustic soda to shrink certain areas.

Plush   See the glossary in Chapter 21.

Pongee   Fabric originally made in China of tan-colored tussah silk. It is plain or printed for summer dresses and suits and is lighter and less slubby than shantung.

Poplin   A crosswise-ribbed cotton fabric similar to cotton broadcloth but with a heavier rib. It may be of rayon, silk, wool, nylon, polyester, or combinations of these fibers. It is used for dresses, coats, jackets, and snowsuits (water-repellent).

Printcloth   Term applied to carded, plain-weave cotton fabrics with single yarns with counts 30s and 40s. Finishes may vary to produce cloths like lawn, percale, cambric, and longcloth.

Power net   An elastic fabric with a two-way stretch used for figure control garments. May be either woven or knitted.

Rep   A silk, rayon, cotton, wool, or mixed fabric in rib construction, heavier than poplin. It is used for draperies and ties, and in lighter weights for blouses and trimmings.

Romain crepe   A semisheer fabric of abraded yarns in warp and filling. It is made of rayon and acetate or wool and is used for street and dressy dresses.

Rough crepe   A heavy fabric of rayon, acetate, or mixtures made with alternately twisted fillings, two right and two left (2 × 2).

Satin   A basic weave in which either the warp or the filling floats. Fabrics made by this weave include

   Antique satin   A heavy, lustrous reversible fabric; one side resembles shantung and the other side silk satin; woven with uneven yarns.

   Baronet satin   A highly lustrous, warp-faced satin with a rayon face and a cotton back.

   Canton satin   A soft fabric with a satin face and a crepe back that has a ribbed effect.

   Charmeuse   A medium- to lightweight satin fabric with a lustrous face and a dull back of crepe yarns. Originally of silk, but now of man-made fibers.

   Ciré satin   A satin fabric finished by the application of wax or resin under heat and pressure.

   Crepe-backed satin   A heavy, reversible satin fabric with a crepe weave on the back.

   Duchess satin   A heavy, stiff, and lustrous satin with a warp float.

   Hammered satin   A satin fabric embossed to give the surface a textured effect.

   Messaline   A lightweight, soft satin dress fabric, loosely woven of rayon or silk.

   Peau d'ange   A dull, waxy, smooth finish usually applied to satin made from acetate fibers. Other fibers may be used. Also called "angel skin."

   Slipper satin   A heavy rayon, acetate, or silk satin usually with a cotton back.

Satin crepe   A heavy reversible fabric with satin on one side and crepe on the other side. It is used in fall and winter dresses and linings.

Satin knit   A knit fabric made to look and feel like (woven) satin by means of yarn modifications.

Seersucker   A cotton, silk, or man-made fibered fabric made by alternating plain and crinkled stripes. It is used for summer dresses, boys' shirts, shorts, men's summer suits, and bedspreads. See *woven seersucker*.

Serge   An even twill-weave worsted fabric with the diagonal wale showing on both sides of the cloth, used for men's and women's suits, coats, and dresses. It is made in cotton or rayon for linings.

Shantung   A plain-weave fabric woven with slub filling yarn made in silk, rayon, cotton, the man-made fibers, or wool. It is used for dresses and suits.

Silhouette   The outline of a garment.

Slipper satin   A heavy rayon, acetate, or silk satin usually with a cotton back. It is used for bedroom and evening slippers and evening dresses.

Splicing (in hosiery)   Reinforcement above the heel and at the toe.

Staple fabrics   Those cloths that, over a period of years, have a steady sale or demand. Such cloths as muslins, flannels, broadcloth, shantung, and taffeta are staples that have to be kept in stock.

Staple names   Name of staple fabrics. See *staple fabrics*.

Stone-washed jeans   Jeans laundered with pumice rock to provide a worn, abraided effect.

Surah   A soft twilled fabric made of silk, rayon, or acetate woven in plaids, stripes, solid color, or print. Since the diagonal of the wale has a flat top, it may be described as a satin-faced twill. It is used for dresses, blouses, trimmings, and neckties. Foulard is often sold as surah.

Taffeta   Plain-weave, smooth, stiffened fabric in silk, rayon, cotton, or man-made fibers, solid colored or printed. It is used for dresses, blouses, and ribbons.

Terry cloth See *terry cloth,* Chapter 5.

Texture See the glossary in Chapter 3.

Tights Skintight garments closely fitting to the figure and extending from the neck down, or from the waist down.

Tricot See the glossary in Chapter 6.

Tweed A rough-surfaced woolen, usually yarn-dyed and often made in two or more colors. In women's wear, a tweed may look rough but feels soft or even spongy. It may be nubbed or slubbed. It is all wool unless otherwise indicated. Now cotton, linen, rayon, synthetics, or blends may be made to resemble wool tweed.

Unbleached muslin Printcloths in gray goods and lightweight sheetings.

Unfinished worsted See the glossary in Chapter 12.

Union suit A one-piece knitted undergarment extending from the neck to the knee or longer.

Velour See the glossary in Chapter 21.

Velvet Silk, rayon, or nylon cut pile fabric made with extra warp yarns. Types of velvet include chiffon, Lyons, transparent, and uncut velvet.

Velveteen A cotton fabric with a filling pile made to look like velvet. It has a cut pile with plain or twill back and is used for dresses, coats, jackets, millinery, and suits.

Viyella flannel See *flannel.*

Voile A low-count, sheer muslin with a thready feel. In better grades, voile is made with ply yarns in counterclockwise twist. It is also made in wool, silk, or rayon and is used for summer dresses and curtains.

Warm-up suit A two-piece knit garment consisting of a short jacket and long pants that is worn by athletes before, after, or during active participation in some sports. It is also worn as apparel for casual relaxation by both males and females.

Whipcord A twill-weave wool or cotton fabric resembling gabardine. The wale is more pronounced on the right side. It is used for riding habits and uniforms.

White-on-white Fabric with a white dobby or Jacquard design on a white ground, common in madras, broadcloth, or nylon. (See *madras,* in the glossary in Chapter 18.)

Wool crepe Made of either woolen or worsted yarns. The crepe texture is produced by keeping the warp yarn slack.

Woven seersucker A crinkled, striped cotton fabric made by weaving some of the yarns in tighter tension than others. See *seersucker.*

Chapter 18

MEN'S AND BOYS' WEAR

Through the years, certain fabrics have remained classic. One of these is the fabric named jean. The French used to identify Genoese sailors by their heavy trousers, which they called *gènes* (after the French *Gènes* for Genoa). The word dungaree (so the story goes) is derived from the Hindustani word dungri. Sailors wore a garment by the same name. Denim, like jean and dungaree, is related to seafaring. The word denim, a contraction of "de Nimes," was named after the French city of Nimes, where the fabric was made for sailcloth and later for sailors' garments.

One of the reasons for jean being a classic fabric over the years is its excellent resistance to wear. But jeans have now become a fashion apparel item not only for sports but for casual wear for men, women, and children alike.

Jeans, as used for trousers, are made not only of jean fabric but also of sateen, denim (sometimes with a brushed surface), twills, and Lycra spandex for stretch jeans. Jeans are often an all-cotton warp (generally blue) with a white filling. A fabric may be made of cotton and man-made fibers such as nylon and/or polyester. This combination of fibers adds resistance to wear, and durable press ensures abrasion resistance and no ironing as well. Not all jeans wear equally well. Generally, the higher the ratio of man-made fiber to cotton, the more durable the fabric.

The trouser jean was first used for work clothes, and jeans were patented by the Levi Strauss Company in 1873 as "riveted clothing." The basic styling of jeans has remained relatively the same, but their use is so universal that they are now worn for almost any occasion. (See Fig. 18.1.) The term "jean" was often used interchangeably with "denim," as for example, the use of the term "blue

Figure 18.1 Early California gold miners wearing Levi jeans (1882), at the Last Chance Mine, Placer County, California. (Photo courtesy of Levi Strauss and Co., Inc.)

jeans." Today, we are more likely to use the term "jeans" to refer to a trouser and "denim" to refer to a popular fabric used for jeans.

Even in such a popular garment as jeans, the consumer should carefully select items of clothing not only for the end use but also for appropriateness in dress, whether for business, leisure, sports, or the college campus. Accessories, too, should be carefully selected to create a harmonious ensemble.

SELECTION OF MEN'S AND BOYS' FURNISHINGS

Men's wear may be classified as (1) men's clothing and (2) men's furnishings. A similar division may be made for boys' wear. Work clothing may be treated as a separate classification.

Both men's and boys' furnishings are composed of similar articles, the chief of which are shirts, sleepwear, underwear, hosiery, robes, ties, handkerchiefs, belts, suspenders, garters, mufflers and scarfs, vests, sweaters, swimwear, warm-up suits, and other sportswear.

Men's clothing includes garments such as suits, topcoats, overcoats, rainwear, jackets, and slacks. Boys' clothing incudes the same general classifications. With the emergence of fashion as a selling force, there are now more divisions of men's and boys' sections in department and specialty stores. Teen sportswear and furnishings departments have often become individual shops or boutiques—that is, sweater, slacks, swimwear, shirt shops.

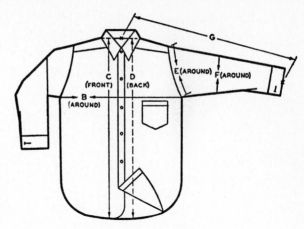

Figure 18.2 Commercial standards for men's shirt sizes call for minimum dimensions in five areas that are important for comfort and appearance. (Reproduced courtesy of Consumers' Research, Inc.)

Shirts

Shirts may be classified according to the occasion for which they are worn: (1) dress (tailored garments worn with a necktie for business, street, and semiformal wear), (2) work, (3) sports, and (4) formal.

Dress Shirts

These can be all white, solid colored, striped, or patterned. For work shirts or one-piece work suits, khaki, dark blue, or color coordinated to pants are common. Sports or leisure shirts may be white, solid colored, plaids, stripes, checks, or figures.

Sizes in dress shirts. Men's dress shirt sizes run 14 to 17 inches or 35.5 to 44.5 cm (neckband measurement). Men who cannot wear standard sizes should buy custom-made shirts. Sleeve lengths come in sizes 32 to 36 inches or 81 to 89 cm. Boys' sizes run 3, 4, 5, 6, and 8, 10, 12, 14, 16, 18, and 20. Sleeve lengths are usually identified as long or short. (See Fig. 18.2).

Cotton and cotton blend shirtings come under FTC rules for shrinkage. That is, if the words "preshrunk" or "full-shrunk" are used, they mean that the fabric will not shrink further. If there is a possibility of residual shrinkage, then the percent to be expected must be stated. It is advisable to buy a half size larger shirt if the residual shrinkage is over 1 percent. For shirts marked "Sanforized," this advice is unnecessary.

Standard commercial sizes for men's shirts, as agreed upon by the trade and published by the National Bureau of Standards, are found in Table 18.1.

Styles in dress shirts. Collars in spread, long, or medium point are attached to the body of the shirt.[1] Button-down collars are popular also. Shirts may have a single or pleated closing that buttons down the front. Cuffs may be single (barrel) or French (double). The latter style has buttonholes for cuff links. The European or continental style is moderately tapered through the body.

[1]See collar styles in illustration, Fig. 18.3.

Table 18.1 Standard Minimum Measurements for Men's Shirts

	In.	Cm	In.	Cm	In.	Cm	In.	Cm	In.	Cm	In.	Cm	In.	Cm
Stamped neckband (A) sizes	14	35.5	14½	37	15	38	15½	39.5	16	40.5	16½	42	17	43
Chest, total circumference (B)	42	87	44	92	46	97	48	102	50	107	52	112	54	117
Front, length of (C)	33	84	33	84	33	84	33	84	33	84	33	84	33	84
Back, length of (D)	33	84	33	84	33	84	33	84	33	84	33	84	33	84
Armholes, length around curve (E)	19½	49.5	20	51	20½	52	21	53	21½	53	22	56	22½	57
Sleeve, width around (F)	14¾	37.5	15¼	39	15¾	40	16¼	41	16¾	43	17¼	44	17¾	45

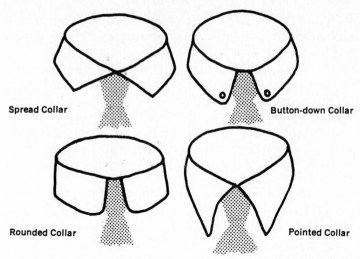

Figure 18.3 Basic collar styles. (Courtesy of the Celanese Fibers Marketing Co.)

Fabrics for dress shirts, including formal shirts. All-cotton or polyester/cotton blends are commonly used for dress shirtings in broadcloth construction. All-rayon or polyester/rayon may be used. Best quality domestic broadcloth is made of 2 × 2 combed pima cotton with a count of 144 × 76, mercerized, and shrinkage-controlled. Poorer grades may have the following weaknesses: 2 × 1 (two-ply warp and single filling) or single-carded yarns in both warp and filling, a count as low as 100 × 56, little or no mercerization, and preshrunk fabric with residual shrinkage declared.

Chambray, a staple yarn-dyed fabric with colored warp and white filling, is also suitable for dress shirts. In better grades are found yarns single and combed, a balanced count 84 × 76, and shrinkage control. Tricot is a knit in 100 percent polyester or 80 percent polyester/20 percent cotton that is quick drying and has minimum-care properties.

Shirts for formal wear are usually pleated or plain, sometimes ruffled with a starched or soft bosom, depending on the current mode. Fabrics include piqué, batiste, broadcloth, silk, or man-made fibered crepe and blends.

Requirements for good workmanship. To ensure good wearing quality, a dress shirt's seams should be stitched firmly but should not pucker (14 to 18 close, even stitches to the inch). Buttons (ocean pearl in better grades because they do not melt as plastic buttons do) should be stitched firmly; buttonholes should be evenly cut and firmly bound; collar points should be even, sharp, and neatly sewn. Double needle (two rows of stitching) is stronger than single needle.

Appearance and comfort. In addition to size and good workmanship, the careful buyer is generally interested in the appearance of the shirt, its comfort, durability, launderability, and suitability. The customer looks for style, color, and cleanness (even the neatness of the cellophane wrapping). A shiny cotton surface created by mercerization is more attractive and easier to care for than a dull fuzzy surface. For comfort, a shirt should be cut full across the chest. Boys and heavier men, especially, need full-cut shirts and correct collar size. Length of sleeves and size of armholes also affect comfort.

Men are frequently exasperated because shirts do not stay tucked in after they have been washed; the shirt tail has shrunk. Shrinkage, already discussed in connection with size, is a major consideration if a garment is purchased for comfort. Some shirts are designed to be longer in the back so that they stay tucked in more easily.

Men's dress shirts now come in durable-press treatments. The 100 percent cotton durable-press shirts have an advantage over blends in that white cotton shirts, being opaque, are whiter; they are also more comfortable, since they absorb perspiration more readily. However, cotton durable-press white shirts are subject to yellowing; they also have reduced wear qualities owing to the loss of tensile strength and abrasion resistance caused by the durable-press treatment.

On the other hand, the cotton/polyester durable-press shirt is subject to oil staining and odor absorption. The odor of perspiration may dissolve in the man-made fiber and be difficult to remove. Oil staining is a problem because polyester has an affinity for oil and does not release it readily. Soil-release finishes have been discovered but have not proved as important in the clothing category as they have in home furnishings. Frequent laundering of the durable-press shirts with oil stains such as mayonnaise and salad dressings is necessary.

Boys' Shirts

For young boys, a long shirt that will stay tucked into the pants is appropriate. School-aged boys should wear shirts with tails or polo shirts sufficiently long to allow an active child to bend over easily. Convertible collars and open-neck styles with short sleeves are appropriate for a growing boy. (See Fig. 18.4.)

Boys' shirt sizes 6 to 20 are usually tailored like men's, with similar-style collars, tailored fronts, fullness at center back, and barrel-style cuffs. A few details in tailoring may be omitted from these shirts. Suitability of material and style of cut determine the use of a shirt.

Body shirts styled for the teenaged male are shaped for close, body hugging fit. The wide chest tapers down to suppressed sides and long shirttails, worn with jeans and often with a sleeveless pullover rib knitted sweater.

Work Shirts

Work shirts, for utility wear, are made of sturdy fabrics, such as mercerized cotton/polyester and 35 percent cotton chambray, all-cotton chino, 65 percent polyester and 35 percent combed cotton gabardine, all-cotton denim, and all-

Figure 18.4 Casual jersey shirts from Ocean Pacific Sunwear are appropriate for any age group. Comfortable corduroy shorts in blends of Trevira® polyester and cotton complete the outfit. (Photo courtesy of Hoechst Fibers Industries. Trevira is a registered trademark of Hoechst AG.)

cotton drill. The emphasis in selecting work shirts should be suitability rather than style. Nowadays, the work shirt is not unattractive, because collar styles may be those of the dress shirt or convertible sport shirt that can be worn with a tie. For comfort, shirts usually have long tails that stay tucked in. Sleeves may be long or short, and sizes are based on the neck size.

Sports Shirts

Styles in sport shirts.   Although sport shirts vary in style, a common feature is that they are made to be worn without a tie. They may or may not have a collar and may have either short or long sleeves. Since sport shirts are intended for active sports and for casual wear, a comfortable, easy-to-care-for fabric is suitable. In general, sport shirt fabrics are classified as knitted or woven. Knitted constructions include jersey and various types of fancy knits and meshes of cotton, polyester, acrylic, nylon, and blends. Woven fabrics may include cotton jean, flannel (wool or cotton and blends with man-made fibers), cord, chambray, gingham, broadcloth, corduroy, woven stretch and blends of polyester and cotton, cotton and rayon, polyester and rayon and others. Neck sizes include small (14 to 14½ inches or 35.5 to 37 cm), medium (15 to 15½ inches or 38 to 39.5 cm), large (16 to 16½ inches or 40.5 to 42 cm), and extralarge (17 to 17½ inches or 43 to 44.5 cm).

Sweat shirts, also known as warm-up clothing, with or without hoods, are usually classified as active sportswear and are used to protect the body from

Figure 18.5 Loungewear/warm-up suit of 1005 polyester creates a sleek look with a hooded jacket and pants. (Photo courtesy of Men's Fashion Association/Arthur Ashe for Le Coq Sportif.)

sudden chill. (See Fig. 18.5.) They may be pullover or jacket style, of fleece-lined cotton knit or double- or triple-knit nylon. Cardigan and sweater shirt sets, sweat shirts and jackets, or sweat pants are worn for sports. The terry-cloth-lined gingham jacket or double-knit polyester beach jacket and trunks may constitute a set for beachwear. Trunks of this set, which may match or contrast with the jacket, may be made of spandex, nylon stretch yarn, polyester double knit, and polyester/cotton poplin.

Factors in Shirt Selection

Durability of shirts. The durability of a shirt is determined by the grade of fabric (judged according to the quality of the fibers, yarns, weaves, and finishing processes).

Workmanship also affects durability. Stitching and buttons have been discussed under requirements for good workmanship. In addition, the following tips will help the consumer find satisfaction in purchasing shirts:

1. Stripes or patterns in sport shirts should match at seams.
2. A center pleat ensures a good anchorage for buttons.
3. A shirt with six or seven buttons stays tucked in better than one with five.
4. A band inside the collar is highly desirable.
5. Thread should match the predominant color of the shirt.
6. Wide seams and reinforcements increase the length of life of a shirt.
7. Everyday shirts and work shirts for men and boys should be made with a button fastening at the cuff to avoid the inconvenience of cuff links.
8. The lining materials should be shrunk to the same extent as the shirt fabric so that the collar will stay flat after laundering and avoid wrinkles and folds.

Ease in laundering. Ease in laundering is also a factor in durability. Single-cuffed shirts are easier to iron than are those with double cuffs, but the latter are usually more durable. For traveling, the polyester/cotton durable-press or knitted shirts are popular. They can be washed at night and hung to drip dry overnight with no ironing required. (See Chapters 7 and 16). Since the collars and cuffs of shirts of polyester/cotton blends soil more quickly than the body of the shirt, a small nail brush can be used effectively to apply a liquid detergent to soiled areas. Sometimes a ring around the collar cannot be entirely removed by this method. One needs a soil-release technique with polyester/cotton blends with durable-press finishes. As recommended in Chapter 16, soaking the shirt in an enzyme product for 30 minutes or overnight will break down or digest into small particles (by chemical means) the various kinds of organic matter—protein, starch, or the like.

Launderability.   Recently, the International Fabricare Institute conducted wash tests on all-cotton men's shirts compared with 65 percent polyester/35 percent cotton blends. The cotton shirts retained much more soil than did the polyester blends. After twenty washings, the cotton shirts were so badly worn as to be no longer acceptable, whereas the polyester/cotton shirts retained their appearance with no fraying of collars or cuffs; they also retained their whiteness, whereas the cotton shirts were yellowed.[2]

Brands.   Some men prefer to buy a shirt of a familiar nationally known brand. Although there may be a lesser known brand that is more suited to their needs, some men refuse to switch from a brand to which they have become accustomed. Among the national brands are Gant, Soro, Arrow, Van Heusen, Manhattan, Marlboro, Truval, National, A.M.C., Towncraft (J. C. Penney), Hathaway, and Pilgrim (Sears).

Price.   With the escalation of prices in the 1980s, price becomes an important factor in the purchase of a shirt. If the consumer knows that a dress shirt to his liking may cost $15 to $35, he expects comfort, dimensional stability, attractiveness (neat and style-right appearance), as well as ease of care and durability.

Formal Shirts

The formal shirt continues to be highly standardized: white, polyester/cotton or all cotton, heavily starched, stiff plain front or pleats, jeweled studs down the front, and matching cuff links.

While this is the classic formal shirt garb, older boys and more fashion attuned males wear formal shirts in a variety of colors and with ruffles down the front, at the neck, and at the wrists. Sociologists note that this gives some young men the trappings of the male peacock.

Neckties

There are two main styles in men's ties: formal and informal. Formal ties include bow ties, which may be tied by hand or bought ready-tied, long ties, and ascots or scarf ties, the end of which, being tied once, can be crossed in front

---

[2]International Fabricare Institute, *Bulletin TN 119* (1982).

and fastened with a scarf pin. The bow tie is worn for formal occasions with dinner jackets and with full dress and also with business attire. When fashion decrees, ascots may be worn for formal or semiformal morning or afternoon wear occasions with a cutaway or frock coat or informally with a sport shirt. Informal ties are usually the long type, sometimes a knitted construction, with pointed or straight ends. (See Fig. 18.6.)

In addition to the style and suitability of a tie, the durability of the material and the construction are important. The fibers, yarns, weave, and finishing processes affect the wearing quality.

The two types of construction are resilient and rigid. The tie with resilient construction is sewn by machine with long, bastinglike stitches that allow greater elasticity in tying than do the short, rather tight, machine stitches of the rigid construction. The rigid type are inexpensive ties. To determine whether a tie has a resilient construction, check to see if the fabric was cut on the bias by grasping it with thumb and forefinger of each hand, pulling it gently in opposite directions along with length of the tie, and noting whether or not it gives. Other points to consider in workmanship are the stitching along the edge and the evenness of the hems.

A tie made of a fabric cut on the bias will hold its shape better than one cut on the straight of the material. If the outer fabric is cut on the bias, the lining should be cut on the bias too. Also, a tie that is lined with wool has greater elasticity and therefore holds its shape longer than one that is lined with cotton. A well-made tie has four or five folds at the broad end. A tie with facing at the ends has an improved appearance because no stitching shows.

Figure 18.6 Casual knitted ties can be worn with button-down collar shirts. (Photo courtesy of Men's Fashion Association/Excello.)

Ties made from woven goods stay tied better than do those made from knitted fabrics. There is less slippage of the knot. Knitted ties wear well and do not wrinkle.

Acetate, cotton, and weighted silk wrinkle badly, and the wrinkles do not hang out. Wool and pure silk are excellent as tie fabrics, because they are wrinkle-resistant and resilient. Polyester, which is both resilient and spot-resistant, makes a good woven or knitted tie fabric, as do many fabrics in polyester blends.

Sweaters

Many consumers are interested in style when they buy a sweater. The two classic styles for men as well as for women are the pullover, which pulls over the head and generally has no buttons but may have a short zipper, and the cardigan, which fastens down the front, generally with buttons or a zipper. The pullover without sleeves is popular because it is more comfortable under jackets or coats. Necklines of the pullover may be V-shaped, round, boat, turtle, or crew. (See Fig. 18.7.) Sizes are 36 to 46 or small through extra-large. The cardigan may be made with or without shawl collar and two lower pockets.

Sweaters are made in smooth and in bulky, shaggy, hairy, nubbed, and linenlike textures. The smooth type is more comfortable under a jacket, whereas the others are particularly suited to sportswear.

Patterns in sweaters are created by variations in the knitted stitch and by color contrast in body, collars, and cuffs. The three classic stitches for sweaters are (1) jumbo, a coarse stitch with large, heavy yarn; (2) gauze, a close stitch with

Figure 18.7 Boys' designer sweater by Polo. (Photo courtesy of Polo/Ivey's.)

fine, thin yarn; and (3) shaker knit, a weight between jumbo and gauze. Other knitted stitches include interlock, links, cable, waffle, pineapple, fisherman's knit, and bulky rib. Sweaters are made of all wool or all cashmere, acrylic, polyester, nylon, cotton, and blends. (See women's sweaters, Chapter 17.)

Underwear

Garments sold in men's and boys' underwear departments include T-shirts, undershirts, drawers, shorts, briefs, and union suits (knitted one-piece garments with sleeves and legs in varied lengths). The most popular styles in underwear for men and boys are athletic or T-shirts and athletic shorts or briefs.

T-shirts and Undershirts

For boys, T-shirts or athletic shirts come in sizes 2 and 4 and in sizes small (6 to 8), medium (10 to 12), and large (14 to 16). Some size ranges run to 20. T-shirt and undershirt sizes for men are small (34 to 36), medium (38 to 40), large (42–44), and extra-large (46–52).

Men's underwear is the latest convert to style, color, and pattern. Until 1935, the drop-seat style predominated. Now styles range from an all-in-one stretch mesh union suit to a modified G-string known as "jock sock." Bikini styles have arrived. While they may seem uncomfortable and impractical for men who are overweight, there is a trend away from loose-fitting garments to those that hug the body closely and smoothly and provide greater warmth. For example, there are (1) A-line undershirts and bikini outfits and (2) brief and top combinations in colorful cotton blends. (See Fig. 18.8.)

Selection

The male consumer should buy for:[3]

1. *Comfort* by checking the length, width, size of neckband and armhole opening; seams smooth next to the skin.
2. *Cleanliness* in keeping outer clothes clean.
3. *Durability* by having taped or overcast seams to resist snagging.

Shorts and Briefs

Styles in men's woven shorts are (1) boxer, which has an all-around elastic waist and (2) yoke, which has a snap fastener and elastic inserts in the waist. Sizes, based on waist measurement, run in even numbers 28 to 44 inches (71 to 112 cm). These garments are commonly made of cotton or cotton and polyester blends in broadcloth or percale. Many fabrics are durable press.

Briefs are knitted articles of underwear of rib-knitted cotton or polyester and cotton flat knit. A nylonized finish on combed cotton adds strength and wear; a sanitized finish gives hygienic protection. The better qualities are made of cotton yarns like Durene, which is combed, two ply, mercerized for strength

[3]*Moneysworth*, January 21, 1974.

Figure 18.8   New contemporary styles in men's underwear. (Photo courtesy of Kodel polyester 451, Eastman Chemical Products, Inc.)

and luster, highly absorbent, and sanitized to check perspiration odor and to arrest growth of bacteria. A durable blend is 80 percent cotton and 20 percent nylon.

Support briefs may be made of 94 percent combed cotton and 6 percent spandex, with a belt of 64 percent acetate, 28 percent rayon, and 8 percent spandex. A reinforced double crotch and front-panel reinforced seams, nonbinding bound elasticized leg openings, and elastic waistband are considerations in comfort and wear. Sizes in briefs are also by waist measurement.

Probably the most comfortable underwear is made of a knitted fabric, because it gives with movements of the body, ventilates the skin, keeps the body warm in winter and cool in summer, is easily washed, and needs no ironing. It is especially suitable for active sportswear. Some men prefer a short cap sleeve in knitted undershirts to protect the outer shirt from perspiration. Since cotton absorbs perspiration better than silk, rayon, or nylon, many men prefer cotton for underwear in all climates. Both woolen and worsted yarns can be used in knit underwear. The woolen yarn is soft and pliable and makes a good napped or fleecy surface. Worsted yarn is smooth and lustrous and makes a fine, even, smooth-knitted structure. Wool knitted underwear is very warm.

One hundred percent nylon knitted underwear, although it is very strong and quick drying, does not absorb perspiration. Nylon or polyester thread can be used for sewing seams of underwear because of its strength. A knitted fabric made of a layering of cotton (75 percent) and Merino wool (25 percent) is comfortable. Since the wool, buried between two layers of cotton,[4] does not touch the skin, the underwear does not cause itching.

In winter, quilted or thermal Raschel knits are often worn for sports, especially in colder climates. This type of underwear is enjoying a recent upsurge in sales due to the lower room temperatures being maintained in energy-conserving homes and increased interest in winter sports. The quilted type may consist of jacket and drawers made with a cotton shell, modacrylic batting, and cotton interlining. This set is made flame-retardant. The Raschel knits are 100 percent cotton or 75 percent cotton/25 percent Acrilan acrylic. Heavy stretch thermal knits may be 94 percent cotton/6 percent spandex. Recently, thermal underwear of a blend of vinyon and acrylic fiber has been well received. (See Chapter 15 for details.)

Launderability is an important factor in underwear. Both wash-and-wear cotton and the noncellulosic man-made fibers are easy to care for and require little or no pressing. The trademark Sanfor-Knit assures the consumer lasting comfort and fit. The man-made fibers have the added advantage of drying quickly, but some men say that these fibers feel clammy because they do not have the absorptive quality of cotton.

Hosiery

Men want socks to fit well and to wear well. A comfortable sock is soft, fits smoothly over the instep, ankle, and heel, does not pinch the toes, does not slip or roll down, and is smooth on the sole of the foot. There are three main styles in men's socks: (1) dress for street wear, (2) casual socks for sport, and (3) work socks. Each style comes in lengths from over the calf (executive length) and midcalf to just above the ankle. The sock for street wear usually comes in solid colors in stockinette or rib knit. Clocks and small patterns often enhance it. Sport or casual socks are usually worn with a sport jacket and slacks or sweater and slacks. They can be made cushion soft by using 70 percent acrylic bulky textured yarn, 20 percent cotton, and 10 percent nylon. A kind of casual sock in white with colored stripe top, called a "crew sock," may be made of bulky textured acrylic 69 percent, stretch nylon 29 percent, and nylon reinforcement 2 percent in toe and heel. A second type of casual sock is the argyle with the familiar Jacquard plaid pattern. A third type is novelty, with varied designs and colors. And a fourth type is thermal for winter, made of stretch nylon outside (lined with 50 percent olefin/50 percent cotton) or 80 percent worsted wool/20 percent stretch nylon.

For comfort and wear, a sanitized finish inhibits germ growth, which helps feet to stay fresh longer.

Ingrain-dyed (yarn-dyed) color is a selling point. Bulky acrylic blends that feel woolly and are shrink-resistant are suitable for sportswear. Also, a 50 percent lamb's wool and 50 percent nylon blend and an 80 percent wool and 20 percent stretch nylon are appropriate. (See *stretch yarn*, Chapter 3.)

---

[4]This fabric is Innerwool by the William Carter Company.

Tops of socks are frequently made of spandex yarn in rib knit. Since these yarns keep the sock from slipping, the wearer need not use garters. When labeled antistatic it means the socks have been finished to keep them from clinging to the trouser legs and from collecting lint. An acrylic/stretch nylon blend ensures a good fit. A 100 percent stretch nylon or textured nylon/spandex blend with an elastic top is called "support hosiery."

Work socks are intended to be long wearing—suitable for workmen, schoolboys, and the home owner who "does it himself." A sock made of 95 percent cotton/5 percent spandex with nylon reinforcements is durable and suitable for hard wear. Also the all-cotton sock with reinforced heel and toe is popular. For absorbency and softness, the sole of the sock may be made of terry cloth. For cold weather, wool may be blended with nylon. For extra support, some work socks have a support section in the calf area.

Men's hosiery sizes run from 9 to 13. Three stretch sizes will cover the entire size range. Boys' sizes commonly come in three sizes: medium to fit children's shoe sizes, large to fit boys' shoe sizes, and extra-large to fit men's shoe sizes.

Slippers and slipper socks are often made mostly of fabric for both men and women.

Sleepwear

Just as men seek comfort in underwear, they also want comfort in sleeping garments. If a garment feels smooth and soft, if it is easy to put on and take off, and if it has a full cut and smooth seams, it will generally prove comfortable.

Probably the next most important consideration in sleepwear is durability, which includes launderability. Shrinkage of less than 5 percent is considered satisfactory. Durable press is a valued selling point. For some men the appearance of the garment is more important than comfort or durability. In such cases, decoration, trimming, or quality of workmanship are noticed.

Pajamas generally include a coat-style, or pullover top with or without collar, and pants. Small children often wear the same styles as adults, or they may wear one piece, sometimes with feet attached. The separate coat is buttoned down the front, whereas the pullover needs no front closing. The pants are fastened at the waist with an elastic band or drawstring. For summer, short-length pajama pants and short sleeves are comfortable. For winter, two-piece pajamas made in ski-suit style (with elastic waist and fitted wristlets and anklets) are warm. Other styles may include the long knitted or woven nightshirt.

Pajamas are made of the following materials:

Balbriggan	Knitted jersey
Broadcloth	Tricot knit
Chambray	Percale
Cotton crepe	Pongee
Flannelette	

The sizes in men's pajamas are indicated by the letters A, B, C, D. These sizes are limited because pajamas do not have to be so form-fitting as underwear. Size A generally fits a 34 or smaller; B, a 34 to 36; C, a 38 to 40, and D, a 42 to 44. Size E is an oversize. In sizes B, C, and D extra lengths can be procured. Boys' and students' sizes run 8 to 20.

In more recent years pajamas have become popular for lounging. The lounging type, generally made of luxurious materials such as silk, rayon, or the man-made fibers, has more ornamentation than the sleeping pajamas. Such fabrics as satins, corduroy, Jacquard, nylon or silk tricot, and crepe are also used.

Lounging Robes, Jackets, and Bathrobes

If a man is interested primarily in appearance as opposed to comfort, he will generally purchase a lounging robe rather than a bathrobe. Both garments serve almost the same purpose. In a lounging robe a man expects a good-looking fabric, the latest style of cut, rich coloring, and excellent workmanship. Lounging robes are usually made of plush velour, brocade, or flannel, trimmed with the same fabric in a contrasting color, a cord, braid, or satin. Jackets, shorter than robes, are made of the same fabrics as lounging robes. Most bathrobes are made of terry, flannelette (especially for boys), and corduroy. The sizes in robes run small, medium, large, and extra-large.

Accessories

Handkerchiefs

Handkerchiefs for men may be classified as monogram, plain white, and fancy (colored handkerchiefs with patterns). High-quality handkerchiefs that are made of pure linen (Belgian or Irish) and have fine line yarns are called *linen lawn* or *handkerchief linen*. The count of cloth is high and well balanced (sometimes as high as 1,200). The hems are usually hand-rolled (hand-stitched). A handkerchief may be labeled "pure Irish linen," yet may not be the best quality from the standpoint of yarn, weave, and workmanship. (It may be hemstitched instead of hand-rolled.) Linen (55 percent) and cotton (45 percent) in a blend, or 65 percent polyester/35 percent cotton, are commonly used for handkerchiefs. If fibers, yarns, construction, and workmanship are good, the article may be higher quality than a poor grade of all linen. The United States imports cotton handkerchiefs from Switzerland that are long-stapled Egyptian cotton, combed yarn, closely woven, and mercerized with hand-rolled edges. Some handkerchiefs are made of combed domestic cotton yarn that is sent to the Philippines to be woven, finished, cut, and sewn, and then shipped back to this country. Such merchandise constitutes the low end of the price scale for serviceable goods. Pure Italian silk handkerchiefs are sold for decorative use only. They are more expensive than a good grade of pure linen. A polyester fabric is also used for the decorative-type handkerchief and is generally lower in price than linen or silk. Sizes of handkerchiefs vary from 17-inch or 43-cm squares.

Belts

Although most belts are made of leather or a nontextile plastic, some are made of a heavy cotton called *belting,* which is made with very heavy fillingwise ribs or cords. Belting may also have silk or nylon running one way to cover the cords. Fancy belts are made of cord in knitted or crocheted effects. Some belts are made of the same material as the slacks.

Belts differ in the kind of material used and also in length, width, shape (some are curved at the side), color, and design (of buckle as well as material).

Neckwear and Gloves

The scarf, thrown around the neck and crossed at the front, is worn under the coat. Scarfs may be long and narrow or square. For formal wear, luxurious fabrics of silk, acetate, nylon, and polyester are used. Wool flannel, knitted wool, cashmere, and blends are warm for winter wear. Lighterweight scarfs are made of surah, twills, and crepe in silk or man-made fibers.

When buying a scarf, a man thinks of warmth and weight, color and design, grade of material, workmanship (including hemming, fringe, and embroidery), size, and use.

Cotton, wool, and acrylic knitted gloves are suitable for sportswear when warmth is important. They come in varied colors, in sizes small, medium, and large. While leather is more popular than fabric for gloves, sometimes fabric (acrylic/nylon) is combined with leather in gloves used for driving. A wool or acrylic knit may line a leather glove. Work gloves are comfortable and economical when made of cotton flannel, cotton canvas, fleece-lined cotton, and nylon jersey. Mittens, sized like gloves, are in much less demand in men's wear but are particularly suited for small children.

Hats

For men who wear hats, fur felt made with wool is the traditionally accepted material for everyday wear. (See *felting,* Chapter 6.) Fur felt is made of Australian rabbit, nutria, and beaver blends. Widths of the brim and bands, the height and width of the hat, and the tapering of the crown vary according to style.

Straw is traditionally worn during the summer months. While for formal wear a man may wear a Homburg, bowler, or derby, a top hat is seldom worn except for very formal state occasions. For casual country wear, there has been considerable use of fabric hats of tweed, velour, corduroy, or blend of 90 percent wool/10 percent nylon knit. The visored cap of tweed, corduroy, flannel, or twilled cotton is adapted to sightseeing and to sportswear. The cowboy hat, cap, and softer dress hats are popular today.

Very small boys wear brimmed fabric hats of wool, cotton, or synthetics with or without earlaps for play in mild weather. For dress-up they may wear a flannel Eton style. Older boys often go hatless except in cold weather, when they may pull the hood of a parka or jacket over the head or may don a bulky knitted cap.

Men's hat and cap sizes run 6¾, 6⅞, 7, 7⅛, 7¼, 7⅜, 7½, 7⅝, and 7¾; boys' sizes from from 6⅛ to 7¼, all with one-eighth of an inch jump in measurement.

SELECTION OF MEN'S AND BOYS' OUTERWEAR

Suits

Although men may buy their suits, women often have much to say when a selection is made, and women do most of the buying of boys' clothing. Therefore, it is important for men and women to know a tweed from a gabardine, a woolen from a worsted, and as much as possible about the textiles involved.

Brands

Historically, brands have been more important in men's wear than in women's wear, but brand names, including designer names, are now important to many women. An example is Hart Schaffner & Marx, one of the major manufacturers and retailers of quality men's wear. It sells through some 275 of its own retail outlets, as well as through many other retailers, many labels, including its own name. Others of its brands are Hickey-Freeman, Jaymar-Ruby, M. Wite, Christian Dior, John Nicklaus, Johnny Carson, and Playboy. It has entered aggressively into the women's wear field, where it enjoys about a quarter of its total volume

Suit Styling

In general, today's suit can be defined as a garment composed of at least two matching pieces: a jacket and tailored trousers for everyday business wear or jeans with matching short jacket for casual or leisure wear. But recently, vests have been returning to their former favor. Nearly every businessman has at least one suit with a vest. One popular suit ensemble includes four pieces: a jacket, a reversible vest, and two pairs of trousers. One side of the vest matches the jacket and the other side is of a plaid that matches one of the two pairs of trousers. Thus with one suit jacket, a variety of looks can be achieved.

One who is fashion conscious will notice that designers may change from time to time either/or both the style of the jacket and/or the trousers. (see Fig. 18.9.) The style of the jacket may be changed by

1. Shortening or lengthening.
2. Varying the widths of the collar and lapels—notched, peaked, or L-shaped.
3. Shortening or lengthening the sleeves (two or more buttons on cuff).

Figure 18.9 The traditional double-breasted jacket features peak lapels, three flap pockets, and a double vented back. (Photo courtesy of Men's Fashion Association/Daks.)

4. Using natural or padded shoulders.
5. Changing the waistline (loose or fitted).
6. Making the jacket with straight or flared lines.
7. Making the front a straight line or rounded closing.
8. Using single- (two or three buttons) or double-breasted closing (four to six buttons).
9. Slanting the two front pockets or making them straight—with or without flaps—breast pockets (none, one or two) one or two inside breast pockets.
10. Using one center back vent or two side back vents.

The designer may change the style of the trousers by

1. Making them with or without cuffs.
2. Fitting the legs and buttocks tightly or loosely.
3. Making a high or low rise (the measurement extending from the crotch to the waist or above—low or high rise, respectively).
4. Varying the size, depth, and number of pockets.[5]

Table 18.2 gives the specifications of the three recognized suit styles.

A knowledgeable clothing salesperson will direct the customer's attention to changes in style as well as to color, price, and weight, since these factors are usually key considerations in selecting suits and jackets.

---

[5]May have two side pockets—one may have a button closing. Possible change pocket at right front waistline.

Table 18.2 Types of Men's Suits

	American	International (Continental)	Natural Shoulder
Shoulder	Lightly padded	More heavily padded	Unpadded and unconstructed
Waistline	Follows body line	Tapered	Straight
Vents	Center or side	Deep side, resulting in flared effect	Center
Closures	Two or three	One, two, or three	Three
Trousers	Cuffed, straight leg	Cuffless, tapered leg	Cuffed, straight leg

Fibers and Fabrics in Suits

Two weights of suit are usually carried by retail stores located in the same latitude as the Middle Atlantic states—a lightweight for spring and summer and a regular weight for fall and winter. The summer weight is generally 4 to 5 ounces and is minimum care, made of polyester and blends with cotton or other man-made fibers. The heavier weight is about 7 ounces and may be all-wool or blends of wool and polyester.

Both natural and man-made fibers are used for suits and jackets. Cotton and wool are the most frequently used natural fibers. Cotton is both comfortable and absorbent, while wool is warm and long-wearing.

As mentioned previously, there are two main types of all-wool yarns and wool fabrics—woolens and worsteds. (See Chapter 12.) Generally speaking, woolens are made of fibers of varied lengths averaging less than 2 inches. The yarns are carded and are rather rough, and the finishing is customarily done by fulling and then brushing up a nap (it may be sheared). Worsteds are usually made of fibers more than 2 inches or 5 cm long (all the short fibers have been removed). The yarns are carded and combed and even and smooth; the finishing consists of mending, scouring, shearing, and pressing. Only unfinished and semifinished worsteds are fulled and slightly napped.

The man-made fibers used alone or in blends for men's suitings, both woven or knitted, are polyester, acrylic, nylon, and triacetate. When polyester is used alone or blended with cotton, wool, or other man-made fibers, it has wrinkle resistance, strength, crease retention, and durability and requires minimum care. The blending of polyester staple with wool or acrylic makes fabrics with a worsted appearance. When blended with cotton or rayon, a cotton look and hand is produced. Acrylic fibers produce light weight, brilliant colors, bulk, and softness. Triacetate used alone or in blends is found in knitted jackets, blazers, and shirts that are cool and comfortable.[6] Fabrics made of man-made fiber are generally washable. However, one should always consult the care label.

---

[6]"Today's Fashions in Men's Wear," a pamphlet by Celanese Fibers Marketing Co., Consumer and Retail Information Dept.

Table 18.3 Standard Body Sizes for Boys

Height		Girth (Hips)		Average Age (Years)
In.	Cm	In.	Cm	
43	109	22½	57	5½
45½	115.5	23	58	6½
47½	120.5	24	61	7½
50	127	25	63.5	8½
52	132	26	66	9½
54½	138	27½	70	10½
57	145	28½	72	12

Sizes and Fit of Suits and Jackets

Criteria for determining size are chest, waist, and height measurements. For boys' and girls' clothing, the U.S. Agricultural Research Service has done some research on sizes. From this study, the United States of America Standards Institute has formulated standard sizes of clothing for boys from kindergarten to junior high school. The committee of the Institute chose height and hip measurements because (1) hips are better than the chest as an indicator of the other girth measurements, (2) the hips can be more accurately measured than the chest, and (3) a tape measure is the only equipment needed to make these two measurements.

Table 18.3 gives seven standard body sizes for boys as set up by the U.S.A. Standards Institute.

These standard sizes should make shopping easier and lessen the number of return goods. Manufacturers should find them advantageous in making better fitting children's garments. (See Fig. 18.10.) Mail-order catalogs give measurements of height in inches, centimeters, and average, slim, and husky chest and waist measurements to facilitate ordering the proper size to fit. (See page 466.)[7]

Other points to check are (1) the buttons, buttonholes, or zippers to see if they are stout and properly attached; (2) the adequacy of pockets and their depth and width; and (3) the durability of the material used for the lining and the pockets—will they last as long as the outer material will?

Formal Evening Wear

The traditional tuxedo, appropriate when the occasion calls for "black tie," has a black jacket with satin or faille lapels, black cuffless trousers with satin or faille stripes along the outer seams, and a cummerbund. (See Fig. 18.11.) The current tuxedo is made of colorful and fancier fabric, such as brocade and satin. Trousers

---

[7]Similar information is available from mail-order catalogs for men's suits.

Figure 18.10 Designer sports coat for boys. (Photo courtesy of Polo/Ivey's.)

need not match the jacket material. The evening shirt styles have already been discussed.

For very formal evening wear, "white tie," a jacket with tails, and a white, rather than black tie is required.

Casual Wear

Garments designed for informal use known as "casuals" are coordinates or separates that consist of two or more items of apparel with the same or contrasting fabrics, colors, patterns, and trimmings that are grouped together for coordinated selling. For instance, jackets and pants, shirts and jeans, shirts and pullovers may be coordinated. Some stores coordinate these pieces of apparel for ease in customer selection or leave it to the customers to do their own coordinating in the store.

Coordinates first appeared in casual sportswear. Today, the blazer or sport jacket and slacks are a perennial outfit for casual and business wear. The popularity of this attire has tended to reduce the number of suits in a man's wardrobe. Likewise, jeans and coordinated jackets have become outfits for casual wear. The leisure suit is so called because the male customer creates his own relaxed suit, which is a separate or coordinate. The suit may consist of a

Figure 18.11 Fall and winter formal wear. A black cashmere overcoat tops a wool tuxedo jacket with a satin shawl lapel. Plain-front trousers utilize the traditional satin striping. (Photo courtesy of Men's Fashion Association/Emanuel Ungaro.)

safari jacket with epaulets, patch pockets, button cuffs, and belted. The jacket may be made in twill of polyester and cotton, and the trousers in flare-bottom or straight-bottom jeans of polyester and rayon in navy blue or tan. Designer jeans have become especially popular for casual wear and may be made of 100 percent cotton or cotton/polyester blends. (See Fig. 18.12.)

A word of caution in selecting the correct size (see Table 18.4) for permanent-press garments: be sure the garment is comfortable. If it is not, select a larger size because when man-made fibers are heat-set for durable press, a crease mark will remain when seams are let out.

Fabrics for casual slacks can be woven or knitted. Woven types include blends of polyester and cotton, nylon and cotton, or 100 percent cotton. For winter, the fabric may be a blend in which there is some wool or 100 percent wool.

Men like polyester and wool worsted blends because these blends have inherent wrinkle-resistant properties and durability and hold their shape well. When acrylic fibers are blended with wool, the acrylic gives strength, crease and shrink resistance, minimum-care properties, and dimensional stability. Nylon

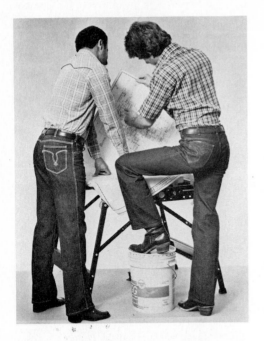

Figure 18.12 Stretch denim jeans (78 percent cotton, 22 percent nylon) with Western detailing are worn here with a plaid Western shirt and a short-sleeved shirt. (Photo courtesy of Levi Strauss & Co.)

when blended with wool for boys' pants gives increased strength and abrasion resistance. (See Fig. 18.13 for an example of a casual sportswear style.)

Boys also wear slacks and sports jackets. Madras, seersucker, and cords are appropriate for summer, whereas flannel and tweed are typical winter materials. The toddler wears overalls of corduroy, cord, denim, or seersucker. For rough play, boys wear jeans like their fathers'.

Fit of Slacks

No matter whether slacks are tailored, casual, hip-fitting, fitted at the waist, cuffed, or uncuffed, they will fit properly and be comfortable if there is[8]

1. Accurate sizing at the waist.
2. Proper length of inseam and outseam.
3. No puckering in the cuff.
4. Correct length (touch top of shoes for straight pants and top of heel for flared pants) and proper fit by hanging straight from the hips.
5. Correct depth of crotch for comfort.
6. Room for uninhibited movement and for sitting comfortably, increasingly realized by the use of stretch fabric. This is often achieved by the use of a small percentage of spandex, such as Lycra.

[8]"Today's Fashions in Men's Wear."

Table 18.4 Jean Sizes[a]

Inseam		Waist							
	In. Cm	32 81	33 84	34 86	36 91	38 96.5	40 102	41 104	44 112
In.	Cm								
29	74			X	X	X	X	X	
30	76		X	X	X	X	X	X	
31	79		X	X	X	X	X	X	X
32	81		X	X	X	X	X	X	X
34	86		X	X	X	X			

[a]The X's indicate the combinations of inseam and waist normally made available.

Active Sportswear

The word "active" as used here means that the man is to be a participant in a sports event. However, there are so many active sports in which men and boys participate that a discussion of each one and the attire appropriate for it would

Figure 18.13 A twill jacket of polyester/wool, gingham shirt, and polyester/wool pants make up an authentic Western look in casual wear. (Photo courtesy of Men's Fashion Association/Stetson.)

Figure 18.14 Swimwear coordinates. (Photo courtesy of Catalina.)

be impossible. Accordingly, only the attire for the following sports will be considered: jogging, swimming, golf, and skiing.

Jogging

Running or jogging clothes vary according to both the climate and the season. In warm climates and seasons, a loose boxer-type short is comfortable for strenuous physical activity and is worn with a knitted sports shirt of cotton or cotton and polyester blend. Some runners prefer the protective and absorptive knitted "warm-up" pants and sweaters for both cold- and hot-weather seasons. Cotton and cotton/polyester blends are the two most popular fibers.

Swimming

Swim trunks are shorts in varied lengths. Men's and boys' styles are similar. They may be boxer style with belt, zip front with tab closing, and have a drawstring or stretch waist. A loose style is most comfortable. Many styles have an inside lining and tricot-knit supporter.[9] A fully lined trunk wears longer and keeps its shape after swimming. Fabrics for men and boys are similar: polyester 65 percent/35 percent stretch-knit nylon and 100 percent polyester double knit. These modern fabrics are considered machine washable in warm water and tumble dried.

The swimwear garment (see Fig. 18.14) should not cramp the swimmer's movement, yet should give support; it should dry quickly and have colors that are fast to light, to salt water, and to chlorine in pools. Sizes of trunks are based on waist measurements. Consult the care label for washing instructions.

---

[9]The surfing trunk is especially styled for the sport of surfing.

Golf

Slacks in woven or knitted stretch and a sport shirt and/or sweater are comfortable for this sport. A snap- or zip-front flannel-lined or unlined nylon taffeta jacket is worn in colder rainy weather. A solid-color polyester blazer with plaid or checked pants is also appropriate. Shorts may be worn instead of slacks during the summer.

Skiing and Other Cold-Weather Activities

Skiing is a winter sport that has become so popular that special equipment and attire are essential. A water-repellent jacket of the parka type is desirable.

The parka, a long, lightweight jacket for cold-weather wear, is commonly hooded.[10] While originally a pullover, it now is designed in jacket form with a front zipper. For warmth, it does not depend on weight or thickness of material but rather on trapping body heat so that the heat remains around the body. The outer shell is usually nylon or a mixture of cotton and nylon or polyester. It is treated with a water-resistant finish. (See Chapter 7.) A virtually waterproof fabric called Gore-tex is now available treated with a fluorocarbon finish with tiny holes too small for water to penetrate but large enough for vapors of perspiration to escape. A similar fabric may be used for the pants of the complete outfit.

The insulating material is ideally either goose or duck down, both of which are light, fluffy, and highly resilient. But the price is very high, so adequate substitutes are commonly used. One such substitute is a combination of down and feathers, but down lumps up when wet or even when damp and must be dried carefully after use. Accordingly, a fill of polyester, such as DuPont's Hollofill and Celanese's Polorguard, is used; these do not deflate like down and dry more quickly. A newer material is 3M's Thinsulate, which combines polyester fill with olefin fiber that traps more air than polyester alone and needs a layer of fill that is thinner than that otherwise required.[11]

To ensure warmth, the design of the parka is important. The hood should be insulated, and the body should close tightly at the collar, front, waist, bottom, and wrists. A heavy nylon zipper is desirable. Pants to supplement the outfit should have an inside storm cuff of nylon and elastic that fits over the boot to keep out snow and cold. Zippers at the sides are a convenience in dressing.

Work Clothes

For hard work as well as for general sportswear, men prefer overalls or jeans (sometimes with jackets to match). Since the prime requisites of these garments are durability and comfort, fabrics such as cotton/polyester twill and cotton/poly-

---

[10]See *Consumer Reports*, November 1981, p. 642, for further details.

[11]Down garments for both men and women can be cleaned best by the professional cleaner, but home washing is possible where manufacturers' instructions are followed carefully.

ester denim (usually navy blue warps and white fillings) are used. Denim overalls with bibs are especially designed for painters, carpenters, iron workers, and welders and are considered *avant* (advanced) fashion by some style setters.

For less arduous work, a work shirt of luster twill described previously may be matched to heavy pants of the same material. Stretch fabrics of 65 percent polyester/35 percent cotton are used for both the work shirt and the pants. A one-piece, long-sleeved work suit is both comfortable and absorbent when made of all cotton or cotton/polyester. This garment may be worn over shirt and pants.

Overalls and jeans are measured by the size of the waist and inseam. For the one-piece garment, often called a coverall, the chest measurement should be added to that of the waist and inseam. The waist is measured over the pants without a belt; the inseam is the measurement from the crotch to the desired length. The coverall, too, can be considered sportswear when it is made in less durable fabric and features decorative trim, such as oversized industrial zippers, monogramming, and fancy finishing.

School Clothes

For the schoolboy who gives his clothes very hard wear and the young man who works his way through college, sturdy tweeds, sharkskin, or worsteds (cheviot, covert, or serge in all wool or blends with polyesters and acrylics) are appropriate, for they give him his money's worth in service and comfort. Poplins, cotton twills, corduroys, and denims are also durable fabrics.[12]

Outer Coats and Jackets

For outerwear, men and boys wear coats or jackets in various styles.

Topcoats

A topcoat, which is generally worn in fall and spring, and in warm climates all winter, differs from the overcoat in the weight of the fabric used. The topcoat of 13 to 20 ounces per square yard has virtually replaced the heavier 23-ounce cloth. With a zip-out lining of 70 percent acrylic/30 percent modacrylic, or 50 percent polyester/35 percent rayon, this coat can be worn as an all-weather coat for at least three seasons of the year in a moderate climate. The coat proper may be made of water-repellent poplin, gabardine, 100 percent polyester with acrylic-coated inner surface, 50 percent polyester/50 percent cotton, or 80 percent polyester/20 percent combed cotton. Actually, the all-weather coat with an acrylic zip-out lining has virtually replaced the topcoat. Little boys and youths also wear the all-weather coat. It may be in the Balmacaan style with raglan sleeves or the double-breasted trench style with belt. (See Fig. 18.15.)

---

[12]See the glossary in this chapter.

Figure 18.15 A taupe wool British warmer topcoat over a plaid wool suit typifies warmth and elegance in business wear. (Photo courtesy of Men's Fashions Association/Daks.)

Overcoats

An overcoat is usually identified with cold-weather wear. Cashmere (100 percent) or cashmere and wool, camel and wool, fleece, heavy tweeds, reversible double cloth, worsted covert, and melton are found in men's overcoats. Furlike fabrics may be used for the outside or as collars and for linings. The length of a topcoat or overcoat depends on the weather conditions in which it will be worn and how it becomes the wearer.

Overcoats vary little in styling, color, and fabric from season to season. The sport coat such as the duffle coat is made of rainwear and overcoat fabrics, and in many cases replaces the overcoat in male attire.

Rainwear

Probably the all-weather coat should be considered the most popular garment for men's rainwear, with water- and stain-repellent finishes. Since these finishes differ in efficiency, one should read the label carefully for specific data on performance. The familiar finishes like Scotchgard and Zepel are chemical finishes given the fabric before the garment is constructed. Such treatments retain their repellency through several washings or dry cleanings. Liquids that are water- or oil-based can often be blotted off the fabric. They leave no mark. Water or cleaning solvent will often remove a stubborn stain without

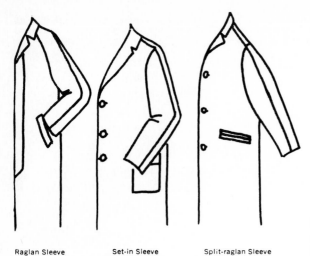

Raglan Sleeve   Set-in Sleeve   Split-raglan Sleeve

Figure 18.16 Sleeve types in rainwear and outerwear. (Courtesy of Celanese Fibers Marketing Co.)

leaving a ring. One should realize that fabrics so finished are water-repellent and not waterproof. The former type has the pores of the weave open so the skin can "breathe." The latter type has closed pores and is, therefore, hot. Waterproofing rainwear does not prevent shrinkage, as many customers have thought. The outer fabric, if not preshrunk or otherwise stabilized, tends to shrink more than the lining, with puckering and excessive fullness in the lining when dry cleaned and steam finished. (Figure 18.16 illustrates sleeve types in rainwear and outerwear.)

Boys and students wear vinyl parkas for rainwear. They may have adjustable drawstring hoods. Since these raincoats are waterproof, air holes under the arms provide ventilation. A waterproof suit with hood can be worn for work or sport. It may be nylon with polyurethane coating that makes it lightweight and stronger than rubber or neoprene-coated rainwear. It resists both oils and chemicals and will not stiffen in cold weather. Its seams are electrothermo-welded.

Knitted fabrics of 100 percent textured polyester are comfortable, wrinkle-resistant, and durable for rainwear.

Casual Coats

These are leisure types of coats suitable for all occasions. They are more casual than a sport coat, dressier than a jacket. This type of coat may be worn with a turtleneck or sport shirt and tie for summer. A cotton and acetate seersucker or a textured polyester is appropriate.

For cool weather, the rugged "bush coat" in Western style resembling an old rancher's jacket may be worn. It may be made of stitch-trimmed cotton sateen in waist or hip length. It usually has flap patch pockets with buttons and a snap front with shirred elastic waist in back. Another ranch style may be made of split leather (nontextile) with leather buttons and an acrylic pile body lining, sleeves lined with acetate over fiber batting, and collar of acrylic pile on a cotton back. A variation of the ranch-style coat is the split cowhide shirt jacket with nylon body and sleeve lining. Trimming may consist of white stitching around the collar, a front snap closing, cuffs, and patch pockets.

Outer Jackets

Most of these jackets consist of a nylon shell (outer fabric) that may be coated for water repellency and lined with a deep acrylic pile. Polyester/cotton in chambray with a denim look on one side is reversible. A nylon quilted to a polyester fiber-filled inner lining is on the other side.

Sizes are

Regular	5'7" to 5'11" (1.7 to 1.8 m)
Tall	5'11" to 6'3" (1.8 to 1.9 m)
Extra tall	6'3" to 6'7" (1.9 to 2.0 m)

A waist-length, pile-lined, or unlined jacket of denim with or without a pile-lined vest can top jeans in a Western-style outfit, a popular style found throughout both mens' and boys' wear classifications.

Windbreakers and battle or bomber jackets are usually made from rainwear or skiwear fabrics.

Fitting Overcoats and Outer Jackets

Rainwear and outerwear are easier to fit properly than are suits and jackets. A good rule is to have adequate room in the shoulders when worn over other garments. When the buttons are closed, there should be no strain on the fabric. Sleeves should cover the jacket sleeves.

Linings

Linings for suits, overcoats, all-weather coats, and jackets must be durable, attractive, and easy to slip on. Fabrics in satin weave with short floats or twill constructions in rayon, acetate, silk, nylon, or polyester offer attractive appearance and slip on easily. An acetate warp and rayon filling is a relatively inexpensive lining. Due to abrasion, this fabric often wears out before the suiting proper. Satins, sateens, brocades, and twills are common lining materials. For rainwear, a water-repellent shell with polyester lining is serviceable. All-weather and ranch-style coats often have zip-out acrylic pile linings. Suit pockets are usually lined with a closely woven cotton twill (not heavily sized in good grades). All cotton linings should be preshrunk and colorfast.

Interfacings for suits and coats are, for the most part, shrinkage controlled, and some are machine washable. Better suits have coat fronts lined with a good quality of hair canvas. The shoulders are lined with a fine haircloth covered with flannel or thin felt. Interlinings for collars are made of firm linen. Armholes are taped with thin, strong, preshrunk tape. Fine, soft, flexible padding that does not feel bulky composes the shoulder padding.

Canvas interfacing for sportswear is sheer and may be made of 60 percent cotton/40 percent spun rayon. A nonwoven fabric can be obtained in several weights for this purpose. There are also iron-on interfacings that are both woven and nonwoven, such as Staflex and Pellonite.

Since interlinings are intended to give warmth to the garment, an all-wool woven fabric is highly desirable.

SUMMARY

The increasing use of blends in men's and boys' wear has changed the fabric picture in this area. When wool was plentiful at a moderate price, suits, jackets, slacks, and overcoats were made of all wool. As a general rule, one finds summer clothing made of the man-made fibers, often blended with cotton. For winter, nylon, acrylic, and modacrylic furlike fabrics are to be found almost exclusively in sportswear. An acrylic sweater is the rule rather than the exception. Even in winter suits, sports jackets, and slacks, one finds polyester, acrylic, nylon, and triacetate often blended with wool.

Since knitted fabrics are comfortable because of their stretch, wrinkle resistance, and ease of care, the knitted construction has become popular. Knitted fabrics when made of man-made fibers do not stretch out of shape when washed or dry-cleaned.

It is advisable to save the care label attached to the garment in case the article does not perform in use as claimed. The garment should then be returned to the store.

PROJECTS

1. Plan a complete wardrobe for a boy age twelve who is going to a summer camp in New England. Give names and quantities of the articles needed, the fabrics of which each item is made, and approximate retail prices of each.
2. Assume you are planning a weekend skiing outing. You will stay at a ski lodge for two nights.
   (a) List the articles of apparel in the quantities that you would need to take with you.
   (b) Give the names of the fabrics used in each garment and the approximate retail prices.
3. Plan a wardrobe for a male college student who is going to attend a small campus college in Minnesota.
   (a) List the articles of apparel in the quantities that will be required.
   (b) Give the names of the fabrics used in each garment and approximate retail prices.

4. A blazer is advertised as having the following fiber content: polyester/nylon/rayon.
   (a) What particular attribute does each fiber add to the utility of the blazer.
   (b) Since the percentages of each fiber in a garment do not have to be revealed in the ad but must normally appear on the label, locate in a store or stores two blazers composed of two or more fibers. Then estimate the advantages of the blends and suggest the lowest ratio of any one fiber to make its presence significant.

GLOSSARY

A-line The style of garment that flairs from the top down, like the letter A.

Balbriggan A tubular knitted fabric of all-cotton or blend for winter sports and underwear. Origin: Ireland.

Balmacaan (named after an estate near Inverness) Swagger-style coat with slash pockets and no belt. It has a raglan sleeve and military collar. Fabrics used are gabardine, tweed, and cashmere (in solid colors for dress).

Barathea A silk, rayon, and cotton or rayon and wool mixed fabric with a pebbly texture in a fine woven design resembling a brick wall. It is used for ties, women's dresses, and trimmings.

Batiste A very sheer muslin used for men's summer shirts. See the glossary in Chapter 17.

Belting A heavy cotton, rayon, silk, or mixed fabric with large fillingwise ribs. It may be knitted. See *webbing*.

Blazer A casual sport-type jacket with metal, pearl or leatherlike buttons on the front closing and cuffs. Suede or flannel are popular fabrics.

Box coat A single- or double-breasted straight-hanging coat with notch or peak lapels. It generally has a regulation sleeve. Occasionally, it is half-belted in back.

Broadcloth See the glossary in Chapter 17.

Brocade Used for ties, loungewear, vests, and robes. See the glossary in Chapter 17.

Burlap A coarse rough fabric often called gunny sacking, made of jute, hemp, or cotton. It is used as interlining in men's suits. This is a poorer fabric than hair canvas for the purpose.

Camel's hair The soft lustrous underhair of a camel. Light tan to brownish black. Often combined with wool or acrylic fibers.

Canvas A firm, heavy cotton or linen fabric. The unbleached fabric is used for coat fronts, lapels, and linings of men's suits. Hair canvas for interlinings is made of goat's hair and wool.

Cashmere A fabric made of soft fibers of the Indian Kashmir goats that may be combined with sheep's wool. It is used for men's sweaters, scarfs, and coats. See Chapter 12.

Cavalry twill See *elastique*.

Challis Lightweight wool or man-made fibers for a tie. See the glossary in Chapter 17.

Chambray See the glossary in Chapter 17.

Chesterfield (adapted from the style worn by Lord Chesterfield). It has a very long skirt, single- or double-breasted, with or without a velvet collar.

Cheviot A woolen or worsted with a slightly rough texture in a twill weave. It is used for suits and coats.

Chinchilla A men's overcoating. See the glossary in Chapter 17.

Chino cloth   A twill-weave cotton originally used for slacks, sport shirts, and summer army uniforms. It is made of two-ply cotton combed yarns, is of vat-dyed khaki color, and is mercerized and Sanforized.

Corduroy   A pile fabric with wales warpwise used for jackets, slacks, sport shirts, and bathrobes.

Covert   A medium-heavy cotton or wool fabric in twill weave. It originally had a flecked appearance because one of the ply yarns was white and the other one colored; now it is generally made in solid color (in wool or mixtures). Wool covert may be used for suits, topcoats, raincoats and uniforms; cotton covert is used for work clothes.

Crochet knit   Machine-knitted tie fabric made to resemble hand knitting.

Cummerbund   A wide fabric belt that fastens in the back, worn with a tuxedo evening suit.

Denim   See the glossary in Chapter 17.

Donegal tweed   A thick woolen tweed in plain or twill weave with a blend of colors in the filling yarn. Originally hand-woven in Donegal County, Ireland.

Drill   A heavy, durable twilled cotton suitable for slacks, uniforms, overalls, and work shirts.

Dungaree   A heavy, coarse cotton or blended twill fabric woven from colored yarns. Heavier than jean.

Elastique   A firmly woven, clear-finished worsted with a steep double twill that is used for riding breeches, army uniforms, and slacks. It is similar to cavalry twill.

End-to-end   A colored warp yarn alternating with a white warp yarn; fillings are white. There is end-to-end broadcloth and end-to-end chambray, which is frequently sold as end-to-end madras. It is synonymous with *end-on-end* or *end-and-end*.

Faille   A tie fabric with fillingwise ribs. See the glossary in Chapter 17.

Fedora   A soft felt hat with crown creased lengthwise.

Flannel   See the glossary in Chapter 17. Also see *flannelette*. See *outing flannel* in this glossary.

Foulard   Soft, lightweight silk, mercerized cotton, or rayon fabric in fine twill weave used for men's ties and women's dresses. It is frequently sold as surah.

Gabardine   Steep-twilled wool, cotton, or rayon mixed or blended fabric, on which the back is flat. It is used for sport shirts, slacks, coats, and suits.

Haircloth   A stiff, wiry cloth of cotton with a mohair or horsehair filling. It is used for interfacing and stiffening.

Harris tweed   Fabric identified by the label "Harris tweed," which is required as a protective device by the British association of that name. Originated in the Isle of Harris and other islands of the Hebrides group. Originally, hand-woven and dyed with color pigments that were cooked over peat fires by cottagers—hence the distinctive odor.

Jean   See the glossary in Chapter 17.

Jersey   See the glossary in Chapter 13.

Macclesfield   Hand-woven silk or rayon fabric with small overall Jacquard patterns. Macclesfield, England, is the town of origin. See *Spitalfields*.

Madras   A muslin shirting with a woven-in pattern or stripe in balanced count. The designs may be dobby or Jacquard. White-on-white madras has a white figure on a white ground. Indian madras has rather subdued colors, usually in plaid design.

Melton   See the glossary in Chapter 17.

Mesh   Used for summer sport shirts and underwear. See the glossary in Chapter 17.

Mogadore   A corded silk or rayon fabric with wide ridges and often with wide stripes that is used for ties.

Moleskin finish   A cotton fleece-lined with close, soft, thick nap that is used for underwear in cold climates.

Outing flannel   A lightweight, soft plain- or twill-weave cotton fabric generally napped on both sides, often with stripes. It is used for pajamas, interlinings, and diapers.

Oxford   See the glossary in Chapter 17.

Parka   A lightweight cold-weather jacket dependent on trapped air to keep the body warm.

Percale   A muslin used for inexpensive shirts, shorts, and pajamas. See the glossary in Chapter 17.

Piqué   Used for shirts. See the glossary in Chapter 17.

Plush velour   A pile-weave fabric with especially long shaggy pile, used for robes and loungewear.

Pongee   Suitable for scarfs, sport shirts, and pajamas. See the glossary in Chapter 17.

Poplin   Used for shirts, ski jackets, and sports jackets. See the glossary in Chapter 17.

Raincoat   A water-repellent or waterproof coat usually of poplin or gabardine.

Rep   A heavily ribbed fabric in silk, rayon, cotton, wool, or a mixture. Fabric may be solid or striped. It is used for ties, robes, drapery, and upholstery.

Sateen   A cotton fabric in the satin weave. It is usually mercerized and is used for linings, draperies, comforters.

Satin   Silk or man-made fabric in the satin weave. It has a smooth, lustrous surface, because the warp or filling floats. It is used for linings of coats, jackets, facings, and ties. See satin crepe in the glossary in Chapter 17.

Serge   Used for men's suits and slacks. See the glossary in Chapter 17.

Shantung   See the glossary in Chapter 17.

Sharkskin   A worsted fabric originally made in two colors. It is so called because it resembles leather sharkskin in durability. Now made in glen plaids, stripes, bird's-eye, and nail-head patterns; it is used for men's and women's suits, coats, and slacks.

Spitalfields   An English town, home of Huguenot weavers, now a lace-making center. The hand-woven Jacquard silk Spitalfields tie originated here.

Tank top   A snug-fitting, knitted garment, styled like a man's T-shirt. It may be worn as a top with pants. Named for tank suit or swim suit.

Trench coat   The officer's coat worn during World War I. It is double-breasted and belted. It has a high-closing collar and shoulder flaps.

Tropical   A plain-weave, lightweight summer suiting in worsted or blends with man-made fibers; it is also used for women's suits.

T-shirt   A knitted cotton undershirt with short sleeves that may be worn for sports or work without an outer garment.

Tweed   A rough-surfaced woolen, usually yarn-dyed. It is generally twill or a variation in men's wear and is used for coats, suits, jackets, and slacks.

Unfinished worsted   A suiting fabric in twill weave, finished with a nap longer than that of other worsteds.

Webbing   A strong, tightly woven narrow fabric for straps or belts.

White-on-white   A fabric in any fiber mixture or blend that has a white woven-in design on a white background.

Wool broadcloth   A smooth, silky napped woolen in twill weave. Nap obliterates the weave. It is used for men's dinner jackets and formal evening wear—also for women's coats and suits.

Woolen   A class of wool fabrics made of short fibers of varied lengths and carded yarns.

Worsted   A class of wool fabrics made of long fibers and combed yarns.

Worsted flannel   See *flannel,* in the glossary in Chapter 17.

Chapter 19

HOME FURNISHINGS TEXTILES

Home furnishings textiles, also called linens and domestics, as well as household textiles, have broad general usage both on the home front and in commercial and institutional use. They dry dishes and bodies and cover beds and tables. Wherever people furnish a living environment, one finds home furnishings textiles—at home, in hotels, motels, hospitals, college dormitories, and in a host of other places. The trend in the production and shipment in the United States of the chief home furnishings textiles appears in Fig. 19.1.

In small retail establishments, one buyer generally has charge of all home furnishings textiles. Larger stores have two buyers, usually one for domestics and linens and another for blankets and bedspreads. Even larger department, chain, and mass merchandising stores may have a buyer for each of the major product classifications. A typical merchandise classification used in retailing follows:

For linens:

1. Towels (bathroom, beach, and kitchen and kitchen accessories)
2. Shower curtains
3. Bathroom ensembles
4. Table linen/damask (cloths and sets, placemats, doilies, runners, napkins)
5. Embroidery and lace (for fancy linen)

For domestics:

1. Sheets and pillowcases, yard goods (most stores no longer stock sheeting by the yard)
2. Mattress pads

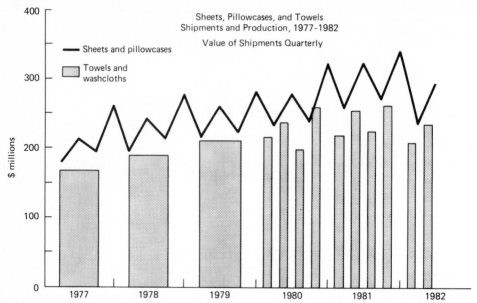

Figure 19.1 Shipments and production of sheets, pillowcases, and towels, 1977 to 1982. (Courtesy of the American Textile Manufacturers Institute.)

3. Blankets and blanket covers
4. Comforters and quilts (also covers for these products)
5. Bedspreads

THE LINEN CLASSIFICATION

Towels

Towels, which make up a large category in many retail stores, are an essential part of any linen closet and should be chosen with the same care as sheets, pillow slips, and other home furnishings textiles. (Towels will be discussed according to the above linen classification.)

Bath Towels

Bath towels come in terry cloth and are usually made of a blend of cotton with polyester selvage yarns or of 100 percent cotton yarns. An insignificant number have some linen in their construction. (See *friction towels*.) Unusual textures and decorative effects can be produced in terry cloth, since this fabric is characterized by a surface of looped pile. It is this looped-pile construction that increases absorbency; an increase in the number of loops will increase the absorbency of the towel. ("Terry cloth" and its construction are explained in Chapter 5.)

The construction, when on the loom, consists of a formation of ground warps in tension, arranged alternately with pile warps that form loops as tension is released. By removing pile warps from a section of the cloth, the ground weave is visible. In a three-pick towel, the filling yarns are grouped in threes: two fillings are shot through the same shed and one filling is then shot through to interlace with the ground warps. This construction of fillings grouped in threes denotes a three-pick and are of medium grade. One- and two-pick towels are considered of poor quality; towels of more than three picks are better than average. The quality of a terry cloth depends upon the following factors:

1. *Number and length of the pile loops.* The purpose of pile loops is to increase the surface area and thereby increase the absorptive power of the towel. For this purpose, loops should be reasonably close together, soft, and not twisted too tightly. A bath towel will have over 500,000 loops and 5 miles of yarn in it.

In more expensive towels, pile loops are longer. Long loops in double-thread construction improve absorptive quality, but they catch and pull out easily. (For an explanation of double thread, *see strength of yarns.*) On the other hand, too short loops do not increase the surface area sufficiently. A loop about one-eighth inch deep seems to be generally the best.

So-called "friction towels" are made with all-linen pile or a row of linen pile alternating with a cotton pile.

2. *The tightness of the weave.* Some loops pull out very easily in laundering and in use, so that the towel become unattractive and weak. The greater the pickage, the less likely are loops to pull out. A groundwork of twill weave is more durable than a groundwork of plain or basket weave. A tight weave with balanced count is important.

3. *The strength of the yarns.* The tensile strength of the ground warp should be great enough to withstand the tension of the loom and the strain met in use; so the better towels are made with ground warps of ply yarns. Proper balance in tensile strength between ground warps and fillings is equally important. Poorer towels are made by the *single-thread* method; better grades are made by the *double-thread* method, in which each loop is made of two parallel threads not twisted together. These two threads come out of the same space between two filling threads. Double threads provide durability and, particularly, absorbency.

A more recent development has been the addition of polyester yarns in the warp direction, thereby increasing the overall durability of the towel, especially in the towel selvage. Most manufacturers have converted to polyester/cotton blends for ground warps, while using cotton yarns for pile (or surface warps).

4. *The selvage.* It should be firm and even. It is important that filling yarns bind in the warps used for the selvage. Sometimes only one filling out of three goes out to bind the edges of the fabric. Since yarns used in towels have to be loosely twisted to be absorbent, it is imperative that all fillings continue out to, and loop around, the very edge.

5. *Workmanship.* The hems at both ends of the towel should be even (all raw edges should be turned under at least one-quarter inch), carefully sewed with comparatively short, regular stitches, and finished at the sides so they will not pull out.

Although a consumer purchaser cannot mutilate a towel to determine pickage, number of threads, and strength of yarns, one can observe the closeness and length of the loops, tightness of weave, firmness and evenness of selvages, and workmanship. Features such as pickage, double thread, ply ground warp, and twist of yarn are important specifications for a retail store buyer to understand. A project to determine these features can be carried out by students who have access to a textile laboratory.

The attractiveness of a bath towel has been greatly enhanced by the introduction of interesting solid colors, prints, and sheared loops on one side of the towel. When so done, the fabric is called velour terry or a sheared towel. Shearing tends to reduce the absorbency ability of the sheared side of the towel; thus, it is advisable to use the unsheared side for more effective drying and blotting. Towels may be monogrammed in schiffli embroidery. After many years of all-white and color-bordered towels, solid colors appeared, followed by gaily printed fabrics and elaborate Jacquard-woven designs. (See Figs. 19.2 and 19.3.) Solid colors that mix or match with prints and two-tone effects are featured. All-

Figure 19.2 Marimekko towel designs for Dan River. (Photo by Robert Grant for Dan River.)

Figure 19.3 Paddington™ Bear (Eden Toys, Inc.) towels by Dan River in a variety of sizes. (Photo by Robert Grant for Dan River.)

white towels, however, are still an important part of basic stock and in decorating are used much the same way as colors.

Sizes. Bath towels are made in a range of sizes to please any personal taste. Medium sizes for the bath are 20 × 40 and 22 × 44 inches; the largest are 24 × 46 and 32 × 64, although beach towels, which come in solid colors and Jacquard prints, are even larger. Probably the largest volume of business is done in the 20 × 40 and 22 × 44 sizes, because medium-sized towels are less expensive than the large size, lighter in weight, and easier to handle. Heavy towels weigh more and thereby increase the drying time. Also, small- or medium-sized towels are easiest for children to manage. Baby's bath towels come in size 36 × 36 inches and washcloths in sizes 9 × 9 inches.

Consumers should be aware of possible shrinkage before purchasing towels. Shrinkage occurs for the most part in the first five launderings; after that, it is negligible. For some towels, residual shrinkage can be as high as 10 percent, although this represents but a fraction of manufactured towels in the United States. An average dimensional change—shrinkage—is in the 3 to 4 percent range. Laundering with an adequate amount of detergent or soap in warm water is recommended, followed by two rinses in clean warm water. Fabric softeners used to increase the softness of hand should be sparingly used, as they tend to reduce absorbency with overuse. Towels should be shaken before they are hung to dry, preferably on a windy day; tumble drying improves absorption by fluffing the loops.

Hand Towels

Terry cloth is also a popular fabric for the smaller hand towel. They appear in sizes 16 × 26 and 18 × 36 inches and in fingertip size 11 × 18 inches. When made in colors and patterns that match bath towel and washcloth, they compose a set, often sold as a gift item. Huck face towels may be made wholly of cotton or of linen or of cotton warp and linen or rayon filling. Cottons and mixtures are less expensive than are linens, but the former are more apt to become linty after several washings.

The huckaback or honeycomb weave is done on the dobby loom. The grade of the fabric is determined by the quality of the fibers and of the yarns used and the construction. At present, very few stores carry huck towels, and 100 percent linen hucks are imported.

Washcloths

Since the primary purpose of a washcloth is to give friction for cleansing the skin, a terry cloth with loops on both sides is better than a knitted back. Knitted washcloths are softer than woven ones, but they are more likely to stretch out of shape, although a locking stitch will prevent this problem from occurring. (Knitted washcloths are appropriate for infants.) Durability depends upon firm, even-weave, stitching of edges so that corners will not fray or stitching unravel. Washcloths range in size from 8 to 13 inches square.

Dish Towels

Regular dish towels may be made of (1) cottonade, a coarse, heavy cotton resembling woolens and worsteds in weave and finish; (2) crash, a rough-textured cotton or linen in plain weave with novelty yarns; (3) damask, a cotton fabric in Jacquard pattern; (4) glass cloth, a cotton fabric with smooth, hard-twisted yarns that do not lint; (5) Osnaburg, a plain, strong cotton fabric with a crashlike appearance, having very coarse yarns in both warp and filling and made of low-grade, short-staple cotton; (6) linen crash, a rather heavy, plain-weave linen made from tow yarns; and (7) terry cloth. Kitchen towels may be a two-fiber blend of linen and rayon or linen and cotton or a three-fiber blend of cotton, rayon, and linen in terry cloth.

Crash is excellent for dish and glass towels. It has a hard texture that prevents it from linting and is still rough enough to be absorbent. Linen crash is preferable to cotton for dish towels because it does not lint badly, does not seem to wet quickly, and dries faster than cotton does. Linen crash towels are generally made of rather poorly hackled tow yarns. These yarns are naturally coarse and bumpy; hence, they give the desired texture. Cotton crash is also made of irregular, coarse yarns that are spun to resemble linen. Short fibers are singed in the finishing process to prevent linting as much as possible. Beetling is also used to make cotton resemble linen. An attractively printed linen crash makes an effective "show towel" (one to be seen but seldom, if ever, used).

A fairly high, well-balanced count—comparable to terry cloth in tensile strength of warp and filling—and workmanship are important for dish towels. Although the designs of crashes are not so intricate as those of terry towel fabrics, almost any color desired can be found to harmonize with a kitchen ensemble. Crash toweling can be purchased by the yard in some stores and by mail order. Ready-made crash dish towels come in sizes 15 × 30, 17 × 32, and 18 × 32 inches.

Pot holders of terry cloth and quilted cottons and quilted mitts for handling hot dishes are usually found in the store near the dish towels.

Glass Towels

Glass towels are intended for drying glasses and thus should be free of lint. They are lighter in weight than regular dish towels. An all-linen crash makes a satisfactory glass towel. Usual sizes of Irish linen glass towels are 20½ × 31½ and 22½ × 33 inches. Glass toweling is also sold by the yard in some fabric and department stores and occasionally through mail-order firms.

Shower Curtains

Since the advent of fashion color and pattern in the bathroom in the early 1950s, shower curtains have become as fashionable as the towels and other bath products they complement. They are made in solid colors, patterns that either match or coordinate with towels, and in novelty patterns that express current fashion. It is wise to keep in mind the limited space in a typical bathroom when selecting a shower curtain, as the proportionateley large size of the curtain (anywhere from 68 × 72 inches to 72 inches square) can create an unbalanced look if an inappropriate pattern is used. Some fabrics of which shower curtains are made are taffeta, satin (in acetate, rayon, nylon, polyester), moiré, cotton and cotton blends, and novelties such as polyester schiffli-embroidered marquisette curtain over a plastic liner.

Fabrics for shower curtains may be either water-resistant (water-repellent) or waterproof. All-plastic curtains (nontextile), plastic-coated fabrics, and cloths with plastic liners are waterproof. Printed all-plastic and plastic-coated shower curtains have become prominent items in a wide variety of patterns in retail stores.

Bathroom Ensembles

Bath and hand towels, washcloths, tank toppers, lid covers, window and shower curtains, and bathmats are sold separately or in sets. A typical set may include bath and hand towels and washcloths. Bathmats are made of terry cloth (pure cotton or cotton blends), chenille, modacrylic, or rubber. Bath rugs are made of nylon and polyester primarily, with only a very small amount in cotton. A dense plush pile is locked with rubber coating to a backing to hold the pile

Figure 19.4 The high-fashion "glitter" look is brought into the area of bedroom and bathroom by Fieldcrest with this two-toned rug with Lurex on either side of a contrasting inset. Center portion is sheared, with the outside frame left in the high-loft weave. Made from 100 percent nylon with Latex Diamondback™. (Photo courtesy of Fieldcrest Mills, Inc.)

tufts in place and to make the rug skid-resistant. Wall-to-wall carpeting also in both nylon and polyester has become increasingly popular in bathroom decor. (See Figs. 19.4 and 19.5.)

Table Linen

People often speak of their "table linen" and their "bed linen," although actually much of it is cotton and blends of cotton, rayon, and polyester. Yet linen is used extensively for dining tablecloths because (1) it looks clean, (2) it is somewhat lustrous, (3) stains can be removed from it easily, and (4) it wears and washes well, retaining its luster and beauty after many washings.

Cloths for Dining Tables

Cloths for dining tables include dinner cloths, banquet cloths, luncheon cloths, dinette and tea sets, placemats, napkins, table pads (made of felt or baize—a loose, plain-weave, napped fabric in imitation of felt—or a quilted material similar to that used for mattress covers), and hot spots (heavy, novelty mesh or doily material placed over pads of cork or made of silver finish).

The chief selling points for the cloths and sets mentioned here are appearance, suitability, serviceability, durability, minimum care, and size. For example, if a customer wants a cloth for a dinette where small children have their meals, the salesperson might show her a screenprinted, cotton woven cloth covered with a coat of vinyl plastic that can be wiped off or a 65 percent polyester/35 percent cotton that is machine washable and durable press. In some instances, a soil-release finish lets stains wash out quickly and thoroughly. A small square cloth, 54 × 54 or even 45 × 45 inches, might suffice. A vinyl-faced laminated cloth would be equally suitable. Placemats of plastic-coated fabric

Figure 19.5 Bathroom ensemble of "Royal Velvet," a quality towel made of 100 percent combed cotton; it is unsheared with a dobby border. Bath carpet, tank and lid covers, and bath rugs, all of 100 percent DuPont nylon by Fieldcrest, are in the same color range as the towels. Here, bath carpeting is used to face the side of the bath in a step arrangement as well as to cover the bathroom floor. (Photo courtesy of Fieldcrest Mills, Inc.)

might also be suggested. (One hundred percent plastic mats are also appropriate, but they are non-textiles.)

Placemats have become varied and imaginative in design and are used for both formal and informal dining. For a patio or barbecue pit, the homemaker might want a light, bright, gay, carefree touch. For indoor dining, one might prefer a richer, more elegant mat. Juvenile placemats should have a design that appeals to the child and can be easily laundered or cleaned.

Table covers for outdoor dining are frequently made of laminated rayon, cotton terry, and flannel-backed polished cotton in solid color, gay prints, checkerboards, and stripes. For informal dining indoors, a solid or printed cotton, rayon and cotton, all-linen crash cloth, or Fiberglas Beta (no-iron, soil-release), with or without napkins, are appropriate. Sizes are 54 × 54, 54 × 72, or 63 × 80 inches.

Luncheon and bridge sets, doilies, runners, and napkins are often made of linen crash cloth. Characteristics to look for in selecting linen cloths for dining are

1. Smooth yarns of even diameter.
2. Count and balance: excellent grade, 80 yarns per square inch; medium grade, 64 yarns per square inch; poor grade, 55 yarns per square inch.

3. Dyes fast to sunlight and to washing.
4. Hems evenly turned and firmly stitched.
5. The amount of sizing. Although good-quality linens are not heavily sized, a little starch may be added in the finish to give the leathery stiffness common to new linens. Flimsy cotton crash is often heavily sized to resemble heavy linen. The friction test will reveal the presence of excessive sizing.
6. Amount of bleaching. Although snow-white linens are beautiful, it is often advisable to buy linen cloth that is not fully bleached when it is purchased. Each time a full-bleached linen is laundered, the chemical bleaches used by the laundry overbleach the cloth, thereby tendering it. To ensure long service, linen cloths should be oyster-bleached (slightly bleached) or silver-bleached (deep cream color) when purchased.
7. Minimum-care finishes, such as durable press and soil release.

Cocktail-size napkins are small, ranging from 5 to 7 inches square to a 5 × 8 inch measurement. Fabrics used are much the same as those in table covers, and fancy styles in embroidery and appliqué are available. Their use has decreased with the increased availability of disposable paper products in a variety of pattern and color.

Textiles Used for Table Linen

With the advent of improved minimum-care finishes, the tablecloth has become more popular for informal as well as for formal dining. (See Figure 19.6.)

For formal dining, a lace cloth of cotton, polyester, or nylon or a cloth of embroidered linen or linen damask is appropriate. Machine-made lace cloths in ivory, ecru, white in Venetian motifs, filet, and novelty patterns can be used. A discussion of laces of various types is to be found at the end of this section.

Damask

Damask tablecloths come in standard sizes, and the choice of size depends on the number of people to be seated at the table. A damask cloth 72 × 90 inches comfortably accommodates eight people; a cloth 82 × 108 inches seats twelve. Banquet cloths are 60 × 116, 72 × 126, or 72 × 144 inches. Dinner napkins generally match the tablecloth and may be 18 or 22 inches square.

Table damasks are pure linen, pure cotton, or mixtures of these fibers. Sometimes rayon is included to make the design more prominent and lustrous. Damasks are made in Jacquard weave with a warp satin design and a filling satin ground. The twill weave is sometimes used for the design and the satin weave for the ground.

From the standpoint of construction, there are two types of damask: simple or single and compound or double. Both types are woven single; the same applies to the type of weave. Single damask has a four-float construction, whereas double damask has a seven-float construction. The count of cloth of double damask is higher than that of single damask (some authorities say double damask should have a count of 180 with at least 50 percent floating yarn).

Figure 19.6 Table linens may actually be made of cotton and blends of cotton, rayon, and polyester. This "table linen" is made of 50 percent polyester and 50 percent cotton. The appearance is lustrous; stains can be removed from it easily; and it wears and washes well, retaining its luster and beauty after many washings. "Songbirds," by Springs Mills, is from the Metropolitan Museum of Art design collection. (Photo courtesy of Springs Industries, Inc.)

Quality of damask. To judge the wearing quality of a damask, the following factors should be considered:

1. *The length of the fibers.* Since damasks are woven in a satin construction necessitating floats, long fibers do not pull out and fuzz as quickly as short ones; and since linen fibers are generally longer than cotton fibers, they are more adaptable to satin weaves.

2. *The evenness of yarns.* If yarns are unevenly spun, then the cloth will be thick and thin in spots. Such a cloth presents a poor appearance and also gives poorer service.

3. *The closeness of the weave.* A loose weave is a weakness in a damask because it allows yarns to slip and thereby wear out the float. A close, firm weave is necessary if a damask is to be durable.

4. *The length of the floats.* Floats in this construction may pass over four to twenty yarns. A float that passes over four yarns is considered short. Although they will wear well, short floats do not give lustrous surface. The longer the float, the greater the light reflection and the more beautiful the cloth. For elaborate leaf and floral designs, a long float (at least eighteen or twenty yarns) is necesary. These allow a great amount of yarn to be exposed to friction on the surface. Consequently, long floats are not durable.

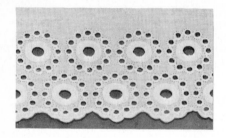

Figure 19.7 Machine embroidery with punchwork. (Photo courtesy of Max Mandel Laces, Inc.)

EMBROIDERY AND LACE

Not only are laces and embroideries used for apparel, but they are also used for the table covers, doilies, scarfs, and trimming of home furnishings textiles.

Embroidery

Embroidery is ornamental needlework done on the fabric itself, whereas lace is a fabric created by looping, interlacing, braiding, or twisting threads. Embroidery can be done by machine (see Fig. 19.7) or by hand. The latter method, if the work is done well, is preferable but generally more expensive than the machine product. Machine embroidery is often rather coarse, and the wrong side may not be well finished. A few common types of embroidery follow:

1. Japanese hand embroidery—large designs.
2. Philippine embroidery—very small designs.
3. Mexican drawnwork—lacy, spiderweb effects.
4. French embroidery—silky looking with small designs.
5. Madeira—floral patterns with punchwork.
6. Appenzell—Swiss embroidery in geometrical punchwork designs.

Much of the eyelet all-over needlework and edges for trimming on tablecloths, curtains, spreads, dresses, lingerie, and blouses is embroidered by a machine called the Schiffli. This machine can embroider almost any design on either woven cloth or net. The machine itself is a double-decker about 15 yards long. It is equipped with boat-shaped shuttles (*schiffli* means "little boat") and needles, and it operates somewhat like a sewing machine. The design is controlled by punched Jacquard cards. Eyelets are punched by a separate operation.

Batiste, lawn, organdy, nylon sheers, cotton piqués, edgings, and flouncings are but a few of the fabrics that may be Schiffli embroidered. Since Schiffli designs are more intricate than swivel, clip spot, or lappet, they are also more expensive.

Lace[1]

This is an important trimming, for it is used for tablecloths, curtains, handkerchiefs, dresses, and underwear. Lace consists of two elements: (1) the pattern, flower, or group, which forms the closer-worked and more solid portion, and (2) the ground or filling, which serves to hold the pattern together. The two main types of laces are "real," or handmade, and machine made. Linen thread is usually used for real lace, but cotton, rayon, nylon, or silk may be used for machine lace. The former is softer, more irregular in mesh and pattern, and more expensive. There are five kinds of real laces: (1) needlepoint, (2) bobbin (pillow), including Duchesse, (3) darned, including some filet lace, (4) crocheted, and (5) knotted. All these patterns are also made or imitated by machine.

Real Laces

Needlepoint lace. The design for needlepoint is drawn on parchment stitched to a backing of stout linen, and the lace is made by filling in the pattern with buttonhole stitches. When the lace is completed, the parchment is removed. Two of the most common needlepoint laces are Venetian and Alençon. See the illustrations on pp. 526–528.

Bobbin lace. Sometimes called pillow lace, the lace design is drawn either on a pillow or on a paper that is placed over the pillow. Small pegs or pins are stuck into the pillow along the design, and a large number of small bobbins of thread are manipulated around the pegs or pins to produce the lace. As the lace is completed, the pins are pulled out and the lace is removed from the pillow. Making pillow lace requires great skill and dexterity, for as many as three hundred bobbins may be needed to make some patterns.

Duchesse. Because of its exquisite large, clothy design, duchesse is the queen of the bobbin laces. Other bobbin laces are Binche, Val, Chantilly, Torchon, and Cluny. (See the illustrations and accompanying descriptions on pp. 526–528.)

Darned lace. When made by hand, the design of darned lace is sewn with thread and needle passed in and out of a square mesh net.

Crocheted lace. When handmade, this is made with a crochet hook, working usually with specially twisted cotton thread. It is a comparatively inexpensive heavy lace. Irish crocheted lace (not necessarily made in Ireland) is typified by a rose or shamrock design that stands out from the background.

Filet lace. Characterized by a flat, geometrical design, this lace may be either crocheted or darned. It is very common for household use, particularly for

[1]See "Lace," *Fairchild's Dictionary of Textiles*, 6th ed. (New York: Fairchild Publications, Inc., 1979).

doilies, runners, antimacassar sets, and tablecloths. It may also be used for dress trimming.

Knotted lace. This is made by twisting and knotting thread by means of a shuttle. When made by passing a shuttle in and out of loops in a thread, it is called *tatting.* It is identified by a circlelike motif and picots around the edge of the motif.

Machine-Made Laces

Nearly all the laces classified as "real laces" can be duplicated by machine with slight variations and simplifications.

Machinery for making looped net was invented about 1764. But the forerunner of the present lace machine, the bobbinet machine, was patented by John Heathcote in the early 1800s and was later modified by several other inventors, one of whom was John Levers, whose name has come down to us via the Levers machine we now use.

Bobbinet. The design is embroidered on a plain hexagonal mesh cotton or rayon net. The embroidery is done primarily by the Levers machine, but the Schiffli machine may be used for certain types, and the net is sometimes embroidered by hand. Bobbinet, which comes in wide widths like dress goods, is often imported from France. Bobbinet is sold by the hole count. To compute hole count, count the actual number of holes to an inch in a straight line; then repeat the count of the last hole and count the holes on the diagonal to an inch. Multiply the first figure by the second figure. (See Fig. 19.8.) The greater the hole count, the finer the quality. Bobbinet, when stiffened, is used for veiling, evening gowns, and dress linings. Nylon bobbinet has become popular.

Tulle. This is similar to bobbinet but is made in silk, rayon, or nylon and has a higher hole count. Tulle is stiffened. The nylon tulle, very sheer and rip-resistant, can be made fireproof, permanently crisp, and resistant to steam or rain.

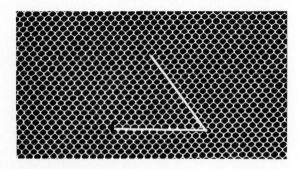

Figure 19.8 In this bobbinet, there are thirteen holes to the inch horizontally and sixteen holes to the inch (counting the corner hole twice) on the diagonal. Therefore, 13 × 16 = 208 hole count of this fabric.

Point d'esprit. Point d'esprit is an embroidered tulle or net. When made by hand, the dots or squares are embroidered into the net with point stitches. Point d'esprit (machine-made) is usualy higher priced than bobbinet of the same grade.

Breton. A heavy thread is used for the design of this embroidered net. When embroidered by hand, the net is sold as *hand run.* This net is used for trimming slips and nightgowns.

Princess. Although real princess lace can be made by bobbins, it is usually an embroidered net made on the Schiffli machine. As an embroidered net, it can be used for bridal gowns and veils and is comparatively inexpensive.

Some of the most common laces, both machine- and handmade, are illustrated in Fig. 19.9.

Uses of Laces

Laces are made in different widths for different uses. For example, a narrow lace with a scalloped edge is used for trimming a baby's dress; a lace with slits or eyelets is so made that ribbon may be run through it. There are seven major uses of laces:[2]

1. *All-over laces.* An all-over lace is a fabric up to 36 inches wide with the pattern repeated over the entire surface. The fabric is cut and sold from the bolt like woven dress goods. The dressmaker cuts it to pattern and makes it up into formal evening, dinner, and cocktail dresses and blouses.
2. *Flouncing.* Flouncing applies to laces 18 to 36 inches wide with a plain edge at the top and a scalloped edge at the bottom of the fabric. It is used for wide ruffles or flounces. Often these flounces are arranged in tiers to form a skirt.
3. *Galloon.* A galloon is a lace up to 18 inches wide with a scalloped edge at top and bottom. It may be used as an insertion between two cut edges of fabric, or it may be appliquéd to a fabric in bands or as a border.
4. *Insertion.* Insertion is a band of lace sewn between two pieces of fabric or on a fabric at the straight top or bottom edges. A variety of insertion is *footing,* which has a straight edge at top and bottom but no pattern. Footing is often used at the bodice or at the bottom hem of a slip.
5. *Beading.* Beading has slots through which ribbon may be run. These slots may be found in edgings or galloons but are much more common in insertions.
6. *Edging.* An edging is a lace never more than 18 inches wide that is straight at the top and scalloped at the bottom. It is sewn to the edge of a dress, gown, blouse, or handkerchief.
7. *Medallion.* A medallion is a lace in a single design that can be appliquéd to a fabric ground for ornamentation. It is sometimes used in the corners of napkins, or towels or as an ornament for a dress.

[2]The first six classifications and their descriptions are adapted from *Lace,* a pamphlet by Max Mandel Laces, Inc.

Carrickmacross, an Irish appliquéd lace with a floral design. The pattern of handmade Carrickmacross is cut from fine cambric and appliquéd to the ground by point stitches. The pattern and ground of machine-made Carrickmacross are made at the same time.

Alençon, a needlepoint lace. Fine loops of thread form the background and produce a double-thread. Natural floral patterns are outlined by heavy threads.

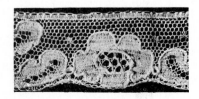

Breton, embroidered net. The design is made of heavy thread embroidered on net. This lace is used for trimming women's underwear.

Chantilly, a bobbin lace made of silk. The pattern is usually a rather simple branch design, but sometimes Chantilly has vine or spray motifs. It usually comes in white or black. This lace has long been a favorite trimming for bridal veils.

Cluny, a rather geometric bobbin lace. The design is so open that the finished product is light and pleasing. Cluny is used to trim dresses, luncheon sets, and so forth.

Figure 19.9 Types of laces.

Duchesse, an exquisite bobbin lace. The design is large and clothy. Brides, or threads, join the various parts of the design. The lace is usually made in wide widths.

Binche, a bobbin lace. Real Binche is made by appliquéing the flat sprig-like design to a rather coarse net ground, the mesh of which resembles a cane chair set. The design and background of machine-made Binche are made at the same time.

Tatting, a knotted lace. The knots are made by passing a shuttle in and out of loops in the thread.

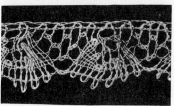

Torchon (beggar's lace), a coarse pillow lace made with a loosely twisted thread. A shell pattern is a common design. It is an inexpensive, common lace—hence the name *beggar's lace*. Machine-made cotton torchon laces are quite durable, and they wash well.

Figure 19.9 Continued.

Val (Valenciennes), a flat bobbin lace with a diamond or lozenge-shaped mesh ground. The lace is worked in one piece, and just one kind of thread is used for the outline of the design and every part of the fabric. The pattern is usually sprig-like or floral. Val comes in narrow widths for trimming babies' garments.

Irish, a fine crocheted lace with rose or clover-leaf patterns that stand out from the background. It is a heavy lace that is comparatively inexpensive. Irish crochet lace is easily made by hand.

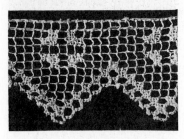

Filet, a darned lace with a square mesh. It is made by darning the thread in and out of the meshes. The pattern and background of machine-made filet are made in the same operation. Filet comes in narrow widths for trimming, and is also made in large pieces such as table covers, runners, and bedspreads.

Point d'esprit, an embroidered tulle or net used to trim evening gowns. The dots or small squares are closely set at regular intervals.

Figure 19.9 Continued.

Venetian point, a needlepoint lace that is sometimes known as *raised point* because the design is thrown into relief by a sort of embroidery or buttonhole stitching. The pattern, in the form of flowers, is rather large, and is united by brides, or bars. When the pattern is in the form of a rose, the lace is called *rose point*. Venetian point is usually wide and quite heavy. In all-over patterns it makes very attractive blouses.

Care of Lace

As was just indicated, lace is important in both clothing and home furnishings. The International Fabricare Institute suggests to consumers the following guidelines for the wear and care of clothing containing lace:[3]

1. Laces snag and tear easily; even your jewelry can snag delicate lace. For this reason, extreme care must be used when wearing lace. Laces are difficult to mend and the mend is usually visible.
2. Lace clothing should have ample side and underarm seams which are well bound. Narrow seams will pull out with strain in wear.
3. Unfinished or machine-stitched buttonholes fray readily.
4. Protect lace, especially silk lace, from perspiration, deodorant, and antiperspirant damage, as this may weaken the fibers.
5. Lace garments should be folded and placed in drawers to relieve points of strain.

DOMESTIC CLASSIFICATION

Sheets and Pillowcases

The word "muslin," as we have noted, is derived from the French word *mousseline*, which in turn originated with the city of Mosul in Mesopotamia. We often hear of *mousseline de soie* (silk muslin), which is a very thin, crisp silk organdy. Muslin is the name commonly applied to various cotton cloths in plain weave ranging in weight from thin batiste and nainsook to heavy sheetings, such as longcloth and percale. The lightweight muslins, called print cloths, have been discussed in Chapter 17 under fabrics for women's apparel; the heavier, sheeting-weight muslins will be discussed here.

Although we speak of "bed linen," it would be difficult to find a home whose occupants use real linen sheets or pillow slips. Most sheetings sold are cotton muslins or blends. There are also nonwoven (disposable) and rubber sheetings, often with a cotton back for babies and the sickroom; acetate and nylon satin; and cotton flannel and cotton blend flannel sheets (used in cold climates and for light summer blankets). Rayon and nylon satin sheets as well as cotton/polyester-blended knits have a wide range of colors that give them gift appeal. Pillowcases with nylon face and slip-resistant back of no-iron polyester, nylon, and cotton reduce the problem of mussing up one's hair-do. All-cotton sheets with permanent-press finishes have recently been introduced for consumers who prefer sheets in natural fibers. Two sheet blends have become quite popular in the United States: the 50/50 and 65/35 polyester and cotton blends. (See Figs. 19.10 and 19.11.) These are weight proportions, and the blending takes place during the spinning preparatory process by combining card slivers at the drawframe. A newer development in sheeting is the cotton sheet with a polyester fiber core, providing the comfort features of cotton and the durability

---

[3]International Fabricare Institute *News Column* (NC–37), February 1982.

Figure 19.10 "Morning," a Marimekko design for Dan River. Sheets are made of 65 percent polyester/35 percent cotton percale. (Photo by Robert Grant for Dan River.)

of polyester. Minimal or no ironing is required, and machine washing and drying are recommended.

There are two kinds of sheet construction—muslin and percale. Percale is the better grade and has the higher thread count. It is known that the typical consumer buys sheets and pillow slips without first consideration of durability. A no-iron finish, size, price, brand, and general appearance are considered, however. In fact, many women know very little about sheets—younger customers especially. For example, few women are aware that the standard

Figure 19.11 "Grace," from the Danville Collection by Dan River, is made of 65 percent polyester/35 percent cotton muslin. (Photo by James Levin for Dan River.)

twin-bed flat sheet size is 66 × 104 inches. When 5- to 6-inch hems are made (3 inches at the top, 2 inches at the bottom), the finished size is 66 × 96 inches. Most mills package sheets with both finished size and torn (unfinished) size on the label.

Sheets are sold today primarily on the basis of design and of the no-iron feature rather than on durability. Consumers want a sheet that is smooth and nonwrinkled after washing and drying and a colored sheet fast to repeated washings. Consumers' Research (CR) believes that the wise consumer would do well to take into consideration the construction and probable life of a sheet.

Wearing Quality of Sheets

How long will a sheet last? The life of a sheet is related to its breaking strength. The USA Standard L22.30.8 calls for a minimum breaking strength of 55 pounds for the 180 (B grade) and 200 (A grade) percales. (See Fig. 19.12.) This standard for new sheets has been lowered from 60 pounds minimum breaking strength to 55 pounds. There is some question whether this standard is too low. However, it should be noted that CR found, in some cases, that a sheet can increase in breaking strength as much as 15 percent after twenty launderings. In other cases, a sheet may lose as much as 10 percent in one direction. But in the CR test of thirteen brands of polyester/cotton blends that originally met the standard of 55 pounds minimum for new sheets, no sheet fell below the standard.

Tests conducted by the International Fabricare Institute (IFI) on polyester/cotton-blended sheets versus all-cotton products provided similar results. Following 175 launderings, the all-cotton sheet was discarded due to product failure; the polyester/cotton sheets were still intact after 300 launderings (the tests were concluded with the three-hundredth cycle).

Two sheets of different brands may be purchased at the same time and be given the same number of washings; yet one sheet may outwear the other. A study of the fibers, yarns, weave, and finish will reveal the reason.

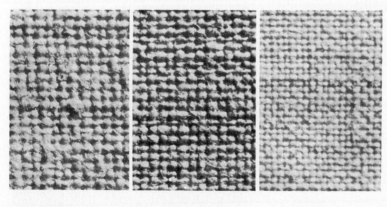

TYPE 128   TYPE 140   TYPE 200

Figure 19.12 Sheetings with grades.

1. Cotton fibers should be of good quality and as long as possible if they are to be spun into regular, even, strong yarn. The best sheets contain cotton fibers at least 1 inch in length. An even yarn will stand washing better than an uneven one. A bumpy yarn may protrude on the surface, and, besides making an unsightly appearance, will be subjected to more friction and wear than will an unprotruding yarn. Uneven yarns are apt to break in laundering and so make a hole in the cloth.

2. To be durable, yarns should be spun tightly. Since most sheets contain fibers that are comparatively short, a tight twist will keep the fibers from pulling out with wear. The tensile strength of tightly spun yarns is greater than that of loosely spun yarns.

3. To be considered "first" or "standard" quality, a sheet should be free from imperfections in the weave, such as thick and thin spots due to uneven yarns. *Run-of-the-mill* means that the defects are due either to imperceptible uneven threads or to little oil spots that occurred in the manufacturing process. These defects do not affect the wearing quality of the sheet. Sheets are marked "seconds" if there are some defects in weave or imperfections in the yarns. All manufacturers have their own rules of what constitutes a second. If a manufacturer's standards are high, then slight flaws will not seriously affect the durability. Such a second, sold at a lower price than first quality, may be an economical purchase.

4. The count is also important. The number of warp and filling yarns to the inch determines the count of the cloth; the proportion of warps to fillings indicates the balance. A high-count cloth with a good balance will generally outwear a low-count cloth with poor balance. To illustrate, a high-count sheet of good balance would be 108 × 102; a low-count sheet with poorer balance would be 76 × 60. In each case, the warp yarns are expressed first. Counts may vary from 54 × 47 for a sleazy sheet to 109 × 104 for a very fine one; the average count is 73 × 62 for muslins.

USA Standard specifications for bleached bed sheets and pillowcases (L22.30.8) appear in Table 19.1.[4]

5. Tensile or breaking strength is an important factor in durability. The number of pounds required to break a strip of cloth an inch wide is called the *tensile strength* of that cloth. Since the warp is usually stronger than the filling, it has a slightly higher breaking strength. If in one sheet warps break at 62 pounds and fillings at 56 pounds, that sheet will wear better than one whose breaking strength is 47 pounds for warp and 34 pounds for filling. Furthermore, a sheet may have a well-balanced count and still have a low breaking strength. The two factors, count and tensile strength, must be considered separately. In general, sheets with satisfactory thread counts have been found to have good tensile strength, and vice versa. Polyester adds additional tensile and breaking strength.

[4]All standards are minimum specifications, with the exception of sizing, which is maximum.

Table 19.1 Standards in Bed Sheets and Pillowcases

	Type 200[a] Combed Yarn	Type 180 Combed or Carded Yarn	Type 140 Carded Yarn	Type 128 Carded Yarn
Combined thread count: warp and filling (per inch square)	200	180	140	128
Warp breaking strength (pounds)	60	60	70	55
Filling breaking strength (pounds)	60	60	70	55
Maximum added sizing (percent	1	2	4	6
Weight (ounces per square yard)	3.6	3.6	4.6	4.0

[a]"200" and other numbers represent types or grades (by counts) of the U.S. Bureau of Standards and L22. Type 200 and 180 are called percale and type 140 and 128 are called muslin.

6. When sheets were made primarily of cotton, they often had a great deal of sizing. Sizing in the form of starch or China clay was commonly used for finishing poor-quality sheets. Sizing makes the finish appear smooth, seems to give weight to the cloth, and covers up imperfections in construction. However, after a heavily sized sheet has been washed, it looks flimsy and fuzzy. With the polyester/cotton blends, sizing is not present in appreciable amounts. In all thirteen brands tested by CR, sizing amounted to less than 4 percent, the maximum sizing permitted by the industry standard. The chemicals applied in durable-press treatments do not wash out because they become a part of the fabric.

Sheets vary in weight. According to industry standards, a type 180 percale sheet should weigh a minimum of 3.6 ounces per square yard. The type 140 muslin weighs 4.6 ounces per square yard. Most all-cotton sheets shrink somewhat in laundering. Loosely woven sheets shrink more than closely woven ones. Unless shrinkage-controlled, an allowance of 4½ to 5 percent should be made for shrinkage. There was no appreciable shrinkage (1.5 percent) in the CR tests cited.

Consumers have discovered the comfort of smooth durable-press sheets. These sheets make a more tailored-looking bed, and they dry wrinkle-free with little or no ironing needed.

Determining Quality

To be sure, a consumer cannot use a tensile tester or a counting glass, but laboratory tests can be made by any testing bureau for the benefit of the store's buyer.

Most national and private brands of sheets now bear informative labels that specify size, thread count, tensile strength, weight, and percent of shrinkage. But what does a thread count of 128 mean to the consumer? One must be able to interpret that figure to know whether it specifies a grade A or a grade B muslin.

The appearance and feeling of the sheeting can be noted easily by the consumer. Bumpy yarns can be detected at a glance. By holding the cloth to the light, one may notice any streaked effect. If there is a predominance of warp, there will be a heavy lengthwise streaking. One should also notice the closeness of weave. The closer the weave, the higher the count, and other factors being equal, the stronger the cloth.

If the sheet is hemmed, the stitching should be noticed. A fairly short, even machine stitch is preferable to a long or an uneven stitch. A minimum of eight even stitches per inch is recommended.

Strong thread should be used, and the ends of thread should be fastened securely. Evenness of hems is ensured if the sheeting used has been torn and not cut into lengths. Furthermore, hems with closed ends are to be preferred.

The selvage should be examined carefully, because it may be the first place to show wear. The edge should be firm, with all the yarns caught in securely. The taped selvage is recommended for added wear.

Sizes, Serviceability, and Comfort

The choice of size is really dependent on individual preference. But, largely through ignorance, many consumers buy flat sheets too short. If a bed is about 6 feet long, the consumer is apt to think that a 90-inch sheet allows ample coverage. A standard mattress is 75 inches long and 5 inches thick. Therefore 10 inches should be allowed to cover the mattress at head and foot. In addition, tests show that the average all-cotton sheet shrinks 4½ percent after seventy-five washings.[5] If shrinkage-controlled, the sheet will shrink 2 percent or less. A 108-inch sheet, then, would shrink about 5 inches. This shrinkage should be considered in deciding size. Hems are generally 3 inches at the top and 2 inches at the bottom. Also, some allowance should be made for tucking in at top and bottom—about 13 inches. Accordingly, 75 inches (mattress) plus 5 inches plus 5 inches (thickness of mattress at both ends) plus 5 inches (allowance for shrinkage) plus 5 inches (for hems) plus 6 to 7 inches (tuck-in allowance for each end) equals 108 inches. The sheet required here is the 108-inch length (108 inches is the torn length before the sheet is hemmed). Since a polyester/cotton blend's shrinkage is negligible, the 104-inch length would be adequate.

To make flat sheets wear evenly, some buyers prefer hems of the same width at top and bottom; either end may be used as the top and both ends wear evenly. Others prefer a wider hem at one end to distinguish top from bottom.

Top and bottom flat sheets are usually the same size. The bottom sheet should be long enough to tuck in at the head and foot and thus cover the whole mattress. The top sheet should tuck in 6 or 7 inches at the end and should fold back over the blanket about half a yard. The sizes of flat sheets sold in most stores are shown in Table 19.2.[6]

---

[5]Tests of forty-five sheets of different brands were made in a laundry under methods approved by the Laundry Owners' National Association.

[6]Top sheet sizes were reduced in the seventies by practically every producer.

Table 19.2 Sizes of Flat Sheets

Type of Bed	Size of Sheet (inches)
Crib	42 × 72
Youth bed	63 × 96
Twin bed or three-quarter bed	66 × 104
Double bed	81 × 104
Queen size	90 × 110
King or Hollywood size	108 × 110

Fitted or contour sheets are made for both top and bottom use, although the large majority are produced in bottom styles. Manufacturers note the following selling features of fitted sheets: (1) they will not wrinkle appreciably, (2) they do not toss and turn with you, (3) beds need little remaking, (4) a better fit is assured, (5) corners slip on quickly and easily, (6) they need no ironing, (7) mattress lifting is eliminated, and (8) they hold mattress pad in place. However, this contour or fitted feature also has one notable disadvantage: the stretch and tension exerted in pulling and fitting the contour end over the mattress edge produces more wear and tear on this type sheet than on a flat bottom one. Therefore, a consumer should inspect carefully the construction of the contour corners. An improvement in fitted bottom sheets is the use of a stretch material (rubber, latex, or a similar stretch fiber) around the full corner, providing ease of bed making without reducing the strength of the corners of the sheet.

Bottom fitted sheets come in mattress sizes shown in Table 19.3. Top fitted styles have two slip-on corners with "kick room" allowance; they are usually available only in twin and full (double) sizes and in limited color and patterns.

Color

Prior to the early 1950s, sheets were all made of bleached white fabric and sold by the pound as a commodity product. Solid colors and prints brought fashion to this home textile product and subsequently dramatically changed the

Table 19.3 Sizes of Bottom Fitted Sheets

Type of Bed	Size of Sheet (inches)
Cot	30 × 75
Youth or day bed	33 × 76
Twin bed	39 × 75
Three-quarter bed	48 × 75
Full (double)	54 × 75
Extralarge twin	39 × 80
Queen size	60 × 80
King	78 × 80
California king	72 × 84

nature of merchandising for sheets and products closely related, such as bedspreads, blankets, and comforters.

There are solids in virtually every color that can be coordinated with printed sheets as well as the standard bleached white. There are stripes and florals and combinations of these designs. There are also embroidered sheets and pillowcases, sold separately or in sets. It is a well-documented fact that color and pattern far outweigh durability in consumer choice of sheets, and it is thought by many retailers that pattern and color also are more important to consumers than the muslin or percale construction of bed sheets. With the advent of designer sheets and high-fashion merchandising and promotional campaigns, consumers now may select from a vast array of both pattern and color in coordinated bed linens.

Brands

Some customers say, "I know what brands are good, so I buy one of them. If I can afford to pay more, I select *X* brand; if I cannot, I buy *Y* brand." These buyers are doubtless buying satisfactory goods. The best standard brands are backed by years of reliable service and sustained high standards of quality. Probably many customers do better if they buy by brand than by quality, because many of them do not know the factors determining wearing quality.

Some of the large department stores and major chain stores have private brands that they sell in preference to the nationally advertised brands; and many of these stores do have a product as good as those nationally advertised and possibly cheaper. If the consumer is able to judge quality, she may get a bargain in the private brand.

The intelligent consumer should learn how to judge quality and other factors making for value in use and thus choose the brand, style, or line number that best suits the combination of personal requirements.

Sheeting by the Yard

Most consumers today prefer made-up sheets, so the sale of sheeting by the yard is negligible. Pillow tubing and ticking is also sold by the yard in a few major department stores.

Linen Sheets and Sheeting

Although there is almost no demand for linen sheets, there are some distinct advantages in buying them. Linen sheets of good grade outwear cotton of good grade, but the cost of linen is considerably higher. After a linen sheet has served its life as a sheet, it may be cut up into doilies, hand towels, and dress trimmings. Even if linen is old, it has a rich brilliance that an old cotton or cotton/polyester blend does not have.

The wearing quality of linen sheeting is determined by the grades of fiber, yarn, weave, and finish. A sheeting should wear well if it has long, even fibers of good tensile strength; well-hackled, even yarns; a close, firm weave; and a smooth beetle finish—and if it is not overbleached. Hems should be even and hemstitching of good quality. Finished sizes are 72 × 108 for twin and 90 × 108 for double and queen beds and 108 × 122 for a king size bed.

Pillowcases

Most pillowcases are made to match the sheet and usually are packaged two to a set. The two may be bought in attractive packages and make desirable gift items. Bolster pillows, when in style, lead to sales of pillow protectors and bolster pillowcases.

Pillowcases should be 8 to 9 inches longer than the pillow and about 1 to 2 inches larger around. Table 19.4 shows the size of the pillow and the appropriate size for a pillowcase. The length is the torn length before hemming.

The same points to be considered in judging the wearing quality of sheets should be applied to the selection of pillowcases and bolster cases. The hems should be 2 to 3 inches wide, straight and even. Seams should be firmly and evenly stitched (14 stitches to the inch) and finished to prevent raveling.

Disposable pillowcases and sheets may be made of a layered fabric, with strong yarns bonded between layers of cellulose wadding. For hygienic utility in hospitals, sickrooms, and clinics, these pillowcases have proved acceptable. They can also be used as laundry and shoe bags and as wastebasket liners. They come in white and a few colors.

Obtaining Longer Wear from
Sheets and Pillowcases

Many times customers complain that sheets in service only three or four months show signs of wear. The customer blames her laundry, and the laundry claims the fault lies in the poor quality of the sheet. It is difficult to determine which is at fault. Accordingly, salespeople should give customers a few hints that will help to get longer wear from sheets.

1. Sheets wear out where shoulders rub. Experiments made in hotels show that most sheets wear out first at this point. If the sheets have hems of the same width at both ends, head and foot can be reversed to equalize wear. If hems are wider at the top, the lower sheet may be turned head to foot.

2. A sheet that is the right size for the bed will wear longer than one that is too short or too narrow. Sheets too small for a bed are subjected to unnecessary strain.

Table 19.4 Pillow and Pillowcase Sizes

Size of Pillow (inches)	Size of Pillowcase (inches)
Standard 20 × 26	21 × 35
Queen 20 × 30	21 × 39
King 20 × 36	21 × 44

3. Bed springs, splinters, and nails on the bed may snag a sheet. A loose nail may work its way through the covering of a box spring; a projecting sliver of wood may catch a sheet when it is pulled off; the threads may become weakened and a hole may consequently appear. In short, a bed may be giving a sheet harder wear than the laundry.

4. Mattress pads or covers prolong the life of both the sheet and the mattress.

5. Sheets and cases will wear longer if all holes and tears are mended before they are laundered.

6. Whether sheets and cases are laundered at home or by a commercial laundry, strong undiluted bleaches should not be used because they weaken the cloth.

7. Folds of sheets and pillowcases should not be ironed. It weakens the fabric. No-iron sheets obviate this problem.

8. The bed should be made with a light touch rather than with force.

9. Laundries may wear out sheets and cases by putting them through the ironer too fast. As a result the selvage may roll or fold. Continued mangling in this manner may wear the sheet out along these folds in the selvage before the body of the sheet shows wear. Shrinkage is minimized if sheets are laundered at home.

10. Sheets should be rotated. Discarded sheets should be replaced immediately. By so doing, the homemaker will get better wear than to continue to use a smaller and smaller number of sheets until they are all worn out.

Mattresses and Pillows

Mattresses

Although most consumers buy mattresses only a few times in their lives, when they do buy they want a mattress that is comfortable and durable. Probably comfort in some minds is associated with softness. Certainly in the days of feather beds, softness and warmth were considerations. But there is much to be said for the firm, level mattress that does not let the sleeper sink down deeply into it and that provides good support for the body. This type will buoy up the small of the back and will be apt to keep the spine in a straight line rather than a sagging one. Beds that are too soft often restrict the normal body movements of a sleeper; beds that are too hard do not permit perfect relaxation and often restrict circulation.

Health experts say that a mattress should be adjustable; that is, the mattress should adjust itself to various degrees of pressure from different parts of the body. The body should not be required to adjust itself to an unyielding mattress.

The filling is largely responsible for comfort and durability. Probably the inner-spring mattress retains its resiliency longest (with the exception of the foam rubber). In the inner-spring or polyurethane plastic foam mattress there are approximately 200 to 850 coil springs mounted in a steel-wire frame. This spring unit is contained between two layers of padding (generally cotton) and insulating materials consisting usually of fiber pads. All these units are encased in a ticking. The durability of the inner-spring mattress depends, in a large measure, on the quality of steel used in the springs. A large number of springs is not necessarily a measure of good performance. A smaller number of well-designed springs, suitably tied and combined with padding and insulation, should give comfort, firmness, and good performance.

The majority of these mattresses have their coil springs tied with twine, wire, metal or plastic clips in a manner to permit individual springs to move independently up and down. This movement helps the mattress to conform to and support the human body. The most popular bedsprings are box springs, in which the springs are stapled to wooden slats that are tied together at the top and fastened to an outer frame. In good-grade mattresses, the springs are wrapped in muslin to prevent the wear of friction and also to eliminate creaking.

Mattresses without inner springs are filled with horsehair, kapok, polyester batting, felted cotton, loose cotton, or foam rubber. South American horsehair is the most durable, most resilient, and most expensive. Cattle hair is considered next best to horsehair. Kapok is less resilient than horsehair but is well suited to damp climates, because it throws off moisture and dries quickly. Felt fillings of combed cotton felted into strips and laid in layers are slightly less resilient than kapok. Loose cotton, which is often used for inexpensive mattresses, becomes lumpy in time.

Ever since the 1940s, foam rubber mattresses have been used in homes and hospitals. They are simpler in construction than inner-spring mattresses—just a rectangular slab of foam encased in ticking. A foam rubber mattress conforms to the contour of the body and supports it at all points, even the small of the back. These mattresses are about half as heavy as inner springs and never should be turned. They are expensive, but they have the advantage of being nonallergenic and not unduly hot in summer or cold in winter. They do not mildew or harbor insects; there are no buttons or tufting. Since foam rubber tears easily, any moving of the mattress should be done by its cover, the ticking. Foam rubber should never be soaked to clean it. Removing the ticking and washing the rubber with a dampened cloth is sufficient. The mattress should not be exposed to the sun, because the ultraviolet light deteriorates it.

The plastic polyurethane foam mattress, which is light and less expensive than foam rubber, assures firm, healthful support. It is very light (only 15 pounds) compared with foam rubber or inner-spring mattresses. The homemaker can easily lift it.

The mattress covering or bag that holds the filling is called *ticking*. It comes in twill weave, with variations of herringbone and Jacquard, and less frequently in satin weaves.

The color of the covering may sell the mattress to the consumer who must have a harmonious color scheme in the bedroom. Drill—a stout, medium-weight twilled cotton—and cotton and rayon mixed fabrics are used. A slightly undersized ticking is preferable with the foam rubber filler to keep the filler from spreading.

Tufting, a brushlike button of clipped cotton yarn, appears at regular intervals on some mattresses. These buttons, or tufts, are the ends of yarns that are drawn straight through the mattress to prevent the filling from slipping or becoming lumpy. In a good mattress, tufts are directly opposite each other on either side and are about 12 inches apart. Deep indentations at the point of tufting are noticeable. Tufts that are merely sewed on the surface of the ticking are found in the poorer grades of mattresses. Handles on either side of a mattress facilitate easy turning.

Air mattresses for station wagons and for camping are made of double-coated, rubberized woven nylon or cotton, often with built-in pillows. Also, they may be made of embossed vinyl plastic (nontextile), water-repellent poplin, or vinyl-plastic-coated cotton sheeting. Liners are cotton broadcloth, cotton flannel, or oxford. Sleeping bags may be filled with layers of polyester or goose down and polyester for insulation.

Another requisite of a good mattress is a firm edge that will hold its shape. Felted cotton used as the core of a cord stitched around the edge of the mattress ensures firmness. Better grades may also have the sidewalls reinforced with filling and cloth stitched together. A selling point of the inner-spring variety is the small, screened, hole ventilator. The air drawn into the mattress every time weight is removed keeps it sanitary and prolongs its life. A cloth tape is frequently bonded to the foam rubber edges to add strength. A zipper or chain-stitched seam permits removal of ticking for cleaning.

A cover protects the mattress and also keeps sheets and blankets from soiling if the mattress is dusty. Mattress covers come in all mattress sizes. They are made of muslin (unbleached, printed, or in pastel shades), taffetized 100 percent vinyl plastic, cotton muslin bonded to foam rubber, and bleached white cotton quilted pads and polyester/cotton blends. The plastic-foam-filled quilted mattress pad is easy to care for, nonallergenic, mildewproof, and fire- and liquid-resistant, and it will not sag because it has a strong, elasticized tuck-under to prevent slipping. It may fit over the mattress with elasticized corners or around the entire mattress surface with a zippered or snapped closing. A recent innovation is the quilted box spring cover made to coordinate with a quilted mattress cover that encases the entire mattress. The effect achieved with matching mattress and box spring covers is a tailored, padded appearance that alleviates the need for a box spring skirt. Brand names such as Bedsack feature wide color choices along with fancy quilting designs and are made in the standard mattress and box spring sizes. (See Fig. 19.13.)

Although mattress covers should not be used primarily to cover a dirty mattress, they can often be used to cover an old, faded one. Covers should be

Figure 19.13 A new concept in mattress and box spring covers, Bedsack adds an upholstered look to the bed. The cotton-polyester blended cover fabrics are ultra-sonically quilted and filled with Kodel polyester. (Photo courtesy of Perfect Fit Industries, Inc.)

removed and laundered at regular intervals. At this time a thorough vacuum cleaning will help keep the mattress completely dry and will prolong its life. Vacuum cleaning is even more important when covers are not used.

Pillows

The factors of comfort and durability considered in buying a mattress are also considered in purchasing pillows. Some people prefer loosely filled pillows in which the head sinks deeply; others feel smothered by a soft pillow and prefer a thin, hard one. But most people seem to prefer a soft, plump one that is very resilient and light in weight.

The kind of filling used determines the comfort, wearing quality, and price. Fillings may be graded in order of excellence, beginning with the best: (1) down from the breasts of geese or ducks, (2) goose feathers, (3) duck feathers, (4) kapok, (5) fine chicken and turkey feathers, (6) mixed down and feathers, (7) acrylic or polyester staple fibers, and (8) foam rubber.

Of the feathers, white ones are considered best because they are apt to be finer, softer, and lighter in weight than dark ones. Down from the breasts of geese or ducks is very light, soft, spineless, and resilient. A pillow plumply stuffed with crushed goose down is a real sleep inducer. It is most expensive, however. Goose or duck feathers with quills are heavier and less resilient than down. They can be felt through the pillow casing if it is not of close construction. Turkey and hen feathers are about twice as heavy as down and are stiffer, less soft, and less buoyant. Different kinds of feathers may be mixed in the same pillow. Hen feathers are comparatively inexpensive but, like goose and duck feathers, the quills may come through the casing if it is not sufficiently close in weave.

Kapok and foam rubber are real boons to sufferers from asthma or hay fever. Feathers often irritate people with these afflictions, whereas kapok (a vegetable fiber) or foam rubber does not. Kapok is also suitable for pillows used at the seashore, since it does not feel damp quickly, and if it becomes wet, it dries in a short time. Cushions for canoes, cruisers, and yachts are satisfactory when stuffed with kapok, because if they fall into the water they float. Kapok-filled pillows are inexpensive, but they mat or become lumpy in time.

Synthetic staple fiberfill is nonallergenic, buoyant, odorless, and moth- and mildewproof. Better qualities of bed pillows are covered with tightly woven ticking in floral, stripes, or all-over printed patterns. Medium and poorer quality covers are made of percale. Any cover should be closely woven and seamed, so that stuffing does not come through. Corded edges make for durability. Separate zippered pillow protectors can be purchased to protect covers.

Foam latex pillows are springy and durable, cool for the summer months, and nonallergenic. Urethane foam is a synthetic material available in one piece or chopped form.

The following list should serve as a guide in buying pillows:[7]

1. Balance the pillow on the hands. The lighter pillow is usually the better choice.
2. Press both hands into the center of the pillow. When the hands are lifted, the pillow should spring back.
3. Hold one end of the pillow and shake it vigorously. Filling should not shift easily and pack at one end.[8]
4. Pound the pillow with the fist to see if dust emerges or lumps appear. These are undesirable features.
5. Sniff the pillow for odor. If there is odor, do not buy it.
6. Notice whether the cover is closely woven and seams are welted (reinforced with a double edge) for durability.

[7]Anne Sterling, *Buying and Care of Pillows* (International Fabricare Institute, Silver Spring, Md.: 1968). Merchandise bearing the seal of this organization has passed extensive tests for washability and wear.

[8]According to Cameron A. Baker, research director of Better Fabrics Testing Bureau (New York), pillows properly selected do not need to be punched and tucked under for individual comfort. He has developed a device to measure filling materials, which enables a manufacturer to standardize production methods with the result that gives consumers the degree of firmness or resiliency they prefer. It is possible that performance evaluation will appear on a tag or label. The best fillers, according to Mr. Baker, are Polish goose down and Taiwan duck down (both expensive). Other fillers include chicken and turkey feathers, solid and shredded foams and rubber, man-made fibers, cotton batting, and kapok. From *Consumer Bulletin,* January 1969.

A few suggestions for the care of pillows follow:[9]

1. All rips and tears in a pillow ticking should be repaired immediately to prevent loss of filling.
2. All pillows should be cleaned after an illness.
3. Should a pillow sag when placed over one's arm, it needs cleaning and professional renovation.
4. Soiled tickings soil pillowcases. The use of a washable, zippered pillow cover is suggested.

Blankets

Blankets, like sheets, are an essential item of bed covering. Although blankets are purchased less frequently than are sheets, consumers are just as anxious to get their money's worth when they do buy.

Blankets may be made of 100 percent wool, cotton, rayon, acrylic, nylon, and polyester fibers, or blends of these with other man-made fibers. Wool and cotton, longtime blanket fabrics, now meet competition from the man-made fibers and blends. Nearly 90 percent of all blankets in the United States are now constructed of man-made fibers, with acrylic and polyester the dominant; white cotton blankets account for approximately 7 percent and wool 4 percent.[10] In 1967 an all-Dacron polyester unnapped Fiberwoven blanket apeared in Chatham Manufacturing Company's line followed by West Point-Pepperell's nylon flocked polyurethane core blanket in the late 1960s.[11] This nonwoven construction was quickly accepted by consumers and it was soon adopted by several major textile manufacturers. It continues to be of major importance in the blanket market. The general appearance is a velvetlike pile fabric that is light in weight and has a soft luxurious hand. Machine launderability is excellent.

A polyester blend or 100 percent Sanforized cotton has a soft, warm feel that makes it increasingly popular in homes where energy-conscious consumers have lowered thermostats and thus sleep in cooler bedrooms. Many are now available in solid pastel colors as well as screen printed floral and geometric patterns.

Warmth

The weight of a blanket is not a true indication of its warmth. Blankets average three to five pounds in weight, but very lightweight wool blankets may be just as warm as, or warmer than, heavy, tightly woven felted ones. The lighter the blanket, the more comfortable it is as a bed covering. The warmth of a blanket is determined largely by its thickness and nap, not by weight and fiber

[9]Sterling, *Pillows.*
[10]Man-Made Fiber Producers Association, 1980.
[11]Fiberwoven is the Chatham registered trade name of a nonwoven process fabric that eliminates yarn making and weaving.

Figure 19.14 Thermal blanket fabric of acrylic fiber in leno weave. (Photo by Jonas Grushkin.)

content. Since a closely napped cloth traps more still air than an unnapped cloth, it should be warmer. Pockets of still air act as insulation against cold air.

Loosely twisted filling yarns can be napped more successfully than can tightly twisted yarns. The amount of twist in the filling yarns is a factor in warmth. To improve the napping of a cloth without jeopardizing durability, the core of the filling yarn may be tightly spun and the fibers then twisted loosely about the core. Cotton blankets may feel damper and therefore colder than wool if they are used in damp climates, especially at the seashore. Cotton holds moisture on the surface and therefore feels damp more quickly than does wool, which can absorb much moisture before it begins to feel wet.

After several washings, cotton blankets may shrink or felt to such an extent that they feel heavy, but they are no warmer than they were at first. A "pouflike" finish can be applied to blankets of 100 percent Acrilan acrylic, rayon, and blends to keep them from shedding, pilling, and matting. It is claimed that softness and loft are retained after repeated washings.[12]

If one is looking for a very lightweight, durable, lint-free covering, then a thermal-weave blanket should be considered. (See Fig. 19.14.) Many look like the afghans of Grandma's day.

In winter, a cover is placed on top of the thermal-weave blanket so that air warmed by body heat is trapped between the yarns. In summer, the cover is omitted and body heat is permitted to escape through tiny "air cells." Consumers' Research tests revealed that the thermal-weave blankets with a cover were not as warm as a heavy wool blanket (4½ pounds). All the thermal-weave blankets tested with a cover were as warm as, or warmer than, a lightweight (2½ pounds) acrylic blanket.[13] Furthermore, all the thermal-weave blankets without a cover were cooler than the woven wool blanket, but only five of the nine brands tested were cooler than the woven acrylic blanket. In this CR study, the napped blankets lost lint in laundering, but not enough to affect their original weight. Blankets were rated good to fair after three launderings. Some of these thermal weaves are known to withstand two hundred launderings.

[12]This protective finish is Nap-Guard, by West Point-Pepperell, Inc., and Neva-Shed by Fieldcrest Mills, Inc.
[13]*Consumer Bulletin*, December 1965.

Attractiveness

Color, design, and the finishing of the edges make for attractiveness. Blankets are made in solid colors, plain white, plaid, checks, and novelty color combinations, and some have colored borders. If a blanket is to be used as an extra "throw" (folded on the bed during the day), the color selected should harmonize with the furnishings in the room. Even if blankets are covered by a bedspread, the color-conscious consumer will want the colors in blankets to be harmonious. The edges of blankets may be whipped (a kind of scalloped machine embroidery) or bound with cotton, acetate, or nylon bindings.

Blankets with a soft texture are usually the most attractive. If wool fibers are fine, of sufficiently long staple, and smooth, the blanket is sure to be soft. Acrylic fibers have an almost cashmerelike softness, while some of the newer flocked blankets have velvety suedelike textures. Some luxury-type specialty shops, special boutiques within department stores, and specialty mail-order firms sell limited assortment of blankets made from pure cashmere or blends of cashmere and Merino wool. Such items are, of course, very expensive and can retail at five to twenty times the price of more widely used acrylic or other blended blankets.

Durability

Whether a blanket is wool, cotton, acrylic, rayon, or a blend, certain factors are important in judging the wearing quality:

1. *Length of the fibers.*   Long fibers do not pull out or slip so readily as short fibers. If fibers are too short, they often pull out in the napping process, thereby weakening the yarn. The quality of the fibers is also important.

2. *Tensile strength of the fibers.*   If fibers in a yarn are weak, the yarn is correspondingly weak. Therefore, the first requisites for a long-wearing blanket are good-quality fibers sufficiently long and strong to make strong yarns.

3. *Tensile strength of yarns.*   It is particularly important that warps have sufficient strength to withstand the tension in the loom and also to bear the weight of water in washing. Fillings are generally spun more loosely than are the warps so that fibers may be brushed up for the nap. Some manufacturers, however, sacrifice durability for appearance by spinning fillings too loosely and by making too thick a nap. Ply yarns usually have greater tensile strength than single yarns and so are often used for warp.

4. *Construction.*   This factor depends upon the balanced strength of warp and filling—that is, a balanced count together with firm, even weaving. In considering the proportionate strength of warp to filling, it should be understood that the warp must be stronger than the filling to withstand the friction and tension of the loom. But if fillings are spun too loosely, they may be proportionately so much weaker than the warps that the blanket may split or shred when it is washed. This shredding occurs when strong cotton warps are

used with short-staple filling fibers made of slack-twisted yarn. A well-balanced count ensures an even distribution of warps and fillings and longer wear. Most blankets for home use are twill or a variation of the twill. This construction throws more filling to the surface for the purpose of napping.

One of the best ways to test the uniformity of the weave is to hold the blanket to a strong light. Thick and thin spots indicate poor construction. If there is a border, the weave should be the same in the border as in the rest of the blanket. A difference in closeness of the weave in the border may result in ripples or puckers after laundering.

When the blanket is held toward the light, one can see whether it has been cut straight. The ends of the blanket should run parallel to the filling yarns.

A process of tufting blankets has been developed that may, in time, compete costwise with woven blankets. (For tufted bedspreads, see *tufted fabric*, glossary in this chapter; for tufted rugs, see Chapter 20.)

Nonwoven constructions are later innovations in blankets. One process, called Fiberwoven, converts fiber directly into fabric. Invented by Dr. Alexander Smith, a former professor at the Massachusetts Institute of Technology, the process is conducted by interlocking many loops of fibers, shaped or entangled by fast-moving rows of barbed needles. Blankets so constructed are claimed to be warm and strong, to shrink less, and to last longer than commercially woven blankets.

One nonwoven blanket is produced by West Point-Pepperell, Inc., under a patented process called "Vellux." The blanket is built around an inner core of man-made foam that has special thermal qualities that trap warmth despite the lightness of the fabric. Nylon fiber is electrostatically bonded permanently to both sides of the core. The fabric is claimed to be soft, warm, lightweight, velvety, and luxurious. It will not shrink when laundered and is very durable; it is moth-resistant; it comes in solid colors and prints; and it can be reversed. Carved dimensional effects are available in this construction in the luxury price range. Several other blanket producers now have similarly constructed products in their lines.

5. *Amount of nap raised.* As has been stated, a heavy nap of short fibers pulled out from loosely twisted yarn decreases durability. If filling yarns have sufficient tensile strength and fibers are long, a moderate nap makes a blanket attractive and warm and does not affect durability. To determine the durability of the nap, rub the surface of the blanket. If little balls of fiber roll up, the nap is made of too short fibers, and the blanket will lose its warmth. Nap should be uniform in thickness and in coverage of the surface. Another way in which to test the durability of the nap is to take a pinch of it between the thumb and forefinger and lift the blanket slightly. If the nap does not pull out, the fibers are long and well anchored in the yarn.

6. *Bindings and finishes of the ends.* These should be neat and strong. Bindings should be eased onto the edge of a blanket and should be firmly stitched with two or three rows of parallel stitching or with close featherstitch-

ing. Some blanket corners fit closely like fitted sheets. Nylon makes a durable binding. Rayon and acetate are very attractive but have to be replaced sooner than nylon. Sateen is inexpensive and usually wears well.

Automatic Blankets

When a person is asleep, he or she is unable to adjust to the loss of body heat by putting on more blankets, changing the room temperature, or exercising. Uniform sleeping comfort can be provided by an automatic blanket. There are three kinds: the thermostat blanket, the automatic sheet, and the solid-state blanket.

1. The thermostat blanket consists of four units:
    a. The blanket unit that has a fabric woven so as to provide many small lengthwise channels. A network of parallel heating wires is shuttled through these channels. The wires terminate in a male plug at the bottom of the blanket. Double-bed and larger-sized blankets may be provided with dual controls to heat each side separately.
    b. A heater element consisting of conductor wires around a fiber core of polyester yarn. The core and wires are insulated and protected with vinyl plastic.
    c. A number of protective thermostats to prevent overheating. Even with excess folding or bunching, at least one or two of the elements will operate.
    d. A control unit that maintains the desired temperature, which is set manually by operating a dial. Somewhat like a home furnace control, a heater coil activates a bimetal switch.
2. The automatic sheet is similar in operation to the thermostat blanket, but it is lighter and the wires are not set in channels in the fabric, but rather are covered with tapes sewn to the sheet. These take less wattage than the blankets, yet with average room temperature provide adequate heat.
3. The solid-state blanket differs from the thermostat blanket in that electronic components modulate the energy, somewhat as a light dimmer switch does. It substitutes precise electronic elements for the manually adjusted bimetal switch. This assembly eliminates bimetal clicking and produces more uniform temperature than the thermostat.

Comforters

Comforters are stuffed or quilted bed coverings. (See Fig. 19.15.) In parts of New England, and elsewhere, a soft, lightweight, very resilient comforter with a removeable cover is called a puff. In Europe this comforter is often known as a *duvet* (France), *fedderbett* (German), and *pouff* (Finland).

A consumer may be attracted to a beautiful brocaded satin comforter; the covering is all that she knows or cares about. It will look attractive in her room; her friends will admire it; so she buys it. But, although the covering is an important consideration, this customer has neglected a vital factor from the standpoint of comfort and wear—the filling. Just as in mattresses and pillows, the filling can make the comforter light or heavy, soft or hard, resilient or not. No one wants to be weighed down with heavy bed coverings that are hard and

Figure 19.15 Bill Blass designs, including a fitted bedspread, comforter, and matching sheets and pillowcases. Sheets are made of no-iron Wondercale of 65 percent Kodel polyester and 35 percent cotton percale. Comforter facing and backing is 65 percent polyester and 35 percent cotton. Fiberfill is of 100 percent polyester. (Photo courtesy of Spring Industries, Inc.)

possibly lumpy. Heaviness generally does not make the comforter warm, for a resilient comforter, like a blanket, enmeshes air to retain warmth; thus a lighter weight is achieved.

To test the amount of resiliency or buoyancy of a comforter, put one hand on the top and the other hand on the bottom of the comforter and press them together. Note how much it can be compressed and how fast it returns to its original shape. If it does not spring back to shape, it can become bunchy and misshapen in a comparatively short time when in use. If two comforters of the same thickness are compared, one may compress greatly and spring back quickly, whereas the other may compress very little and return to shape slowly. The former is usually the lighter in weight and retains its resilience longer while in use.

Fillings

Fillings for comforters can be made of cotton, acetate and cotton, wool, down, feathers, acrylic, and polyester fibers. Long-staple cotton of good grade is resilient and wears well. Short-staple cotton, a coarser and poorer grade than the long staple, is the second best type of cotton filling. Short fibers, because they do not cling together as well as long ones, lump or bunch more readily. Cotton linters are poor because they do not have sufficient resiliency.

Fine, long-staple Australian wool makes a soft filling. The first shearing from the lamb is particularly fine and soft. The better grade fillings are made of carefully scoured and carded wool. Poorer grades are grayish in color, poorly scoured, poorly carded, and less soft. Poor scouring leaves burrs and foreign substances in the filling, which in time may work through the covering of the comforter. Short ends removed from the sliver in the carding of wool are often used for poor-grade fillings. These short fibers are wool waste and are often coarse. Recycled wool may also be used.

The types of filling and care in selection, presented in connection with pillows, apply equally well to comforters. Man-made fibers are increasingly used in comforters, with polyester fiberfill the most widely used. Some advantages are moderate prices, and the properties of being allergy-free, snow white, mildewproof, and odorless. Their resiliency has been greatly improved with plumper, lighterweight fills that have the added advantage of generally being machine- or hand-washable (making their maintenance less expensive). An innovation in fiberfill is the use of polyester fibers that are either in continuous-filament form or have a hollow construction. This permits even greater shape recovery and softness of the fill, more closely resembling the characteristics of down and feathers.

Coverings

Comforter coverings should be soft and pliable, with good draping qualities; that is, they should cling to the other coverings on the bed and not look too bulky. A stiff, harsh material makes a cover that is hard to quilt—that is, to sew in a pattern or design. Corners may also appear bulky if the covering is too stiff.

Some fabrics slip easily, and no matter how well they are tucked in they do not seem to adhere to the bed. Rayons made in long-float satin weave have this undesirable characteristic. In fact, any satin of silk, acetate, or rayon will slip more than a fabric with a ribbed or dull surface will. A closely woven nylon tafetta is both attractive and durable, but it too may slip. A fabric made of tightly twisted yarns in a firm weave is best. Brocaded satins are luxurious in appearance and adhere better than plain satins. Sateen and polished cotton are both practical and less expensive. Cotton corduroy and percale can also be used for less expensive coverings. A wrinkle-resistant fabric is desirable for a covering. If washable, a durable-press fabric is desirable.

Coverings should be made with finishes permanent enough to dry-clean or launder. A homemaker should save and follow instructions for care given on the attached label. *Removable comforter covers,* widely used in Europe for several hundred years, are now being manufactured in the United States as an added benefit in both use and care and decorating of comforters. These covers, generally made of sheeting fabric to coordinate with bed sheets are of an envelope-type construction, with the botton end open for ease of removal and laundering. Closing devices are made of buttons, grip-snap fasteners, hand ties, or in some cases, a full-width zipper. These covers, also referred to as duvet or puff covers, sometimes have openings or slits in the sides near the top of the cover to facilitate the placement of the cover within the comforter.

Quilts

Quilts are thinner and less expensive than comforters. Antique patchwork quilts, pieced by hand, in some instances are works of art. Artistic, well-made ones are collectors' items and, if in good condition, are expensive. Favorite designs were the star, the wedding ring, or conventionalized florals, frequently in handmade designs. Pieces were cut, sewn together in blocks or motifs, and the blocks were sewn together to form the top covering of the quilt. Generally, these covers were brightly colored solid or printed cotton, occasionally silk. When the covering was finished, a fabric the exact size for the back was cut and made ready for the next step—quilting. Cotton batting was placed between the covering and the backing. Then the quilters were ready for their quilting party. Friends came in for the afternoon to help the quilt designer sew the three layers (cover, batting, and back) together. Geometric or floral patterns were made with fine quilting stitches. Quilting was done on a frame to keep the fabrics smooth and in shape. The edges of the fabric were bound with bias-cut strips of cloth.

There are no standard sizes for antique patchwork quilts. Size was governed by the size of the bed to be covered and by the pieces of fabric available for the purpose.

Designs of modern patchwork quilts are frequently copies of old designs. Modern quilts may not have the sentiment connected with the old quilts, but their colors are faster. The machine stitching makes them firm, yet gives the homemade effect. Some so-called patchwork quilts have covers made of one piece of cloth printed to resemble small pieces sewed together. They are quilted or tufted. This type of quilt is quite inexpensive. Filling may be cotton or polyester.

Modern cotton patchwork quilts can be laundered at home or can be sent to the laundry. Antique quilts should be dry-cleaned, because there is no assurance of the fastness of the colors. Furthermore, the fabric may have tendered with age.

A stitchless, threadless quilting technique recently introduced produces a quilted look to fabric. Through an electronic process a quilted design is created that simulates the "puffy" look of machine- and hand-quilted fabrics. The process is said to be relatively inexpensive.

Bedspreads

One who is beginning to furnish a new home decides what type each room is to be—formal or informal—and what period or periods are most appropriate to each room. The consumer usually buys large pieces of furniture first. The accessories, such as bedding, curtains, and pillows, come next. Although the average consumer may not think of style or appearance first when buying pillows or a mattress for a bed, appearance is the first consideration in purchasing a bedspread. The intelligent buyer tries to visualize the bedspread in its intended setting: "Will it harmonize with my curtains, rugs, and upholstered chairs?" Fortunate is the person who has this power of visualization.

Principles of Selection

A few simple principles will guide the consumer in the selection of bedspreads:

1.   Materials should be of a texture that will not wrinkle or crush easily. This is particularly important when beds are to be used as seats during the day.

2.   Materials should be cleanable by automatic washing or dry cleaning. Preshrunk fabrics that require no ironing are desirable.

3.   The spread should be large enough for the bed. If pillows are to be covered so that they give the effect of a bolster, the length should be 105 or 108 inches. The sizes (without flounce ruffles) stocked in stores are shown in Table 19.5.

4.   The spread should be cut and sewed so that it has a trim appearance, whether tailored or boxlike. Flat spreads often have rounded corners. A spread of heavy material generally fits better if the corners are cut out for a fourposter bed. Split corners and corner inserts help to give a good fit.

5.   In tailored spreads, double interlocked seams and cord welt edges ensure serviceability. Matching the bedspread with draperies, upholstered chairs, or cushions can have a pleasing effect. The modern homemaker considers the design as well as the function of the bedroom and chooses draperies, curtains, bedspread, blankets, sheets, and accessories accordingly. Cooperation of manufacturers in ensembling their related products makes shopping quick and easy.

Flounce ruffles, pillow shams, and draperies may be made of the same fabric as the spreads. These items can be purchased separately as well as in ensembles.

Table 19.5   Sizes of Bedspreads

Type of Bed	Size of Spread (inches)
Bunk	63 × 100
Twin	76 × 105, 79 × 108
Double	88 × 105, 96 × 108
Queen size	102 × 120
King size	120 × 120

The following fabrics are used for bedspreads:

Washable corduroy
Loop woven cotton Jacquards with
  knotted fringe
Candlewick (cotton)
Broadcloth (cotton/polyester)*
Chenille (cotton, rayon)
Embroidered fabrics
Polished cotton*
Regular sheeting fabric

Cotton sailcloth
Quilted rayon, acetate, nylon
Textured cotton and blends
Tufted cotton (see *tufted fabric* in the
  glossary)
Embossed cotton*
Crocheted lace
Taffeta (rayon, acetate, nylon)
Elaborate Jacquards (Old World look)

*Particularly well suited for children's spreads.

Novelty Items

During recent years new quilted products have been introduced as alternatives to the traditional comforter and bedspread. Among these innovative products is the quilted "garment bag" introduced by Heritage Quilts in 1977. The trade name Snug Sack was advertised initially to be worn for warmth around a cooler-temperature home. Many other manufacturers subsequently followed suit, and there are now numerous versions of these products, principally in the same blends and constructions as their "sister" counterparts, the quilted bedspread and comforter.

Table 19.6 Production of Major Home Furnishings Textiles (million dozens)

Period	Sheets Flat and Fitted[a]	Pillowcases	Terry Woven Towels	Huck and Crash[b] Towels and Terry Washcloths
1972	18.0	14.1	47.7	30.1
1973	16.4	14.4	47.6	28.3
1974	15.8	13.8	42.2	29.0
1975	15.5	12.3	41.4	105.8
1976	16.8	13.0	45.6	94.8
1977	16.3	14.0	45.1	94.2
1978	16.8	13.7	45.0	92.7
1979	15.9	14.3	47.1	55.0
1980	16.5	14.7	44.0	49.8
1981	16.8	14.4	44.9	48.6
1982				
1st Q	3.5	3.0	9.4	11.3
2nd Q	3.8	3.2	11.0	12.9

[a]Excludes crib sheets.

[b]Prior to 1975 these figures excluded huck and crash towels.

Source: U.S. Department of Commerce, Bureau of the Census.

SUMMARY

Bed coverings, towels, and table coverings are a very important part of home furnishings. Now that dyes are fast, printing more attractive, and woven designs more varied, fashion has really entered the domestic field. Table 19.6 gives the trend in production of some of the major home furnishings textiles discussed in this chapter.

Department stores and specialty retailers of many types feature ensembles for different rooms in a special departments, such as the bath shop. Consumers should give as much consideration to the assembling of bed and table coverings and towels as they do to the buying of personal wardrobes. Care in selection and proper care in use ensure the durability and long life of home furnishings textiles.

PROJECTS

1. Plan a color-coordinated ensemble for a bathroom that has one window, beige tile walls, pink fixtures and red wall-to-wall carpeting.
   (a) List all the household textiles you will need in this room for a family of two adults and two children (aged four and six).
   (b) Include the names of each fabric, its size, color, and design.
   (c) In a few paragraphs, give the reasons for your choices.
2. Plan the household textiles of either a college girl's or a college boy's bedroom.
   (a) Accurately describe or draw a floor plan of the room.
   (b) Accurately describe fabric or include swatches of fabric that you would suggest for bedspread, curtains or draperies, and accessories.
   (c) Draw or accurately describe the style and size of each item.
   (d) In a few short paragraphs, give the reasons for your choices.
3. Plan a table setting for a Sunday dinner for a family of two adults and four children of high school and college age.
   (a) Describe the table covering and napkins with regard to fabric name, texture, size, color, and price.
   (b) List and describe the household textiles used for the occasion.
4. (a) Make a count of colors, sizes, and prices of terry cloth bath towels sold in three retail stores.
   (b) Tabulate the results of your findings.
   (c) Analyze your data, and come to some conclusions as to how well these stores are meeting customer demand in the community.

GLOSSARY

Bath rug Usually a comparatively small rug with cotton, rayon, or nylon pile suitable for a bathroom.

Bed linen Any cotton, linen, nylon, polyester, or blended sheeting for use on a bed.

Beetle finish   See the glossary in Chapter 7.

Blanketing   A heavily napped fabric of wool, cotton, or man-made fibers in blends or mixtures, woven 60 or 80 inches or more in size in plain or twill weave.

Bolster   A long, rectangular pillow the width of the bed.

Candlewick   See *tufted fabric.*

Cheesecloth   A sheer, very low count, slackly twisted, carded cotton fabric.

Chenille   See *tufted fabric.*

Chintz   See Chapter 21.

Comfortable   Synonym for *comforter.*

Comforter   A quilted bed covering made with a layer of stuffing between two fabrics of taffeta, brocaded satin, sateen, or printed muslin.

Comforter cover   A removable cover for a comforter.

Contour sheets   See *fitted sheets.*

Crash   A linen, cotton, or mixture suitable for dish, glass, and kitchen towels. Better grades may be used for luncheon sets, doilies, and bureau scarfs. See the glossary in Chapter 17.

Cretonne   See the glossary in Chapter 21.

Crocheted lace   For bedspread or table cover. See *Lace*

Damask   A fabric for table cloth and napkins in Jacquard weave. The pattern is reversible. Linen, cotton, rayon, or a combination of fibers are made in double or single damask.

Dimity   See the glossary in Chapter 17.

Domestics   A classification of textile merchandise that includes towels, table covers, and all bed coverings.

Drill   A strong warp-faced twilled cotton fabric, commonly used as covering for box springs, mattresses, and pillows.

Duvet   A French term for a comforter, usually down-filled.

Duvet cover   A comforter cover used for a duvet.

Embroidery   Ornamental needlework done on the fabric itself.

Felt   Used for table covers. See Chapter 12.

Fitted sheets   Those whose corners are made to fit the mattress. Both bottom and top fitted sheets are available.

Gingham   A fabric used for bedspreads. See the glossary in Chapter 17.

Glass towels   Towels made of linen crash, cotton, or mixtures suitable for drying glasses because they are lint free.

Guest towels or fingertip towels   Towels that are lightweight and smaller than hand towels. They are made of lightweight linen crash, huck, damask, terry, in white, solids, and designs.

Huck towels   Cotton, linen, or mixtures, occasionally with rayon in honeycomb dobby weave. They may have Jacquard borders. Face or hand towels in white or colors are available.

Lace   A fabric created by looping, interlacing, braiding, or twisting threads.

Longcloth   Synonym for *muslin sheeting.*

Muslin   See the glossary in Chapter 17.

Muslin sheeting   A carded muslin for bed sheets in white or colors made in types 140 (A grade), 128 (B grade), and 112 (C grade).

Patchwork quilts   Made of small pieces of cotton or silk fabric cut in various shapes and sewn together to form patterns. They are quilted on a frame when done by hand. Modern patchwork quilts may be printed to resemble the hand-sewn.

Percale sheeting   A combed muslin (may be carded in poorer grade) for bed sheets, in white or colors, made in type 200 (A grade) and 180 (B grade). See *percale* for dresses, in the glossary in Chapter 17.

Pickage   The number of fillings that pass between two rows of pile yarns plus the number of fillings under the pile loops. Two fillings shot through the same pile shed and one filling shot through to interlace with the ground warps (2 + 1) equals three picks.

Plastic-coated fabric   Used for shower curtains and dress covers. It is a plastic film supported by fabric or coating covering a textile fabric.

Quilt   A bed covering, usually thinner and less resilient than a comforter, made of two thicknesses of printed cotton muslin with cotton, wool, or polyester batting between. Fabrics and batting are sewn together with fine quilting (running) stitches.

Seersucker   Used for bedspreads. See the glossary in Chapter 17.

Silence cloth   A padding placed under the tablecloth on a dining table.

Table linen   Any fabric, regardless of fiber content, that is suitable for a table covering.

Taffeta   Used for bedspreads and shower curtains. See the glossary in Chapter 17.

Tapestry   Used for table covers. See the glossary in Chapter 21.

Terry cloth   A cotton pile fabric commonly made with uncut or cut loops on one or both sides of the fabric. It may have linen pile in a "friction" towel. It is used for bath and face towels, face cloths, bath rugs and beach robes. See Chapter 5.

Thermal woven   A porous cloth so constructed that air warmed by the body is trapped between the yarns. First used in underwear, now also used for blankets and the reverse sides of comforters.

Thread   In towels (double or single). In double thread, each loop is made of two parallel threads not twisted together, and these threads come out of the same space between two fillings. Single thread is made of a single yarn and is less durable and absorbent.

Ticking   A heavy, tightly woven carded cotton fabric in alternate stripes of white and colors, suitable for pillow and mattress covers. It is usually twill but may be in satin weave.

Tufted fabric   A fabric ornamented with soft, fluffy, slackly twisted ply yarns (usually cotton). Most tufts are inserted by needles into a woven fabric like unbleached muslin, textured cotton, and rayon plain-weave cloth. When tufts are spaced (as coin dots), the bedspread is called *candlewick;* when placed in close rows, the fabric is *chenille.* "Loom tufted" means tufts woven in as the cloth is woven. Tufted fabrics are used for bedspreads, mats, and robes. See *rugs,* Chapter 20.

Tufting   A brushlike button of clipped cotton yarn that appears at regular intervals on mattresses. Also used for rugs.

Turkish towel   A bath towel, face towel, or washcloth made of terry cloth.

Unbleached muslin   A cotton plain-weave fabric used for ironing-board covers, dust covers, and dustcloths. See the glossary in Chapter 17.

Chapter 20

PERIOD STYLES IN HOME FURNISHINGS AND SOFT FLOOR COVERINGS

PART I: PERIOD STYLES

If a room is to be newly furnished, you first should decide what sort of atmosphere you wish to create—formal or informal. Consideration should also be given to the various roles that the room will assume in the life of the occupants.

CREATING AN ATMOSPHERE

The living room is what the name implies—a place in which to live. It should be warm, comfortable, and hospitable—an appropriate background for entertaining guests or for normal household life.

Rooms that are used less frequently may be a little bold or dramatic. Foyers, halls, and dining rooms come under this description. A bedroom should be more serene; a child's room, restful but bright; a dinette, inviting and cheerful; a kitchen, efficient and colorful.

In decorating, it is helpful to be familiar with period furnishings, not to reproduce exactly the era desired, but rather to convey the spirit of the period while designing a room that is appropriate to its particular purpose and up-to-date in comfort and style. Different periods of furniture can be used together effectively. This avoids the monotony of everything looking alike and endows the room with the unique personality of the homeowner. An occasional traditional piece mixed with modern furniture lends warmth and a sense of heritage. Oriental antiques or reproductions mingled with contemporary furnishings suggest sophistication and elegance. This juxtaposition of styles calls for taste refined by exposure to a variety of settings. In choosing to mix periods, the combined styles should have some similarity or they should be very different. This eclectic decorating trend has no hard and fast rules, but rather, pieces are selected to complement each other, to soften hard modern lines, to dramatize beauty or individuality, and to offset and differentiate the ordinary.

The use of the room must be considered in the light of the kind of atmosphere the owner wishes to create: formal or informal, elaborate or simple. There are a few other points to be considered, however.

Massive furniture makes a small room seem smaller, whereas a few pieces of small furniture and small designs make a small room seem more spacious than it really is. In short, furniture and designs should be in proportion to the size of the room. (See Chapter 21 for other factors in creating a harmonious setting.)

An awareness of the history of furniture and an appreciation of design ingenuity and craftsmanship will pay dividends in the perceptive selection and enjoyment of such furnishings. Although furniture is not a textile, and so does not technically come within the scope of this book, it is helpful to be able to recognize the most common styles in order to select appropriate fabrics for draperies, upholsteries, and rugs, as well as for accessories.

PERIOD FURNITURE AND DESIGN

There are many long-standing styles in furniture and home furnishings that are in use today: Italian, Spanish, French, English, American, Modern, Contemporary, and Oriental. (See Fig. 20.1.) From such a general classification, each style group may be subdivided into periods named for the king, queen, or cabinetmaker whose style in furnishings typified those times. See Appendix H for appropriate period styles in woods, rugs, upholstery, and drapery fabrics.

Italian Style

Large, massive furniture ornately carved—with vivid, striking designs in upholstery, hangings, and draperies—is characteristic of the Italian style in general. Luxury and magnificence controlled the furnishings and the fabric decorations in the days of Italy's grandeur. The Italian Renaissance (1400–1643) marked the revival of the classic arts.

Woods used for the furniture were dark finish with geometric carvings. The designs in fabrics were large, raised, and impressive, consisting of flowers in vases or baskets or the fluorescent artichoke or pineapple motifs and clusters of round dots. Brocades, damasks, velvets, and velours are all suited to the Italian style. Fabric colors were dark green, burgundy, cream, and gold.

Figure 20.1a An ornate lampas, which is a silk, rayon, cotton, wool, or mixed-fiber fabric similar to satin damask. Lampas has two sets of warps and one filling. The heraldic influence is seen in the architectural motifs consisting of castles. Italy, early sixteenth century.

Figure 20.1b A modern composite American design based mostly upon the Italian Renaissance. Note the parapeted castle treated in the modern manner by placing it on the bias and forgetting all the rules of gravitation. The slender, needlelike tower is inspired from the "Trylon," the theme motif of the 1939 New York World's Fair. The ever-popular tulip motif has been utilized together with stylized Persian cone motifs. (Photo courtesy of the Scalamandré Museum of Textiles.)

This style requires large, preferably formal, rooms. An upholstered sofa and a Jacobean chair would harmonize with the Italian style, for these pieces have a quality of massiveness. Venetian style favored painted finishes and mirrored walls. Decorative fringes were used.

Spanish Style

The days of Ferdinand and Isabella—and the Italian-born Columbus (1451–1504)—are recollected in the Spanish decoration of today. Designs are large, bold in outline, and often a combination of the Moorish and the Italian. Like the Italian, Spanish interiors should be spacious, since furniture and designs tend to be large, striking, and imposing. Adaptations of ship designs and appropriate white scrolls and motifs similar to the Italian types are used. Fabrics suitable for a Spanish-style room include leathers, damasks, and velvets. Fringes and nailheads frequently serve as decorative elements. For an informal room, printed linens or coarse cottons in colorful stripes or Spanish motifs are suitable. Off-white walls with green and/or orange furnishings are often seen.

French Styles

The accepted French periods of design are French Renaissance (latter half of the fifteenth century), Louis XIV (1643–1715), Louis XV (1723–1774), Louis XVI (1774–1793), Directoire (1795–1799), and Empire (1804–1825).

French Renaissance

The Renaissance was an intellectual movement with a revival in the arts. It marked the transition from medieval to modern times. In Italy, Renaissance architecture and art succeeded the Gothic and spread to France during the latter half of the fifteenth century. It was expressed in great castles, such as Chambord and Fontainebleau, and in the interior decorations French furniture showed a marked Italian influence.

Louis XIV

So far as the cultivation of the arts is concerned, the Grand Monarch, Louis XIV, is the most important of the French kings. Furniture of the time was in a grand style called *baroque*. Massive and symmetrical, the woods were carved, gilded, inlaid with tortoise shell or metals, and ornamented with marquetry.

During the reign of Louis XIV, renewed interest was taken in the arts and fabric weaving. The silk industry at Lyons flourished under the patronage of the king, and France became a producer of fine fabrics. French brocades and damasks were known for their fine quality throughout Europe. Probably the artistic interest of Louis XIV was fired by the woman whom he was courting, Louise de la Valliére, the woman who had called his hunting lodge crude and bare. In reply to this jibe, Louis built the palace of Versailles.

Louis himself loved brilliance and so was often called *le roi soleil*—the Sun

King. He preferred very large designs, such as flowers in baskets, immense fleurs de lis, and feather and flower motifs. Rich colors borrowed from Italy— dark red, blue, dark green, and old gold—were his favorites. But a woman's choice again influenced color preference, and new, delicate colors such as yellowish pink (called aurora), plum, yellow, and flame appeared.

In the French furniture of this period, flat, boxlike lines of the sixteenth century were replaced by framework with rounded contours, characterized by much ornamentation, such as elaborate scrolls, engraved white metal ornaments, inlays of tortoise shell, and mountings in bronze. André Charles Boulle (1642–1732) was the outstanding furniture maker of the time.

Louis XV

Du Barry and Madame de Pompadour, the latter a woman of superb taste and accomplishments, greatly influenced the design and ornamentation of this period. Actually, the transition to the softer, gentler style began during the eight years from 1715 to 1723 when the Duc d'Orleans was regent. French furniture of this period is called Regence. It shows the flowing lines and charming decorative touches typical of furniture in Louis XV style. These years marked the introduction of the Chinese influence, later to become known as "the craze for Chinoiserie."

There were bombé (convex) fronts and sides on cabinets and chests. Many more pieces of small-in-scale furniture were used in this period, and fabric decoration favored realistic flowers, scrolls, and chinoiseries. Beauvais tapestry was frequently used for upholstering fine sofas and chairs. Later Louis XV, called *rococo*, was extravagant in detail—not balanced or symmetrical. The two famous furniture makers of this period, who continued to be famous during the reign of Louis XVI, were Jean Riesener (1734–1806) and David Roentgen (1743–1807).

Louis XVI

The reign of Louis XVI is marked by less ornate design and a more delicate and refined treatment. Designs of this period were influenced by furniture and murals excavated at Pompeii and Herculaneum. The lines of Louis XVI furniture and designs are straight and symmetrical. Chair legs are usually straight and fluted longitudinally like columns, tapering to the base. Ornamentation was of classical Greek influence and was used to emphasize beauty of line.

Marie Antoinette, wife of Louis XVI, was interested in a rural life. Pastoral scenes, interlocked rings, musical instruments, turtle doves, bowknots, and gardeners' tools were popular motifs for upholstery and hangings. Bows of ribbon often surmounted furniture panels and chair backs. Brocade, satin, damask, and *toile de Jouy* prints were common upholstery coverings and draperies. More background and less design is shown in this period. The Jouy prints were the first roller prints (made by direct printing) and became so much the vogue that they rivaled the brocades of Lyons.

The Directoire Period

This era was a transition in design from Louis XVI to Empire. Napoleon emerged as the central figure after the French Revolution ended the monarchy. He admired Rome and so had the French palace redecorated in formal styles. The bee and the butterfly were his symbols. Designs were rich in color and perfectly balanced. Motifs were classical, from Roman influence and the Egyptian campaign. Stripes, medallions, cornucopias, circles, and squares were typical designs. Napoleon preferred golden yellow, red, and green; his wife, Josephine, liked pale blue, white, yellow, mauve, and gray. Woods commonly used in furniture were ebony, mahogany, and satinwood. For upholstery, heavy brocades, silks, and satins were evident. Military objects such as drums, stars, and wrought iron trimmed with bronze were popular.

The Empire Period

Furniture became more massive and heavy and was frequently ornamented with brass or bronze mountings. Mahogany, ebony, and rosewood, often inlaid with ivory, were used for furniture. Tables had marble tops and metal feet; chair legs were fluted in front, somewhat like the Louis XVI type, but they were heavier. The back legs were curved in the classic mode. Some legs were made in the form of bundles of arrows, or fasces. Laurel wreaths, torches, eagles, lions, and sphinx served as ornamentation. Upholstery was heavy, consisting of damasks, velvets, and prints. A simplified Empire style, suited to the less pretentious life of the provinces, is called *Biedermeier* in Germany. Usually furniture combined two tones of wood.

French Provincial

Traditionally, furniture and furnishings used in the provinces in France were usually copies of that found in royal palaces and the chateaux of the nobility. Furniture was made from local fruitwoods by country craftsmen and frequently was on a smaller scale than the massive furniture made for the larger, grander dwellings. Such furniture integrates beautifully into American interiors—in towns as well as country areas, bringing warmth and adding an architectural element very often lacking from today's contemporary interiors.

Original pieces from France, though they might have started life in a Normandy farmhouse, are now extremely expensive and often hard to find at any price. But many American manufacturers do excellent adaptations of eighteenth- and nineteenth-century French country pieces; they have often been rescaled by perceptive designers and so fit better into our homes than do the authentic pieces from which they are derived.

Chairs are comfortable with wide rush seats and padded backs, and tables are spacious. Floral or pastoral designs in chintz, cretonne, linen crash, and rough-textured peasant linens are in good taste. *Italian Provincial* is a more formal adaptation of the French style, with straighter lines and geometric designs of triangles and squares.

English Styles

The periods of English decoration may be separated into four main classifications: Early English, Georgian, Regency, and Victorian.

Early English

These styles may be subdivided into Jacobean (1603–1688), William and Mary (1689–1702), and Queen Anne (1702–1714).

During the Tudor days, when Henry VIII reigned, portable furniture and decorative refinements were rare. Cushions and fragments of cloth were used for decoration, if any cloth was used. But when Elizabeth I became queen in 1558, she encouraged all forms of needlecraft and weaving. Velvets and tapestries were imported. She had walnut trees planted abundantly so that succeeding generations might profit and not be dependent upon oak for furniture. So, although the Jacobean style of decoration did not begin until 1603, the foundation was laid in Elizabeth's time; her interest in window, bed, and wall hangings spurred textile imports and encouraged weaving and needlework at home.

Elizabeth's successor, James I, furthered the new movement by interesting himself in embroideries and tapestries; the result was that handsome designs prevailed in Jacobean hangings and upholsteries. The Jacobean floral is the characteristic design of the period. It is a rather large pattern full of gorgeous colors that emphasize movement and rhythm. English traders were bringing fabrics home from the Far East, especially India—fabrics that English designers copied. The Tree of Life design and crewel embroidery were introduced into England in this manner. Heraldic insignia were important patterns for wall hangings.

Lines in furniture were straight or classically curving, with vigorous scrollwork and trimmings; pieces were consequently sturdy and heavy and often massive. Geometric paneling and furniture with stubby feet and turned legs were used. Oak and some walnut were popular. Embroideries, printed fabrics, needlepoint, brocade, velvet, and leather comprise the leading upholstery fabrics.

The next important period in Early English styles is that of William and Mary.[1] The ruggedness of Jacobean styles was modified by a Dutch influence that lent a more homelike and cheerful effect. Straight lines changed to sweeping curves; ball or bun feet and slender legs; stretcher connectors; caning; teardrop pull hardware; and finer proportions. Walnut was the principal wood used in furniture. Needlework, chintz, damask, and leather were the common upholstery fabrics.

---

[1] Some authorities place the elegant, gay Carolean style between the Jacobean and the William and Mary.

In the period during which Queen Anne reigned (1702–1714), there was a continuing trend toward comfort, grace and a generally "English" look. The flowing line was still there, but there was unity, evident in the association of the cabriole leg with other parts of a piece of furniture—chair backs and the shapes of seats, for instance. A new way of life was also beginning; this was reflected in the furniture that was designed. The fashion for tea drinking brought forth a plethora of small tables; the mania for buying and collecting fine china also brought a demand for vitrines and curio cabinets; the craze for card playing was responsible for the designing and making of gaming and card tables. Such motifs as the scallop shell and the classical acanthus leaf are typical of the Queen Anne period, and walnut was much used and cherished for its fine surface. Perceptive scaling is however the most notable feature of Queen Anne furniture. Perhaps never before or since has there been more charming, better proportioned furniture than was crafted in this period in England.

Rooms of that time were spacious, sometimes with ornamented ceilings and the furniture shows a marked tendency toward comfort. The "easy chair" came into use; one type is the wing chair. These chairs were upholstered and often overstuffed. Love seats also came into being. Common upholstery fabrics were petit point, needlepoint, and gros point. The period marked the popularity of the highboy (made in two sections for convenience in moving), the kneehole desk with hidden drawers, writing tables, secretaries, curved cabriole legs ending in pad feet, and decorative fan or sunburst embellishments.

For hangings, Chinese embroideries and India prints were popular, and chintz in Oriental designs was used for window draperies. Some authorities credit Queen Anne with originating the fashion of covering furniture entirely with fabric. At any rate, the idea was a good one.

The Georgian Period

This era (1710–1806) was marked by the expert craftsmanship of a new group of cabinetmakers and designers: Chippendale, Hepplewhite, Sheraton, and the Adam brothers. During this period, as was true in France at the time of Louis XV, rooms became smaller, less like Roman temples, and pieces of furniture became more numerous. This was an era of chairs. Whereas chests, benches, and stools were sufficient as seats for lesser members of a household in earlier days, chairs now became essential for all. This demand for chairs afforded Chippendale an opportunity to express his ability. Mahogany supplanted walnut and oak. Some of Chippendale's furniture stressed the Chinese influence, but he also utilized Gothic and French styles. Chippendale was the chief exponent of eighteenth-century English rococo expressed by naturalistic motifs, curves and scrolls. Characteristics of this designer's style are cabriole leg, claw and ball foot, and serpentine or ox-bow design.

One of the four Adam brothers (all architects) became interested in travel and studied Roman ruins extensively. He introduced the classical feeling later expressed in their work. He also created the interest in exquisitely decorated painted furniture and popularized the use (in England) of satinwood and inlay. The Adam brothers are particularly well known for artistic chairs and sofas. They designed complete interiors with elaborate but symmetrical plaster ceilings and mantels. French brocades and moirés were favorite upholsteries. Colors were pale gray, blue, and white.

Hepplewhite and Sheraton were contemporaries of the Adam brothers. Furniture became delicate in proportion, more slender and refined. Mahogany, satinwood, and rosewood inlay were used. Fabrics for the Hepplewhite period took on a French appearance. The French satin stripe became popular, together with silks and satins and designs of festoons, tassels, and ribbons. The designs that Sheraton approved were more conservative and classical than Hepplewhite's. Lightweight silks, damasks, and printed linens in designs of urns, musical instruments, and medallions were favored by Sheraton. He also favored tapering fluted legs and straight-back chairs. Hepplewhite used curved lines and designed chairbacks in shield shapes.

Regency Period

The Prince of Wales served as regent for his deranged father, George III, from 1780 to 1820, but the Regency era is listed as being from 1793 to 1820. The Brighton Pavilion, an extravagant and beautiful palace, was designed by John Nash, the great architect of the period, to reflect the future George IV's interest in Oriental and Indian decorative styles. Flamboyance became fashionable, and there was considerable copying and borrowing from exotic sources. Bamboo furniture was introduced in England, and black lacquer was generously used with mother of pearl or gilt decoration. Eccentric shapes, contrasting textures, and richness of pattern abounded. Swagged draperies and shirred fabric tents contributed to the rich effect. The use of pattern that was popular in Victorian times began with George IV.

Victorian Period

Queen Victoria of Great Britain had the longest reign in English history. The Victorian era (1837–1901) was the day of the horsehair sofa, the very high architectural headboard on beds, wax flowers covered with glass, the parlor with its mantelpiece and whatnot covered with bric-a-brac, red plush seats in chairs and railroad coaches, and the marble-top table, cluttered rooms, heavy draperies, large patterned wallpaper and rugs, oval or horseshoe-shaped chair backs. In short, there was much gingerbread work. Black walnut, oak, and mahogany were commony used woods. Some of the architecture and furniture of the period is considered by many to be overly ornate, heavy, ponderous, and cluttered, but revivals of Victorian styles take the most attractive elements and eliminate the gewgaws. Victorian red velvet has been revived in dress and home furnishings. Many of the old horsehair sofas and chairs sell at a premium. Edwardian styles, immediately following the Victorian, are often considered a distinct period with emphasis on lighter, leaner styles with straight lines, little decoration, and simple form.

American Styles

American styles begin with Early American (1607–1725), the period of early colonization, and continue through the period 1725 to 1790, often called Colonial. These two periods before the colonies became states will be discussed together.

Early American and Colonial

Much of the early furniture and furnishings used in America was essentially English: Jacobean, Queen Anne, Chippendale, Hepplewhite, and Sheraton. Some furniture was brought from England, and the rest was made here in reproduction of the styles with which the colonists were familiar. English oak and walnut were used, as were woods from native forests, such as maple, pine, cedar, cherry, ash, and hickory. The fact that the colonists were lacking in tools for making elaborate styles in furniture, and the great necessity for thrift, created a style that is plain and sometimes crude, yet individual. Chairs had wooden, leather, or rush seats with narrow vertical slats or horizontal ladder backs. Serviceability and sturdy construction were emphasized. Ingenuity produced many unusual pieces.

The first fabrics used in this country were imported from England, Italy, and France; it was not until the colonists had become fairly securely established that they began to make their own. In the first efforts of the colonial craftsman, present-day interior designers/decorators find their models of Early American interiors. Homespun, damask, chintz in small designs, and quilted cottons were made. In the latter part of the eighteenth century, more fabrics were imported from England and the Continent, with the result that homes became more elaborate, with silk damasks, brocatelles, Genoese velvets, and Chinese brocades. In general, Colonial styles were Georgian, Chippendale, Hepplewhite, and Sheraton.

Then came the Federal period, following the signing of the Constitution, made memorable with respect to furniture by our own great cabinetmaker Duncan Phyfe (fl. 1795–1847). He was often called "the American Sheraton." His mastery of carving and his skill in making curved lines did much to establish the Sheraton influence in America. Furniture became slender and graceful. Mahogany and walnut were the favorite woods. Striped brocades, satins, damasks, and haircloth were common upholstery fabrics.

Many of Duncan Phyfe's styles are reproduced in fine furniture of today. Some of the most common are the sectional dining table, each part of which, when not in use for dining, can be used as a separate table tilted back against the wall, and the lyre-back side chairs and sofas. The furnishings of the White House are typical of the early Federal period. (See Figs. 20.2 and 20.3.)

Figure 20.2 The Green Room of the White House, early nineteenth century.

Figure 20.3 One of a pair of early nineteenth-century sofas covered in embroidered cotton of the period, the White House.

American Victorian

In the 1850s, John Belter developed his process of lamination, which made it possible to bend and shape wood and carve intricate designs. Wood was given a dark, almost black finish and was upholstered in brilliant jeweltone velvets or tapestries. Light-colored marble table tops served as a contrast to the deep colors.

Art Nouveau

Originally developed as a renewed interest in the decorative arts, this period (1875–1900) gave rise to a rebellion against the stale copying of classicism and was based on natural growing forms and a whiplike sharp curve. Furniture resembled flowers, trees, ferns, or animals. Wood appeared sculpted, combining light, dark, and painted finishes. Louis Comfort Tiffany (1848–1933), son of the famed American jeweler, had a profound influence on this era, especially for his creations in stained glass.

Early Modern and Modern

A reaction against the Victorian ornamental excesses and the commercialization of the natural forms developed an impetus toward a simpler, more rational type of expression, known as Early Modern (1911–1920s). As early as 1911, the Bauhaus school in Germany was applying an architectural approach to furniture. Straight lines replaced curves. In the United States, architects such as Louis Sullivan and later his star pupil Frank Lloyd Wright called for honesty in design, where extraneous details were eliminated and the simple utilitarian form was considered beautiful. Chairs, beds, couches, and storage units were slung close to the floor and appeared as architectural elements of the room.

Modern has gone through several periods of popularity since its inception. In the 1930s, there was a resurgence of Art Nouveau, called Art Deco or Moderne. Geometric or American Indian patterns abounded. Colors were light, lots of mirrors were used, and lucite was introduced. Fabrics were smooth, soft, and shiny.

As the Bauhaus influence grew, the post–World War I furniture designers used such building materials as glass, chrome, and steel. Architects who also designed furniture that became modern classics were Mies Van der Rohe for his leather sling chair and Marcel Breuer for his cane and chrome chairs.

But to the average family, Early Modern design was cold and bizarre looking. It took many years before the public accepted the modern credo that form follows function, that extraneous details are eliminated, and that beauty is the result of the innate qualities of the materials used in the clarity of design. Eventually, modifications were made and modern pieces gained in popularity as buyers came to appreciate the comfort, simplicity, utility, and economy inherent in this furniture.

In the 1950s Scandinavian designers developed a lighter modular look with pieces that could be easily reassembled if the homeowner moved. Wood was light in color, of bleached mahogany or limed oak. Fabric was heavily textured wool or cotton and rayon.

In the 1960s, with technological advancements, plastic came to rival wood in furniture construction. New production techniques encouraged ingenuity and innovation. Charles Eames designed a lightweight, plastic-coated, bucket-seat chair that could be readily mass-produced. Eero Saarinen developed a line of pedestal tables and chairs that has become a design classic. In fabrics, textures have predominated—rough linen weaves, wool and man-made fiber blends, velvets, modern tapestries, and tweeds. Patterns involved mechanical symbols, simple geometrics, and later bolder free forms and florals. As more window was exposed, textured but translucent casement cloth was used as a simple window treatment, eliminating heavy, ornate hangings.

Figure 20.4 Contemporary style in home furnishings. Milo Baughman designed this modular group for Thayer Coggin to provide a clean, new look with chintz fabric, quilted in a block pattern. (Photo courtesy of Southern Furniture Manufacturers Association.)

Contemporary

But modern was not, and is not, to everyone's taste, and so Contemporary furnishing has proven a safe haven for those looking for a more traditional appearance. Period styling has been adapted to modern comfort and convenience with deep and softly covered couches and chairs. Heavy features have been lightened, scaled down in size, and simplified. A hint of an era is sufficient to recall the past and warm the future. (See Fig. 20.4.)

Oriental Influences

Since the time of Marco Polo, almost every period of furniture has responded to the exotic inspiration of drawings, screens, and chinaware that were exported from China and much later from Japan. Furniture makers usually borrowed Oriental details that could easily be transposed to the traditional period desired. Chippendale, in the 1750s, used fanciful chinoiseries to lend a sophisticated flavor to his designs. Pagodas, Chinese latticework, and lacquer finishes were used extensively.

Today, with the opening of trade with China, there is a greater appreciation for the structural beauty of Chinese furniture. The classical serenity, simplicity of line, and flawless proportions are especially suited to contemporary furniture. The integration of detail and sparse decoration within the furniture have provided particular inspirations to modern designers.

Japan, where comparatively little furniture is used, has lent an air of spaciousness and lightness to design. A room divider, whether a low squarish chest or an arrangement of shelves, allows a flexibility of use derived from the Japanese.

PART II: SOFT FLOOR COVERINGS (CARPETS AND RUGS)

Soft (textile) floor coverings are considered a requirement in most American homes today. It is estimated that virtually all living rooms have them and that four-fifths of the bedrooms and three-fourths of the dining areas in America are carpeted. (See Fig. 20.5 for U.S. carpet shipments in a recent six-year period.) Carpets and rugs are also used in many bathrooms and in some kitchens. They eliminate floor noise and absorb airborne noise; if wall to wall, they reduce danger of slippage; they provide warmth and comfort; and they add beauty and harmony to the home. They are also used in indoor-outdoor living areas in sunrooms, patios, and around swimming pools; they may also be found on boats.

Not only are soft floor coverings important in residences, but they also serve a function in public places, such as schools, offices, hospitals, restaurants, stores, and airports. In fact, these commercial carpet installations now account

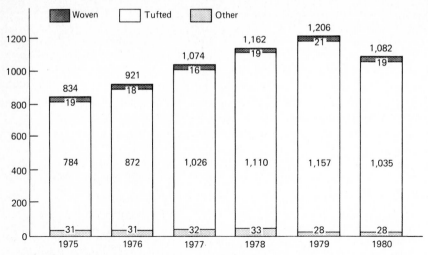

Figure 20.5 Total industry shipments of carpets and rugs in the United States, 1975–1980 (millions of square yards). (Courtesy of the Carpet and Rug Institute.)

for about 40 percent of all the carpeting sold in the United States. This is due to a variety of factors, including durability, ease of maintenance, absorption of noise, sure (not slippery) footing, and colorful and exciting surroundings *or* quiet and restful ones.

CLASSIFICATION OF SOFT FLOOR COVERINGS

Textile floor coverings are classified broadly as rugs and carpets, although in common parlance the two words are used synonymously. They may also be classified as machine-made versus handmade and as domestic versus imported.

Rugs are soft floor coverings laid on the floor but not fastened to it. A rug does not usually cover the entire floor. Scatter rugs are small rugs, about 2 feet × 3 feet and 4 feet × 6 feet, which can be placed in front of doors, couches, and on stairs. Usual sizes of rugs (in feet) are 2½ × 4¼, 9 × 6, 9 × 10½, 9 × 12, 9 × 13½, 9 × 15, 9 × 18, 12 × 12, 12 × 13½, 12 × 15, 12 × 18, and 12 × 21.

A carpet is a soft covering fastened to the entire floor. Wall-to-wall, stair, and hall carpets are examples. Many hall carpets are 27 inches wide, not covering the entire floor.

A broadloom is a seamless carpeting of any weave or style, 6 to 18 (or more) feet wide. Most production today is in the form of roll goods, generally 12 to 15 feet wide, that can be bought to install as wall-to-wall carpeting. Broadloom is also cut into rugs of all sizes and shapes.

Broadlooms are popular because there are no visible seams to break the attractive pile surface. A solid-colored broadloom or one that has a two-tone effect will blend nicely with any period of furnishings.

SELECTION OF FLOOR COVERINGS

In addition to size requirements, the consumer is interested in the nature of the space to be covered. A salesclerk may ask the customer, "Do you live in the room or just walk through it?" If there is heavy traffic, as in an entrance hall, a durable floor covering that will not show soil should be selected. The salesperson may show the customer a *twist,* a broadloom made with uncut pile, in which yarns of different colors may be twisted together to form the pile. The resultant blending of colors is attractive, and the carpet does not show footmarks so quickly. For a bedroom, where there is little traffic, a cotton rug or a hooked rug may be appropriate. For the living room, the "heart" of the home, a softer, more luxurious surface of high-quality man-made fibers or even wool is generally to be preferred.

Indoor-outdoor carpets are floor coverings that are suitable both inside the house and out of doors—for example, carpets for boats, patios, terraces, miniature golf courses, kitchens, and bathrooms. They are made in tufted construction of 100 percent olefin in dense pile plush-type or in a grasslike carpet. They are also made of acrylics.

For commercial use, a careful selection should be made, since once installed, the carpet may remain in use for years.

Beyond considerations of size and type of covering, most modern consumers have aesthetic concerns: they want coverings that appeal to the eye—color and design—and those that appeal to the sense of touch—the body and depth of the pile. Economic considerations are also important to most: wearlife, ease of care, and price. In the case of antiques, as in some Orientals, rarity is another consideration.

Color

Although the consumer often turns to the salesperson for advice, choosing colors is really a personal problem. In general, it may be said that colors harmonize if they have something in common. For instance, they may belong to the same hue or color family. Colors, like people, have personalities. Some colors are gay, light, and airy; others are heavy and ponderous. The extent to which colors are used and the way of using them are considerations. In some combinations, one color dominates but does not overpower the color scheme, because balance is emphasized by visualizing where the colors are to be used and the relative size of ceiling, floor, upholstery, draperies, and accents. Furthermore, there is a tendency today to stress those colors that emphasize informality and easy living. Home and women's magazines, furnishing displays in retail stores, home pages of newspapers, and salespeople's advice will help consumers answer their color questions.

Design or Pattern and Texture

Floor coverings are solid-colored, two-toned, or varicolored and are sometimes called *sculptured* or *carved*. The carved rug is made with different heights of pile; for example, the design may have a deeper pile than the ground. Sculpturing may also combine cut pile with uncut loops for a multitextured effect. Carved rugs have become popular in contemporary styles. The choice of design in a rug is contingent upon other factors, such as use and size of the room, style of decorations, and colors and designs already present in the draperies and upholstery. Generally speaking, solid-colored floor coverings show footfalls more than two-toned or varicolored types do.

Sometimes, a pattern in a carpet is not readily obvious, yet there is the semblance of a pattern. Three versions of this type have emerged: the shag, the random-tipped sheer, and the plush. The nylon, polyester, or wool pile in the shag and random-tipped is long, loose, and resilient, with the high pile of the random sheer cut at varied lengths. They have proven difficult to clean, since cleaning solution may remain deep in the pile and cause a change in color. Currently, these types are out of style and have been replaced by a plush construction with a single level of shorter cut pile of soft twist yarn or of nubby and heat-set yarn (to prevent slipping).

Wool Rya rugs come from Denmark. They are made of blended wools from New Zealand and Scotland in patterns suited to contemporary décor. The pile is thick and strong for luxury and wear. The designs are woven through to the back, achieving the effect of hand craftsmanship. Rya rugs are advertised as colorfast and mothproof.

A newer application of color and design to rugs is done by printing. This technique was introduced in 1968. At that time, one type of printing machine produced copies of linoleum patterns. Today, carpet printing can produce near perfect register for up to ten colors. In 1973 about 25 percent of carpet yardage was printed in color patterns. By the mid-1980s, it is estimated that 50 percent of floor coverings will be printed.

Fabrics that are printable are level loop pile and frieze in all types of fibers (acrylics, nylons, and polyesters). In fact, the designs found in woven Axminster and Wilton can be reproduced in prints at appreciably lower prices. The homespun quality of authentic colonial American patterns, colors, and designs has been adapted to room size rugs as well as to wall-to-wall installations.

Body and Depth of Pile

Carpet yarns are made in different bulks and weight; also, in single yarns, two-ply, and three- and even four-ply. The major production is probably in two- and three-ply yarns. Three- and four-ply are used for striated effects: for very heavy

Table 20.1 Market Share of Fibers in Carpets and Rugs, 1975–1985F (as a percentage of total market)[a]

	1975	1976	1977	1978	1979	1980	1981	1985F
Acrylic	6	6	4	4	3	2	2	2
Nylon BCF	37	33	34	35	38	43	40	41
Nylon staple	39	41	43	44	43	40	43	42
Polyester staple	10	13	12	11	10	7	8	8
Polypropylene BCF/slit film	4	4	4	4	4	5	5	5
Polypropylene staple	2	2	2	2	2	2	2	2
Others	2	1	1	—	—	1	—	—
Total	100	100	100	100	100	100	100	100

[a]Figures through 1981 are rounded and are from the U.S. Department of Commerce, Bureau of the Census.
F – Forecast.

fabrics, three- and four-ply yarns are necessary. Since most wear is on the pile, the yarn used should give excellent coverage of the surface, good appearance, and adequate tensile strength. Texturized and bulky yarns of man-made fibers, including bicomponents, allow interesting possibilities for styling.

In general, the greater the closeness of the pile, the better the wearing quality. Both pile density and pile depth are factors to consider in quality, even though some of the finest rugs have very short pile. Pile density depends upon the closeness of the tufts of yarn to each other. Pile depth (also called height) signifies the length of the pile yarn from the backing to the surface. In general, deep pile rugs flatten and show footfalls more quickly than do those with short (or loop) pile; but this depends somewhat upon the resiliency of the fibers themselves. Deep pile is also usually more difficult to clean. Its softness makes it more suitable for minimum-traffic rooms, such as bedrooms and dens.

CARPET AND RUG FIBERS

While the quality of a soft floor covering is determined in part by the density and depth of the pile, quality also depends (1) upon the fiber used—its strength, resilience, luster, and resistance to moisture, stains, and other outside elements—and (2) upon the method of construction—a matter to be discussed in the section following this one.

Man-made fibers today dominate the pile face market, with 99 percent of the total for the United States. The natural fibers, including wool, account for hardly 1 percent of the total. (See Appendix B for trade names.)

The major man-made fibers are nylon, polyester, olefin, and acrylic. They are made from special types of these fibers growing out of years of research by the leading fiber producers. The man-mades are today's answer to the small world supply of wool and its high cost. (See Table 20.1.)

Nylon

Nylon accounts for over 80 percent of the fibers used in face yarns. Over half of this is in *bulked continuous-filament* form, called BCF. The rest is in staple yarns (cut into short lengths and spun). The BCF yarns are treated, while in solution form, before extrusion through the spinneret, so as to provide extra bulk. They do not require spinning and go directly to the construction process. Thus, cost is kept low.

Nylon is one of the strongest man-made fibers. It has excellent resistance to stains and abrasion, withstands crushing, and has good fastness to color. It can be treated to provide antistatic and soil-hiding qualities and can be dyed to achieve many interesting effects.

Polyester

Polyester accounts for less than 10 percent of the fibers used in face yarns for carpets. It is strong, has excellent abrasion resistance, and possesses antistatic quality. It has especially good pattern and texture retention. It may be treated for both fire and crush resistance and for improved dyeability and softer face.

Olefin (largely polypropylene)

Olefin is in third place among the carpet fibers, with about 7 percent of the carpet face yarn market. Its use has increased considerably since the early 1970s. It is used for the pile mostly in filament rather than in staple form. Olefin floor coverings are strong and resistant to water and dampness and abrasion; they are also antistatic.

Olefin's main use is for indoor-outdoor carpeting. But the fastest-growing segment of the recent market has been for artificial grass. The pile, generally green, looks like grass. It is used on patios and decks of swimming pools, cruise ships, in hotel lobbies, on some restaurant floors, and on tennis courts and other athletic fields. It is easy to maintain; resists water, stain, mildew, and fading; and never needs mowing or watering.

Acrylic

Acrylic accounts for little more than 2 percent of the surface fiber applications. It is the most woollike of all the man-made fibers. Its resistance to crushing is very good, the yarn has fire resistance, and its durability has been improved. Among the leading brands are Acrilan by Monsanto and Orlon by DuPont.

Wool

Before the 1960s, wool was the dominant face fiber. It accounted in 1961 for nearly two-thirds of total U.S. volume. But, with the improvements in the man-made fibers and the rising cost of wool, already noted, wool has dropped to less than 1 percent of the carpet market. Its resilience and dyeability are excellent; so is its resistance to soil.

The wool produced in the United States is too fine for floor coverings in moderate price ranges. The wool carpet yarns used in this country are from coarse, wiry, tough, low-grade wool, imported largely from New Zealand and Australia. High-grade wools are used abroad for hand-tied Orientals that are discussed later in this chapter.

Cotton

All-cotton yarns are seldom used for soft floor coverings. They do not wear well, they are not resilient, and they are hard to walk on. But small cotton rugs, with rubberized backing, are readily washable and highly absorbent; thus they are useful in bathrooms and some playrooms. Interesting colors and patterns are available. Cotton yarns are also used for chain warps, those that bind together the front and back of a rug.

CONSTRUCTION OF CARPETS

Tufted

Over 95 percent of the machine-made carpets in this country are now made by a relatively new method called tufted. Nearly ninety years ago (in 1895), a teenager in Georgia was working on a wedding dress when she accidentally completed a stitch that locked into the fabric. When she snipped off the thread, she noticed that the end standing up looked like a tuft of grass. This gave her the idea of making a tufted spread. The idea caught on and tufted spreads became popular. Many years later, this led to the invention of a machine that would do the tufting job. In the mid-1950s, the carpet industry experimented with the idea of using various fibers, and the tufted carpet became a reality, virtually replacing the established woven carpet. Figure 20.6 explains the tufting process.

The tufting process, as performed mechanically, requires needles to carry the yarn for the pile through the backing material where a "looper" catches the yarn as the needle is withdrawn to form a loop of pile. The loop may be cut by a knife to produce cut pile or it may be left uncut. (See Fig. 20.7.)

Tufted carpets can be produced not only with either cut or uncut pile of equal length but also with pile of varying lengths: high/low pile and floral/geometric and floral effects. These variations are accomplished by means of a pattern attachment to the basic tufting machine that controls the quantity of yarn supplied to the tufting needles. If less yarn is fed to the needles, the difference is "robbed" from the previously formed loop, thus shortening the height of that loop. Changes in the amount of yarn supplied to the needles brings about the desired pattern.

In practice, wide multiple-needle machines are used to punch an entire

Short-Loop Tufting

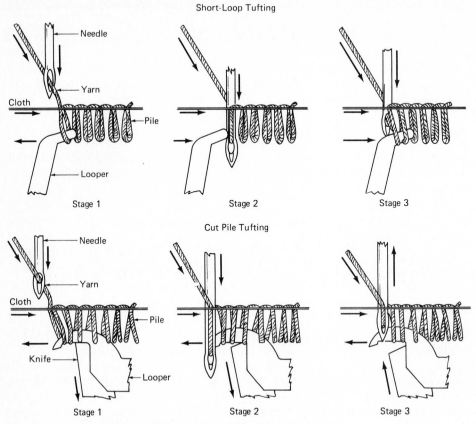

Cut Pile Tufting

Figure 20.6 The tufting process. (Courtesy of The Hoover Company.)

row of tufts across the entire width of the carpet in a single operation. For example, a quality carpet of three-ply yarn that is 12 feet wide requires about 970 needles (roughly 80 to the inch) and five to eight rows are punched for every inch of length. An area 9 × 15 feet can be punched in about 4 minutes—a rate that is about twenty-five times as fast as weaving.

The customer can get some idea as to whether the rows of tufts are close enough by bending a segment of the carpet to separate the rows. If the backing is clearly visible, so that the separation seems to "grin," the rows are probably too far apart for long wear and durability.

It is interesting to note that a chance observation by a young woman many years ago has initiated a series of events that has revolutionized a great industry and has been instrumental in keeping the cost of soft floor coverings low compared with the prices of other consumer goods. In fact, in a recent ten-year period, carpets increased in price only 20 percent, whereas apparel, other home furnishings, and autos increased more than 40 percent and foodstuffs much more.

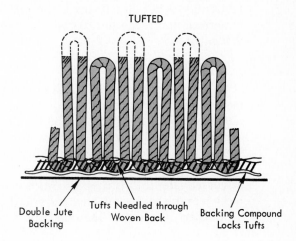

COMBINATION LOOP/CUT PILE

TUFTED

Figure 20.7   Tufting construction.

Double Jute
Backing

Tufts Needled through
Woven Back

Backing Compound
Locks Tufts

Tufted Carpet Backing

The backing for the tufted carpet is generally of olefin, but other fibers, such as jute, may be used. It may be a woven or nonwoven fabric constructed before the tufts of pile are inserted. This feature distinguishes it from the backing of woven carpets, to be discussed shortly, where certain warp or filling yarns used in the weaving process constitute the pile.

In tufting, the fabric backing is treated with a heavy coating of foam (latex) that holds the tufts in place. The carpet is usually provided with a secondary backing laminated to the primary backing to provide added strength and dimensional stability.

Dyeing and Printing Tufted Carpets

Carpets can be dyed and figured in various ways. Probably the most durable is to color the pile yarns before tufting. Yarns are printed in color segments determined by computer, so that each segment of the colored yarn is tufted to the backing at the precise point necessary to complete a pattern design, either free flowing or geometric.

After construction, the pile, if level and looped, can be printed in many different colors. The rotary screen printing technique, which uses a different screen for each color, has proven especially efficient. Improvements in printing machinery have increased speed, flexibility, and color changeover. Quicker-drying dyes and improved shearing equipment are employed.

An important recent development eliminates screen printing: controlled by magnetic tape and a so-called "chromotronic" computer, patterns are transferred to the pile by means of jets of dyestuffs. The elimination of screens has reduced costs by as much as 85 percent. The process has been found suitable for all types of carpet and allows exceptional repeat variations.

Where only a single solid color is to be applied with no design, a new economical method is to spread a foam carrying the dye over the surface of the fabric that penetrates through the pile. However, if the foam or the printed pattern do not reach the base of the pile, color and pattern renditions may be inadequate.

The Karacrest Process

This is a new and unique system for preparing multicolored pile yarns and feeding them onto a backing where they are fusion-bonded. The pile ends are not woven into the backing; rather, they are dipped into polyvinyl chloride, cured, and bonded securely to the substrate. In 1978, the Karastan Rug Mills bought the world-wide rights to this system. The system is limited to eight colors, but it provides for many patterns, including some Oriental rug designs, discussed later in this chapter. Since virtually all the pile is on the surface, not hidden in the back, and since the speed of the loom operation is faster than the Axminster, the cost of manufacture is considerably reduced.

Woven Machine-Made Carpets and Rugs

Although woven rugs currently account for less than 2 percent of total shipments of soft floor coverings in this country, they are prized in many homes and commercial and business establishments for their long-lasting quality and beauty. This group includes the Wilton, the Axminster, the Oriental design (basically Wilton or Axminster in construction), the velvet, the tapestry, the chenille, and the Karaloc. (See Figs. 20.8 (a), (b), and (c).) Figure 20.5 shows that shipments of wovens are holding at about 18 million square yards a year; however, back in 1969, the volume was twice as great.

Wilton

As early as 1740, weavers were brought from France to England, and a carpet factory was established at Wilton, England. In 1825 the Jacquard loom was adapted to Wilton carpeting. Only the colors required in a row are drawn up as pile, and the other colors are buried beneath the surface. Buried yarn gives body, strength, and resilience to the carpet. The flat wires used to form the pile loops have knives on the ends that cut the top of each loop as the wires are withdrawn. The pile of a Wilton is therefore erect and cut. See Chapter 5 for a more detailed description and Fig. 20.8 (a).

Good-quality Wilton rugs are long-wearing, luxurious carpets with a wide range of solid colors, patterns, and textures. Very little Wilton production is

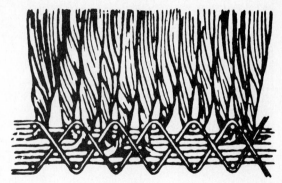

Figure 20.8a The Wilton construction. (Courtesy of the American Carpet Institute.)

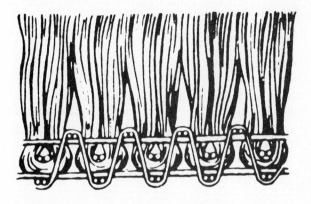

Figure 20.8b The Axminster construction. (Courtesy of the American Carpet Institute.)

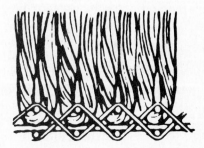

Figure 20.8c The velvet construction. (Courtesy of the American Carpet Institute.)

available for domestic use. Almost all Wiltons are used in the contract business today. (See *contract carpeting* in the glossary; also see the glossary for a similar woven construction, the Brussels, seldom if ever woven today.)

Axminster

Although the Axminster loom was invented by an American, its name comes from a town in England. A special mechanism attached to this loom permits carpets with an almost unlimited number of colors and designs to be constructed with most of the pile on the surface. (See Fig. 20.8 (b).)

Figure 20.9 A spool of yarn with its pile delivery system: Axminster weave. The combination of colored yarns needed for each row of tufts in the pattern is wound on a loom spool. The yarn ends protruding from the tubes are dipped down between the chain warp yarns and are bound in place by filling yarns. The ends are turned up by means of a comblike device to complete the pile. (Courtesy of *Woven Floor Coverings*, Mohawk Carpet Mills.)

The weaving is preceded by an operation called pattern setting. Guided by a point-paper design that indicates the color for each pile in every row of the design, colored yarns are wound on large spools in the proper sequence. If the design calls for 10 rows of pile to the inch and the pattern is to repeat every 36 inches, a total of 360 spools of yarn must be prepared, each with those colors that are to appear as pile in that row. Each yarn on each spool is threaded through a metal tube to guide it to the exact spot that yarn is to appear as pile in the weaving process. The threaded spools are then placed on endless chains arranged in the exact order in which each is to be used in the sequence of rows.

In the weaving process, each spool, in sequence, is automatically removed from the chain, and the pile ends are made to dip into the warp yarns that have been set up in the loom.

A filling yarn is shot across the loom on the top side of the pile and is beaten forward by a reed to bind the pile, and a comblike device turns up the end of the pile yarns to complete a tuft of pile. The loom is raised a short distance, and a knife is moved across the ends of the pile to sever them, at the desired height, from the spool. The spool is then reinserted into its place in the endless chain and the next spool is moved forward to provide the next row of pile. (See Fig. 20.9.)

Thus, most of the pile yarn is used for the tufts of pile rather than being buried in the backing to be used again, as in the Wilton, only when needed for the design. In some Axminsters, the design does not show on the back, but on others, a change in the shedding permits it to be shown. The backing in most Axminsters, other than those of machine-made Oriental designs, is generally made of jute that is heavily ribbed and can be rolled only length-wise, not crosswise.

Axminster can be distinguished from Wilton in that a Wilton construction can be rolled either lengthwise or crosswise, and Axminster, except for some Oriental design rugs, can be rolled only one way.

Machine-Woven Oriental-Design Rugs

These rugs are also called *sheen-type* or *dometic* Orientals. Basically, they are of the Wilton or Axminster construction, mostly the latter, with designs that resemble the hand-tied Orientals but sell at a considerably lower price. In some constructions, the design shows through on the back. The pile is of long skein-dyed worsted or woolen. Washing or brushing in a chemical solution adds luster. (See Fig. 20.10.)

The leading producer in the United States is the Karastan Rug Mills (Eden, North Carolina), a subsidiary of Fieldcrest Mills, Inc. Others are Karagheusian, Cabistan, and Gulistan. These rugs are also made abroad in Belgium, Germany, and France.

The Karastan rugs are made on an Axminster loom of 100 percent worsted skein-dyed pile yarn with 70 tufts of pile to the square inch and with a cotton back that can be rolled in either direction. A chlorinated wash followed by beating with a bundle of old wood, called Sultan Shoes, gives the rugs a remarkably lustrous quality and a soft coloring.

Because U.S.-grown wool is too soft and lacks the coarseness needed for carpets, the wool used comes from New Zealand, Argentina, Scotland, and parts of the Middle East and North Africa.

Good grades of Oriental-type rugs will stand hard wear. They are moderately priced, and their sheen makes them most suitable for living and

Figure 20.10 A coral Isfahan pattern. (Photo courtesy of Karastan Rug Mills.)

dining rooms. These rugs have been a boon to those who appreciate Oriental designs and colorings but cannot afford the genuine articles. The durability of the construction of the pile depends on the density of the pile and closeness of construction.

Velvet

The word "velvet" sounds rich and luxurious when applied to floor coverings. The colors, range, and textures of these rugs are all that the word implies. A plush effect results when the pile is cut and stands erect. (See Fig. 20.8 (c).) Uncut looped pile gives a pebbly surface or may appear in distinct rows like friezes. For these varied effects, a velvet loom (not a Jacquard loom) suffices. It makes use of the wire method of making pile, explained at the outset in Chapter 5.

When closely woven, velvet carpeting is durable as well as rich looking. Nearly all of it is made to order for commercial or public institutions. Few residential styles are available.

The Karaloc Loom

The Karaloc loom is a rug- or carpet-weaving technique invented and patented (in 1948) by Karastan, the Carpet and Rug Division of Fieldcrest Mills, Inc. Production began in 1952. It combines features of the Axminster, Wilton, and velvet looms.

A series of pile wires extends longitudinally or toward the weaver. A device known as a dip needle carries the pile yarn down alongside a pile wire and into the warps. A filling needle carrying a weft or filling yarn crosses the width of the loom and inserts the filling between the pile yarn and the ground warp. Almost simultaneously, the dip needle carrying the pile yarn is made to rise up, cross over the pile, and be reinserted in the warps on the other side of the pile wire. Thus, a loop of pile is formed. The filling yarn is reinserted and binds the other leg of the pile loop to the back of the fabric. The weave shows through to the back. If cut pile is desired, a razor blade is affixed to the end of the pile wire. As the loop is drawn off the pile wire, it is cut. (See Fig. 20.11.)

All dip needles act in unison. They are not individually controlled. In a normal 12-foot loom, there are 720 needles. Each needle is threaded with a yarn color or colors, and all descend into the warps and cross over a pile wire simultaneously. If one needle is threaded with color B and color B is not to show on the next pick, a pile wire is made to retract by means of a Jacquard head. In this case, a two-level wire is used (i.e., one having a low front portion and a high back portion). The retraction of the pile wire causes the loop to weave over the low portion of the pile wire and is thus buried or hidden from view by the high portion of the pile.

Considerable improvements and elaborations have been made over the original method so that the loom can now produce both high and low pile, cut

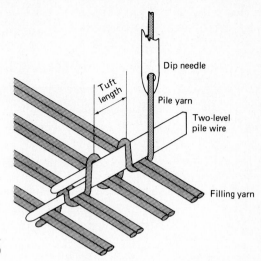

Figure 20.11 Weaving on the Karaloc loom.
(Courtesy of J. E. Troy, Fieldcrest Mills, Inc.)

and uncut pile, and a range of colors and patterned effects in both plain and multicolors. This one loom is alleged to be the most versatile loom on the market.

Tapestry

The pile for these rugs or carpets consists of uncut loops of warp yarn, generally of wool. These are printed before weaving in the desired pattern and colors. By means of a Jacquard control, each segment of the printed warp yarns is brought to the surface at the exact point needed for the surface pattern. The filling and stuffer yarns, generally of another fiber, such as jute, form the backing.

Chenille

This is a luxurious and expensive machine-made woven carpet, seldom manufactured today except for custom designs. The pile consists of fuzzy fillings of chenille yarn. (See Chapter 3.) The warps, the core of the chenille, may be cotton. The backing for the carpet is woolen, worsted, or jute. The weaving process is similar to that of the Axminster. Striking effects are achieved by varying the colors, sizes, and fibers in the filling yarns of the fabrics from which the chenille yarns are made.

MACHINE-MADE CARPETS AND RUGS OTHER THAN THE TUFTED AND THE WOVEN

Figure 20.12 gives the breakdown of shipments of these coverings in millions of square yards. Note that volumes have not changed much since 1974.

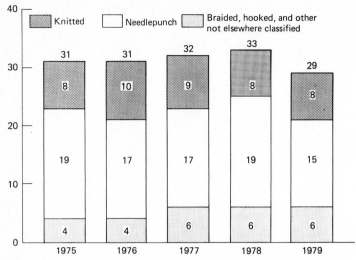

Figure 20.12 All other shipments of carpets and rugs (other than tufteds or wovens), 1975–1979 (in millions of square yards). (Courtesy of the Carpet and Rug Institute.)

Knitted

Like woven carpeting, the knitted type is made in one operation. But unlike the woven, the knitting process loops together the backing yarn, the stitching yarn, and the pile yarn with three sets of needles in much the same way as in hand knitting. Knitted carpeting is usually made with uncut loops, both single and multilevel. For cut pile, modifications must be made in the knitting machine. To give additional body to a carpet, a coat of latex is applied to the back. A second backing may be added. The quality of the carpet depends on the amount of pile yarn on the surface and the strength of attachment of the yarns.

Machine-made knitted carpets were first introduced in 1950 by Mohawk, now Mohasco, under the brand name Trendtex. More than 40 million square yards of this carpeting had been sold up to 1980.

Needlepunched and Flocked (Nonwoven)

This is a nonwoven nonpile carpeting with feltlike surface. A lap, web, or batt of loose fibers is created by needles having downward-facing barbs that entangle the fibers (mostly olefin). The primary use is for indoor-outdoor carpeting. When used indoors, a backing is sometimes applied. It is also used as the backing for some tufted carpets.

Another type of nonwoven pile may be made of precut electrostatically charged fibers that are projected toward a backing fabric that has been coated with an adhesive. The appearance of the rug resembles flocked wallpaper.

Minor Machine-Made Rugs

This category includes rugs made of fiber, grass, sisal, and braided, rag, and hooked rugs, all inexpensive and suited for cottages, porches, and doormats, among other uses.

Carpet Cushions

Carpet or rug cushions, sometimes called underlays, are made of hair, hair and jute, jute, foam rubber, and sponge rubber.

Hair

Made of felted cattle hair, these cushions are the most expensive of those listed, but they have been found most effective in increasing the wear life of carpets.[2] They also have the greatest resistance to burning, but tear resistance is poor.

Hair and Jute

The proportion of hair to jute varies. Some have up to 80 percent hair (a factor in higher cost). The resistance to burning has been found acceptable. However, rubberized hair and fiber foam and fiber combinations were found to be unsatisfactory in this respect. Products in this category are poor in resistance to mildew.

Jute

These cushions are the least expensive. When new they have resilience, but with wear, jute tends to bunch up and break down.

Foam Rubber

This makes for a "quiet" walk. Its natural thermal conductivity makes it good for covering floors that have embedded heating pipes. The wear life of the carpet is not increased by the use of this kind of cushion. Foam rubber has fair resistance to mildew.[3]

Sponge Rubber

Sold in a number of thicknesses, some do not give sufficient support because the cushions are too light. Normal traffic areas should have 60- to 80-ounce weight. Sponge rubber ensures a "soft" walk because it is resilient and it also has good heat conductivity. Slippage of the rug off the cushion is common unless the cushion has a scrim or mesh backing. Sponge rubber is flammable and may contribute to the spread of fire.

---

[2]From a study by the Institutional Research Council, *Consumer Bulletin,* May 1971.
[3]Ibid.

JUDGING THE QUALITY OF DOMESTIC MACHINE-MADE RUGS

In the store before purchase:

1. Look at the pile in the carpet sample. Bend the pile back on itself. The less backing you see, the denser the pile, and the better the quality. (This test does not apply to shags.)
2. Test the tufts by pulling a few to see if they are firmly anchored.
3. Examine the closeness of the weave in the backing.
4. Study the information on the label. Federal regulations require carpets to be labeled to show the generic name of its face fiber(s) and the percentages of each (over 5 percent). The manufacturer's name or the Federal Trade Commission's registration number and the country of origin (if the carpeting is imported) must also be shown.
5. Check flammability. Federal regulations require that soft floor coverings put on sale must have met flammability standards that assure that a flame will not continue to spread from the source of ignition. Large rugs should be labeled with a "T" if the approved retardant finish has been applied, but where the pile fiber is inherently flame-resistant, such as olefin, the designation is not required. Small rugs need not be labeled if fire-resistant, but if not, a warning label should be attached. See Appendix C for further details.
6. Be sure that the construction of the carpet or rug is suited to its intended use. For example, on a damp or exposed floor, olefin is preferable; if subjected to heavy traffic, a printed pattern will show less dirt than a solid one; if there are pets in the home, looped and shag rugs should be avoided, with low pile preferred; for kitchen and dining areas, a short, dense pile treated with a coating, such as Scotchgard, is recommended.
7. Check the reasonableness of the price by comparison shopping and by watching for special sales.

HANDMADE RUGS

The most exciting of all handmade rugs are the Orientals. Therefore, they are discussed separately following this section, according to place of origin, uses, design, color, prices, and selection.

Hooked and Rag Rugs

In the early years of American colonization, hooked and rag rugs were made by hand. They were popular as scatter rugs in New England and Nova Scotia. (See Fig. 20.13.) This handcraft has experienced a "revival" during the 1980s, probably due to the increased popularity of American folk art in many forms. The introduction in 1982 of a number of museum reproductions in the home textile field included many Early American designs.

For the very old handmade hooked rugs, a backing of linen was used; later burlap became common. The pile made of yarn or strips of cloth is pulled through the back by means of a hook. The resulting pile is sometimes cut.

Figure 20.13 Two hand-hooked rugs.

Patterns in hooked rugs may be geometric or floral; animals, ships, and domestic scenes are depicted. The hooked rug made in New England in the early days is considered more valuable than the Nova Scotia rug because of its more intricate designs and more beautiful colorings. Many modern Nova Scotian rugs have geometric designs copied from current linoleum patterns. Japan is a source of many inexpensive hand-hooked rugs. Most modern hooked rugs can be cleaned by shampooing, because the modern textiles from which they are made have generally fast dyes. Old hooked rugs should be sent to a reliable cleaner, for the burlap foundation may be weak and may fall apart when wet. Hooked rugs may be purchased in room size as well as scatter size. Old hooked rugs vary in size and shape, but large machine types are more or less standard.

Rag rugs are made of strips of twisted rags braided, crocheted, or bound together by cotton thread. Handmade rag rugs are becoming more plentiful due to the popularity of American "Country" designs for home interiors in the early eighties. There are no particular patterns and many are now featuring solid colors, including white (for more contemporary interiors). Braided rugs are usually oval or round. Hit-or-miss rugs, made of many-colored twisted rags bound together, are generally oblong.

Navajo Rugs and Mats

Navajo Indians in the western part of the United States originally made blankets and mats for their own use, but now these are made commercially. The Navajo loom consists of warp yarns suspended between two horizontal sticks. The filling is passed over and under the warp yarns by means of a pointed stick on which the yarn is wound. At points where the design is to appear, another color is introduced. Designs are geometric, and favorite colors are bright red on a white or gray ground, or white on a red ground. Originally, the Navajos obtained wool for rugs and blankets from their own flocks, which were carefully tended. Now their fine blankets are made of Germantown wool yarn made ready for weaving.

Weaving by this method is slow. When weavers were more skilled than they are today, it took an expert weaver about a month to make a blanket 5½ × 6¾ feet.

ORIENTAL HAND-TIED RUGS

Origin and Construction

Hand-tied Orientals come from the Near East, India, and China. Most of the Near Eastern rugs come from Iran, Turkey in Asia, and the Caucasus regions, with some from Rumania in the Balkans.

It is believed that carpet weaving by hand originated in southern Persia (now Iran) nearly six thousand years ago. The oldest rug known is the Pazyryk, found in 1953 in a frozen burial mound in the Altai mountains of southern Siberia, where perpetual ice preserved the rug perfectly. It is a hand-knotted rug with 25 knots to the square inch and over 1,250,000 knots in the entire rug.

Oriental rugs are made on a vertical loom, although long ago some were made on horizontal looms. (See Fig. 20.14.) The pile yarns are of wool, silk, mohair, and sometimes silk and wool. The pile is tied to the warp and filling yarns and is cut with a knife to the depth desired. Two major kinds of knots are used: the Ghiordes (Turkish) and the Senna (Iranian). A third knot—the Khorasson (Spanish)—is tied around a single warp. In the Ghiordes, the tufts of pile yarn tie two warps together with both ends standing up between the two warp yarns; in the Senna, the tufts pass singly between two warp yarns. In both cases, the pile does not stand vertically on the ground but, rather, leans toward the end of the rug first woven. Extra filling yarns hold the pile in place. The warp and weft that form the backing are commonly made of cotton, but silk and wool are also used. In a few Anatolian rugs, the pile is also cotton. Rugs made with wool from hides (skin wool), rather than from live sheep, have a fraction of the strength of the usual wool. The fringe of the Oriental is the ends of the warp yarns; it is not sewed on separately unless the original fringe has been badly worn.

Some Orientals are not made with a pile. Rather, a dyed filling thread is

Figure 20.14 Ancient horizontal hand loom. In ancient India, before the birth of Christ, the horizontal hand loom was extensively employed to weave the priceless cotton hangings of that culture. (Courtesy of the Hoover Home Institute, The Hoover Company.)

bound around the warp threads by means of a shuttle or needle. This makes the fabric look much alike on both sides. The construction is like that of tapestry. These coverings are called kilims (ghileems). While used in the Orient as floor coverings as well as spreads, they are not very satisfactory on the floors in this country. Heels and hard soles are likely to damage them, and they will slip unless backed with rug cushioning.

Dates on the origin of handwoven rugs cannot be stated exactly, but probably Oriental rugs are as old as civilization and date back to 5000 B.C. Until we have further evidence, the date of origin must begin with the old Egyptian civilization. Later on, Assyria and Chaldea became the home of Oriental rugs. The Persians, who were the master weavers, probably learned the art from the Babylonians. Some historians believe that the origin of the Oriental rug antedates the early Egyptian times.

Countries of Origin

Oriental rugs may be classified according to their geographical origin and also as to use. (See Fig. 20.15.)

Iranian

Rugs from Iran (formerly Persia) are perhaps the most sought after of the Orientals because of their artistic, intricate designs and fineness of construction. It is said that the Italianesque touch in the design of some Persian rugs is traceable to the time of Shah Abbas, a Turkish ruler of the sixteenth century. He sent some young men to Italy to study art under Raphael, and it is through them that rugs reached their zenith of development. Designs of Persians are usually predominantly floral with now and then a depiction of animals or human figures. Straight fringes, which are the actual continuation of warp yarns, appear at both ends. Sometimes fringes are braided or knotted.

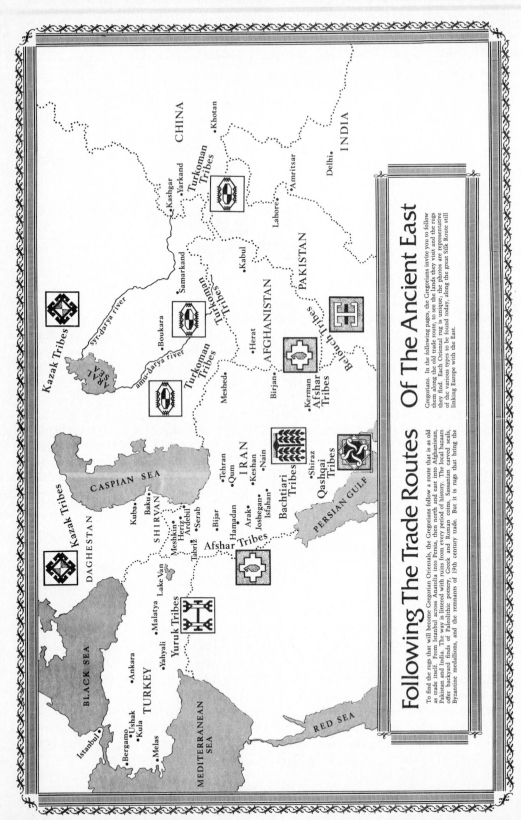

Figure 20.15 The rug centers of the Near East. (Courtesy of Arthur T. Gregorian, Inc., Newton Lower Falls, Mass.)

The names of the rugs are derived from the towns or districts using a particular grade of yarn and particular designs. Among the well-known districts noted for the highest quality are Afshar, Isphahan, Kashan, Nain, Quom (Qum), Tabriz, and Teheran. Two very popular in the United States may be included in this list: Kirman and Sarouk. (See Fig. 20.16.)

Of somewhat lower quality, usually, are the rugs from Gorvan, Dargezin, Hamadan, Heriz, Josheghan, Khorasan, Mahal, Mosel, Hiraz, and Shirvan, among others.

Figure 20.16 Persian (now Iranian) animal rug, Kurdistan; eighteenth century. Animals and birds against a background design of trees and flowers, a type of composition derived from Persian court carpets of the classic period. Colors: field, red; animals, white, rose, light and dark blue; background pattern, white, cream, rose, reds, and blues; border, red and light blue on dark blue. 13′ × 6′7″. (Collection of Mr. and Mrs. Arthur M. Brilant. Photo courtesy of the Asia Society and *Antiques Magazine*.)

Figure 20.17 A Qashqai tribe in southern Iran travels with its rug loom inside the tent. (Photo courtesy of Arthur T. Gregorian, Inc., Newton Lower Falls, Mass.)

The supply of new rugs from Iran and from adjacent countries is dwindling. The disturbed political situation and warfare have interfered with production and export. A more enduring cause is the influence of Western life-styles on the younger generation in the Near East. Many are no longer willing to spend months, even years, sitting at a loom tying knots. (See Fig. 20.17.)

Turkish

The patterns of Turkish rugs (Anatolian) are less intricate than the Persian, and they tend to be more geometric in design. The pile is longer than the Persian, and the rugs are somewhat coarser in construction. Some of the most common types are Bergama, Ladik, Ghiordes, Kula, Milas, and Oushak.

The Turkish prayer rugs (see Fig. 20.18) woven in the seventeenth and eighteenth centuries, in the Ladik, Ghiordes, and Kula districts of Asia Minor, have probably never been surpassed in design and coloring. Rugs of this kind were used by Moslems in their frequent prayers, with the peak of the rug directed toward Mecca, the holy city, in what is now Saudi Arabia.

In recent years, the production of Near Eastern Orientals has spread into the Balkans, especially to Rumania.

Caucasian

These rugs come from Caucasia and Transcaucasia on the Black and the Caspian seas. Characteristics are their geometric patterns with sharp outlines. Blues, yellows, and reds are favorite colors. These rugs seldom come in large

Figure 20.18 Turkish prayer rug, Anatolia, Ghiordes; first half of the eight-eenth century. A floral decoration takes the place of the mosque lamp in the mihrab, or niche; the stylized flowers in the border are derived from Turkish court rugs. Colors: niche, red; spandrels, light blue with yellow; border, dark blue with pattern in white, tan, green, red, and black. (The Metropolitan Museum of Art, Gift of James F. Ballard, 1922. Photo courtesy of the Metropolitan Museum of Art, the Asia Society, and *Antiques Magazine*.)

sizes. It is said that Kazak rugs originated from the word Cossack, the name of a nomadic people. The designs in this type of rug are more geometric and cruder than are those made by other groups. Examples are Chi-Chi, Dagestan, Kabistan, Karaja, Kazak, Kuba, and Shirvan.

Turkoman

Rugs from Turkestan, which is north of Iran and east of the Caspian Sea, are usually characterized by wide webbing at the ends. The designs in the center field are rows of octagonal medallions. Red, white, brown, and green are the principal colors. The most common Turkoman rugs are the Bokhara, Beshir, Tekke Turkoman, and Samarkand. Pakistan is now making many Bokharas. Afghan rugs from Afghanistan, between Turkestan and Baluchistan, may be included.

Baluchistan

Baluchistan is a section extending between Kirman on the west and India on the east, from Afghanistan on the north to the Arabian Sea on the south. Rugs from Baluchistan, often called *Baluchi,* have wide-webbed ends and are similar to the Turkoman. Vivid reds and browns predominate.

Indian

Indian rugs can be classified into three groups: hand-tied rugs, numdahs, and druggets. The hand-tied rugs come from the district around Lahore in the province of Punjab and from Benares and Rajistan. The numdahs come from Punjab and Tibet. The druggets are made throughout India from the fleece of wire-haired sheep.

The numdahs come in different grades. They are made of felted goat's hair, not woven hair. Designs are embroidered by hand, the patterns being generrlly floral or vinelike. The Tree of Life design appears frequently. The usual dimensions of numdahs are 2 × 3, 3 × 4, and 4 × 6 feet. These rugs are comparatively inexpensive.

Druggets also come in different grades. The better ones are all wool; the poorer ones have a pile made of wool mixed with cow's hair. The groundwork of these rugs is jute. Patterns are usually very colorful and quite simple. Druggets are used on sun porches and in summer cottages.

Indian rugs should be dry-cleaned, not washed.

Chinese

The pile is deep and rich. Blue and tan are common colors. Dragons and flowers in circles are characteristic motifs, although when modern furniture came into vogue, Chinese rug manufacturers had their designers create patterns to meet the style. Then, with the demand, they made them in plain colors. However, these rugs are not as durable as the Persian and Turkish. They require much care and may not compete with the domestic American solid color rugs and carpets, both in quality and price.

Since the reopening of trade between the United States and China in the seventies, the once limited supply of Chinese rugs is becoming a major part of many retailers' inventories. This is especially true with large department stores and chains who maintain import divisions for this purpose.

Original Uses of Oriental Rugs

The artistic and poetic temperament of Oriental peoples expresses itself in the beautiful pictures on their rugs. These designs have been copied by Occidental peoples, but the latter have never really been able to duplicate the works of art handed down through the centuries.

Although our present-day rugs are used chiefly as floor coverings or hangings, the old Oriental rugs were created for other purposes as well. These include *prayer rugs,* characterized by a design in the form of an arch directed toward Mecca during prayer; *hearth rugs,* often with a cypress tree design, once used for family prayers; *grave rugs,* used to cover the dead before interment and to cover the grave after burial; *dowry* or *wedding rugs,* considered part of a girl's dowry and woven by the bride herself; *mosque (Mecca) rugs,* taken to Mecca as a gift to the mosque; *saddle bags,* in the form of two pouches joined together by webbing used to transport merchandise (now often cut apart and used as couch pillows); *saddle covers,* to fit the back of the camel; *runners,* made to lay on couches (now used for halls and foyers); *hangings,* either silk rugs or kilims (ghileems); *pillowcases,* now used also on tables and in front of doors; *bath rugs,* originally given to the bride by her parents on her wedding day; and *sample corners,* pieces about two feet square used to show the quality of weaving to wealthy buyers (very rare today).

Although it is romantic to think of the original uses of Oriental rugs, it should be remembered that in our modern civilization the old uses have in many cases disappeared. In the selling or buying of rugs, then, the salesperson or customer should try to visualize a rug in use in a home, not a mosque in Turkey. Salespeople should remember that modern Orientals are made solely "for the trade" and are not intended to be used in places of worship or for transporting merchandise.

Design of Oriental Rugs

The geometric designs are the most primitive. Not so complicated as the floral types, their simplicity makes them popular. Authorities on designs in rugs believe that geometric patterns originated with the rug itself. It must be remembered that the whole family used to weave rugs. The mother would tend the baby while weaving and, to keep the child amused, would often weave into her rug some figures or symbols especially for the child. Possibly some of the irregularities in antique rugs are due to interruptions of the weaver, although the story is that no faithful Mohammedan would wish to make a rug perfect in symmetry of design and weaving because he might offend Allah, who alone is the symbol of perfection. Furthermore, the representation of human figures, birds, or beasts was forbidden in strict observance of Mohammedan laws. Consequently, the original geometric designs were perpetuated.

Floral patterns are now identified with Persian rugs, but the oldest floral patterns were not developed in Persia. Greece and neighboring countries borrowed simple geometric designs from Egypt and Assyria and developed beautiful, complicated floral designs. Persia received this art centuries later.

The present designs in our modern Oriental rugs are copies of old pieces. The symbolism attached to designs in antique rugs no longer exists. Swastikas for happiness, latch-hooks for good luck, a geometric figure supposed to represent a dog who preceded Mohammed when he first entered Mecca are all symbols of the early rugmakers, who also wove their life histories into their rugs. The same designs are present today, but no symbolic meaning is intended by the weaver.

Antique versus Modern Orientals

A rug, to be considered antique, should be at least one hundred years old.[4] Colors of antiques have been softened and subdued by constant wear and by dirt, and the pile is worn down in places, with the result that there is an effect of light and shadow on the surface. These mellow colors are quite different from the garish brillance of some recently loomed Orientals.

The yarns used in the antiques were dyed with natural coloring matter, for example, ox blood or madder for red, the saffron crocus for yellow, the indigo plant for blue, and walnut shells for brown and black. These have great depth, natural sheen, and softness; they are also colorfast.

While the first aniline dyes were developed over a hundred years ago, they were of poor quality and did not come into general use until after World War I, when they were greatly improved. In early days, the Persian government outlawed the use of aniline dyes to protect the country's reputation for quality rugs. It is reported that the government threatened to cut off the hand of any rugmaker who attempted to use the new synthetic dyes.

Today, excellent synthetic dyes from benzine, obtained in turn from coal tar, have replaced the natural dyes. They are colorfast to light and to shampooing but tend to lack the softness of the antiques. To emulate the old coloring, the new Orientals are frequently subjected to chemical washes of chlorine or an acetic acid to mute the vivid colors. Glycerine may also be applied to give sheen. Coloring matter in the desired hues is often applied to the washed rugs by a hand-operated dye pencil. The pencil may also be used to cover worn spots on used rugs.

A chemical wash can be detected by comparing the wrong side with the top side. If the former is brighter, the rug has probably been washed. Sniffing

---

[4]At the British Dealers' Antique Fair, the term "antique" has been limited to rugs made not later than 1830. In the U.S. there is no import duty on rugs 100 years old.

the rug may detect the chemical odor. Repainted rugs often have shiny areas that give off color when rubbed with a wet finger or tissue.

Values in Oriental Rugs

As noted earlier, Oriental rugs are classified by age as antiques, over one hundred years old (at present, made before 1880); semiantiques, between fifty and one hundred years old; and moderns, less than fifty years old, many of them new.

While age is a factor in value, other considerations are often of equal importance: the yarn (silk being more expensive than wool and fine wool from the chest of baby sheep being more expensive than wool from other parts), the design, the colors, the place of origin, the rarity, and the closeness of the weave, measured by the number of knots to the square inch. It is said that some of the ancient weavers went blind at their looms.[5] Great rugs dating back to the sixteenth, seventeenth, and eighteenth centuries are museum pieces valued as art treasures.

Semiantiques are valued more by condition, place of origin, and appearance than by age. New modern rugs of excellent quality are worth more than many semiantiques. The good moderns are becoming scarce due to the turmoil in the Near East and the changing life-styles there.

A comparison of the price of modern or new Orientals with machine-made tufted domestics is of interest. High-quality new Orientals usually sell for more than $100.00 a square yard, or over $11.00 a square foot. Broadlooms are sold by the square yard and seldom (as of 1982) sell for much more than $45.00 a square yard, or $5.00 a square foot. Orientals are sold by the piece and are measured by the foot and inch. Some "prized" Orientals bring as much as $100.00 a square foot, but they are not sold on that basis.

Factors to Consider in the Selection of an Oriental Rug

In buying an Oriental rug, first consider the interior in which it is to be used. For example, Oriental rugs fit into nearly every type of living room except possibly one with Colonial, French Provincial, or Directoire furniture. They are not, as a rule, used in bedrooms, where softer, more resilient carpets are recommended. Floors in dining rooms, halls, and libraries are usually appropriately covered with machine-made or real Orientals. In decorating a room, remember that the rug usually covers the largest or second largest area. Accordingly, if one already has chairs upholstered in vivid, patterned fabrics, and draperies in patterned materials, it would be wise and in good taste to select a plain-colored rug, possibly a domestic.

[5]A skilled craftsman can tie 8,000 to 12,000 knots in one day. Thus, a 9 × 12 rug with 150 knots to the square inch will take one person about nine months of steady work with some allowance for loom set-ups and adjustments.

Figure 20.19 Buying An Oriental. An Oriental rug dealer discussing a rug purchase with prospective buyers. (Photo courtesy of Arthur T. Gregorian, Inc., Newton Lower Falls, Mass.)

When deciding to buy an Oriental rug, the consumer should consider these points as well:

1. *Authenticity.* Be sure that the rug is a genuine Oriental, with the design on the back as clear as that on the face.

2. *Detection of worn areas.* Careful inspection is necessary by running the hand over the surface of the entire rug to detect low or worn spots. If the rug is small enough, hold it up to the light. If you can see light through the rug, it is badly worn.

3. *The size best suited to the space.* If the room is large, a rug at least 9 × 12 feet in size would be advisable, because too many small scatter rugs seem to cut up the floor space. One large rug with smaller ones in front of doors, the fireplace, or stairs is a better arrangement, because the large rug forms a center for the room. Some people prefer a room-sized carpet in a neutral shade over which they throw small scatter-sized Orientals. With this plan, the small rugs do not slip on hardwood floors, whereas small rugs alone require a felt or rubber mat under them. However, small orientals may slip when placed on a long-piled acrylic broadloom.

4. *The design.* If one has no furniture or draperies as yet, any appealing designs or colors may be used. But if there are other furnishings, their color and

type must be considered to make a harmonious ensemble. The outline of the design should be distinct, and whites should be clear.

5. *The closeness of construction and evenness of weave.* Turn the rug over on the back and notice the closeness of the weave. The more knots to the inch, the stronger the rug. An evenly woven rug will be flat on the floor and will not pucker at the ends. The thickness of the rug and the depth of the pile have no definite bearing on durability; some of the thinnest Orientals with short pile wear longest, because they are very closely woven of grade A wool. A new rug should have even pile, and the color should be the same on the surface as it is at the knot.

6. *The country and district of origin.* This reflects the quality of the wool, the tightness and evenness of the weave, and the beauty of coloring and design.

7. *Place of purchase.* To acquire a thorough knowledge of Orientals would take a lifetime. It is therefore advisable to go to a reliable department store or importer who will stand behind the merchandise. A guarantee by an unethical merchant is meaningless. Some so-called antiques are really modern; they may have been treated with chemicals and filled with dust to make them appear old. Good buys can be obtained at auctions, but considerable expertise is needed in selection. If the customer can spot the dealers present and is careful to bid only slightly higher than a dealer, he or she may do better than in the stores, but a good deal of time has to be spent consummating the purchase. (See Fig. 20.19.)[6]

CARE OF RUGS

If they are to give long service, all rugs should have proper care. A rug cushion should always be placed under a rug, and it should be turned around occasionally to equalize wear.

When a domestic rug is new, a certain amount of fiber may brush out of it. This is to be expected, for in the process of shearing, particles often fall back into the pile. The regular vacuuming will, in time, remove all the excess fiber.

If the surface of the pile is not even, however, any long ends, tufts, or knots projecting above the surface should be cut off. Pulling out long ends may injure the construction.

Sometimes a solid-colored rug seems to have dark and light spots in it. These marks are called *shading*, which is due to a crushing of the pile in spots—often caused by someone walking or moving furniture on the rug. The crushing

[6]One auctioneering firm, Germezian Bro., New York City, represents Iranian weavers and sells directly to the public. It has a price guarantee "to be less than the fair retail value" and also an exchange policy that the price paid may be applied against another selection if the customer is not wholly satisfied.

of the pile may be reduced somewhat if the rug is turned around occasionally; the wear is thus distributed evenly. Running the sweeper or vacuum cleaner in the direction of the pile will decrease shading. Professional cleaning may be the cure.

Soft floor coverings can be kept reasonably clean by going over them once a day lightly (three strokes) with a carpet sweeper or suction-only vacuum cleaner and once a week vacuuming more thoroughly (seven or more strokes) to remove more imbedded dirt. In vacuuming Orientals, avoid going over the fringes. A stiff broom may injure the pile of the rug and so should be used lightly. The sweeping should be in the direction of the pile, not against it. New rugs should be vacuumed as often as old rugs. Hand-hooded rugs should not be shaken or cleaned with a vacuum, as the pile may be loosened by the suction; the old-fashioned carpet sweeper or broom is the best cleaner.

In the case of indoor-outdoor carpeting used outdoors, hosing down is a good cleaning method. If used indoors, the carpeting should be sponged with a detergent solution.

Rugs are best kept free of moths by hard use. Rugs used for hangings should be examined frequently to see that moths are not in them. A weekly spraying with an insecticide will generally keep rugs free of moths during the summer months, and vacuum cleaning is also helpful. In the South, where the woodworm sometimes eats the jute back of rugs, naphthalene can be used as a preventative.

For storage, rugs should be rolled up, not folded, preferably around a pole, and sprinkled with a moth crystal that should be changed every few months.

Professional Cleaning Methods
Used in the Home

Soap, water, or chemicals may injure domestic wool rugs unless one knows how to use them. Soil embedded in carpets and rugs can best be thoroughly cleaned by commercial cleaning services. Domestic and Oriental rugs and carpets that can be removed from the floor may be sent to a rug-cleaning plant for most thorough and efficient cleaning. Wall-to-wall coverings can be done professionally in the home. Care in selection of a commercial rug-cleaning establishment is important. However, cleaning equipment can be rented in many stores for use by the consumer.[7]

Spot Removal

Unless a rug is made of fibers that soil easily, shampooing is not required very often. Prompt and careful treatment of stains is important for good serviceability in any carpet or rug.

---

[7]See *Carpet Rug and Care Guide*, The Carpet and Rug Institute, Dalton, Georgia. This pamphlet presents an excellent coverage of the care and cleaning of carpets and rugs.

For removing spots from acrylic and nylon pile carpets, use a dull-edged spoon to dilodge as much of the soil as possible. With tissues or white cloth, blot up all you can of the soil. Apply a detergent or cleaner sparingly. To avoid spreading the stain, work from the edge to the center. Rinse with water and blot with tissues after each application of cleaner. Then put a half-inch stack of tissues, weighted down with a heavy object, on the cleaned area and leave it overnight. Remove the tissues, which have absorbed moisture from the carpet. Brush up the carpet pile lightly. The spot should have disappeared.

SUMMARY

The decoration of an interior should grow out of the use to which the rooms are put and the personal preferences of the occupants; but a knowledge of period styles in furniture and furnishings is useful and necessary.

Since the rug takes up a large area in a room, it is a very important consideration in decoration. A rug usually proves to be a good buy if it is carefully selected and properly cared for. In modern domestic rugs, colors and patterns can be found that fit with any decorative scheme. If one can afford to possess an Oriental, there are innumerable designs from which to choose. Again, care in selection repays the buyer many times over.

PROJECTS

1. Visit a first-class furniture or department store and, by observation and questioning, find out whether it carries any of the French, English, and Early American furniture styles discussed in this chapter. Also question the buyer in charge as to whether many customers ask to see specific styles representing periods such as Victorian or designers such as Duncan Phyfe. Observe, also, whether any of the contemporary styles in stock seem to replicate the features of previous fashions. Prepare a report of your findings covering the importance, if any, of period styles in today's stock offerings.

2. Draw the layout of a department that sells soft floor coverings in a large retail store.
   (a) Classify carpets and rugs sold in each section; give their names, sizes, colors, approximate prices.
   (b) Constructively criticize the layout and stock assortment.

3. Clip advertisements for rugs in your local newspaper.
   (a) Classify carpets and rugs offered by various stores.
   (b) Tabulate fiber contents, sizes, colors, and prices of each article.
   (c) Analyze your data to determine which floor covering is the best value for the price. Which is the poorest value? Rate articles in order from best to poorest.
   (d) Support your conclusions.
   Alternate: If advertisements of soft floor coverings cannot be obtained, visit a large department or specialty store that carries carpets and rugs. Follow steps (a), (b), (c), and (d).

4. Select and defend the appropriate choice of carpeting under the following six conditions:
   (a) For a den with children but no pets in the home:
       _____ A dense, tightly tufted carpet
       _____ A loosely tufted carpet
   (b) For a basement to be turned into a playroom:
       _____ Wool carpet
       _____ Nylon carpet
   (c) For a kitchen with two children in the house:
       _____ Carpet with a high pile to ease the feet
       _____ White shag to match the appliances
       _____ Low-pile carpeting
   (d) For the bathroom:
       _____ To match the carpeting in the hall off the bathroom
       _____ To be machine washable
   (e) For a small studio apartment just occupied and filled with Early American furniture lent temporarily by your folks:
       _____ A deep-colored carpet to match the furniture
       _____ A reasonably light color to offset the furniture
   (f) For the bedroom, decorated in shades of orange, for a young working couple living and working in New York City:
       _____ A luxurious cantaloupe-colored plush carpet that fits into the wall decorations
       _____ Something in dark orange
       _____ Charcoal-colored carpeting preferred by their folks who are paying the rent.

5. Visit a store that carries both domestic wall-to-wall carpeting and Oriental rugs. Determine the price per square yard of the store's best wall-to-wall carpeting and compare it with the price (on a square-yard basis) of a room-size hand-tied Oriental rug. On what bases may the difference in price be justified? Discuss thoroughly.

6. Make a study of Oriental rugs as an investment by reading and talking to some dealers and other knowledgeable people. Write a report of your findings.

GLOSSARY

Antique Oriental rug   A hand-tied Oriental rug at least one hundred years old.

Aubusson carpet   A heavy handwoven fabric in scenic design formed by filling threads. Famous from the seventeenth century, now machine-made imitation produced on the Jacquard loom.

Axminster   A cut pile woven rug made with a spool-like tufting device that inverts rows of pile yarn between warp yarns bound by extra filling yarns.

Baluchistan rug   A hand-tied Oriental rug from Baluchistan, commonly called *Baluchi*.

Bath mat   A covering of tufted chenille yarn stitched to a backing. See Chapter 19.

Broadloom   A seamless woven carpet 6 to 18 feet or more in width.

Brussels carpet   A woolen or worsted warp pile woven carpet no longer made. Each warp is in one of three to five colors. A loop of each colored warp is carried into the face of the carpet at the point required for a simple design; much of the warp is "buried" in the back.

Carpet rayon   A specially constructed fiber and yarn for carpets that has greater tensile strength and is coarser than rayon for clothing.

Carpeting   A soft floor covering that can be made of a variety of different fibers. It is sold by the yard and can be cut to any size.

Carved rug   See *sculptured rug.*

Caucasian rug   Hand-tied Oriental from Caucasia and Transcaucasia on the Black and Caspian seas. Names include Kabistan, Shirvan, Kazak, and Karaja.

Chain warp   A warp that joins or binds together the upper and lower surfaces of a rug.

Chenille blanket   A loosely woven fabric (often cotton warps and large woolen fillings); it is cut into narrow strips that are pressed V-shaped and form the filling yarn for a chenille rug.

Chenille rug   A floor covering made with chenille (caterpillar) yarn used as a filling. It may be carved. See *chenille blanket.*

Chinese rug   A hand-tied Oriental rug made in China, often characterized by dragons and flowers in circles.

Contemporary style   A present style in home furnishings that emphasizes mobile and functional furniture.

Contract carpeting   Floor covering in considerable yardage contracted for by motels, bowling alleys, schools, and institutions.

Domestic rugs   Floor coverings manufactured in the United States.

Drugget   A rug of all wool or wool and cow's hair mixed pile with a ground of jute. It is used for sun porches and summer cottages.

Embossed type rug   See *sculptured rug.*

Fiber rug   A floor covering made of tightly twisted strips of paper, finished to repel friction and moisture.

Flocked carpet   See *nonwoven floor coverings.*

Frame   Denotes the number of colors possible in a Wilton rug; for example, five frames means five colors are possible, one frame for each color yarn. Frame holds spools of colored pile yarn in Axminster construction.

Ghiordes   Type of knot used to make pile in Turkish hand-tied rugs.

Grass rug   Made of cured prairie grass.

Hearth rug   A hand-tied Oriental-type rug characterized by designs in the form of arches, one at either end.

Hit-or-miss rug   A floor covering made of many colored twisted rags bound together.

Hooked rug   Handmade by using a large hooked needle to pull yarn or bias-cut strips of fabric through a coarse burlap fabric. Some types are made on the Jacquard loom in round wire construction to imitate the hand-hooked type.

India rug   Hand-tied rugs made in India in the province of Lahore, numdahs, and druggets.

Indoor-outdoor carpeting   Floor coverings suitable for both inside the house and outdoors.

Kilim (ghileem)   Near Eastern Oriental woven with a shuttle or needle, with no pile. Kilims are used by the Orientals as portières, couch covers, and table covers.

Looper   The unit of a tufting machine that forms a loop in the pile yarn that is thrust by a needle through the backing. The loop may be left as uncut pile or cut to form cut pile.

Luster rugs   Rugs that are chemically washed to give them sheen. They may be Wilton,

Axminster machine-made rugs with Oriental designs or velvet construction, and are frequently referred to as sheen-type rugs.

Modern style   A style in home furnishings that emphasized simplicity, angularity, and straight lines in furniture.

Mohair rug   Floor covering with mohair pile and jute back.

Needlepunched carpeting (needle loom)   A nonwoven nonpile carpeting with a feltlike surface. A lap, web, or batt of loose fibers is applied to a base of cotton fabric, burlap, plastic, rubber, etc. Needles having downward-facing barbs are forced into the base, thus causing the tufts of fiber to adhere to the base.

Nonwoven floor coverings   Carpets having tufts that are usually punched through a burlap backing. Flocked carpets are made of precut electronically charged fibers that are stuck to a backing coated with adhesive.

Numdah rug   A rug from India, made of felted goat's hair. Designs are embroidered on the rug by hand.

Oriental rug   Hand-tied rug made in the Near East, India, or China.

Patent back   Carpeting that has its tufts locked in place by a mixture of latex or pyroxylin.

Persian (Iranian) rug   A hand-tied Oriental rug made in Iran. Names of Persian rugs include Kirman, Kashan, Shiraz, Teheran, Saraband, Isfahan, Sarouk, Hamadan, Meched, Tabriz, Nain, and Qum.

Pile warp   The warp yarn in a carpet that forms the looped pile.

Pitch   The number of pile yarns to the 27-inch width.

Plush carpet   Floor covering with one level of cut pile made of soft twisted yarns that do not show any yarn texture.

Prayer rug   A hand-tied Near Eastern Oriental rug characterized by a design in the form of an arch.

Rag rug   Floor covering made of strips of twisted rags braided, crocheted, or bound together by cotton thread or cord.

Random-tip shears   Carpets and rugs with a high pile sheared at random.

Round-wire carpet   A Wilton construction in which a round wire is used instead of a flat wire to make the pile. Pile is therefore uncut.

Rows to the inch   Rows of yarn tufts to the inch lengthwise.

Rug   A thick, heavy fabric that can be made of a variety of different fibers and textures. Term is often used synonymously with carpet. Rugs are made with ends finished with binding or fringe.

Rug cushion   A fabric of sponge rubber or hair felt placed under the rug to prevent the rug from slipping and to made the rug more soft and cushiony.

Savonnerie   A French rug made in imitation of Oriental knotted rugs with rococo patterns.

Sculptured rug   A floor covering with a Jacquard design made with different heights of pile.

Semiantique Oriental   An Oriental rug at least fifty years old but not old enough to be classified as an antique Oriental.

Senna knot   Type of knot used to make pile in Persian hand-tied rugs.

Shading   Crushing of the pile of a rug so that it seems to have light and dark spots in it.

Shag   A floor covering with relatively long, loose wool or man-made fibered pile.

Stuffer warp   A warp that passes straight through the carpet to form a stuffing.

Toile de Jouy   Used for draperies. See the glossary in Chapter 21.

Tufted carpet   Made by needling pile yarns into a previously woven backing of jute or cotton.

Turkish rug   A hand-tied Oriental rug made in Turkey. Names of Turkish rugs include Bergama, Ladik, Ghiordes, Kulah, and Oushak.

Turkoman rug   A hand-tied Oriental rug from Turkestan. Names include Bokhara, Beshir, Tekke Turkoman, and Samarkand.

Tweed   Heavy wool, cotton, or man-made fibered fabric in handwoven effects, used for draperies and upholstery primarily.

Twist   A carpet made with uncut pile. Yarns of different colors may be twisted together to form pile loops.

Underlay   See *rug cushion*.

Velvet rug   A floor covering woven in the pile weave (see Chapter 5) with cut pile that is dyed or printed.

Wall-to-wall carpeting   A carpet of any fiber or fibers and in any construction that covers the entire floor.

Wilton   A woven rug (usually woolen or worsted) with portions of the pile yarn not needed for the design buried in the back.

Wire   1. Each row of pile or tufts on the surface of a rug; see *rows to the inch*. 2. A wire inserted through the shed in weaving that holds up the warp yarns that form the pile in a row across the fabric.

Chapter 21

DRAPERIES AND CURTAINS, UPHOLSTERY, AND TAPESTRY

More interest is being directed to the design and redecoration of homes as people attempt to escape everyday pressures and create a truly personal environment.

No successful interior scheme comes into being without thought. A carefully considered plan must be worked out before a satisfactory living area or an efficient working space can be created. Each individual reacts in a different way to the design of a space where he or she will live or work. Consequently, each person involved in using these areas should be considered both by the fabric designer and the interior designer/decorator or salesperson.

WHAT IS DESIGN?

Design is the knowledgeable selection and manipulation of the basic art elements—line, shape, light, color, and texture—to produce a unified expressive visual statement. The process must consider the elements as related and integral parts that combine into a harmonious whole to satisfy a function.

In designing a room, it is important to see the whole rather than only the parts—the furniture, the colors, and the decorations. For instance, if one has only a floor plan without wall elevations, one cannot determine the height of the ceiling, door openings, windows, and the like. Function must be a factor of every single object in the decorating and furnishing scheme.

The design of drapery and curtain fabrics is an important way of creating a harmonious whole in any interior. While the design may be printed, structural designs are of great importance today. These are built into the construction of

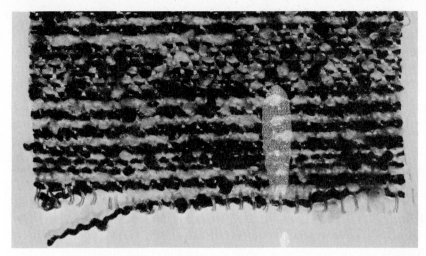

Figure 21.1 Construction of a visual design.

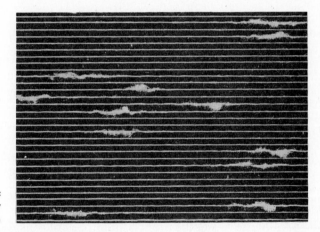

Figure 21.2 Curtain and drapery fabric
of acetate random slub yarns. (Courtesy
of Eastman Chemical Corp.)

the fabric by weaving or knitting. When these designs cause an optical effect where the combination of elements seems to change color and texture, the design is often called a visual design. (See Figs. 21.1 and 21.2.)

CREATING A SUCCESSFUL COMBINATION

To create a successful interior scheme, there are six essential points to be kept in mind:

1. The atmosphere to be created
2. The uses of the room
3. The size of the room

4. The style of furniture
5. The size and shape of the windows
6. Energy efficiency

Atmosphere and Environs

Is the room to become dignified, dramatic, cottagelike, theatrical, or masculine? These factors naturally have more bearing on the choice of hangings than on the grade of the fabric. Draperies, an intrinsic part of home furnishings, help to build up the character and mood of each room, whether it is a room in a home, office, theater, hotel, or restaurant.

Depending on the choice of fabric for draperies, one can make a room formal or informal. A formal room would require a fine fabric: velvet, damask, taffeta, satin, or antique satin. Choice of color can depend on exposure of the room or personal likes or dislikes of the occupant. A scheme may be built around a fine Oriental rug or an antique Aubusson rug that the individual owns or wishes to acquire.

Use of the Room

Some rooms are used much more than others. Much used rooms include living rooms, nurseries, and bedrooms; those used less frequently include foyers, dining rooms, and guest rooms. Appropriate color schemes are based on the use for which the room is intended. In general, rooms lived in most of the time should be decorated in muted tones.

The color scheme for a house or an apartment should be thought of as a whole, not room by room. A feeling of shock is experienced by the visitor who walks from a red hall into a lavender living room or into a rose or blue dining room. It is like looking at a display of model rooms in a department store.

Size of the Room

The size of the room is an important consideration in the selection of appropriate furniture and also in the selection of a drapery design. Ordinarily, small designs are best for a small room and large designs for a large room. A striped pattern hung horizontally normally makes a room appear lower and broader. Mirrors on one side of the room with draperies on the opposite side tend to make the room seem larger and more luxuriously draped.

Style of the Furniture

In Chapter 20 the different period styles in furniture were discussed. To select suitable draperies, one needs to know the fabric with the exact design and texture that best typifies the spirit of the period represented by one's furniture. (Appendix H gives the fabrics appropriate to different historical periods.)

Curtains and draperies are usually a background for the style of furniture, the rug or carpet, and the upholstery to be used. The exception would be a room where a fine designer or period fabric is used. The colors in the drapery would be a guide for the carpet, wall color, and upholstery.

The consumer can very often be influenced by current fashion trends, which may be only fleeting fads. An interior designer/decorator should offer suggestions on items of major expense, such as carpeting, lighting, and draperies. He or she is trained to aid the client in the selection of quality carpeting and fabrics that will withstand the test of time and serve as a good background for the changing values and taste in furniture selections that come with maturity.

It is important for the skilled and trained designer/decorator as well as for the client to exercise great control in combining colors. There are very real psychological reactions to color, and one cannot presume to dictate taste in color to another person. It is too subtle and too personal a matter for mathematical formulas.

Size and Shape of the Windows

There are various sizes and shapes of windows that have to be draped, curtained, or both. Some windows are tall and narrow, some are short and wide, and some are arranged in groups. Each shape is a problem in decoration.

In general, a high, narrow window looks wider if the drapery extends beyond the window on the wall at either side. The amount of widening would depend on the architectural features of the wall space; for example, the draperies might be brought out six to ten inches on either side of the window frame for balance. However, there is no set rule. One might want to cover as much as three or more feet of wall to balance the room.

Energy Considerations

The textiles components of the interior environment may play another very important role, that of thermal comfort and energy conservation. Energy-conscious consumers will want to consider the insulating properties of different window treatments.

A combination of drapery and roller shades can reduce energy costs and create interior spaces that are more comfortable for the inhabitants. Use of liners and the addition of roller shades to the drapery help to retain heat in the room or keep sunlight out. Best effects occur when the drapery is closed at the top, sides, and bottom. This may influence a return to a style where the drapery rests on the floor several inches to help prevent room heat from circulating between the fabric and the glass where it is cooled. (See *Other Treatments*, page 612, for additional energy considerations.)

DRAPERIES AND CURTAINS

The types of draperies and curtains are classified on the following pages. (See Figs. 21.3 (a)–(d), which show the optical effect of drapery lines.)

Draperies or Overhangings

These are decorative fabrics that are hung at the sides of the windows or doors for artistic effects. They may soften the line of the doors and windows or screen a doorway. They also add a note of color and interest. Draperies may be made of cotton, linen, rayon, silk, wool, man-made fibers, or mixtures of these fibers. (See the glossary for the names of fabrics commonly used for draperies.) In the choice of draperies, as in that of upholsteries, the fabric should correspond with furnishings in the room. Textures in a formal room should be woven in silklike surfaces in acetates and polyesters. Cotton blended with polyester or rayon or acrylic textures may be used in informal rooms. Linens are more formal, durable, serviceable, and vigorous. Silks are formal, suggesting regalness and luxury. Rayons, acetates, polyesters, acrylics, and glass fibers are used in the same weaves and textures as silks.

Most newer man-made fibers can be laundered or dry-cleaned. Wools are especially appropriate for masculine decoration, such as in hunting lodges, libraries, and dens. Wools and nylons are also adaptable for fabrics used as curtains and seat covers in vehicles of transportation and hotel lobbies and rooms, and in clubs. Wool, a heavy fabric, drapes beautifully but requires care insofar as it attracts moths unless treated. Wools are informal, suggesting warmth, orderliness, and masculinity.

Because of the trend to casual living and informal decoration, satins and Jacquards are declining, whereas open weaves, knits, and sheer panels in natural colors are increasing in demand.

While the terms draperies and curtains are often used interchangeably, the trade tends to limit the use of curtains for the home to fabrics that cover the inside of the window, also called inner curtains. These are usually of light weight material and cut off the view, both without and within. Heavier insulated material is increasingly used to conserve energy.

Inner Curtains

Since these are hung next to the window frame or glass, they may also be called glass curtains. They may be divided into four groups: sheer, tambour, draw, and sash.

Sheer Curtains

Made of very thin materials and hung on a rod by hooks or casings, they average 1½ to 3 yards in length and usually hang loosely to the sill. A casement curtain is a type of glass curtain hung from an inside rod, the outside rod

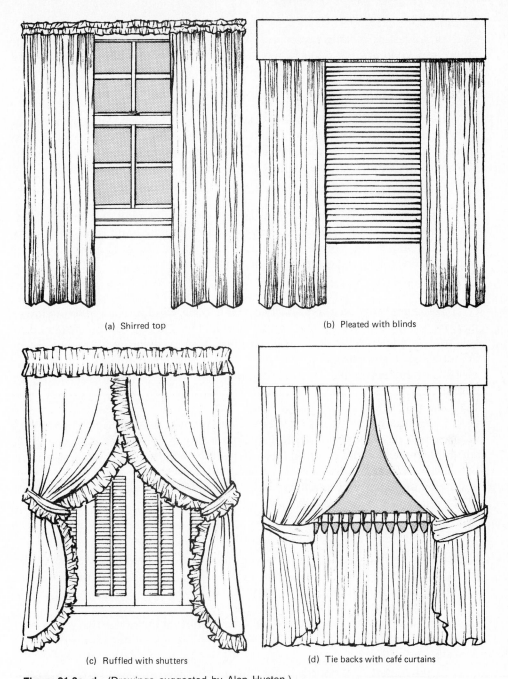

(a) Shirred top

(b) Pleated with blinds

(c) Ruffled with shutters

(d) Tie backs with café curtains

Figure 21.3a–d (Drawings suggested by Alan Huston.)

holding the overdraperies. Casement curtains are usually made of casement cloth of polyester, acetate, rayon, or silk gauze. Fiber glass, heavy lace, filet net, lawn, and voile are particularly well suited to windows where neighbors are close and privacy is a requirement.

Tambour Curtains

Heavily embroidered curtains made of Swiss batistes, lawns, or net in elaborate and exquisite designs (white on white), these curtains can take the place of glass curtains or draperies, and they may be formal or informal. The net style is often used for ecclesiastical purposes.

Draw Curtains

Used as window shades, they ensure privacy or shut out bright light. Equipped with a draw cord or traverse rod, they usually hang from an outside rod to the sill, to the bottom of the apron, or to the floor. They are made of opaque fabrics and are often lined or foam backed.

Sash, Tier, or Café Curtains

These are hung on a rod attached to the lower window sash or to the lower half of the window casing. Bathroom or kitchen windows can be curtained in this way so that curtains do not hinder the raising or lowering of the windows. Windows that are opened frequently are best treated in this manner so that curtains do not soil or tear by blowing out of the window. French doors may be curtained with a sheer fabric, such as marquisette, ninon, voile, or batiste, held taut at top and bottom by small brass rods.

Café curtains (originally styled in France) consist of one, two, or three tiers of fabric that can be installed with (1) plain heading with brass rings sewn on, (2) clips, (3) shirred headings, or (4) fabric loops. The length of the tiers depends on the number of tiers desired; usually tiers overlap each other 3 inches. Headings and hems of the café curtains may be cut in scallops or squares or left straight. These curtains can be made of any informal fabric.

Other Treatments

Curtains for French doors or in-swinging casements are held firmly down at the top and bottom of the door or window by small brass rods. If the doors open into another room, the upper panes may be left bare, but if they open to the outdoors, the curtain might cover the entire door.

French doors may be treated with draperies to ensure privacy and add color to the room. They may be made so that they can be drawn and treated as a window.

Two long panel draperies that hang at either side of a window or at either end of a group treatment for side decoration is a popular window treatment.

Other window treatments to consider are shades of several varieties.

Shades fit windows of all sizes and can be made from many types of fabrics, like draperies, to suit any decorating treatment. The most common type available is the roller shade, usually made of stiffened fabric and controlled by a spring inside the roller. These can either be pulled down or from the bottom up, which allows light to enter through the upper portion of the window.

Drapery alone does not prevent heat loss if simply hung on a traverse rod. It allows a gap which cools warm interior air as it passes behind the drapery. Shades can be a most effective treatment for insulating windows if mounted properly. They should be installed with brackets inside the window frame so that when the shade is lowered it is as close as possible to the glass without touching it. These trapped air spaces act as excellent insulators.

Roman, Austrian, and woven wood shades are lowered or raised by a cord. The Roman and Austrian shade is usually made of a decorative fabric, and their purpose is to enhance the interior scheme.

There is an insulating Roman shade available which is made of polyester Fiberfil material lined on the outside with a sun resistant fabric and on the room side with a vapor barrier and decorative fabric. Another special insulating shade, Window Quilt[R] (Appropriate Technology Corp., Brattleboro, Vt.), consists of five layers of quilted material ultrasonically bonded together. The edges of the shade ride up and down on a track system providing greater energy savings. (See Fig. 21.4.)

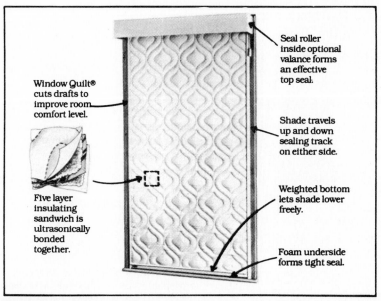

Window Quilt® cuts drafts to improve room comfort level.

Five layer insulating sandwich is ultrasonically bonded together.

Seal roller inside optional valance forms an effective top seal.

Shade travels up and down sealing track on either side.

Weighted bottom lets shade lower freely.

Foam underside forms tight seal.

Figure 21.4 Window Quilt®, an insulating window shade designed for energy conservation. (Courtesy of Appropriate Technology Corp.)

Estimating for Draperies and Curtains

Although curtains and draperies can be purchased ready-made, consumers may prefer to make their own to achieve greater individuality.

Estimate correctly the amount of material needed. This estimate requires careful measuring of the window with a metal rule. (A string or tape stretches and is therefore likely to be inaccurate.) In estimating, add 9 inches to each curtain length: 5 inches for a bottom hem and 4 inches for a top hem. Sheer materials look best when the hem is turned over three times.

Sheer inner curtains usually just clear the sill or hang to the bottom of the apron. A graceful drapery reaches to the bottom of the apron or to the floor. Very formal draperies can spread out on the floor.

When sheer materials are shirred on rods, a fullness of three times the width of the window should be allowed, and for heavy fabrics a fullness of one and a half times. (See Fig. 21.5.) Curtains or draperies may also be pleated at the top. A Flemish or a French pleat is a box pleat with three loops caught together about 4 inches from the top and hung by a hook or ring. Seven pleats are

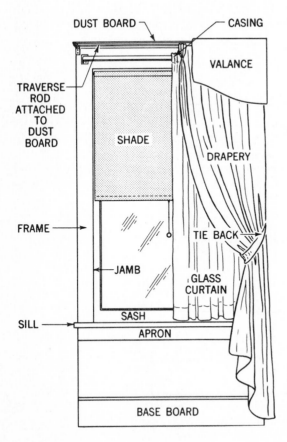

Figure 21.5 The parts of a window. Drapery should be pleated at top and hung on track that is on dust board. Draperies can be either stationary or draw. (Adapted from illustration produced by Singer Sewing Machine Company.)

generally made in 50-inch materials, which leaves a panel 25 inches wide. Five pleats in a 36-inch fabric leave an 18-inch panel. When using a 36-inch width, allow one-third again as much fabric as you need for a 50-inch material, whether for draperies, upholstery, or slipcovers. If you are using a patterned fabric, allow for repeat of the pattern.

The valance or decoration of ornamental material hung at the top of the window may be of these types:

1. Shirred on an outside rod (not on same rod as the side draperies).
2. Flat (pulled straight, no fullness).
3. French-pleated (three small pleats pinched together at intervals).
4. Box pleated (pleats spread flat and pressed, sewed at even intervals).
5. Side pleated (pleats basted at even intervals and pressed in one direction).
6. Dutch (valance shirred on same rod and placed between the side draperies).
7. Cornice board (a piece of wood carved or cut to serve as a valance and painted in the color scheme of the room).
8. Swag and jabots (hangs in draped curves between two or more points). See the glossary.

Sometimes a wide valance is hung across the top of several panels in a group to make them look like one.

Ready-Made Curtains

Nearly every type of curtain or casement curtain is available ready-made. Ready-made draperies can also be purchased. The most common types of ready-made curtains are

1. Ruffled (with tie-backs, with or without valance; well suited to informal rooms, bedrooms, nurseries, and so forth; also called Priscilla curtains).
2. Crisscross (two panels cross each other at the top and are tied back; appropriate for colonial rooms; also called Priscilla curtains).
3. Sash curtains (cover the bottom sash of the window; appropriate for kitchens and bathrooms).
4. Plain pairs of curtains (sold in pairs; narrow hems down the sides and wider hems across the bottom; may or may not have fringes).
5. Panels (single curtains; one panel is made to cover the entire window).
6. Café (consist of one, two, or three tiers of fabric that usually overlap about 3 inches; sometimes known as tier curtains).

Selection of Materials for Draperies

There are so many types of drapery fabrics that at first it may seem difficult to make an appropriate selection. But if three important factors are considered, *color, texture,* and *design,* the task should be easier. Color having been determined, texture can next be settled. Texture means the roughness or smoothness of the surface of a fabric. The one rule that governs texture combination is that textures should be neither too much alike nor too dissimilar.

Figure 21.6 Toile de Jouy: a pictorial design fabric. (Photo by Jack Pitkin.)

For example, silk velvet should not be combined with rough linen-like textures or taffeta with monk's cloth. On the other hand, there should be enough textural contrast to create interest. In a room in which the draperies are of damask and the curtains are of gauze, the upholstery may be of brocade, striped taffeta, plain taffeta, or velvet. For an informal room a pleasant combination might be achieved by combining a toile de Jouy for draperies and bedspread with a solid-color antique satin for a wing chair and a small bench. (See Fig. 21.6.) (See the glossary at the end of this chapter for names and identifying features of drapery fabrics.)

In selecting appropriate designs, remember that too much pattern in a room is tiresome and should be avoided. The same principle that applies to color applies to one's selection of design. (See Figs. 21.7 and 21.8.)

In choosing drapery materials, a practical consideration is the effect of sunlight on the different fibers. Window fabrics can be subjected to up to 300°F temperature that builds up between fabric and glass. Nearly all fabrics are weakened somewhat by sunlight. Rayon is about as resistant to sunlight as cotton, and bright acetate is more resistant than cotton. Sunlight decreases the strength of pure silk. Strong sunlight also injures nylon. Since both polyester and acrylic fibers are highly resistant to sunlight, they are seldom lined and are good choices.

Drapery linings will protect fabrics as well as provide uniform external appearance and improved draping quality.

Most casements used in windows with western or southern exposure may need the extra protection of blinds, shades, or blackout curtains. In a survey by Owens-Corning, women were found to look for the following traits (in order of

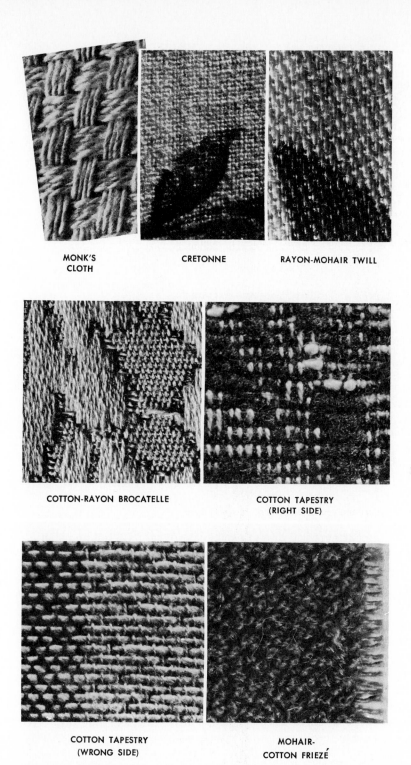

MONK'S
CLOTH

CRETONNE

RAYON-MOHAIR TWILL

COTTON-RAYON BROCATELLE

COTTON TAPESTRY
(RIGHT SIDE)

COTTON TAPESTRY
(WRONG SIDE)

MOHAIR-
COTTON FRIEZÉ

Figure 21.7 Selection of fabrics used for draperies. (Photos by Jack Pitkin.)

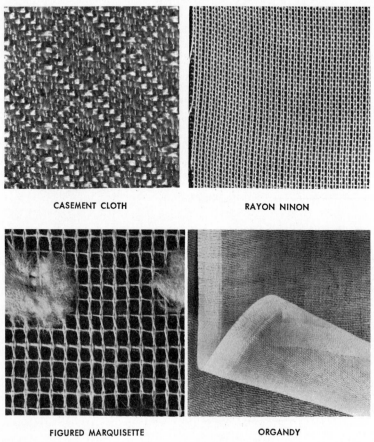

CASEMENT CLOTH RAYON NINON

FIGURED MARQUISETTE ORGANDY

Figure 21.8 Selection of fabrics for inner curtains. (Photos by Jack Pitkin.)

preference) in buying curtains and draperies: (1) ease of care, (2) holding shape, (3) resistance to fading, (4) fire resistance, (5) protection of furniture from sunlight, and (6) assurance of privacy.[1]

Care of Draperies and Curtains

If instructions for care of draperies and curtains appear on a label attached to the merchandise when purchased, that label should be saved for reference when the curtains must be cleaned.

Most cottons, particularly those blended with polyesters, can be washed in an automatic washer. Many curtains today have durable-press performance and can be tumble-dried. No ironing is required. Some all-cotton curtains require starching to give them a crisp finish. If the label indicates that they are

---

[1]*The New York Times,* September 22, 1974, Sec. 3, p. 12.

permanent starchless finish, then starching is unnecessary. Curtains that require minimum care usually should be thrown over a line or hung at the window (with paper underneath to catch the water) to drip dry. Little if any ironing is generally needed. All-cotton velveteen, velour, and tapestry should be dry-cleaned.

Should the label indicate that the article is hand-washable, a neutral soap solution of lukewarm water should be used. Cotton fabrics containing rayon should be dried flat or hung over a line with edges straight, away from heat or sun. The strain of drying should come on the cotton (the warp), not on the rayon. Since clothespins may cause threads or bulge of break, they should not be used on delicate fabrics. There is no problem with polyesters or acrylics. Fabrics containing man-made fibers should be pressed with a warm, not a hot, iron.

Linen draperies are usually washable, provided that the dyes are fast. They are usually fairly heavy, sturdy cloths and so do not require special treatment in laundering. If ironing is required to remove wrinkles, it is advisable to do so while the fabric is still damp. Most silk fabrics should be dry-cleaned. Sheer fabrics made of polyester and acrylic fibers are usually machine-washable and machine-dryable. Glass-fibered curtains are hand-washable and do not wrinkle. When washed by hand, such sheer curtains should be dipped in a soap solution, rinsed, and hung to dry. Since glass fibers do not absorb moisture, fabrics should be cleaned and dried quickly, without wrinkling, shrinking, or losing their shape. When used in sheer curtains, glass fibers are smooth and may slip in laundering unless care is taken. Hems may need hand smoothing after washing to prevent puckering.

Wool fabrics and blends should be dry-cleaned. To keep moths from attacking the wool in upholsteries and draperies, vacuum and treat for moth prevention. A thorough cleaning of wool fabrics at regular intervals will rid them of odors, dirt, and moths.

Before curtains or draperies of any fabric are stored for a season they should be laundered or cleaned. Dirt and grit tend to rot cotton fabrics.

Curtains or draperies of any fabric should be laundered or cleaned, according to use, probably at least once a year. Soiled silks and rayons look much better when they have been dry-cleaned, for then their natural luster returns.

The Curtain and Drapery Market

Between 1975 and 1979, annual retail sales of home textiles rose from about $4.7 billion to over $8 billion. Of that figure, the curtain and drapery market made up $1.5 billion, with alternative window treatments accounting for $1 billion. Much of the buying is done by those in the 25- to 35-year-old age group. It is expected that over the next several years, there will be more individual household units, a growing number of women in the work force, and more families with incomes in excess of $25,000 a year. The annual retail sales of curtains, draperies, casements, and other window treatments are expected to grow approximately 2.8 percent annually through the 1980s.[2]

UPHOLSTERY

Fabrics used for covering upholstered furniture and cushions and for slipcovers are classified as upholstery fabrics. They include the following types: light-weight, medium weight, and heavyweight.

Lightweight is suitable for upholstery if heavier grades of the following are selected: antique satin, broadcloth, chintz, homespun, moiré, oxford cloth, poplin, rep, and stretch.

Medium-weight coverings include brocade, brocatelle, canvas, cretonne, crewel, damask, denim, embroidery, mohair, monk's cloth, satin, serge, and ticking.

Heavyweight upholstery coverings are ideal because of their weight and durability. These include bouclé, corduroy, frieze, matelassé, needlepoint, plastic, plush, tapestry, tweed, twill, velour, velvet, velveteen, and vinyl.

Any textile fiber can be used for upholstery, provided that the cloth is sturdy enough to resist friction, sunlight, dry cleaning, and, in some cases, laundering. Wool, cotton, nylon, and polypropylene are probably the most satisfactory upholstery fibers. Nylon is strong, resists abrasion, and is easily cleaned. Nylon, acrylic, and polyester appear to be taking over the upholstery market traditionally held by wool.

If upholstery is to have hard usage, inconspicuous patterns and colors that will not show soil should be chosen. A few silk, rayon, or metal threads shot through a cotton or wool upholstery fabric give it luster and additional beauty. For durability, yarns should be tightly twisted and the weave close.

Upholstery fabric retains its freshness longer if it is covered during the summer months. Linen and cotton fibers are excellent for summer use as slipcovers; they make a chair or divan upholstered in wool seem cooler. Bright, cheerful designs in chintz or cretonne can change a formal room into an informal one. If upholstery is somewhat shabby, new slipcovers will freshen it. Some of the fabrics commonly used for slipcovers are chintz, cretonne, linen crash, cotton rep, nylon and cotton blends with rayon or polyester, cotton broadcloth, denim, and knitted stretch fabrics.

Some of the most commonly used fabrics for covering upholstered furniture and cushions are textures (in wool or cotton), brocade, damask, plush velvet, velour, mohair, leather and its substitutes, tapestry, needlepoint, and laminated fabrics. (A description of the fabrics listed here appears in the glossary.)

The relation between the style, size, and use of the piece of furniture to be

[2]"Inside Furniture," *Home Furnishings Daily,* Section C, January 7, 1980, p. 31.

Figure 21.9 The use of nonwoven fabrics under the upholstery covering. (Photo courtesy of Southern Furniture Manufacturers Association.)

covered and the selection of fabrics is the same as that between the room and the draperies and curtains.

Care of Upholstery

Upholstery should be brushed and vacuumed frequently, not only to remove dirt but to prevent attacks by moths on wool.

To guard against moths, when a new piece of furniture is bought, make sure that the upholstery fabric is treated chemically to make it mothproof. A muslin covering inside the upholstery fabric will keep moths from the inside of the furniture. (See Fig. 21.9.)

If moths do get into an upholstered chair, spread paradichlorobenzene crystals (two to three pounds) over it. Then carefully wrap the chair in paper to confine the odor.

Spots should be removed when they first appear, with either soap and water (if the fabric is washable) or a dry-cleaning fluid. A white fabric often can be cleaned at home. Sprinkle dry powdered magnesia on it, rub the magnesia in, and then brush it off. If upholstery is badly soiled, take it to a reliable upholsterer for cleaning.

Consumers also can find in stores many different kinds of upholstery cleaners suitable for home cleaning and spot removal.

TAPESTRY

Tapestry is an ornamental textile with a long service record. It is basically a handwoven fabric made with a bobbin worked from the wrong side on a warp stretched vertically or horizontally. The bobbin is carried only to the edge of the pattern and not from selvage to selvage. The surface consists entirely of filling threads. If the warp is stretched vertically, the loom is called *high warp;* if horizontally, *low warp.* In the high-warp loom, the outline is designed in ink on the warp; in the low-warp loom, the weaver places a cartoon (sketch of the design) under and close up to the warp, making inking unnecessary.

The warp yarns may be of wool, linen, or cotton. The warp of wool is elastic and is likely to produce a cloth with a crooked shape; warp of linen or cotton is stiffer. The filling yarn is generally wool, except in Chinese tapestry. Although silk is attractive in satin and brocade, it is flat and uninteresting in the interpretation of large pictures. The texture and vibrant character of tapestry is caused by three factors: the ribs formed by the covered warps, which form the highlights; the hatchings, the fine filling threads in vertical series, which form the middle lights; and last, the slits (holes grouped in diagonal series), which form the shadows.

Handmade tapestries are still produced, and machine-made reproductions are woven on Jacquard looms. Two sets of warp and filling yarns are used. The wrong side is smoother than that of a handmade tapestry.

Figure 21.10 An Aubusson tapestry.

Tapestries are distinguished according to period and origin as follows:

1. Primitive—from Egypt; woven as early as 1500 B.C.
2. Gothic—from France; about the fourteenth century.
3. Renaissance—from France; wide borders, composition clear and picturesque, texture inferior to Gothic.
4. Gobelin (early)—from France; seventeenth century; Gobelins originally a family of dyers who added a tapestry factory; Louis XIV in 1662 made the factory a state institution; early Gobelin tapestries characterized by solemnity, conformity, and dignity; inspired by paintings of Rubens and LeBrun.
5. Gobelin (later)—brightness, individuality, and grace replaced earlier characteristics; inspired by Watteau and Boucher.
6. Beauvais—from a famous factory north of Paris; private but backed by Louis XIV; coarser and less expensive than Gobelin tapestries; mostly landscapes.
7. Aubusson—from the city of Aubusson, 207 miles south of Paris; less expensive than Beauvais; depict especially groups of personages; coarse, loose texture. (See Fig. 21.10.)
8. Tapestries produced outside France—German, Swiss, English, Spanish, Russian, Turkish, and Chinese.

Tapestries were used in the Middle Ages as a protection against drafts and as wall decorations. In modern homes, where there is a concern for energy conservation, consumers can once again use tapestries as protection against drafts. We still use tapestries for hangings, either as a background or as pictures. Modern tapestries woven on the Jacquard loom are suitable for fire-screen covers, covers for benches or stools, reupholstering of furniture, and knitting or shopping bags.

SUMMARY

One who prefers individuality in home furnishing may follow that preference by using his or her own taste in choosing fabrics for draperies and curtains. Those who favor period styles may follow that inclination in decoration, provided that appropriate fabrics are coordinated with the furniture and rugs. The most important thought to bear in mind is that harmony of design, color, and the texture of the fabrics must be maintained. In addition, the style of furniture, the size of the room, the use of the room, and the size and shape of the windows as well as energy usage are important considerations.

PROJECTS

1. Plan the fabric decorations for a master bedroom (18 × 13 feet) of a suburban home. Two windows face north, and walls are painted in a grayish, pale, warm beige. Furniture is Chippendale. If possible, include swatches of actual fabric with prices for ready-made articles or for fabric by the yard.

2. Plan the décor for a living room (20 × 18 feet) of a city apartment. Casement windows open onto an unsightly, dark court. Walls are painted a light gray. Furniture is contemporary with an Oriental influence. Wherever possible, the prices of fabric by the yard or of the ready-made article should be included.

3. Plan the fabric decorations for a teenage boy's or a teenage girl's sunny bedroom in a small ranch-type home of five rooms. The wallpaper in the boy's room is patterned with large motifs of sailing vessels. The wallpaper in the girl's room has a spaced design of varicolored flowers. The rooms each have a square, medium-sized window with louvers of clear glass. Furniture is contemporary.

GLOSSARY

Antique satin A fabric made to resemble a silk satin of an earlier century. Has a slub face and a satin back.

Antique taffeta Originally pure silk fabric with a nubby texture. Now usually polyester warps and silk fillings.

Bouclé A fabric made of novelty yarn that is characterized by tight loops projecting from the body of the yarn at fairly regular intervals.

Brocade A drapery or upholstery fabric in Jacquard weave with raised designs. It has contrasting surfaces or colors that emphasize the pattern. Metallic threads may be shot through the fabric.

Brocaded satin A satin fabric with raised designs in Jacquard weave.

Brocatelle A drapery and upholstery fabric made in double-cloth construction with a silk- or rayon-fibered face. Best grades have linen back. The design stands in relief from the ground, giving a padded effect.

Burlap A coarse, stiff fabric in plain weave. It is made of jute, hemp, or cotton and is used for draperies.

Café curtains Consist of one, two, or three tiers of fabric that usually overlap abut three inches.

Canvas A heavy cotton cloth in plain weave. Used for awnings, upholstery covers, and whenever a coarse, heavy fabric is needed.

Casement cloth Any medium-sheer drapery fabric suitable for casement windows and draperies.

Chenille Fabric of silk, wool, cotton, or man-made fibers, made with chenille yarns or tufts, used for draperies and bedspreads. See Chapter 19, *tufted fabric.*

Chintz Glazed cotton and blends of polyester/cotton fabric, often printed in gay colors, used for draperies, slipcovers, bedspreads, and upholstery.

Contemporary style See the glossary in Chapter 20.

Corduroy In cotton blended with polyester for draperies; upholstery and other home furnishings items in cotton or cotton/polyester blends. See the glossary in Chapter 17.

Cretonne A plain-weave carded cotton fabric, usually printed with large designs. Cretonne is unglazed and is used for draperies and slipcovers.

Crewel A type of embroidery using varicolored wools worked on unbleached cotton or linen. The spreading design covers only a part of the background and is often a Tree of Life motif.

Curtain (as used in home decoration) A relatively sheer hanging that covers a window next to the glass or hangs against another opening.

Damask   A drapery or upholstery fabric of silk, rayon, and cotton, or other combinations of fibers, woven in Jacquard weave with reversible flat designs.

Denim   Twilled cotton fabric made of single hard-twisted yarns. Staple type has colored warp and white filling. Woven-in stripes and plaids are popular for draperies, upholstery, and bedspreads.

Design   The orderly process of functional and/or aesthetic elements in space that achieves a sense of unity or harmony.

Direct designing   A trial-and-error method in the use of yarns of different fibers and blends to create a visual design. It is done directly on a hand loom with no point-paper pattern.

Drapery   A relatively heavy fabric hung on both sides or across a window or other opening.

Embroidery   A fabric with surface decorations done with needle and thread, either by hand or by machine.

Faille   Used for draperies. See the glossary in Chapter 17.

Fiberglas   See *glass fibers* in the glossary in Chapter 15.

Fishnet   Large novelty mesh fabric of cotton or linen, acrylic, or polyester, made to resemble fishing nets in white or colors. It is used for curtains.

Frieze   Heavy pile fabric with rows of uncut loops. It is made of mohair, wool, cotton, or man-made fibers and is used for draperies and upholsteries.

Fringes   Thread or cords of any fibers grouped or bound together and loose at one end, used for trimming draperies and upholstery.

Gauze   Sheer, loosely woven plain-weave fabric suitable for curtains. It is made in wool, silk, or man-made fibers.

Gingham   Used for curtains. See the glossary in Chapter 17.

Homespun   A very coarse, rough linen, wool, cotton, or man-made fiber or blend in varied colors; generally in plain weave resembling wool homespun. It is used for draperies and upholstery.

Hopsacking   A coarse, loosely woven fabric in basket or novelty weave. The original hopsacking was used for sacking hops. Now made to resemble the original of linen, spun rayon, or cotton, and used in blends. Also used for dresses and coats.

Jabot   A pleated fan-shaped side panel attached at the top of a drapery, a type of valance. For women's wear, a pleated fabric edging attached down the center front of a blouse or dress.

Lace   See *laces*, Chapter 19.

Laminated fabric   (for upholstery) A fabric with a sheet of plastic bonded on its surface.

Louver   A fitted window frame with slatted panels.

Marquisette   A sheer curtaining material of silk, rayon, nylon, polyester, or acrylic fibers woven in leno weave.

Matelassé   A heavy Jacquard double cloth with quilted appearance that is used for draperies and upholstery. See *matelassé* for dresses, glossary in Chapter 17.

Mohair   A yarn or cloth made from the fleece of the Angora goat. The fiber is strong and makes one of the most durable of all textiles.

Monk's cloth   A heavy cotton fabric in basket weave (4×4 or 8×8). It comes in natural color, solid, or stripes, and is used for draperies and couch covers.

Monochromatic scheme   The use of a combination of different shades of one color.

Needlepoint   An upholstery fabric. Designs are usually floral, embroidered with yarn on coarse canvas.

Net   See the glossary in Chapter 17.

Ninon   A sheer plain-weave glass curtaining made in polyester or other man-made fibers. The warp yarns are arranged in pairs.

Organdy   Sheer, crisp, cotton or polyester in plain weave. See the glossary in Chapter 17.

Oxford cloth   Plain basket or twill weave, lightweight to rather heavyweight. Durable and launders well.

Percale   Plain weave, closely woven fabric in cotton or man-made blends in dull finish that may be dyed or printed. It is used for curtains and bedspreads.

Petit point   Similar to needlepoint but with a finer slanting stitch.

Plastics   Fabrics made of plastic-impregnated or plastic-coated yarns (core of yarn made of cotton, rayon, linen, silk, glass, nylon), plastic-finished fabrics, and all-plastic extruded fibers and yarns suitable for webbing and woven fabrics for porch and beach furniture. (See *saran*, Chapter 15).

Plush   A heavy-pile fabric with deeper pile than velvet or velour. It may be mohair, silk, rayon, acrylic, or polyester, and it is used for upholstery.

Pongee   Used for draperies and casement curtains. See the glossary in Chapter 17.

Poplin   See the glossary in Chapter 17.

Rep or repp   Heavy fillingwise corded fabric, heavier than poplin. It may be silk, rayon, or other man-made fibers, wool, or cotton. It is used for draperies and upholstery.

Sailcloth   A generic name for fabrics used for sails. May be made of cotton, linen, jute, nylon, or polyester. Sailcloth is also used for draperies, upholstery, and sportswear.

Sateen   A mercerized fabric of cotton or cotton blended with polyester in satin weave used for lining draperies. It may be printed for draperies.

Satin   Silk and cotton, acetate and cotton, or other man-made fiber combinations woven in satin weave. It is used for draperies, upholsteries, bedspreads, and sheets.

Satin antique   See *antique satin*.

Seersucker   See the glossary in Chapter 17.

Serge   Silk, wool, cotton, or rayon twill weave, with a clear and hard finish.

Shantung   Used for draperies. See the glossary in Chapter 17.

Sheer curtains   Thin fabrics of polyester, cotton, and blends that hang next to the window glass.

Shiki (shiki rep)   Heavy rayon, acetate, and cotton, or other mixtures identified by wavy fillingwise cords. It is used for draperies.

Stretch   Knit or woven with special stretch properties or of spandex. Smooth to rough in texture. Good for slipcovers and contoured shapes.

Structural design   A woven-in or knitted-in pattern as opposed to a printed one.

Swag   A draped ornamental fabric hanging at the top of the drapery, may be a type of valance.

Swiss (dotted or figured)   Used for curtains. See *dotted swiss* in the glossary in Chapter 17.

Synthetic fibers   Man-made fibers. See Chapter 2.

Taffeta   A plain-weave, stiff-finished fabric in silk or the man-made fibers. Used for draperies and bedspreads. See *antique taffeta*.

Tambour curtains   Imported Swiss, heavily embroidered batiste, lawn, or polyester curtains, originally embroidered by hand on a kind of drum, now machine made.

Tapestry   A Jacquard woven fabric in cotton, wool, or man-made fibers. The design is woven in by means of colored filling yarns. On the back, shaded stripes identify this fabric. It is used for draperies and upholstery.

Textured   A surface that is woven with a nubby yarn construction. May be made in any fiber.

Ticking   Closely woven cotton in twill or satin weave with woven or printed stripes.

Toile de Jouy   Cotton fabric printed in pictorial designs. The original toile was printed by Oberkampf in 1759 at Jouy, France. It is used for draperies and bedspreads.

Tweed-textured   An exaggerated chevron or tweedlike structural design with accentuated nubs.

Twill   A basic weave; also the fabric woven in that manner. It has a diagonal rib effect.

Valance   A decorative fabric or board that is installed across the top of a window.

Velour   A smooth, closely woven pile fabric usually of cotton, wool, or man-made fibers. The fabric is heavier than velvet and is used for draperies, upholstery, and bedspreads.

Velvet   Silk, rayon, nylon, acrylic cut pile fabrics. When used for draperies and upholstery it is somewhat heavier than dress velvet.

Velveteen   An all-cotton pile fabric for draperies and upholstery that is heavier than dress velveteen. See the glossary in Chapter 17.

Vinyl   Textile fused or coated with vinyl plastic.

Visual design   A structural design where unusual optical effects are created by combinations of different colors and types of yarns.

Voile   A sheer plain-weave curtain fabric of cotton, rayon, or polyester fibers made of hard-twisted yarns.

Whipcord   Hard-woven worsted fabric with fine diagonal cords on the face that is used for draperies and upholstery.

Chapter 22

THE PRODUCTION AND MARKETING CHANNELS FOR TEXTILE PRODUCTS AND CAREER OPPORTUNITIES

No field of merchandise better deserves the attention of producers, distributors, and consumers than does that of textiles. In the United States, about 2.6 million people depend upon the various textile industries for their jobs. About half of these work in the apparel industry, nearly a third in the textile mills that construct the fabrics, and the rest in fiber and machinery construction.

Measured in pounds per capita, the 1982 U.S. annual consumption of textile products was about 60, compared with a world average of only 15. The four end-use classifications of textile products, measured in millions of pounds, has increased materially over the past two decades as the following table indicates.[1]

	1960	1980
Apparel	20	25
Home furnishings	7	8
Carpeting (for homes, vehicles, and public places)	2	8
Industry	9	12
Total (in millions of pounds)	38	53

[1]See *America's Textiles'* special study of the American textile industry, August 1982.

TEXTILE PRODUCTION AND DISTRIBUTION CHANNELS

As you have read in earlier chapters, the American textile industry is composed of many components, but there are principal ones that dominate because of their size and importance. These components form a channel or pipeline of industrial activity often performed by independent processors that, in turn, create the fibers and carry them through the stages of yarn making, fabric construction, and fabric finishing (converting). They also manufacture fabrics into consumer products and distribute them to "wholesale" distributors and to retailers and then to the final users (household consumers and users of industrial, commercial, and institutional kinds). See Fig. 22.1 for the steps involved in transforming textile fiber to finished product and delivering it to the consumer; see Fig. 22.2 for the steps involved in garment construction and ultimate sale (with accompanying explanations).

In practice, there are many variations in the production and marketing channel. For example, the fiber producers may also produce the yarn, especially in the case of man-made fibers; the fabric mills may also do their own finishing and some may also manufacture the consumer product. This is especially true in the case of household textiles, such as sheets, towelings, and other coverings. At times, smaller manufacturers may sell directly to household consumers, bypassing distributors and retailers.

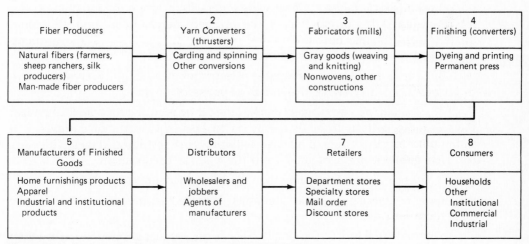

Figure 22.1 From textile fiber to finished product and to consumer.

A. Construction

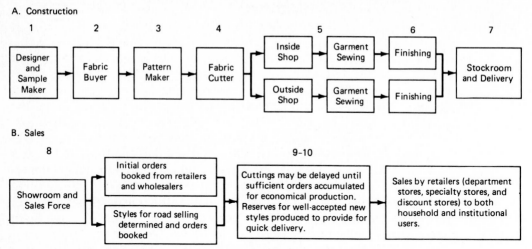

Figure 22.2 Flow chart of garment construction and sale.

Explanation of Steps in Figure 22.2

1. *The Designer.* Bases work on research and intuition. Clothing designers work out ideas by draping fabrics on live models. When satisfied with the results, the designer has assistants finish each garment by hand from which patterns are made for mass production. Some designers become manufacturers, going into the business of selling their own creations.

2. *The Fabric Buyer.* Deals with orders from fabric manufacturers, the fabrics required for production of the ordered merchandise, and additional quantity for probable new orders and reorders. To avoid overstock, arrangements may be made for reorders contingent on need.

3. *The Pattern Maker.* Prepares patterns for all parts of the styles that are to be produced in view of the initial response of buyers.

4. *The Cutter.* Arranges layers of the fabric required for a style and size. Lays out the pattern in such a way as to keep the waste of cuttings at a minimum. Cuts the layers of material with powerful revolving knives. The parts for each garment are separated from the pile for construction.

5. *Inside Shop.* Sews together the pieces cut for each garment.

6. *The Finisher.* Checks for faults. Presses and prepares goods for the stockroom and delivery.

Alternate to 5 and 6: *The Outside Shop.* Cuts parts of garments that are then delivered to an outside contractor who performs the sewing and finishing operations. The contractor also returns the goods to the manufacturer, who owns and sells the new merchandise.

7. *Stockroom and Delivery Staff.* Handles the packing and shipment.

8. *The Showroom with Sales Personnel.* Presents the styles created for the new season by means of live models and then by showing on the hanger. Next, store buyers and wholesale buyers visit the showroom and place orders.

9. Reorders may be handled in one of two ways—by a reserve stock, beyond immediate requirements prepared and drawn on as needed, or by accumulation, until enough reorders are gathered to warrant a new cutting and production. Only if enough reorders are received are they put into manufacture.

10. Styles stocked by both retailers and wholesalers with the former selling them to consumers.

The function performed by the garment manufacturer is often supplemented by small specialized firms that may be called upon by the manufacturers to perform in a subcontracting capacity.

Table 22.1 explains the functions of five specialized firms or workers found in the garment industry. These are a declining breed as some of the functions are performed by mills in the South that manufacture the cloth and so are less important in the United States as more garments are manufactured abroad.

Marketing the Textile Output Through the Channels

In each of the various channels of production and marketing (fiber, yarn, fabric, or finished goods), the product is actively marketed by sales representatives, sales managers, and advisers. Fiber producers actively solicit the business of yarn spinners.

Next it is the responsibility of the sales department in the yarn mill to sell the yarn output to various fabric mills. Likewise, if the fabric mill's output is only gray, unfinished goods, this mill's output must be sold, or at least assigned, to

Table 22.1 Specialized Workers in the Garment Industry

The Pleater	Spreads fabric across a table between layers of prepleated paper and gathers it into folds and places it in a steam box for about 20 minutes.
The Shrinker	Preshrinks the cloth before cutting by blasting it with live steam over a frame. The cloth may also be dunked in soapy cold water. It is then pressed and dried under 280°F.
The Weaver	Repairs pulled threads and tiny holes in garments by picking threads from the seams and weaving them into the flaw. Loose threads are shaved off.
The Swatcher	By means of a pinking machine, cuts small squares of cloth for manufacturers of fashion garments to show their customers.
The Ragman	Buys by the pound clippings and scraps from the cutting tables and sells them, usually abroad, for reprocessing the fibers into yarns for use in new fabrics and garments.

converters to finish the fabric according to the needs of the next processor in the channel: the manufacturer of the finished product ready for consumption. While the manufacturer's immediate customers are mainly retailers and distributois, those who use brand names and sell under their own brands advertise heavily to consumers to *pull* their products through the pipeline rather than to *push* them through. This means that customer demand created by advertising influences retailers to stock the line.

Every unit in the channel is involved not only with production and moving the product line to the next unit in the channel, but also with buying: raw materials, machinery, supplies, yarns, unfinished fabric, finished fabrics, and manufactured products in the form ready for use. Thus, buyers and purchasing agents are found all along the line. Many of these are only concerned with the technical requirements of their companies' production processes. The manufacturers of consumer goods and the distributors and retailers employ buyers who adjust their purchasing to every change in consumer demand. The retail store buyers, in particular, are guided in their selections by their estimate of the consumer demand that is subject to fashion dictates as well as the many vagaries of the marketplace. Many buyers are both sales managers for their lines as well as selectors of what they buy and make available.

The Marketing Manager and the Marketing Plan

Overall responsibility for planning and managing the marketing program of a textile company is usually assigned to a marketing manager. He or she can be involved in activities as diverse as planning with the design department, manufacturing operations, market research, consumer relations, and the promotional areas of advertising, fashion merchandising, and, of course, sales.

A market plan, such as that outlined in Table 22.2, shows how a new textile product is conceived, designed, developed, tested, priced, packaged, advertised, promoted, and evaluated. Each stage of the plan is a necessary step in preparation for the essential function of marketing—getting the product to the ultimate consumer. As many experienced businesspeople know, nothing really happens until somebody sells something. Thus, the ultimate goal of any marketing plan is to maximize sales—at the right time, in the right place, to the right customer, and at the right price. Meeting consumer needs and desires, anticipating such needs, and motivating people to purchase products are all important parts of the marketing plan.

Goal Development

As the model in Table 22.2 indicates, the planning process in the marketing of a new product line starts with the development of goals, both for materials (product) and human capital (personnel) of the company. In many companies, this may be a part of a larger or long-range planning document already in place. If not, this goal planning will probably occur in the upper ranks of management

Table 22.2 Model of a Marketing Plan to Introduce a New Textile Product Line

---

 I. Long- and short-range goals of the company (division, department)
   A. Product line: philosophical statement
   B. Human resources: maximizing human capital
   C. Financial planning: maximizing profit
 II. Scope of the market
   A. Competition: market share
   B. Competition in relation to situation after product introduction
III. The product line: strategies for development and pricing
   A. Classification/type and price points
   B. Design: strategic planning (long and short range)
   C. Quality development: standards and controls
   D. Projected selling costs and cost analyses (with manufacturing)
 IV. Channels of distribution (COD): sales strategy
   A. Identification of domestic and international CODs
   B. Marketing practices of COD selected (including confinements)
   C. Company selling policies versus competition
   D. Introduction of product (internal): sales meetings and product training
   E. Credit control and management
 V. Advertising and promotion of product line
   A. Identifying ultimate consumer: targeting the retail market
   B. Segmenting the market through advertising and promotion
   C. Market research, making it work for the retailer
   D. Public relations: policy and program
   E. Sales training: program development and coordination with retailer advertising plans
   F. Sales promotion and fashion coordination
   G. Packaging and labeling of product: policy and program
   H. Marketing research: consumer feedback followed by evaluation of the marketing plan
 VI. Marketing liaison with manufacturing
   A. Production scheduling: strike-offs to finished product
   B. Delivery systems (including shipping, warehousing, and distribution points)
   C. Service and product warranties and guarantees
   D. Quality-control feedback: from marketing to manufacturing

---

and may require the approval of the governing board (e.g., directors) or the chief executive officer of the company.

Survey of the Market

Surveying the market with respect to present and potential competition enables the planner to project the volume of sales that can be expected, especially if the new product is a variation of one currently being marketed. A case in point was the introduction of a new fiber blend for bed sheets, in which the new product had a different proportion of fibers than others on the market. The overall sheet market was surveyed, using statistics from government sources such as that in Fig. 19.1 and information from other trade publications and associations. Data such as these give the planner a historical overview of sales by product and year, thus providing a sound point of reference from which to project potential sales for similar products.

The Product Line and Its Promotion

Developing the product line requires the cooperative efforts of designers, merchandising personnel, sales, and manufacturing specialists. Determining the selling costs is also cooperatively managed by both those who produce the product (the manufacturing division) and those who sell the product (the marketing division). In most major textile companies, the product manager of each product division or department serves in a liaison role between the sales and the manufacturing division, quite often commuting between the two divisions if they are located in the typical arrangement (marketing in New York City and manufacturing in a Southern city or town).

Distribution Channels

Channels of distribution will be decided upon and may include chain stores, department stores, discount stores, specialty shops, and catalog stores, among other kinds of retail stores. In some instances, a few major or very important retail accounts may be given an "exclusive" or "confinement," namely, the right to sell (or market) exclusively a product for a specific period of time and within a specified geographical area. This allows, for example, one store in a city to advertise and promote the fact that is is the only retailer in the area where consumers can buy the new product.

Advertising and Promotion

While the new product is in the early developmental stages, many other activities simultaneously take place. The timing of the new product introduction is of strategic importance, and thus the advertising and promotional strategies are planned at the same time that other marketing personnel are testing the product, designing packaging, and determining the selling tactics that will be used to achieve maximum desirable market exposure. Selling personnel will be given special sales training on the new product while developing their own retail training program for sales personnel.

Communication is the underlying consideration in planning, developing, and executing programs to announce new products to the trade (retailers and wholesalers) and ultimate consumers. Such communication tools as newspaper and magazine advertisements, television commercials, fashion shows, and other special events with retail stores may be used to communicate the features and selling points that will stimulate consumers to purchase.

Liaison with Manufacturing and New Product Introduction

Once production schedules have been determined with the manufacturing division, sales managers in the marketing division prepare for the introduction of the product to retail accounts, usually during a major market period when there will be the largest number of retailers shopping the market. Sales presentations will be developed, polished, and presented to selling personnel, the sales force. This will often take the form of a national sales meeting, planned to bring together the company's sales force to unveil to them the new product and to stimulate their enthusiasm for the job ahead, presenting and selling the line to their retail accounts.

In other parts of the marketing division, there will be planning for the announcement to the press, whether it be an elaborate press party at a luxury hotel, a showing of the line in the showroom, or simply a concisely worded press release. The public relations department will also attempt to maximize the response of the media—newspapers, magazines, radio, and television being the major ones.

Market Research

Market research will have preceded many of the steps in developing the new textile product. It is important for planners and managers to have as much information as possible to avoid the costly mistakes that prior information could obviate. Consumer test panels, organized by market researchers, are often used to predict the acceptance of new products. Market surveys and test marketing will also spot potential problem areas involving competitive products as well as feedback to the marketers of their own merchandise. This information, in turn, is communicated to manufacturing personnel and is of major importance to maintaining quality-control standards.

The marketing of textiles is a complex, integrative, and vital part of business and requires a vast assemblage of people with skills, imagination, creativity, and competitive spirit! It is ever-changing, for the consumer is forever changing—and thus it responds to the needs and wants of consumers.

Competitive Practices and Policies

There are a number of techniques in promotion that deserve special consideration, as explained below:

Brands

Many of the man-made fiber and yarn manufacturers, the manufacturers of finished cloth, and those producing the final consumer textile product brand their products with names and symbols that they own. This establishes a standard of quality that will come to be recognized by their customers, retailers, and distributors as well as by the general consuming public. But many have excess capacity and accept orders from their customers to carry private brands that are owned by companies who may be distributors or retailers. These brands may differ in minor respects from the sellers' national brands, perhaps eliminating some relatively minor details that add to the cost of the articles, thus making a lower price possible. Some manufacturers produce goods only for private branding, with the distributors or retailers providing the exact specifications that are to be followed as well as a company's particular brand labels.

Cooperative Advertising

A practice of great significance in buying and selling activities of each textile segment in the channel is cooperative advertising (also called in the trade *co-op* advertising). For example, the manufacturer of man-made fibers may grant a customer, the fabric manufacturer, advertising money to be used by the latter in advertising the product (or brand name) to the next segment in the channel. Sometimes the fiber producer provides advertising allowances to manufacturers of the finished article (i.e., carpets) to make retailers aware of the fiber's brand name, such as Anso Nylon. These allowances are sometimes assigned by the product producer to the retail accounts, if they include the producer's fiber brand names in their advertisements. Where there are adequate controls to assure that advertising co-op money is used as intended, the practice is an important sales promotion device, supplementing what the retailer would spend independently and reducing the advertising costs of the end-product manufacturer, since retailers pay historically lower advertising rates than do manufacturers or fiber producers. Also, the consumer reading the advertisement knows where to find the goods advertised and is given additional prepurchasing information regarding the fiber as well as other product information.

Regional Concentrations

The production of textile fabrics was once concentrated in New England. DuPont in Delaware is still a key textile fiber center, but most major fiber production has now moved to the South with centers in North and South Carolina, particularly in the vicinities of Charlotte and Greensboro, North Carolina. Major yarn and fabric mills with their plants in this area are Celanese, Milliken, Springs Industries, J. P. Stevens, Lowenstein, Cannon Mills, Burlington, and Fieldcrest. (See Fig. 22.3.)

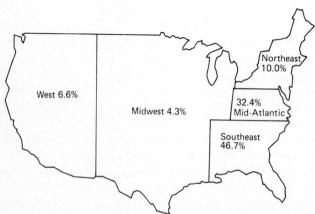

Figure 22.3 Textile plant locations. (Courtesy of the American Textile Manufacturers Institute.)

The marketing of textile fabrics, particularly those sold under the brand names of the producers, remains in New York City. Large showrooms are the focal point for two major semiannual market periods in May and November, at which time retail store buyers come to New York to make their selections for the coming selling seasons. Minimarkets were introduced in the seventies by a few major producers and are usually scheduled for February and August or September. Clearances are also held late in each season. The industry is highly competitive, and care must be taken to avoid agreement among competing sellers as to prices on identical goods and agreement of the timing, clearance offerings, and favoritism in assigning clearance merchandise to certain buyers.

White Sales

One of the most criticized policies in home furnishings marketing, especially from the consumer's viewpoint, has been the practice of "white sales," which historically evolved from inventory closeouts.

More recently, the white sale has evolved into an almost continuous sale period for many major stores, and whereas it was formerly a January and August month-long sale, it now is quite often of a two- to three-month duration. Consumer advocate groups have charged the industry with "artificial pricing policies" and generally have criticized manufacturers and retail stores for perpetuating this practice. During the last two years, several of the major producers have switched their price lists to a "year-round" single pricing policy, thus allowing retailers to schedule sales periods at their discretion.

Outlet Stores: A New Phenomenon
in Textile Marketing

A new development in marketing textile products is of notable interest, namely, the emergence of the "outlet store" or the manufacturer's retail outlet store. In these, producers sell their surplus merchandise—goods for which there is no ready buyer. Outlet stores are mostly concentrated in and near large manufacturing concerns. They are, in many instances, outgrowths of the "employee store," the "mill store," and the "company store." Many different names are used to designate the place where employees of a producing concern can buy their company's goods at special discounted prices or "employee prices."

Outlet stores also sell merchandise that the producer has identified as "seconds" (or less than first-quality goods). In addition, patterns, colors, and styles of discontinued or "dropped" products are sold in these outlets. Most important to the consumer are the deeply discounted prices usually assigned to merchandise in outlet stores. The outlet store has become so popular in the southern part of the United States (where mills are concentrated) that shopping malls featuring many different manufacturers' outlet stores have developed into

Figure 22.4 The Mills mill, in Greenville, South Carolina, now functions as an outlet complex. (Courtesy of *America's Textiles*.)

major retailing complexes. Sometimes manufacturers' outlet stores operate in old, antiquated textile mills that have been converted to attractive retail stores. (See Fig. 22.4.) Today, the mill in Fig. 22.4 provides modernized space for some thirty manufacturers to sell their surplus output at sharply reduced retail prices. The assortments include "seconds," styles being replaced by new ones, and often regular goods carrying labels different from those used for the same merchandise sold to department and specialty stores. These outlets are no longer just piles of odds and ends but, rather, modern merchandising establishments with assortments carefully displayed to appeal to today's customers.

CAREERS IN TEXTILES: A GROWING FASHION INDUSTRY

What Kinds of Jobs Are There?

As you have read in earlier chapters, the textile industry is one of the most important in the United States, being one of the largest employers of people and producing products that touch every life every moment of the day. If you were to calculate the thousands of textile items in each household, you would perceive quickly the major impact that the world of textiles has on everyday living. From the clothes we wear to the furnishings in our homes, to automobile interiors and tires, to the core of baseballs, to the fabric of camping tents, to parachutes, to surgical threads and many more products, we depend upon textile technology to enhance our lives with comfort, functionality, and aesthetic pleasure. No wonder, then, that such a vital industry offers so many different and exciting career possibilities for the student with a textiles background.

There are many different paths to follow in pursuing a career in textiles, and the path selected depends upon which part of the textile pipeline one follows.

Opportunities in Production

Fiber and Yarn Producers

Starting with the very beginning of the textile production process is the fiber producer, the farmer who grows cotton or the rancher who raises sheep or the producer of man-made fibers. Obviously, careers with fiber producers are distinctly different from those found in a modern man-made fiber-producing plant. Farming involves quite varied technical skills and competencies. Students should be aware that with the development of recent trends in agribusiness, the raising of cotton, or the ranching of sheep is quite frequently "big business," requiring the agriculturalist to have a high degree of business expertise as well as knowledge of agricultural subjects. Adding to this a general knowledge of textiles, one sees the comprehensive background necessary for a cotton farmer or sheep rancher. For those interested in agricultural careers, the addition of textile subjects in a program of study seems sound. It is recommended that such students seek the advice of persons in several other areas of agricultural professions, namely, the county or state extension agricultural agent and land grant university's School or College of Agriculture.

Man-made fiber producers offer a myriad of career choices for textile students, from the laboratories to the sales department. A number of possible entry-level positions are obtainable for those holding a college degree (baccalaureate) in textiles. Two distinctly different kinds of career preparation can be followed: (1) the marketing/sales management approach in business programs or (2) the technological approach of college textile science majors which leads to careers in (a) research and development labs, (b) production technology in all its stages from the mixing of chemicals to the extrusion and finishing of the synthetic fiber ready for fabric production, and (c) the quality-control laboratory found in even the smallest fiber-producing mill.

Yarn Spinners and Converters

As with the producer of the man-made fiber, the yarn conversion process offers challenging career opportunities for the textile major. Much, of course, depends on a student's academic orientation and personal preference as to which of the two general approaches to a textile career is taken. Both require college preparation if one is to move through higher levels of responsibility than entry-level positions require. It is for this reason that the serious student of textiles should be aware that, although there are many entry-level positions open to noncollege graduates, advancement beyond the first or second level is limited without the baccalaureate degree. It is possible that nondegree textile workers can obtain additional training on the job, or even in a company-financed college degree program, once competence on the job has been demonstrated. Major career opportunities in converting follow much the same lines as with the fiber producer for production, technology, and research and development as well as those in yarn design, construction, and fabrication. The yarn designer would be well served with a degree program with emphasis on textile design or a related applied arts area.

Textile Fabric/Product Producers

One of the major sources of job opportunities is in the textile mills where fabric is usually woven, knitted, or produced in nonwoven production facilities. Most of the manufacturing divisions of these textile "giants" are located in the southeastern part of the United States. (See Fig. 22.3.) These companies are employers of large numbers of skilled workers. Textile students may use their scientific training in numerous technological positions such as quality control and product testing.

Figure 22.5 A process-control technician in a textile mill. (Photo courtesy of Springs Industries, Inc.)

For production, the plant needs textile engineers, specialists in fabric development and design, chemists and assistants, physicists and assistants, department directors, and managers in many administrative roles. (See Fig. 22.5.) A field that has experienced fast growth over the past decade is data processing, which includes programming, analysis, sales and profit forecasting, estimating, and inventory control. The student who combines the study of textiles with computer science should enjoy entrée into many different kinds of textile producing firms.

The Textile Designer

For students with a background in color and design, the field of textile design holds great interest and opportunity and, therefore, is given special attention here.

There are two types of professional designers: (1) those who plan and execute designs for garments, usually draping on live figures from which patterns are drawn for mass production, known also as apparel designers (see Fig. 22.2), and (2) those who prepare designs to be printed on a fabric or to be built into the fabric in the weaving and knitting process (structural designers).

Printing of patterns has already been discussed in Chapter 8, on dyeing and printing, and in Chapters 5 and 6, that include fancy weaves and knits.

Since structural design is of special interest to consumers today, its creation deserves special attention.

An intricate structural design made for Jacquard or dobby weave or for a knitted construction is first worked out in point paper or on a computer. (See Fig. 22.6.) Then cards (narrow wooden strips) or computer tapes are made to govern the loom operation. These structural designs may be called visual designs when they produce an optical effect. For instance, if one pure color is

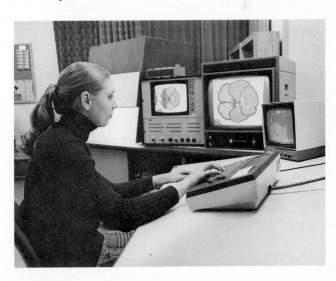

Figure 22.6 Computers can be used to express a design electronically in terms of the sequence of stitches. A scanning unit reads the design very rapidly and produces a point pattern of the stitch formation on a color television set. (Photo courtesy of American Textile Manufacturers Institute.)

used in the warp and another pure color is used in the filling, the effect is an iridescent one or even a new shade. This combination of colors in a weave may create a sheen; or a black warp and a gold filling may give a metallic gold appearance. Visual designs are popular in contemporary styles because of their textural interest.

Any natural or man-made-fibered yarn or blend may be used for a structural design. The designer tries, on a hand loom, the fiber and the color in the warp that will give the effect desired. This trial-and-error method is called direct designing; no point-paper patterns are drawn because the weave is usually a basic one. There are unexpected hazards, however, in such an approach to designing. For example, a designer working with spun saran found that its static electricity caused it to pick up pieces of varicolored lint around the plant. As a result, the woven cloth appeared to be multicolored and not the two-colored construction as planned.

Some designers who are novices in weaving may sacrifice certain basic qualities in a cloth just for the visual effect. When this occurs, the manufacturer can experience a loss of profits due to the poor selection of fiber and no consideration of function.

When a designer for a fabric house is satisfied with the design that has been created on the hand loom, the design is approved by the chief designer. Next the design is checked by the testing laboratory to see if it performs adequately for its intended uses. If it qualifies, it is sent to a mill to be power-woven or knitted on a commercial basis.

In addition to designs created by its own staff, a fabric house may buy designs from free-lance designers. There seems to be no sure way of patenting or trademarking a structural or visual design, for by merely changing the count of the cloth, the fiber content, or the color of the yarn, the design can be shown not to be a copy. It is disheartening to a fabric house to find another manufacturer adding one insignificant metallic yarn to a "borrowed" design so as to make it different from the original.

Opportunities in Marketing

Fiber and Yarn Marketers

The marketing approach is the second of the career patterns one can follow in preparing for a career in textiles. As indicated earlier in this chapter, marketing includes every process employed in the sale and distribution of the product to the ultimate user. In the case of the man-made fiber producer, the ultimate user is generally a yarn producer or a vertically integrated producer of an end product that includes spinning or other yarn preparation processing. It is to these yarn processors that the major sales of man-made fibers are made; thus, the marketing division projects its planning to these customers. Careers in marketing fibers include advertising, promotion, selling, sales training, fashion coordination, and market research. A heavy emphasis in communication skills is considered highly desirable for the textile marketing major who enters this aspect of the industry, as a large part of a marketer's time is spent in communicating information to clients and other users.

The Marketers of Textile Fabrics and
Finished Goods

The marketing divisions of the major textile mills are usually located in New York City, where buyers of textile products from across the United States "come to market" on a regularly scheduled basis to buy for their retail stores. Thus, New York City is a hub of textile marketing activity throughout the year, but especially during "market weeks" when thousands of retailers descend upon the city to "shop the market" for the newest and latest in consumer textile goods. Both home furnishings and apparel producers maintain showrooms, generally in their New York marketing headquarters, for the express purpose of providing a showcase for the goods they produce and a central location to which buyers travel to do much of their buying and marketing planning. These marketing headquarters most often provide full marketing support services to their retail customers, such as advertising, sales promotion, sales training, fashion coordination, publicity, product training, consumer education, and interior space planning or visual merchandising. Career potential in these areas is considered by many to be one of the best for the textiles student with respect to the wide variety of interesting career paths. For example, the advertising department may need an ad layout designer (or graphics artist), preferably with some textiles background, as well as a strong foundation in the applied arts areas.

For the graduate with a textiles background combined with special communications skills these merchandising areas offer numerous career paths such as advertising copy writing. The advertisement in Figure 22.7 is an excellent example of an informative and educational ad that provides the consumer with pertinent information concerning both fabric and construction. Interior design students (who usually study textiles as part of their professional training) also find career opportunities in the space planning of showroom facilities and in visual merchandising programs in both wholesale and retail programs, especially large department and other chain stores.

To the students of fashion merchandising and retailing, their textiles background will serve them well in marketing positions throughout the textile pipeline. Among those career track positions in manufacturers' marketing headquarters are fashion coordinating, visual merchandising, sales training, sales promotion and advertising, consumer affairs, product development, market research, and public relations.

Opportunities in Retailing

In retailing there are excellent career opportunities for the student of textiles who has also had related courses in such areas as retail operations and management. Selling experience, even part-time, in a department or specialty store is usually the first step. The direct contact with customers who are the final

When we found we could offer this quality herringbone jacket for only $115, we got into traditional clothes.

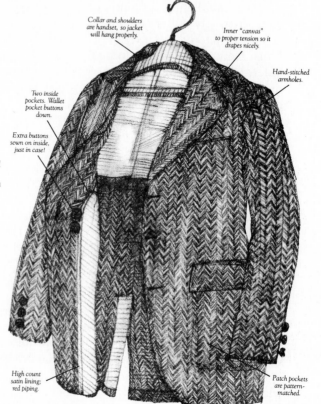

Collar and shoulders are handset, so jacket will hang properly.

Inner "canvas" to proper tension so it drapes nicely.

Hand-stitched armholes.

Two inside pockets. Wallet pocket buttons down.

Extra buttons sewn on inside, just in case!

High count satin lining; red piping.

Patch pockets are pattern-matched.

What first led us to think about tailored clothing was your active response to our Oxford button downs, our Lands' End knit ties, and other classic items like our Lands' End turtlenecks.

We reasoned you might like suitable jackets to wear over these items, *provided* —and this was a big "if"—we could offer them with the kind of quality features you expect from Lands' End, and at Lands' End prices.

Then we went to work.

We sent our buyers on the prowl for fabrics. We challenged our tailors to add quality features, not eliminate them for cost reasons. And, finally, we encouraged them to practice their Old World tailoring skills; and how they responded when they realized we were serious!

The results are now in.

The herringbone classic described above is typical of what Lands' End now offers in our *Charter Collection.* A small but excellent group of traditional jackets, plus some well-tailored slacks that harmonize with them, and some appropriate shirts and ties.

There's no way we can properly describe the look and feel and fit of this clothing. You need to experience it, yourself. Even then you'll find it hard to believe prices like $95 for a serviceable corduroy jacket, to $148.50 for a glen plaid import.

Open our catalog.

See the complete *Charter Collection* in our Winter Catalog. Shop us for sweaters, ski wear, deck wear and soft luggage, too. And, remember, everything Lands' End offers carries our incredible guarantee:

"If you are not completely satisfied with any item you buy from us at any time during your use of it, return it and we will refund your full purchase price."

Send the coupon for a free catalog or

call for one toll-free at 800-356-4444 (except in Wisconsin where the number is 608-935-2788). One of our 86 operators will answer you in person, 24 hours a day.

LANDS' END
DIRECT MERCHANTS

of fine wool and cotton sweaters, Oxford buttondown shirts, traditional dress clothing, snow wear, deck wear, original Lands' End soft luggage and a multitude of other quality goods from around the world.

Figure 22.7 An advertisement that guides the consumer in selecting a quality herringbone jacket. (Photo courtesy of Lands' End, Dodgeville, Wisconsin.)

arbiters of which products will sell and which will fail is essential. Even successful retailing executives who have many other responsibilities spend some time on the selling floor, contacting and observing customers in order to adjust the merchandise and services of the store to the requirements of these customers. (See Fig. 22.8.)

The college graduate, ready for a full-time job, may apply for a place in a store organization's executive training program. Here, selling experience will be augmented by classroom training and, often, experience in nonselling departments. This is commonly followed with appointment as assistant department manager in one of the organization's branch stores. This leads typically to the position of sales manager in a department or group of departments in the branch. If the employee exhibits merchandising ability, the next step may be that of assistant buyer for a department, such as women's coats, men's furnishings, or domestics, that buys the merchandise for all the stores in the chain or branch organization. Successful performance in this position leads to that of full-fledged buyer with major responsibility to procure products that will sell readily.

While for many this is the peak of their careers, some buyers do go on to become divisional merchandise managers and even a general merchandise manager who may also be an officer in the company.

But buyers and merchandise managers are not limited to positions in retailing. Many become senior executives and even owners of manufacturing firms that produce textile products.

Figure 22.8 Consumers may look for brand-name merchandise or they may ask for sales advice in choosing garments. (Photo courtesy of American Textile Manufacturers Institute.)

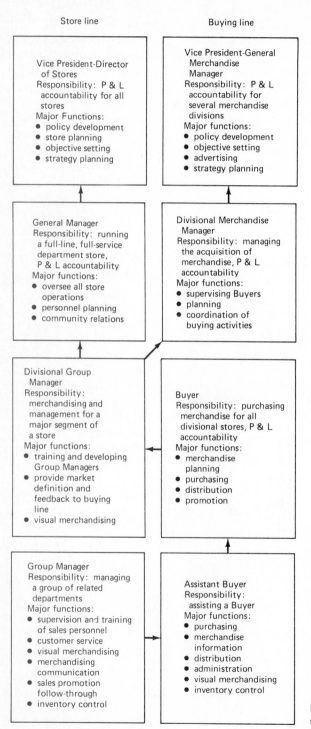

Figure 22.9 Career paths in retailing. (Courtesy of Gimbels, Philadelphia.)

Those who do not find the buying line compatible may be given the opportunity of moving into another area, such as advertising and promotion, store operations, personnel management, or control. While textile knowledge is not of first importance in these fields, it is likely to prove of great value, especially in advertising and promotion and in customer service departments.

Figure 22.9. presents the career opportunities in one leading department store. The career track begins with the position of group (or department) manager. A college degree is recommended for entry level.

SUMMARY

On their way to the final consumer, textiles pass through two channels: production and distribution. The first includes (1) the harvesting of the natural fiber and the chemical construction of the man-made fiber, (2) the preparation and spinning of the fiber (to be made ready for the next step), (3) the construction of the fabric, (4) the finishing process, (5) dyeing and printing, and (6) manufacturing the finished product.

The distribution channel, of which there are many variations, has two aspects: (1) the physical movement of the textile material as it progresses through the construction process and then through the hands of the distributors toward the ultimate consumer and (2) the promotion and selling activities that accompany the major steps in the production process and the steps in the distribution process of the finished product as it moves toward the ultimate consumer (household or industrial, commercial, or institutional). Moving goods through the distribution channel requires both a seller and a buyer, since at each stage of the process, the seller must buy the materials or the finished goods from the previous producer or handler. Thus the entire cycle of production and distribution involves the coordinated activities of many firms and of many individuals in each firm.

The textile industry requires a continual influx of new people who are trained in the special requirements for diverse and challenging careers by means of organized study and firsthand work experience. Every person interested in the field should make a study of his or her interest and special abilities to determine where he or she could make a contribution to the field and at the same time achieve a good living. The opportunity to serve the consumer with better products at affordable prices is great, especially because of the tremendous technological, creative, and managerial advances being made today in both production and distribution.

PROJECTS

1. As a member of a class committee, visit (a) a large local store that distributes textile products primarily or (b) a manufacturer of a textile line, such as clothing or housewares or even an industrial textile line.

Determine what opportunities exist for a career in the field. Obtain the details of any executive training program that may be available. Findings should be reported to the class, followed by a discussion.

2. You have developed a line of placemats with unusual structural designs that you have made on large hand looms. You have trained a number of people to do the weaving and finishing so that you can develop your distribution systems.

Develop a marketing plan suitable to your small operation, but base it on the plan given in the text.

3. Conduct a market research study of the kinds of winter (or fall or spring) coats worn by women (or men) for daytime wear in your community. Observe the outer attire of at least one hundred well-dressed women (or men) at a place where many people pass or congregate, such as a bus station, a restaurant, a department or specialty store entrance, or a theater.

Draw up a form (see the one given here) and check every coat you observe under the nine headings provided. Since it is likely to be difficult to observe nine features almost at once, two observers may work as a team, one checking length,

Form for Reporting Readily Observable Coat Features

Date and hour of count: _____
Place: _____
Number of men or women: _____

Type	Collar and lapels
Casual	Narrow
Dressy	Medium
Raincoat type	Wide
Length of coat	Hood attached
Short (just below hips)	No lapels
Medium (about the knee)	Fur (or textile body)
Long, with vent	Color
Long, no vent	Black
Line of coat	Brown
Straight line	Blue, dark
Slight flair	Gray
Other (explain)	Green, dark
Front closing	Others (list
Single breasted	Material
Double breasted	Smooth
Zipper	Rough texture
No front fastening	Quilted
Belting	Pile (including fake fur)
All-around belt	Fur
No belt	Sleeves
Half belt	Fitted, wrist length
	Loose shoulders
	Loose at wrist
	Two-thirds length
	Elbow length

line, front closing, and belting and the other collar, color, material, and sleeves. Both should agree on type.

Count and tabulate your checks. Can you come to any sound conclusion as to local preference? What suggestions would you make to the management of a clothing store in your community?

4. Due largely to lower production costs in the Far East, imports account for nearly 40 percent of all textiles and apparel sold in the U.S. (See *The New York Times,* July 16, 1983, p. 1). This has led to unemployment in the U.S. apparel and textile industries and to government intervention to restrict imports by quotas established through international agreements. Collect current information about this major marketing problem, including the effect on retail prices.

GLOSSARY

Brand   A name or symbol, generally registered, owned by a manufacturer, wholesaler, or retailer to differentiate his or her product line from those of others.

Cooperative advertising   An arrangement between a manufacturer (or wholesale distributor) of a branded product and a retailer to reimburse the retailer, either partially or wholly, for advertising the product under the manufacturer's (or wholesaler's) brand name. Also known as "co-op" advertising.

Cutter   A specialist in a clothing manufacturer's establishment who cuts up layers of fabric, guided by the patterns made available to him or her.

Designer   An artist who creates or modifies designs so that they can be reproduced on fabrics or on finished goods, such as styles in apparel.

Fabric buyer   An executive employed by a manufacturing company of finished goods, such as apparel, who buys appropriate fabrics needed for production from fabric producers and wholesalers.

Inside shop   An apparel manufacturer who performs the sewing and finishing of the styles to be incorporated in his or her line on the firms own premises.

Marketing   All business activities involved in the distribution of merchandise from producer to consumer or other ultimate customers.

Marketing plan   A detailed plan developed by management for the introduction of a new product line. It includes goals, the features of the line itself, the selection of channels of distribution, the promotion and selling, and the liaison between production and marketing activities.

Market research   An organized study of the market for a product or service, such as potential for consumer acceptance, segments of the market, and consumer response to advertising and promotional efforts.

Outlet store   A retail store that specializes in selling manufacturers' surplus products, including irregulars and discontinued styles, at reduced prices.

Outside shop   An apparel manufacturer who arranges for the sewing and finishing of the product line to be done at a shop outside the manufacturer's establishment on a contract basis. The term may also be applied to the contractor's establishment.

White sale   Periodic special sales of home furnishings textiles conducted by the retailer, commonly made possible by special price concessions provided by the manufacturer or wholesale distributor.

Appendix A

PHOTOMICROGRAPHS OF TEXTILE FIBERS

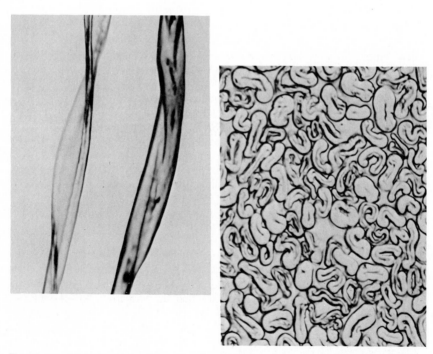

Figure A.1 Unmercerized native cotton: longitudinal and cross-sectional views. (Photomicrographs courtesy of the Southern Regional Research Laboratory of the U.S. Department of Agriculture.)

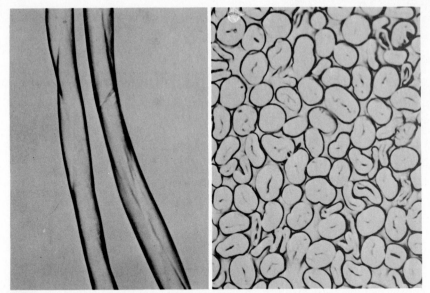

Figure A.2 Mercerized cotton: longitudinal and cross-sectional views. (Photomicrographs courtesy of the Southern Regional Research Laboratory of the U.S. Department of Agriculture.)

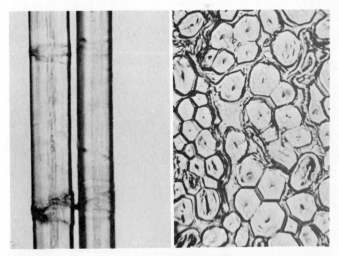

Figure A.3 Flax fibers: longitudinal and cross-sectional views magnified 500 times. (Photomicrographs courtesy of the Southern Regional Research Laboratory of the U.S. Department of Agriculture.)

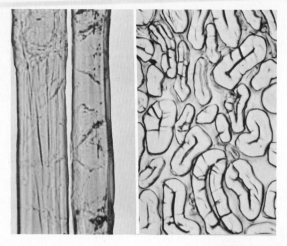

Figure A.4 Ramie fibers: longitudinal and cross-sectional views magnified 500 times. (Photomicrographs courtesy of the Southern Regional Research Laboratory of the U.S. Department of Agriculture.)

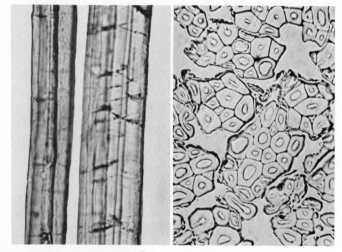

Figure A.5 Jute fibers: longitudinal and cross-sectional views magnified 500 times. (Photomicrographs courtesy of the Southern Regional Research Laboratory of the U.S. Department of Agriculture.)

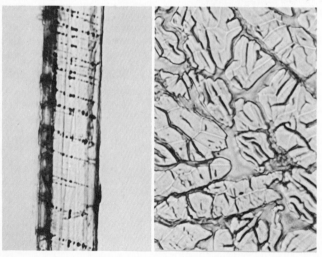

Figure A.6 Hemp fibers: longitudinal and cross-sectional views magnified 500 times. (Photomicrographs courtesy of the Southern Regional Research Laboratory of the U.S. Department of Agriculture.)

Figure A.7 Cultivated raw silk. Left: Longitudinal view of silk fibers, showing the sericin, which forms an outer layer around the fibroin, or main core, of the fiber. Right: cross sections of raw silk threads reeled from six cocoons. Since each thread is doubled, there are actually twelve filaments bound together by the natural gum, or sericin. (Photomicrographs courtesy of the Southern Regional Research Laboratory of the U.S. Department of Agriculture.)

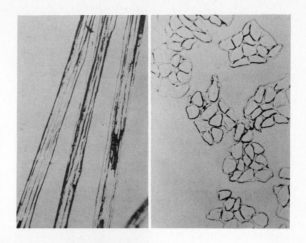

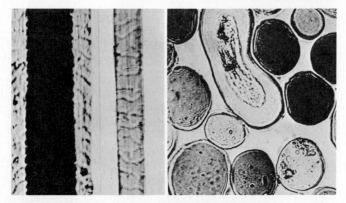

Figure A.8 Mohair: longitudinal and cross-sectional views. (Photomicrographs courtesy of the Forstmann Woolen Company.)

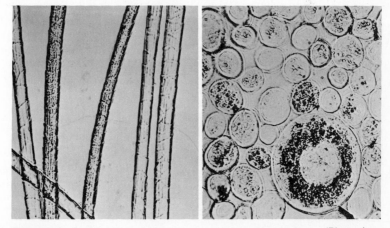

Figure A.9 Cashmere: longitudinal and cross-sectional views. (Photomicrographs courtesy of the Forstmann Woolen Company.)

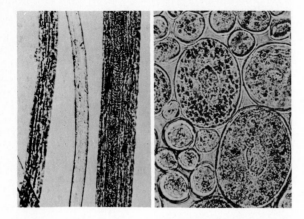

Figure A.10 Camel's hair: longitudinal and cross-sectional views. (Photomicrographs courtesy of the Forstmann Woolen Company.)

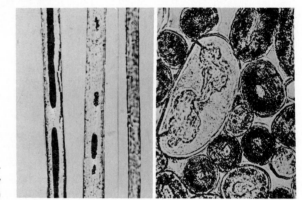

Figure A.11 Alpaca: longitudinal and cross-sectional views. (Photomicrographs courtesy of the Forstmann Woolen Company.)

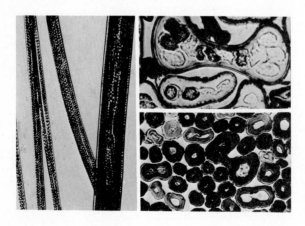

Figure A.12 Rabbit's hair: longitudinal and cross-sectional views. (Photomicrographs courtesy of the Forstmann Woolen Company.)

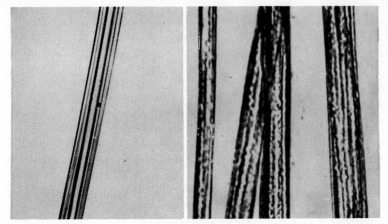

Figure A.13   Vicose rayon. Left: Bright. Right: Delustered. (Photomicrographs courtesy of the United States Testing Company, Inc.)

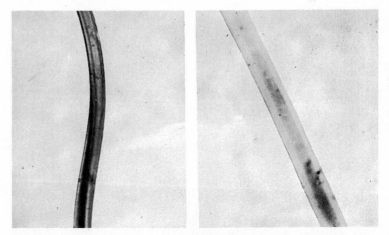

Figure A.14   Left: Cuprammonium rayon (bright). Right: Acetate (bright). (Photomicrographs courtesy of the United States Testing Company, Inc.)

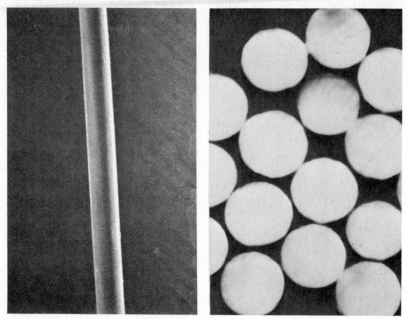

Figure A.15 Nylon. Left: Longitudinal view of a semidull nylon filament (3-3 grams per denier) magnified 400 times. (Photomicrograph courtesy of Allied Chemical.) Right: Cross-sectional view magnified 660 times. The seventeen filaments are almost perfectly round and very smooth. This is a thread used in sheer stockings and fine knit goods. (Photomicrograph courtesy of E. I. DuPont de Nemours & Company, Inc.)

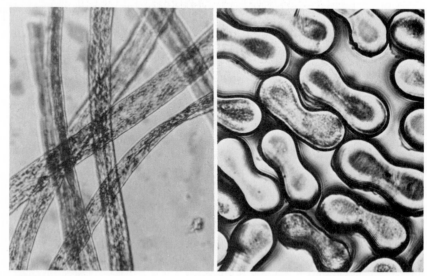

Figure A.16 Orlon acrylic. Left: Longitudinal view of continuous filament yarn shows the striated surface of the fiber. Right: Cross-sectional view of staple yarn magnified 500 times. (Photomicrographs courtesy of E. I. DuPont de Nemours & Company, Inc.)

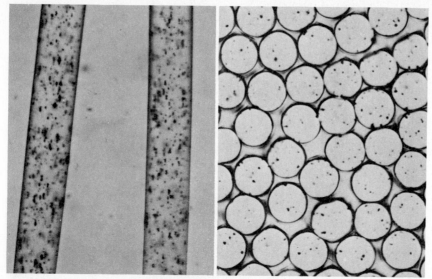

Figure A.17 Dacron polyester: longitudinal and cross-sectional views magnified 1,000 times. (Photomicrographs courtesy of E. I. DuPont de Nemours & Company, Inc.)

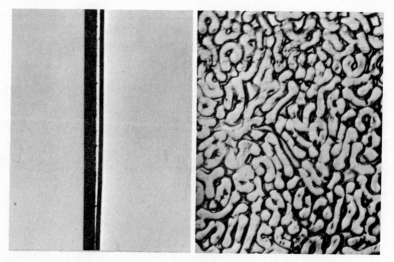

Figure A.18 Dynel modacrylic: longitudinal and cross-sectional views. (Photomicrographs courtesy of Carbide and Carbon Chemicals Company.)

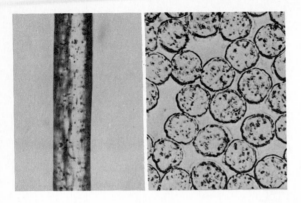

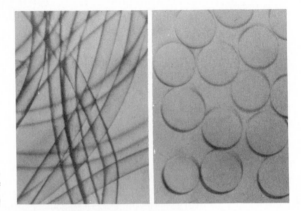

Figure A.19 Acrilan acrylic: longitudinal and cross-sectional views. (Photomicrographs courtesy of the Chemstrand Corporation.)

Figure A.20 Saran: longitudinal and cross-sectional views. (Photomicrographs courtesy of the National Plastic Products Company.)

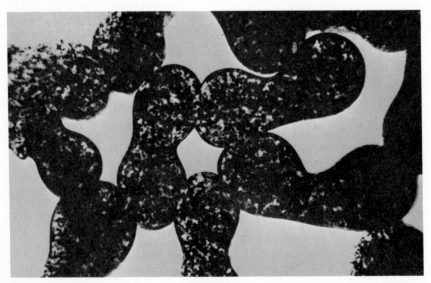

Figure A.21 Lycra spandex: cross-sectional view magnified 500 times. (Photomicrograph courtesy of E. I. DuPont de Nemours & Company, Inc.)

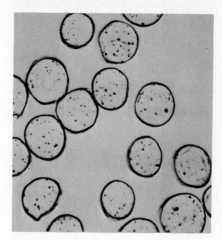

Figure A.22 Polypropylene olefin: cross-sectional view magnified 500 times. (Photomicrograph courtesy of E. I. DuPont de Nemours & Company, Inc.)

Appendix B

REPRESENTATIVE FIBER TRADEMARKS LISTED BY GENERIC FIBER NAME

Generic Name	Trade Names	Features	Producers
Acetate	Acetate by Avtex	Filament yarn	Avtex Fibers, Inc.
	Ariloft	Filament yarn	Eastman Chemical Products, Inc.
	Celanese	Staple, filament, cigarette filter tow, and fiberfill	Celanese Fibers Marketing Co., Celanese Corporation
	Chromspun	Solution-dyed filament yarn	Eastman Chemical Products, Inc.
	Estron	Filament yarn and cigarette filter tow	Eastman Chemical Products, Inc.
	Lanese	Bulk acetate with polyester core	Celanese Fibers Marketing Co., Celanese Corporation
	Loftura	Slub voluminized filament yarn	Eastman Chemical Products, Inc.
Acrylic	Acrilan	Staple and tow	Monsanto Fibers and Intermediates Company
	Bi-Loft	Fibers, filaments	Monsanto Fibers and Intermediates Company
	Creslan	Staple and tow	American Cyanamid Company
	Fina	Fine-denier fiber	Monsanto Fibers and Intermediates Company
	Orlon	Staple and tow	E. I. DuPont de Nemours & Co., Inc.
	So-Lara	Producer-colored	Monsanto Fibers and Intermediates Company
	Zefran	Dyeable and producer-colored	Badische Corporation
Aramid	Kevlar	Filament	E. I. DuPont de Nemours & Co., Inc.
	Nomex	Filament and staple	E. I. DuPont de Nemours & Co., Inc.

Generic Name	Trade Names	Features	Producers
Fluorocarbon	Teflon	Filament, staple, tow, and flock	E. I. DuPont de Nemours & Co., Inc.
Modacrylic	Acrilan	Staple and tow	Monsanto Fibers and Intermediates Company
	SEF	Staple	Monsanto Fibers and Intermediates Company
	Verel	Staple	Eastman Chemical Products, Inc.
Nylon	A.C.E.	High-tenacity filament industrial yarns	Allied Chemical Corporation, Fibers and Plastics Company
	Anso	Filament and staple carpet yarns for residential and commercial applications	Allied Chemical Corporation, Fibers and Plastics Company
	Antron	Filament, staple, tow, and bulk, continuous filament, and antistatic	E. I. DuPont de Nemours & Co., Inc.
	Blue "C"	Staple	Monsanto Fibers and Intermediates Company
	Cadon	Filament yarn and multilobal monofilament	Monsanto Fibers and Intermediates Company
	Cantrece	Self-bulking filament	E. I. DuPont de Nemours & Co., Inc.
	Caprolan	Mono- multifilament textile denier yarns	Allied Chemical Corporation, Fibers and Plastics Company
	Celanese	Staple filament, cigarette filter tow, and fiberfill	Celanese Fibers Marketing Co., Celanese Corporation
	Cordura	High-tenacity industrial filament	E. I. DuPont de Nemours & Co., Inc.
	Courtaulds Nylon	Filament yarn	Courtaulds North America Inc.
	Crepeset	Patented continuous monofilament that develops a regular crimp, also available in anticling yarn	American Enka Company
	Cumuloft	Textured filament carpet yarn	Monsanto Fibers and Intermediates Company
	Eloquent Luster	15 denier continuous multifilament, bulked continuous filament and staple, carpet yarns for residential and commercial applications	Allied Chemical Corporation, Fibers and Plastics Company
	Eloquent Touch	12-denier continuous multifilament, bulked continuous filament and staple, carpet yarns for residential and commercial applications	Allied Chemical Corporation, Fibers and Plastics Company
	Enka 10-10	Bulked continuous filament and modified cross section	American Enka Company
	Enkaloft	Textured multilobal continuous-filament carpet yarn and staple	American Enka Company
	Enkalure	Multilobal continuous-filament apparel yarn and textured delayed soiling carpet yarn	American Enka Company

Generic Name	Trade Names	Features	Producers
	Enkasheer	Continuous multi- or monofilament torque yarn for ladies' stretch hosiery (patented process)	American Enka Company
	Lusterloft	Modified cross section carpet staple fiber	American Enka Company
	Natura Luster	Continuous multifilament, bulked continuous filament and staple, carpet yarns for residential and commercial applications	Allied Chemical Corporation, Fibers and Plastics Company
	Multisheer	Multifilament producer-textured stretch yarn for panty hose	American Enka Company
	Qiana	Filament	E. I. DuPont de Nemours & Co., Inc.
	Shareen	Monofilament and multifilament textured yarn	Courtaulds North America Inc.
	Silver Label	Patented continuous monofilament that develops a regular crimp, also available in anti-cling yarn	American Enka Company
	Softalon	Producer-textured nylon filament.	American Enka Company
	Ulstron	Polypropylene fibers, threads, and yarns	Monsanto Fibers and Intermediates Company
	Ultron	Filament, staple	Monsanto Fibers and Intermediates Company
	Vive La Crepe	Patented continuous monofilament that develops a regular crimp, also available in anti-cling yarn	American Enka Company
	Zeflon	Staple and bulked continuous filament	Badische Corporation
	Zefran	Staple and bulked continuous filament	Badische Corporation
Olefin	Herculon	Continuous multifilament, bulked continuous multifilament, staple, and tow	Hercules Incorporated, Fibers Marketing Division
	Marquesa	Continuous multifilament, bulked continuous multifilament staple	Amoco Fabrics Company, Fibers & Yarn Division
	Marvess	Staple, tow, and filament yarn	Phillips Fibers Corporation, subsidiary of Phillips Petroleum Company
	Pation	Fiberillated yarn	Amoco Fabric Company, Fibers & Yarn Division
	Polyloom	Fiberillated yarn	Chevron Chemical Company
	Vectra	Continuous multifilament, bulked continuous multifilament, staple	Vectra Corporation, subsidiary of Chevron Chemical Company
Polyester	A.C.E.	High-tenacity filament industrial yarns	Allied Chemical Corporation, Fibers and Plastics Company
	Avlin	Filament yarn and staple	Avtex Fibers, Inc.
	Blue "C"	Staple	Monsanto Fibers and Intermediates Company

Generic Name	Trade Names	Features	Producers
	Caprolan	Yarns, monofilaments, and textured yarns	Allied Chemical Corporation, Fibers & Plastics Company
	Crepesoft	Multifilament polyester	American Enka Company
	Dacron	Polyester filament yarn staple, tow, and fiberfill	E. I. DuPont de Nemours & Co., Inc.
	Encron	Continuous filament yarn, staple, fiberfill	American Enka Company
	Fortrel	Filament yarn, staple, tow, and fiberfill	Fibers Industries, Inc.; marketed by Celanese Fibers Marketing Co., Celanese Corporation
	Golden Glow	Filament yarns	American Enka Company
	Golden Touch	High filament yarns	American Enka Company
	Hollofil	Filling fibers	E. I. DuPont de Nemours & Co., Inc.
	Kodel	Filament yarn, staple, tow	Eastman Chemical Products, Inc.
	KodOfill	Fiberfill	Eastman Chemical Products, Inc.
	KodOsoff	Fiberfill	Eastman Chemical Products, Inc.
	PBI[a]	High-performance nonflammable fiber	Celanese Fibers Marketing Co., Celanese Corporation
	Plyloc	Producer-textured two-ply yarn	American Enka Comparny
	Polyextra	Producer-textured filament	American Enka Company
	Silky Touch	Filament yarns	American Enka Company
	Spectran	Staple	Monsanto Fibers and Intermediates Company
	Strialine	Slub-effect, variable dyeing, Encron polyester	American Enka Company
	Trevira	Filament yarn, staple, and fiberfill monofilament	Hoechst Fibers Industries
	Twisloc	Yarns and threads made from tangled/entrapped filaments and fibers	Monsanto Fibers and Intermediates Company
Rayon	Absorbit	Modified rayon staple for absorbency	American Enka Company
	Avril	High-wet-modulus staple	Avtex Fibers, Inc.
	Avsorb	Staple, high-fluid-holding fiber	Avtex Fibers, Inc.
	Beau-Grip	Specially treated viscose high-tenacity yarn	North American Rayon Corporation
	Coloray	Solution-dyed staple	Courtaulds North America Inc.
	Enkaire	Flat-filament rayon staple	American Enka Company
	Enkrome	Patented acid-dyeable staple and continuous-filament yarn	American Enka Company
	Fibro	Staple	Courtaulds North America Inc.
	Rayon by Avtex	Staple, filament	Avtex Fibers, Inc.
	Zantrel	High-wet-modulus staple	American Enka Company
Spandex	Lycra	Filament	E. I. DuPont de Nemours & Co., Inc.
Triacetate	Arnel	Filament yarn and staple	Celanese Fibers Marketing Company, Celanese Corporation
Vinyon	Vinyon by Avetx	Staple	Avtex Fibers, Inc.

[a]Unclassified—market introduction in 1983.

Source: Man-Made Fiber Producers Association, *Man-Made Fibers Fact Book Update,* 1980.

Appendix C

FEDERAL FLAMMABILITY REGULATIONS

The following are summaries of the federal regulations that are implemented under the Flammable Fabrics Act.[1] The numbers used are from the code of federal regulations.

   1.   *General Wearing Apparel* (16-CFR 1610). Exclusive of interlining fabrics, certain hats, gloves, and footwear. Tests required to meet the standards: a piece of fabric in a holder at a 45° angle be exposed to a flame for 1 second. Flame must not spread a distance of 5 inches up the sample in 3.5 seconds for smooth fabrics and 4.0 seconds for napped fabrics. Special regulations exist for vinyl plastic film used in wearing apparel.

   2.   *Large Carpets and Rugs* (carpets with areas of over 24 square feet) (16-CFR 1630). Excludes linoleum vinyl tile and asphalt tile (nontextiles). Tests required 9 inch by 9 inch samples that are exposed to a burning tablet on the center of each sample must not have a char length of more than 3 inches in any direction. Test to simulate burning match dropped on carpet. Test must be passed to permit marketing. Label carpet with "T" if flame retardant has been applied. Fibers inherently flame-retardant do not require labeling; neither do one-of-a-kind merchandise such as Orientals.

   3.   *Small Carpets and Rugs* (16-CFR 1631). Refers to carpets with less than 24 square feet of surface area. Nontextile hard floor coverings are excluded. Same tablet test as used for large carpets and rugs. Small carpets and rugs that do not

---

[1]Based on *Fact Sheet* (on flammability regulations) of the U.S. Consumer Product Safety Commission, Washington, D.C. 20207.

pass this test may be marketed but must be labeled as flammable and not be used near sources of ignition. Same requirement for labeling with letter "T" is prescribed for small rugs and carpets.[2]

4. *Mattresses and Mattress Pads* (16-CFR 1632). Includes ticking filled with a resilient material intended or promoted for sleeping upon, including mattress pads, but excludes pillows, box springs, and upholstered furniture. Requires that the smooth, tape, and quilted or tufted mattress surfaces be exposed to a total of nine burning cigarettes on the bare mattress and that the char length on the mattress surface be not more than 2 inches in any direction from any cigarette. Two-sheeted tests are also conducted with nine burning cigarettes placed between the sheets on surfaces as described for mattresses. A sampling plan provides for premarket testing to detect noncomplying mattresses.

Mattresses that meet the standard are not required to have a label, although many manufacturers may attach a voluntary label stating that the mattress meets the standard.

Mattress pads must also pass the test. Those that have had a flame-retardant treatment must be labeled with the letter "T," and care labeling is required on the treated mattress pads to inform the consumer how to protect the pad against loss of flame retardance.

5. *Children's Sleepwear, Sizes 0–6x* (16-CFR 1615). Includes any garment (sizes 0–6x) worn primarily for sleeping (such as nightgowns, pajamas, robes, and sleepers) but excludes diapers and underwear. Fabrics intended for use in children's sleepwear must also meet the standard.

Each of five samples is hung in a cabinet and is exposed to a gas flame along its bottom edge for 3 seconds. The samples cannot have an average char length of more than 7 inches; no single sample can have a char length of 10 inches. This is required for both the new fabric or garment and after the fabric or garment has been laundered fifty times. A sampling provides for premarket testing of fabrics and garments.

Sleepwear manufactured after July 29, 1973 must meet the standard. The manufacturer is not required to label the garment, but many manufacturers are voluntarily labeling, as follows:

Flame-Retardant Fabric

This garment meets flammability requirements of federal Children's Sleepwear Standard 16-CFR 1615 for sizes 0–6x.

Care labels must be attached if any agent or treatment could adversely affect the flame-retardant qualities of the fabric.

---

[2]One-of-a-kind carpets or rugs, such as an antique, Oriental, or hide, may be excluded from the testing requirements, for both large and small carpets and rugs.

6. *Children's Sleepwear, Sizes 7–14* (16-CFR 1616). Includes any garment (sizes 7–14) worn primarily for sleeping (such as nightgowns, pajamas, robes, and sleepers) but excludes underwear. Fabrics intended for use in children's sleepwear must also meet the standard. Similar requirements as those for sleepwear sizes 0–6x are mandated, although this standard is not quite as rigorous in its required tests.

The detailed regulations outlined here are found in the "Code of Federal Regulations: 16 Commercial Practices 1000 to End," published by the *Federal Register*, General Services Administration, Washington, D.C. This publication explains each test completely, with diagrams of equipment required, selection of samples, and disposition of goods that fail to pass the appropriate tests.

Imported goods are subject to the same tests as those for domestic products. But goods for export, unless to U.S. nationals, are not regulated for flammability; neither are those imported to this country for finishing or storage under bond to be subsequently exported.

Appendix D

CARE LABELING REGULATIONS[1]

Section 423.2   Textile Wearing Apparel; Draperies and Curtains; Slipcovers; Linens[2]

(a) It is an unfair or deceptive act or practice for the manufacturer or importer of any textile product in the form of a finished article of wearing apparel, drapery, curtain, slipcover or linen to sell, in or affecting commerce as "commerce" is defined by the Federal Trade Commission Act, any such article which does not have a permanent label[3] affixed or attached thereto, which clearly discloses instructions for the care and maintenance of such article.

(b) Instructions for the care and maintenance of any item within the scope of this section shall conform to the following:

(1) *General rule.* Fully and completely inform the purchaser of such regular care and maintenance procedures necessary to the ordinary use and enjoyment of the item. In order to constitute full and complete information, such instructions shall comply with, but need not necessarily be limited to, the provisions set forth below:

(i) *Washing.* In any washing instruction each of the following topics must be clearly disclosed:

(A) Method of washing and adjectival description of water temperature, *e.g.,* hot, warm, cold;

(B) Method of drying and, if by machine, adjectival description of temperature, *e.g.,* high, medium, low;

[1]Digested from Federal Trade Commission rulings.

[2]Linens include any bed covering or any bath, kitchen, or table accessory, including towels, shower curtains, doilies, tablecloths, placemats, or napkins, where the manufacture is complete and where the article is customarily used as an interior appointment.

[3]A "permanent label" is one attached or affixed in such a manner that it should not in ordinary use become separated from the item during the useful life of the item, except that a label attached to upholstered furniture in accordance with this part should not, in ordinary use, become separated from the furniture during the useful life of the outer covering of the furniture.

(C) Use of iron and adjectival description of ironing temperature, *e.g.*, hot, warm, cool, when necessary to the ordinary use and enjoyment of the item;

(D) Bleaching method in accordance with the following provisions set forth below:

(aa) Where all commercially available bleaches can be used without damage or substantial impairment to the labeled article, the phrase "bleach only when needed" or its precise equivalent must be included;

(bb) Where not all commercially available bleaches can be used without damage or substantial impairment to the labeled article but some can be so used, the type of bleach which can be used, followed by the phrase "only when needed" or its precise equivalent, must be included;

(cc) Where no commercially available bleaches can be used without damage or substantial impairment to the labeled article, an appropriate warning as required by section 423.2(b) (2) must be included;

(dd) *Provided, however, that* where the party responsible for care instructions under this part has a reasonable basis for determining that bleach, under all foreseeable circumstances, will *never* be necessary to the ordinary use and enjoyment of an article covered by this section during its useful life (assuming ordinary wear and tear) and a warning against the use of bleach is not appropriate, no bleaching instructions need be included.

(ii) *Drycleaning.* In any drycleaning instruction, each of the following topics must be clearly disclosed:

(A) The type of drycleaning solvent to be used when not all commercially available drycleaning solvents can be used;

(B) Any other modifications to the drycleaning process, as defined herein, when necessary to the ordinary use and enjoyment of the item, *provided, however, that* the words "commercial(ly)" and "drycleanable" may not be used in any drycleaning instruction.

In addition to the general rules just given for permanent-care labels, there are special rules for the following:

1. *The labeling of alternate-care information.* If any item may be washed or dry-cleaned, both methods of care must be disclosed, but if one method is clearly superior to the other, from the consumer's point of view, only that method need be disclosed.

2. *The labeling of piece goods and yarns for sale to the ultimate consumer.* Conspicuous description of care information at the end of each bolt of cloth or attached to the skein of yarn. Also, the provision of an adequate supply of labels to give to the consumer to attach to the finished article.

3. *Labeling of upholstered furniture.* The general-care labeling rules apply, but hangtags may be substituted where labels would impair utility and appearance.

4. *Carpets and rugs.* Permanent-care labels or tags are not required, but clearly stated information on care must be available at or before the time of purchase by the ultimate consumer. However, where the carpet or rug is subject to washing, drying, ironing, and bleaching described in Section 423.2b, the general rules apply.

Appendix E

EFFECT OF HEAT AND FLAME ON THE MAJOR TEXTILE FIBERS[1]

Fiber	Effect of Heat[a]	Effect of Flame	Characteristics of Ash or Other Residue
Acetate	Sticks at 350–375°F; softens at 400–445°F; melts at 500°F	Near flame, fuses with melting; in flame, burns with melting; after flame, continues to burn	Brittle, black, irregular bead
Acrylic	Sticks at 420–490°F; does not melt; iron at 300°F	Near flame, fuses; in flame, burns with melting	Hard, brittle, black, irregular bead
Aramid	Does not melt; decomposes at 700–930°F	Difficult to ignite	Chars and retains shape
Fluorocarbon*	Melts at 550–620°F (no degradation at 400–500°F)	Does not burn	*
Glass*	Softens at 1350°F; melts at 2050–2720°F	Does not burn	*
Modacrylic	May be slippery at 300°F; does not melt; resistant to shrinkage	After flame, does not support combustion	Hard, black, irregular bead
Nylon 6	Slight discolorization at extended heat of 300°F; melts at 419–430°F; decomposes at 600–739°F	Near flame, fuses and shrinks away; in flame, burns slowly with melting; after flame, usually self-extinguishing	Hard, tough, gray, round bead
Nylon 6.6	Yellows slightly at 300°F; sticks at 445°F; melts at 480–525°F	Same as above	Same as above
Olefins Polyethylene	Softens at 225–235°F; melts at 230–280°F; decomposes at 550°F	Near flame, fuses and shrinks away; in flame, burns with melting; after flame, continues to burn	Hard, tough, tan, round bead

Appendix E (continued)

Fiber	Effect of Heat[a]	Effect of Flame	Characteristics of Ash or Other Residue
Polypropy-lene	Softens at 285–330°F; melts at 320–350°F; decomposes at 500°F	Same as above	Same as above
Polyester	Sticks at 440–445°F; melts at 475–500°F	Near flame, fuses and shrinks away; in flame, burns slowly with melting; after flame, usually self-extinguishing	Hard, tough, black, round bead
Rayon	Does not soften, stick, or melt; decomposes at 350°F	Near flame, does not soften or shrink away; in flame, burns without melting; after flame, continues to burn	Does not leave a bead or nob
Viscose	Does not soften, stick, or melt, but loses strength at 300°F and, depending on type, may decompose above this point	Same as above	Same as above
Spandex	Sticks at 347–446°F; melts at 446–518°F	Near flame, fuses but does not shrink away; in flame, burns very slowly with melting; after flame, continues to burn without melting	Soft, fluffy, black ash
Cotton	Does not melt; gradual decomposition over 300°F; may scorch with very hot iron	Near flame, does not fuse or shrink away; in flame, burns without melting; after flame, continues to burn without melting	Does not leave a bead or nob but does leave a fluffy gray ash
Flax	Same as above, but requires much higher temperatures for scorching	Same as above	Same as above
Silk	Dry heat damages the fiber	Near flame, fuses and curls away; in flame, burns slowly with some melting; after flame, burns slowly, sometimes self-extinguishing	Black beads
Wool	Same as above	Same as above	Brittle black ash

[1]Data for this appendix are from Textile World's *Behavior of Major Fibers 1961* and *Man-Made Fiber Chart 1980*, with permission.

[a]The variations in the effect of heat are caused by variations in types of fiber manufactured by the producers under various trade names.

*These two fibers are not included in the *Man-Made Fibers Chart.*

Appendix F

SCHOOLS AND COLLEGES PROMINENT IN ADVANCING TEXTILE EDUCATION

Auburn University (formerly Alabama Polytechnic Institute, School of Textile Technology), Auburn, Ala. (B.S., M.S.)

Clemson University, College of Industrial Management and Textile Science, Clemson, S.C. (B.S., M.S., Ph.D.)

Cornell University, College of Human Ecology, Ithaca, N.Y. (B.S., M.S., Ph.D.)

Fashion Institute of Technology, New York, N.Y. (A.A.S. graduates at FIT may apply for the B.S.)

Georgia Institute of Technology, The A. French Textile School, Atlanta, Ga. (B.S., M.S., Ph.D., evening, extension)

Institute of Textile Technology, Charlottesville, Va. (education and training in the physical sciences and textile technology leading to the M.S.)

Kansas State University, School of Home Economics, Manhattan, Ks. (B.S., M.S., Ph.D.)

Lowell Technological Institute, Lowell, Mass.

Massachusetts Institute of Technology, Cambridge, Mass. (B.S., M.S., D.Sc., Ph.D.)

North Carolina State University, School of Textiles, Raleigh, N.C. (B.S., M.S., Ph.D.)

Philadelphia College of Textiles and Science, Philadelphia, Pa. (B.S., M.S.)

Purdue University, School of Consumer and Family Sciences, Lafayette, Ind. (B.S., M.S., Ph.D.)

Rhode Island School of Design, Providence, R.I. (B.S. or B.F.A.)

Southeastern Massachusetts Technological Institute, New Bedford, Mass., and Fall River, Mass. (formerly Bradford Durfee Institute of Technology and New Bradford Institute of Technology, now combined) (B.S., M.S.)

Southern Technical Institute, Marietta, Ga. (B.A., A.A.S.)

Texas Technological College, Lubbock, Tex. [Bachelor of Textile Engineering (B.T.E.) and Bachelor of Textile Chemistry (B.T.C.)]

Textile Research Institute, Princeton, N.J. (Ph.D.)

University of Maryland, Department of Textiles and Consumer Economics, College Park, Md. (B.S., M.S., Ph.D.)

All schools with majors in textile design; textile majors in college departments and/or schools of home economics, human ecology, consumer science; special textile courses in retailing, fashion merchandising, and apparel college programs; and specialized adult courses in extension and continuing education divisions of colleges.

Appendix G

MAJOR TRADE ASSOCIATIONS AND RESEARCH INSTITUTES

ASSOCIATIONS

American Apparel Manufacturers Association
1611 N. Kent St., Arlington, Va. 22209

American Association of Textile Chemists and Colorists
P.O. Box 12215, Research Triangle Park, Durham, N.C. 27709

American Association of Textile Technology, Inc.
1040 Avenue of the Americas, New York, N.Y. 10018

American Society for Textile Testing and Materials (Committee on Textiles)
1916 Race Street, Philadelphia, Pa. 19103

American Textile Manufacturers Institute
1101 Connecticut Avenue, N.W., Washington, D.C. 20036

American Textile Machinery Association
1730 M Street, N.W., Washington, D.C. 20036

American Yarn Spinners Association
601 West Franklin Avenue, Gastonia, N.C. 28052

Bed, Bath and Linen Association
437 Fifth Avenue, New York, N.Y. 10016

Belgian Linen Association
Brussels, Belgium

Carpet and Rug Institute
P.O. Box 2048, 208 West Cuyler Avenue, Dalton, Ga. 30720
In Washington, D.C.: 1629 K Street, Suite 700, Office 9, Washington, D.C. 20006

Cotton Incorporated
1370 Avenue of the Americas, New York, N.Y. 10019

INDA (International and Nonwoven Disposables Association)
1700 Broadway, 25th floor, New York, N.Y. 10019

International Fabricare Institute
12251 Tech Road, Silver Spring, Md. 20904

Knitted Textile Association
51 Madison Avenue, New York, N.Y. 10010

Man-Made Fiber Producers Association
1150 17th Street, N.W., Washington, D.C. 20036

National Association of Hosiery Manufacturers
516 Charlottetown Mall, P.O. 4098, Charlotte, N.C. 28204

National Knitwear Manufacturers Association
350 Fifth Avenue, New York, N.Y. 10001

National Knitwear & Sportswear Association
51 Madison Avenue, New York, N.Y. 10010

Northern Textile Association
211 Congress Street, Boston, Mass. 02110

Southern Furniture Manufacturers Association
Box 2436, High Point, N.C. 27261

Southern Textile Association
P.O. Box 190, Cary, N.C. 27511

Textile Designers Guild
30 East 20th Street, New York, N.Y. 10003

Textile Distributors Association, Inc.
1040 Avenue of the Americas, New York, N.Y. 10018

Textile Fibers and Bi-Products Association, Inc.
P.O. Box 11065, Charlotte, N.C. 28220

Textured Yarn Association of America
P.O. Box 1013, Monroe, N.C. 28110

The Wool Bureau
360 Lexington Avenue, New York, N.Y. 10017

RESEARCH INSTITUTES[1]

Calloway Institute
La Grange, Ga. 30240

Cotton Incorporated
Research Triangle Park, N.C., 27709

Fabric Research Laboratories
Dedham, Mass. 02026

Southern Research Institute
2000 Ninth Avenue, Birmingham, Ala. 35205

U.S. Department of Agriculture[2] Regional Laboratories
Northeastern: Bldg. 003, Agricultural Research Center, Beltsville, Md. 20705
North Central: 200 W. Pioneer Parkway, Peoria, Ill. 61616
Southern: P.O. Box 53326, New Orleans, La. 70153
Western: 1333 Broadway, Oakland, Calif. 94612

U.S. Army Quartermaster Corps, Natick, Mass., 01760.

---

[1]See Appendix F for schools and colleges, many of which conduct textile research.

[2]USDA supports cooperative research in textiles with many land-grant colleges and universities through state and federally supported Agricultural Experiment Stations.

Appendix H

PERIOD STYLES WITH APPROPRIATE WOODS, RUGS, AND UPHOLSTERY AND DRAPERY FABRICS

| | Type of Furniture | | | | Upholstery and |
Period	Lines	Proportions	Woods	Rugs	Drapery Fabrics
Italian					
Renaissance 1400–1643	Curved and straight	Massive	Chestnut Ebony Lime, Oak Sycamore Walnut Painted finish; gilt trim; mirrored furniture	Oriental designs rich in coloring, with ruby red dominant	Brocade, damask, satin, tapestry, velour, velvet; large expanse of background in fairly rich colors
Venetian	Curved and flowing	Large			Same as above; decorative fringes
Spanish					
1451–1504	Similar to Italian	Similar to Italian		Similar to Italian	Brocade, cottons (coarse), damask, linen (printed), velvet, plastic-coated fabrics to resemble leather
French 1643–1825					
Louis XIV 1643–1715	Straight, also rounded	Massive	Chestnut Ebony Oak Walnut	Plain carpeting and designs of the period; also Chinese and some Near East Oriental designs	Brocade, damask, satin, tapestry, velvet
Louis XV 1723–1774	Curves	Small and graceful	Mahogany Oak Rosewood Walnut	Plain carpeting and designs of the period; some Oriental designs	Brocade, damask, cretonnes, moiré, needlepoint, prints, satin, taffeta, tapestry, toile de Jouy, velvet; pastel grounds, ribbons and flowers, swags, bouquets, medallions, vases; naturalistic flower designs important

Period	Lines	Feel	Woods	Floor Coverings	Fabrics
Louis XVI 1774–1793	Straight, a few curves	Small, dainty, and light	Mahogany, Rosewood, Satinwood, Walnut	Same as Louis XV	Similar to above; classic influence beginning to be felt; stripes
Directoire 1795–1799	Transition from straight to straight with ovals, classic influence	Small and graceful	Ebony, Mahogany, Satinwood	Plain carpeting and designs of the period; fairly strong colors; Near Eastern Oriental and Chinese designs not suitable	Materials same as Louis XIV; fabric designs classic; also stripes and small floral motifs
Empire 1804–1825	Straight with ovals	Heavy and massive	Ebony, Mahogany, Satinwood	Plain carpeting or Empire designs in strong, full colors	Damask, brocade, moiré, satin, taffeta; medallions, swags, tassels, vase motifs, wreaths, arrow motifs, vertical stripes, scenic chintz, Indian printed cottons
French Provincial	Straight, some curves	Simple and sturdy	Beech, Fruit woods, Maple, Walnut	Hooked, fiber, and rag rugs	Crash (linen), cretonnes, homespuns; small wild flowers, gay plaids
English					
Jacobean 1603–1688	Straight	Strong and sturdy	Oak, Walnut	Oriental patterns with distinct, vigorously drawn motifs, reds predominating	Brocade, chenille, corded fabrics, leather upholstery, needlepoint, velour, velvet
William and Mary 1689–1702	Straight, changing to curves	Lighter	Walnut	Chinese designs with blue and old-gold grounds; oriental designs in softened colors and small motifs	Chintz, cretonne, damask, leather upholstery, needlepoint
Queen Anne 1702–1714	Curved, little carving	Light and graceful	Walnut, some mahogany	Similar to William and Mary	Brocade, Chinese embroidery, chintz, gros point, needlepoint, petit point, India prints

| | | Type of Furniture | | | |
Period	Lines	Proportions	Woods	Rugs	Upholstery and Drapery Fabrics
Georgian 1710–1806					
Chippendale 1750–1775	Straight with flowing lines, more carving	Light and graceful	Mahogany	Oriental designs, small patterns; with Chinese Chippendale, Chinese designs with blue grounds	Brocade, damask, leather upholstery, needlepoint, satin, tapestry, velour, velvet
Hepplewhite 1765–1795	Curved, except chair legs	Small, slender, and sturdy	Mahogany Rosewood inlay Satinwood	Plain carpeting or contemporary French designs; oriental designs light in coloring with fine patterns and texture	Damask, haircloth, striped and figured moiré and satin, trimmings of ribbons and tassel; classic designs
Sheraton 1757–1806	Straight, a few curves	Delicate, slender, narrow, and refined	Mahogany Rosewood inlay Satinwood	Similar to Hepplewhite	Brocade, damask, haircloth, linens (printed), silks (lightweight); floral motifs on small scale
Adam Brothers 1760–1792	Straight, rectangular	Graceful	Mahogany Maple Pine Satinwood	Carpeting matching walls in darker tones	Brocade, moiré, silks (lightweight)
Regency 1793–1820	Curved	Flamboyant	Bamboo Black lacquer Mother-of-pearl decorations	Oriental and Indian rug designs	Contrasting textures
Victorian 1837–1901	Curved	Fairly large with much ornamentation	Black walnut Mahogany Oak	Brussels carpeting, tapestry rugs, Wiltons; in floral designs	Brocade, damask, horsehair upholstery, plush, velour, velvet
American					
Early American 1607–1725	Straight	Simple and sturdy	Ash Cherry Maple Oak Pine	Hooked rug designs, rag rugs, plaid carpeting	Chintz, crash, cretonne, denim, dotted Swiss, homespun, marquisette (dotted), monk's cloth, novelty cottons, organdy, rep

Period					
Colonial 1725–1790	Curved and straight	Solid and substantial	Black walnut Mahogany	As above; also oriental rugs in close, quiet patterns	Same as Early American; also brocades and velvets being introduced
Federal 1795–1847	Curved and straight	Graceful and slender	Mahogany Walnut	Plain carpeting or designs of the period; oriental patterns with well-colored designs	Similar to Georgian
American Victorian 1850s	Curved	Intricate carving	Bent and shaped wood Dark, black finishes	Brussels and Axminster carpets and rugs	Plush, velvet, velour, damask, tapestry, horsehair
Art Nouveau 1875–1900	Ship-lash curve	Natural growing forms	Sculped, combining dark, light, and painted finishes	Brussels, Wilton, Axminster carpets	Frieze, plush, velvet, damask
Modern					
Early Modern 1911–1920 Moderne 1930–1940s	Straight, angular, and sharp pointed	Solid, substantial, and simple	Metal Metallic-painted woods Inlaid woods	Plain carpeting in light and soft colors; modern designs	Armure, casement cloth, chenille, corded fabrics, gauze, modern tapestry, mohair, monk's cloth, rough linens and cottons; large sweeping and block designs, exaggerated in size but simplified in line
Contemporary 1948–	Sophisticated simplicity	Sturdy, mobile, functional	Grained plywoods, glass brick, unbreakable sheet glass Plastics	Carved and textured; geometric designs; cotton, wool, and synthetic blends	Antique satin, bouclé, hand-woven effects, textured cottons, linens, gauze for curtains
Oriental	Classical serenity	Structural beauty	Latticework Lacquered finished wood	Chinese Orientals; Near East Orientals; tufted rugs and carpets	Gauze, ninon, bouclé, textured cottons, linens, polyesters, glass fibers

Appendix I

AUDIOVISUALS

American Textile Manufacturers Institute
1101 Connecticut Ave., N.W.
Washington, D.C. 20036

"Textiles—Magic in the Making." Color. Sound filmstrip, cassette, and script (fibers moved through stages to fabric).

"Textiles—The Design Story." Color. Sound filmstrip, cassette, and script.

"Textiles—Always in Fashion." Color. Filmstrip, cassette, and script. (Ways of expressing fashion in apparel and home furnishings).

"Textiles—It's All in the Finish." Color. Sound filmstrip, cassette, and script (tour of a finishing plant).

"What About the Fabric?" Color, three filmstrips, cassette, and script (how the finished fabric is affected by fiber, yarn, construction, design, and finish).

"Pick the Fabric to the Job." Filmstrip, tape cassette, and script (buying considerations for apparel, home furnishings, and home sewing).

"Wear and Care of Textiles." Color. Sound filmstrip, cassette, and script (built-in quality, cleaning, and storage).

Prices are $5.00 each except for "What About the Fabric?" which is $15.00.

America's Textiles, the magazine for textile executives, has recently introduced a video film service covering many topics such as employee training and orientation, sales promotion, and product identification. The address is 106 E. Stone Avenue, P.O. Box 88, Greenville, S.C. 29602.

Association Films
866 Third Avenue
New York, NY 10022

The Cotton Belt: Yesterday and Today. 17-minute color film (for rent).
Pioneer Spinning and Weaving, 10-minute color film (for rent).

Celanese Fibers Marketing Co.
Public Relations Department
1211 Avenue of the Americas
New York, N.Y. 10036

> *The Shape of Polyester.* 15-minute color film on the uses of polyester in the industrial
> market (free rental).

E. I. DuPont de Nemours & Company, Inc.
G.S. Department
Motion Pictures
Wilmington, Dela. 19898

> *Nomex III, A Material Difference.* 15 minutes, color (on protective clothing).
> *The Way It Is with Man-Made Fibers.* 27 minutes, color (natural and man-made fibers
> classified and compared).
> *Knitting Is Fun.* 30 minutes each, color.
> > *Hand Knitting* (in three parts)
> > *Crocheting* (in three parts)
> *Antron III Carpets—Good Looks That Last.* 15 minutes, color.

> These are free on short-term loan.

Fairchild Publications
7 East 12th Street
New York, N.Y. 10003

> "Fashion in the Making," by Jeffrey Tracktenberg. 35 mm slides. Part I: "The
> Manufacturer's Role," 36 slides. Part II: "The Retailer's Role," 24 slides (for sale).
> "Great Developments in Fashion Series," by Rosalie Kolodny. 35 mm slides. In
> three programs: (1) the dome skirt, (2) the peg skirt, (3) the dolman sleeve (for
> sale).
> "Textiles from Source to Consumer," by Isabel B. Wingate. 35 mm colored slides,
> script, swatches, and glossary.
> > Set   I: "Classifications and Uses of Textile Fibers"
> > Set II: "Yarns"
> > Set III: "Weaving, Knitting, and Other Constructions"
> > Set IV: "Finishing of Cloth"
> > Set V: "Coloring of Cloth"
> > Set VI: "Care of Textile Fabrics"
> Each set may be purchased separately or as a unit.

> *How to Choose a Fabric.* 16 mm color film, 8 to 10 minutes (home sewing).

Karastan Rug Mills
Marketing Services Division
919 Third Avenue
New York, N.Y. 10022

> On a limited-loan basis, 16 mm films on Oriental rugs and on carpet construction
> are available.

Man-Made Fiber Producers Association, Inc.
1150 Seventeenth St., N.W.
Washington, D.C. 20036

> "Interplay—The Story of Man-made Fibers." Filmstrip in color, 140 frames, 20
> minutes, record or cassette, lesson plan, fact book, 50 student review books.
> Moderately priced.

Modern Talking Picture Service
5000 Park Avenue N.
St. Petersburg, Fla. 33709

Stitches in Time (creation of machine-made Schiffli embroidery). 22 minutes, color film, free loan. Also available are films on clothing.

Appendix J

METRIC CONVERSIONS

	When You Know the	You Can Find the	If You Multiply by
Length	inches	millimeters	25
	feet	centimeters	30
	yards	meters	0.9
	millimeters	inches	0.04
	centimeters	inches	0.4
	meters	yards	1.1
Area	square inches	square centimeters	6.5
	square feet	square meters	0.09
	square yards	square meters	0.8
	square centimeters	square inches	0.16
	square meters	square inches	1.2
	square kilometers	square miles	0.4
	square hectometers (hectares)	acres	2.5
Mass	ounces	grams	28
	pounds	kilograms	0.45
	short tons	megagrams (metric tons)	0.9
	grams	ounces	0.035
	kilograms	pounds	2.2
	megagrams (metric tons)	short tons	1.1
Liquid Volume	ounces	milliliters	30
	pints	liters	0.47
	quarts	liters	0.95
	gallons	liters	3.8
	milliliters	ounces	0.034
	liters	pints	2.1
	liters	quarts	1.06
	liters	gallons	0.26
Temperature	degrees Fahrenheit	degrees Celsius	5/9 (after subtracting 32)
	degrees Celsius	degrees Fahrenheit	9/5 (then add 32)

REFERENCES

GENERAL REFERENCE WORKS AND TEXTS

Alexander, P. R. *Textile Products: Selection Use and Care.* Boston: Houghton-Mifflin Company, 1977.

American Fabrics. *A. F. Encyclopedia of Textiles,* 2nd ed. Englewood Cliffs, N.J.: Prentice-Hall, Inc., 1973.

American Home Economics Association, *Textile Handbook,* 4th ed. Washington, D.C.: AHEA, 1970.

Chambers, Helen G., and Verna Moulton. *Clothing Selection.* Philadelphia: J. B. Lippincott Company, 1969.

Collier, A. M. *A Handbook of Textiles* New York: Pergamon Press, 1976.

Corbman, B. P. *Textiles, Fiber to Fabric,* 5th ed., rev. New York: McGraw-Hill Book Company, 1975.

Dembeck, A. A. *A Guide to Man-made Textiles Fabrics and Texture Yarns of the World.* New York: United Piece Dye Works, 1964.

Dictionary of Textile Terms, George E. Linton, ed., 11th ed., Danville, Va.: Dan River Mills, 1971.

Garrett, Pauline C., *You Are a Consumer of Clothing.* Waltham, Mass.: Ginn & Co., 1967.

Gioello, Debbie. *Profiling Fabrics: Properties, Performance, and Construction Techniques.* New York: Fairchild Publication, Inc., 1981.

Hall, A. J. *The Standard Handbook of Textiles,* 8th ed. New York: Halstead Press, Inc., 1975.

Harries, N., and T. Harries. *Textiles: Decision Making for the Consumer.* New York: McGraw-Hill Book Company, 1974.

Hollen, M., and J. Saddler. *Textiles,* 5th ed. New York: Macmillan Publishing Co. Inc., 1979.

Holt, J. M. *Fabrics and Clothing.* Plainfield, N.J.: Textile Book Service, 1957.

Joseph, Marjory L. *Introductory Textile Science*, 4th ed. New York: Holt, Rinehart and Winston, Inc., 1981.

Klapper, Marvin. *Fabric Glossary*. New York: Fairchild Publications, Inc., 1973.

Labarthe, J. *Elements of Textiles*. New York: Macmillan Publishing Co., Inc. 1975.

Linton, George E. *Applied Basic Textiles*, 2nd ed. rev. Plainfield, N.J.: Textile Book Service, n.d.

Linton, George E. *The Modern Textile and Apparel Dictionary*, 4th ed. Plainfield, N.J.: Textile Book Service, 1972.

Lyle, D. S. *Modern Textiles*. New York: John Wiley & Sons, Inc., 1978.

Ontiveros, J. R. *Panamerican Textile Dictionary*, Spanish-English, English-Spanish, 2nd ed. Plainfield, N.J.: Textile Book Service, 1971.

Pizzuto, Joseph J. *Fabric Science*, rev. by Arthur Price and Allen C. Cohen. New York: Fairchild Publications, Inc., 1980.

Potter, M. D., and B. P. Corbman. *Textiles: Fiber to Fabric*. New York: McGraw-Hill Book Company, 1967.

Smith, Betty F., and Ira Block. *Textiles in Perspective*. Englewood Cliffs, N.J.: Prentice-Hall, Inc., 1982.

Stout, Evelyn. *Introduction to Textiles*, 3rd ed. New York: John Wiley & Sons, Inc., 1970.

Tate, Mildred T., and Otis Gibson. *Family Clothing*. New York: John Wiley & Sons, Inc., 1961.

Textile Institute. *Textile Terms and Definitions*, 6th ed. Plainfield, N.J.: Textile Book Service, 1970.

Tortora, Phyllis G. *Understanding Textiles*, 2nd ed. New York: Macmillan Publishing Co., Inc., 1982.

Wingate, Isabel B. *Fairchild's Dictionary of Textiles*, 6th ed. New York: Fairchild Publications, Inc., 1979.

REFERENCES TO SPECIFIC SUBJECTS

Fibers and Yarns

Cook, J. Gordon. *Handbook of Textile Fibers*, 4th ed., 2 vols. Plainfield, N.J.: Textile Book Service, 1968.

Glossary of Industrial Fiber Terminology. Celanese Fibers Marketing Company, 1211 Avenue of the Americas, New York, N.Y. 10036.

Man-Made Fiber Fact Book and Guide to Man-Made Fibers. Man-Made Fiber Producers Association, 1150 17th St., N.W., Washington, D.C. 20036.

Man-Made Fiber and Textile Dictionary. Celanese Fibers Marketing Co., 1211 Avenue of the Americas, New York, N.Y. 10036.

Moncrief, R. W. *Man-Made Fibers*. New York: John Wiley & Sons, Inc., 1966.

Textile Fibers and Their Properties. Greensboro, N.C.: Burlington Industries, Inc., 1970.

Construction of Cloth

Computer Technology for Textiles. Atlanta Ga.: W. E. Smith Publishing Co., 1970.

Handbook of Bonded and Laminated Fabrics. Research Triangle Park, N.C.: American Association of Textile Chemists and Colorists, 1974.

Hathorne, B. L. *Woven Stretch and Textured Fabrics*. New York: John Wiley & Sons, Inc., 1964.

Held, S. B. *Weaving*. New York: Holt, Rinehart and Winston, 1972.

The Knitter. 106 East Stone Avenue, Greenville, S.C. 29602.

Lord, P. R., and M. H. Mohamed. *Weaving: Construction of Yarn to Fabric*. Watford, England: Merrow Publishing Co., 1973.

McDonald, M. *Non-Woven Fabric Technology*. Plainfield, N.J.: Textile Book Service, 1971.

Reichman, Charles, et al. *Knitted Fabric Primer, 1967*, and *Knitting Encyclopedia, 1972*. New York: National Knitted Outerwear Association, 1967 and 1972.

Robinson, A. T. C. and R. Marks. *Woven Cloth Construction*. London: Butterworth, 1967.

Schwab, F. R. *The Story of Lace and Embroidery*. New York: Fairchild Publications, Inc., 1951.

Wheatley, B. *Raschel Lace Production*. New York: National Knitted Outerwear Association, 1968.

Finishing

Hall, A. J. *Textile Finishing*. New York: Chemical Publishing Co., 1966.

Harper, P. J. *Durable Press Cotton Goods*. Watford, England: Merrow Publishing Co., 1971.

Marsh, J. T. *An Introduction to Textile Finishing*. Plainfield, N.J.: Textile Book Service, 1966.

Stout, E. E. *Textile Finishing Glossary*. Greensboro, N.C.: Cone Mills Corp., 1967.

Dyeing, Printing, and Design

AATCC Glossary of Printing Terms. Research Triangle Park, N.C.: American Association of Textile Chemists and Colorists, 1980.

Albers, Ani. *On Designing*. Wesleyan, Conn.: Wesleyan University Press, 1965.

Brookman, Helen. *The Theory of Fashion Design*. New York: John Wiley & Sons, Inc., 1965.

Melas, J. W. T., *Textile Printers*. Watford, England: Merrow Publishing Co., 1971.

Proud, Nora. *Textile Printing and Dyeing*. New York: Van Nostrand Reinhold Company, 1965.

Storey, Joyce. *Textile Printing*. New York: Van Nostrand Rheinhold Company, 1974.

Tilton, John K. *The Development of the Modern in Textile Design*. New York: Scalamandré Museum of Textiles, 1959.

Ward, N. *Art and Design in Textiles*. New York: Van Nostrand Reinhold Company, 1972.

Textile Clothing

The Art of Sewing (series). New York: Time-Life Books, Inc., 1969.

The Boys' Outfitter. 71 West 35 Street, New York, N.Y. 10001.

Calasibetta, Charlotte. *Fairchild's Dictionary of Fashion*. New York: Fairchild Publications, Inc., 1975.

Deranian, Helen. *Finishing Techniques for the Textile Maintenance Industry*. New York: Barclay Publishing Co., Inc., 1968.

Fourt, Lyman, and Norman Hollies. *Clothing: Comfort and Function*. New York: Marcel Dekker, Inc., 1970.

Flugel, J. C. *The Psychology of Clothes*. London: Hogarth Press, 1966.

Jaffee, Hilde. *Children's Wear Design*. New York: Fairchild Publications, Inc., 1972.

Lyle, Dorothy S. *Focus on Fabrics*. Silver Spring, Md.: International Fabricare Institute, 1964.

Mathisen, M. P. *Apparel and Accessories*. New York: McGraw-Hill Book Company, Gregg Division, 1979.

Moss, A. J. Earnest. *Textiles and Fabrics, Their Care and Preservation*. New York: Tudor Publishing Co., 1961.

Newburth, L. H., ed. *Physiology of Heat Regulation and the Science of Clothing*. New York: Hefner Book Co., 1971.

Sewing and Threads. New York: Coats & Clark, Inc., Educational Bureau, 1979.

Textiles for the Home

Easy Guide to Carpets and Rugs (cu-54). Celanese Fibers Marketing Co., Customer Information Services Department, 1211 Avenue of the Americas, New York, N.Y. 10036.

Easy Guide to Curtains and Draperies, Upholstery and Bedspreads (cu-93). Celanese Fibers Marketing Co., Customer Information Services Department, 1211 Avenue of the Americas, New York, N.Y. 10036.

Guide to Sheets, Pillow Cases, Pillows and Mattresses Pads. Celanese Fibers Marketing Co., 1211 Avenue of the Americas, New York, N.Y. 10036.

Hoffman, Emanuel F. *Fairchild's Dictionary of Home Furnishings*. New York: Fairchild Publications, Inc., 1974.

Household Textiles (pamphlets). Good Housekeeping Institute, 939 8th Avenue, New York, N.Y. 10019.

How to Care for Your Rugs and Carpets. Dalton, Ga.: Carpet and Rug Institute, 1971.

Instant Table Decoration with 60 Ideas for Table Setting (pamphlet for distribution in U.S. only). Belgian Linen Association, Brussels, Belgium.

Pianzola, M., and J. Coffinet. *Tapestry*. New York: Van Nostrand Reinhold Company, 1974.

Robinson, G. *Carpets and Other Textile Floor Coverings*. 2nd ed. Plainfield, N.J.: Textile Book Service, 1972.

Schlosser, Ignace. *The Book of Rugs: Oriental and European*, trans. from German. New York: Crown Publishers, Inc., 1963.

Upholstery Fabrics. Hercules Incorporated, Fibers Division, 910 Market Street, Wilmington, Del. 19879.

Vollbach, W. F. *Early Decorative Textiles*. New York: Paul Hamlyn, Inc., 1969.

Care of Textiles

The International Fabricare Institute. Publications, especially *Fabricare News, TABS Bulletins,* and *IFI Bulletins;* also a *Selling Sense* series for salespeople on care. 12251 Tech Road, Silver Spring, Md. 20904.

Moss, A. G. E. *Textiles and Fabrics: Their Care and Preservation*. New York: Chemical Publishing Co., 1969.

Soap and Detergent Association. Publications. 475 Park Avenue South, New York, N.Y. 10016.

"Soaps and Detergents for Home Laundering." *Home and Garden Bulletin #139.* Washington, D.C.: U.S. Department of Agriculture, 1973.

American Association for Textile Technology. *The Technique of Home Laundering,* Textile Monograph #108. New York: AATT, 1973.

GOVERNMENT BULLETINS

Catalog of government bulletins on textiles (fibers, fabrics and sewing aids). Also *Consumers Guide*. U.S. Government Printing Office, Superintendent of Documents, Washington, D.C. 20207.

Compilation of laws administered by the U.S. Consumer Product Safety Commission (includes Flammable Fabrics Act), Washington, D.C. 20207.

Rules and regulations under the Textile Fiber Products Identification Act, and the Wool Products Labeling Act, Federal Trade Commission, Washington, D.C. 20250.

U.S. Department of Agriculture, Office of Information, Washington, D.C. (Numerous bulletins.)

TEXTILE TESTING

References

AATCC Technical Manual. Research Triangle Park, N.C.: American Association of Textile Chemists and Colorists, 1980.

American Society for Testing and Materials. *Book of ASTM Standards*, Parts 24, 25, and 30. Philadelphia: ASTM, published annually.

Booth, John E. *Principles of Textile Testing*, 3rd ed. New York: Chemical Publishing Co., 1969.

"Federal Test Method Standard No. 191," Textile Test Methods. Washington, D.C.: General Service Administration, 1968.

Pizzuto, Joseph J. *Fabric Science*, rev. by A. Price and A. C. Cohen. New York: Fairchild Publications, Inc., 1974, Chapter 10.

United States of America Standards Institute. *U.S.A. Standard Performance Requirements for Textile Fabrics* (U.S.A.S. L22, 1968). New York: USASI, 1968.

Weaver, J. W. *Analytical Methods for a Textile Laboratory*. Triangle Park, N.C. AATCC, 1968.

Wingate, Isabel B., and Ralph Burkholder. *Laboratory Swatch Book for Textile Fabrics*, 7th ed. Dubuque, Iowa: W. C. Brown Publishers, 1970.

Laboratories

American Institute of Flammability Testing, Inc., 960 Avenue of the Americas, New York, N.Y. 10001.

Better Fabrics Testing Bureau, 101 West 31st St., New York, N.Y. 10001.

Flammability Consulting Service, 960 Allen Boulevard, Farmingdale, N.Y. 11735.

Hatch Textile Research, Inc., 25 East 26th Street, New York, N.Y. 10010.

International Fabricare Institute. Textile Testing and Approval Laboratories, 12251 Tech Road, Silver Spring, Md. 20904.

Kimtex Service Laboratories, Inc., 108 North 7th St., Paterson, N.J. 07509.

United States Testing Company, Inc., and Nationwide Consumer Testing Institute, 1405 Park Ave., Hoboken, N.J. 07030.

Private testing laboratories are also operated by a number of retail chain stores, including Macy, Sears, and Penney.

TRADE PERIODICALS

General

American Dyestuff Reporter, 630 Third Avenue, New York, N.Y. 10010 (monthly).

American Fabrics and Fashions, 24 East 38th Street, New York, N.Y. 10016 (quarterly).

American Society for Testing and Materials, 1916 Rice Street, Philadelphia, Pa. 19103 (monthly).

America's Textiles, bulletin edition and knitting edition, 106 East Stone Avenue, P.O. Box 88, Greenville, S.C. 29602 (monthly).

Daily News Record, Fairchild Publications, Inc., 7 East 12th Street, New York, N.Y. 10003 (daily).

Home Economics Research Journal, American Home Economics Association, 2010 Massachusetts Ave., N.W., Washington, D.C. 20036 (quarterly).

International Textiles, 17 East 45th Street, New York, N.Y. 10017 (monthly.)

Journal of Home Economics, American Home Economics Association, 2010 Massachusetts Ave., N.W., Washington, D.C. 20036 (bimonthly).

Modern Textiles Magazine, 303 Fifth Avenue, New York, N.Y. 10016 (monthly).

Textile Asia, Tak Yan Commercial Building, 11/F, 30–32 d'Aguilas St., Hong Kong (monthly).

Textile Directions, P.O. Box 928, New York, N.Y. 10010 (quarterly).

Textile Chemist and Colorist (journal of the AATCC), Box 12215, Research Triangle Park, N.C. 27709 (monthly).

Textile Products and Processes, 1175 Peachtree St., N.E., Atlanta, Ga. 30361 (monthly).

Textile Research Journal, P.O. Box 625, Princeton, N.J. 08540 (monthly).

Textile Technology Digest, Institute of Textile Technology, P.O. Box 31, Charlottesville, Va. 22902 (monthly).

Textile World, McGraw-Hill, 1221 Avenue of the Americas, New York N.Y. 10020 (monthly).

WWD (Women's Wear Daily), Fairchild Publications, Inc., 7 East 12th Street, New York, N.Y. 10003 (daily).

Specific Consumer Goods

Outer Clothing

Infants' and Children's Review, Earnshaw Publications, 393 7th Avenue, New York, N.Y. 10001.

Knitting Times, 51 Madison Avenue, New York, N.Y. 10016.

Sportswear on Parade, 60 East 42 Street, New York, N.Y. 10017.

Underwear

Corset, Brassiers and Lingerie Magazine, 95 Madison Avenue, New York, N.Y. 10016.

Men's and Boys' Wear

The Boys' Outfitter, 71 West 35 Street, New York, N.Y. 10010.

Men's Wear, Fairchild Publications, 7 East 12 Street, New York, N.Y. 10003 (monthly).

Home Furnishings

Carpet & Rug Industry, Denville, N.J. 07834.

Curtain and Drapery Magazine, 370 Lexington Avenue, New York, N.Y. 10017.

HFD Home Furnishings Daily, Fairchild Publications, Inc., 7 East 12th Street, New York, N.Y. 10003.

Linens, Domestics and Bath Products, 370 Lexington Avenue, New York, N.Y. 10017.

News from West Point-Pepperell Inc., 1221 Avenue of the Americas, New York, N.Y. 10036.

INDEX